D1556216

Criminal Law: Cases and Commentary
2020 Edition

Professor Lore Rutz-Burri, J.D.

Photo Credit: Severin Burri, 2019

Acknowledgements
This edition is dedicated to my 2019 student assistants--Robert Close, Megahn Distefeno, Andrew Pinedo, and Sami Whitmore—great students and extraordinary people.
With much gratitude and thanks. LRB

TABLE OF CONTENTS

INTRODUCTION

This text is a casebook containing cases from state and federal appellate courts. These cases explore the substantive criminal law—that is, the law that defines crimes and establishes the punishment for crimes. Chapters One and Two explore the limits the Constitution places on lawmakers. Chapter Three covers the elements of crimes in general. It also examines statutes that allow criminal convictions without proof of criminal action or criminal mindset on the part of the actor—that is, strict or vicarious liability crimes. Chapter Four focuses on the inchoate (incomplete) offense of attempt, conspiracy, and solicitation. Chapter Five examines accomplice liability (when multiple people take part in a crime.)

Chapter Six starts the exploration of specific crimes, beginning with criminal homicide. Chapter Seven continues with other crimes against persons and covers sexual crimes, assault and battery, mayhem, kidnapping and false imprisonment. Chapter Eight examines crimes against habitation -- burglary, trespass, arson, and criminal mischief. Chapter Nine then discusses myriad property crimes such as larceny, embezzlement, false pretenses, robbery, carjacking, forgery, uttering a forged document, and receiving stolen property.

Chapters Ten and Eleven discuss the affirmative defenses that a person may raise when he or she is charged with a crime. Some of these defenses allow the offender to completely evade any liability, and some of these defenses merely allow mitigated criminal liability (that is, being convicted of a lesser crime). Chapter Ten focuses on the justification defenses of execution of public duties, self-defense, defense of others, defense of habitation, defense of property, necessity, and consent. Chapter Eleven focuses on the excuse defenses of insanity and diminished capacity, age, mistake of fact, intoxication, duress, and entrapment.

Chapter One: Constitutional Limits on Criminal Law—Part I

OVERVIEW

State and federal constitutions limit the ability of the legislative and executive branch to pass certain types of criminal laws. The drafters of the federal Constitution[1] were so concerned about two historic abuses by English Parliament--ex post facto laws and bills of attainder--that they prohibited Congress from passing these types of laws in original body of the Constitution. See, Const. Art. I, § 9. Most of the other limitations discussed in this chapter and the next are found within the Bill of Rights--the first eight amendments to the Constitution. The states adopted the Bill of Rights in 1791.[2] These amendments added several constraints on Congress that had not yet been worked out yet at the time of the Constitutional Convention. The impact of the Bill of Rights was to place substantial checks on the federal government's ability to define crimes.

This chapter explores the Second, and Eighth Amendments' impact on federal substantive law. When drafted and passed, the U.S. Constitution and the Bill of Rights applied only to the federal government. Individual states each had their own guarantees found in their own state constitutions. Since 1868, the Fourteenth Amendment has become an important tool for making states also follow the provisions of the Bill of the Rights. It was drafted to enforce the Civil Rights Act passed in 1866 in the post-Civil War states. Section 1 of the Fourteenth Amendment enjoins the states from depriving any person of life, liberty, or property, without due process of law. It prohibits states from adopting any laws that abridge the privileges and immunities of the citizens of the United States and requires that states not deny any person equal protection under the law. U.S. Const. amend. XIV, § 2.

Making the states follow provisions of the Bill of Rights is known as incorporation. Over decades, the Court[3] debated whether the Bill of Rights should be incorporated all together in one-fell swoop (called total incorporation) or piece-by-piece (called selective incorporation). The case-by-case, bit-by-bit approach won out. In a series of decisions, the Supreme Court has held that the Due Process Clause of the Fourteenth Amendment makes enforceable against the states those provisions of the Bill of Rights that are "implicit in the concept of ordered liberty." *Palko v. Connecticut*, 302 U.S. 319 (1937). For example, in 1925 the Court recognized that the First Amendment protections of free speech and free press apply to states as well as to the federal government. *Gitlow v. New York,* 268 U.S. 652 (1925). In the 1960s, the Court selectively incorporated many of the *procedural guarantees*[4] of the Bill of Rights. The Court also used the Fourteenth

---

[1] This text will use the term "Constitution" to mean the federal, United States Constitution. State constitutions will be distinguished and specifically identified. Instead of referring to the Amendments to the United States Constitution by number and full title "First Amendment to the Constitution of the United State" in sentences, they will simply be referred to as "the First Amendment." In citing to specific article and section numbers of provisions of the United States Constitution, they will similarly be abbreviated (for example, Const. Art I, Sec. 9 or Art I, § 9, or U.S. Const. amend. XIV, §2).

[2] There is a rich history about the political squabbles and compromises that existed when the federal constitution took effect, but it is beyond the scope of this text. Essentially, the statesmen had opposing viewpoints concerning how strong the national government should be and how strong state governments should be. Even as the original federal constitution was being circulated and ratified, the framers were thinking about the provisions that became known as the Bill of Rights.

[3] This text will use "Court" refers to the United States Supreme Court, and will sometimes, for clarity, refer to the U.S. Supreme Court as "the Supreme Court." All other state and federal courts will be distinguished and specifically identified.

[4] Procedural guarantees include, for example, freedom from unreasonable search and seizure, the right to a fair trial, the right to a jury trial, or due process.

Amendment to extend *substantive guarantees*[5] of the Bill of Rights to the states. More recently, the Court, in *McDonald v. City of Chicago,* 561 U.S. 742 (2010), held that the Second Amendment's right to bear arms also applied to the states. Scheb noted,

> McDonald was the latest, and quite possibly the last, in a series of decisions incorporating provisions of the Bill of Rights into the Fourteenth Amendment. With the exception of the Fifth Amendment's Grand Jury Clause and the Eighth Amendment's prohibitions of excessive bail and excessive fines, all the provisions of the Bill of Rights have been incorporated into the Fourteenth Amendment making them applicable to state and local governments. Thus, the U.S. Constitution and the Bill of Rights, now stands as a barrier to unreasonable or oppressive criminal laws, whether they are enacted by Congress, a state's legislature, or a local governing body. John Scheb, *Criminal Law and Procedure*, 65-66 (10th ed., 2013).

It turns out that Professor Scheb was not so prophetic. In 2019 the Court decided *Timbs v. Indiana*, 586 U.S. ___ (2019). The government seized Timbs' Land Rover worth over $42,000 claiming it was connected to his crime of dealing heroin—a crime with a maximum fine of only $10,000. The Court not only incorporated the Excessive Fines Clause of the Eighth Amendment and said it was "fundamental to our scheme of ordered liberty" and "deeply rooted in our nation's history and tradition," Justice Ginsberg writing for the unanimous court stated, "[i]f a Bill of Rights protection is incorporated, there is no daylight between the federal and state conduct it prohibits or requires." Indeed, the Court seems likely to hold that the jury unanimity required in federal cases is also required in state cases (the Sixth Amendment right to a jury trial was incorporated in the 1960s) in an upcoming decision in *Ramos v. Louisiana*, ___ U.S. ___ (20XX) (argued in October 2019). One of the arguments presented in *Ramos* was that, under *Timbs*, there can be no difference between how a right is implemented in state cases (Louisiana allowed a nonunanimous verdict) and how that same right is implemented in federal case (federal juries must render unanimous verdict in criminal cases).

EX POST FACTO LAWS

Ex post facto laws are ones that are applied retroactively. For example, assume that Cheryl catches and squashes a centipede on January 1st; in response the city council, on January 2nd, passes a law that makes centipede-squashing a misdemeanor. The prohibition against ex post facto laws protects Cheryl from being prosecuted under this new law. Any attempt by the state to prosecute Cheryl using the new law applied retroactively would violate the provision against ex post facto laws. One of the reasons that ex post facto laws are problematic is because they violate the principle of legality which holds that individuals are entitled to know, in advance, what the law prohibits. Without the protection against ex post facto laws, Cheryl would only be able to guess at what types of laws could ensnare her at any time in the future.

Modern legislatures are generally careful not to draft statutes that violate ex post facto prohibitions. However, courts occasionally find a law to be retroactive in ways that the legislature failed to consider. When that happens, the court will strike down the law. For example, the Court struck down Florida sentencing guidelines in 1987 to the extent they reduced time off for an inmate's good behavior because it had the effect of increasing the punishment for those who committed crimes before the enactment of the guidelines. *Miller v. Florida*, 482 U.S. 423 (1987). Conversely, in *Smith v. Doe*, 538 U.S. 84 (2003), defendants who had committed crimes before Alaska Sex Offender Registration Law (Megan's Law) was passed were nevertheless required to register under the act. The Court held that the act was not punitive in nature, and therefore the ex post facto limitation did not apply.

---

[5] Substantive guarantees include, for example, equal protection of law, the right to be free from cruel and unusual punishment.

CARMELL v. TEXAS,
529 U.S. 513 (2000)

FACTS (Official Summary)

In 1996, petitioner was convicted on 15 counts of committing sexual offenses against his stepdaughter from 1991 to 1995, when she was 12 to 16 years old. Before September 1, 1993, Tex. Code Crim. Proc. Ann., Art. 38.07, specified that a victim's testimony about a sexual offense could not support a conviction unless corroborated by other evidence or the victim informed another person of the offense within six months of its occurrence, but that, if a victim was under 14 at the time of the offense, the victim's testimony alone could support a conviction. A 1993 amendment allowed the victim's testimony alone to support a conviction if the victim was under 18. The validity of four of petitioner's convictions depends on which version of the law applies to him. Before the Texas Court of Appeals, he argued that the four convictions could not stand under the pre-1993 version of the law, which was in effect at the time of his alleged conduct, because they were based solely on the testimony of the victim, who was not under 14 at the time of the offenses and had not made a timely outcry. The [trial] court held that applying the 1993 amendment retrospectively did not violate the Ex Post Facto Clause, and the State Court of Criminal Appeals denied review.

RULING

Petitioner's convictions on the counts at issue, insofar as they are not corroborated by other evidence, cannot be sustained under the Ex Post Facto Clause.

OPINION

JUSTICE STEVENS delivered the opinion of the Court. (Official Summary)

(a) In *Calder v. Bull*, 3 Dall. 386, 390, Justice Chase stated that the proscription against ex post facto laws was derived from English common law well known to the Framers, and set out four categories of ex post facto criminal laws: "1st. Every law that makes an action done before the passing of the law, and which was innocent when done, criminal; and punishes such action. 2d. Every law that aggravates a crime, or makes it greater than it was, when committed. 3d. Every law that changes the punishment, and inflicts a greater punishment, than the law annexed to the crime, when committed. 4th. Every law that alters the legal rules of evidence, and receives less, or different, testimony, than the law required at the time of the commission of the offence, in order to convict the offender." The Court has repeatedly endorsed this understanding, including the fourth category. Both Justice Chase and the common-law treatise on which he drew heavily cited the case of Sir John Fenwick as an example of the fourth category. England charged Fenwick with high treason in the late 17th century, but, under an Act of Parliament, he could not be convicted without the testimony of two witnesses. Parliament passed a bill of attainder making the two-witness rule inapplicable, and Fenwick was convicted on the testimony of only one witness.

(b) Article 38.07 plainly fits within Calder's fourth category. Requiring only the victim's testimony to convict, rather than that testimony plus corroborating evidence, is surely "less testimony required to convict" in any straightforward sense of those words. Indeed, the circumstances here parallel those of Fenwick's case. That Article 38.07 neither increases the punishment for, nor changes the elements of, the offense simply shows that the amendment does not fit within Calder's first or third categories.

(c) The fourth category resonates harmoniously with one of the principal interests that the Ex Post Facto Clause was designed to serve, fundamental justice. A law reducing the quantum of evidence required to convict is as grossly unfair as retrospectively eliminating an element of the offense, increasing punishment for an existing offense, or lowering the burden of proof. In each instance, the government refuses, after the fact, to play by its own rules, altering them in a way that is advantageous only to the State, to facilitate an easier conviction. There is plainly a fundamental fairness interest in having the government abide by the rules of law it establishes to govern the circumstances under which it can deprive a person of his or her liberty or life. Indeed, Fenwick's case itself illustrates this principle.

(d) None of the reasons that the United States as amicus advances for abandoning the fourth category is persuasive. It asserts that the fact that neither Blackstone nor ex post facto clauses in Ratification-era state constitutions mention the fourth category shows that Justice Chase simply got it wrong. Accepting this assertion would require the Court to abandon the third category as well, for it is also not mentioned in any of those sources. And it does not follow from the fact that Fenwick was convicted by a bill of attainder that his case cannot also be an example of an ex post facto law. In fact, all of the specific examples that Justice Chase listed in Calder were passed as bills of attainder. Nor, as the United States and Texas argue, was the fourth category effectively cast out in *Collins v. Youngblood*, 497 U. S. 37, which actually held that it was a mistake to stray beyond Calder's four categories, not that the fourth category was itself mistaken.

(e) Texas' additional argument that the fourth category is limited to laws that retrospectively alter the burden of proof is also rejected. The Court's decision in *Cummings v. Missouri*, 4 Wall. 277, nowhere suggests that a reversal of the burden of proof is all the fourth category encompasses; and laws that lower the burden of proof and laws that reduce the quantum of evidence necessary to meet that burden are indistinguishable in all meaningful ways relevant to concerns of the Ex Post Facto Clause. Texas' assertion that Fenwick's case concerns only a reduction in the burden of proof is based on a mistaken historical premise. . . . Unlike the witness competency rules at issue there, Article 38.07 is a sufficiency of the evidence rule. It does not merely regulate the mode in which the facts constituting guilt may be placed before the jury, but governs the sufficiency of those facts for meeting the burden of proof.

Indeed, *Hopt* expressly distinguished witness competency laws from laws altering the amount or degree of proof needed for conviction. Moreover, a sufficiency of the evidence rule resonates with the interests to which the Ex Post Facto Clause is addressed, in particular the elements of unfairness and injustice in subverting the presumption of innocence.

JUSTICE GINSBURG, with whom THE CHIEF JUSTICE, JUSTICE O'CONNOR, and JUSTICE KENNEDY join, **dissenting.**

The Court today holds that the amended version of Article 38.07 of the Texas Code of Criminal Procedure reduces the amount of proof necessary to support a sexual assault conviction, and that its retroactive application therefore violates the Ex Post Facto Clause. In so holding, the Court misreads both the Texas statute and our precedents concerning the Ex Post Facto Clause. Article 38.07 is not, as the Court would have it, most accurately characterized as a "sufficiency of the evidence rule"; it is in its essence an evidentiary provision dictating the circumstances under which the jury may credit victim testimony in sexual offense prosecutions. The amended version of Article 38.07 does nothing more than accord to certain victims of sexual offenses full testimonial stature, giving them the same undiminished competency to testify that Texas extends to witnesses generally in the State's judicial proceedings. Our precedents make clear that such a witness competency rule validly may be applied to offenses committed before its enactment. I therefore dissent.

. . .

II

The Ex Post Facto Clause, this Court has said repeatedly, furthers two important purposes. First, it serves "to assure that legislative Acts give fair warning of their effect and permit individuals to rely on their meaning until explicitly changed." Second, it "restricts governmental power by restraining arbitrary and potentially vindictive legislation." The latter purpose has much to do with the separation of powers; like its textual and conceptual neighbor the Bill of Attainder Clause, the Ex Post Facto Clause aims to ensure that legislatures do not meddle with the judiciary's task of adjudicating guilt and innocence in individual cases.

The Court does not even attempt to justify its extension of the Clause in terms of these two fundamental purposes. That is understandable, for today's decision serves neither purpose. The first purpose (fair warning and reliance), vital as it is, cannot tenably be relied upon by Carmell.

He had ample notice that the conduct in which he engaged was illegal. He certainly cannot claim to have relied in any way on the preamendment version of Article 38.07: He tendered no reason to anticipate that K. M. would not report the assault within the outcry period, nor any cause to expect that corroborating evidence would not turn up sooner or later. Nor is the Clause's second purpose relevant here, for there is no indication that the Texas Legislature intended to single out this defendant or any class of defendants for vindictive or arbitrary treatment. Instead, the amendment of Article 38.07 simply brought the rules governing certain victim testimony in sexual offense prosecutions into conformity with Texas law governing witness testimony generally.

In sum, it is well settled (or was until today) that retroactive changes to rules concerning the admissibility of evidence and the competency of witnesses to testify cannot be ex post facto. Because Article 38.07 is in both function and purpose a rule of admissibility, *Thompson v. Missouri, Hopt, Beazell,* and *Collins* dictate that its retroactive application does not violate the Ex Post Facto Clause. That conclusion comports perfectly with the dual purposes that underlie the Clause: ensuring fair notice so that individuals can rely on the laws in force at the time they engage in conduct, and sustaining the separation of powers while preventing the passage of vindictive legislation. The Court today thus not only brings about an "undefined enlargement of the Ex Post Facto Clause," *Collins,* … that conflicts with established precedent, it also fails to advance the Clause's fundamental purposes.

STOGNER v. CALIFORNIA, 539 U.S. 607 (2003)

JUSTICE BREYER delivered the opinion of the Court.

California has brought a criminal prosecution after expiration of the time periods set forth in previously applicable statutes of limitations. California has done so under the authority of a new law that (1) permits resurrection of otherwise time-barred criminal prosecutions, and (2) was itself enacted *after* pre-existing limitations periods had expired. We conclude that the Constitution's *Ex Post Facto* Clause, Art. I, §10, cl. 1, bars application of this new law to the present case.

I

In 1993, California enacted a new criminal statute of limitations governing sex-related child abuse crimes. The new statute permits prosecution for those crimes where "[t]he limitation period specified in [prior statutes of limitations] has expired"--provided that (1) a victim has reported an allegation of abuse to the police, (2) "there is independent evidence that clearly and convincingly corroborates the victim's allegation," and (3) the prosecution is begun within one year of the victim's report. A related provision, added to the statute in 1996, makes clear that a prosecution satisfying these three conditions "shall revive any cause of action barred by [prior statutes of limitations]." The statute thus authorizes prosecution for criminal acts committed many years beforehand--and where the original limitations period has expired--as long as prosecution begins within a year of a victim's first complaint to the police.

In 1998, a California grand jury indicted Marion Stogner, the petitioner, charging him with sex-related child abuse committed decades earlier--between 1955 and 1973. Without the new statute allowing revival of the State's cause of action, California could not have prosecuted Stogner. The statute of limitations governing prosecutions at the time the crimes were allegedly committed had set forth a 3-year limitations period. And that period had run 22 years or more before the present prosecution was brought.

Stogner moved for the complaint's dismissal. He argued that the Federal Constitution's *Ex Post Facto* Clause, Art. I, §10, cl. 1, forbids revival of a previously time-barred prosecution. The trial court agreed that such a revival is unconstitutional. But the California Court of Appeal reversed, citing a recent, contrary decision by the California Supreme Court. Stogner then moved to dismiss his indictment, arguing that his prosecution is unconstitutional under both the *Ex Post Facto* Clause and the Due

Process Clause, Amdt. 14, §1. The trial court denied Stogner's motion, and the Court of Appeal upheld that denial. . . . We granted certiorari to consider Stogner's constitutional claims.

II

The law at issue here created a new criminal limitations period that extends the time in which prosecution is allowed. It authorized criminal prosecutions that the passage of time had previously barred. Moreover, it was enacted after prior limitations periods for Stogner's alleged offenses had expired. Do these features of the law, taken together, produce the kind of retroactivity that the Constitution forbids? We conclude that they do.

First, the new statute threatens the kinds of harm that, in this Court's view, the *Ex Post Facto* Clause seeks to avoid. Long ago the Court pointed out that the Clause protects liberty by preventing governments from enacting statutes with "manifestly *unjust and oppressive*" retroactive effects. *Calder* v. *Bull*, 3 Dall. 386, 391 (1798). Judge Learned Hand later wrote that extending a limitations period after the State has assured "a man that he has become safe from its pursuit ... seems to most of us unfair and dishonest." *Falter* v. *United State.* In such a case, the government has refused "to play by its own rules," *Carmell* v. *Texas.* It has deprived the defendant of the "fair warning," that might have led him to preserve exculpatory evidence. ... And a Constitution that permits such an extension, by allowing legislatures to pick and choose when to act retroactively, risks both "arbitrary and potentially vindictive legislation," and erosion of the separation of powers. ...

Second, the kind of statute at issue falls literally within the categorical descriptions of *ex post facto* laws set forth by Justice Chase more than 200 years ago in *Calder* v. *Bull* --a categorization that this Court has recognized as providing an authoritative account of the scope of the *Ex Post Facto* Clause. ...

In his alternative description, Chase traced these four categories back to Parliament's earlier abusive acts, as follows:

Category 1: "Sometimes they respected the crime, by declaring acts to be treason, which were not

treason, when committed."

Category 2: "[A]t other times they inflicted punishments, where the party was not, by law, liable to any punishment."

Category 3: "[I]n other cases, they inflicted greater punishment, than the law annexed to the offence."

Category 4: "[A]t other times, they violated the rules of evidence (to supply a deficiency of legal proof) by admitting one witness, when the existing law required two; by receiving evidence without oath; or the oath of the wife against the husband; or other testimony, which the courts of justice would not admit." 3 Dall., at 389.

The second category--including any "law that *aggravates a crime,* or makes it *greater* than it was, when committed," --describes California's statute as long as those words are understood as Justice Chase understood them--*i.e.,* as referring to a statute that "inflict[s] *punishments,* where the party was not, by *law,* liable to *any punishment,*" ... After (but not before) the original statute of limitations had expired, a party such as Stogner was not "liable to any punishment." California's new statute therefore "aggravated" Stogner's alleged crime, or made it "greater than it was, when committed," in the sense that, and to the extent that, it "inflicted punishment" for past criminal conduct that (when the new law was enacted) did not trigger any such liability. ...

So to understand the second category (as applying where a new law inflicts a punishment upon a person not then subject to that punishment, to any degree) explains why and how that category differs from both the first category (making criminal noncriminal behavior) and the third category (aggravating the punishment). And this understanding is consistent, in relevant part, with Chase's second category examples--examples specifically provided to illustrate Chase's *alternative* description of laws " 'inflict[ing] *punishments,* where the party was not, by *law,* liable to *any punishment.*' " ...

In finding that California's law falls within the literal terms of Justice Chase's second category, we do not deny that it may fall within another category as well. Justice Chase's fourth category, for example, includes any "law that alters the *legal* rules of *evidence*, and receives less, or different, testimony, than the law required at the time of the commission of the offence, *in order to convict the offender*." This Court has described that category as including laws that diminish "the quantum of evidence required to convict."...

Significantly, a statute of limitations reflects a legislative judgment that, after a certain time, no quantum of evidence is sufficient to convict. And that judgment typically rests, in large part, upon evidentiary concerns--for example, concern that the passage of time has eroded memories or made witnesses or other evidence unavailable. ...

Consequently, to resurrect a prosecution after the relevant statute of limitations has expired is to eliminate a currently existing conclusive presumption forbidding prosecution, and thereby to permit conviction on a quantum of evidence where that quantum, at the time the new law is enacted, would have been legally insufficient. And, in that sense, the new law would "violate" previous evidence-related legal rules by authorizing the courts to " 'receiv[e] evidence . . . which the courts of justice would not [previously have] admit[ted]' " as sufficient proof of a crime. ... Nonetheless, given Justice Chase's description of the second category, we need not explore the fourth category, or other categories, further.

In sum, California's law subjects an individual such as Stogner to prosecution long after the State has, in effect, granted an amnesty, telling him that he is "at liberty to return to his country ... and that from henceforth he may cease to preserve the proofs of his innocence," It retroactively withdraws a complete defense to prosecution after it has already attached, and it does so in a manner that allows the State to withdraw this defense at will and with respect to individuals already identified. "Unfair" seems to us a fair characterization.

IV

The statute before us is unfairly retroactive as applied to Stogner. A long line of judicial authority supports characterization of this law as *ex post facto.* For the reasons stated, we believe the law falls within Justice Chase's second category of *ex post facto* laws. We conclude that a law enacted after expiration of a previously applicable limitations period violates the *Ex Post Facto* Clause when it is applied to revive a previously time-barred prosecution.

THE VOID-FOR-VAGUENESS DOCTRINE

No specific constitutional provision bans overly vague laws. Instead, the Due Process Clauses of the Fifth and Fourteenth Amendments require clarity in criminal statutes. Due process requires that individuals receive notice of criminal conduct, and vaguely written laws result in individuals having to guess at whether their behavior is allowed or prohibited. The Court has repeatedly struck down laws that are so vague that a person of ordinary intelligence could not reasonably understand them or determine when they applied. The Court will also strike down laws that give excessive discretion to law enforcement officials to decide who can be arrested or prosecuted. When dealing with statutes that may be too vague, the Court will sometimes throw the statute a lifeline by upholding them if, through judicial interpretation, they can be construed with sufficient specificity. *See, e.g., Rose v. Locke*, 423 U.S. 48 (1975). Police, prosecutors, judges, and jurors must have a reasonably clear statement of what is prohibited behavior. The "definite standard" requirement ensures the uniform and nondiscriminatory enforcement of law.

The court presumes laws are constitutional. The burden of proving otherwise falls on the defendant. In the context of claiming void-for-vagueness, the defendant,

> [M]ust show that upon examining the statute, an individual of ordinary intelligence would not understand what he is required to do under the law. Thus, to escape responsibility . . . [the defendant] must prove that he could not reasonably understand that . . . [the law in question] prohibited the acts in which he is engaged. ... The party alleging that a statute is unconstitutional must prove this assertion beyond a reasonable doubt. *State v. Anderson*, 566 N.E. 2d 1224 (Ohio, 1991).

Void-for-vagueness cases have historically fallen into two categories—those dealing with obscenity laws and those dealing with loitering and vagrancy statutes. *State v. Metzger*, below, deals with whether a statute criminalizing immodest, indecent and filthy acts is too vague. *City of Chicago v. Morales* addresses whether a statute prohibiting criminal gang members from loitering on the streets is too vague (it also involves the First Amendment right to assemble discussed above).

STATE v. METZGER,
319 N.W. 2d 459 (Neb. 1982)

KRIVOSHA delivered the opinion of the court.

FACTS

Metzger lived in a garden-level apartment located in Lincoln, Nebraska. A large window in the apartment faces a parking lot which is situated on the north side of the apartment building. At about 7:45 a. m. on April 30, 1981, another resident of the apartment, while parking his automobile in a space directly in front of Metzger's apartment window, observed Metzger standing naked with his arms at his sides in his apartment window for a period of 5 seconds. The resident testified that he saw Metzger's body from his thighs on up.

The resident called the police department and two officers arrived at the apartment at about 8 a. m. The officers testified that they observed Metzger standing in front of the window eating a bowl of cereal. They testified that Metzger was standing within a foot of the window and his nude body, from the mid-thigh on up, was visible.

The pertinent portion of § 9.52.100 of the Lincoln Municipal Code, under which Metzger was charged, provides as follows:

> It shall be unlawful for any person within the City of Lincoln ... to commit any indecent, immodest or filthy act in the presence of any person, or in such a situation that persons passing might ordinarily see the same.

OPINION

…The…issue presented to us by this appeal is whether the ordinance, as drafted, is so vague as to be unconstitutional. We believe that it is. There is no argument that a violation of the municipal ordinance in question is a criminal act. Since the ordinance in question is criminal in nature, it is a fundamental requirement of due process of law that such criminal ordinance be reasonably clear and definite….

A criminal statute cannot rest upon an uncertain foundation. The crime and the elements constituting it must be so clearly expressed that the ordinary person can intelligently choose in advance what course it is lawful for him to pursue. Penal statutes prohibiting the doing of certain things and providing a punishment for their violation should not admit of such a double meaning that the citizen may act upon one conception of its requirements and the courts upon another. A statute which forbids the doing of an act in terms so vague that men of common intelligence must necessarily guess as to its meaning and differ as to its application violates the first essential elements of due process of law. It is not permissible to enact a law which in effect spreads an all-inclusive net for the feet of everybody upon the chance that, while the innocent will surely be entangled in its meshes, some wrongdoers may also be caught….

Several other jurisdictions which have viewed ordinances with the same general intent in mind have reached similar conclusions. In the case of *State v. Sanders*, 245 S.E.2d 397 (1978), the South Carolina Court of Appeals was presented with a statute making it a misdemeanor for members of the opposite sex to occupy the same bedroom at a hotel for "any immoral purpose." In finding the ordinance too vague and indefinite to comply with constitutional due process standards, the court said:

> A criminal statute or ordinance must be sufficiently definite to inform citizens of common intelligence of the particular acts which are forbidden. [The statute] fails to define with sufficient precision exactly what the term "any immoral purpose" may encompass. The word *immoral* is not equivalent to the word *illegal*; hence, enforcement of [the statute] may

involve legal acts which, nevertheless, are immoral in the view of many citizens. One must necessarily speculate, therefore, as to what acts are immoral. If the legislative intent of [the statute] is to proscribe illicit sexual intercourse the statute could have specifically so provided.

...The ordinance . . . makes it unlawful for anyone to commit any 'indecent, immodest or filthy act.' We know of no way in which the standards required of a criminal act can be met in those broad, general terms. . . . The dividing line between what is lawful and what is unlawful in terms of 'indecent,' 'immodest,' or 'filthy' is simply too broad to satisfy the constitutional requirements of due process. Both lawful and unlawful acts can be embraced within such broad definitions. That cannot be permitted. One

is not able to determine in advance what is lawful and what is unlawful.

We do not attempt . . . to determine whether Metzger's actions in a particular case might not be made unlawful, nor do we intend to encourage such behavior. Indeed, it may be possible that a governmental subdivision using sufficiently definite language could make such an act as committed by Metzger unlawful. We simply do not decide that question at this time because of our determination that the ordinance in question is so vague as to be unconstitutional.

We therefore believe. . . [that the ordinance] . . . must be declared invalid. Because the ordinance is therefore declared invalid, the conviction cannot stand.

CITY OF CHICAGO v. MORALES et al., 527 U.S. 41(1999)

FACTS
In 1992, the Chicago City Council enacted the Gang Congregation Ordinance, which prohibits "criminal street gang members" from "loitering" with one another or with other persons in any public place. The question presented is whether the Supreme Court of Illinois correctly held that the ordinance violates the Due Process Clause of the Fourteenth Amendment to the Federal Constitution.

I

Before the ordinance was adopted, the city council's Committee on Police and Fire conducted hearings to explore the problems created by the city's street gangs, and more particularly, the consequences of public loitering by gang members. Witnesses included residents of the neighborhoods where gang members are most active, as well as some of the aldermen who represent those areas. Based on that evidence, the council made a series of findings that are included in the text of the ordinance and explain the reasons for its enactment.

The council found that a continuing increase in criminal street gang activity was largely responsible for the city's rising murder rate, as well as an escalation of violent and drug related crimes. It noted that in many neighborhoods throughout the city, "the burgeoning presence of street gang members in public places has

intimidated many law abiding citizens." Furthermore, the council stated that gang members "establish control over identifiable areas ... by loitering in those areas and intimidating others from entering those areas; and . . . [m]embers of criminal street gangs avoid arrest by committing no offense punishable under existing laws when they know the police are present . . . ." It further found that "loitering in public places by criminal street gang members creates a justifiable fear for the safety of persons and property in the area" and that "[a]ggressive action is necessary to preserve the city's streets and other public places so that the public may use such places without fear." Moreover, the council concluded that the city "has an interest in discouraging all persons from loitering in public places with criminal gang members."

The ordinance creates a criminal offense punishable by a fine of up to $500, imprisonment for not more than six months, and a requirement to perform up to 120 hours of community service. Commission of the offense involves four predicates. First, the police officer must reasonably believe that at least one of the two or more persons present in a "public place" is a "criminal street gang membe[r]." Second, the persons must be "loitering," which the ordinance defines as "remain[ing] in any one place with no apparent purpose." Third, the officer must then order "all" of the persons to disperse and remove themselves "from the area." Fourth, a person must disobey the officer's order. If any person, whether a gang member or not, disobeys the officer's order, that person is guilty of violating the ordinance.

Two months after the ordinance was adopted, the Chicago Police Department promulgated General Order 92-4 to provide guidelines to govern its enforcement. That order purported to establish limitations on the enforcement discretion of police officers "to ensure that the anti-gang loitering ordinance is not enforced in an arbitrary or discriminatory way." The limitations confine the authority to arrest gang members who violate the ordinance to sworn "members of the Gang Crime Section" and certain other designated officers, and establish detailed criteria for defining street gangs and membership in such gangs. In addition, the order directs district commanders to "designate areas in which the presence of gang members has a demonstrable effect on the activities of law abiding persons in the surrounding community," and provides that the ordinance "will be enforced only within the designated areas. The city, however, does not release the locations of these "designated areas" to the public.

II

During the three years of its enforcement, the police issued over 89,000 dispersal orders and arrested over 42,000 people for violating the ordinance. In the ensuing enforcement proceedings, two trial judges upheld the constitutionality of the ordinance, but eleven others ruled that it was invalid. In respondent Youkhana's case, the trial judge held that the "ordinance fails to notify individuals what conduct is prohibited, and it encourages arbitrary and capricious enforcement by police."

The Illinois Appellate Court affirmed the trial court's ruling . . . persuaded that the ordinance impaired the freedom of assembly of non-gang members in violation of the First Amendment to the Federal Constitution and Article I of the Illinois Constitution, that it was unconstitutionally vague, that it improperly criminalized status rather than conduct, and that it jeopardized rights guaranteed under the Fourth Amendment.

The Illinois Supreme Court affirmed. It held "that

the gang loitering ordinance violates due process of law in that it is impermissibly vague on its face and an arbitrary restriction on personal liberties." The court did not reach the contentions that the ordinance "creates a status offense, permits arrests without probable cause or is overbroad."

In support of its vagueness holding, the court pointed out that the definition of "loitering" in the ordinance drew no distinction between innocent conduct and conduct calculated to cause harm. "Moreover, the definition of `loiter' provided by the ordinance does not assist in clearly articulating the proscriptions of the ordinance." Furthermore, it concluded that the ordinance was "not reasonably susceptible to a limiting construction which would affirm its validity."

We granted certiorari and now affirm. Like the Illinois Supreme Court, we conclude that the ordinance enacted by the city of Chicago is unconstitutionally vague.

OPINION (Summaries)
JUSTICE STEVENS concluded that the ordinance's broad sweep violates the requirement that a legislature establish minimal guidelines to govern law enforcement. *Kolender v. Lawson.*

The ordinance encompasses a great deal of harmless behavior: In any public place in Chicago, persons in the company of a gang member "shall" be ordered to disperse if their purpose is not apparent to an officer. Moreover, the Illinois Supreme Court interprets the ordinance's loitering definition--"to remain in any one place with no apparent purpose"--as giving officers absolute discretion to determine what activities constitute loitering. This Court has no authority to construe the language of a state statute more narrowly than the State's highest court. The three features of the ordinance that, the city argues, limit the officer's discretion-- (1) it does not permit issuance of a dispersal order to anyone who is moving along or who has an apparent purpose; (2) it does not permit an arrest if individuals obey a dispersal order; and (3) no order can issue unless the officer reasonably believes that one of the loiterers is a gang member--are insufficient. Finally, the Illinois Supreme Court is correct that General Order 92-4 is not a sufficient limitation on police discretion.

JUSTICE STEVENS, joined by JUSTICE SOUTER and JUSTICE GINSBURG, concluded:
1. It was not improper for the state courts to conclude that the ordinance, which covers a significant amount of activity in addition to the intimidating conduct that is its factual predicate, is invalid on its face. An enactment may be attacked on its face as impermissibly vague if, inter alia, it fails to establish standards for the police and public that are sufficient to guard against the arbitrary deprivation of liberty. The freedom to loiter for innocent purposes is part of such "liberty." The ordinance's vagueness makes a facial challenge appropriate. This is not an enactment that simply regulates business behavior and contains a scienter requirement. It is a criminal law that contains no mens rea requirement, and infringes on constitutionally protected rights.

2. Because the ordinance fails to give the ordinary citizen adequate notice of what is forbidden and what is permitted, it is impermissibly vague. See, e.g., *Coates v. Cincinnati*. The term "loiter" may have a common and accepted meaning, but the ordinance's definition of that term--"to remain in any one place with no apparent purpose"--does not. It is difficult to imagine how any Chicagoan standing in a public place with a group of people would know if he or she had an "apparent purpose." This vagueness about what loitering is covered and what is not dooms the ordinance. The city's principal response to the adequate notice concern--that loiterers are not subject to criminal sanction until after they have disobeyed a dispersal order--is unpersuasive for at least two reasons. First, the fair notice requirement's purpose is to enable the ordinary citizen to conform his or her conduct to the law.
See *Lanzetta v. New Jersey*. A dispersal order, which is issued only after prohibited conduct has occurred, cannot retroactively provide adequate notice of the boundary between the permissible and the impermissible applications of the ordinance. Second, the dispersal order's terms compound the inadequacy of the notice afforded by the ordinance, which vaguely requires that the officer "order all such persons to disperse and remove themselves from the area," and thereby raises a host of questions as to the duration and distinguishing features of the loiterers'

separation.

JUSTICE O'CONNOR, joined by JUSTICE BREYER, concluded that, as construed by the Illinois Supreme Court, the Chicago ordinance is unconstitutionally vague because it lacks sufficient minimal standards to guide law enforcement officers; in particular, it fails to provide any standard by which police can judge whether an individual has an "apparent purpose." This vagueness alone provides a sufficient ground for affirming the judgment below, and there is no need to consider the other issues briefed by the parties and addressed by the plurality. It is important to courts and legislatures alike to characterize more clearly the narrow scope of the Court's holding. Chicago still has reasonable alternatives to combat the very real threat posed by gang intimidation and violence, including, e.g., adoption of laws that directly prohibit the congregation of gang members to intimidate residents, or the enforcement of existing laws with that effect. Moreover, the ordinance could have been construed more narrowly to avoid the vagueness problem, by, e.g., adopting limitations that restrict the ordinance's criminal penalties to gang members or interpreting the term "apparent purpose" narrowly and in light of the Chicago City Council's findings. This Court, however, cannot impose a limiting construction that a state supreme court has declined to adopt.
See, e.g., *Kolender v. Lawson*. The Illinois Supreme Court misapplied this Court's precedents, particularly *Papachristou v. Jacksonville*, to the extent it read them as requiring it to hold the ordinance vague in all of its applications.

JUSTICE KENNEDY concluded that, as interpreted by the Illinois Supreme Court, the Chicago ordinance unconstitutionally reaches a broad range of innocent conduct, and, therefore, is not necessarily saved by the requirement that the citizen disobey a dispersal order before there is a violation. Although it can be assumed that disobeying some police commands will subject a citizen to prosecution whether or not the citizen knows why the order is given, it does not follow that any unexplained police order must be obeyed without notice of its lawfulness. The predicate of a dispersal order is not sufficient to eliminate doubts regarding the adequacy of notice under this ordinance. A citizen, while engaging in a wide array of innocent conduct, is not likely to know when he may be subject to such an order based on the officer's own knowledge of the identity or affiliations of other persons with whom the citizen is congregating; nor may the citizen be able to assess what an officer might conceive to be the citizen's lack of an apparent purpose.

JUSTICE BREYER concluded that the ordinance violates the Constitution because it delegates too much discretion to the police, and it is not saved by its limitations requiring that the police reasonably believe that the person ordered to disperse (or someone accompanying him) is a gang member, and that he remain in the public place "with no apparent purpose." Nor does it violate this Court's usual rules governing facial challenges to forbid the city to apply the unconstitutional ordinance in this case. There is no way to distinguish in the ordinance's terms between one application of unlimited police discretion and another. It is unconstitutional, not because a policeman applied his discretion wisely or poorly in a particular case, but rather because the policeman enjoys too much discretion in every case. And if every application of the ordinance represents an exercise of unlimited discretion, then the ordinance is invalid in all its applications. See *Lanzetta v. New Jersey.* Contrary to Justice Scalia 's suggestion, the ordinance does not escape facial invalidation simply because it may provide fair warning to some individual defendants that it prohibits the conduct in which they are engaged. This ordinance is unconstitutional, not because it provides insufficient notice, but because it does not provide sufficient minimal standards to guide the police. See Coates v. Cincinnati.

JUSTICE SCALIA, **dissenting**.
The citizens of Chicago were once free to drive about the city at whatever speed they wished. At some point Chicagoans (or perhaps Illinoisans) decided this would not do, and imposed prophylactic speed limits designed to assure safe operation by the average (or perhaps even subaverage) driver with the average (or perhaps even subaverage) vehicle. This infringed upon the "freedom" of all citizens, but was not unconstitutional.

Similarly, the citizens of Chicago were once free to stand around and gawk at the scene of an accident. At some point Chicagoans discovered that this obstructed traffic and caused more accidents. They did not make the practice unlawful, but they did authorize police officers to order the crowd to disperse, and imposed penalties for refusal to obey such an order. Again, this prophylactic measure infringed upon the "freedom" of all citizens, but was not unconstitutional.

Until the ordinance that is before us today was adopted, the citizens of Chicago were free to stand about in public places with no apparent purpose--to engage, that is, in conduct that appeared to be loitering. In recent years, however, the city has been afflicted with criminal street gangs. As reflected in the record before us, these gangs congregated in public places to deal in drugs, and to terrorize the neighborhoods by demonstrating control over their "turf." Many residents of the inner city felt that they were prisoners in their own homes. Once again, Chicagoans decided that to eliminate the problem it was worth restricting some of the freedom that they once enjoyed. The means they took was similar to the second, and more mild, example given above rather than the first: Loitering was not made unlawful, but when a group of people occupied a public place without an apparent purpose and in the company of a known gang member, police officers were authorized to order them to disperse, and the failure to obey such an order was made unlawful. See Chicago Municipal Code §8-4-015 (1992). The minor limitation upon the free state of nature that this prophylactic arrangement imposed upon all Chicagoans seemed to them (and it seems to me) a small price to pay for liberation of their streets.

The majority today invalidates this perfectly reasonable measure by ignoring our rules governing facial challenges, by elevating loitering to a constitutionally guaranteed right, and by discerning vagueness where, according to our usual standards, none exists.
. . .
The fact is that the present ordinance is entirely clear in its application, cannot be violated except with full knowledge and intent, and vests no more discretion in the police than innumerable other measures authorizing police orders to preserve the public peace and safety. As suggested by their tortured analyses, and by

their suggested solutions that bear no relation to the identified constitutional problem, the majority's real quarrel with the Chicago Ordinance is simply that it permits (or indeed requires) too much harmless conduct by innocent citizens to be proscribed. . . .

But in our democratic system, how much harmless conduct to proscribe is not a judgment to be made by the courts. So long as constitutionally guaranteed rights are not affected, and so long as the proscription has a rational basis, all sorts of perfectly harmless activity by millions of perfectly innocent people can be forbidden--riding a motorcycle without a safety helmet, for example, starting a campfire in a national forest, or selling a safe and effective drug not yet approved by the FDA. All of these acts are entirely innocent and harmless in themselves, but because of the risk of harm that they entail, the freedom to engage in them has been abridged. The citizens of Chicago have decided that depriving themselves of the freedom to "hang out" with a gang member is necessary to eliminate pervasive gang crime and intimidation--and that the elimination of the one is worth the deprivation of the other. This Court has no business second-guessing either the degree of necessity or the fairness of the trade. I dissent from the judgment of the Court.

Other Cases—Void for Vagueness

Johnson v. United States, 135 S.Ct. 2551 (2015)
Defendant was convicted of being a felon in possession of a firearm. Prosecution sought to increase his sentence under the act based on prior firearm possession convictions. Court concluded that the residual clause of the Career Armed Criminal Act, 18 U.S. C. 924 was so unclear and uncertain that it was unconstitutionally vague. Court found that the clause failed to give any guidance on what degree of potential risk was enough to make the act applicable in a given case.

Coates v. Cincinnati, 402 U.S. 611 (1971)
Defendant was convicted of violating an ordinance that made it illegal for three or more people gathered on a sidewalk to "annoy" passersby. Court held that because what annoys one person may not annoy the other, "the ordinance was vague . . . in the sense that no conduct is specified at all. "

Papachristou v. City of Jacksonville, 405 U.S. 156 (1972)
Defendant was convicted of violating an ordinance that made being a "vagrant" a crime and defining vagrants as "rogues and vagabonds" "disosolute persons," or "common night walkers." In this landmark decision, the Court struck down a Jacksonville, Florida ordinance that prohibited various forms of vagrancy, including loitering and "prowling by auto." Court held the ordinance was unconstitutional because it did not give fair notice of prohibited conduct. Justice Douglas objected to the unfettered discretion the ordinance placed in the hands of the police, saying it allowed for "arbitrary and discriminatory enforcement of the law."

Kolender v. Lawson, 461 U.S. 352 (1983)
The Court struck down a statute criminalizing any person who "loiters or wanders upon the streets or from place to place without apparent reason or business and who refuses to identify himself and to account for his presence when requested to do so."

"As presently drafted and as construed by the state courts, [the statute] contains no standard for determining what a suspect has to do in order to satisfy the requirement to provide a "credible and reliable" identification. As such, the statute vests virtually complete discretion in the hands of police to determine whether the suspect has satisfied the statute and must be permitted to go on his way in the absence of probable cause to arrest. An individual, whom police may think is suspicious, but do not have probable cause to believe has committed a crime, is entitled to walk the public streets 'only at the whim of any police officer' who happens to stop that individual under [the statute]."

See also, **Warren v. State**, 572 So.2d 1376 (Fl. S. Ct., 1991) (Statute making it a crime to keep a "house of ill fame" was unconstitutionally vague); **State v. Lara**, 853 P.2d 1168 (Kan. Ct. App., 1993) (Statute making criminal "excessive and unusual" motor vehicle noises held not void for vagueness); **State v. Bohannon**, 814 P.2d 694 (Wash. Ct. App, 1991)(Statute making it a crime for causing a minor to engage in "sexually explicit conduct" held not void for vagueness); **United States v. White**, 882 F.2d 250, 252 (7th Circuit, 1989)(The "vagueness doctrine" is "designed more to limit the discretion of police and prosecutors than to ensure that statutes are intelligible to persons pondering criminal activity.")

RIGHT TO BEAR ARMS

The poorly-drafted Second Amendment to the U.S. Constitution states, "A well regulated Militia, being necessary to the security of a free state, the right of the people to keep and bear arms shall not be infringed." There are thousands of local, state, and federal prohibitions against the sale, possession, and use of certain firearms and ammunition. Arguably, these laws seem to conflict with the Second Amendment's "right to keep and bear arms." Thus, Courts and commentators have been left debating its reach and application to modern circumstances.

In *United States v. Miller,* 307 U.S. 174 (1939), the Court upheld a federal law criminalizing the interstate shipment of sawed-off shotguns. The Court held the phrase "to keep and bear arms shall not be infringed" needed to be interpreted in context with the phrase "a well-regulated militia." Since possession of sawed-off shotguns had no reasonable relationship to serving the militia, the statute (regulating shotguns) was not unconstitutional. In 1980 the Court reaffirmed this reasoning in *Lewis v. United States*, 445 U.S. 55, 58 (1980) stating, "The Second Amendment guarantees no right to keep and bear a firearm that does not have some reasonable relationship to the preservation of efficiency of a well-regulated militia."

In *District of Columbia v. Heller*, 554 U.S. 570 (2008), however, the Court declared the right to keep and bear arms was a personal right tied to a natural right of self-defense that had nothing to do with being part of a militia. Washington, D.C. had enacted an ordinance that created a complete ban on handguns and required that any weapons kept at home must be unloaded and non-functional. Heller, a special police officer in D.C., was authorized to carry a handgun at his job at the Federal Judicial Center. He applied to register his personal gun, but the government refused. He sued to enjoin the District of Columbia from enforcing the ordinance, arguing that he (and others) had a constitutional right to possess a weapon in his home for his personal safety. The Court did not define the scope of the right to keep and bear arms, nor did it indicate whether the Second Amendment was applicable to the states through the Fourteenth Amendment, but it did hold that the D.C. ordinance was too restrictive, nevertheless noting that the right to bear arms was subject to reasonable government regulations.

Several suits were filed after *Heller* was decided. In Chicago, gun owners challenged Chicago ordinances which were virtually identical to the ordinance in *Heller*. They asked the Court to hold that the Second Amendment applied to the states through the Fourteenth Amendment. In a five-four decision, the U.S. Supreme Court held that an individual's right to keep and bear arms is incorporated and applicable to the states through the 14th Amendment's Due Process Clause. Writing for the majority in *McDonald v. City of Chicago*, Justice Alito observed: "It is clear that the Framers and ratifiers of the Fourteenth Amendment counted the right to keep and bear arms among those fundamental rights necessary to our system of ordered liberty. ... The Fourteenth Amendment makes the Second Amendment right to keep and bear arms fully applicable to the States."

The Court majority did not ultimately rule on the constitutionality of this gun ban; however, the Court made it clear that such restrictive bans are unconstitutional. The *McDonald* Court reiterated what it said in Heller -- the Second Amendment only protects a right to possess a firearm in the home for lawful uses such as self-defense. It stressed that some firearm regulation is constitutionally permissible and the Second Amendment right to possess firearms is not unlimited. The Second Amendment does not guarantee a right to possess any firearm, anywhere, and for any purpose. The dissent argued that the right to own guns was not "fundamental" and therefore states and localities should be free to regulate, or even ban, them. Dissenting justices maintained that *Heller* was incorrectly decided, and--even if correct--they would not have extended its applicability to states.

Other Cases—Right to Bear Arms

United States v. Miller, 307 U.S. 174 (1939)
Federal law prohibited shipping sawed-off shotguns interstate. The Court upheld the constitutionality of the federal law holding that the Second Amendment protections are limited to gun ownership that has

some reasonable relationship to the preservation or efficiency of a well-regulated militia.

Moore v. Madigan, 708 F.3d 901 (2013) (7th Cir).
Court of Appeals found unconstitutional a flat ban by Illinois statute on carrying a loaded firearm within accessible reach outside the home. The law allowed exceptions by police officers, security personnel, hunters and members of target shooting clubs. The Court, found that although the need for self-defense noted in *Heller* and *McDonald* was most acute inside a home, this did not mean that it was not acute outside the home.

Young v. State, 896 F.3d 1044 (9th Cir. 2018), reh'g en banc granted, 915 F.3d 681 (9th Cir. 2019)
Ninth Circuit Court of Appeals struck down Hawaii's "place to keep" statutes which required that gun owners keep their firearms at the place of business, residence, or sojourn. Individuals could petition chief of police for license for concealed carry based on reason to fear injury to person or property and could obtain open license carry permit based on urgency or need to protect. 2-1 majority found that under the statute, law-abiding citizens in Hawaii were foreclosed from exercising the core Second Amendment right to bear arms in self-defense.

Gun Owners of America v. Barr, ___ U.S. ___ (March 2019)
In March 2019, the Supreme Court refused to block a federal ban on bumpstocks.

> "The court's action, in a one-sentence order, means that the regulation will remain in force while challenges to it move forward in the courts. …
>
> The case concerns executive power, not the Second Amendment. The lead plaintiff, Gun Owners of America, which describes itself as "the 'no compromise' gun lobby," argued that the administration had exceeded its authority by banning bump stocks under federal laws that largely ban machine guns." See, https://www.nytimes.com/2019/03/28/us/politics/supreme-court-bump-stocks.html

THE RIGHT TO PRIVACY

The Constitution also limits government's ability to pass laws that violate a person's right to privacy. If you were to scour the Constitution you would not find the words "right to privacy," but the Court has held that the right to privacy is inherent in several of the Amendments and thus falls in the "penumbra" of the Constitution. Having the right to privacy has been equated to being free from governmental intrusion over certain areas of one's life.

The right to privacy is a fundamental right. As such, courts employ strict scrutiny over statutes that would limit a person's right to be free from governmental intrusion in a private matter. Even employing strict scrutiny, sometimes the government can enact laws (such as laws that criminalize the possession of child pornography) which pass constitutional muster. The test of whether a statute passes a strict scrutiny exam is whether the state can show a compelling state interest in regulating the behavior, and show there is no more suitable means of control. The state obviously has a compelling interest in protecting children from being victimized by the pornography industry. (And yet, as seen in the next chapter, Congress has had difficulty crafting statutes that address child pornography that are not too broad and do not violate the First Amendment.

LAWRENCE v. TEXAS,
539 U.S. 558 (2003)

Justice Kennedy delivered the opinion of the Court.

Liberty protects the person from unwarranted government intrusions into a dwelling or other private places. In our tradition the State is not omnipresent in the home. And there are other spheres of our lives and existence, outside the home, where the State should not be a dominant presence. Freedom extends beyond spatial bounds. Liberty presumes an autonomy of self that includes freedom of thought, belief, expression, and certain intimate conduct. The instant case involves liberty of the person both in its spatial and more transcendent dimensions.

I

The question before the Court is the validity of a

Texas statute making it a crime for two persons of the same sex to engage in certain intimate sexual conduct.

In Houston, Texas, officers of the Harris County Police Department were dispatched to a private residence in response to a reported weapons disturbance. They entered an apartment where one of the petitioners, John Geddes Lawrence, resided. The right of the police to enter does not seem to have been questioned. The officers observed Lawrence and another man, Tyron Garner, engaging in a sexual act. The two petitioners were arrested, held in custody overnight, and charged and convicted before a Justice of the Peace.

The complaints described their crime as "deviate sexual intercourse, namely anal sex, with a member of the same sex (man)." The applicable state law is Tex. Penal Code Ann. §21.06(a) (2003). It provides: "A person commits an offense if he engages in deviate sexual intercourse with another individual of the same sex." The statute defines "[d]eviate sexual intercourse" as follows:
   "(A) any contact between any part of the genitals of one person and the mouth or anus of another person; or
   "(B) the penetration of the genitals or the anus of another person with an object."
   §21.01(1).

The petitioners exercised their right to a trial *de novo* in Harris County Criminal Court. They challenged the statute as a violation of the Equal Protection Clause of the Fourteenth Amendment and of a like provision of the Texas Constitution. Those contentions were rejected. The petitioners, having entered a plea of *nolo contendere*, were each fined $200 and assessed court costs of $141.25.

The Court of Appeals for the Texas Fourteenth District considered the petitioners' federal constitutional arguments under both the Equal Protection and Due Process Clauses of the Fourteenth Amendment. After hearing the case en banc the court, in a divided opinion, rejected the constitutional arguments and affirmed the convictions. The majority opinion indicates that the Court of Appeals considered our decision in *Bowers* v. *Hardwick*, 478 U.S. 186 (1986), to be controlling on the federal due process aspect of the case. *Bowers* then being

authoritative, this was proper.

We granted certiorari to consider three questions:
   "1. Whether Petitioners' criminal convictions under the Texas "Homosexual Conduct" law–which criminalizes sexual intimacy by same-sex couples, but not identical behavior by different-sex couples–violate the Fourteenth Amendment guarantee of equal protection of laws?
   "2. Whether Petitioners' criminal convictions for adult consensual sexual intimacy in the home violate their vital interests in liberty and privacy protected by the Due Process Clause of the Fourteenth Amendment?
   "3. Whether *Bowers* v. *Hardwick* … should be overruled?"

The petitioners were adults at the time of the alleged offense. Their conduct was in private and consensual.

II

We conclude the case should be resolved by determining whether the petitioners were free as adults to engage in the private conduct in the exercise of their liberty under the Due Process Clause of Fourteenth Amendment to the Constitution. For this inquiry we deem it necessary to reconsider the Court's holding in *Bowers*.

There are broad statements of the substantive reach of liberty under the Due Process Clause, . . . but the most pertinent beginning point is our decision in *Griswold* v. *Connecticut*, 381 U.S. 479 (1965).

In *Griswold* the Court invalidated a state law prohibiting the use of drugs or devices of contraception and counseling or aiding and abetting the use of contraceptives. The Court described the protected interest as a right to privacy and placed emphasis on the marriage relation and the protected space of the marital bedroom. *Id.*, at 485.

After *Griswold* it was established that the right to make certain decisions regarding sexual conduct extends beyond the marital relationship. In *Eisenstadt* v. *Baird*, 405 U.S. 438 (1972), the Court invalidated a law prohibiting the distribution of contraceptives to unmarried persons. The case was decided under the Equal Protection Clause, but with respect to unmarried persons, the Court went on to state the fundamental proposition that the law impaired the exercise of their personal rights. It … [stated]:

> "It is true that in *Griswold* the right of privacy in question inhered in the marital relationship… . If the right of privacy means anything, it is the right of the *individual*, married or single, to be free from unwarranted governmental intrusion into matters so fundamentally affecting a person as the decision whether to bear or beget a child." *Id.,* at 453.

Roe v. Wade . . . recognized the right of a woman to make certain fundamental decisions affecting her destiny and confirmed once more that the protection of liberty under the Due Process Clause has a substantive dimension of fundamental significance in defining the rights of the person.

In *Carey* v. *Population Services Int'l.* (1977), the Court confronted a New York law forbidding sale or distribution of contraceptive devices to persons under 16 years of age. Although there was no single opinion for the Court, the law was invalidated. Both *Eisenstadt* and *Carey*, as well as the holding and rationale in *Roe*, confirmed that the reasoning of *Griswold* could not be confined to the protection of rights of married adults. This was the state of the law with respect to some of the most relevant cases when the Court considered *Bowers* v. *Hardwick*.

The facts in *Bowers* had some similarities to the instant case. A police officer, whose right to enter seems not to have been in question, observed Hardwick, in his own bedroom, engaging in intimate sexual conduct with another adult male. The conduct was in violation of a Georgia statute making it a criminal offense to engage in sodomy. One difference between the two cases is that the Georgia statute prohibited the conduct whether or not the participants were of the same sex, while the Texas statute, as we have seen, applies only to participants of the same sex. Hardwick was not prosecuted, but he brought an action in federal court to declare the state statute invalid. He alleged he was a practicing homosexual and that the criminal prohibition violated rights guaranteed to him by the Constitution. The Court . . . sustained the Georgia law.

The Court began its substantive discussion in *Bowers* as follows: "The issue presented is whether the Federal Constitution confers a fundamental right upon homosexuals to engage in sodomy and hence invalidates the laws of the many States that still make such conduct illegal and have done so for a very long time." *Id.,* at 190. That statement, we now conclude, discloses the Court's own failure to appreciate the extent of the liberty at stake. To say that the issue in *Bowers* was simply the right to engage in certain sexual conduct demeans the claim the individual put forward, just as it would demean a married couple were it to be said marriage is simply about the right to have sexual intercourse. The laws involved in *Bowers* and here are, to be sure, statutes that purport to do no more than prohibit a particular sexual act. Their penalties and purposes, though, have more far-reaching consequences, touching upon the most private human conduct, sexual behavior, and in the most private of places, the home. The statutes do seek to control a personal relationship that, whether or not entitled to formal recognition in the law, is within the liberty of persons to choose without being punished as criminals.

This, as a general rule, should counsel against attempts by the State, or a court, to define the meaning of the relationship or to set its boundaries absent injury to a person or abuse of an institution the law protects. It suffices for us to acknowledge that adults may choose to enter upon this relationship in the confines of their homes and their own private lives and still retain their dignity as free persons. When sexuality finds overt expression in intimate conduct with another person, the conduct can be but one element in a personal bond that is more enduring. The liberty protected by the Constitution allows homosexual persons the right to make this choice.

[The Court discusses the history of sodomy laws as set forth in *Bowers*]

Laws prohibiting sodomy do not seem to have been enforced against consenting adults acting in private. A substantial number of sodomy prosecutions and convictions for which there are surviving records were for predatory acts against those who could not or did not consent, as in the case of a minor or the victim of an assault. As to these, one purpose for the prohibitions was to ensure there would be no lack of coverage if a predator committed a sexual assault that did not constitute rape as defined by the criminal law.

The policy of punishing consenting adults for private acts was not much discussed in the early legal literature. We can infer that one reason for this was the very private nature of the conduct. Despite the absence of prosecutions, there may have been periods in which there was public criticism of homosexuals as such and an insistence that the criminal laws be enforced to discourage their practices. But far from possessing "ancient roots," *Bowers*, 478 U.S., at 192, American laws targeting same-sex couples did not develop until the last third of the 20th century.

In summary, the historical grounds relied upon in *Bowers* are more complex than the majority opinion and the concurring opinion by Chief Justice Burger indicate. Their historical premises are not without doubt and, at the very least, are overstated.

It must be acknowledged, of course, that the Court in *Bowers* was making the broader point that for centuries there have been powerful voices to condemn homosexual conduct as immoral. The condemnation has been shaped by religious beliefs, conceptions of right and acceptable behavior, and respect for the traditional family. For many persons these are not trivial concerns but profound and deep convictions accepted as ethical and moral principles to which they aspire and which thus determine the course of their lives. These considerations do not answer the question before us, however. The issue is whether the majority may use the power of the State to enforce these views on the whole society through operation of the criminal law. "Our obligation is to define the liberty of all, not to mandate our own moral code." *Planned Parenthood of Southeastern Pa.* v. *Casey*, 505 U.S. 833, 850 (1992).

… In all events we think that our laws and traditions in the past half century are of most relevance here. These references show an emerging awareness that liberty gives substantial protection to adult persons in deciding how to conduct their private lives in matters pertaining to sex.

This emerging recognition should have been apparent when *Bowers* was decided. In 1955 the American Law Institute promulgated the Model Penal Code and made clear that it did not recommend or provide for "criminal penalties for consensual sexual relations conducted in private." ALI, Model Penal Code §213.2, Comment 2, p. 372 (1980). It justified its decision on three grounds: (1) The prohibitions undermined respect for the law by penalizing conduct many people engaged in; (2) the statutes regulated private conduct not harmful to others; and (3) the laws were arbitrarily enforced and thus invited the danger of blackmail. ALI, Model Penal Code, Commentary 277–280 (Tent. Draft No. 4, 1955

…

The doctrine of *stare decisis* is essential to the respect accorded to the judgments of the Court and to the stability of the law. It is not, however, an inexorable command. *Payne* v. *Tennessee*, 501 U.S. 808, 828 (1991) ("*Stare decisis* is not an inexorable command; rather, it 'is a principle of policy and not a mechanical formula of adherence to the latest decision' ") (quoting *Helvering* v. *Hallock*, 309 U.S. 106, 119 (1940))). …

The rationale of *Bowers* does not withstand careful analysis. In his dissenting opinion in *Bowers* Justice Stevens came to these conclusions:

"Our prior cases make two propositions abundantly clear. First, the fact that the governing majority in a State has traditionally viewed a particular practice as immoral is not a sufficient reason for upholding a law prohibiting the practice; neither history nor tradition could save a law prohibiting miscegenation from constitutional attack. Second, individual decisions by married persons, concerning the intimacies of their physical relationship, even when not intended to produce offspring, are a form of "liberty" protected by the Due Process Clause of the Fourteenth Amendment. Moreover, this protection extends to intimate choices by unmarried as well as married persons."
478 U.S., at 216 (footnotes and citations

omitted).

Justice Stevens' analysis, in our view, should have been controlling in *Bowers* and should control here.

Bowers was not correct when it was decided, and it is not correct today. It ought not to remain binding precedent. *Bowers* v. *Hardwick* should be and now is overruled.

The present case does not involve minors. It does not involve persons who might be injured or coerced or who are situated in relationships where consent might not easily be refused. It does not involve public conduct or prostitution. It does not involve whether the government must give formal recognition to any relationship that homosexual persons seek to enter. The case does involve two adults who, with full and mutual consent from each other, engaged in sexual practices common to a homosexual lifestyle. The petitioners are entitled to respect for their private lives. The State cannot demean their existence or control their destiny by making their private sexual conduct a crime. Their right to liberty under the Due Process Clause gives them the full right to engage in their conduct without intervention of the government. "It is a promise of the Constitution that there is a realm of personal liberty which the government may not enter." *Casey, supra*, at 847. The Texas statute furthers no legitimate state interest which can justify its intrusion into the personal and private life of the individual.

. . .

[The Court reversed the judgement of the Court of Appeals of Texas]

Other Cases—Right to Privacy

Stanley v. Georgia, 384 U.S. 557 (1969).
The court found that individuals have the right to privacy in possessing pornography depicting adult subjects.

Griswold v. Connecticut, 381 U.S. 479 (1965).
First case to recognize a constitutional right to privacy. The Court, in that case, struck down a statute that punished using or assisting someone to use birth control. Physicians had been found guilty and ordered to pay a $100.00 fine for providing counseling and contraceptives to married people. Court noted that the Ninth Amendment means that rights not spelled out in the in the Constitution (enumerated rights), nevertheless exist. The Court held that a married couple's use of contraceptives was protected by the constitutional right to privacy.

In re Quinlan, 355 A.2d 647 (N.J. 1976).
The Court upheld, as a matter of constitutionally protected privacy, the right of family members of a comatose woman to remove extraordinary means of life support

Richmond Newspapers, Inc. v. Virginia, 448 U.S. 555 (1980).
Court held that "certain unarticulated rights . . . [including the right to privacy] . . . are implicit in the enumerated guarantees."

Satz v. Perlmutter, 379 So.2d 359 (Fla.1980).
The Court found that an adult with a terminal illness had a protected right of privacy in the decision to refuse medical treatment that would unnaturally prolong life.

Gilbert v. State, 487 So. 2d 1185 (Fla. App. 1986).
The Court refused to extend the right to privacy as a justification for euthanasia or doctor-assisted suicide.

Gonzalez v. Oregon, 546 U.S. 243 (2006).
The Court held that Oregon's Death with Dignity Act survived challenges by the U.S. Attorney General who had attempted to invalidate the law arguing that physicians were violating the Federal Controlled Substance Act when they prescribed drugs that would be used to commit suicide. The Court held that the U.S. Attorney General was encroaching on the practice of medicine-- traditionally a state regulated profession. Although not necessarily a right to privacy case, this decision limits the federal government's ability to regulate in this area which most would hold to be a private decision.

Roe v. Wade, 410 U.S. 113 (1973). Stenberg v. Carhart, 530 U.S. 914 (2000); Gonzales v. Carhart, 550 U.S. 124 (2007)
Series of cases in which the Court held that the right to privacy included a woman's right to terminate an unwanted pregnancy.

.

EQUAL PROTECTION UNDER THE LAW

The Fourteenth Amendment tells state governments that they should not deprive their citizens of equal protections of law. Unlike most of the Bill of Rights which have been incorporated and applied to the states, the Bill of Rights contains no Equal Protection Clause. In 1954, however, the Court employed a "reverse incorporation" theory and found that the protection was implied within the Due Process Clause of the Fifth Amendment. Justice Warren wrote, "The concepts of equal protection and due process, both stemming from our American ideal of fairness, are not mutually exclusive." Equal protection is more explicit safeguard against discrimination but "discrimination may be so unjustifiable as to be violative of due process." He opined that it would be unthinkable that the Equal Protection Clause applied to the states, but did not apply to the federal government. See, *Bolling v. Sharpe, 347 U.S. 497 (1954)*.

Basically, equal protection of laws means legislators cannot write laws that treat people differently. But obviously, in some circumstances, they do. It is one thing to treat people differently based on age or employment or educational level, and the government may do so if it has a good reason, but it is quite another to treat people differently because of their sex or race. Courts employ three levels of scrutiny in deciding whether a law violates equal protections: rational basis scrutiny, heightened scrutiny, or strict scrutiny. The level of scrutiny courts employ is contingent upon the nature of the classification. (Who is being treated differently than whom.)

Most classifications will be governed by rational basis scrutiny. The classifications are presumed valid so long as they are rationally related to a constitutionally permissible state interest. In *Westbrook v. Alaska*, for example, the issue was whether the state could permissibly restrict underage drinking and impose a minimum age of 21. (Westbrook was convicted of underage drinking). The Court held that the state had shown a reasonable interest in regulating and ensuring responsible drinking and that the age requirement was rationally related to that interest. Accordingly, it upheld the statute.

Classifications based on sex or other "quasi-suspect classifications" are subjected to heightened, intermediate scrutiny. These laws will only survive challenge when they bear a fair and substantial relationship to a legitimate state end or "important government interest."

Classifications involving race or ethnicity are inherently suspect, subject to strict scrutiny, and are unlikely to survive challenge--the state must have a compelling state interest in singling out a racial or ethnic minority and there must be no alternative approach to advancing a compelling state interest. This is the same "strict scrutiny" review that the court engages in when examining a fundamental right such as freedom of speech, freedom of religion, or due process. In order to survive strict scrutiny, the statute must be narrowly tailored to address the compelling state interest. It is a very heavy, but not impossible burden for the government to carry as it is presumed that laws limiting fundamental rights are unconstitutional.

LOVING v. VIRGINIA,
388 U.S. 1 (1967)

MR. CHIEF JUSTICE WARREN delivered the opinion of the Court.

This case presents a constitutional question never addressed by this Court: whether a statutory scheme adopted by the State of Virginia to prevent marriages between persons solely on the basis of racial classifications violates the Equal Protection and Due Process Clauses of the Fourteenth Amendment. For reasons which seem to us to reflect the central meaning of those

constitutional commands, we conclude that these statutes cannot stand consistently with the Fourteenth Amendment.

In June 1958, two residents of Virginia, Mildred Jeter, a Negro woman, and Richard Loving, a white man, were married in the District of Columbia pursuant to its laws. Shortly after their marriage, the Lovings returned to Virginia and established their marital abode in Caroline County. At the October Term, 1958, of the Circuit Court of Caroline County, a grand jury issued an indictment charging the Lovings with violating Virginia's ban on interracial marriages. On January 6, 1959, the Lovings pleaded guilty to the charge and were sentenced to one year in jail; however, the trial judge suspended the sentence for a period of 25 years on the condition that the Lovings leave the State and not return to Virginia together for 25 years. ...

After their convictions, the Lovings took up residence in the District of Columbia. On November 6, 1963, they filed a motion in the state trial court to vacate the judgment and set aside the sentence on the ground that the statutes which they had violated were repugnant to the Fourteenth Amendment. . . . On January 22, 1965, the state trial judge denied the motion to vacate the sentences, and the Lovings perfected an appeal to the Supreme Court of Appeals of Virginia. On February 11, 1965, the three-judge District Court continued the case to allow the Lovings to present their constitutional claims to the highest state court.

The [Virginia] Supreme Court of Appeals upheld the constitutionality of the antimiscegenation statutes and, after modifying the sentence, affirmed the convictions. The Lovings appealed this decision. ...

[The statutes under which appellants were convicted and sentenced were part of a comprehensive statutory scheme aimed at prohibiting and punishing interracial marriages and punishing individuals violating the statute by incarceration in a penitentiary for a minimum of one year and a maximum of five years. The laws also voided without judicial proceedings all interracial marriages.]

The Lovings have never disputed in the course of this litigation that Mrs. Loving is a "colored person" or that Mr. Loving is a "white person" within the meanings given those terms by the Virginia statutes.

Virginia is now one of 16 States which prohibit and punish marriages on the basis of racial classifications. ...

I

In upholding the constitutionality of these provisions in the decision below, the Supreme Court of Appeals of Virginia referred to its 1955 decision in *Naim v. Naim* as stating the reasons

supporting the validity of these laws. In Naim, the state court concluded that the State's legitimate purposes were "to preserve the racial integrity of its citizens," and to prevent "the corruption of blood," "a mongrel breed of citizens," and "the obliteration of racial pride," obviously an endorsement of the doctrine of White Supremacy. The court also reasoned that marriage has traditionally been subject to state regulation without federal intervention, and, consequently, the regulation of marriage should be left to exclusive state control by the Tenth Amendment.

While the state court is no doubt correct in asserting that marriage is a social relation subject to the State's police power, the State does not contend in its argument before this Court that its powers to regulate marriage are unlimited notwithstanding the commands of the Fourteenth Amendment. ... Instead, the State argues that the meaning of the Equal Protection Clause, is only that state penal laws containing an interracial element as part of the definition of the offense must apply equally to whites and Negroes in the sense that members of each race are punished to the same degree. Thus, the State contends that, because its miscegenation statutes punish equally both the white and the Negro participants in an interracial marriage, these statutes, despite their reliance on racial classifications, do not constitute an invidious discrimination based upon race. The second argument advanced by the State assumes the validity of its equal application theory. The argument is that, if the Equal Protection Clause does not outlaw miscegenation statutes because of their reliance on racial classifications, the question of constitutionality would thus become whether there was any rational basis for a State to treat interracial marriages differently from other marriages. On this question, the State argues, the scientific evidence is substantially in doubt and, consequently, this Court should defer to the wisdom of the state legislature in adopting its policy of discouraging interracial marriages.

Because we reject the notion that the mere "equal application" of a statute containing racial classifications is enough to remove the classifications from the Fourteenth Amendment's proscription of all invidious racial discriminations, we do not accept the State's contention that these statutes should be upheld if there is any possible basis for concluding that they serve a rational purpose. The mere fact of equal application does not mean that our analysis of these statutes should follow the approach we have taken in cases involving no racial discrimination. ... In these cases, involving distinctions not drawn according to race, the Court has merely asked whether there is any rational foundation for the discriminations, and has deferred to the wisdom of the state legislatures. In the case at bar, however, we deal with statutes containing racial classifications, and the fact of equal application does not immunize the statute from the very heavy burden of justification which the Fourteenth Amendment has traditionally required of state statutes drawn according to race.

... We have rejected the proposition that ... the requirement of equal protection of the laws is satisfied by penal laws defining offenses based on racial classifications so long as white and Negro participants in the offense were similarly punished.

... [T]he Equal Protection Clause requires the consideration of whether the classifications drawn by any statute constitute an arbitrary and invidious discrimination. The clear and central purpose of the Fourteenth Amendment was to eliminate all official state sources of invidious racial discrimination in the States.

There can be no question but that Virginia's miscegenation statutes rest solely upon distinctions drawn according to race. The statutes proscribe generally accepted conduct if engaged in by members of different races. Over the years, this Court has consistently repudiated "[d]istinctions between citizens solely because of their ancestry" as being "odious to a free people whose institutions are founded upon the doctrine of equality." At the very least, the Equal Protection Clause demands that racial classifications, especially suspect in criminal statutes, be subjected to the "most rigid scrutiny," Korematsu v. United States, and, if they are ever to be upheld, they must be shown to be necessary to the accomplishment of some permissible state objective, independent of the racial discrimination which it was the object of the Fourteenth Amendment to eliminate. Indeed, two members of this Court have already stated that they "cannot conceive of a valid legislative

purpose ... which makes the color of a person's skin the test of whether his conduct is a criminal offense."

There is patently no legitimate overriding purpose independent of invidious racial discrimination which justifies this classification. The fact that Virginia prohibits only interracial marriages involving white persons demonstrates that the racial classifications must stand on their own justification, as measures designed to maintain White Supremacy. We have consistently denied the constitutionality of measures which restrict the rights of citizens on account of race. There can be no doubt that restricting the freedom to marry solely because of racial classifications violates the central meaning of the Equal Protection Clause.

II

These statutes also deprive the Lovings of liberty without due process of law in violation of the Due Process Clause of the Fourteenth Amendment. The freedom to marry has long been recognized as one of the vital personal rights essential to the orderly pursuit of happiness by free men.

Marriage is one of the "basic civil rights of man," fundamental to our very existence and survival. To deny this fundamental freedom on so unsupportable a basis as the racial classifications embodied in these statutes, classifications so directly subversive of the principle of equality at the heart of the Fourteenth Amendment, is surely to deprive all the State's citizens of liberty without due process of law. The Fourteenth Amendment requires that the freedom of choice to marry not be restricted by invidious racial discriminations. Under our Constitution, the freedom to marry, or not marry, a person of another race resides with the individual and cannot be infringed by the State.

These convictions must be reversed.
...
MR. JUSTICE STEWART, concurring.

I have previously expressed the belief that "it is simply not possible for a state law to be valid under our Constitution which makes the criminality of an act depend upon the race of the actor." Because I adhere to that belief, I concur in the judgment of the Court.

CRAIG v. BOREN,
429 U.S. 190 (1976)

[Summary: An Oklahoma law prohibited the sale of "nonintoxicating" 3.2 percent beer to males under the age of 21 and to females under the age of 18. Curtis Craig, a male then between the ages of 18 and 21, and Carolyn Whitener, a licensed vendor challenged the law as discriminatory. The Court was faced with the question of whether the statute violated the Fourteenth Amendment's Equal Protection Clause by establishing different drinking ages for men and women.

The Court discussed *Reed v. Reed* and later cases that established that examined classification by gender noting that those cases held that the state must substantially further important governmental objectives. The three-judge District Court held that appellees' statistical evidence regarding young males' drunk-driving arrests and traffic injuries demonstrated that the gender-based discrimination was substantially related to the achievement of traffic safety on Oklahoma roads. And the Supreme Court had to decide whether this was correct.]

MR. JUSTICE BRENNAN delivered the opinion of the Court.

Oklahoma's gender-based differential constitutes an invidious discrimination against males 18-20 years of age in violation of the Equal Protection Clause. Appellees' statistics (the most relevant of which show only that .18% of females and 2% of males in the 18-20-year-old age group were arrested for driving while under the influence of liquor) do not warrant the conclusion that sex represents an accurate proxy for the regulation of drinking and driving.

The operation of the Twenty-first Amendment does not alter the application of equal protection standards that otherwise govern this case. The Court has never recognized that application of that Amendment can defeat an otherwise established claim under the Equal Protection Clause, the principles of which cannot be rendered inapplicable here by reliance upon statistically measured but loose-fitting generalities concerning the drinking tendencies of aggregate groups.

II
A

[The court traced Oklahoma's history concerning age of majority (with regard to criminal responsibility) for females and males prior to 1972, and then after 1972's *Reed* decision.]

... *Reed* emphasized that statutory classifications that distinguish between males and females are "subject to scrutiny under the Equal Protection Clause." To withstand constitutional challenge, previous cases establish that classifications by gender must serve important governmental objectives and must be substantially related to achievement of those objectives. Thus, in *Reed*, the objectives of "reducing the workload on probate courts," and "avoiding intrafamily controversy were deemed of insufficient importance to sustain use of an overt gender criterion in the appointment of administrators of intestate decedents' estates. Decisions following *Reed* similarly have rejected administrative ease and convenience as sufficiently important objectives to justify gender-based classifications. And only two Terms ago, *Stanton v. Stanton* held that Reed required invalidation of a Utah differential age-of-majority statute, notwithstanding the statute's coincidence with and furtherance of the State's purpose of fostering "old notions" of role typing and preparing boys for their expected performance in the economic and political worlds.

Reed v. Reed has also provided the underpinning for decisions that have invalidated statutes employing gender as an inaccurate proxy for other, more germane bases of classification. Hence, "archaic and overbroad" generalizations, concerning the financial position of servicewomen and working women could not justify use of a gender line in determining eligibility for certain governmental entitlements. Similarly, increasingly outdated misconceptions concerning the role of females in the home rather than in the "marketplace and world of ideas" were rejected as loose-fitting characterizations incapable of supporting state statutory schemes that were premised upon their accuracy. In light of the weak congruence between gender and the characteristic or trait that gender purported to represent, it was necessary that the legislatures choose either to realign their substantive laws in a gender-neutral fashion, or to adopt procedures for identifying those instances where the sex-centered generalization actually comported with fact.

In this case, too, "*Reed*, we feel, is controlling . . .." We turn then to the question whether, under *Reed*, the difference between males and females with respect to the purchase of 3.2% beer warrants the differential in age drawn by the Oklahoma statute. We conclude that it does not.

. . .

C

[The Court wasn't persuaded by the statistics presented].

MR. JUSTICE POWELL, **concurring**.

. . .

With respect to the equal protection standard, I agree that Reed v. Reed is the most relevant precedent. But I find it unnecessary, in deciding this case, to read that decision as broadly as some of the Court's language may imply. Reed and subsequent cases involving gender-based classifications make clear that the Court subjects such classifications to a more critical examination than is normally applied when "fundamental" constitutional rights and "suspect classes" are not present. *

I view this as a relatively easy case. No one questions the legitimacy or importance of the asserted governmental objective: the promotion of highway safety. The decision of the case turns on whether the state legislature, by the classification it has chosen, has adopted a means that bears a "fair and substantial relation" to this objective.

It seems to me that the statistics offered by appellees and relied upon by the District Court do tend generally to support the view that young men drive more, possibly are inclined to drink more, and - for various reasons - are involved in more accidents than young women. Even so, I am not persuaded that these facts and the inferences fairly drawn from them justify this classification based on a three-year age differential between the sexes, and especially one that is so easily circumvented as to be virtually

meaningless. Putting it differently, this gender-based classification does not bear a fair and substantial relation to the object of the legislation.

[Footnote *] As is evident from our opinions, the Court has had difficulty in agreeing upon a standard of equal protection analysis that can be applied consistently to the wide variety of legislative classifications. There are valid reasons for dissatisfaction with the "two-tier" approach that has been prominent in the Court's decisions in the past decade. Although viewed by many as a result-oriented substitute for more critical analysis, that approach - with its narrowly limited "upper-tier" - now has substantial precedential support. As has been true of *Reed* and its progeny, our decision today will be viewed by some as a "middle-tier" approach. While I would not endorse that characterization and would not welcome a further subdividing of equal protection analysis, candor compels the recognition that the relatively deferential "rational basis" standard of review normally applied takes on a sharper focus when we address a gender-based classification. So much is clear from our recent cases.

MR. JUSTICE STEVENS, **concurring**.

There is only one Equal Protection Clause. It requires every State to govern impartially. It does not direct the courts to apply one standard of review in some cases and a different standard in other cases. Whatever criticism may be leveled at a judicial opinion implying that there are at least three such standards applies with the same force to a double standard.

I am inclined to believe that what has become known as the two-tiered analysis of equal protection claims does not describe a completely logical method of deciding cases, but rather is a method the Court has employed to explain decisions that actually apply a single standard in a reasonably consistent fashion. I also suspect that a careful explanation of the reasons motivating particular decisions may contribute more to an identification of that standard than an attempt to articulate it in all-encompassing terms. It may therefore be appropriate for me to state the principal reasons which persuaded me to join the Court's opinion.

In this case, the classification is not as obnoxious as some the Court has condemned, nor as inoffensive as some the Court has accepted. It is objectionable because it is based on an accident of birth, because it is a mere remnant of the now almost universally rejected tradition of discriminating against males in this age bracket, and because, to the extent it reflects any physical difference between males and females, it is actually perverse. The question then is whether the traffic safety justification put forward by the State is sufficient to make an otherwise offensive classification acceptable.

The classification is not totally irrational. For the evidence does indicate that there are more males than females in this age bracket who drive and also more who drink. Nevertheless, there are several reasons why I regard the justification as unacceptable. It is difficult to believe that the statute was actually intended to cope with the problem of traffic safety, since it has only a minimal effect on access to a not very intoxicating beverage and does not prohibit its consumption. Moreover, the empirical data submitted by the State accentuate the unfairness of treating all 18-20-year-old males as inferior to their female counterparts. The legislation imposes a restraint on 100% of the males in the class allegedly because about 2% of them have probably violated one or more laws relating to the consumption of alcoholic beverages. It is unlikely that this law will have a significant deterrent effect either on that 2% or on the law-abiding 98%. But even assuming some such slight benefit, it does not seem to me that an insult to all of the young men of the State can be justified by visiting the sins of the 2% on the 98%.

Opinions Omitted:
MR. JUSTICE BLACKMUN, **concurring** in part.
MR. JUSTICE STEWART, **concurring** in the judgment. (Omitted).
MR. CHIEF JUSTICE BURGER, **dissenting**. (Omitted)

MR. JUSTICE REHNQUIST, **dissenting**.
The Court's disposition of this case is objectionable on two grounds. First is its conclusion that men challenging a gender-based statute which treats them less favorably than women may invoke a more stringent standard of judicial review than pertains to most other types of classifications. Second is the Court's enunciation of this standard, without citation to any source, as being that "classifications by

gender must serve important governmental objectives and must be substantially related to achievement of those objectives." The only redeeming feature of the Court's opinion, to my mind, is that it apparently signals a retreat . . . from [the] view that sex is a "suspect" classification for purposes of equal protection analysis. I think the Oklahoma statute challenged here need pass only the "rational basis" equal protection analysis . . . , and I believe that it is constitutional under that analysis.

. . .

The Court's conclusion that a law which treats males less favorably than females "must serve important governmental objectives and must be substantially related to achievement of those objectives" apparently comes out of thin air. The Equal Protection Clause contains no such language, and none of our previous cases adopt that standard. I would think we have had enough difficulty with the two standards of review which our cases have recognized - the norm of "rational basis," and the "compelling state interest" required where a "suspect classification" is involved - so as to counsel weightily against the insertion of still another "standard" between those two. How is this Court to divine what objectives are important? How is it to determine whether a particular law is "substantially" related to the achievement of such objective, rather than related in some other way to its achievement? …

I would have thought that if this Court were to leave anything to decision by the popularly elected branches of the Government, where no constitutional claim other than that of equal protection is invoked, it would be the decision as to what governmental objectives to be achieved by law are "important," and which are not. As for the second part of the Court's new test, the Judicial Branch is probably in no worse position than the Legislative or Executive Branches to determine if there is any rational relationship between a classification and the purpose which it might be thought to serve. But the introduction of the adverb "substantially" requires courts to make subjective judgments as to operational effects, for which neither their expertise nor their access to data fits them. And even if we manage to avoid both confusion and the mirroring of our own preferences in the development of this new doctrine, the thousands of judges in other courts who must interpret the Equal Protection Clause may not be so fortunate.

II

The applicable rational-basis test is one which

"permits the States a wide scope of discretion in enacting laws which affect some groups of citizens differently than others. The constitutional safeguard is offended only if the classification rests on grounds wholly irrelevant to the achievement of the State's objective. State legislatures are presumed to have acted within their constitutional power despite the fact that, in practice, their laws result in some inequality. A statutory discrimination will not be set aside if any state of facts reasonably may be conceived to justify it." McGowan v. Maryland.

Our decisions indicate that application of the Equal Protection Clause in a context not justifying an elevated level of scrutiny does not demand "mathematical nicety" or the elimination of all inequality. Those cases recognize that the practical problems of government may require

rough accommodations of interests, and hold that such accommodations should be respected unless no reasonable basis can be found to support them. Whether the same ends might have been better or more precisely served by a different approach is no part of the judicial inquiry under the traditional minimum rationality approach.

. . .

. . . [T]he present equal protection challenge to this gender-based discrimination poses only the question whether the incidence of drunk driving among young men is sufficiently greater than among young women to justify differential treatment. Notwithstanding the Court's critique of the statistical evidence, that evidence suggests clear differences between the drinking and driving habits of young men and women. Those differences are grounds enough for the State reasonably to conclude that young males pose by far the greater drunk-driving hazard, both in terms of sheer numbers and in terms of hazard on a per-driver basis. The gender-based difference in treatment in this case is therefore not irrational. . . .

MICHAEL M. v. SONOMA COUNTY SUPERIOR COURT, 450 U.S. 464 (1981)

[Summary: At approximately midnight on June 3, 1978, Michael M. and two friends approached Sharon, a 16 1/2-year-old female, and her sister as they waited at a bus stop. Michael M and Sharon, who had already been drinking, moved away from the others and began to kiss. After being struck in the face for rebuffing petitioner's initial advances, Sharon submitted to sexual intercourse with petitioner. Michael M., a 17 and 1/2 year-old male, was found guilty of violating California's "statutory rape" law. The law defined unlawful sexual intercourse as "an act of sexual intercourse accomplished with a female not the wife of the perpetrator, where the female is under the age of 18 years." The statute made men alone criminally liable for such conduct. Michael M. challenged the constitutionality of the law. The Court had to decide whether California's statutory rape law violated the Fourteenth Amendment's Equal Proection Clause and unconstitutionally discriminated on the basis of gender?

In a plurality [split] decision, the Court held that

the law did not violate the Equal Protection Clause of the Fourteenth Amendment, noting that "young men and young women are not similarly situated with respect to the problems and the risks of sexual intercourse." The Court found that the state had a strong interest in preventing "illegitimate pregnancy." The Court also noted that "[i]t is hardly unreasonable for a legislature acting to protect minor females to exclude them from punishment. Moreover, the risk of pregnancy itself constitutes a substantial deterrence to young females. No similar natural sanctions deter males."]

JUSTICE REHNQUIST announced the judgment of the Court and delivered an opinion, in which THE CHIEF JUSTICE, JUSTICE STEWART, and JUSTICE POWELL joined.

. . .

As is evident from our opinions, the Court has had some difficulty in agreeing upon the proper approach and analysis in cases involving

challenges to gender-based classifications. . . .
Our cases have held, however, that the
traditional minimum rationality test takes on a
somewhat "sharper focus" when gender-based
classifications are challenged. In *Reed v. Reed*, for
example, the Court stated that a gender-based
classification will be upheld if it bears a "fair and
substantial relationship" to legitimate state ends,
while in *Craig v. Boren* the Court restated the test
to require the classification to bear a "substantial
relationship" to "important governmental
objectives."

Underlying these decisions is the principle that a
legislature may not "make overbroad
generalizations based on sex which are entirely
unrelated to any differences between men and
women or which demean the ability or social
status of the affected class." But because the
Equal Protection Clause does not "demand that a
statute necessarily apply equally to all persons"
or require "`things which are different in fact . . .
to be treated in law as though they were the
same,'" this Court has consistently upheld
statutes where the gender classification is not
invidious, but rather realistically reflects the fact
that the sexes are not similarly situated in certain
circumstances. As the Court has stated, a
legislature may "provide for the special problems
of women."
. . .

The justification for the statute offered by the
State, and accepted by the Supreme Court of
California, is that the legislature sought to
prevent illegitimate teenage pregnancies. That
finding, of course, is entitled to great deference.
And although our cases establish that the State's
asserted reason for the enactment of a statute
may be rejected, if it "could not have been a goal
of the legislation," this is not such a case.

We are satisfied not only that the prevention of
illegitimate pregnancy is at least one of the
"purposes" of the statute, but also that the State
has a strong interest in preventing such
pregnancy. At the risk of stating the obvious,
teenage pregnancies, which have increased
dramatically over the last two decades, have
significant social, medical, and economic
consequences for both the mother and her child,
and the State. Of particular concern to the State is
that approximately half of all teenage
pregnancies end in abortion. And of those

children who are born, their illegitimacy makes
them likely candidates to become wards of the
State.

We need not be medical doctors to discern that
young men and young women are not similarly
situated with respect to the problems and the
risks of sexual intercourse. Only women may
become pregnant, and they suffer
disproportionately the profound physical,
emotional, and psychological consequences of
sexual activity. The statute at issue here protects
women from sexual intercourse at an age when
those consequences are particularly severe.

The question thus boils down to whether a State
may attack the problem of sexual intercourse and
teenage pregnancy directly by prohibiting a male
from having sexual intercourse with a minor
female. We hold that such a statute is sufficiently
related to the State's objectives to pass
constitutional muster.

Because virtually all of the significant harmful
and inescapably identifiable consequences of
teenage pregnancy fall on the young female, a
legislature acts well within its authority when it
elects to punish only the participant who, by
nature, suffers few of the consequences of his
conduct. It is hardly unreasonable for a
legislature acting to protect minor females to
exclude them from punishment. Moreover, the
risk of pregnancy itself constitutes a substantial
deterrence to young females. No similar natural
sanctions deter males. A criminal sanction
imposed solely on males thus serves to roughly
"equalize" the deterrents on the sexes.

. . .

There remains only petitioner's contention that
the statute is unconstitutional as it is applied to
him because he, like Sharon, was under 18 at the
time of sexual intercourse. Petitioner argues that
the statute is flawed because it presumes that as
between two persons under 18, the male is the
culpable aggressor. We find petitioner's
contentions unpersuasive. Contrary to his
assertions, the statute does not rest on the
assumption that males are generally the
aggressors. It is instead an attempt by a
legislature to prevent illegitimate teenage
pregnancy by providing an additional deterrent
for men. The age of the man is irrelevant since

young men are as capable as older men of inflicting the harm sought to be prevented.
. . .

JUSTICE STEWART, **concurring**.
. . .

B

The Constitution is violated when government, state or federal, invidiously classifies similarly situated people on the basis of the immutable characteristics with which they were born. Thus, detrimental racial classifications by government always violate the Constitution, for the simple reason that, so far as the Constitution is concerned, people of different races are always similarly situated. By contrast, while detrimental gender classifications by government often violate the Constitution, they do not always do so, for the reason that there are differences between males and females that the Constitution necessarily recognizes. In this case we deal with the most basic of these differences: females can become pregnant as the result of sexual intercourse; males cannot.

. . . Gender-based classifications may not be based upon administrative convenience, or upon archaic assumptions about the proper roles of the sexes. But we have recognized that in certain narrow circumstances men and women are not similarly situated; in these circumstances a gender classification based on clear differences between the sexes is not invidious, and a legislative classification realistically based upon those differences is not unconstitutional. "[G]ender-based classifications are not invariably invalid. When men and women are not in fact similarly situated in the area covered by the legislation in question, the Equal Protection Clause is not violated."

. . .

E

In short, the Equal Protection Clause does not mean that the physiological differences between men and women must be disregarded. While those differences must never be permitted to become a pretext for invidious discrimination, no such discrimination is presented by this case. The Constitution surely does not require a State to pretend that demonstrable differences between men and women do not really exist.

JUSTICE BLACKMUN, **concurring** in the

judgment. Omitted.

JUSTICE BRENNAN, with whom JUSTICES WHITE and MARSHALL join, **dissenting**.

I

It is disturbing to find the Court so splintered on a case that presents such a straightforward issue: Whether the admittedly gender-based classification … bears a sufficient relationship to the State's asserted goal of preventing teenage pregnancies to survive the "mid-level" constitutional scrutiny mandated by *Craig v. Boren*. Applying the analytical framework provided by our precedents, I am convinced that there is only one proper resolution of this issue: the classification must be declared unconstitutional. I fear that the plurality opinion and JUSTICES STEWART and BLACKMUN reach the opposite result by placing too much emphasis on the desirability of achieving the State's asserted statutory goal - prevention of teenage pregnancy - and not enough emphasis on the fundamental question of whether the sex-based discrimination the California statute is substantially related to the achievement of that goal.

It is perhaps because the gender classification in California's statutory rape law was initially designed to further these outmoded sexual stereotypes, rather than to reduce the incidence of teenage pregnancies, that the State has been unable to demonstrate a substantial relationship between the classification and its newly asserted goal. But whatever the reason, the State has not shown that Cal. Penal Code 261.5 is any more effective than a gender-neutral law would be in deterring minor females from engaging in sexual intercourse. It has therefore not met its burden of proving that the statutory classification is substantially related to the achievement of its asserted goal.

I would hold that 261.5 violates the Equal Protection Clause of the Fourteenth Amendment, and I would reverse the judgment of the California Supreme Court.

JUSTICE STEVENS, **dissenting**.
. . .

In my judgment, the fact that a class of persons is especially vulnerable to a risk that a statute is designed to avoid is a reason for making the statute applicable to that class. The argument that a special need for protection provides a rational explanation for an exemption is one I simply do not comprehend.

In this case, the fact that a female confronts a greater risk of harm than a male is a reason for applying the prohibition to her - not a reason for granting her a license to use her own judgment on whether or not to assume the risk. Surely, if we examine the problem from the point of view of society's interest in preventing the risk-creating conduct from occurring at all, it is irrational to exempt 50% of the potential violators. And, if we view the government's interest as that of a *parens patriae* seeking to protect its subjects from harming themselves, the discrimination is actually perverse. Would a rational parent making rules for the conduct of twin children of opposite sex simultaneously forbid the son and authorize the daughter to engage in conduct that is especially harmful to the daughter? That is the effect of this statutory classification.

If pregnancy or some other special harm is suffered by one of the two participants in the prohibited act, that special harm no doubt would constitute a legitimate mitigating factor in deciding what, if any, punishment might be appropriate in a given case. But from the standpoint of fashioning a general preventive rule - or, indeed, in determining appropriate punishment when neither party in fact has suffered any special harm - I regard a total exemption for the members of the more endangered class as utterly irrational.

In my opinion, the only acceptable justification for a general rule requiring disparate treatment of the two participants in a joint act must be a legislative judgment that one is more guilty than the other. The risk-creating conduct that this statute is designed to prevent requires the participation of two persons - one male and one female. In many situations it is probably true that one is the aggressor and the other is either an unwilling, or at least a less willing, participant in the joint act. If a statute authorized punishment of only one participant and required the prosecutor to prove that participant had been the aggressor, I assume that the discrimination would be valid. Although the question is less

clear, I also assume, for the purpose of deciding this case, that it would be permissible to punish only the male participant, if one element of the offense were proof that he had been the aggressor, or at least in some respects the more responsible participant in the joint act. The statute at issue in this case, however, requires no such proof. The question raised by this statute is whether the State, consistently with the Federal Constitution, may always punish the male and never the female when they are equally responsible or when the female is the more responsible of the two.

It would seem to me that an impartial lawmaker could give only one answer to that question. The fact that the California Legislature has decided to apply its prohibition only to the male may reflect a legislative judgment that in the typical case the male is actually the more guilty party. Any such judgment must, in turn, assume that the decision to engage in the risk-creating conduct is always - or at least typically - a male decision. If that assumption is valid, the statutory classification should also be valid. But what is the support for the assumption? It is not contained in the record of this case or in any legislative history or scholarly study that has been called to our attention. I think it is supported to some extent by traditional attitudes toward male-female relationships. But the possibility that such a habitual attitude may reflect nothing more than an irrational prejudice makes it an insufficient justification for discriminatory treatment that is otherwise blatantly unfair. For, as I read this statute, it requires that one, and only one, of two equally guilty wrongdoers be stigmatized by a criminal conviction.

. . .

Finally, even if my logic is faulty and there actually is some speculative basis for treating equally guilty males and females differently, I still believe that any such speculative justification would be outweighed by the paramount interest in evenhanded enforcement of the law. A rule that authorizes punishment of only one of two equally guilty wrongdoers violates the essence of the constitutional requirement that the sovereign must govern impartially.
I respectfully dissent.

CABRET, ASSOCIATE JUSTICE delivered the opinion of the court:

Patrick Webster, Jr., was convicted in the Superior Court of aggravated assault and battery and disturbing the peace, both as acts of domestic violence, and unauthorized use of a vehicle. Webster appeals, arguing that the aggravated assault statute contains unconstitutional sex-based classifications and that the evidence was insufficient to establish the other charges. For the reasons that follow, we reverse Webster's assault conviction and affirm his convictions for disturbing the peace and unauthorized use of a vehicle.

FACTS

On May 4, 2011, at approximately 1 a.m., Webster went into the bedroom of his mother Vernice Webster while she was sleeping to ask for the keys to her car. When she refused, Webster searched the room for the keys while his mother went to the kitchen. When he could not find the keys, Webster grabbed Vernice by the throat and the wrap she was wearing, pulling her back into the bedroom and then repeatedly pushing her down onto her bed, demanding the keys. Still refusing to give Webster the keys, Vernice returned to the kitchen, ending up on the floor with Webster standing over her holding a wine bottle. Webster once again dragged his mother into the bedroom and threw her onto her mattress several more times. Vernice finally retrieved the keys from a bathroom cabinet and gave them to Webster, who disabled the house phone and took Vernice's cell phone before leaving with the car.

After he left, Vernice went to a neighbor to call 911. Once police arrived, they noticed bruises and minor scratches on her collarbone and forearm, and observed that the bedroom was "ransacked." The responding officers took Vernice to her sister's house for the night because she was afraid that Webster would return to the house. She returned home in the morning with Officer Vernon Williams, where they found the car outside and Webster asleep in his bedroom. Williams then arrested Webster. The following day, Vernice went to the hospital complaining of back pain caused by the altercation.

. . .

. . . [T]he trial concluded . . . there was not enough evidence to support a conviction for third-degree assault with a deadly weapon or the use of a dangerous weapon during a crime of violence, but entered convictions against Webster for aggravated assault and battery, disturbing the peace, and unauthorized use of a vehicle. The court also found that aggravated assault and disturbing the peace were acts of domestic violence as defined by 16 V.I.C. § 91(b). . . . [T]he Superior Court sentenced Webster to a suspended ten-month prison sentence and a $1,000 fine for aggravated assault and battery, a concurrent sixty-day sentence for disturbing the peace, a concurrent one-year suspended sentence for unauthorized use of a vehicle, and placed him on supervised probation for one year. Webster filed a timely notice of appeal on February 8, 2012

DISCUSSION

Webster argues that his conviction for aggravated assault must be reversed because the statute under which he was convicted, 14 V.I.C. § 298(5), violates constitutional principles assuring equal protection of the laws. He further asserts that the evidence was insufficient to support his convictions for disturbing the peace and unauthorized use of a vehicle. We address each argument in turn.

14 V.I.C. § 298(5)

For the first time on appeal, Webster argues that because 14 V.I.C. § 298(5) enhances simple assault to aggravated assault based only on the respective sexes of the attacker and the victim, it violates the Equal Protection Clause of the Fourteenth Amendment to the United States Constitution. Because he did not raise this argument before the Superior Court, we review it only for plain error. "Under plain error review, there must be an error, that was plain, that affected the defendant's substantial rights." "Even then, this Court will only reverse where the error seriously affects the fairness, integrity, or public reputation of judicial proceedings." ... In conducting this review, we must first determine whether the Superior Court erred by entering a conviction against Webster under an unconstitutional statute.

The Superior Court entered the conviction under section 298, which enumerates nine aggravating circumstances that enhance a simple assault to an aggravated assault. ... Webster argues that by making his sex an aggravating factor, section 298(5) denies him equal protection of the law.

"The Equal Protection Clause of the Fourteenth Amendment 'is essentially a direction that all persons similarly situated should be treated alike.'" *Lawrence v. Texas.* Here, it is evident that section 298(5) creates a sex-based classification on its face, upgrading an assault from simple to aggravated in all instances in which the defendant is male and the victim is female. While most statutory classifications—such as those contained in tax policy and economic regulations—must meet only rational basis review, *see Heller v. Doe* (rational basis review is satisfied by "any reasonably conceivable state of facts that could provide a rational basis for the classification"), an explicitly sex-based statutory classification—like those based on race, national origin, or alienage—must satisfy heightened constitutional scrutiny.

In the case of a sex-based classification, this heightened level of scrutiny is intermediate. Unlike rational basis review—where it is the defendant's burden to "negat[e] every conceivable basis that might support the government's statutory classification,"— intermediate scrutiny requires the People to carry the burden of establishing that there is an "exceedingly persuasive justification" for the classification by showing that it "serves important governmental objectives and that the discriminatory means employed are substantially related to the achievement of those objectives." We must closely examine the People's justifications "free of fixed notions concerning the roles and abilities of males and females," as generalizations and stereotypes about the respective characteristics of men and women cannot satisfy intermediate scrutiny.

The People concedes that it bears the burden of demonstrating the constitutionality of section 298(5) and asserts that "the statute identifies men because of the demonstrable fact that they are physically different from women." The People also contends that "[t]he Government's objective in having a gender based statute is to protect women from physically aggressive and overpowering men as was the situation in this case." The People further insists that the "[L]egislature could easily have determined that assaults and batteries by physically larger and stronger men are more likely to cause greater physical injuries to women than similar assaults by females." While the People may be correct that the Legislature *could* have enacted section 298(5) with the aim of protecting women from assaults by physically larger and stronger men, a justification "hypothesized or invented *post hoc* in response to litigation" cannot meet intermediate scrutiny. Instead, "a tenable justification must describe actual state purposes, not rationalizations for actions in fact differently grounded."

. . .

... While it is undoubtedly true that the Legislature "can take into account . . . physical differences when classifying crimes relating to physical violence," section 298(5) does not do this. Instead, this provision makes any assault committed by a man upon a woman an aggravated assault regardless of the physical differences between the attacker and the victim, providing no additional protections to a man assaulted by a physically stronger woman, or a woman assaulted by a physically stronger woman. By using sex as a proxy for the relative physical characteristics of the attacker and the victim, section 298(5) rests entirely on "archaic and stereotypic notions" that have been specifically rejected by the United States Supreme Court. As the Supreme Court explained, "if the statutory objective is to . . . 'protect' members of one gender because they are presumed to suffer from an inherent handicap or to be innately inferior, the objective itself is illegitimate." Legislative classifications such as this "carry the inherent risk of reinforcing stereotypes about the 'proper place' of women and their need for special protection." Finally, it would seem apparent that if the Legislature's objective was to take into account "physical differences when classifying crimes relating to physical violence," this purpose would have been better served by enacting a statute that actually takes into account physical differences in classifying violent crimes. And when governmental objectives are as well-served by a sex-neutral law that does not "carr[y] with it the baggage of sexual stereotypes," the government "cannot be permitted to classify on the basis of sex." Therefore, even if the Legislature enacted 14 V.I.C. § 298(5) with the objective of providing greater protections to women who are attacked by physically stronger men, because the statute fails to take into account the relative physical prowess of the attacker and the victim, we cannot say that the "discriminatory means employed are substantially related to the achievement of those objectives." In arguing that section 298(5) does not violate equal protection, the People relies heavily on *Gov't of the V.I. v. Prescott*. But *Prescott* . . . applied rational basis review long after the United States Supreme Court held that sex-based statutory classifications must satisfy intermediate scrutiny. ... The only recent case cited is *State v. Wright*, 563 S.E.2d 311 (S.C. 2002), in which the South Carolina Supreme Court upheld a sex-based sentencing enhancement. But despite appropriately identifying intermediate scrutiny, the *Wright* court relied almost entirely on cases utilizing rational basis review in upholding that statute. ...

Accordingly, by providing that any assault committed by a male upon a female is automatically aggravated in nature, 14 V.I.C. § 298(5) violates the Equal Protection Clause of the Fourteenth Amendment, and the Superior Court committed error in entering a conviction against Webster under this section.

Despite this error, because Webster failed to raise the constitutionality of section 298(5) before the Superior Court, we will only exercise our discretion to reverse his conviction if the Superior Court's error was plain and affected Webster's substantial rights, and affirming Webster's conviction would "seriously affect[] the fairness, integrity, or public reputation of judicial proceedings."

... In the case of sex-based statutory classifications, the United States Supreme Court has repeatedly instructed that courts must apply heightened constitutional scrutiny, requiring a careful examination of whether an "exceedingly persuasive justification" motivated the Legislature's use of this otherwise impermissible classification. ... Given this longstanding precedent from the United States Supreme Court, the Superior Court's error in entering a conviction under section 298(5) — a statute containing an explicit sex-based classification — is plain under current law.

Furthermore, there is no doubt that this error affected Webster's substantial rights . . . and that affirming Webster's conviction under a facially unconstitutional statute would clearly affect the integrity and public reputation of judicial proceedings. . . . Accordingly, because the Superior Court committed plain error in entering a conviction against Webster under a statute that violates the Equal Protection Clause of the Fourteenth Amendment, we reverse Webster's conviction for aggravated assault under 14 V.I.C. § 298(5).

Other Cases: Equal Protections

United States v. Windsor, 570 U.S. ___ (2013) The U.S. Supreme Court struck down part of the Defense of Marriage Act (Doma), a federal law which defined marriage as "only a legal union between one man and one woman." The law had in effect denied federal benefits to same-sex couples whose marriages were recognized under state law. The Court found no legitimate purpose of the law overcomes the purpose and effect of the law which	was to injure demean and deny equal statutes to same sex marriages. **Obergefell v. Hodges, 576 U.S. ___ (2015)** The U.S. Supreme Court held that the Fourteenth Amendment's Equal Protection Clause (and the Due Proces Clause) guarantee same-sex couples the same fundamental right to marry as is afforded to opposite sex couples and ruled that the state prohibitions on same-sex marriage were unconstitutional.

CRUEL AND UNUSUAL PUNISHMENT

The Eighth Amendment tells the government that it cannot make punishment cruel or unusual. The terms "cruel and unusual," according to the Court, may change over time. In *Trop v. Dulles*, 356 U.S. 86

(1958), Chief Justice Warren wrote that the Cruel and Unusual Punishments Clause "must draw its meaning from the evolving standards of decency that mark the progress of a maturing society." *Trop* involved removing a soldier's citizenship after he had been found guilty of desertion. The Court found the penalty too extreme. The Court has cited extensively to *Trop* in cases in which it interprets what the words "cruel and unusual" mean. Professor LaFave lists three approaches the Court has used in interpreting the clause:

> ➢ limiting the methods employed to inflict punishment,
> ➢ restricting the "amount of punishment" that may be imposed, and
> ➢ prohibiting the criminal punishment of certain acts. LaFave, at 187.

Barbaric Punishment

Punishment that is "barbaric" (meaning it involves needless pain) is cruel and unusual punishment. Barbaric punishment describes the form of punishment. "The Eighth Amendment was designed to prohibit certain forms of punishment, such as torture, that had been practiced in England and were widely viewed as reprehensible." Kerper, *supra* at 334. When the Eighth Amendment passed, barbaric punishment included: burning at the stake, crucifixion, breaking on the wheel, drawing and quartering, the rack and the thumbscrew. Now most courts are willing to consider that some punishments that were not included in that original list may, nevertheless, be cruel and unusual. The passage of time may alter whether a type of punishment is considered cruel and unusual. For example, corporal punishment was acceptable when the Eighth Amendment was passed in 1791, but was abolished in 1972 when Delaware, the last state to allow corporal punishment, repealed its statute allowing whipping.

Capital punishment has been challenged as inherently barbaric, but the death penalty has historically been viewed as a constitutionally acceptable form of punishment. The Court has noted that punishments are "cruel when they involve torture or lingering death; but the punishment of death is not cruel within the meaning of that word or as used in the constitution. Cruelty implies there is something inhuman or barbarous—something more than the mere extinguishment of life." *In re Kemmler*, 136 U.S. 436, at 436 (1897) (electrocution was unusual, but not cruel.) Even the *Furman v. Georgia*, the case which temporarily invalidated all death sentences, did not find that capital punishment was inherently unconstitutional. The five methods of execution used in the United States (hanging, firing squad, electrocution, the gas chamber, and lethal injection) have all been found by the Court to not be inherently cruel and unusual. In *Coker v. Georgia*, 433 U.S. 584 (1977), the Court held that a punishment is unconstitutional if it (1) makes no measurable contribution to acceptable goals of punishment and hence is nothing more than the purposeless and needless imposition of pain and suffering."

IRICK v. TENNESSEE,
585 U.S. ____ (2018)

JUSTICE SOTOMAYOR, dissenting from the denial of the application for stay.

Tonight the State of Tennessee intends to execute Billy Ray Irick using a procedure that he contends will amount to excruciating torture. During a recent 10-day trial in the state court, medical experts explained in painstaking detail how the three-drug cocktail Tennessee plans to inject into Irick's veins will cause him to experience sensations of drowning, suffocating, and being burned alive from the inside out. . . . The entire process will last at least 10 minutes, and perhaps as many as 18, before the third drug (potassium chloride) finally induces fatal cardiac

arrest. Meanwhile, as a result of the second drug (vecuronium bromide), Irick will be "entirely paralyzed, unable to move or scream."

But Irick may well be aware of what is happening to him. In theory, the first drug in the three-drug protocol, midazolam, is supposed to render a person unable to feel pain during an execution. But the medical experts who testified here explained that midazolam would not work, and the trial court credited that testimony. If the drug indeed fails, the consequences for Irick will be extreme: Although the midazolam may temporarily render Irick unconscious, the onset of pain and suffocation will rouse him. And it may do so just as the paralysis sets in, too late for him to alert bystanders that his execution has gone horribly (if predictably) wrong.

...[T]he trial court credited the evidence put on by Irick and his co-plaintiffs, finding that they "established that midazolam does not elicit strong analgesic [i.e., pain-inhibiting] effects," and that therefore Irick "may be able to feel pain from the administration of the second and third drugs." Id., at 21. Those are the drugs that will paralyze him and create sensations of suffocation and of burning that "'may well be the chemical equivalent of being burned at the stake'" before eventually stopping his heart. Accounts from other executions carried out using midazolam lend troubling credence to the trial court's finding. See No. 18–183–II(III), at 28 (noting testimony describing inmates' "grimaces, clenched fists, furrowed brows, and moans" during lethal injection executions, including by use of midazolam); Glossip, 576 U. S., at ___ (SOTOMAYOR, J., dissenting) (slip op., at 19–20).

Given the Eighth Amendment's prohibition on "cruel and unusual punishments," one might think that such a finding would resolve this case in Irick's favor. And to stay or delay Irick's execution, the Tennessee Supreme Court needed only to conclude that it is likely (not certain) that Irick can persuade an appellate court that his claim has merit.

But the Tennessee Supreme Court did not find any such likelihood and declined to postpone Irick's execution to allow appellate review of his claims. Id., at 3–5. The court instead effectively let stand the trial court's order, which held that Irick's extensive and persuasive evidence describing the ordeal that awaits him raised no constitutional concerns. The trial court offered two independent reasons for its holding: first, that Irick had not proven that another, less painful method of killing him was available to the State; and second, even assuming Irick had proven a readily available alternative, that this Court would not consider the painful ordeal that

Irick faces sufficiently torturous to violate the Eighth Amendment. Thereafter, the Tennessee Supreme Court refused to postpone Irick's execution on the ground that he was unlikely to succeed in disturbing the trial court's no-available-alternative holding on appeal. The court did not directly address the trial court's second rationale, but implied that it agreed. See id., at 5.
. . .
As to the prediction that this Court would deem up to 18 minutes of needless torture anything less than cruel, unusual, and unconstitutional, I fervently hope the state courts were mistaken. At a minimum, their conclusion that the Constitution tolerates what the State plans to do to Irick is not compelled by Glossip, which did not categorically determine whether a lethal injection protocol using midazolam is a constitutional method of execution. Glossip's majority concluded only that, based on the evidence presented in that case, there was no clear error in the District Court's factual finding that midazolam was highly likely to prevent a person from feeling pain. As noted, the trial court here came to a different factual conclusion based on a different factual record, as have others. ...

If it turns out upon more sober appellate review that this case presents the question, I would grant certiorari to decide the important question whether the Constitution truly tolerates executions carried out by such quite possibly torturous means.

In refusing to grant Irick a stay, the Court today turns a blind eye to a proven likelihood that the State of Tennessee is on the verge of inflicting several minutes of torturous pain on an inmate in its custody, while shrouding his suffering behind a veneer of paralysis. I cannot in good conscience join in this "rush to execute" without first seeking every assurance that our precedent permits such a result. If the law permits this execution to go forward in spite of the horrific final minutes that Irick may well experience, then we have stopped being a civilized nation and accepted barbarism. I dissent.

Other Cases—Barbaric Punishment

Hope v. Pelzer, 536 U.S. 730 (2002).
Hope's, a prisoner in Alabama, was handcuffed to a hitching post for seven-hours in the hot sun; he was painfully handcuffed at shoulder level to a horizontal bar without a shirt, taunted, and provided with water only once or twice and denied bathroom breaks. There was no effort to monitor his condition despite the risks of dehydration and sun damage. The Court held that Alabama's use of the "hitching post" to discipline inmates constituted "wanton and

unnecessary pain." The Court held that the use of the hitching post was painful and punitive retribution which served no legitimate and necessary penal purpose

Brown v. Plata,
593 U.S. 493 (2011)

FACTS (Official Summary)
Marciano Plata and other prisoners filed a class action suit against California prison alleging that due to serious and continued overcrowding, lack of proper health care, serious mental health care in California prisons was deteriorating. They argued that these conditions amounted to cruel and unusual punishment and that California was violating their constitutional rights under the Eighth Amendment to the U.S. Constitution.

OPINION
If a prison deprives prisoners of basic sustenance, including adequate medical care, the courts have a responsibility to remedy the resulting Eighth Amendment Violation. "The trial record documents the severe impact of burgeoning demand on the provision of care. The evidence showed that there were high vacancy rates for medical and mental health staff and that the numbers understated the severity of the crisis because the State has not budgeted sufficient staff to meet demand. … Such a shortfall contributes to significant delays in treating mentally ill prisoners, who are housed in administrative segregation for extended periods while awaiting transfer to scarce mental health treatment beds. There are also backlogs of up to 700 prisoners waiting to see a doctor for physical care. Crowding creates unsafe and unsanitary conditions that hamper effective delivery of medical and mental health care. It also promotes unrest and violence and can cause prisoners with latent mental illnesses to worsen and develop overt symptoms. Increased violence required increased reliance on lockdowns to keep order, and lockdowns further impede the effective delivery of care. Overcrowding's effects are particularly acute in prison reception centers, which process 140,000 new or returning prisoners annually, and which house some prisoners for their entire incarceration. Numerous experts testified that crowding is the primary cause of the constitutional violations.

The Prison Litigation Reform Act (PLRA) requires courts to set a population limit at the lightest level consistent with an efficacious remedy and order the population reduction to be achieved in the shortest time reasonably consistent with public safety. The Court upheld the three-judge court's order releasing enough prisoners to bring the inmate population to 137.5% of the prison's total design capacity and establishing a 2-year deadline for relief.

Disproportionate Punishment

Disproportionate punishment also violates the Cruel and Unusual Punishment Clause of the Eighth Amendment to the U.S. Constitution. In *Coker*, the Court looked at whether the death penalty was grossly out of proportion to the severity of the crime when the defendant had raped an adult woman. The Court found that it was. In striking down the death penalty, Justice White wrote, "The death penalty, which is unique in its severity and its irrevocability, is an excessive penalty for a rapist who does not take a human life." 433 U.S. at 598 (1977). *Coker* left open the question of whether death was an appropriate sentence for rape of a child victim. *Kennedy v. Louisiana*, 554 U.S. 407 (2008), involving a horrific rape of a twelve-year-old girl by her step-father, answered that question. The Court decided that Kennedy's death sentence also was disproportionate since the crime did not result in the death of the victim. So, what we know from those cases is that the Court will likely find that a sentence of death for a crime that does not result in the victim's death is cruel and unusual because it is grossly disproportionate and therefore violates the Eighth Amendment.

Punishment may also be disproportionate if it is imposed in an uneven manner. The 1970s' death penalty cases before the Court highlight this. In *Furman v. Georgia,* 408 U.S. 238 (1972), the Court ultimately struck down capital punishment laws across the nation, finding they were applied in an uneven, arbitrary and capricious manner. The states immediately reacted by enacting mandatory death penalty laws that required capital punishment for all defendants convicted of intentional homicide. The Court held that these mandatory laws were similarly unconstitutional--mandatory death for all homicides may not be arbitrary punishment, but these statutes may result in death being inflicted on undeserving defendants.

Instead, the Court held, the jury must fit the punishment to the circumstances of the particular offense and the character and record of the individual offender. *Woodson v. North Carolina*, 438 U.S.280 (1976).

The Court has also grappled with the question of whether a lengthy sentence (not a death sentence) of incarceration could be considered cruel and unusual punishment under the disproportionality test. Some federal appellate judges believe that it is perfectly acceptable for federal courts to evaluate states' non-death penalty statutes to determine if they impose disproportionate punishment. Other disagree, believing that the length of a criminal sentence is the province of the elected state legislators and that judicial intervention should be extremely rare.

HUMPHREY v. WILSON,
228 Ga. 520 (Ga.Sup.Ct., 2007)

In Case No. S07A1481, the appellant, Warden Carl Humphrey, appeals from the grant of habeas corpus relief to the appellee, Genarlow Wilson, by the Superior Court of Monroe County (hereinafter referred to as the "habeas court"). For the reasons that follow, we conclude that the habeas court properly ruled that Wilson's sentence of ten years in prison for having consensual oral sex with a fifteen-year-old girl when he was only seventeen years old constitutes cruel and unusual punishment, but erred in convicting and sentencing Wilson for a misdemeanor crime that did not exist when the conduct in question occurred. Because the minimum punishment for the crime for which Wilson was convicted constitutes cruel and unusual punishment, this case must be remanded to the habeas court for it to enter an order reversing Wilson's conviction and sentence and discharging him from custody.
Accordingly, in Case No. S07A1481, we affirm the habeas court's judgment in part and reverse it in part.

FACTS:
1. In February 2005, Wilson was found guilty in Douglas County for the aggravated child molestation of T.C. Wilson was seventeen years old at the time of the crime, and the victim was fifteen years old. The sexual act involved the victim willingly performing oral sex on Wilson. At the time of Wilson's trial, the minimum sentence for a conviction of aggravated child molestation was ten years in prison with no possibility of probation or parole; the maximum sentence was thirty years in prison. The trial court sentenced Wilson to eleven years, ten to serve and one year on probation. In addition to the foregoing punishment, Wilson was also subject to registration as a sex offender. In this regard, under OCGA §42-1-12, Wilson would be required, before his release from prison, to provide prison officials with, among other things, his new address, his fingerprints, his social security number, his date of birth, and his photograph. Prison officials would have to forward this information to the sheriff of Wilson's intended county of residence, and Wilson, within seventy-two hours of his release, would have to register with that sheriff, and he would be required to update the information each year for the rest of his life. Moreover, upon Wilson's release from prison, information regarding Wilson's residence, his photograph, and his offense would be posted in numerous public places in the county in which he lives and on the internet. Significantly, Wilson could not live or work within 1,000 feet of any child care facility, church, or area where minors congregate.

After the trial court denied Wilson's motion for new trial, Wilson filed a notice of appeal to this Court. This Court transferred the appeal to the Court of Appeals, and that Court affirmed Wilson's conviction on April 28, 2006. On appeal, Wilson claimed that his trial counsel was ineffective for failing to contend that OCGA §16-6-4 violated equal protection by imposing a minimum sentence of ten years in prison on a seventeen-year-old male who engages in oral sex with a female under the age of sixteen when a seventeen-year-old male who engages in intercourse with the same female is guilty of only misdemeanor statutory rape under OCGA §16-6-3(b). Wilson also contended that his sentence constituted cruel and unusual punishment. In addressing Wilson's equal protection claim, the Court of Appeals stated that Wilson's equal protection challenge was effectively resolved against him in Odett v. State, and that, in any event, this Court's transfer order meant that "Wilson's constitutional challenge is untimely and thus waived." The Court of Appeals did not address Wilson's contention that his sentence constituted cruel and unusual punishment. In a motion for reconsideration filed on May 8, 2006, Wilson stated that, two days before the Court of Appeals issued its opinion, Georgia Governor Sonny Perdue signed House Bill 1059, which amended OCGA §16-6-4 effective July 1, 2006, by adding a new subsection (d)(2) to make conduct such as Wilson's a misdemeanor and which amended OCGA § 42-1-12 to relieve him from having to register as a sex offender. Wilson contended that this new law should lead to a different outcome on his equal protection and ineffective assistance of counsel claims. The Court of Appeals denied Wilson's motion for reconsideration. Wilson thereafter petitioned this Court for certiorari, contending that this Court should review his equal protection claim Wilson did not pursue his cruel and unusual punishment claim on certiorari. This Court subsequently denied Wilson's petition for certiorari.

On April 16, 2007, Wilson filed the present application for writ of habeas corpus, contending that his sentence constituted cruel and unusual punishment due in large part to the fact that the 2006 Amendment to OCGA §16-6-4 makes conduct such as his a misdemeanor, while the 2006 Amendment to OCGA § 42-1-12 relieved him from the requirements of the sex offender registry. In this regard, the 2006 Amendment to OCGA §16-6-4 provides that, if a person engages in sodomy with a victim who "is at least 13 but less than 16 years of age" and, if the person who engages in the conduct is "18 years of age or younger and is no more than four years older than the victim," the person is guilty of the new crime of misdemeanor aggravated child molestation. Moreover, the 2006 Amendment to OCGA § 42-1-12 provided that teenagers whose conduct is a misdemeanor under the 2006 Amendment to OCGA § 16-6-4 do not have to register as sex offenders.

On June 11, 2007, the habeas court ruled that Wilson's claim of cruel and unusual punishment was not procedurally barred, reasoning that since "the aggravated child molestation statute was not amended until after [Wilson's] direct appeal was filed, [Wilson] could not have reasonably argued that the amended statute resulted in a constitutional violation of his right to be free from cruel and unusual punishment."

Concluding that the extraordinary changes in the law reflected in the 2006 Amendments to OCGA § 16-6-4 and OCGA § 42-1-12 reflected this State's contemporary view of how Wilson's conduct should be punished, the habeas court ruled that Wilson's punishment was cruel and unusual. Finally, the habeas court, as a remedy, ruled that Wilson was guilty of misdemeanor aggravated child molestation under the 2006 Amendment to OCGA § 16-6-4, and it sentenced Wilson to twelve months to serve with credit for time served. On June 11, 2007, the warden filed a notice of appeal from the habeas court's grant of relief to Wilson.

That same day, pursuant to OCGA § 9-14-52(c), Wilson filed a motion to be released on bond pending the warden's appeal. As required by OCGA § 9-14-52(c), Wilson filed the motion for bond in the trial court. On June 27, 2007, the trial court denied Wilson's motion for bond on the ground that OCGA § 17-6-1(g) precludes the grant of an "appeal bond" when a person has been convicted of aggravated child molestation. Wilson appealed the denial of his motion. This Court subsequently expedited both the warden's appeal from the habeas court's grant of relief to Wilson and Wilson's appeal from the denial of his motion for bond pending the warden's appeal.

. . .

The warden . . . contends that the habeas court erred in ruling that Wilson's sentence constituted cruel and unusual punishment. We disagree.

(a) Under the Eighth Amendment to the United States Constitution and under Art. I, Sec. I, Par. XVII of the Georgia Constitution, a sentence is cruel and unusual if it " ' "is grossly out of proportion to the severity of the crime." ' " Moreover, whether "a particular punishment is cruel and unusual is not a static concept, but instead changes in recognition of the ' "evolving standards of decency that mark the progress of a maturing society." ' " Legislative enactments are the clearest and best evidence of a society's evolving standard of decency and of how contemporary society views a particular punishment.
In determining whether a sentence set by the legislature is cruel and unusual, this Court has cited with approval Justice Kennedy's

concurrence in Harmelin v. Michigan. Under Justice Kennedy's concurrence in *Harmelin*, as further developed in *Ewing v. California*, in order to determine if a sentence is grossly disproportionate, a court must first examine the "gravity of the offense compared to the harshness of the penalty" and determine whether a threshold inference of gross disproportionality is raised. In making this determination, courts must bear in mind the primacy of the legislature in setting punishment and seek to determine whether the sentence furthers a "legitimate penological goal" considering the offense and the offender in question. If a sentence does not further a legitimate penological goal, it does not "reflect [ ] a rational legislative judgment, entitled to deference," and a threshold showing of disproportionality has been made. If this threshold analysis reveals an inference of gross disproportionality, a court must proceed to the second step and determine whether the initial judgment of disproportionality is confirmed by a comparison of the defendant's sentence to sentences imposed for other crimes within the jurisdiction and for the same crime in other jurisdictions.

(b)

. . .

(c) We turn now to the threshold inquiry of disproportionality as developed in *Harmelin* and *Ewing*. [W]e conclude that . . . considering the nature of Wilson's offense, his ten-year sentence does not further a legitimate penological goal and thus the threshold inquiry of gross disproportionality falls in Wilson's favor.

In *Fleming*, this Court addressed whether the execution of mentally retarded offenders constituted cruel and unusual punishment. At the time of Fleming's trial, Georgia did not have any prohibition against executing the mentally retarded, but in 1988, the Georgia legislature added such a prohibition to OCGA § 17-7-131. Although this Court rejected Fleming's claim that the new statute should be applied retroactively to him, we ruled in Fleming's favor on his claim that executing him would amount to cruel and unusual punishment. Recognizing that recent legislative enactments constitute the most objective evidence of a society's evolving standards of decency and of how a society views a particular punishment, this Court held that this State's recent legislative enactment prohibiting

the execution of the mentally retarded "reflect[ed] a decision by the people of Georgia that the execution of mentally retarded offenders makes no measurable contribution to acceptable goals of punishment." We thus concluded that *Fleming's* punishment was cruel and unusual.

In *Dawson*, we . . . [held]. . . that death by electrocution was cruel and unusual. In 2001, our General Assembly amended OCGA § 17-10-38 to provide that lethal injection would replace electrocution as this State's method of execution. We noted that this amendment constituted a significant change in the law and that it represented a shifting societal consensus on electrocution and constituted clear and objective evidence that our contemporary society condemned this method of punishment. We thus concluded that death by electrocution "makes no measurable contribution to accepted goals of punishment" and constituted cruel and unusual punishment.

Here, the legislature has recently amended OCGA § 16-6-4 to substitute misdemeanor punishment for Wilson's conduct in place of the felony punishment of a minimum of ten years in prison (with the maximum being 30 years in prison) with no possibility of probation or parole. Moreover, the legislature has relieved such teenage offenders from registering as a sex offender. It is beyond dispute that these changes represent a seismic shift in the legislature's view of the gravity of oral sex between two willing teenage participants. Acknowledging, as we must under Fleming, that no one has a better sense of the evolving standards of decency in this State than our elected representatives, we conclude that the amendments to OCGA §§ 16-6-4 and 42-1-12 reflect a decision by the people of this State that the severe felony punishment and sex offender registration imposed on Wilson make no measurable contribution to acceptable goals of punishment.

Stated in the language of *Ewing* and *Harmelin*, our legislature compared the gravity of the offense of teenagers who engage in oral sex but are within four years of age of each other and determined that a minimum ten-year sentence is grossly disproportionate for that crime. This conclusion appears to be a recognition by our General Assembly that teenagers are engaging in oral sex in large numbers; that teenagers should not be classified among the worst offenders because they do not have the maturity to appreciate the consequences of irresponsible sexual conduct and are readily subject to peer pressure; and that teenage sexual conduct does not usually involve violence and represents a significantly more benign situation than that of adults preying on children for sex. Similarly, the Model Penal Code adopted a provision de-criminalizing oral or vaginal sex with a person under sixteen years old where that person willingly engaged in the acts with another person who is not more than four years older. The commentary to the Model Penal Code explains that the criminal law should not target "[s]exual experimentation among social contemporaries"; that "[i]t will be rare that the comparably aged actor who obtains the consent of an underage person to sexual conduct . will be an experienced exploiter of immaturity"; and that the "more likely case is that both parties will be willing participants and that the assignment of culpability only to one will be perceived as unfair."

In addition to the extraordinary reduction in punishment for teenage oral sex reflected in the 2006 Amendment to OCGA § 16-6-4, the 2006 Amendment to that statute also provided for a large increase in the punishment for adults who engage in child molestation and aggravated child molestation. The new punishment for adults who engage in child molestation is ten years to life in prison, whereas the punishment under the prior law was imprisonment "for not less than five nor more than 20 years." For aggravated child molestation, the punishment for adults is now twenty-five years to life, followed by life on probation, with no possibility of probation or parole for the minimum prison time of twenty-five years. The significant increase in punishment for adult offenders highlights the legislature's view that a teenager engaging in oral sex with a willing teenage partner is far from the worst offender and is, in fact, not deserving of similar punishment to an adult offender.

Although society has a significant interest in protecting children from premature sexual activity, we must acknowledge that Wilson's crime does not rise to the level of culpability of adults who prey on children and that, for the law to punish Wilson as it would an adult, with the extraordinarily harsh punishment of ten years in prison without the possibility of probation or parole, appears to be grossly disproportionate to his crime.

Based on the foregoing factors and, in particular, based on the significance of the sea change in the General Assembly's view of the appropriate punishment for teenage oral sex, we could comfortably conclude that Wilson's punishment, as a matter of law, is grossly disproportionate to his crime without undertaking the further comparisons outlined in *Harmelin* and *Ewing*. However, we nevertheless will undertake those comparisons to complete our analysis.

(d) A comparison of Wilson's sentence with sentences for other crimes in this State buttresses the threshold inference of gross disproportionality. For example, a defendant who gets in a heated argument and shoving match with someone, walks away to retrieve a weapon, returns minutes later with a gun, and intentionally shoots and kills the person may be convicted of voluntary manslaughter and sentenced to as little as one year in prison. A person who plays Russian Roulette with a loaded handgun and causes the death of another person by shooting him or her with the loaded weapon may be convicted of involuntary manslaughter and receive a sentence of as little as one year in prison and no more than ten years. A person who intentionally shoots someone with the intent to kill, but fails in his aim such that the victim survives, may be convicted of aggravated assault and receive as little as one year in prison. A person who maliciously burns a neighbor's child in hot water, causing the child to lose use of a member of his or her body, may be convicted of aggravated battery and receive a sentence of as little as one year in prison. Finally, at the time Wilson committed his offense, a fifty-year-old man who fondled a five-year-old girl for his sexual gratification could receive as little as five years in prison, and a person who beat, choked, and forcibly raped a woman against her will could be sentenced to ten years in prison. There can be no legitimate dispute that the foregoing crimes are far more serious and disruptive of the social order than a teenager receiving oral sex from another willing teenager. The fact that these more culpable offenders may receive a significantly smaller or similar sentence buttresses our initial judgment that Wilson's sentence is grossly disproportionate to his crime.

(e) Finally, we compare Wilson's sentence to sentences imposed in other states for the same conduct. A review of other jurisdictions reveals that most states either would not punish Wilson's conduct at all or would, like Georgia now, punish it as a misdemeanor. Although some states retain a felony designation for Wilson's conduct, we have found no state that imposes a minimum punishment of ten years in prison with no possibility of probation or parole, such as that provided for by former OCGA § 16-6-4. This review thus also reinforces our initial judgment of gross disproportionality between Wilson's crime and his sentence.

(f) At this point, the Supreme Court's decision in *Weems v. United States*, merits discussion. In that case, Weems forged signatures on several public documents. The Supreme Court found that a minimum sentence of twelve years in chains at hard labor for falsifying public documents, combined with lifetime surveillance by appropriate authorities after Weems's release from prison, constituted cruel and unusual punishment. The Court stated that, because the minimum punishment imposed on Weems was more severe than or similar to punishments for some "degrees of homicide" and other more serious crimes, Weems's punishment was cruel and unusual. According to the Court,

> [t]his contrast shows more than different exercises of legislative judgment. It is greater than that. It condemns the sentence in this case as cruel and unusual. It exhibits a difference between unrestrained power and that which is exercised under the spirit of constitutional limitations formed to establish justice.

(g) All of the foregoing considerations compel the conclusion that Wilson's sentence is grossly disproportionate to his crime and constitutes cruel and unusual punishment under both the Georgia and United States Constitutions. We emphasize that it is the "rare case [ ]" in which the threshold inference of gross disproportionality will be met and a rarer case still in which that threshold inference stands after further scrutiny. The present case, however, is one of those rare cases. We also emphasize that nothing in this opinion should be read as

endorsing attempts by the judiciary to apply statutes retroactively. As in *Fleming* and *Dawson*, in which this Court did not apply the legislative amendments retroactively, we are not applying the 2006 Amendment retroactively in this case. Instead, as in *Fleming* and *Dawson*, we merely factor the 2006 Amendment into the evaluation of whether Wilson's punishment is cruel and unusual.

As a final matter, the dissent's concerns about the impact of today's opinion are unfounded. In point of fact, today's opinion will affect only a small number of individuals whose crimes and circumstances are similar to Wilson's, i.e., those teenagers convicted only of aggravated child molestation, based solely on an act of sodomy, with no injury to the victim, involving a willing teenage partner no more than four years younger than the defendant. For example, in this regard, Widner was convicted not only of aggravated child molestation but also of statutory rape.

4. The State contends that, even if the habeas court properly concluded that Wilson's punishment was cruel and unusual, it had no authority to resentence Wilson for a lesser crime. We agree that the trial court did not grant the proper relief to Wilson.

In *Weems*, after concluding that the minimum sentence of twelve years in chains at hard labor constituted cruel and unusual punishment, the Court ruled that, because the minimum punishment was unconstitutional and because there was no other law under which Weems could be sentenced, Weems's " judgment [had to] be reversed, with directions to dismiss the proceedings." Similarly, in the present case, Wilson stands convicted of aggravated child molestation, and, as in *Weems*, we have determined that, under the statute then in effect, the minimum punishment authorized by the legislature for that crime is unconstitutional. Because *Weems* was decided on direct appeal, and the present case stems from Wilson's habeas petition, we cannot direct the trial court to set aside the judgment and to dismiss the proceedings against Wilson. Instead, the corresponding and appropriate habeas relief would be for the habeas court to set aside Wilson's sentence and to discharge Wilson from custody.

MILLER v. ALABAMA,
567 U.S. 460 (2012)

FACTS (Official Summary)
In each of these cases, a 14-year-old was convicted of murder and sentenced to a mandatory term of life imprisonment without the possibility of parole. In No. 10–9647, petitioner Jackson accompanied two other boys to a video store to commit a robbery; on the way to the store, he learned that one of the boys was carrying a shotgun. Jackson stayed outside the store for most of the robbery, but after he entered, one of his co-conspirators shot and killed the store clerk. Arkansas charged Jackson as an adult with capital felony murder and aggravated robbery, and a jury convicted him of both crimes. The trial court imposed a statutorily mandated sentence of life imprisonment without the possibility of parole. Jackson filed a state habeas petition, arguing that a mandatory life-without-parole term for a 14-year-old violates the Eighth Amendment. Disagreeing, the court granted the State's motion to dismiss. The Arkansas Supreme Court affirmed.

In No. 10–9646, petitioner Miller, along with a friend, beat Miller's neighbor and set fire to his trailer after an evening of drinking and drug use. The neighbor died. Miller was initially charged as a juvenile, but his case was removed to adult court, where he was charged with murder in the course of arson. A jury found Miller guilty, and the trial court imposed a statutorily mandated punishment of life without parole. The Alabama Court of Criminal Appeals affirmed, holding that Miller's sentence was not overly harsh when compared to his crime, and that its mandatory nature was permissible under the Eighth Amendment.

KAGAN, J., delivered the opinion of the Court, in which KENNEDY, GINSBURG, BREYER, and SOTOMAYOR, JJ., joined.

HELD: The Eighth Amendment forbids a sentencing scheme that mandates life in prison without possibility of parole for juvenile homicide offenders.

(a) The Eighth Amendment's prohibition of cruel and unusual punishment "guarantees individuals the right not to be subjected to excessive

sanctions." *Roper* v. *Simmons*, 543 U. S. 551, 560. That right "flows from the basic 'precept of justice that punishment for crime should be graduated and proportioned' " to both the offender and the offense.

Two strands of precedent reflecting the concern with proportionate punishment come together here. The first has adopted categorical bans on sentencing practices based on mismatches between the culpability of a class of offenders and the severity of a penalty. See, *e.g., Kennedy* v. *Louisiana*. Several cases in this group have specially focused on juvenile offenders, because of their lesser culpability. Thus, *Roper* v. *Simmons* held that the Eighth Amendment bars capital punishment for children, and *Graham v. Florida*, 560 U. S. ___, concluded that the Amendment prohibits a sentence of life without the possibility of parole for a juvenile convicted of a nonhomicide offense. *Graham* further likened life without parole for juveniles to the death penalty, thereby evoking a second line of cases. In those decisions, this Court has required sentencing authorities to consider the characteristics of a defendant and the details of his offense before sentencing him to death. Here, the confluence of these two lines of precedent leads to the conclusion that mandatory life without parole for juveniles violates the Eighth Amendment.

As to the first set of cases: *Roper* and *Graham* establish that children are constitutionally different from adults for sentencing purposes. Their " 'lack of maturity' " and " 'underdeveloped sense of responsibility' " lead to recklessness, impulsivity, and heedless risk-taking. *Roper.* They "are more vulnerable . . . to negative influences and outside pressures," including from their family and peers; they have limited "contro[l] over their own environment" and lack the ability to extricate themselves from horrific, crime-producing settings. And because a child's character is not as "well formed" as an adult's, his traits are "less fixed" and his actions are less likely to be "evidence of irretrievabl[e] deprav[ity]." *Roper* and *Graham* emphasized that the distinctive attributes of youth diminish the penological justifications for imposing the harshest sentences on juvenile offenders, even when they commit terrible crimes.

While *Graham's* flat ban on life without parole was for nonhomicide crimes, nothing that *Graham* said about children is crime-specific. Thus, [*Graham's*] reasoning implicates any life-without-parole sentence for a juvenile, even as its categorical bar relates only to nonhomicide offenses. Most fundamentally, *Graham* insists that youth matters in determining the appropriateness of a lifetime of incarceration without the possibility of parole. The mandatory penalty schemes at issue here, however, prevent the sentencer from considering youth and from assessing whether the law's harshest term of imprisonment proportionately punishes a juvenile offender. This contravenes *Graham's* (and also *Roper's*) foundational principle: that imposition of a State's most severe penalties on juvenile offenders cannot proceed as though they were not children.

Graham also likened life-without-parole sentences for juveniles to the death penalty. That decision recognized that life-without-parole sentences "share some characteristics with death sentences that are shared by no other sentences." 560 U. S., at ___. And it treated life without parole for juveniles like this Court's cases treat the death penalty, imposing a categorical bar on its imposition for nonhomicide offenses. By likening life-without-parole sentences for juveniles to the death penalty, *Graham* makes relevant this Court's cases demanding individualized sentencing in capital cases. In particular, those cases have emphasized that sentencers must be able to consider the mitigating qualities of youth. In light of *Graham's* reasoning, these decisions also show the flaws of imposing mandatory life-without-parole sentences on juvenile homicide offenders.

(1) The State first contend that *Harmelin* v. *Michigan* forecloses a holding that mandatory life-without-parole sentences for juveniles violate the Eighth Amendment. *Harmelin* declined to extend the individualized sentencing requirement to noncapital cases "because of the qualitative difference between death and all other penalties." But *Harmelin* had nothing to do with children, and did not purport to apply to juvenile offenders. Indeed, since *Harmelin*, this Court has held on multiple occasions that sentencing practices that are permissible for adults may not be so for children.

The States next contend that mandatory life-without-parole terms for juveniles cannot be unconstitutional because 29 jurisdictions impose them on at least some children convicted of murder. In considering categorical bars to the death penalty and life without parole, this Court asks as part of the analysis whether legislative enactments and actual sentencing practices show a national consensus against a sentence for a particular class of offenders. But where, as here, this Court does not categorically bar a penalty, but instead requires only that a sentencer follow a certain process, this Court has not scrutinized or relied on legislative enactments in the same way.

In any event, the "objective indicia of society's standards," that the States offer do not distinguish these cases from others holding that a sentencing practice violates the Eighth Amendment. Fewer States impose mandatory life-without-parole sentences on juvenile homicide offenders than authorized the penalty (life-without-parole for nonhomicide offenders) that this Court invalidated in *Graham*. And as *Graham* and *Thompson* v. *Oklahoma* explain, simply counting legislative enactments can present a distorted view. In those cases, as here, the relevant penalty applied to juveniles based on two separate provisions: One allowed the transfer of certain juvenile offenders to adult court, while another set out penalties for any and all individuals tried there. In those circumstances, this Court reasoned, it was impossible to say whether a legislature had endorsed a given penalty for children (or would do so if presented with the choice). The same is true here.

(2) The States next argue that courts and prosecutors sufficiently consider a juvenile defendant's age, as well as his background and the circumstances of his crime, when deciding whether to try him as an adult. But this argument ignores that many States use mandatory transfer systems. In addition, some lodge the decision in the hands of the prosecutors, rather than courts. And even where judges have transfer-stage discretion, it has limited utility, because the decisionmaker typically will have only partial information about the child or the circumstances of his offense. Finally, because of the limited

sentencing options in some juvenile courts, the transfer decision may present a choice between a light sentence as a juvenile and standard sentencing as an adult. It cannot substitute for discretion at post-trial sentencing.

BREYER, J., **concurring** opinion in which SOTOMAYOR, J., joined, omitted.

ROBERTS, C. J., **dissenting** opinion, in which SCALIA, THOMAS, and ALITO, JJ., joined, omitted.
THOMAS, J., **dissenting** opinion, in which SCALIA, J., joined., omitted.
ALITO, J., **dissenting** opinion, in which SCALIA, J., joined, omitted.

EWING v. CALIFORNIA,
538 U.S. 11 (2003)

FACTS (Official Summary)
Under California's three strikes law, a defendant who is convicted of a felony and has previously been convicted of two or more serious or violent felonies must receive an indeterminate life imprisonment term. Such a defendant becomes eligible for parole on a date calculated by reference to a minimum term, which, in this case, is 25 years. While on parole, petitioner Ewing was convicted of felony grand theft for stealing three golf clubs, worth $399 apiece. As required by the three strikes law, the prosecutor formally alleged, and the trial court found, that Ewing had been convicted previously of four serious or violent felonies. In sentencing him to 25 years to life, the court refused to exercise its discretion to reduce the conviction to a misdemeanor--under a state law that permits certain offenses, known as "wobblers," to be classified as either misdemeanors or felonies--or to dismiss the allegations of some or all of his prior relevant convictions. The State Court of Appeal ... rejected Ewing's claim that his sentence was grossly disproportionate under the Eighth Amendment and reasoned that enhanced sentences under the three strikes law served the State's legitimate goal of deterring and incapacitating repeat offenders. The State Supreme Court denied review.

OPINION (Official Summary)
Justice O'Connor, joined by The Chief Justice and Justice Kennedy, concluded that Ewing's sentence is not grossly disproportionate and therefore does not violate the Eighth Amendment's prohibition on cruel and unusual punishments.

(a) The Eighth Amendment has a "narrow proportionality principle" that "applies to noncapital sentences." *Harmelin v. Michigan*. The Amendment's application in this context is guided by the principles distilled in Justice Kennedy's concurrence in *Harmelin:* "[T]he primacy of the legislature, the variety of legitimate penological schemes, the nature of our federal system, and the requirement that proportionality review be guided by objective factors" inform the final principle that the "Eighth Amendment does not require strict proportionality between crime and sentence [but] forbids only extreme sentences that are 'grossly disproportionate' to the crime."

(b) State legislatures enacting three strikes laws made a deliberate policy choice that individuals who have repeatedly engaged in serious or violent criminal behavior, and whose conduct has not been deterred by more conventional punishment approaches, must be isolated from society to protect the public safety. Though these laws are relatively new, this Court has a longstanding tradition of deferring to state legislatures in making and implementing such important policy decisions. The Constitution "does not mandate adoption of any one penological theory," and nothing in the Eighth Amendment prohibits California from choosing to incapacitate criminals who have already been convicted of at least one serious or violent crime. Recidivism has long been recognized as a legitimate basis for increased punishment and is a serious public safety concern in California and the Nation. Any criticism of the law is appropriately directed at the legislature, which is primarily responsible for making the policy choices underlying any criminal sentencing scheme.

(c) In examining Ewing's claim that his sentence is grossly disproportionate, the gravity of the offense must be compared to the harshness of the penalty. Even standing alone, his grand theft should not be taken lightly. The California Supreme Court has noted that crime's seriousness in the context of proportionality review; that it is a "wobbler" is of no moment, for it remains a felony unless the trial court imposes a misdemeanor sentence. The trial judge justifiably exercised her discretion not to extend lenient treatment given Ewing's long criminal history. In weighing the offense's gravity, both his current felony and his long history of felony recidivism must be placed on the scales. Any other approach would not accord proper deference to the policy judgments that find expression in the legislature's choice of sanctions. Ewing's sentence is justified by the State's public-safety interest in incapacitating and deterring recidivist felons, and amply supported by his own long, serious criminal record. He has been convicted of numerous offenses, served nine separate prison terms, and committed most of his crimes while on probation or parole. His prior

strikes were serious felonies including robbery and residential burglary. Though long, his current sentence reflects a rational legislative judgment that is entitled to deference.

Justice Scalia agreed that petitioner's sentence does not violate the Eighth Amendment's prohibition against cruel and unusual punishments, but on the ground that that prohibition was aimed at excluding only certain modes of punishment. This case demonstrates why a proportionality principle cannot be intelligently applied.

Justice Thomas concluded that petitioner's sentence does not violate the Eighth Amendment's prohibition against cruel and unusual punishments because the Amendment contains no proportionality principle.

Other Case—Cruel and Unusual Punishment

Weems v. United States, 217 U.S. 349 (1910).
Court held that a 12-year-sentence of hard labor for the crime of passing a forged check was cruel and unusual punishment.

Lockyer v. Andrade, 563 U.S. 63 (2003).
Decided on the same day as Ewing v. California. The Court affirmed two 25-year-to-life sentences for stealing videotapes totaling $150.00 under California's "three strikes law."

Madison v. Alabama 586 U.S. ___ (2019) (same case as above, but revisited.
Vernon Madison had been on death row for over 30 years for killing a police officer. While on death row, he suffered a series of strokes, was diagnosed with vascular dementia, and could not remember killing the police officer. The Court held that the Eighth Amendment does not prohibit a state from executing a prisoner who, due to mental disability, cannot remember committing the crime. The Court also had to decide whether it was cruel and unusual punishment to execute a prisoner who cannot rationally understand the reasons for his execution whether that inability is due to psychosis or dementia. The Court found that it was. Justice Kagan's opinion stated,

> First, a person lacking in memory of his crime may yet rationally understand why the State seeks to execute him; if so, the Eighth Amendment poses no bar to his execution. Second a person suffering from dementia ma be unable to rationally

understand the reasons for his sentence; if so, the Eighth Amendment does not allow his execution. What matters is whether a person has the a rational understanding. . .not whether he has any particular memory or any particular mental illness.

Bucklew v. Precythe, 587 U.S. ___ (2019)
Bucklew ws convicted by a state court jury and sentenced to death. He was scheduled to be executed in 2014. In federal court he claimed that Missouri's lethal injection protocol would constitute cruel and unusual punishment as applied to him because of his unique congenital medical condition. He claimed that the injection would likely cause him to hemorrhage during the execution causing him to choke on his own blood. He proposed nitrogen hypoxia as an alternative method for his execution. A state court prisoner can successfully request an alternative method (or claim that the state's method constitutes a violation of the Eighth Amendment) if he can show that there is a feasible and readily implemented alternative that would significantly reduce a substantial risk of pain, and that the state had refused to adopt it without any legitimate penological reason. The Court held 5-4 that Bucklew had failed to meet his burden in proving that nitrogen hypoxia was a viable, readily implemented alternative…And, even if he had, he had failed to show that it would significantly reduce a substantial risk of severe pain.

WRAP UP

Legislators must be very careful when making new laws: they cannot make laws that are drafted so that a person of ordinary intelligence would not understand the law or that would allow police too much discretion in how they will interpret and apply the law. Such laws would be considered void for vagueness. Legislators cannot make laws that apply retroactively (ex post facto laws); make laws that allow the government to invade people's privacy. Legislatures can place restrictions on weapons and ammunitions purchase and possession, but they cannot completely restrict people's ability to possess guns for the purpose of self-defense. Generally, legislatures can make laws that treat people differently if the laws are rationally related to a legitimate government interest. But, when laws treat people differently based upon their sex, then the lawmakers have to have even a compelling reason to do so. When laws treat people different because of their race, the courts, employing "strict scrutiny" are likely to declare such laws unconstitutional. Finally, legislators cannot pass laws (and courts cannot tolerate laws) that make the punishment for a crime barbaric or disproportionate to the crime committed.

Chapter Two: Constitutional Limits Part II (First Amendment Issues)

The First Amendment lists several restrictions on Congress's power to create legislation. Through the Fourteenth Amendment's Due Process Clause, these restrictions also apply to state legislation. As you have read in Chapter One, when the government creates laws that run up against some constitutional protections, courts may strike down those statutes. Thus, we refer to these protections as constitutional limits (on the government's ability to regulate certain types of behavior. The First Amendment provides,

> Congress shall make no law respecting an establishment of religion, or prohibiting the free exercise thereof; or abridging the freedom of speech, or of the press; or the right of the people peaceably to assemble, and to petition the Government for a redress of grievances.

One court-created doctrine that defendant's also raise that is closely related to the First Amendment and is often raised in attacks on a statute that impacts a First Amendment right is that of "void for overbreadth." Although a law may technically be impermissibly overbroad for a variety of reasons, the void for overbreadth claim frequently involves scenarios in which the defendant is claiming a statute is overbroad because it violates his or her freedom of speech or expression.

FREEDOM OF RELIGION

Religious freedom was particularly important to the new colonists, and it is the first right set forth in the Bill of Rights. The First Amendment prohibits Congress from making laws that restrict the freedom of religion. It comprises two separate clauses: The Establishment Clause and the Exercise Clause.

The Establishment Clause

The First Amendment states, "Congress shall make no law respecting an establishment of religion." The "Establishment Clause" has little to do with criminal law or procedure and basically means that Congress cannot create a national church or prescribe a religion; government cannot set up a religion and require people to be part of that religion.

It is, however, impossible to completely separate the church and the state. For example, even church buildings have to conform to building codes. Nevertheless, the First Amendment tries to ensure that government neither favors, nor is hostile toward, one religion over another. Questions raised by cases interpreting the Establishment Clause is how much governmental interaction is necessary for one to conclude it is establishing a religion? Is providing federal financial aid to students who want to go to a private religious based school sufficient connection? (Generally, no). Is it okay for a school to have a Christmas tree? A minute of prayer?

Generally, when studying substantive criminal law, we get to dodge the bullet on these questions because they are beyond the scope of the criminal law. But essentially, in order to survive an Establishment Clause challenge, the state law must: (1) have a primary secular (non-religious) purpose; (2) have a principle effect that neither advances nor inhibits religion; and (3) not generate excessive entanglement between government and religion. The cases in the Establishment Clause area show the struggle between changing norms and constitutional interpretations

Other Cases—Establishment Clause

Everson v. Board of Education, 330 U.S. 1 (1947). Court held that the Establishment Clause of the Constitution was applicable to the states through the Fourteenth Amendment and found that a state statute allowing reimbursement to parents for money spent to transport their children to parochial schools on the public bus system did not constitute the establishment of religion. The Court noted that the reimbursement policy applied to parents of both public and parochial school students and conformed to the intent of the clause. It likened the statute to general public welfare legislation.

Stone v. Graham, 449 U.S. 39 (1980).
The Court struck down a Kentucky law requiring the posting of the Ten Commandments in all classrooms.

Town of Greece v. Galloway, 572 U.S. ____ (2014).
The Court upheld a town's practice of beginning the monthly town board meetings with a prayer given by clergy selected from the congregations listed in a local directory. It found that this practice did not violate the First Amendment's Establishment Clause where 1) legislative prayer is not required to be nonsectarian; 2) absent a pattern of prayers that over time denigrate, proselytize, or betray an impermissible government purpose, a challenge based solely on the content of particular prayer will not likely establish a constitutional violation; and 3) so long as the town maintains a policy of nondiscrimination, the Constitution does not require it to search beyond its borders for non-Christian prayer givers in an effort to achieve religious balancing.

The American Legion v. American Humanist Association, 588 U.S. ___ (2019)
The Court held that when a local government displays and maintains a large memorial cross, it does not violate the Establishment Clause. This case reiterated the three-prong analysis courts employ when evaluating whether a law establishes a religion in violation of the First Amendment.

The Exercise Clause

The second aspect of religious freedom has a much clearer connection to the criminal law. The First Amendment states, "Congress shall make no law . . . prohibiting the free exercise [of religion]." The free exercise of religion involves the freedom to believe and the freedom to act.

> The First Amendment was intended to allow every one under the jurisdiction of the United States to entertain such notions respecting his relations to his Maker and the duties they impose as may be approved by his judgment and conscience, and to exhibit his sentiments in such form of worship, as he may think proper, not injurious to the rights of others. *Davis v. Beason,* 133 U.S. 33 (1890).

A few examples highlight how the substantive criminal law can impact a person's exercise of his or her religion. Is Edie entitled to smoke peyote as part of her religious practice while incarcerated or does the correctional staff have a right to deny her that right even assuming it is a legitimate exercise of her religion? Can the court force parents who are practicing Jehovah's Witnesses to allow a life-saving blood transfusion for their minor child? If they refuse, and their child dies will they successfully be prosecuted for criminally negligent homicide? Note that courts generally recognize the right of adults to refuse medical treatment for themselves based on their personal religious beliefs, but when adults make similar decisions for their children, they may violate the criminal law. "Parents may be free to become martyrs themselves. But it does not follow that they are free in identical circumstances to make martyrs of their children before they have reached the age of full legal discretion when they can make that choice for themselves." *Prince v. Massachusetts,* 321 U.S. 158 (1944).

WHEN FREE EXERCISE OF RELIGION CONFLICTS WITH CRIMINAL LAW

When religion and criminal law conflict, the courts will generally look at whether the criminal statute is one of general applicability (for example, criminally negligent homicide) or whether it is more inclined to target religious practices. The Constitution permits the former but not the latter. The courts have distinguished between laws which incidentally prohibit some exercise of religious practice and laws which are written specifically to stop a religious practice.

CANTWELL v. CONNECTICUT,
10 U.S. 296 (1949)

MR. JUSTICE ROBERTS, delivered the opinion of the Court.

Newton Cantwell and his two sons, Jesse and

Russell, members of a group known as Jehovah's witnesses, and claiming to be ordained ministers, were arrested in New Haven, Connecticut, and each was charged by information in five counts, with statutory and common law offenses. After trial in the Court of Common Pleas of New Haven County each of them was convicted on the third count, which charged a violation of 6294 of the General Statutes of Connecticut, and on the fifth count, which charged commission of the common law offense of inciting a breach of the peace. On appeal to the Supreme Court the conviction of all three on the third count was affirmed. The conviction of Jesse Cantwell, on the fifth count, was also affirmed, but the conviction of Newton and Russell on that count was reversed and a new trial ordered as to them.

[T]he appellants pressed the contention that the statute under which the third count was drawn was offensive to the due process clause of the Fourteenth Amendment because, on its face and as construed and applied, it denied them freedom of speech and prohibited their free exercise of religion. In like manner they made the point that they could not be found guilty on the fifth count, without violation of the Amendment.

. . .

. . . On the day of their arrest the appellants were engaged in going singly from house to house on Cassius Street in New Haven. They were individually equipped with a bag containing books and pamphlets on religious subjects, a portable phonograph and a set of records, each of which, when played, introduced, and was a description of, one of the books. Each appellant asked the person who responded to his call for permission to play one of the records. If permission was granted he asked the person to buy the book described and, upon refusal, he solicited such contribution towards the publication of the pamphlets as the listener was willing to make. If a contribution was received a pamphlet was delivered upon condition that it would be read.

Cassius Street is in a thickly populated neighborhood, where about ninety per cent of the residents are Roman Catholics. A phonograph record, describing a book entitled 'Enemies', included an attack on the Catholic religion. None of the persons interviewed were members of Jehovah's witnesses.

The statute under which the appellants were charged [in count three] provides:

'No person shall solicit money, services, subscriptions or any valuable thing for any alleged religious, charitable or philanthropic cause, from other than a member of the organization for whose benefit such person is soliciting or within the county in which such person or organization is located unless such cause shall have been approved by the secretary of the public welfare council. Upon application of any person in behalf of such cause, the secretary shall determine whether such cause is a religious one or is a bona fide object of charity or philanthropy and conforms to reasonable standards of efficiency and integrity, and, if he shall so find, shall approve the same and issue to the authority in charge a certificate to that effect. Such certificate may be revoked at any time. Any person violating any provision of this section shall be fined not more than one hundred dollars or imprisoned not more than thirty days or both.'

The appellants claimed that their activities were not within the statute but consisted only of distribution of books, pamphlets, and periodicals. The State Supreme Court construed the finding of the trial court to be that 'in addition to the sale of the books and the distribution of the pamphlets the defendants were also soliciting contributions or donations of money for an alleged religious cause, and thereby came within the purview of the statute. It overruled the contention that the Act, as applied to the appellants, offends the due process clause of the Fourteenth Amendment, because it abridges or denies religious freedom and liberty of speech and press. The court stated that it was the solicitation that brought the appellants within the sweep of the Act and not their other activities in the dissemination of literature. It declared the legislation constitutional as an effort by the State to protect the public against fraud and imposition in the solicitation of funds for what purported to be religious, charitable, or philanthropic causes.

The facts which were held to support the conviction of Jesse Cantwell on the fifth count were that he stopped two men in the street, asked, and received, permission to play a phonograph record, and played the record 'Enemies', which attacked the religion and church of the two men, who were Catholics. Both were incensed by the contents of the record and were tempted to strike Cantwell unless he went away. On being told to be on his way he left their presence. There was no evidence that he was personally offensive or entered into any argument with those he interviewed.

The court held that the charge was not assault or breach of the peace or threats on Cantwell's part, but invoking or inciting others to breach of the peace, and that the facts supported the conviction of that offense.

First. We hold that the statute, as construed and applied to the appellants, deprives them of their liberty without due process of law in contravention of the Fourteenth Amendment. The fundamental concept of liberty embodied in that Amendment embraces the liberties guaranteed by the First Amendment. The First Amendment declares that Congress shall make no law respecting an establishment of religion or prohibiting the free exercise thereof. The Fourteenth Amendment has rendered the legislatures of the states as incompetent as Congress to enact such laws. The constitutional inhibition of legislation on the subject of religion has a double aspect. On the one hand, it forestalls compulsion by law of the acceptance of any creed or the practice of any form of worship. Freedom of conscience and freedom to adhere to such religious organization or form of worship as the individual may choose cannot be restricted by law. On the other hand, it safeguards the free exercise of the chosen form of religion. Thus the Amendment embraces two concepts, -freedom to believe and freedom to act. The first is absolute but, in the nature of things, the second cannot be. Conduct remains subject to regulation for the protection of society. The freedom to act must have appropriate definition to preserve the enforcement of that protection. In every case the power to regulate must be so exercised as not, in attaining a permissible end, unduly to infringe the protected freedom. No one would contest the proposition that a state may not, by statute, wholly deny the right to preach or to disseminate religious views. Plainly such a previous and absolute restraint would violate the terms of the

guarantee. It is equally clear that a state may by general and non-discriminatory legislation regulate the times, the places, and the manner of soliciting upon its streets, and of holding meetings thereon; and may in other respects safeguard the peace, good order and comfort of the community, without unconstitutionally invading the liberties protected by the Fourteenth Amendment. The appellants are right in their insistence that the Act in question is not such a regulation. If a certificate is procured, solicitation is permitted without restraint but, in the absence of a certificate, solicitation is altogether prohibited.

The appellants urge that to require them to obtain a certificate as a condition of soliciting support for their views amounts to a prior restraint on the exercise of their religion within the meaning of the Constitution. The State insists that the Act, as construed by the Supreme Court of Connecticut, imposes no previous restraint upon the dissemination of religious views or teaching but merely safeguards against the perpetration of frauds under the cloak of religion. Conceding that this is so, the question remains whether the method adopted by Connecticut to that end transgresses the liberty safeguarded by the Constitution.

The general regulation, in the public interest, of solicitation, which does not involve any religious test and does not unreasonably obstruct or delay the collection of funds, is not open to any constitutional objection, even though the collection be for a religious purpose. Such regulation would not constitute a prohibited previous restraint on the free exercise of religion or interpose an inadmissible obstacle to its exercise.

It will be noted, however, that the Act requires an application to the secretary of the public welfare council of the State; that he is empowered to determine whether the cause is a religious one, and that the issue of a certificate depends upon his affirmative action. If he finds that the cause is not that of religion, to solicit for it becomes a crime. He is not to issue a certificate as a matter of course. His decision to issue or refuse it involves appraisal of facts, the exercise of judgment, and the formation of an opinion. He is authorized to withhold his approval if he determines that the cause is not a religious one.

Such a censorship of religion as the means of determining its right to survive is a denial of liberty protected by the First Amendment and included in the liberty which is within the protection of the Fourteenth.

The State asserts that if the licensing officer acts arbitrarily, capriciously, or corruptly, his action is subject to judicial correction. ...

. . . The line between a discretionary and a ministerial act is not always easy to mark and the statute has not been construed by the State court to impose a mere ministerial duty on the secretary of the welfare council. Upon his decision as to the nature of the cause, the right to solicit depends. Moreover, the availability of a judicial remedy for abuses in the system of licensing still leaves that system one of previous restraint which, in the field of free speech and press, we have held inadmissible. A statute authorizing previous restraint upon the exercise of the guaranteed freedom by judicial decision after trial is as obnoxious to the Constitution as one providing for like restraint by administrative action.

. . . Even the exercise of religion may be at some slight inconvenience in order that the state may protect its citizens from injury. Without doubt a state may protect its citizens from fraudulent solicitation by requiring a stranger in the community, before permitting him publicly to solicit funds for any purpose, to establish his identity and his authority to act for the cause which he purports to represent. The state is likewise free to regulate the time and manner of solicitation generally, in the interest of public safety, peace, comfort or convenience. But to condition the solicitation of aid for the perpetuation of religious views or systems upon a license, the grant of which rests in the exercise of a determination by state authority as to what is a religious cause, is to lay a forbidden burden upon the exercise of liberty protected by the Constitution.

Second. We hold that, in the circumstances disclosed, the conviction of Jesse Cantwell on the fifth count must be set aside. Decision as to the lawfulness of the conviction demands the weighing of two conflicting interests. The fundamental law declares the interest of the United States that the free exercise of religion be not prohibited and that freedom to communicate information and opinion be not abridged. The state of Connecticut has an obvious interest in the preservation and protection of peace and good order within her borders. We must determine whether the alleged protection of the State's interest, means to which end would, in the absence of limitation by the federal Constitution, lie wholly within the State's discretion, has been pressed, in this instance, to a point where it has come into fatal collision with the overriding interest protected by the federal compact.

Conviction on the fifth count was not pursuant to a statute . . . [rather] . . . the judgment is based on a common law concept of the most general and undefined nature. The court below has held that the petitioner's conduct constituted the commission of an offense under the State law, and we accept its decision as binding upon us to that extent.

The offense known as breach of the peace embraces a great variety of conduct destroying or menacing public order and tranquility. It includes not only violent acts but acts and words likely to produce violence in others. No one would have the hardihood to suggest that the principle of freedom of speech sanctions incitement to riot or that religious liberty connotes the privilege to exhort others to physical attack upon those belonging to another sect. When clear and present danger of riot, disorder, interference with traffic upon the public streets, or other immediate threat to public safety, peace, or order, appears, the power of the state to prevent or punish is obvious. Equally obvious is it that a state may not unduly suppress free communication of views, religious or other, under the guise of conserving desirable conditions. Here we have a situation analogous to a conviction under a statute sweeping in a great variety of conduct under a general and indefinite characterization, and leaving to the executive and judicial branches too wide a discretion in its application.

Having these considerations in mind, we note that Jesse Cantwell, on April 26, 1938, was upon a public street, where he had a right to be, and where he had a right peacefully to impart his views to others. There is no showing that his deportment was noisy, truculent, overbearing or offensive. He requested of two pedestrians permission to play to them a phonograph record. The permission was granted. It is not claimed that he intended to insult or affront the hearers by playing the record. It is plain that he wished only to interest them in his propaganda. The sound of the phonograph is not shown to have disturbed residents of the street, to have drawn a crowd, or to have impeded traffic. Thus far he had invaded no right or interest of the public or of the men accosted.

The record played by Cantwell embodies a general attack on all organized religious systems as instruments of Satan and injurious to man; it then singles out the Roman Catholic Church for strictures couched in terms which naturally would offend not only persons of that persuasion, but all others who respect the honestly held religious faith of their fellows. The hearers were in fact highly offended. One of them said he felt like hitting Cantwell and the other that he was tempted to throw Cantwell off the street. The one who testified he felt like hitting Cantwell said, in answer to the question 'Did you do anything else or have any other reaction?' 'No, sir, because he said he would take the victrola and he went.' The other witness testified that he told Cantwell he had better get off the street before something happened to him and that was the end of the matter as Cantwell picked up his books and walked up the street.

Cantwell's conduct, in the view of the court below, considered apart from the effect of his communication upon his hearers, did not amount to a breach of the peace. One may, however, be guilty of the offense if he commits acts or make statements likely to provoke violence and disturbance of good order, even though no such eventuality be intended. Decisions to this effect are many, but examination discloses that, in practically all, the provocative language which was held to amount to a breach of the peace consisted of profane, indecent, or abusive remarks directed to the person of the hearer. Resort to epithets or personal abuse is not in any proper sense communication of information or opinion safeguarded by the Constitution, and its punishment as a criminal act would raise no question under that instrument.

We find in the instant case no assault or threatening of bodily harm, no truculent bearing, no intentional discourtesy, no personal abuse. On the contrary, we find only an effort to persuade a willing listener to buy a book or to contribute money in the interest of what Cantwell, however misguided others may think him, conceived to be true religion.

In the realm of religious faith, and in that of political belief, sharp differences arise. In both fields the tenets of one man may seem the rankest error to his neighbor. To persuade others to his own point of view, the pleader, as we know, at times, resorts to exaggeration, to vilification of men who have been, or are, prominent in church or state, and even to false statement. But the people of this nation have ordained in the light of history, that, in spite of the probability of excesses and abuses, these liberties are, in the long view, essential to enlightened opinion and right conduct on the part of the citizens of a democracy.

The essential characteristic of these liberties is, that under their shield many types of life, character, opinion and belief can develop unmolested and unobstructed. Nowhere is this shield more necessary than in our own country for a people composed of many races and of many creeds. There are limits to the exercise of these liberties. The danger in these times from the coercive activities of those who in the delusion of racial or religious conceit would incite violence and breaches of the peace in order to deprive others of their equal right to the exercise of their liberties, is emphasized by events familiar to all. These and other transgressions of those limits the states appropriately may punish. Although the contents of the record not unnaturally aroused animosity, we think that, in the absence of a statute narrowly drawn to define and punish specific conduct as constituting a clear and present danger to a substantial interest of the State, the petitioner's communication, considered in the light of the constitutional guarantees, raised no such clear and present menace to public peace and order as to render him liable to conviction of the common law offense in question.

[The Court reversed Cantwell's convictions.]

RELIGIOUS FREEDOM RESTORATION ACT OF 1993

In 1990 the Court decided *Employment Division v. Smith* (see below). In response, Congress passed, and President Clinton signed, the Religious Freedom Restoration Act of 1993; Pub. L. No. 103-141, 107 Stat. 1488 (November 16, 1993) the explicit purpose of which was to overturn the *Smith* holding. Congress intended to limit government's interference with religious practices. The Court, however, struck down this act holding that it was a legislative encroachment on the judicial right of the courts to interpret the U.S. Constitution. See, *City of Boerne, Texas v. Flores*, 521 U.S. 507 (1997).

Recently, Congress has again attempted to limit government's ability to impede the exercise of religion. Under the Religious Land Use and Institutionalized Persons Act of 2000 (RLUIPA) no government shall impose a substantial burden on the religious exercise of an institutionalized person unless the government demonstrates that the burden is the least restrictive means of furthering a compelling governmental interest. In January 2015 the Court decided *Holt v. Hobbs,* 574 U.S. ___ (2015), in which a devout Muslim inmate wished to grow a 1/2-inch beard in accordance with his religious beliefs but against prison policy.

HOLT v. HOBBS,
574 U.S. ____ (2015)

FACTS (Official Summary)

Section 3 of the Religious Land Use and Institutionalized Persons Act of 2000 (RLUIPA) provides that "[n]o government shall impose a substantial burden on the religious exercise" of an institutionalized person unless the government demonstrates that the burden "is the least restrictive means of furthering [a] compelling governmental interest."

Petitioner is an Arkansas inmate and devout Muslim who wishes to grow a ½-inch beard in accordance with his religious beliefs. Respondent Arkansas Department of Correction (Department) prohibits its prisoners from growing beards, with the single exception that inmates with diagnosed skin conditions may grow ¼-inch beards. Petitioner sought an exemption on religious grounds and, although he believes that his faith requires him not to trim his beard at all, he proposed a compromise under which he would be allowed to maintain a ½-inch beard. Prison officials denied his request, and petitioner sued in Federal District Court. At an evidentiary hearing before a Magistrate Judge, Department witnesses testified that beards compromised prison safety because they could be used to hide contraband and because an inmate could quickly shave his beard to disguise his identity. The Magistrate Judge recommended dismissing petitioner's complaint, emphasizing that prison officials are entitled to deference on security matters and that the prison permitted

petitioner to exercise his religion in other ways. The District Court adopted the recommendation in full, and the Eighth Circuit affirmed, holding that the Department had satisfied its burden of showing that the grooming policy was the least restrictive means of furthering its compelling security interests, and reiterating that courts should defer to prison officials on matters of security.

JUSTICE ALITO, J., **delivered the opinion for a unanimous Court.**

(a) Under RLUIPA, the challenging party bears the initial burden of proving that his religious exercise is grounded in a sincerely held religious belief and that the government's action substantially burdens his religious exercise. Here, petitioner's sincerity is not in dispute, and he easily satisfies the second obligation. The Department's policy forces him to choose between "engag[ing] in conduct that seriously violates [his] religious belie[f]," or contravening the grooming policy and risking disciplinary action. In reaching the opposite conclusion, the District Court misunderstood the analysis that RLUIPA demands. First, the District Court erred by concluding that the grooming policy did not substantially burden petitioner's religious exercise because he could practice his religion in other ways. Second, the District Court erroneously suggested that the burden on petitioner's religious exercise was slight because petitioner testified that his religion would "credit" him for attempting to follow his religious beliefs, even if that attempt proved unsuccessful. RLUIPA, however, applies to religious exercise regardless of whether it is "compelled." Finally, the District Court improperly relied on petitioner's testimony that not all Muslims believe that men must grow beards. Even if petitioner's belief were idiosyncratic, RLUIPA's guarantees are "not limited to beliefs which are shared by all of the members of a religious sect."

(b) Once the challenging party satisfies his burden, the burden shifts to the government to show that substantially burdening the religious exercise of the "particular claimant" is "the least restrictive means of furthering [a] compelling governmental interest." The Department fails to show that enforcing its beard prohibition against petitioner furthers its compelling interests in preventing prisoners from hiding contraband and disguising their identities.

(i) While the Department has a compelling interest in regulating contraband, its argument that this interest is compromised by allowing an inmate to grow a ½-inch beard is unavailing, especially given the difficulty of hiding contraband in such a short beard and the lack of a corresponding policy regulating the length of hair on the head. RLUIPA does not permit the unquestioning deference required to accept the Department's assessment. Even if the Department could show that denying petitioner a ½-inch beard furthers its interest in rooting out contraband, it would still have to show that its policy is the least restrictive means of furthering that interest, a standard that is "exceptionally demanding" and requires the government to "sho[w] that it lacks other means of achieving its desired goal without imposing a substantial burden on the exercise of religion by the objecting part[y]." Here, the Department fails to establish that its security concerns cannot be satisfied by simply searching a ½-inch beard.

(ii) Even if the Department's grooming policy furthers its compelling interest in prisoner identification, its policy still violates RLUIPA as applied in the present circumstances. As petitioner argues, requiring inmates to be photographed both with and without beards and then periodically thereafter is a less restrictive means of solving the Department's identification concerns. The Department fails to show why its prison system is so different from the many institutions that allow facial hair that the dual-photo method cannot be employed at its institutions. It also fails to show why the security risk presented by a prisoner shaving a ½-inch beard is so different from the risk of a prisoner shaving a mustache, head hair, or ¼-inch beard.

(c) In addition to the Department's failure to prove that petitioner's proposed alternatives would not sufficiently serve its security interests, the Department also fails to adequately explain the substantial underinclusiveness of its policy, since it permits ¼-inch beards for prisoners with medical conditions and more than ½ inch of hair on the head. Its failure to pursue its proffered objectives with regard to such "analogous nonreligious conduct" suggests that its interests "could be achieved by narrower ordinances that burdened religion to a far lesser degree." Nor does the Department explain why the vast majority of States and the Federal Government can permit inmates to grow ½-inch beards, either for any reason or for religious reasons, but it cannot. Such evidence requires a prison, at a minimum, to offer persuasive reasons why it believes it must take a different course.

The Department's grooming policy violates RLUIPA insofar as it prevents petitioner from growing a ½-inch beard in accordance with his religious beliefs.

Other Cases—Free Exercise of Religion

People v. Woody, 394 P.2d 813 (Cal. 1964). Several members of the Native American Church were convicted for possession of peyote. The California Supreme Court reversed the convictions, finding that the defendants' sacramental use of peyote was central for the members of that church and thus was protected by the First Amendment.

Church of the Lukimi Babalu Aye, Inc. v. City of Hialeah, 508 U.S. 520 (1993)

The Court invalidated a city ordinance directed at a church sect that used snakes in its religious practices because the statute specifically outlawed the use of live snakes in a ceremony. The statute made it an offense to "unnecessarily kill, torment, torture, or mutilate an animal in a public or private ritual or ceremony not for the primary purpose of food consumption." The Court found that the "laws in question were enacted by officials who did not understand, failed to perceive or chose to ignore the fact that their official actions violated the Nation's essential commitment to religious freedom." The Court specifically noted that the City of Hialeah had criminalized and targeted activity practiced by a religious group and was not enacting a general criminal prohibition against the slaughter of animals.

Employment Division v. Smith, 492 U.S. 872 (1990)
Two American Indian drug counselors in Oregon lost their jobs because they used peyote as part of a religious ritual in their church. They sought unemployment benefits, but the State refused to pay. The Court upheld the Employment Division's refusal. It reasoned that because respondents' ingestion of peyote was constitutionally prohibited under Oregon law, Oregon could deny respondents unemployment compensation when they were dismissed from their jobs because of their drug use. The Court tried to make clear in *Smith* that the Free Exercise Clause does not allow individuals to avoid the responsibilities and consequences of a generally applicable criminal statute.

Griffin v. Coughlin, 88 N.Y.2d 674, 673 N.E.2d 98, 649 N.Y.S.2d 903 (1996); Kerr v. Farrey 95 F.3d 472 (1996); Warner v. Orange County Department of Probation, 115 F.3d 1068 (1996).
Lower appellate court opinions which have struck down sentences that mandated participation in Alcoholics Anonymous or Narcotics Anonymous, saying these sentences violate the Establishment Clause because of the religious components of the 12-step programs (The Supreme Court has, to date, declined to review cases contesting court-mandated participation in AA or NA.)

FREEDOM OF SPEECH

In general, the government may neither require, nor substantially interfere with, individual expression. Most First Amendment cases do not involve the government compelling expression—for example a student may not be compelled to pledge allegiance to the American Flag. Justice Jackson observed,

> If there is any fixed star in our constitutional constellation, it is that no official, high or petty, can prescribe what shall be orthodox in politics, nationalism, religion, or other matters of opinion or force citizens to confess by word or act their faith therein. If there are any circumstances which permit an exception, they do not now occur to us.

> We think the action of the local authorities in compelling the flag salute and pledge transcends constitutional limitations on their power, and invades the sphere of intellect and spirit which it is the purpose of the First Amendment to our Constitution to reserve from all official control. *West Virginia State Board of Education v. Barnette*, 319 U.S. 624, 642 (1943).

Instead, most cases involve a statute that limits an individual's expression. Although the First Amendment's protection of free speech is broad, it is not absolute. In the case below, the Court indicated certain types of speech that are not considered worthy of protection.

CHAPLINSKY v. NEW HAMPSHIRE, 315 U.S. 568 (1942)

MR. JUSTICE MURPHY delivered the opinion of the Court.

Appellant, a member of the sect known as Jehovah's Witnesses, was convicted in the municipal court of Rochester, New Hampshire, for violation of Chapter 378, Section 2, of the Public Laws of New Hampshire: 'No person shall address any offensive, derisive or annoying word to any other person who is lawfully in any street or other public place, nor call him by any offensive or derisive name, nor make any noise or exclamation in his presence and hearing with intent to deride, offend or annoy him, or to prevent him from pursuing his lawful business or occupation.'

The complaint charged that appellant 'with force and arms, in a certain public place in said city of Rochester, to wit, on the public sidewalk on the easterly side of Wakefield Street, near unto the entrance of the City Hall, did unlawfully repeat, the words following, addressed to the complainant, that is to say, 'You are a God damned racketeer' and 'a damned Fascist and the whole government of Rochester are Fascists or agents of Fascists' the same being offensive, derisive and annoying words and names'.

Upon appeal there was a trial de novo of appellant before a jury in the Superior Court. He was found guilty and the judgment of conviction was affirmed by the Supreme Court of the State.

By motions and exceptions, appellant raised the questions that the statute was invalid under the Fourteenth Amendment of the Constitution of the United States in that it placed an unreasonable restraint on freedom of speech, freedom of the press, and freedom of worship, and because it was vague and indefinite. These contentions were overruled and the case comes here on appeal.

There is no substantial dispute over the facts. Chaplinsky was distributing the literature of his sect on the streets of Rochester on a busy Saturday afternoon. Members of the local citizenry complained to the City Marshal, Bowering, that Chaplinsky was denouncing all religion as a 'racket'. Bowering told them that Chaplinsky was lawfully engaged, and then warned Chaplinsky that the crowd was getting restless. Some time later a disturbance occurred and the traffic officer on duty at the busy intersection started with Chaplinsky for the police station, but did not inform him that he was under arrest or that he was going to be arrested. On the way they encountered Marshal Bowering who had been advised that a riot was under way and was therefore hurrying to the scene. Bowering repeated his earlier warning to Chaplinsky who then addressed to Bowering the words set forth in the complaint.

Chaplinsky's version of the affair was slightly different. He testified that when he met Bowering, he asked him to arrest the ones responsible for the disturbance. In reply Bowering cursed him and told him to come along. Appellant admitted that he said the words charged in the complaint with the exception of the name of the Deity.

Over appellant's objection the trial court excluded as immaterial testimony relating to appellant's mission 'to preach the true facts of the Bible', his treatment at the hands of the crowd, and the alleged neglect of duty on the part of the police. This action was approved by the court below which held that neither provocation nor the truth of the utterance would constitute a defense to the charge.

It is now clear that 'Freedom of speech and freedom of the press, which are protected by the First Amendment from infringement by Congress, are among the fundamental personal rights and liberties which are protected by the Fourteenth Amendment from invasion by state action'. Freedom of worship is similarly sheltered.

Appellant assails the statute as a violation of all three freedoms, speech, press and worship, but only an attack on the basis of free speech is warranted. The spoken, not the written, word is involved. And we cannot conceive that cursing a public officer is the exercise of religion in any sense of the term. But even if the activities of the appellant which preceded the incident could be viewed as religious in character, and therefore entitled to the protection of the Fourteenth Amendment, they would not cloak him with immunity from the legal consequences for concomitant acts committed in violation of a valid criminal statute. We turn, therefore, to an examination of the statute itself.

Allowing the broadest scope to the language and purpose of the Fourteenth Amendment, it is well understood that the right of free speech is not absolute at all times and under all circumstances. There are certain well-defined and narrowly limited classes of speech, the prevention and punishment of which has never been thought to raise any Constitutional problem. These include the lewd and obscene, the profane, the libelous, and the insulting or 'fighting' words-those which by their very utterance inflict injury or tend to incite an immediate breach of the peace. It has been well observed that such utterances are no essential part of any exposition of ideas, and are of such slight social value as a step to truth that any benefit that may be derived from them is clearly outweighed by the social interest in order and morality. Resort to epithets or personal abuse is not in any proper sense communication of information or opinion safeguarded by the Constitution. …

The state statute here challenged comes to us authoritatively construed by the highest court of New Hampshire. It has two provisions-the first relates to words or names addressed to another in a public place; the second refers to noises and exclamations. The court said: 'The two provisions are distinct. One may stand separately from the other. Assuming, without holding, that the second were unconstitutional, the first could stand if constitutional.' We accept that construction of severability and limit our consideration to the first provision of the statute. On the authority of its earlier decisions, the state court declared that the statute's purpose was to preserve the public peace, no words being 'forbidden except such as have a direct tendency to cause acts of violence by the person to whom, individually, the remark is addressed'. It was further said: 'The word 'offensive' is not to be defined in terms of what a particular addressee thinks. … The test is what men of common intelligence would understand would be words likely to cause an average addressee to fight. . . . Derisive and annoying words can be taken as coming within the purview of the statute as heretofore interpreted only when they have this characteristic of plainly tending to excite the addressee to a breach of the peace. … The statute, as construed, does no more than prohibit the face-to-face words plainly likely to cause a breach of the peace by the addressee, words whose speaking constitute a breach of the peace by the speaker-including 'classical fighting words', words in current use less 'classical' but equally likely to cause violence, and other disorderly words, including profanity, obscenity and threats.'

We are unable to say that the limited scope of the statute as thus construed contravenes the constitutional right of free expression. It is a statute narrowly drawn and limited to define and punish specific conduct lying within the domain of state power, the use in a public place of words likely to cause a breach of the peace. This conclusion necessarily disposes of appellant's contention that the statute is so vague and indefinite as to render a conviction thereunder a violation of due process. A statute punishing verbal acts, carefully drawn so as not unduly to impair liberty of expression, is not too vague for a criminal law.

Nor can we say that the application of the statute to the facts disclosed by the record substantially or unreasonably impinges upon the privilege of free speech. Argument is unnecessary to demonstrate that the appellations 'damn racketeer' and 'damn Fascist' are epithets likely to provoke the average person to retaliation, and thereby cause a breach of the peace.

The refusal of the state court to admit evidence of provocation and evidence bearing on the truth or falsity of the utterances is open to no Constitutional objection. Whether the facts sought to be proved by such evidence constitute a defense to the charge or may be shown in mitigation are questions for the state court to determine. Our function is fulfilled by a determination that the challenged statute, on its face and as applied, does not contravene the Fourteenth Amendment.

Words Lacking in Value = Unprotected Speech

As you just read, the Court in *Chaplinsky v. New Hampshire* said that certain types of speech are so inherently lacking in value as not to merit any First Amendment protection.

Libel and Slander

One major limitation to the freedom of speech guaranteed by the First Amendment is the civil causes of action known as libel (a written defamatory statement), and slander (a spoken defamatory statement). Libel and slander involve defamatory speech (oral or written) that harms another person's reputation. People can sue others who say something that injures their reputation. Public officials must have a thicker skin, however. In order for public officials to recover damages for slander or liable, the statement made against them must have been made with actual malice (with knowledge that it was false or with reckless disregard whether it was false or not). *New York Times v. Sullivan* , 376 U.S. 254 (1964).

PROFANITY

Although *Chaplinsky* identified profanity as speech not worthy of protection, today courts generally hold that profanity is protected speech. For example, in *Iancu v. Brunetti*, 588 U.S. ___ (2019) the Court held that the trademark office's refusal to register Brunetti's trademark "fuct" under Section 2 of the Lantham Act, which prohibits the federal registration of "immoral" or "scandalous" marks, violated the Free Speech Clause of the First Amendment. Many states' laws and local ordinances still prohibit public profanity, but these provisions are largely unenforced and are likely to be struck down if challenged.

COHEN v. CALIFORNIA,
403 U.S. 15 (1971)

MR. JUSTICE HARLAN delivered the opinion of the Court.

Appellant Paul Robert Cohen was convicted in the Los Angeles Municipal Court of violating that part of California Penal Code 415 which prohibits "maliciously and willfully disturb[ing] the peace or quiet of any neighborhood or person . . . by . . . offensive conduct . . . ." He was given 30 days' imprisonment. The facts [are] as follows:

"On April 26, 1968, the defendant was observed in the Los Angeles County Courthouse in the corridor outside of division 20 of the municipal court wearing a jacket bearing the words `Fuck the Draft' which were plainly visible. There were women and children present in the corridor. The defendant was arrested. The defendant testified that he wore the jacket knowing that the words were on the jacket as a means of informing the public of the depth of his feelings against the Vietnam War and the draft."

"The defendant did not engage in, nor threaten to engage in, nor did anyone as the result of his conduct in fact commit or threaten to commit any act of violence. The defendant did not make any loud or unusual noise, nor was there any evidence that he uttered any sound prior to his arrest."

In affirming the conviction the Court of Appeal held that "offensive conduct" means "behavior which has a tendency to provoke others to acts of violence or to in turn disturb the peace," and that the State had proved this element because, on the facts of this case, "[i]t was certainly reasonably foreseeable that such conduct might cause others to rise up to commit a violent act against the person of the defendant or attempt to forceably remove his jacket.". . . We now reverse.

. . .

I

In order to lay hands on the precise issue which this case involves, it is useful first to canvass various matters which this record does not present.

The conviction quite clearly rests upon the asserted offensiveness of the words Cohen used to convey his message to the public. The only "conduct" which the State sought to punish is the fact of communication. Thus, we deal here with a conviction resting solely upon "speech," not upon any separately identifiable conduct which allegedly was intended by Cohen to be perceived by others as expressive of particular views but which, on its face, does not necessarily convey any message and hence arguably could be regulated without effectively repressing Cohen's ability to express himself. Further, the State certainly lacks power to punish Cohen for the underlying content of the message the inscription conveyed. At least so long as there is no showing of an intent to incite disobedience to or disruption of the draft, Cohen could not, consistently with the First and Fourteenth Amendments, be punished for asserting the evident position on the inutility or immorality of the draft his jacket reflected.

Appellant's conviction, then, rests squarely upon his exercise of the "freedom of speech" protected from arbitrary governmental interference by the Constitution and can be justified, if at all, only as a valid regulation of the manner in which he exercised that freedom, not as a permissible prohibition on the substantive message it conveys. This does not end the inquiry, of course, for the First and Fourteenth Amendments have never been thought to give absolute protection to every individual to speak whenever or wherever he pleases, or to use any form of address in any circumstances that he chooses.

. . .

In this regard, persons confronted with Cohen's jacket were in a quite different posture than, say, those subjected to the raucous emissions of sound trucks blaring outside their residences. Those in the Los Angeles courthouse could effectively avoid further bombardment of their sensibilities simply by averting their eyes. . . . Given the subtlety and complexity of the factors involved, if Cohen's "speech" was otherwise entitled to constitutional protection, we do not think the fact that some unwilling "listeners" in a public building may have been briefly exposed to it can serve to justify this breach of the peace conviction . . . .

II

. . . [The issue in this case] . . . is whether California can excise, as "offensive conduct," one particular scurrilous epithet from the public discourse, either upon the theory of the court below that its use is inherently likely to cause violent reaction or upon a more general assertion that the States, acting as guardians of public morality, may properly remove this offensive word from the public vocabulary.

The rationale of the California court is plainly untenable. At most it reflects an "undifferentiated fear or apprehension of disturbance [which] is not enough to overcome the right to freedom of expression." We have been shown no evidence that substantial numbers of citizens are standing ready to strike out physically at whoever may assault their sensibilities with execrations like that uttered by Cohen. There may be some persons about with such lawless and violent proclivities, but that is an insufficient base upon which to erect, consistently with constitutional values, a governmental power to force persons who wish to ventilate their dissident views into avoiding particular forms of expression. …

Admittedly, it is not so obvious that the First and Fourteenth Amendments must be taken to disable the States from punishing public utterance of this unseemly expletive in order to maintain what they regard as a suitable level of discourse within the body politic. …

At the outset, we cannot overemphasize that, in our judgment, most situations where the State has a justifiable interest in regulating speech will fall within one or more of the various established exceptions . . . to the usual rule that governmental bodies may not prescribe the form or content of individual expression. Equally important to our conclusion is the constitutional backdrop against which our decision must be made. The constitutional right of free expression is powerful medicine in a society as diverse and populous as ours. It is designed and intended to remove governmental restraints from the arena of public discussion, putting the decision as to what views shall be voiced largely into the hands of each of us, in the hope that use of such freedom will ultimately produce a more capable citizenry and more perfect polity and in the belief that no other approach would comport with the premise of individual dignity and choice upon which our political system rests.

To many, the immediate consequence of this freedom may often appear to be only verbal tumult, discord, and even offensive utterance. These are, however, within established limits, in truth necessary side effects of the broader enduring values which the process of open debate permits us to achieve. That the air may at times seem filled with verbal cacophony is, in this sense not a sign of weakness but of strength. We cannot lose sight of the fact that, in what otherwise might seem a trifling and annoying instance of individual distasteful abuse of a privilege, these fundamental societal values are truly implicated. . . .

Against this perception of the constitutional policies involved, we discern certain more particularized considerations that peculiarly call for reversal of this conviction. First, the principle contended for by the State seems inherently boundless. How is one to distinguish this from any other offensive word? Surely the State has no right to cleanse public debate to the point where it is grammatically palatable to the most squeamish among us. Yet no readily ascertainable general principle exists for stopping short of that result were we to affirm the judgment below. For, while the particular four-letter word being litigated here is perhaps more distasteful than most others of its genre, it is nevertheless often true that one man's vulgarity is another's lyric. Indeed, we think it is largely because governmental officials cannot make principled distinctions in this area that the

Constitution leaves matters of taste and style so largely to the individual.

Additionally, we cannot overlook the fact, because it is well illustrated by the episode involved here, that much linguistic expression serves a dual communicative function: it conveys not only ideas capable of relatively precise, detached explication, but otherwise inexpressible emotions as well. In fact, words are often chosen as much for their emotive as their cognitive force. We cannot sanction the view that the Constitution, while solicitous of the cognitive content of individual speech, has little or no regard for that emotive function which, practically speaking, may often be the more important element of the overall message sought to be communicated. . . .

Finally, and in the same vein, we cannot indulge the facile assumption that one can forbid particular words without also running a substantial risk of suppressing ideas in the process. Indeed, governments might soon seize upon the censorship of particular words as a convenient guise for banning the expression of unpopular views. We have been able, as noted above, to discern little social benefit that might result from running the risk of opening the door to such grave results.

It is, in sum, our judgment that, absent a more particularized and compelling reason for its actions, the State may not, consistently with the First and Fourteenth Amendments, make the simple public display here involved of this single four-letter expletive a criminal offense. Because that is the only arguably sustainable rationale for the conviction here at issue, the judgment below must be . . . [r]eversed.

OBSCENITY

Obscene materials are considered to lack "redeeming social importance" and are not constitutionally protected. Distinguishing between obscenity and protected speech is not easy, and the Court has conceded that obscenity cannot be defined with "God-like precision." Justice Stewart pronounced that the only viable test seemed to be that he "knew obscenity when...[he]...saw it." *Jacobellis v. Ohio*, 378 U.S. 184 (1964). In *Miller v. California,* 413 U.S. 15 (1973) the Court finally defined obscenity, holding that it was limited to works that, when "taken as a whole, in light of contemporary community standards, appeal to the prurient interest in sex; are patently offensive; and lack serious literary, artistic, political, or scientific value." Still, the concept remains somewhat vague. Under this definition, for example, a medical textbook portraying individuals engaged in sexual intercourse would probably not constitute obscenity because the book could have scientific value. The Court has found that obscenity refers only to "hard-core" pornography.

The growth of Internet pornography has led to serious national and international child pornography rings, and police and prosecutors no longer target violators of traditional obscenity laws, instead they have directed their resources to aggressively fighting child pornography. Legislators have tried, but found it difficult, to draft child pornography statutes that survive First Amendment challenges. (These laws have been successfully challenged on grounds of overbreadth. See, e.g., *Ashcroft v. American Civil Liberties Union et al.,* 542 U.S. 656 (2004).)

Words That Cause Civil Unrest = Unprotected Speech

WORDS THAT PRESENT A CLEAR AND PRESENT DANGER

Being able to speak against the government has always been recognized as an important right; however, it is not an absolute right. Early on, the Court had to grapple with speech that caused unrest. One of the first tests, enunciated in *Gitlow v. New York*, 268 U.S. 652 (1925), was the "clear and present danger test." This test asks whether words are so potentially dangerous as to not be protected by the First Amendment. In *Gitlow* the Court held that "a state in the exercise of its police power may punish those who abuse this freedom by utterances inimical to the public welfare, tending to corrupt public morals, and incite to crime, or disturbing the public peace" at 667. Gitlow had been indicted under a New York law that prohibited the advocacy of the overthrow of the government by force or violence

INCITEMENT TO VIOLENT ACTION

The Court continued to modify the test after *Chaplinsky*; in the 1950s the Court began to talk in terms of whether the speech "provoked others to imminent violent action." When it did so, it was no longer protected speech. In *Feiner v. New York*, 340 U S 315, 320 (1951), the Court ruled, "when clear and present danger of riot, disorder, interference with traffic upon the public streets, or other immediate threat to public safety, peace, or order, appears, the power of the State to prevent or punish is obvious." On the other hand, in *Terminello v. Chicago*, 337 U.S. 1, 4 (1947), the Supreme Court had stressed that a speaker could not be punished for speech that merely "stirs to anger, invites dispute, brings about a condition of unrest, or creates a disturbance."

FEINER v. NEW YORK,
340 U.S. 315 (1951)

MR. CHIEF JUSTICE VINSON delivered the opinion of the Court.

Petitioner was convicted of the offense of disorderly conduct . . . and was sentenced to thirty days in the county penitentiary. The conviction was affirmed . . . The case is here on certiorari, petitioner having claimed that the conviction is in violation of his right of free speech under the Fourteenth Amendment.

...

On the evening of March 8, 1949, petitioner Irving Feiner was addressing an open-air meeting at the corner of South McBride and Harrison Streets in the City of Syracuse. At approximately 6:30 p. m., the police received a telephone complaint concerning the meeting, and two officers were detailed to investigate. One of these officers went to the scene immediately, the other arriving some twelve minutes later. They found a crowd of about seventy-five or eighty people, both Negro and white, filling the sidewalk and spreading out into the street. Petitioner, standing on a large wooden box on the sidewalk, was addressing the crowd through a loud-speaker system attached to an automobile. Although the purpose of his speech was to urge his listeners to attend a meeting to be held that night in the Syracuse Hotel, in its course he was making derogatory remarks concerning President Truman, the American Legion, the Mayor of Syracuse, and other local political officials.

The police officers made no effort to interfere with petitioner's speech, but were first concerned with the effect of the crowd on both pedestrian and vehicular traffic. They observed the situation from the opposite side of the street, noting that some pedestrians were forced to walk in the street to avoid the crowd. Since traffic was passing at the time, the officers attempted to get the people listening to petitioner back on the sidewalk. The crowd was restless and there was some pushing, shoving and milling around. One of the officers telephoned the police station from a nearby store, and then both policemen crossed the street and mingled with the crowd without any intention of arresting the speaker.

At this time, petitioner was speaking in a "loud, high-pitched voice." He gave the impression that he was endeavoring to arouse the Negro people against the whites, urging that they rise up in arms and fight for equal rights. The statements before such a mixed audience "stirred up a little excitement." Some of the onlookers made remarks to the police about their inability to handle the crowd and at least one threatened violence if the police did not act. There were others who appeared to be favoring petitioner's arguments. Because of the feeling that existed in the crowd both for and against the speaker, the officers finally "stepped in to prevent it from resulting in a fight." One of the officers approached the petitioner, not for the purpose of arresting him, but to get him to break up the crowd. He asked petitioner to get down off the box, but the latter refused to accede to his request and continued talking. The officer waited for a minute and then demanded that he cease talking. Although the officer had thus twice requested petitioner to stop over the course of several minutes, petitioner not only ignored him but continued talking. During all this time, the crowd was pressing closer around petitioner and the officer. Finally, the officer told petitioner he was under arrest and ordered him to get down from the box, reaching up to grab him. Petitioner stepped down, announcing over the microphone that "the law has arrived, and I suppose they will take over now." In all, the officer had asked petitioner to get down off the box three times over a space of four or five minutes. Petitioner had been speaking for over a half hour.

. . .

. . . The trial judge heard testimony supporting and contradicting the judgment of the police officers that a clear danger of disorder was threatened. After weighing this contradictory evidence, the trial judge reached the conclusion that the police officers were justified in taking action to prevent a breach of the peace. The exercise of the police officers' proper discretionary power to prevent a breach of the peace was thus approved by the trial court and later by two courts on review. The courts below recognized petitioner's right to hold a street meeting at this locality, to make use of loud-speaking equipment in giving his speech, and to make derogatory remarks concerning public officials and the American Legion. They found that the officers in making the arrest were motivated solely by a proper concern for the preservation of order and protection of the general welfare, and that there was no evidence which could lend color to a claim that the acts of the police were a cover for suppression of petitioner's views and opinions. Petitioner was thus neither arrested nor convicted for the making or the content of his speech. Rather, it was the reaction which it actually engendered.

The language of *Cantwell v. Connecticut*, 310 U.S. 296 (1940), is appropriate here. "The offense known as breach of the peace embraces a great variety of conduct destroying or menacing public order and tranquility. It includes not only violent acts but acts and words likely to produce violence in others. No one would have the hardihood to suggest that the principle of freedom of speech sanctions incitement to riot or that religious liberty connotes the privilege to exhort others to physical attack upon those belonging to another sect. When clear and present danger of riot, disorder, interference with traffic upon the public streets, or other immediate threat to public safety, peace, or order, appears, the power of the State to prevent

or punish is obvious." 310 U.S. at 308. The findings of the New York courts as to the condition of the crowd and the refusal of petitioner to obey the police requests, supported as they are by the record of this case, are persuasive that the conviction of petitioner for violation of public peace, order and authority does not exceed the bounds of proper state police action. This Court respects, as it must, the interest of the community in maintaining peace and order on its streets. We cannot say that the preservation of that interest here encroaches on the constitutional rights of this petitioner.

We are well aware that the ordinary murmurings and objections of a hostile audience cannot be allowed to silence a speaker, and are also mindful of the possible danger of giving overzealous police officials complete discretion to break up otherwise lawful public meetings. "A State may not unduly suppress free communication of views, religious or other, under the guise of conserving desirable conditions." But we are not faced here with such a situation. It is one thing to say that the police cannot be used as an instrument for the suppression of unpopular views, and another to say that, when as here the speaker passes the bounds of argument or persuasion and undertakes incitement to riot, they are powerless to prevent a breach of the peace. Nor in this case can we condemn the considered judgment of three New York courts approving the means which the police, faced with a crisis, used in the exercise of their power and duty to preserve peace and order. The findings of the state courts as to the existing situation and the imminence of greater disorder coupled with petitioner's deliberate defiance of the police officers convince us that we should not reverse this conviction in the name of free speech.

MR. JUSTICE BLACK, **dissenting**.
The record before us convinces me that petitioner, a young college student, has been sentenced to the penitentiary for the unpopular views he expressed on matters of public interest while lawfully making a street-corner speech in Syracuse, New York. Today's decision, however, indicates that we must blind ourselves to this fact because the trial judge fully accepted the testimony of the prosecution witnesses on all important points. Many times in the past this Court has said that despite findings below, we

will examine the evidence for ourselves to ascertain whether federally protected rights have been denied; otherwise review here would fail of its purpose in safeguarding constitutional guarantees. Even a partial abandonment of this rule marks a dark day for civil liberties in our Nation.

But still more has been lost today. Even accepting every "finding of fact" below, I think this conviction makes a mockery of the free speech guarantees of the First and Fourteenth Amendments. The end result of the affirmance here is to approve a simple and readily available technique by which cities and states can with impunity subject all speeches, political or otherwise, on streets or elsewhere, to the supervision and censorship of the local police. I will have no part or parcel in this holding which I view as a long step toward totalitarian authority.

Considering only the evidence which the state courts appear to have accepted, the pertinent "facts" are: Syracuse city authorities granted a permit for O. John Rogge, a former Assistant Attorney General, to speak in a public school building on March 8, 1948 on the subject of racial discrimination and civil liberties. On March 8th, however, the authorities cancelled the permit. The Young Progressives under whose auspices the meeting was scheduled then arranged for Mr. Rogge to speak at the Hotel Syracuse. The gathering on the street where petitioner spoke was held to protest the cancellation and to publicize the meeting at the hotel. In this connection, petitioner used derogatory but not profane language with reference to the city authorities, President Truman and the American Legion. After hearing some of these remarks, a policeman, who had been sent to the meeting by his superiors, reported to Police Headquarters by telephone. To whom he reported or what was said does not appear in the record, but after returning from the call, he and another policeman started through the crowd toward petitioner. Both officers swore they did not intend to make an arrest when they started, and the trial court accepted their statements. They also said, and the court believed, that they heard and saw "angry mutterings," "pushing," "shoving and milling around" and "restlessness." Petitioner spoke in a "loud, high pitched voice." He said that colored people "don't have equal rights and

they should rise up in arms and fight for them." One man who heard this told the officers that if they did not take that "S*O*B" off the box, he would. The officers then approached petitioner for the first time. One of them first "asked" petitioner to get off the box, but petitioner continued urging his audience to attend Rogge's speech. The officer next "told" petitioner to get down, but he did not. The officer finally "demanded" that petitioner get down, telling him he was under arrest. Petitioner then told the crowd that "the law had arrived and would take over" and asked why he was arrested. The officer first replied that the charge was "unlawful assembly" but later changed the ground to "disorderly conduct."

The Court's opinion apparently rests on this reasoning: The policeman, under the circumstances detailed, could reasonably conclude that serious fighting or even riot was imminent; therefore he could stop petitioner's speech to prevent a breach of peace; accordingly, it was "disorderly conduct" for petitioner to continue speaking in disobedience of the officer's request. As to the existence of a dangerous situation on the street corner, it seems far-fetched to suggest that the "facts" show any imminent threat of riot or uncontrollable disorder. It is neither unusual nor unexpected that some people at public street meetings mutter, mill about, push, shove, or disagree, even violently, with the speaker. Indeed, it is rare where controversial topics are discussed that an outdoor crowd does not do some or all of these things. Nor does one isolated threat to assault the speaker forebode disorder. Especially should the danger be discounted where, as here, the person threatening was a man whose wife and two small children accompanied him and who, so far as the record shows, was never close enough to petitioner to carry out the threat.

Moreover, assuming that the "facts" did indicate a critical situation, I reject the implication of the Court's opinion that the police had no obligation to protect petitioner's constitutional right to talk. The police of course have power to prevent breaches of the peace. But if, in the name of preserving order, they ever can interfere with a lawful public speaker, they first must make all reasonable efforts to protect him. Here the policemen did not even pretend to try to protect petitioner. According to the officers' testimony, the crowd was restless but there is no showing of any attempt to quiet it; pedestrians were forced to walk into the street, but there was no effort to clear a path on the sidewalk; one person threatened to assault petitioner but the officers did nothing to discourage this when even a word might have sufficed. Their duty was to protect petitioner's right to talk, even to the extent of arresting the man who threatened to interfere. Instead, they shirked that duty and acted only to suppress the right to speak.

Finally, I cannot agree with the Court's statement that petitioner's disregard of the policeman's unexplained request amounted to such "deliberate defiance" as would justify an arrest or conviction for disorderly conduct. On the contrary, I think that the policeman's action was a "deliberate defiance" of ordinary official duty as well as of the constitutional right of free speech. For at least where time allows, courtesy and explanation of commands are basic elements of good official conduct in a democratic society. Here petitioner was "asked" then "told" then "commanded" to stop speaking, but a man making a lawful address is certainly not required to be silent merely because an officer directs it. Petitioner was entitled to know why he should cease doing a lawful act. Not once was he told. I understand that people in authoritarian countries must obey arbitrary orders. I had hoped that there was no such duty in the United States.

In my judgment, today's holding means that as a practical matter, minority speakers can be silenced in any city. Hereafter, despite the First and Fourteenth Amendments, the policeman's club can take heavy toll of a current administration's public critics. Criticism of public officials will be too dangerous for all but the most courageous.

. . .

I regret my inability to persuade the Court not to retreat from this principle.

MR. JUSTICE DOUGLAS, with whom MR. JUSTICE MINTON concurs, **dissenting**.
Feiner, a university student, made a speech on a street corner in Syracuse, New York, on March 8, 1949. The purpose of the speech was to publicize a meeting of the Young Progressives of America to be held that evening. A permit authorizing the meeting to be held in a public school auditorium

had been revoked and the meeting shifted to a local hotel.

Feiner delivered his speech in a small shopping area in a predominantly colored residential section of Syracuse. He stood on a large box and spoke over loudspeakers mounted on a car. His audience was composed of about 75 people, colored and white. A few minutes after he started two police officers arrived.

The speech was mainly devoted to publicizing the evening's meeting and protesting the revocation of the permit. It also touched on various public issues.

. . .

There was some pushing and shoving in the crowd and some angry muttering. That is the testimony of the police. But there were no fights and no "disorder" even by the standards of the police. There was not even any heckling of the speaker.
But after Feiner had been speaking about 20 minutes a man said to the police officers, "If you don't get that son of a bitch off, I will go over and get him off there myself." It was then that the police ordered Feiner to stop speaking; when he refused, they arrested him.

Public assemblies and public speech occupy an important role in American life. One high function of the police is to protect these lawful gatherings so that the speakers may exercise their constitutional rights. When unpopular causes are sponsored from the public platform, there will commonly be mutterings and unrest and heckling from the crowd. When a speaker mounts a platform it is not unusual to find him resorting to exaggeration, to vilification of ideas and men, to the making of false charges. But those extravagances, as we emphasized in Cantwell v. Connecticut, 310 U.S. 296, do not justify penalizing the speaker by depriving him of the platform or by punishing him for his conduct.

A speaker may not, of course, incite a riot any more than he may incite a breach of the peace by the use of "fighting words." But this record shows no such extremes. It shows an unsympathetic audience and the threat of one man to haul the speaker from the stage. It is against that kind of threat that speakers need police protection. If they do not receive it and instead the police throw their weight on the side of those who would break up the meetings, the police become the new censors of speech. Police censorship has all the vices of the censorship from city halls which we have repeatedly struck down.

IMMINENT LAWLESS ACTION TEST

In *Brandenburg v. Ohio*, 395 U.S. 444 (1969), the Court reviewed an Ohio statute prohibiting criminal syndicalism which Ohio courts interpreted as advocating violence to achieve political change and announced an "imminent lawless action test." Under this test, if the government demonstrates that (1) the speaker subjectively intended incitement, (2) in context, the words used were likely to produce imminent, lawless action, and (3) the words used by the speaker objectively encouraged and urged incitement, then the words are not protected speech. The Court reversed the conviction of a Ku Klux Klan leader saying that the constitutional guarantees of free speech and free press do not permit a state to forbid advocacy. "People cannot be prosecuted merely for advocating violence; there must be "imminent lawless action" to justify a criminal penalty on public expression."

True Threats

One type of problematic speech is speech involving direct threats. As you will read in Chapter Seven, crimes such as "threatened battery assault" or "menacing" involve using threats to place victims in fear of imminent physical danger. What if the threat is not directly aimed or sent to the victim, but is instead posted on a Facebook page or other social media? Consider the case of Roger Stone who, while awaiting trial for lying to Congress, posted a picture of the judge handling his case with a gun crosshair/scope superimposed on her image. Many states have stalking laws that prohibit repeated and unwanted contact and some of the prohibited contact involves speech. In the Oregon case below, *State v. Rangel*, 328 Or. 224 (1999) the defendant claimed that Oregon's stalking law violated his rights to free speech under the Oregon and federal constitutions. (Note: this case also highlights what courts do when a statute is challenged on the basis of overbreadth—see below).

STATE v. RANGEL,
328 Or. 294, 977 P.2d 379 (1999)

The issue in this criminal case is whether Oregon's stalking statute, ORS 163.732, is overbroad in violation of Article I, section 8, of the Oregon Constitution, or the First Amendment to the United States Constitution. For the reasons discussed below, we hold that the statute is not overbroad under either constitution.
ORS 163.732 provides in part:

"(1) A person commits the crime of stalking if:
"(a) The person knowingly alarms or coerces another person or a member of that person's immediate family or household by engaging in repeated and unwanted contact with the other person;
"(b) It is objectively reasonable for a person in the victim's situation to have been alarmed or coerced by the contact; and
"(c) The repeated and unwanted contact causes the victim reasonable apprehension

regarding the personal safety of the victim or a member of the victim's immediate family or household."

Defendant was charged with stalking by "unlawfully and knowingly alarm[ing the victim] by coming to her place of employment and threatening her" on several occasions.

Before trial, defendant demurred [*made a constitutional challenge to the charging document*], contending that ORS 163.732 is overbroad in violation of Article I, section 8, and the First Amendment. The trial court held that the statute is overbroad, is not capable of judicial narrowing and, thus, is prohibited by Article I, section 8. The Court of Appeals reversed, concluding that ORS 163.732 is akin in virtually all material respects to ORS 166.065(1)(d) (1981), the harassment statute that this court upheld in *State v. Moyle*, 299 Or. 691, 705 P.2d 740 (1985). The court construed and narrowed ORS 163.732 to require proof that the accused made a threat or its equivalent and that the accused intended to cause the victim alarm. The court held that, as so construed and narrowed, the statute is not overbroad under Article I, section 8, or the First Amendment. We allowed defendant's petition for review.

On review, defendant argues that ORS 163.732 is facially overbroad under Article I, section 8, because the alarm element of the statute does not require the state to prove that the defendant made a "threat," and because the statute does not require the state to prove that the defendant "intended" to harm anyone. . . . In the alternative, defendant argues that ORS 163.732 violates the First Amendment. The state responds that the stalking statute is not overbroad, because the narrowing construction of ORS 163.732 adopted by the Court of Appeals follows the constitutional requirements delineated by this court in *Moyle.*

We review a lower court's interpretation of a constitutional provision for legal error. We consider all questions of state law before reaching federal constitutional issues. . . .

Article I, section 8
Our starting point is the analytical framework, first set out in *Robertson,* that this court traditionally has employed in evaluating the constitutionality of laws involving expression. …

… Article I, section 8, forbids the enactment of any statute that is written in terms directed to the restraint of "free expression of opinion" or the restriction of "the right to speak, write, or print freely on any subject" of communication, unless the restraint is wholly confined within some historical exception to the free speech guarantees. … Article I, section 8, does not prohibit the enactment of statutes that focus on forbidden *effects* of expression, if they are not directed at the substance of expression. If the proscribed means include speech or writing, however, even a law written to focus on a forbidden effect must be scrutinized to determine whether it appears to reach privileged communication or whether it can be interpreted to avoid such "overbreadth."… An overbroad statute is one that proscribes speech or conduct that the constitution protects. …

The Court of Appeals concluded, and the parties agree, that ORS 163.732 is directed at the pursuit of forbidden effects (repeated and unwanted "contacts"). We agree. However, because the law identifies expression as one means that may produce those forbidden effects, the law is open to an overbreadth challenge under Article I, section 8.

. . . [A] law written to focus on undesired effects, but that includes speech or writing as the proscribed means of violation, must be examined to determine whether it reaches privileged communication and, if it does so more than rarely, whether a narrowing construction is possible to save it from overbreadth. If a statute passes the first test (which is a determination of whether the statute was directed at the substance of any "opinion" or at the "subject" of communication) it remains open to an overbreadth challenge. A "law is overbroad to the extent that it announces a prohibition that reaches conduct which may not be prohibited." Therefore, a law challenged as overbroad is scrutinized to determine whether it appears to reach communication privileged by Article I, section 8, or whether the law can be interpreted to avoid such overbreadth. Therefore, we examine the stalking statute to determine whether it is overbroad.

To commit the crime of stalking, a person must make unwanted and repeated, i.e., at least two, "contacts" of the kinds set forth in ORS 163.730(3). Several examples of what may constitute a forbidden "contact" under ORS 163.730(3) consist solely of communication, orally or in writing, between the actor and the alleged victim or a third person. ORS 163.730(3)(d), (e), (f), (h), and (i) describe the methods of "contact" that most clearly involve some form of communication, although the statutory list is not exclusive. Our discussion here concerns only the state's invocation of at least one communication-based form of "contact" to establish the repeated and unwanted contact element of stalking. No overbreadth problem arises if none of the contacts on which the state relies to establish stalking involves communication.

The notable characteristic of the crime of stalking is that the victim's apprehension must arise from, and the actor must inflict alarm or coercion through, "repeated and unwanted" contacts. ORS 163.732(1). A single contact that causes apprehension, no matter how severe, does not constitute criminal stalking. But a contact that occurs through communication with the victim or a third person constitutes stalking if the actor also makes at least one other contact, the actor knowingly alarms or coerces the victim by engaging in the repeated contact, and the repeated contact is unwanted, causes the victim reasonable apprehension, and would have alarmed or coerced a reasonable person. The stalking statute does not require that a "contact" that occurs through speech or writing *by itself* (1) must constitute a use of words that the law may prohibit, such as the solicitation of a crime, or blackmail, or (2) cause any particular proscribable effect.

We agree with the Court of Appeals that the stalking statute restricts speech, at least in part, because it criminalizes the inducement of alarm or coercion from the repetition of contacts with a victim and those contacts can include speech or writing. *Moyle* supports that conclusion. In *Moyle,* this court similarly determined that the statute in question, prohibiting harassment, defined the crime to include the communication of verbal threats, and concluded after analysis that some threats constitute protected speech. For similar reasons, the communication-based forms of contact listed in ORS 163.730(3) may constitute protected expression in a variety of political and social settings.

. . . In analyzing criminal statutes that forbid the inducement of undesired effects through communicative acts, this court steadfastly has required a showing that the communicative act itself is unprotected because, for example, it is a prelude to imminent and serious proscribable harm. . . . For example, *Moyle* construed the term "alarm" in the harassment statute to mean "more than mere inconvenience or feelings of anguish which are the result of angry or imposing words; it means being placed in actual fear or terror resulting from a sudden sense of danger."

In *Garcias,* 296 Or. at 701, 679 P.2d 1354, this court upheld the menacing statute against a claim of overbreadth, stating:

> "[t]here is harm to be caused, fear of imminent serious physical injury, and it is specific enough that it can be caused only

by a narrow category of conduct, a face to face confrontation between actor and victim."

…

In *Moyle,* this court concluded that it could adopt several narrowing constructions of the harassment statute that would conform it to the legislature's probable intent, as demonstrated by the statute's words, and still satisfy the following requirements of Article I, section 8:

"`[A]rticle I, section 8, prohibits lawmakers from enacting restrictions that focus on the content of speech or writing, either because that content itself is deemed socially undesirable or offensive, or because it is thought to have adverse consequences. * * * [L]*aws must focus on proscribing the pursuit or accomplishment of forbidden results rather than on the suppression of speech or writing either as an end in itself or as a means to some other legislative end.*' …

For purposes of analysis under Article I, section 8, the Court of Appeals concluded that ORS 163.732 is not distinguishable from the harassment statute considered in *Moyle.* Consequently, the Court of Appeals, addressing two aspects of the stalking statute, applied narrowing constructions that closely resemble the narrowing constructions this court applied in *Moyle.* We turn to an examination of those constructions.

First, the Court of Appeals determined that, although ORS 163.732 does not expressly require that a "threat" be made to the victim, the terms of ORS 163.730 and ORS 163.732 demonstrate that "a threat or its equivalent must have been made in order for the crime of stalking to be found." We agree.

The gist of the crime of stalking is knowingly alarming or coercing another through repeated and unwanted "contacts." Where the state relies on one or more "contacts" that constitute speech or writing, rather than physical force or other behaviors that are beyond the scope of Article I, section 8, the definition of "coerce" in ORS 163.730(2) expressly requires proof of a threat. We conclude that in defining "alarm" in ORS 163.730(1), the legislature also contemplated, as a logical necessity, that a speech-based contact would be punishable as an element of stalking only if it constitutes a threat. If the contact in question amounts to communication by speech or writing, only a threat will be sufficient to "cause apprehension or fear resulting from the perception of danger," as ORS 163.730 requires.

Moyle explains what behavior constitutes a proscribable "threat" in this context. . . . According to *Moyle*, a proscribable threat is a communication that instills in the addressee a fear of imminent and serious personal violence from the speaker, is unequivocal, and is objectively likely to be followed by unlawful acts. . . . Those characteristics of a threat

> "exclud[e] the kind of hyperbole, rhetorical excesses, and impotent expressions of anger or frustration that in some contexts can be privileged even if they alarm the addressee." . . .

Moyle concluded that those characteristics of a proscribable threat were faithful to the legislature's intent by examining the elements of the crime of harassment. Because the material elements of stalking . . . indicate that the legislature intended the term "alarm" in the stalking statute to apply to the same type of communications, we reach the same conclusion here.

Second, in response to defendant's argument that the stalking statute falls short because it requires the actor to induce alarm or coercion "knowingly" rather than intentionally, the Court of Appeals concluded:

> "[W]e interpret the stalking statute to require proof that the alarm as well as the threatened act must be intended by the speaker."

ORS 163.732(1) uses the term "knowingly" to mean that a person acts with an awareness that his or her conduct is of a nature so described or that a circumstances so described exists, as ORS 161.085(8) indicates. The stalking statute also uses "knowingly" with reference to the conscious inducement of an actual effect—fear—by creating a perception of danger in the victim through multiple unwanted contacts. The requirement in ORS 163.732(1)(b) that the perception of danger to personal safety from the actor's contacts be "objectively reasonable" establishes the foreseeability and, thus, the predictability, of the

proscribed harm.

Because ORS 163.732(1) requires both awareness of the nature of the conduct and consciousness that the conduct predictably will lead to a specific result, the statute presents an analytical problem similar to that addressed by this court in the following passage regarding the harassment statute at issue in *Moyle:*

> "The statute, as written, requires neither proof of a specific intent to carry out the threat nor of any present ability to do so. However, the elements—actual alarm and the reasonableness of the alarm under the circumstances—have a similar purpose and effect. These elements limit the reach of the statute to threats which are so unambiguous, unequivocal and specific to the addressee that they convincingly express to the addressee the intention that they will be carried out."

The harassment statute in *Moyle* required communication of a threat "with intent to harass, annoy or alarm another person." That statute, as written, required neither proof of a specific intent to carry out the threat nor of any present ability to do so.

The *Moyle* court concluded, however, that the elements of actual alarm and the reasonableness of the alarm under the circumstances had a similar purpose and effect.

"These elements limit the reach of the statute to threats which are so unambiguous, unequivocal and specific to the addressee that they convincingly express to the addressee the intention that they will be carried out."

The same analysis applies here.

ORS 163.732(1) requires that the actor "knowingly" alarm or coerce another person or a member of that person's immediate family or household. The statute does not expressly require that a contact involving communication be established with proof of a specific intent to carry out the threat or of any present ability to do so. However, we conclude that the requirements in ORS 163.732(1) of actual alarm and the subjective and objective reasonableness of the alarm in the circumstances have the same purpose and effect. Just as in *Moyle,* those elements limit the reach of ORS 163.732(1) to a threat that is so unambiguous, unequivocal, and specific *to the addressee* that it convincingly expresses to the addressee the intention that it will be carried out.

Our analysis does not remove the mental element of "knowingly" from ORS 163.732(1)(a). Instead, we conclude that, under ORS 163.732(3), a contact based on communication must consist of a threat that convincingly expresses *to the addressee* the intention that it will be carried out, and that the actor has the ability to do so. Because that determination leaves the statutory mental element, "knowingly," undisturbed, and construes the contact element consistently with the analysis followed in *Moyle,* defendant's argument fails. Accordingly, we hold that, as construed, ORS 163.732 is not overbroad under Article I, section 8.

First Amendment

Freedom of speech is among the fundamental personal rights and liberties protected by the First and Fourteenth Amendments. *Gitlow v. New York,* 268 U.S. 652 (1925). Defendant argues that ORS 163.732 is overbroad in violation of the First Amendment because it does not require proof that the actor intended to cause harm, does not require proof that the actor made an actual threat, and creates no express exemption for constitutionally protected activity.

Because defendant's first two arguments do not take into account the narrowing constructions

that this court has applied to ORS 163.732, they are unpersuasive. Those constructions supply the requirements of genuine threat and intent to carry out the threat that defendant argues are missing from the statutory text.

. . .

For the purpose of addressing defendant's present argument, it is sufficient to observe that no decision of the United States Supreme Court requires that an express exemption for lawful speech accompany a stalking statute in order to avoid unconstitutional overbreadth.

In *Broadrick v. Oklahoma,* 413 U.S. 601 (1973), the United States Supreme Court set limitations on the invocation of the overbreadth doctrine where conduct and not merely speech is involved. The Supreme Court declared that application of the doctrine is "strong medicine," to be employed "sparingly" and "only as a last resort." Where conduct is regulated, a statute that has constitutional applications is facially invalid only if its overbreadth is "real, [and] substantial as well, judged in relation to the statute's plainly legitimate sweep." We conclude that, as construed, ORS 163.732 is narrowly tailored and does not burden protected speech. See *New York v. Ferber,* 458 U.S. 747, 769, (1982) (only a statute that is substantially overbroad may be invalidated on its face) …

In summary, we hold that, as construed, ORS 163.732 is not facially overbroad under Article I, section 8, or the First Amendment for any of the reasons argued by defendant. Our holding that ORS 163.732 is not overbroad does not preclude a constitutional challenge to the statute "as applied" to specific circumstances.

Hate Speech versus Hate Crimes

Hate speech raises interesting First Amendment concerns. Hate speech is defined as speech that denigrates, humiliates, and attacks individuals on account of some race, religion, ethnicity, nationality, gender, sexual orientation, or other personal characteristics and preferences (hate crimes target categories of people named specifically in the statute). Hate speech can be verbal, written or symbolic. Because it constitutes expression, it is generally protected by the Constitution unless it falls within one of the recognized exceptions to the First Amendment.

Hate speech must be distinguished from hate crimes or criminal offenses directed against a member of a specific groups. Hate crime statutes have been upheld because they target conduct rather than expression. The most important two rulings from the Court that highlight the distinction between hate speech and hate crimes are *R.A.V. v. St. Paul,* 505 U.S. 377 (1992), and *Wisconsin v. Mitchell*, 508 U.S. 475 (1993). They are discussed in the following case of People v. Rokicki, 718 N.E. 2d 333 (Ill. App. 1999).

In *Virginia v. Black*, 538 U.S. 343 (2003), the Court upheld a law banning cross burning with "an intent to intimidate a person or group of persons." Justice O'Connor wrote the plurality decision concluding that "the First Amendment permits Virginia to outlaw cross burnings done with intent to intimidate because burning a cross is a particularly virulent form of intimidation."

PEOPLE v. ROKICKI,
718 N.E.2d 333 (Ill.App. 1999)

JUSTICE HUTCHINSON delivered the opinion of the court

Defendant, Kenneth Rokicki was charged in a single-count indictment with hate crime . . . based on the predicate offense of disorderly conduct. Following a bench trial, defendant was convicted, sentenced to 2 years' probation and ordered . . . to perform 100 hours of community service and attend anger management counseling. [Defendant appealed] contending that the hate crime statute is unconstitutionally overly broad and chills expression protected by the first amendment to the United States Constitution. We affirm.

FACTS
. . .
Donald Delaney testified that he is a store manager of a Pizza Hut in South Elgin. On October 20, 1995 at approximately 1:30 p.m., defendant entered the restaurant. The victim was a server there and took defendant's order. The victim requested payment, and the defendant refused to tender payment to him. Delaney who was nearby, stepped in and completed the sale. Defendant told Delaney not to let "that faggot" touch his food. When defendant's pizza came out of the oven, Delaney was on the telephone, and the victim began to slice the pizza. Delaney saw defendant approaching the counter with an irritated expression and hung up the telephone. Before Delaney could intervene, defendant leaned over the counter and began yelling at the victim and pounding his fist on the counter. Defendant directed a series of epithets at the victim including "Mary," "faggot," and "Molly Homemaker." Defendant continued yelling for 10 minutes and, when not pounding his fist shook his finger at the victim. Delaney asked defendant to leave several times and threatened to call the police. However, Delaney did not call the police because he was standing between the victim and the defendant and feared that the defendant would physically attack the victim if

Delaney moved. Eventually Delaney returned defendant's money and defendant left the establishment.

The victim testified that he was working at the South Elgin Pizza Hut on October 20, 1995. Defendant entered the restaurant and ordered a pizza. When defendant's pizza came out of the oven, the victim began to slice it. Defendant then began yelling at the victim and pounding his fist on the counter. Defendant appeared very angry and seemed very serious. The victim, who is much smaller than defendant, testified that he was terrified by defendant's outburst and remained frightened for several days thereafter. Eventually, the manager gave defendant a refund and defendant left the restaurant. The victim followed defendant into the parking lot, recorded the license number of his car, and called the police.

Christopher Merritt, a sergeant with the South Elgin police department, testified that, at 2:20 P.M. on October 20, 1995, defendant entered the police station and said he wished to report an incident at the Pizza Hut. Defendant told Merritt that he was upset because a homosexual was working at the restaurant and he wanted someone "normal" to touch his food. Defendant stated that he became angry when the victim touched his food. He called the victim a "Mary," pounded on the counter, and was subsequently kicked out of the restaurant. Merritt asked defendant what he meant by a "Mary," and defendant responded that a "Mary" was a homosexual. Merritt conducted only a brief interview of defendant because shortly after defendant arrived at the police station Merritt was dispatched to the Pizza Hut.

Deborah Hagedorn, an employee at the Pizza Hut in St. Charles, testified that in 1995 defendant came into the restaurant and asked for the address of the district manager for Pizza Hut. When asked why he wanted the address, defendant complained that he had been arrested at the South Elgin restaurant because he did not want a "f___g faggot" touching his food.

Defendant testified that he was upset because the victim had placed his fingers in his mouth and had not washed his hands before cutting the pizza. Defendant admitted calling the victim "Mary" but denied that he intended to suggest the victim was a homosexual. Defendant stated that he used the term "Mary" because the victim would not stop talking and "it was like arguing with a woman." Defendant denied yelling and denied directing other derogatory terms toward the victim. Defendant admitted giving a statement to Merritt but denied telling him that he pounded his fist on the counter or used homosexual slurs. Defendant testified that he went to the St. Charles Pizza Hut but that Hagedorn was not present during his conversation with the manager. Defendant testified that he complained about the victim's hygiene but did not use any homosexual slurs.

The trial court found defendant guilty of a hate crime. In a posttrial motion, defendant argued that the hate crime statute was unconstitutional. The trial court denied defendant's motion and sentenced him to two years' probation. As part of the probation, the trial court ordered Defendant not to enter Pizza Hut restaurants, not to contact the victim, to perform 100 hours' community service, and attend anger management counseling. Defendant timely appeals.

ISSUE
On appeal, Defendant does not challenge the sufficiency of the evidence against him. Defendant contends only that the hate crime statute is unconstitutional when the predicate offense is disturbing the peace. Defendant argues that the statute is overly broad and impermissibly chills free speech.

ANALYSIS
. . . The Illinois hate crime statute . . . reads in part as follows:

> A person commits a hate crime when, by reason of the actual or perceived race, color, creed, religion, ancestry, gender, sexual orientation, physical or mental disability, or national origin of another individual or group of individuals, [she or] he commits assault, battery, aggravated

assault, misdemeanor theft, criminal trespass to residence, misdemeanor criminal damage to property, criminal trespass to vehicle, criminal trespass to real property, mob action or disorderly conduct. . . .

. . .

1. Infringement on Free Speech Rights
The issue presented in this case highlights the limits imposed by the first amendment on a state's power to regulate its citizens' speech and thought. In a pair of cases decided in 1992 and 1993, the Supreme Court staked out the boundary between a state's unconstitutional regulation of unpopular beliefs in the market place of ideas and the permissible regulation of conduct motivated by those beliefs. See *R.A.V. v. City of St. Paul*, 505 U.S. 377. . . (1992); Wisconsin v. Mitchell, 508 U.S. 476 . . . (1993). Our analysis of defendant's claims is controlled by these two cases, and we will begin by examining them.

In *R.A.V.*, the petitioner was alleged to have burned a crudely constructed wooden cross on the lawn of the residence of an African-American family and was charged with violating St. Paul's Bias-Motivated Crime Ordinance. The ordinance declared that anyone who places a burning cross, Nazi swastika, or other symbol on private or public property knowing that the symbol would arouse " 'anger, alarm or resentment in others on the basis of race, color, creed, religion, or gender commits disorderly conduct and shall be guilty of a misdemeanor.' " The Minnesota Supreme Court found that the ordinance was constitutional because it could be construed to reach only "fighting words," which are outside the protection of the first amendment. The United States Supreme Court held that, even when a statute addresses speech that is otherwise prescribable, the state may not discriminate on the basis of the content. The *R.A.V.* Court then found that the St. Paul ordinance violated the first amendment because it would allow the proponents of racial tolerance and equality to use fighting words to argue in favor of tolerance and equality but would prohibit similar use by those opposed to racial tolerance and equality.

One year later, the United States Supreme Court revisited the issue in *Mitchell*. The defendant in *Mitchell* was convicted of aggravated battery, which carried a maximum term of two years' incarceration. However, the defendant was sentenced to a term of four years' incarceration under a Wisconsin statute that enhanced the penalty for an offense when the defendant intentionally selected a victim because of his or her " 'race, religion, color, disability, sexual orientation, national origin or ancestry.' " The Wisconsin Supreme Court reversed the conviction and held that the statute was unconstitutional under *R.A.V.*, holding that the legislature cannot "criminalize bigoted thought with which it disagrees."

The *Mitchell* Court held that, unlike the ordinance in *R.A.V.*, the Wisconsin statute was aimed solely at conduct unprotected by the first amendment. The Court noted that, although a defendant may not be punished for his or her abstract beliefs, motive has traditionally been used as a factor in sentencing. The Court also observed that, although the statute punished the defendant for his discriminatory motive, motive played the same role in federal and state antidiscrimination statutes that had withstood first amendment challenges. The Court further held that a state legislature could reasonably conclude that bias-motivated crimes cause greater societal harm warranting stiffer penalties because such offenses are more likely to provoke retaliatory crimes, inflict distinct emotional harms on their victims, and incite community unrest. Consequently, the Court found that the Wisconsin statute did not infringe upon free speech rights.

...

The overbreadth doctrine protects the freedom of speech guaranteed by the first amendment by invalidating laws so broadly written that the fear of prosecution would discourage people from exercising that freedom. A law regulating conduct is facially overly broad if it (1) criminalizes a substantial amount of protected behavior, relative to the law's plainly legitimate sweep, and (2) is not susceptible to a limiting construction that avoids constitutional problems. A statute should not be invalidated for being overly broad unless its overbreadth is both real and substantial.

. . .

In this case, defendant is not being punished merely because he holds an unpopular view on homosexuality or because he expressed those views loudly or in a passionate manner.

Defendant was charged with hate crime because he allowed those beliefs to motivate unreasonable conduct. Defendant remains free to believe what he will regarding people who are homosexual, but he may not force his opinions on others by shouting, pounding on a counter, and disrupting a lawful business. Defendant's conduct exceeded the bounds of spirited debate, and the first amendment does not give him the right to harass or terrorize anyone. Therefore, because the hate crime statute requires conduct beyond mere expression, . . . we . . . conclude that…the Illinois hate crime statute constitutionally regulates conduct without infringing upon free speech.

2. Content Discrimination

Defendant cites *R.A.V.* and argues that the hate crime statute is constitutionally impermissible because it discriminates based on the content of an offender's beliefs. Defendant argues that the statute enhances disorderly conduct to hate crime when the conduct is motivated by, e.g., an offender's views on race or sexual orientation but that it treats identical conduct differently if motivated, e.g., by an offender's beliefs regarding abortion or animal rights. The *R.A.V.* Court invalidated the St. Paul ordinance because it favored some political views over others. The Court stated as follows:

"[T]he ordinance applies only to 'fighting words' that insult, or provoke violence, 'on the basis of race, color, creed, religion or gender.' Displays containing abusive invective, no matter how vicious or severe, are permissible unless they are addressed to one of the specified disfavored topics. Those who wish to use 'fighting words' in connection with other ideas to express hostility, for example, on the basis of political affiliation, union membership, or homosexuality are not covered." *R.A.V.* 505 U.S. at 291 …

. . .

In *R.A.V.*, the Court recognized several limitations to its content discrimination analysis, including statutes directed at conduct rather than speech, which sweep up a particular subset of prescribable speech. … We too decide that the legislature was free to determine as a matter of sound public policy that bias-motivated crimes create greater harm than identical conduct not motivated by bias and should be punished more harshly. Consequently, we reject defendant's content discrimination argument.

3. Chilling Effect

Defendant also argues that the hate crime statute chills free expression because individuals will be deterred from expressing unpopular views out of fear that such expression will later be used to justify a hate crime charge. We disagree. The overbreadth doctrine should be used sparingly and only when the constitutional infirmity is both real and substantial.... The *Mitchell* Court rejected identical arguments and held that any possible chilling effects were too speculative to support an overbreadth claim. ... [W]e find defendant's argument speculative, and we cannot conclude that individuals will refrain from expressing controversial beliefs simply because they fear that their statements might be used as evidence of motive if they later commit an offense identified in the hate crime statute.

CONCLUSION

We hold that the hate crime statute is not facially unconstitutional when the predicate offense is disorderly conduct because (1) the statute reaches only conduct and does not punish speech itself; (2) the statute does not impermissibly discriminate based on content; and (3) the statute does not chill the exercise of first amendment rights. Defendant contends only that the statute is unconstitutional and does not challenge the sufficiency of the evidence against him or assert any other basis for reversal. Accordingly, we affirm defendant's conviction.

Commercial Speech Is Unprotected Speech

The Court has ruled that commercial speech is not protected under the First Amendment. In *Valentine v. Chrestensen, 316* U.S. 52, 54 (1942), the Court stated,

> This Court has unequivocally held that the streets are proper places for the exercise of the freedom of communicating information and disseminating opinion and that, though the states and municipalities may appropriately regulate the privilege in the public interest, they may not unduly burden or proscribe its employment in these public thoroughfares. We are equally clear that the Constitution imposes no such restraint on government as respects purely commercial advertising. Whether, and to what extent, one may promote or pursue a gainful occupation in the streets, to what extent such activity shall be adjudged a derogation of the public right of user, are matters for legislative judgment. The question is not whether the legislative body may interfere with the harmless pursuit of a lawful business, but whether it must permit such pursuit by what it deems an undesirable invasion of, or interference with, the full and free use of the highways by the people in fulfillment of the public use to which streets are dedicated. If the respondent was attempting to use the streets of New York by distributing commercial advertising, the prohibition of the code provision was lawfully invoked against his conduct.

The court explained that advertising was not afforded the same protection as "political speech" under the First Amendment because: 1) advertising is not as important as political speech, 2) it is harder to chill advertising, which has a strong profit motive, and 3) it is easier to verify ad claims than political claims, and therefore we have no need to tolerate false advertising. Courts usually review freedom of speech cases using a strict scrutiny review, but regulations on commercial speech must withstand only intermediate scrutiny. To survive a strict scrutiny challenge, a law must further a "compelling governmental interest," and must be narrowly tailored to achieve that interest; to survive intermediate scrutiny, a law must further an "important government interest" by means that are substantially related to that interest. Thus, it is less likely that laws impacting or regulating commercial speech will be found unconstitutional. Additionally, commercial speech that is false or misleading is not entitled to any protection under the First Amendment, and therefore can be prohibited entirely.

Symbolic Speech and Expressive Conduct = Protected Speech

The Constitution protects symbolic speech and expressive conduct. "Freedom of expression is a broad concept embracing speech, publication, performances, and demonstrations. Even wearing symbols is considered to be constitutionally protected symbolic speech." See, *Tinker v. Des Moines Independent*

Community School District, 393 U.S. 503 (1969). Expressive conduct includes: "sit-ins" to protest racial segregation, civilians wearing American military uniforms to protest the Vietnam War, and "picketing" over a variety of issues. *United States v. O'Brien,* 391 U.S. 367 (1968) established the "test" the Court will use when deciding whether the government impermissibly limited symbolic speech/expressive conduct. David O'Brien burned his draft card at a Boston courthouse and claimed he was expressing his opposition to war when he was charged with violating a federal law making it a crime to mutilate a draft card. The 7-1 opinion in favor of the government and authored by Chief Justice Earl Warren stated, "[W]e think it clear, that a government regulation is sufficiently justified if it is within the constitutional power of the Government; if it furthers an important or substantial governmental interest; if the governmental interest is unrelated to the suppression of free expression; and if the incidental restriction on alleged First Amendment freedoms is not greater than is essential to the furtherance of that interest."

The amount of protection afforded to speech depends, in large part, on where the person is speaking. The Court refers to forums, and has identified three types of forums: traditional public forum, designated public forums, and non-public forums. Some places are not considered forums.

Traditional public forums include public parks, sidewalks, and areas that have been traditionally open to political speech and debate. Speakers in these areas enjoy the strongest First Amendment protections. In traditional public forums, the government may not discriminate against speakers based on their views. This is called "viewpoint discrimination." The government may, however, subject speech to reasonable, content-neutral restrictions on its time, place, and manner. When considering government restrictions of speech in traditional public forums, courts use "strict scrutiny." Under strict scrutiny, restrictions are allowed only if they serve a compelling state interest and are narrowly tailored to meet the needs of that interest.

Sometimes, the government opens public property for public expression even though the public property is not a traditional public forum. These [types of properties] are designated public forums. After opening a designated public forum, the government is not obligated to keep it open. However, so long as the government does keep the forum open, speech in the forum receives the same First Amendment protections as speech in traditional public forums. Examples of designated public forums include municipal theatres and meeting rooms at state universities.

The government may limit access to a designated public forum to certain classes or types of speech. In these "limited forums," although the government may discriminate against classes of speakers or types of speech, it may not exercise viewpoint discrimination. For example, the government may limit access to public school meeting rooms by only allowing speakers conducting school-related activities. It may not, however, exclude speakers from a religious group simply because they intend to express religious views. ...

Nonpublic forums are forums for public speech that are neither traditional public forums nor designated public forums. Government restrictions on speech in nonpublic forums must be reasonable, and may not discriminate based on speakers' viewpoints. Examples of nonpublic forums include airport terminals and a public school's internal mail system. . . .

Finally, some public property is not a forum at all, and thus is not subject to this forum analysis. For example, public television broadcasters are not subject to forum analysis when they decide what shows to air. Http://www.law.cornell.edu/wex/forums.

One form of expressive conduct the Court has frequently considered is flag burning. Scheb noted,

Without question, the most controversial application of the concept of expressive conduct have been the Supreme Court's decisions holding that public burning of the American flag is protected by the First Amendment. In *Texas v. Johnson*, . . . the Court invalidated a Texas statute banning flag desecration. . . . In *United States v. Eichman* . . . the Supreme Court invalidated . . . [the Flag Protection Act of 1989] . . . as well, saying that "punishing desecration of the flag dilutes the very freedom that makes this emblem so revered, and worth revering." . . . On several occasions, Congress has attempted to pass a constitutional amendment to overturn the Supreme Court's flag burning decisions, but in every instance the measure has failed to receive the necessary two thirds vote in the Senate. Scheb, *supra* at 68-69

TEXAS v. JOHNSON,
491 U.S. 397 (1989)

JUSTICE BRENNAN delivered the opinion of the Court.

After publicly burning an American flag as a means of political protest, Gregory Lee Johnson was convicted of desecrating a flag in violation of Texas law. This case presents the question whether his conviction is consistent with the First Amendment. We hold that it is not.

I

While the Republican National Convention was taking place in Dallas in 1984, respondent Johnson participated in a political demonstration dubbed the "Republican War Chest Tour." As explained in literature distributed by the demonstrators and in speeches made by them, the purpose of this event was to protest the policies of the Reagan administration and of certain Dallas-based corporations. The demonstrators marched through the Dallas streets, chanting political slogans and stopping at several corporate locations to stage "die-ins" intended to dramatize the consequences of nuclear war. On several occasions they spray-painted the walls of buildings and overturned potted plants, but Johnson himself took no part in such activities. He did, however, accept an American flag handed to him by a fellow protestor who had taken it from a flagpole outside one of the targeted buildings.

The demonstration ended in front of Dallas City Hall, where Johnson unfurled the American flag, doused it with kerosene, and set it on fire. While the flag burned, the protestors chanted: "America, the red, white, and blue, we spit on you." After the demonstrators dispersed, a witness to the flag burning collected the flag's remains and buried them in his backyard. No one was physically injured or threatened with injury, though several witnesses testified that they had been seriously offended by the flag burning.

Of the approximately 100 demonstrators, Johnson alone was charged with a crime. The only criminal offense with which he was charged was the desecration of a venerated object. ... After a trial, he was convicted, sentenced to one year in prison, and fined $2,000. The Court of Appeals for the Fifth District of Texas at Dallas affirmed Johnson's conviction, but the Texas Court of Criminal Appeals reversed, holding that the State could not, consistent with the First Amendment, punish Johnson for burning the flag in these circumstances.

The Court of Criminal Appeals began by recognizing that Johnson's conduct was symbolic speech protected by the First Amendment: "Given the context of an organized demonstration, speeches, slogans, and the distribution of literature, anyone who observed appellant's act would have understood the message that appellant intended to convey. The act for which appellant was convicted was clearly `speech' contemplated by the First Amendment." To justify Johnson's conviction for engaging in symbolic speech, the State asserted two interests: preserving the flag as a symbol of national unity and preventing breaches of the peace. The Court of Criminal Appeals held that neither interest supported his conviction.

Acknowledging that this Court had not yet decided whether the Government may criminally sanction flag desecration in order to preserve the flag's symbolic value, the Texas court nevertheless concluded that our decision in *West Virginia Board of Education v. Barnette* suggested that furthering this interest by curtailing speech was impermissible. "Recognizing that the right to differ is the centerpiece of our First Amendment freedoms," the court explained, "a government cannot mandate by fiat a feeling of unity in its citizens. Therefore, that very same government cannot carve out a symbol of unity and prescribe a set of approved messages to be associated with that symbol when it cannot mandate the status or feeling the symbol purports to represent." Noting that the State had not shown that the flag was in "grave and immediate danger," of being stripped of its symbolic value, the Texas court also decided that the flag's special status was not endangered by Johnson's conduct.

As to the State's goal of preventing breaches of the peace, the court concluded that the flag-desecration statute was not drawn narrowly enough to encompass only those flag burnings that were likely to result in a serious disturbance of the peace. And in fact, the court emphasized, the flag burning in this particular case did not threaten such a reaction. "`Serious offense' occurred," the court admitted, "but there was no breach of peace nor does the record reflect that the situation was potentially explosive. One cannot equate `serious offense' with incitement to breach the peace." The court also stressed that another Texas statute, prohibited breaches of the peace. . . . [T]he court decided that [this statute] demonstrated Texas' ability to prevent disturbances of the peace without punishing this flag desecration. …

Because it reversed Johnson's conviction on the ground that 42.09 was unconstitutional as applied to him, the state court did not address Johnson's argument that the statute was, on its face, unconstitutionally vague and overbroad. We granted certiorari … and now affirm.

II

Johnson was convicted of flag desecration for burning the flag rather than for uttering insulting words. This fact somewhat complicates our consideration of his conviction under the First Amendment. We must first determine whether Johnson's burning of the flag constituted expressive conduct, permitting him to invoke the First Amendment in challenging his conviction. If his conduct was expressive, we next decide whether the State's regulation is related to the suppression of free expression. If the State's regulation is not related to expression, then the less stringent standard we announced in *United States v. O'Brien* for regulations of noncommunicative conduct controls. If it is, then we are outside of *O'Brien's* test, and we must ask whether this interest justifies Johnson's conviction under a more demanding standard. A third possibility is that the State's asserted interest is simply not implicated on these facts, and in that event the interest drops out of the picture.

The First Amendment literally forbids the abridgment only of "speech," but we have long recognized that its protection does not end at the spoken or written word. While we have rejected "the view that an apparently limitless variety of conduct can be labeled `speech' whenever the person engaging in the conduct intends thereby to express an idea," we have acknowledged that conduct may be "sufficiently imbued with elements of communication to fall within the scope of the First and Fourteenth Amendments,"

In deciding whether particular conduct possesses sufficient communicative elements to bring the First Amendment into play, we have asked whether "[a]n intent to convey a particularized message was present, and [whether] the likelihood was great that the message would be understood by those who viewed it." Hence, we have recognized the expressive nature of students' wearing of black armbands to protest American military involvement in Vietnam, *Tinker v. Des Moines Independent Community School Dist.*; of a sit-in by blacks in a "whites only" area to protest segregation, *Brown v. Louisiana*; of the wearing of American military uniforms in a dramatic presentation criticizing American involvement in Vietnam, *Schacht v. United States*; and of picketing about a wide variety of causes, see, e.g., *Food Employees v. Logan Valley Plaza, Inc.*, [and] *United States v. Grace*.

Especially pertinent to this case are our decisions recognizing the communicative nature of conduct relating to flags. Attaching a peace sign to the flag, refusing to salute the flag, and displaying a red flag, we have held, all may find shelter under the First Amendment. … That we have had little difficulty identifying an expressive element in conduct relating to flags should not be surprising. The very purpose of a national flag is to serve as a symbol of our country; it is, one might say, "the one visible manifestation of two hundred years of nationhood." Thus, we have observed:

> "[T]he flag salute is a form of utterance. Symbolism is a primitive but effective way of communicating ideas. The use of an emblem or flag to symbolize some system, idea, institution, or personality, is a short cut from mind to mind. Causes and nations, political parties, lodges and ecclesiastical groups seek to knit the loyalty of their followings to a flag or banner, a color or design."

…

The State of Texas conceded for purposes of its oral argument in this case that Johnson's conduct was expressive conduct, and this concession seems to us as prudent. Johnson burned an American flag as part - indeed, as the culmination - of a political demonstration that coincided with the convening of the Republican Party and its renomination of Ronald Reagan for President. The expressive, overtly political nature of this conduct was both intentional and overwhelmingly apparent. At his trial, Johnson explained his reasons for burning the flag as follows: "The American Flag was burned as Ronald Reagan was being renominated as President. And a more powerful statement of symbolic speech, whether you agree with it or not, couldn't have been made at that time. It's quite a [juxtaposition]. We had new patriotism and no patriotism." In these circumstances, Johnson's burning of the flag was conduct "sufficiently imbued with elements of communication" . . . to implicate the First Amendment.

III

The government generally has a freer hand in restricting expressive conduct than it has in restricting the written or spoken word. … A law directed at the communicative nature of conduct must, like a law directed at speech itself, be justified by the substantial showing of need that the First Amendment requires." It is, in short, not simply the verbal or nonverbal nature of the expression, but the governmental interest at stake, that helps to determine whether a restriction on that expression is valid.

…

The State offers two separate interests to justify this conviction: preventing breaches of the peace and preserving the flag as a symbol of nationhood and national unity. We hold that the first interest is not implicated on this record and that the second is related to the suppression of expression.

A

Texas claims that its interest in preventing breaches of the peace justifies Johnson's conviction for flag desecration. However, no disturbance of the peace actually occurred or threatened to occur because of Johnson's burning of the flag. Although the State stresses the disruptive behavior of the protestors during their march toward City Hall, it admits that "no actual breach of the peace occurred at the time of the flagburning or in response to the flagburning." The State's emphasis on the protestors' disorderly actions prior to arriving at City Hall is not only somewhat surprising given that no charges were brought on the basis of this conduct, but it also fails to show that a disturbance of the peace was a likely reaction to Johnson's conduct. The only evidence offered by the State at trial to show the reaction to Johnson's actions was the testimony of several persons who had been seriously offended by the flag burning. Id., at 6-7.

The State's position, therefore, amounts to a claim that an audience that takes serious offense at particular expression is necessarily likely to disturb the peace and that the expression may be prohibited on this basis. Our precedents do not countenance such a presumption. On the contrary, they recognize that a principal "function of free speech under our system of government is to invite dispute. It may indeed best serve its high purpose when it induces a condition of unrest, creates dissatisfaction with conditions as they are, or even stirs people to anger." *Terminiello v. Chicago.* … It would be odd indeed to conclude both that "if it is the speaker's opinion that gives offense, that consequence is a reason for according it constitutional protection," and that the government may ban the expression of certain disagreeable ideas on the unsupported presumption that their very disagreeableness will provoke violence.

Thus, we have not permitted the government to assume that every expression of a provocative idea will incite a riot, but have instead required careful consideration of the actual circumstances surrounding such expression, asking whether the expression "is directed to inciting or producing imminent lawless action and is likely to incite or produce such action." *Brandenburg v. Ohio*, (reviewing circumstances surrounding rally and speeches by Ku Klux Klan). To accept Texas' arguments that it need only demonstrate "the potential for a breach of the peace," and that every flag burning necessarily possesses that potential, would be to eviscerate our holding in Brandenburg. This we decline to do.

Nor does Johnson's expressive conduct fall within that small class of "fighting words" that are "likely to provoke the average person to retaliation, and thereby cause a breach of the peace." *Chaplinsky v. New Hampshire*. ... No reasonable onlooker would have regarded Johnson's generalized expression of dissatisfaction with the policies of the Federal Government as a direct personal insult or an invitation to exchange fisticuffs.

We thus conclude that the State's interest in maintaining order is not implicated on these facts. The State need not worry that our holding will disable it from preserving the peace. We do not suggest that the First Amendment forbids a State to prevent "imminent lawless action." And, in fact, Texas already has a statute specifically prohibiting breaches of the peace . . . which tends to confirm that Texas need not punish this flag desecration in order to keep the peace.

B

The State also asserts an interest in preserving the flag as a symbol of nationhood and national unity. In *Spence*, we acknowledged that the government's interest in preserving the flag's special symbolic value "is directly related to expression in the context of activity" such as affixing a peace symbol to a flag. We are equally persuaded that this interest is related to expression in the case of Johnson's burning of the flag. ...

IV

It remains to consider whether the State's interest in preserving the flag as a symbol of nationhood and national unity justifies Johnson's conviction. As in Spence, "[w]e are confronted with a case of prosecution for the expression of an idea through activity," and "[a]ccordingly, we must examine with particular care the interests advanced by [petitioner] to support its prosecution." Johnson was not, we add, prosecuted for the expression of just any idea; he was prosecuted for his expression of dissatisfaction with the policies of this country, expression situated at the core of our First Amendment values.

Moreover, Johnson was prosecuted because he knew that his politically charged expression would cause "serious offense." If he had burned the flag as a means of disposing of it because it was dirty or torn, he would not have been convicted of flag desecration under this Texas law: federal law designates burning as the preferred means of disposing of a flag "when it is in such condition that it is no longer a fitting emblem for display," and Texas has no quarrel with this means of disposal. The Texas law is thus not aimed at protecting the physical integrity of the flag in all circumstances, but is designed instead to protect it only against impairments that would cause serious offense to others. Texas concedes as much: "Section 42.09(b) reaches only those severe acts of physical abuse of the flag carried out in a way likely to be offensive. The statute mandates intentional or knowing abuse, that is, the kind of mistreatment that is not innocent, but rather is intentionally designed to seriously offend other individuals."

Whether Johnson's treatment of the flag violated Texas law thus depended on the likely communicative impact of his expressive conduct. Our decision in *Boos v. Barry* . . . tells us that this restriction on Johnson's expression is content based. In *Boos*, we considered the constitutionality of a law prohibiting "the display of any sign within 500 feet of a foreign embassy if that sign tends to bring that foreign government into 'public odium' or 'public disrepute.'" Rejecting the argument that the law was content neutral because it was justified by "our international law obligation to shield diplomats from speech that offends their dignity," we held that "[t]he emotive impact of speech on its audience is not a 'secondary effect'" unrelated to the content of the expression itself.

According to the principles announced in *Boos*, Johnson's political expression was restricted because of the content of the message he conveyed. We must therefore subject the State's asserted interest in preserving the special symbolic character of the flag to "the most exacting scrutiny."

Texas argues that its interest in preserving the flag as a symbol of nationhood and national unity survives this close analysis. … The State's argument is not that it has an interest simply in maintaining the flag as a symbol of something, no matter what it symbolizes; indeed, if that were the State's position, it would be difficult to see how that interest is endangered by highly symbolic conduct such as Johnson's. Rather, the State's claim is that it has an interest in preserving the flag as a symbol of nationhood and national unity, a symbol with a determinate range of meanings. According to Texas, if one physically treats the flag in a way that would tend to cast doubt on either the idea that nationhood and national unity are the flag's referents or that national unity actually exists, the message conveyed thereby is a harmful one and therefore may be prohibited. …

If there is a bedrock principle underlying the First Amendment, it is that the government may not prohibit the expression of an idea simply because society finds the idea itself offensive or disagreeable. …

In short, nothing in our precedents suggests that a State may foster its own view of the flag by prohibiting expressive conduct relating to it. To bring its argument outside our precedents, Texas attempts to convince us that even if its interest in preserving the flag's symbolic role does not allow it to prohibit words or some expressive conduct critical of the flag, it does permit it to forbid the outright destruction of the flag. The State's argument cannot depend here on the distinction between written or spoken words and nonverbal conduct. That distinction, we have shown, is of no moment where the nonverbal conduct is expressive, as it is here, and where the regulation of that conduct is related to expression, as it is here. …

Texas' focus on the precise nature of Johnson's expression, moreover, misses the point of our prior decisions: their enduring lesson, that the government may not prohibit expression simply because it disagrees with its message, is not dependent on the particular mode in which one chooses to express an idea. If we were to hold that a State may forbid flag burning wherever it is likely to endanger the flag's symbolic role, but allow it wherever burning a flag promotes that role - as where, for example, a person ceremoniously burns a dirty flag - we would be saying that when it comes to impairing the flag's physical integrity, the flag itself may be used as a symbol - as a substitute for the written or spoken word or a "short cut from mind to mind" - only in one direction. We would be permitting a State to "prescribe what shall be orthodox" by saying that one may burn the flag to convey one's attitude toward it and its referents only if one does not endanger the flag's representation of nationhood and national unity.

We never before have held that the Government may ensure that a symbol be used to express only one view of that symbol or its referents. …
. . .
There is . . . no indication … that a separate juridical category exists for the American flag alone. … The First Amendment does not guarantee that other concepts virtually sacred to our Nation as a whole - such as the principle that discrimination on the basis of race is odious and destructive - will go unquestioned in the marketplace of ideas. We decline, therefore, to create for the flag an exception to the joust of principles protected by the First Amendment.

It is not the State's ends, but its means, to which we object. It cannot be gainsaid that there is a special place reserved for the flag in this Nation, and thus we do not doubt that the government has a legitimate interest in making efforts to "preserv[e] the national flag as an unalloyed symbol of our country." We reject the suggestion, urged at oral argument by counsel for Johnson, that the government lacks "any state interest whatsoever" in regulating the manner in which the flag may be displayed. Congress has, for example, enacted precatory regulations describing the proper treatment of the flag, and we cast no doubt on the legitimacy of its interest in making such recommendations. To say that the government has an interest in encouraging proper treatment of the flag, however, is not to say that it may criminally punish a person for burning a flag as a means of political protest.

"National unity as an end which officials may foster by persuasion and example is not in question. The problem is whether under our Constitution compulsion as here employed is a permissible means for its achievement."

. . .

We are tempted to say, in fact, that the flag's deservedly cherished place in our community will be strengthened, not weakened, by our holding today. Our decision is a reaffirmation of the principles of freedom and inclusiveness that the flag best reflects, and of the conviction that our toleration of criticism such as Johnson's is a sign and source of our strength. . . .

The way to preserve the flag's special role is not to punish those who feel differently about these matters. It is to persuade them that they are "wrong." To courageous, self-reliant men, with confidence in the power of free and fearless reasoning applied through the processes of popular government, no danger flowing from speech can be deemed clear and present, unless the incidence of the evil apprehended is so imminent that it may befall before there is opportunity for full discussion. If there be time to expose through discussion the falsehood and fallacies, to avert the evil by the processes of education, the remedy to be applied is more speech, not enforced silence." *Whitney v. California*, 274 U.S. 357, 377 (1927) (Brandeis, J., concurring). And, precisely because it is our flag that is involved, one's response to the flag burner may exploit the uniquely persuasive power of the flag itself. We can imagine no more appropriate response to burning a flag than waving one's own, no better way to counter a flag burner's message than by saluting the flag that burns, no surer means of preserving the dignity even of the flag that burned than by - as one witness here did - according its remains a respectful burial. We do not consecrate the flag by punishing its desecration, for in doing so we dilute the freedom that this cherished emblem represents.

V

Johnson was convicted for engaging in expressive conduct. The State's interest in preventing breaches of the peace does not support his conviction because Johnson's conduct did not threaten to disturb the peace. Nor does the State's interest in preserving the flag as a symbol of nationhood and national unity justify his criminal conviction for engaging in political expression. . . .

JUSTICE KENNEDY, **concurring**.
I write not to qualify the words JUSTICE BRENNAN chooses so well, for he says with power all that is necessary to explain our ruling. I join his opinion without reservation, but with a keen sense that this case, like others before us from time to time, exacts its personal toll. This prompts me to add to our pages these few remarks.

The case before us illustrates better than most that the judicial power is often difficult in its exercise. We cannot here ask another Branch to share responsibility, as when the argument is made that a statute is flawed or incomplete. For we are presented with a clear and simple statute to be judged against a pure command of the Constitution. The outcome can be laid at no door but ours.

The hard fact is that sometimes we must make decisions we do not like. We make them because they are right, right in the sense that the law and the Constitution, as we see them, compel the result. And so great is our commitment to the process that, except in the rare case, we do not pause to express distaste for the result, perhaps for fear of undermining a valued principle that dictates the decision. This is one of those rare cases.

. . .

With all respect to those views, I do not believe the Constitution gives us the right to rule as the dissenting Members of the Court urge, however painful this judgment is to announce. Though symbols often are what we ourselves make of them, the flag is constant in expressing beliefs Americans share, beliefs in law and peace and that freedom which sustains the human spirit. The case here today forces recognition of the costs to which those beliefs commit us. It is poignant but fundamental that the flag protects those who hold it in contempt.

For all the record shows, this respondent was not a philosopher and perhaps did not even possess the ability to comprehend how repellent his statements must be to the Republic itself. But whether or not he could appreciate the enormity of the offense he gave, the fact remains that his acts were speech, in both the technical and the fundamental meaning of the Constitution. So I agree with the Court that he must go free.

CHIEF JUSTICE REHNQUIST, with whom JUSTICE WHITE and JUSTICE O'CONNOR join, **dissenting**.

. . . For more than 200 years, the American flag has occupied a unique position as the symbol of our Nation, a uniqueness that justifies a governmental prohibition against flag burning in the way respondent Johnson did here.
. . .
The American flag . . . has come to be the visible symbol embodying our Nation. It does not represent the views of any particular political party, and it does not represent any particular political philosophy. The flag is not simply another "idea" or "point of view" competing for recognition in the marketplace of ideas. Millions and millions of Americans regard it with an almost mystical reverence regardless of what sort of social, political, or philosophical beliefs they may have. I cannot agree that the First Amendment invalidates the Act of Congress, and the laws of 48 of the 50 States, which make criminal the public burning of the flag.
. . .

...[T]he Court insists that the Texas statute prohibiting the public burning of the American flag infringes on respondent Johnson's freedom of expression. Such freedom, of course, is not absolute.

. . .

. . . Here it may equally well be said that the public burning of the American flag by Johnson was no essential part of any exposition of ideas, and at the same time it had a tendency to incite a breach of the peace. Johnson was free to make any verbal denunciation of the flag that he wished; indeed, he was free to burn the flag in private. He could publicly burn other symbols of the Government or effigies of political leaders. He did lead a march through the streets of Dallas, and conducted a rally in front of the Dallas City Hall. He engaged in a "die-in" to protest nuclear weapons. He shouted out various slogans during the march, including: "Reagan, Mondale which will it be? Either one means World War III"; "Ronald Reagan, killer of the hour, Perfect example of U.S. power"; and "red, white and blue, we spit on you, you stand for plunder, you will go under." For none of these acts was he arrested or prosecuted; it was only when he proceeded to burn publicly an American flag stolen from its rightful owner that he violated the Texas statute.

[Johnson's acts] . . . like *Chaplinsky's* provocative words, conveyed nothing that could not have been conveyed and was not conveyed just as forcefully in a dozen different ways. As with "fighting words," so with flag burning, for purposes of the First Amendment: It is "no essential part of any exposition of ideas, and [is] of such slight social value as a step to truth that any benefit that may be derived from [it] is clearly outweighed" by the public interest in avoiding a probable breach of the peace. The highest courts of several States have upheld state statutes prohibiting the public burning of the flag on the grounds that it is so inherently inflammatory that it may cause a breach of public order. . . .

. . . [F]ive years ago we said . . . that "the First Amendment does not guarantee the right to employ every conceivable method of communication at all times and in all places." The Texas statute deprived Johnson of only one rather inarticulate symbolic form of protest - a form of protest that was profoundly offensive to many - and left him with a full panoply of other symbols and every conceivable form of verbal expression to express his deep disapproval of national policy. Thus, in no way can it be said that Texas is punishing him because his hearers - or any other group of people - were profoundly opposed to the message that he sought to convey. Such opposition is no proper basis for restricting speech or expression under the First Amendment. It was Johnson's use of this particular symbol, and not the idea that he sought to convey by it or by his many other expressions, for which he was punished.
. . .
. . . Surely one of the high purposes of a democratic society is to legislate against conduct that is regarded as evil and profoundly offensive to the majority of people - whether it be murder, embezzlement, pollution, or flag burning.

JUSTICE STEVENS, **dissenting.**

As the Court analyzes this case, it presents the question whether the State of Texas, or indeed the Federal Government, has the power to prohibit the public desecration of the American flag. The question is unique. In my judgment rules that apply to a host of other symbols, such as state flags, armbands, or various privately promoted emblems of political or commercial identity, are not necessarily controlling. Even if flag burning could be considered just another species of symbolic speech under the logical application of the rules that the Court has developed in its interpretation of the First Amendment in other contexts, this case has an intangible dimension that makes those rules inapplicable.

A country's flag is a symbol of more than "nationhood and national unity." It also signifies the ideas that characterize the society that has chosen that emblem as well as the special history that has animated the growth and power of those ideas. The fleurs-de-lis and the tricolor both symbolized "nationhood and national unity," but they had vastly different meanings. The message conveyed by some flags - the swastika, for example - may survive long after it has outlived its usefulness as a symbol of regimented unity in a particular nation.

So it is with the American flag. It is more than a proud symbol of the courage, the determination, and the gifts of nature that transformed 13 fledgling Colonies into a world power. It is a symbol of freedom, of equal opportunity, of religious tolerance, and of good will for other peoples who share our aspirations. The symbol carries its message to dissidents both at home and abroad who may have no interest at all in our national unity or survival.

The value of the flag as a symbol cannot be measured. Even so, I have no doubt that the interest in preserving that value for the future is both significant and legitimate. Conceivably that value will be enhanced by the Court's conclusion that our national commitment to free expression is so strong that even the United States as ultimate guarantor of that freedom is without power to prohibit the desecration of its unique symbol. But I am unpersuaded. The creation of a federal right to post bulletin boards and graffiti on the Washington Monument might enlarge the market for free expression, but at a cost I would not pay. Similarly, in my considered judgment, sanctioning the public desecration of the flag will tarnish its value - both for those who cherish the ideas for which it waves and for those who desire to don the robes of martyrdom by burning it. That tarnish is not justified by the trivial burden on free expression occasioned by requiring that an available, alternative mode of expression - including uttering words critical of the flag. . . .

BARNES v. GLEN THEATRE, INC,
501 U.S. 560 (1991)

FACTS

Respondents, two Indiana establishments wishing to provide totally nude dancing as entertainment and individual dancers employed at those establishments, brought suit in the District Court to enjoin enforcement of the state public indecency law - which requires respondent dancers to wear pasties and a G-string - asserting that the law's prohibition against total nudity in public places violates the First Amendment. The U.S. District court held that the nude dancing involved here was not expressive conduct. The Court of Appeals reversed, ruling that nonobscene nude dancing performed for entertainment is protected expression, and that the statute was an improper infringement of that activity because its purpose was to prevent the message of eroticism and sexuality conveyed by the dancers.

Held (official summary): The enforcement of Indiana's public indecency law to prevent totally nude dancing does not violate the First Amendment's guarantee of freedom of expression.

CHIEF JUSTICE RHENQUIST'S (Official Summary)

OPINION

(a) Nude dancing of the kind sought to be performed here is expressive conduct within the outer perimeters of the First Amendment, although only marginally so.

b) Applying the four-part test of *United States v. O'Brien*, 391 U.S. 367, 376 -377 - which rejected the contention that symbolic speech is entitled to full First Amendment protection - the statute is justified despite its incidental limitations on some expressive activity. The law is clearly within the State's constitutional power. And it furthers a substantial governmental interest in protecting societal order and morality. Public indecency statutes reflect moral disapproval of people appearing in the nude among strangers in public places, and this particular law follows a line of state laws, dating back to 1831, banning public nudity. The States' traditional police power is defined as the authority to provide for the public health, safety, and morals, and such a basis for legislation has been upheld. This governmental interest is unrelated to the suppression of free expression, since public nudity is the evil the State seeks to prevent, whether or not it is combined with expressive activity. The law does not proscribe nudity in these establishments because the dancers are conveying an erotic message. To the contrary, an erotic performance may be presented without any state interference, so long as the performers wear a scant amount of clothing. Finally, the incidental restriction on First Amendment freedom is no greater than is essential to the furtherance of the governmental interest. Since the statutory prohibition is not a means to some greater end, but an end itself, it is without cavil that the statute is narrowly tailored.

JUSTICE SCALIA **concurring** opinion (Official Summary)
[T]the statute - as a general law regulating conduct and not specifically directed at expression, either in practice or on its face - is not subject to normal First Amendment scrutiny, and should be upheld on the ground that moral opposition to nudity supplies a rational basis for its prohibition. . . . There is no intermediate level of scrutiny requiring that an incidental restriction on expression, such as that involved here, be justified by an important or substantial governmental interest.

JUSTICE SOUTER **concurring** opinion (Official Summary)
[T]he nude dancing at issue here is subject to a degree of First Amendment protection, and that the test of *United States v. O'Brien* is the appropriate analysis to determine the actual protection required. [T]he State's interest in preventing the secondary effects of adult entertainment establishments - prostitution, sexual assaults, and other criminal activity - is sufficient under *O'Brien* to justify the law's enforcement against nude dancing. The prevention of such effects clearly falls within the State's constitutional power. In addition, the asserted interest is plainly substantial, and the State could have concluded that it is furthered by a prohibition on nude dancing, even without localized proof of the harmful effects. Moreover, the interest is unrelated to the suppression of free expression, since the pernicious effects are merely associated with nude dancing establishments and are not the result of the expression inherent in nude dancing. Finally, the restriction is no greater than is essential to further the governmental interest, since pasties and a G-string moderate expression to a minor degree when measured against the dancer's remaining capacity and opportunity to express an erotic message.

.

Other Cases—Expressive Conduct

Frederick v. Morse, 551 U.S. 393 (2007)
At a school-supervised event, Frederick held up a banner with the message "Bong Hits 4 Jesus." His school principal, Deborah Morse took away the banner and suspended Frederick for ten day -- citing the school's policy against the display of material that promotes the use of illegal drugs. Frederick sued under 42 U.S.C. 1983, the federal civil rights statute, alleging a violation of his First Amendment right to freedom of speech. The District Court found no constitutional violation, and even if there were, Morse had qualified immunity. The Ninth Circuit, cited the *Tinker* case (above), and found that Frederick was punished for his message rather than for any disturbance, the Circuit Court ruled, the punishment was unconstitutional. Furthermore, the principal had no qualified immunity, because any reasonable principal would have known that Morse's actions were unlawful.

The Court reversed the Ninth Circuit by a 5-4 vote, ruling that school officials can prohibit students

from displaying messages that promote illegal drug use. Chief Justice John Roberts's majority opinion held that although students do have some right to political speech even while in school, this right does not extend to pro-drug messages that may undermine the school's important mission to discourage drug use. The majority held that Frederick's message, though "cryptic," was reasonably interpreted as promoting marijuana use - equivalent to "[Take] bong hits" or "bong hits [are a good thing]." In ruling for Morse, the Court affirmed that the speech rights of public school students are not as extensive as those adults normally enjoy, and that the highly protective standard set by *Tinker* would not always be applied. In concurring opinions, Justice Thomas expressed his view that the right to free speech does not apply to students and his wish to see *Tinker* overturned altogether, while Justice Alito stressed that the decision applied only to pro-drug messages and not to broader political speech. The dissent conceded that the principal should have had immunity from the lawsuit, but argued that the majority opinion was "[...] deaf to the constitutional imperative to permit unfettered debate, even among high-school students [...]."
(https://www.oyez.org/cases/2006/06-278)

Political Speech

In two controversial cases the Court examined political speech—the ability to express political views by contributing financially to a political party. In *Citizens United v. Federal Election Commission*, 558 U.S. 310 (2010), the Court eased restrictions on political and campaign spending by corporations and labor unions, ruling that such restrictions infringe on the organizations' First Amendment free speech rights. In essence, the Court held that for the purposes of speech, a corporation is an "individual." This decision drew sharp criticism across the political spectrum. Four years later, in *McCutcheon v. Federal Election Commission*, 572 U.S. ___ (2014), the Court held that campaign aggregate spending limits are invalid under the First Amendment.

"The right to participate in democracy through political contributions is protected by the First Amendment, but that right is not absolute. Our cases have held that Congress may regulate campaign contributions to protect against corruption or the appearance of corruption. ... At the same time, we have made clear that Congress may not regulate contributions simply to reduce the amount of money in politics, or to restrict the political participation of some in order to enhance the relative influence of others." Id at ___.

FREEDOM OF ASSOCIATION AND ASSEMBLY

The First Amendment protects the right of people to peacefully assemble. *DeYoung v. Oregon,* 299 U.S. 353 (1937), held that freedom of peaceful meeting is as fundamental as freedom of speech and the press to democracy. Although the First Amendment limits the legislature's ability to pass any laws infringing on a person's freedom of assembly, the Court has approved the right of government officials to put limits on the ability to congregate when necessary to maintain public order.

In the same way that courts will often evaluate speech in terms of where and in what form the speaking occurs, courts evaluate the constitutionality of laws regulating public assemblies in terms of the forum in which the assembly occurred. The court uses the same forum designation for the right to assemble as it uses for evaluating political speech:

➢ public forums (like a city park) is property generally used for purposes of public assembly, communicating thoughts between citizens and discussing public questions;
➢ quasi-public forums (like a place in which the public frequently congregates) include areas such as shopping stores and other privately owned building or property to which the public has general access; and
➢ non-public forums (like an individual's home or a business) is privately owned property

Courts will be more likely to strike down ordinances and laws that limit the right to assemble in public forums and less likely to strike down regulations of assemblies in quasi-public and non-public forums. The more public the forum, the less the government will be allowed to restrict people's freedom of assembly.

The right of association is not specifically mentioned in the Constitution; but it is considered a natural right and thus protected by the Constitution.

> Notwithstanding the appropriate caution against reading into the Constitution rights not explicitly defined, this Court has acknowledged that certain unarticulated rights are implicit in enumerated guarantees. For example, the rights of association and of privacy, the right to be presumed innocent, and the right to be judged by a standard of proof beyond a reasonable doubt in a criminal trial, as well as the right to travel, appear nowhere in the Constitution or Bill of Rights. Yet these important but unarticulated rights have nonetheless been found to share constitutional protection in common with explicit guarantees. ... Fundamental rights, even though not expressly guaranteed, have been recognized by the Court as indispensable to the enjoyment of rights explicitly defined. *Richmond Newspapers, Inc. v. Virginia*, 488 U.S. 555, 579 (1980).

Time, Manner, And Place Restrictions

The right of assembly is not absolute. Even at the most public of forums, the government can impose reasonable time, reasonable place, and reasonable manner restrictions on assemblies. Governments may not ban assemblies in the public forum so long as they are peaceful and do not impede the operations of government or the activities of other citizens. [6]

COX V. LOUISIANA, 379 U.S. 536 (1965)

THE FACTS
On December 14, 1961, 23 students from Southern University, a Negro college, were arrested in downtown Baton Rouge, Louisiana, for picketing stores that maintained segregated lunch counters. This picketing, urging a boycott of those stores, was part of a general protest movement against racial segregation, directed by the local chapter of the Congress of Racial Equality, a civil rights organization. The appellant, an ordained Congregational minister, the Reverend Mr. B. Elton Cox, a Field Secretary of CORE, was an advisor to this movement. On the evening of December 14, appellant and Ronnie Moore, student president of the local CORE chapter, spoke at a mass meeting at the college. The students resolved to demonstrate the next day in front of the courthouse in protest of segregation and the arrest and imprisonment of the picketers who were being held in the parish jail located on the upper floor of the courthouse building.

The next morning, about 2,000 students left the campus, which was located approximately five miles from downtown Baton Rouge. Most of them had to walk into the city, since the drivers of their busses were arrested. Moore was also arrested at the entrance to the campus while parked in a car equipped with a loudspeaker, and charged with violation of an anti-noise statute. Because Moore was immediately taken off to jail and the vice-president of the CORE chapter was already in jail for picketing, Cox felt it his duty to take over the demonstration and see that it was carried out as planned. He quickly drove to the city "to pick up this leadership and keep things orderly."

When Cox arrived, 1,500 of the 2,000 students were assembling at the site of the old State Capitol building, two and one-half blocks from the courthouse. Cox walked up and down cautioning the students to keep to one side of the sidewalk while getting ready for their march to

---

[6] Note that recently, the government entities have cancelled planned assemblies across the nation because of the likelihood of potential violence from groups with opposing political viewpoints.

the courthouse. The students circled the block in a file two or three abreast occupying about half of the sidewalk. The police had learned of the proposed demonstration the night before from news media and other sources. Captain Font of the City Police Department and Chief Kling of the Sheriff's office, two high-ranking subordinate officials, approached the group and spoke to Cox at the northeast corner of the capitol grounds. Cox identified himself as the group's leader, and, according to Font and Kling, he explained that the students were demonstrating to protest "the illegal arrest of some of their people who were being held in jail." The version of Cox and his witnesses throughout was that they came not "to protest just the arrest, but . . . [also] to protest the evil of discrimination." Kling asked Cox to disband the group and "take them back from whence they came." Cox did not acquiesce in this request, but told the officers that they would march by the courthouse, say prayers, sing hymns, and conduct a peaceful program of protest. The officer repeated his request to disband, and Cox again refused. Kling and Font then returned to their car in order to report by radio to the Sheriff and Chief of Police, who were in the immediate vicinity; while this was going on, the students, led by Cox, began their walk toward the courthouse.

They walked in an orderly and peaceful file, two or three abreast, one block east, stopping on the way for a red traffic light. In the center of this block, they were joined by another group of students. The augmented group, now totaling about 2,000,
turned the corner and proceeded south, coming to a halt in the next block opposite the courthouse.

As Cox, still at the head of the group, approached the vicinity of the courthouse, he was stopped by Captain Font and Inspector Trigg and brought to Police Chief Wingate White, who was standing in the middle of St. Louis Street. The Chief then inquired as to the purpose of the demonstration. Cox, reading from a prepared paper, outlined his program to White, stating that it would include a singing of the Star Spangled Banner and a "freedom song," recitation of the Lord's Prayer and the Pledge of Allegiance, and a short speech. White testified that he told Cox that "he must confine" the demonstration "to the west side of the street."

White added,

> This, of course, was not -- I didn't mean it in the import that I was giving him any permission to do it, but I was presented with a situation that was accomplished, and I had to make a decision.

Cox testified that the officials agreed to permit the meeting. James Erwin, news director of radio station WIBR, a witness for the State, was present and overheard the conversation. He testified that

> My understanding was that they would be allowed to demonstrate if they stayed on the west side of the street and stayed within the recognized time, and that this was "agreed to" by White.

The students were then directed by Cox to the west sidewalk, across the street from the courthouse, 101 feet from its steps. They were lined up on this sidewalk about five deep and spread almost the entire length of the block. The group did not obstruct the street. It was close to noon and, being lunch time, a small crowd of 100 to 300 curious white people, mostly courthouse personnel, gathered on the east sidewalk and courthouse steps, about 100 feet from the demonstrators. Seventy-five to eighty policemen, including city and state patrolmen and members of the Sheriff's staff, as well as members of the fire department and a fire truck were stationed in the street between the two groups. Rain fell throughout the demonstration

Several of the students took from beneath their coats picket signs similar to those which had been used the day before. These signs bore legends such as "Don't buy discrimination for Christmas," "Sacrifice for Christ, don't buy," and named stores which were proclaimed "unfair." They then sang "God Bless America," pledged allegiance to the flag, prayed briefly, and sang one or two hymns, including "We Shall Overcome." The 23 students, who were locked in jail cells in the courthouse building out of the sight of the demonstrators, responded by themselves singing; this in turn was greeted with cheers and applause by the demonstrators. Appellant gave a speech, described by a State's witness as follows:

> He said that, in effect, that it was a protest

against the illegal arrest of some of their members, and that other people were allowed to picket . . . and he said that they were not going to commit any violence, that, if anyone spit on them, they would not spit back on the person that did it.

Cox then said:

> All right. It's lunch time. Let's go eat. There are twelve stores we are protesting. A number of these stores have twenty counters; they accept your money from nineteen. They won't accept it from the twentieth counter. This is an act of racial discrimination. These stores are open to the public. You are members of the public. We pay taxes to the Federal Government, and you who live here pay taxes to the State.

In apparent reaction to these last remarks, there was what state witnesses described as "muttering" and "grumbling" by the white onlookers.

The Sheriff, deeming, as he testified, Cox's appeal to the students to sit in at the lunch counters to be "inflammatory," then took a power microphone and said,

> Now, you have been allowed to demonstrate. Up until now, your demonstration has been more or less peaceful, but what you are doing now is a direct violation of the law, a disturbance of the peace, and it has got to be broken up immediately.

The testimony as to what then happened is disputed. Some of the State's witnesses testified that Cox said, "don't move"; others stated that he made a "gesture of defiance." It is clear from the record, however, that Cox and the demonstrators did not then and there break up the demonstration. Two of the Sheriff's deputies immediately started across the street and told the group, "You have heard what the Sheriff said, now, do what he said." A state witness testified that they put their hands on the shoulders of some of the students "as though to shove them away."

Almost immediately thereafter -- within a time estimated variously at two to five minutes -- one of the policemen exploded a tear gas shell at the crowd. This was followed by several other shells. The demonstrators quickly dispersed, running back towards the State Capitol and the downtown area; Cox tried to calm them as they ran and was himself one of the last to leave.

No Negroes participating in the demonstration were arrested on that day. The only person then arrested was a young white man, not a part of the demonstration, who was arrested "because he was causing a disturbance." The next day, appellant was arrested and charged with the four offenses above described.

II
THE BREACH OF THE PEACE CONVICTION
Appellant was convicted of violating a Louisiana "disturbing the peace" statute, which provides:

> Whoever with intent to provoke a breach of the peace, or under circumstances such that a breach of the peace may be occasioned thereby . . . crowds or congregates with others . . . in or upon . . . a public street or public highway, or upon a public sidewalk, or any other public place or building . . . and who fails or refuses to disperse and move on . . . when ordered so to do by any law enforcement officer of any municipality, or parish, in which such act or acts are committed, or by any law enforcement officer of the state of Louisiana, or any other authorized person . . . shall be guilty of disturbing the peace.

La.Rev.Stat. § 14:103.1 (Cum.Supp. 1962). It is clear to us that, on the facts of this case, which are strikingly similar to those present in *Edwards v. South Carolina,* and *Fields v. South Carolina,* Louisiana infringed appellant's rights of free speech and free assembly by convicting him under this statute. As in *Edwards,* we do not find it necessary to pass upon appellant's contention that there was a complete absence of evidence so that his conviction deprived him of liberty without due process of law. ... We hold that Louisiana may not constitutionally punish appellant under this statute for engaging in the type of conduct which this record reveals, and also that the statute as authoritatively interpreted by the Louisiana Supreme Court is unconstitutionally broad in scope.

The Louisiana courts have held that appellant's conduct constituted a breach of the peace under state law, . . . but our independent examination of the record, which we are required to make, shows no conduct which the State had a right to prohibit as a breach of the peace.

Appellant led a group of young college students who wished "to protest segregation" and discrimination against Negroes and the arrest of 23 fellow students. They assembled peaceably at the State Capitol building and marched to the courthouse where they sang, prayed and listened to a speech. A reading of the record reveals agreement on the part of the State's witnesses that Cox had the demonstration "very well controlled," and, until the end of Cox's speech, the group was perfectly "orderly." Sheriff Clemmons testified that the crowd's activities were not "objectionable" before that time. They became objectionable, according to the Sheriff himself, when Cox, concluding his speech, urged the students to go uptown and sit in at lunch counters. The Sheriff testified that the sole aspect of the program to which he objected was

> [t]he inflammatory manner in which he [Cox] addressed that crowd and told them to go on up town, go to four places on the protest list, sit down and if they don't feed you, sit there for one hour.

Yet this part of Cox's speech obviously did not deprive the demonstration of its protected character under the Constitution as free speech and assembly. … The State argues, however, that, while the demonstrators started out to be orderly, the loud cheering and clapping by the students in response to the singing from the jail converted the peaceful assembly into a riotous one. The record, however, does not support this assertion. It is true that the students, in response to the singing of their fellows who were in custody, cheered and applauded. However, the meeting was an out-door meeting, and a key state witness testified that, while the singing was loud, it was not disorderly. There is, moreover, no indication that the mood of the students was ever hostile, aggressive, or unfriendly. Our conclusion that the entire meeting, from the beginning until its dispersal by tear gas was, orderly and not riotous is confirmed by a film of the events taken by a television news photographer, which was offered in evidence as a state exhibit. We have viewed the film, and it reveals that the students, though they undoubtedly cheered and clapped, were well behaved throughout. … The singing and cheering do not seem to us to differ significantly from the constitutionally protected activity of the demonstrators in *Edwards,* who loudly sang "while stamping their feet and clapping their hands."

Our conclusion that the record does not support the contention that the students' cheering, clapping and singing constituted a breach of the peace is confirmed by the fact that these were not relied on as a basis for conviction by the trial judge, who, rather, stated as his reason for convicting Cox of disturbing the peace that

> [i]t must be recognized to be inherently dangerous and a breach of the peace to bring 1,500 people, colored people, down in the predominantly white business district in the City of Baton Rouge and congregate across the street from the courthouse and sing songs as described to me by the defendant as the CORE national anthem carrying lines such as "black and white together" and to urge those 1,500 people to descend upon our lunch counters and sit there until they are served. That has to be an inherent breach of the peace, and our statute 14:103.1 has made it so.

Finally, the State contends that the conviction should be sustained because of fear expressed by some of the state witnesses that "violence was about to erupt" because of the demonstration. It is virtually undisputed, however, that the students themselves were not violent, and threatened no violence. The fear of violence seems to have been based upon the reaction of the group of white citizens looking on from across the street. One state witness testified that "he felt the situation was getting out of hand" as, on the courthouse side of St. Louis Street, "were small knots or groups of white citizens who were muttering words, who seemed a little bit agitated." A police officer stated that the reaction of the white crowd was not violent, but "was rumblings." Others felt the atmosphere became "tense" because of "mutterings," "grumbling," and "jeering" from the white group. There is no indication, however, that any member of the white group threatened violence. And this small crowd, estimated at between 100 and 300, was separated from the students by "seventy-five to eighty" armed policemen, including "every available shift of the City Police," the "Sheriff's Office in full complement," and "additional help from the State Police," along with a "fire truck and the Fire Department." As Inspector Trigg testified, they could have handled the crowd

. . .

There is an additional reason why this conviction cannot be sustained. The statute at issue in this case, as authoritatively interpreted by the Louisiana Supreme Court, is unconstitutionally vague in its overly broad scope. The statutory crime consists of two elements: (1) congregating with others "with intent to provoke a breach of the peace, or under circumstances such that a breach of the peace may be occasioned," and (2) a refusal to move on after having been ordered to do so by a law enforcement officer. While the second part of this offense is narrow and specific, the first element is not. The Louisiana Supreme Court in this case defined the term "breach of the peace" as "to agitate, to arouse from a state of repose, to molest, to interrupt, to hinder, to disquiet."

…

[T]he conviction under this statute must be reversed, as the statute is unconstitutional in that it sweeps within its broad scope activities that are constitutionally protected free speech and assembly. Maintenance of the opportunity for free political discussion is a basic tenet of our constitutional democracy. As Chief Justice Hughes stated in *Stromberg v. California*, 283 U.S. 359, 369:

> A statute which, upon its face and as authoritatively construed, is so vague and indefinite as to permit the punishment of the fair use of this opportunity is repugnant to the guaranty of liberty contained in the Fourteenth Amendment.

For all these reasons, we hold that appellant's freedoms of speech and assembly, secured to him by the First Amendment, as applied to the States by the Fourteenth Amendment, were denied by

his conviction for disturbing the peace. The conviction on this charge cannot stand

III
THE OBSTRUCTING PUBLIC PASSAGES
CONVICTION

We now turn to the issue of the validity of appellant's conviction for violating the Louisiana statute, . . . which provides:

Obstructing Public Passages
> No person shall willfully obstruct the free, convenient and normal use of any public sidewalk, street, highway, bridge, alley, road, or other passageway, or the entrance, corridor or passage of any public building, structure, watercraft or ferry, by impeding, hindering, stifling, retarding or restraining traffic or passage thereon or therein.

> Providing however nothing herein contained shall apply to a bona fide legitimate labor organization or to any of its legal activities such as picketing, lawful assembly or concerted activity in the interest of its members for the purpose of accomplishing or securing more favorable wage standards, hours of employment and working conditions.

Appellant was convicted under this statute not for leading the march to the vicinity of the courthouse, which the Louisiana Supreme Court stated to have been "orderly," but for leading the meeting on the sidewalk across the street from the courthouse. In upholding appellant's conviction under this statute, the Louisiana Supreme Court thus construed the statute so as to apply to public assemblies which do not have as their specific purpose the obstruction of traffic. There is no doubt from the record in this case that this far sidewalk was obstructed, and thus, as so construed, appellant violated the statute.

Appellant, however, contends that, as so construed and applied in this case, the statute is an unconstitutional infringement on freedom of speech and assembly. This contention, on the facts here presented, raises an issue with which this Court has dealt in many decisions, that is, the right of a State or municipality to regulate the use of city streets and other facilities to assure the safety and convenience of the people in their use and the concomitant right of the people of free speech and assembly.

. . . The rights of free speech and assembly, while fundamental in our democratic society, still do not mean that everyone with opinions or beliefs to express may address a group at any public place and at any time. The constitutional guarantee of liberty implies the existence of an organized society maintaining public order, without which liberty itself would be lost in the excesses of anarchy. The control of travel on the streets is a clear example of governmental responsibility to insure this necessary order. A restriction in that relation, designed to promote the public convenience in the interest of all, and not susceptible to abuses of discriminatory application, cannot be disregarded by the attempted exercise of some civil right which, in other circumstances, would be entitled to protection. One would not be justified in ignoring the familiar red light because this was thought to be a means of social protest. Nor could one, contrary to traffic regulations, insist upon a street meeting in the middle of Times Square at the rush hour as a form of freedom of speech or assembly. Governmental authorities have the duty and responsibility to keep their streets open and available for movement. A group of demonstrators could not insist upon the right to cordon off street, or entrance to a public or private building, and allow no one to pass who did not agree to listen to their exhortations.

We emphatically reject the notion urged by appellant that the First and Fourteenth Amendments afford the same kind of freedom to those who would communicate ideas by conduct such as patrolling, marching, and picketing on streets and highways, as these amendments afford to those who communicate ideas by pure speech. ... We reaffirm the statement of the Court in *Giboney v. Empire Storage & Ice Co.,* that

> it has never been deemed an abridgment of freedom of speech or press to make a course of conduct illegal merely because the conduct was in part initiated, evidenced, or carried out by means of language, either spoken, written, or printed.

We have no occasion in this case to consider the constitutionality of the uniform, consistent, and nondiscriminatory application of a statute forbidding all access to streets and other public facilities for parades and meetings. Although the statute here involved on its face precludes all street assemblies and parades, it has not been so applied and enforced by the Baton Rouge authorities. . . . From all the evidence before us, it appears that the authorities in Baton Rouge permit or prohibit parades or street meetings in their completely uncontrolled discretion.

...

This Court has recognized that the lodging of such broad discretion in a public official allows him to determine which expressions of view will be permitted and which will not. This thus sanctions a device for the suppression of the communication of ideas and permits the official to act as a censor. Also inherent in such a system allowing parades or meetings only with the prior permission of an official is the obvious danger to the right of a person or group not to be denied equal protection of the laws. ... It is clearly unconstitutional to enable a public official to determine which expressions of view will be permitted and which will not or to engage in invidious discrimination among persons or groups either by use of a statute providing a system of broad discretionary licensing power or, as in this case, the equivalent of such a system by selective enforcement of an extremely broad prohibitory statute.

It is, of course, undisputed that appropriate, limited discretion, under properly drawn statutes or ordinances, concerning the time, place, duration, or manner of use of the streets for public assemblies may be vested in administrative officials, provided that such limited discretion is exercised with "uniformity of method of treatment upon the facts of each application, free from improper or inappropriate considerations and from unfair discrimination" . . . [and with] a "systematic, consistent and just order of treatment, with reference to the convenience of public use of the highways. . . ."

But here it is clear that the practice in Baton Rouge allowing unfettered discretion in local officials in the regulation of the use of the streets for peaceful parades and meetings is an unwarranted abridgment of appellant's freedom of speech and assembly secured to him by the First Amendment, as applied to the States by the

Fourteenth Amendment. It follows, therefore, that appellant's conviction for violating the statute as so applied and enforced must be reversed.

DeJoung v. Oregon , 299 U.S. 353 (1937)
On July 27, 1934, at a meeting held by the Communist Party, Dirk De Jonge addressed the audience regarding jail conditions in the county and a maritime strike in progress in Portland. While the meeting was in progress, police raided it. De Jonge was arrested and charged with violating the State's criminal syndicalism statute. The Oregon law defined criminal syndicalism as "the doctrine which advocates crime, physical violence, sabotage or any unlawful acts or methods as a means of accomplishing or effecting industrial or political change or revolution." De Jonge was convicted and argued at the State Supreme Court there was insufficient evidence to justify his conviction. The State Supreme Court disagreed noting that the the indictment did not charge De Jonge with criminal syndicalism, but rather that he presided at, conducted and assisted in conducting an assemblage of persons, organization, society and group called by the Communist Party, which was unlawfully teaching and advocating in Multnomah county the doctrine of criminal syndicalism and sabotage. The U.S. Supreme Court held that the Oregon statute, as applied, violated the due process clause of the Fourteenth Amendment. After reviewing the record, the Court determined that De Jonge's sole offense was assisting in a public meeting held under the auspices of the Communist Party. The Court reasoned that to preserve the rights of free speech and peaceable assembly - principles embodied in the Fourteenth Amendment - not the auspices under which a meeting is held, but the purpose of the meeting and whether the speakers' remarks transcend the bounds of freedom of speech must be examined, which had not occurred in De Jonge's case.

Wood v. Moss, et al. 572 U.S. ___ (2014).

(Official Summary)
While campaigning for a second term, President George W. Bush was scheduled to spend the night at a Jacksonville, Oregon, cottage. Local law enforcement officials permitted a group of Bush supporters and a group of protesters to assemble on opposite sides of a street along the President's motorcade route. When the President made a last-minute decision to have dinner at the outdoor patio area of the Jacksonville Inn's restaurant before resuming the drive to the cottage, the protesters moved to an area in front of the Inn, which placed them within weapons range of the President. The supporters remained in their original location, where a two-story building blocked sight of, and weapons access to, the patio. At the direction of two Secret Service agents responsible for the President's security, petitioners here (the agents), local police cleared the area where the protesters had gathered, eventually moving them two blocks away to a street beyond weapons reach of the President. The agents did not require the guests already inside the Inn to leave, stay clear of the patio, or go through a security screening. After the President dined, his motorcade passed the supporters, but the protesters, now two blocks from the motorcade's route, were beyond his sight and hearing.

The protesters sued the agents for damages, alleging that the agents engaged in viewpoint discrimination in violation of the First Amendment when they moved the protesters away from the Inn but allowed the supporters to remain in their original location. The District Court denied the agents' motion to dismiss the suit for failure to state a claim and on qualified immunity grounds, but on interlocutory appeal, the Ninth Circuit reversed. The court held that the protesters had failed to state a First Amendment claim .

Held: The agents are entitled to qualified immunity.

Government officials may not exclude from public places persons engaged in peaceful expressive activity solely because the government actor fears, dislikes, or disagrees with the views expressed. … The fundamental right to speak, however, does not leave people at liberty to publicize their views " 'whenever and however and wherever they please.' "

The doctrine of qualified immunity protects government officials from liability for civil damages "unless a plaintiff pleads facts showing (1) that the official violated a statutory or constitutional right, and (2) that the right was 'clearly established' at the time of the challenged conduct." … The "dispositive inquiry . . . is whether it would [have been] clear to a reasonable officer" in the agents' position "that [their] conduct was unlawful in the situation [they] confronted." … This Court has recognized the overwhelming importance of safeguarding the President . . . . Mindful that officers may be faced with unanticipated security situations, the key question addressed is whether it should have been clear to the agents that the security perimeter they established violated the First Amendment.

(b) The protesters assert, and the Ninth Circuit agreed, that the agents violated clearly established federal law by denying them "equal access to the President." No decision of which the Court is aware, however, would alert Secret Service agents engaged in crowd control that they bear a First Amendment obligation to make sure that groups with conflicting views are at all times in equivalent positions. Nor would the maintenance of equal access make sense in the situation the agents here confronted, where only the protesters, not the supporters, had a direct line of sight to the patio where the President was dining. The protesters suggest that the agents could have moved the supporters out of the motorcade's range as well, but there would have been no security rationale for such a move.

(c) The protesters allege that, in directing their displacement, the agents acted not to ensure the President's safety, but to insulate the President from their message. These allegations are undermined by a map of the area, which shows that, because of the protesters' location, they posed a potential security risk to the President, while the supporters, because of their location, did not. The protesters' counterarguments are unavailing. They urge that, had the agents' professed interest in the President's safety been sincere, the agents would have screened or removed from the premises persons already at the Inn when the President arrived. But staff, other diners, and Inn guests were on the premises before the agents knew of the President's plans, and thus could not have anticipated seeing the President, no less causing harm to him. The agents also could keep a close watch on the relatively small number of people already inside the Inn, surveillance that would have been impossible for the hundreds of people outside the Inn. A White House manual directs the President's advance team to "work with the Secret Service . . . to designate a protest area . . . preferably not in view of the event site or motorcade route." The manual guides the conduct of the political advance team, not the Secret Service, whose own written guides explicitly prohibit "agents from discriminating between anti-government and pro-government demonstrators." Even assuming, as the protesters maintain, that other agents, at other times and places, have assisted in shielding the President from political speech, this case is scarcely one in which the agents lacked a valid security reason for their actions.

THE OVERBREADTH (DUE PROCESS) DOCTRINE

Generally limited to statutes which implicate the First Amendment, but closely related to the void-for-vagueness doctrine is the doctrine of overbreadth. The Court first discussed the overbreadth doctrine in *Thornhill v. Alabama*, 310 U.S. 88 (1940). Under this doctrine, the Court should strike down criminal laws that are written so broadly that they infringe on a person's constitutionally protected right. "The overbreadth doctrine encourages legislatures consider free speech issues when drafting legislation because these statutes will be especially vulnerable to constitutional challenges. The threat of a court invalidating a statute as overbroad incentivizes the legislatures to narrowly tailor their statutes." Id.

A law is overbroad when it prohibits what the constitution protects. For example, In *Coates (supra)* --in addition to finding the statute too vague--the Court found that the ordinance was overly broad because it criminalized speech and assembly that are protected by the First Amendment. The cases of *R. A.V.* and *Mitchell* discussed in *Rokicki* (supra) also addressed the primary concern of the overbreadth doctrine and the chilling effect that their relevant statutes had on people's behavior. If a statute seems to prohibit what is protected (speech), then individuals will refrain from engaging in that type of speech, even though the Constitution considers it a fundamental right. Because statutes that are overbroad have a "chilling effect" on people's behavior, they may be challenged even by persons not charged with violating the law. (Note: this is contrary to the general holding that a person must have standing—a specific personal interest in the outcome of the case--before he or she can challenge a statute.) "The overbreadth doctrine creates a distinct exception to the standing requirement, which, in effect, allows any litigant willing to challenge an allegedly overbroad statute to bring suit." Christopher Pierce, *The "Strong Medicine" of the Overbreadth Doctrine: When Statutory Exceptions Are No More than a Placebo,* 64 (1) Fed. Comm. L.J. at 182.

When applying the overbreadth doctrine, a court considers the constitutionality of a statute on its face (rather than as it is applied under these facts). However, the Court will not necessarily declare a statute automatically void when it is overbroad. For example, the Court refused to strike down a child pornography statute that defendant argued was overbroad in *New York v. Ferber,* 458 U.S. 747 (1982). The court believed the statute might possibly be applied to punish constitutionally protected artistic expression but held that a statute should not be invalidated for overbreadth if its legitimate reach "dwarfs its arguably impermissible applications." Fifteen years later, however, the Court struck down the Communications Decency Act of 1996 in *Reno v. American Civil Liberties Union,* 521 U.S. 844 (1997), finding that Congress had attempted to ban "indecent" as well as "obscene" speech from the Internet and thus swept within its ambit constitutionally protected speech as well as obscenity. [7]

As you can see in the case of *State v. Rangel* (supra), courts will analyze what aspects of a statute may make it potentially overbroad and then will, to the extent possible, narrow that statute without necessarily declaring it void.

HOUSTON v. HILL,
482 U.S. 451 (1987)

JUSTICE BRENNAN delivered the opinion of the Court.

This case presents the question whether a municipal ordinance that makes it unlawful to interrupt a police officer in the performance of his or her duties is unconstitutionally overbroad under the First Amendment.

I

[Appellee Raymond Wayne Hill is a lifelong resident of Houston, Texas working as a paralegal and as executive director of the Houston Human Rights League. Hill helped found and was a board member of the Gay Political Caucus. Hill was also affiliated with a Houston radio station, and had carried city and county press passes since 1975. He lived in Montrose, a "diverse and eclectic neighborhood" that is the center of gay political and social life in Houston.]

The incident that sparked this lawsuit occurred in the Montrose area on February 14, 1982. Hill observed a friend, Charles Hill, intentionally stopping traffic on a busy street, evidently to enable a vehicle to enter traffic. Two Houston police officers, one of whom was named Kelley, approached Charles and began speaking with him. According to the District Court, "shortly thereafter" Hill began shouting at the officers "in an admitted attempt to divert Kelley's attention from Charles Hill." Hill first shouted: "Why don't

---

[7] In response to this decision, Congress passed the Child Online Protection Act in 1998, but it never took effect due to a series of permanent injunctions granted by the Third Circuit Court of Appeals. In *Ashcroft v. Free Speech Coalition,* 535 U.S. 234 (2002), the U.S. Supreme Court struck down the federal child pornography law because it intruded on free speech rights. In 2004, the Supreme Court once again faced this issue (see, *Ashcroft v. American Civil Liberties Union,* 542 U.S. 656 (2004)). The Court upheld the injunction granted by the lower court stopping the implementation of COPA. The Court stated,

"Content-based prohibitions, enforced by severe criminal penalties, have the constant potential to be a repressive force in the lives and thoughts of a free people. To guard against that threat the Constitution demands that content-based restrictions on speech be presumed invalid, *R. A. V.* v. *St. Paul* and that the Government bear the burden of showing their constitutionality. *United States* v. *Playboy Entertainment Group, Inc..* This is true even when Congress twice has attempted to find a constitutional means to restrict, and punish, the speech in question."

you pick on somebody your own size?" After Officer Kelley responded: "[A]re you interrupting me in my official capacity as a Houston police officer?" Hill then shouted: "Yes, why don't you pick on somebody my size?" Hill was arrested under Houston Code of Ordinances, 34-11(a), for "wilfully or intentionally interrupt[ing] a city policeman . . . by verbal challenge during an investigation." Charles Hill was not arrested. Hill was then acquitted after a nonjury trial in Municipal Court.

Code of Ordinances, City of Houston, Texas, 34-11(a) (1984), reads:

"Sec. 34-11. Assaulting or interfering with policemen.

"(a) It shall be unlawful for any person to assault, strike or in any manner oppose, molest, abuse or interrupt any policeman in the execution of his duty, or any person summoned to aid in making an arrest."

Following his acquittal in the Charles Hill incident, Hill brought the suit in the Federal District Court for the Southern District of Texas, seeking (1) a declaratory judgment that 34-11(a) was unconstitutional both on its face and as it had been applied to him, (2) a permanent injunction against any attempt to enforce the ordinance, (3) an order expunging the records of his arrests under the ordinance, and (4) damages and attorney's fees under 42 U.S.C. 1983 and 1988.

At trial, Hill introduced records provided by the city regarding both the frequency with which arrests had been made for violation of the ordinance and the type of conduct with which those arrested had been charged. He also introduced evidence and testimony concerning the arrests of several reporters under the ordinance. Finally, Hill introduced evidence regarding his own experience with the ordinance, under which he has been arrested four times since 1975, but never convicted. The District Court held that Hill's evidence did not demonstrate that the ordinance had been unconstitutionally applied. The court also rejected Hill's contention that the ordinance was unconstitutionally vague or overbroad on its face. The ordinance was not vague, the court stated, because:

"[t]he wording of the ordinance is

sufficiently definite to put a person of reasonable intelligence on fair notice of what actions are forbidden. In particular, the Court finds that the use of words such as `interrupt' are sufficiently clear by virtue of their commonly-understood, everyday definitions. Interrupt commonly means to cause one to cease, such as stopping someone in the middle of something. The Plaintiff, for example, clearly `interrupted' the police officers regarding the Charles Hill incident."

The court also held that the statute was not overbroad because "the ordinance does not, at least facially, proscribe speech or conduct which is protected by the First Amendment."

A panel of the Court of Appeals reversed. The city's suggestion for rehearing en banc was granted, and the Court of Appeals, by a vote of 8-7, upheld the judgment of the panel. The Court of Appeals agreed with the District Court's conclusion that the ordinance was not vague, and that it "plainly encompasse[d] mere verbal as well as physical conduct." Applying the standard established in *Broadrick v. Oklahoma*, 413 U.S. 601 (1973), however, the Court of Appeals concluded that the ordinance was substantially overbroad. It found that "[a] significant range of protected speech and expression is punishable and might be deterred by the literal wording of the statute."

The Court of Appeals also reviewed the evidence of the unconstitutional application of the ordinance which Hill had introduced at trial. The court did not disturb the District Court's ruling that the statute had not been unconstitutionally applied to Hill or to the reporters. It did conclude, however, that other evidence not mentioned by the District Court revealed "a realistic danger of, and a substantial potential for, the unconstitutional application of the ordinance." This evidence showed that the ordinance "is officially regarded as penalizing the mere interruption of a policeman while in the line of duty," and has been employed to make arrests for, inter alia, "arguing," "[t]alking," "[i]nterfering," "[f]ailing to remain quiet," "[r]efusing to remain silent," "[v]erbal abuse," "[c]ursing," "[v]erbally yelling," and "[t]alking loudly, [w]alking through scene."

The city appealed, claiming that the Court of Appeals erred in holding the ordinance facially overbroad and in not abstaining until the ordinance had been construed by the state courts. We noted probable jurisdiction and now affirm.

II

The elements of First Amendment overbreadth analysis are familiar. Only a statute that is substantially overbroad may be invalidated on its face. "We have never held that a statute should be held invalid on its face merely because it is possible to conceive of a single impermissible application . . . ." Instead, "[i]n a facial challenge to the overbreadth and vagueness of a law, a court's first task is to determine whether the enactment reaches a substantial amount of constitutionally protected conduct." Criminal statutes must be scrutinized with particular care; those that make unlawful a substantial amount of constitutionally protected conduct may be held facially invalid even if they also have legitimate application.

The city's principal argument is that the ordinance does not inhibit the exposition of ideas, and that it bans "core criminal conduct" not protected by the First Amendment. In its view, the application of the ordinance to Hill illustrates that the police employ it only to prohibit such conduct, and not "as a subterfuge to control or dissuade free expression." Since the ordinance is "content-neutral," and since there is no evidence that the city has applied the ordinance to chill particular speakers or ideas, the city concludes that the ordinance is not substantially overbroad.

We disagree with the city's characterization for several reasons. First, the enforceable portion of the ordinance deals not with core criminal conduct, but with speech. . . . Accordingly, the enforceable portion of the ordinance makes it "unlawful for any person to . . . in any manner oppose, molest, abuse or interrupt any policeman in the execution of his duty," and thereby prohibits verbal interruptions of police officers.

Second, contrary to the city's contention, the First Amendment protects a significant amount of verbal criticism and challenge directed at police officers. "Speech is often provocative and challenging. . . . [But it] is nevertheless protected against censorship or punishment, unless shown likely to produce a clear and present danger of a serious substantive evil that rises far above public inconvenience, annoyance, or unrest." *Terminiello v. Chicago*, 337 U.S. 1, 4 (1949). In *Lewis v. City of New Orleans*, 415 U.S. 130 (1974), for example, the appellant was found to have yelled obscenities and threats at an officer who had asked appellant's husband to produce his driver's license. Appellant was convicted under a municipal ordinance that made it a crime "`for any person wantonly to curse or revile or to use obscene or opprobrious language toward or with reference to any member of the city police while in the actual performance of his duty.'" We vacated the conviction and invalidated the ordinance as facially overbroad. Critical to our decision was the fact that the ordinance "punishe[d] only spoken words" and was not limited in scope to fighting words that "`by their very utterance inflict injury or tend to incite an immediate breach of the peace.'" Moreover, in a concurring opinion in Lewis, JUSTICE POWELL suggested that even the "fighting words" exception recognized in *Chaplinsky v. New Hampshire*, 315 U.S. 568(1942), might require a narrower application in cases involving words addressed to a police officer, because "a properly trained officer may reasonably be expected to `exercise a higher degree of restraint' than the average citizen, and thus be less likely to respond belligerently to `fighting words.'"

The Houston ordinance is much more sweeping than the municipal ordinance struck down in Lewis. It is not limited to fighting words nor even to obscene or opprobrious language, but prohibits speech that "in any manner . . . interrupt[s]" an officer. The Constitution does not allow such speech to be made a crime. The freedom of individuals verbally to oppose or challenge police action without thereby risking arrest is one of the principal characteristics by which we distinguish a free nation from a police state.

The city argues, however, that even if the ordinance encompasses some protected speech, its sweeping nature is both inevitable and essential to maintain public order. . . .

The city further suggests that its ordinance is comparable to the disorderly conduct statute upheld against a facial challenge in *Colten v. Kentucky*. . . . This Houston ordinance, however, is not narrowly tailored to prohibit only disorderly conduct or fighting words, and in no way resembles the law upheld in Colten. Although we appreciate the difficulties of drafting precise laws, we have repeatedly invalidated laws that provide the police with unfettered discretion to arrest individuals for words or conduct that annoy or offend them. . . .

Houston's ordinance criminalizes a substantial amount of constitutionally protected speech, and accords the police unconstitutional discretion in enforcement. The ordinance's plain language is admittedly violated scores of times daily, yet only some individuals - those chosen by the police in their unguided discretion - are arrested. . . . We conclude that the ordinance is substantially overbroad, and that the Court of Appeals did not err in holding it facially invalid.

III

The city has also urged us not to reach the merits of Hill's constitutional challenge, but rather to abstain. . . . In its view, there are certain limiting constructions readily available to the state courts that would eliminate the ordinance's overbreadth.

. . .

Even if this case did not involve a facial challenge under the First Amendment, we would find abstention inappropriate. In cases involving a facial challenge to a statute, the pivotal question in determining whether abstention is appropriate is whether the statute is "fairly subject to an interpretation which will render unnecessary or substantially modify the federal constitutional question." If the statute is not obviously susceptible of a limiting construction, then even if the statute has "never [been] interpreted by a state tribunal . . . it is the duty of the federal court to exercise its properly invoked jurisdiction."

This ordinance is not susceptible to a limiting construction because, as both courts below agreed, its language is plain and its meaning unambiguous. Its constitutionality cannot "turn upon a choice between one or several alternative meanings." Nor can the ordinance be limited by

severing discrete unconstitutional subsections from the rest. . . . The enforceable portion of this ordinance is a general prohibition of speech that "simply has no core" of constitutionally unprotected expression to which it might be limited. The city's proposed constructions are insufficient, and it is doubtful that even "a remarkable job of plastic surgery upon the face of the ordinance" could save it. In sum, "[s]ince `the naked question, uncomplicated by [ambiguous language], is whether the Act on its face is unconstitutional,' abstention from federal jurisdiction is not required."

. . .

IV

Today's decision reflects the constitutional requirement that, in the face of verbal challenges to police action, officers and municipalities must respond with restraint. We are mindful that the preservation of liberty depends in part upon the maintenance of social order. But the First Amendment recognizes, wisely we think, that a certain amount of expressive disorder not only is inevitable in a society committed to individual freedom, but must itself be protected if that freedom would survive. We therefore affirm the judgment of the Court of Appeals.
It is so ordered.

JUSTICE BLACKMUN, **concurring**. (Omitted).

JUSTICE SCALIA, **concurring** in the judgment. . . . Because I do not believe that the Houston ordinance is reasonably susceptible of a limiting construction that would avoid the constitutional question posed in this case, I agree with the Court that certification would also be inappropriate

JUSTICE POWELL, with whom JUSTICE O'CONNOR joins, and with whom THE CHIEF JUSTICE joins as to Parts I and II, and JUSTICE SCALIA joins as to Parts II and III, **concurring in the judgment in part and dissenting in part**. (Omitted).

WRAP UP

Legislators must be very careful when creating laws that limit individuals' speech--although some speech is deemed not worthy of protection. Likewise, they must be careful not to write laws that create a religion or laws that target and interfere with a person's exercise of their own religion. Legislatures should not create laws that completely limit people's ability to gather together peaceably – although reasonable time and manner limitations are permissible. When defendant believes that a statute prohibits behavior that the constitution protects, he or she may file an "overbreadth challenge" to the charges (called a demurrer.) One option the court has in lieu of striking down a statute that may, on its face, infringe on a person's rights is to narrowly construe the statute.

Chapter Three: Elements of a Crime

OVERVIEW

When charged with a crime, the first thing a defendant might do is to assert that there is something constitutionally wrong with the law he is alleged to have violated. Did the people passing the law get it right? Does the law in some way violate the state or federal constitution? The second challenge the defendant will make is to assert that the government cannot prove everything this law requires it to prove. This chapter examines what the government must prove to convict someone of a crime—the elements of the crime. [In later chapters we will examine carefully the specific crimes and each of their specific requirements, so this chapter will deal only with the elements of the crime in a general sense.] The elements of legality and punishment are presumed—meaning that generally the state need not prove those to a jury in order to obtain a conviction. Except in the special cases of strict and vicarious liability crimes, the state must prove the defendant had the required actus reus, mens rea, and concurrence of mens rea and actus reus in all crimes; and in crimes of result, the state must also prove the defendant caused the proscribed harm.

How do we know what exactly the state must prove? Historically, substantive law (that is, the set of laws that define crimes, identify permissible defenses, and indicate the maximum penalties for the crime) was comprised of the common law. Today, however, the great majority of substantive law is codified and found in the state's particular criminal code[8] or in the federal code—meaning you will be able to tell what the state must prove by looking at the statute setting out the crime.

Much of the work of "codification" of the substantive law came about following the publication of the Model Penal Code (MPC) in 1962. The MPC has had significant impact on legislative drafting of criminal statutes. Every state has adopted at least some provisions of the MPC; some states have adopted many of the provisions; but no state has adopted the MPC in its entirety. You will find many provisions of the MPC throughout this text. Although many textbooks provide sample statutes from the states as illustrations, this text does not do so. Instead, you will be able to glean from the cases presented the variety of state approaches to their substantive law by looking at the language of the statute the defendant was charged with.

Note that even if the state is able to prove all the elements of the crime, the defendant may nonetheless raise defenses that may keep him or her from being convicted—these defenses, called justifications or excuses, are explored in Chapters Ten and Eleven.

LEGALITY AND PUNISHMENT

The legality requirement stems from the legal maxim "no crime without law." Substantive criminal law must be properly enacted, and the legislature in passing the statute must jump through all the hoops required of law-making in that particular jurisdiction. Proper enactment involves following law-making procedure -- for example, the required quorum, a proper recording of the law. That said, the state spends no time during the criminal trial discussing whether the crime was lawfully enacted because the state benefits from a presumption that the law was validly enacted (known as the presumption of regularity), and any challenges to the law's valid enactment would occur before the trial.

Second, the law must contain a statement of how a violation of the law will be punished. This requirement is known as the punishment element, and it stems from the legal maxim, "no punishment without law." A law that forbids certain behavior but does not have a specified punishment is really just a guideline since there can be no crime without a punishment. Any challenge to a lack of specified punishment would also be addressed in advance of the trial.

---

[8] Laws created through the initiative and referendum process are typically adopted into these codes.

Before we blame an individual for bad behavior, he or she must be put on notice of what counts as bad behavior. Fair warning requires that the individual is able to determine whether his or her behavior will be illegal and the maximum punishment that may be imposed for such behavior.

> If the criminal law is to deter antisocial activity, it should provide persons who might engage in such activity with a warning that their actions will be subject to punishment. Advance notice as to the scope of the law is also relevant to the criminal law's emphasis upon blameworthiness as the basis for imposing retribution. Kerper, at 82.

States have taken two approaches in dealing with incorporating the punishment element in their codes. About half the states, specify the punishment in the statute that defines the crime. For example, the statute might read,

> A person commits the crime of harassment when he or she intentionally subjects another to offensive physical contact. Harassment is punishable by up to 6 months' incarceration and a fine in the amount of $2500.

The other half of the states follows Model Penal Code approach. The MPC defines the individual crimes without reference to a specific punishment. Instead the crime will indicate its classification as either a felony or misdemeanor or sub-classification of these. There is then a separate provision that states how those classifications of felonies and misdemeanors are punished. (So, someone looking to find out the punishment for harassment would need to look in two different places). In the special part of the code the statute might read,

> A person commits Harassment when he or she intentionally subjects another to offensive physical contact. Harassment is a Class B misdemeanor.

In the general part of the code, the punishment scheme for felonies and misdemeanors would be stated. For example, that part might read:

> Misdemeanors: Class A, punishable by up to one year of incarceration and a fine in the amount of $5000.00; Class B, punishable by up to six months incarceration and a fine in the amount of $2500.00; Class C, punishable by up to 30 days incarceration and a fine in the amount of $1250.00.

ACTUS REUS

The Latin phrase actus reus means "the act of a criminal," and in order to convict, the government must prove beyond a reasonable doubt the actus reus element specified for the crime. Actus reus includes voluntary acts, failures to act when there was a legal duty to do so, or possessing something criminally.

Actus Reus: Voluntary Act

Most acts are voluntary. When you move your hand to put your pencil on the desk, it is a voluntary act. If, however, you move your hand because of a muscle spasm or someone bumping you, then your act is not voluntary. Frequently people think of voluntariness as meaning wishing something to occur. But, when dealing with actus reus, voluntariness looks at whether the action is a product of a reflex or physical response to an outside force. Consider this example: Kirk sees a group of children walking on the sidewalk and decides it would be fun to drive his car toward them to scare them, but he does nothing. Seconds later, the passenger in his car grabs his arm causing him to drive into the children. Kirk has not committed a voluntary act.

People v. Decina,
2 N.Y.2d 133 (1956)

At about 3:30 P.M. on March 14, 1955, a bright, sunny day, defendant was driving, alone in his car, in a northerly direction on Delaware Avenue in the city of Buffalo. The portion of Delaware Avenue here involved is 60 feet wide. At a point south of an overhead viaduct of the Erie Railroad, defendant's car swerved to the left, across the center line in the street, so that it was completely in the south lane, traveling 35 to 40 miles per hour.

It then veered sharply to the right, crossing Delaware Avenue and mounting the easterly curb at a point beneath the viaduct and continued thereafter at a speed estimated to have been about 50 or 60 miles per hour or more. During this latter swerve, a pedestrian testified that he saw defendant's hand above his head; another witness said he saw defendant's left arm bent over the wheel, and his right hand extended towards the right door.

A group of six schoolgirls were walking north on the easterly sidewalk of Delaware Avenue, two in front and four slightly in the rear, when defendant's car struck them from behind. One of the girls escaped injury by jumping against the wall of the viaduct. The bodies of the children struck were propelled northward onto the street and the lawn in front of a coal company, located to the north of the Erie viaduct on Delaware Avenue. Three of the children, 6 to 12 years old, were found dead on arrival by the medical examiner, and a fourth child, 7 years old, died in a hospital two days later as a result of injuries sustained in the accident.

After striking the children, defendant's car continued on the easterly sidewalk, and then swerved back onto Delaware Avenue once more. It continued in a northerly direction, passing under a second viaduct before it again veered to the right and remounted the easterly curb, striking and breaking a metal lamppost. With its horn blowing steadily — apparently because defendant was "stooped over" the steering wheel — the car proceeded on the sidewalk until it finally crashed through a 7¼-inch brick wall of a grocery store, injuring at least one customer and causing considerable property damage.

When the car came to a halt in the store, with its horn still blowing, several fires had been ignited. Defendant was stooped over in the car and was "bobbing a little". To one witness he appeared dazed, to another unconscious, lying back with his hands off the wheel. Various people present shouted to defendant to turn off the ignition of his car, and "within a matter of seconds the horn stopped blowing and the car did shut off".

Defendant was pulled out of the car by a number of bystanders and laid down on the sidewalk. To a policeman who came on the scene shortly he appeared "injured, dazed"; another witness said that "he looked as though he was knocked out, and his arm seemed to be bleeding". An injured customer in the store, after receiving first aid, pressed defendant for an explanation of the accident and he told her: "I blacked out from the bridge".

When the police arrived, defendant attempted to rise, staggered and appeared dazed and unsteady. When informed that he was under arrest, and would have to accompany the police to the station house, he resisted and, when he tried to get away, was handcuffed. The foregoing evidence was adduced by the People, and is virtually undisputed — defendant did not take the stand nor did he produce any witnesses.

…

We turn first to the subject of defendant's cross appeal, namely, that his demurrer should have been sustained, since the *indictment* here does not charge a crime. The indictment states essentially that defendant, *knowing* "that he was subject to epileptic attacks or other disorder rendering him likely to lose consciousness for a considerable period of time", was culpably negligent "in that he *consciously* undertook to and *did operate* his Buick sedan on a public highway" and "while so doing" suffered such an attack which caused said automobile "to travel at a fast and reckless rate of speed, jumping the curb and driving over the sidewalk" causing the death of 4 persons. In our opinion, this clearly states a violation of section 1053-a of the Penal Law. The statute does not require that a defendant must deliberately intend to kill a human being, for that would be murder. Nor does the statute require that he knowingly and consciously follow the precise path that leads to death and destruction. It is sufficient, we have said, when his conduct manifests a "disregard of the consequences which may ensue from the act, and indifference to the rights of others. No clearer definition, applicable to the hundreds of varying circumstances that may arise, can be given. Under a given state of facts, whether negligence is culpable is a question of judgment."

Assuming the truth of the indictment, as we must on a demurrer, this defendant knew he was subject to epileptic attacks and seizures that might strike *at any time*. He also knew that a moving motor vehicle uncontrolled on a public highway is a highly dangerous instrumentality capable of unrestrained destruction. With this *knowledge*, and without anyone accompanying him, he deliberately took a chance by making a conscious choice of a course of action, in disregard of the consequences which he knew might follow from his conscious act, and which in this case did ensue. How can we say as a matter of law that this did not amount to culpable negligence within the meaning of section 1053-a?

To hold otherwise would be to say that a man may freely indulge himself in liquor in the same hope that it will not affect his driving, and if it later develops that ensuing intoxication causes dangerous and reckless driving resulting in death, his unconsciousness or involuntariness at that time would relieve him from prosecution under the statute. His awareness of a condition which he knows may produce such consequences as here, and his disregard of the consequences, renders him liable for culpable negligence. … To have a sudden sleeping spell, an unexpected heart or other disabling attack, without any prior knowledge or warning thereof, is an altogether different situation … and there is simply no basis for comparing such cases with the flagrant disregard manifested here.

DESMOND, J. (dissenting in part).

The indictment charges that defendant knowing that "he was subject to epileptic attacks or other disorder rendering him likely to lose consciousness" suffered "an attack and loss of consciousness which caused the said automobile operated by the said defendant to travel at a fast and reckless rate of speed" and to jump a curb and run onto the sidewalk "thereby striking and causing the death" of 4 children. Horrible as this occurrence was and whatever necessity it may show for new licensing and driving laws, nevertheless this indictment charges no crime known to the New York statutes. Our duty is to dismiss it.

Section 1053-a of the Penal Law describes the crime of "criminal negligence in the operation of a vehicle resulting in death". Declared to be guilty of that crime is "A person who operates or drives any vehicle of any kind in a reckless or culpably negligent manner, whereby a human being is killed". The essentials of the crime are, therefore, first, vehicle *operation* in a culpably negligent *manner*, and, second, the resulting death of a person. This indictment asserts that defendant violated section 1053-a, but it then proceeds in the language quoted in the next-above paragraph of this opinion to describe the way in which defendant is supposed to have offended against that statute. That descriptive matter … shows that defendant did *not* violate section 1053-a. No *operation* of an automobile in a reckless manner is charged against defendant. The excessive speed of the car and its jumping the curb were "caused", says the indictment itself, by defendant's prior "attack and loss of consciousness". Therefore, what defendant is accused of is *not* reckless or culpably negligent driving, which necessarily connotes and involves consciousness and volition. The fatal assault by this car was after and because of defendant's failure of consciousness. To say that one drove a car in a reckless manner in that his unconscious condition caused the car to travel recklessly is to make two mutually contradictory assertions. One cannot be "reckless" while unconscious. One cannot while unconscious "operate" a car in a culpably negligent manner or in any other "manner". The statute makes criminal a particular kind of knowing, voluntary, immediate operation. It does not touch at all the involuntary presence of an unconscious person at the wheel of an uncontrolled vehicle. To negative the possibility of applying section 1053-a to these alleged facts we do not even have to resort to the rule that all criminal statutes are closely and strictly construed in favor of the citizen and that no act or omission is criminal unless specifically and in terms so labeled by a clearly worded statute. …

Tested by its history section 1053-a has the same meaning: penalization of conscious operation of a vehicle in a culpably negligent manner. It is significant that until this case … no attempt was ever made to penalize, either under section 1053-a or as manslaughter, the wrong done by one whose foreseeable blackout while driving had consequences fatal to another person.

The purpose of and occasion for the enactment of section 1053-a is well known. It was passed to give a new label to, and to fix a lesser punishment for, the culpably negligent automobile driving which had formerly been prosecuted under section 1052 of the Penal Law defining manslaughter in the second degree. It had been found difficult to get manslaughter convictions against death-dealing motorists. But neither of the two statutes has ever been thought until now to make it a crime to drive a car when one is subject to attacks or seizures such as are incident to certain forms and levels of epilepsy and other diseases and conditions.

Now let us test by its consequences this new construction of section 1053-a. Numerous are the diseases and other conditions of a human being which make it possible or even likely that the afflicted person will lose control of his automobile. Epilepsy, coronary involvements, circulatory diseases, nephritis, uremic poisoning, diabetes, Meniere's syndrome, a tendency to fits of sneezing, locking of the knee, muscular contractions — any of these common conditions may cause loss of control of a vehicle for a period long enough to cause a fatal accident. An automobile traveling at only 30 miles an hour goes 44 feet in a second. Just what is the court holding here? No less than this: that a driver whose brief blackout lets his car run amuck and kill another has killed that other by reckless driving. But any such "recklessness" consists necessarily not of the erratic behavior of the automobile while its driver is unconscious, but of his driving at all when he knew he was subject to such attacks. Thus, it must be that such a blackout-prone driver is guilty of reckless driving whenever and as soon as he steps into the driver's seat of a vehicle. Every time he drives, accident or no accident, he is subject to criminal prosecution for reckless driving or to revocation of his operator's license . And how many of this State's 5,000,000 licensed operators are subject to such penalties for merely driving the cars they are licensed to drive? No one knows how many citizens or how many or what kind of physical conditions will be gathered in under this practically limitless coverage of section 1053-a of the Penal Law and section 58 and subdivision 3 of section 71 of the Vehicle and Traffic Law . A criminal statute whose reach is so unpredictable violates constitutional rights . . . .

When section 1053-a was new it was assailed as unconstitutional on the ground that the language "operates or drives any vehicle of any kind in a reckless or culpably negligent manner" was too indefinite since a driver could only guess as to what acts or omissions were meant. Constitutionality was upheld. . . . The then Justice LEWIS, later of this court, wrote that the statutory language was sufficiently explicit since "reckless driving" and "culpable negligence" had been judicially defined in manslaughter cases as meaning the operation of an automobile in such a way as to show a disregard of the consequences … The *manner* in which a car is driven may be investigated by a jury, grand or trial, to see whether the manner was such as to show a reckless disregard of consequences. But giving section 1053-a the new meaning assigned to it permits punishment of one who did not drive in any forbidden manner but should not have driven at all, according to the present theory. No motorist suffering from any serious malady or infirmity can with impunity drive any automobile at any time or place, since no one can know what physical conditions make it "reckless" or "culpably negligent" to drive an automobile. Such a construction of a criminal statute offends against due process and against justice and fairness. . . .

A whole new approach may be necessary to the problem of issuing or refusing drivers' licenses to epileptics and persons similarly afflicted … But the absence of adequate licensing controls cannot in law or in justice be supplied by criminal prosecutions of drivers who have violated neither the language nor the intendment of any criminal law. Entirely without pertinence here is any consideration of driving while intoxicated or while sleepy, since those are conditions presently known to the driver, not mere future possibilities or probabilities. The demurrer should be sustained and the indictment dismissed

I suggest that *Decina* presents sloppy legal overreaching. The law requires a voluntary act. But, unlike the recent incidents where drivers apparently drove into crowds of people with terroristic intent, Decina's actions were shown to be the result of a convulsion or seizure. Although the consequences were horrible (which is probably why the court's majority was reluctant to let him evade criminal responsibility), there was no indication that at the time of his seizure he had any control over his muscles. Why is it important that Decina knew he was subject to seizure, knew that he might suffer a convulsion at any time, and knew that he was driving a car? This knowledge does not change the fact that he had an inability to control his movements. Convulsions are not voluntary acts. Whether the defendant knew he or she was prone to seizures, should not matter one iota in determining the voluntariness of the act. If the act is a product of a reflex, there is nothing the defendant's awareness about his situation can do to change that. Although, it may be understandable that the court wished to punish Decina for placing himself in a position where he knew he could cause such a horrible result, the state could deal harshly with people who voluntarily get behind a wheel knowing that they are subject to seizures. The legislature could pass a serious felony law prohibiting just that. For example the statute could read:

> "No person shall knowingly drive a vehicle having advanced knowledge that they may possibly have a seizure...Such offense is a Class A felony, punishable by. . . ."

My opinions notwithstanding, the trend has been to hold people responsible for getting themselves in positions where things can go wrong—particularly if they know in advance that something bad could happen. Courts have embraced the theory that these are "voluntarily induced involuntary acts," and may find that the actus reus requirement is satisfied--this is particularly true when defendant's action results from voluntary consumption of an intoxicating substance.

Other behaviors considered not to be voluntary acts include: acts done while unconscious, asleep, or in a state of automatism. An act performed during a state of "unconsciousness" does not meet the actus reus requirement. But what is unconsciousness? What if the defendant testifies that he "blacked out?" Most courts agree that amnesia itself doesn't constitute a defense, but if the defendant can show that he or she was "on automatic pilot" and not conscious of what he or she was doing, then there is a chance that his act will be held to be involuntary. The MPC notes that an act is not involuntary simply because the individual acted out of the habit and therefore was not conscious of what he was doing. In such a case, the act clearly was within the actor's physical control if he simply would have paid more attention. See, Kerper, *supra* at 98.

MPC §2.01 Requirement of a Voluntary Act; Omission as Basis of Liability; Possession as an Act

(1) A person is not guilty of an offense unless his liability is based on conduct which includes a voluntary act or the omission to perform an act of which he is physically capable.

(2) The following are not voluntary acts within the meaning of this Section:
(a) a reflex or convulsion;
(b) a bodily movement during unconsciousness or sleep;
(c) conduct during hypnosis or resulting from hypnotic suggestion;
(d) a bodily movement that otherwise is not a product of the effort or determination of the actor, either conscious or habitual.

. . .

(4) Possession is an act, within the meaning of this Section, if the possessor knowingly procured or received the thing possessed or was aware of his control thereof for a sufficient period to have been able to terminate his possession.

Although the MPC holds that acts performed under hypnosis are involuntary, some states hold that defendants who are hypnotized are nevertheless liable for their voluntary acts because of the view that nobody will perform acts under hypnosis that are deeply repugnant to them.

BROWN v. STATE, 955 S.W.2d 276 (Tex.Crim.App.)

Appellant was charged by indictment with the offense of murder, . . . was found guilty by a jury. . . [and was sentenced to] . . . 12 years confinement. . . . [We granted review to determine] . . . whether the District Court was correct in holding that the trial court should have submitted jury instructions on voluntary conduct.

FACTS
The record reflects that on the evening of July 17, 1992, appellant was drinking beer and talking with friends in the parking lot of an apartment complex. Appellant was involved in an altercation with James McLean, an individual with whom he had an encounter one week prior, in which McLean and some other individuals had beaten appellant. Appellant testified that following the altercation on the day in question, he obtained a .25 caliber handgun in order to protect himself and his friends from McLean and his associates, who were known to possess and discharge firearms in the vicinity of the apartment complex. Appellant, who is right-handed, testified that he held the handgun in his left hand because of a debilitating injury to his right hand. Appellant testified that during the course of the events in question, the handgun accidentally fired when he was bumped from behind by another person, Coleman, while raising the handgun. Coleman testified that he bumped appellant and the handgun fired. Appellant testified that the shot that fatally wounded the victim, Joseph Caraballo, an acquaintance and associate of appellant, was fired accidentally. Caraballo was not one of the individuals who posed a threat to Brown.

OPINION
Appellant testified at trial that the handgun in his possession accidentally discharged after he was bumped from behind by Ryan Coleman. Coleman also testified at trial that his bumping appellant precipitated the discharge of the gun and that idiosyncrasies of the handgun may

have also allowed its discharge.

Section 6.01(a) of the Texas Penal Code states that a person commits an offense only if he engages in voluntary conduct, including an act, an omission, or possession. Only if the evidence raises reasonable doubt that the defendant voluntarily engaged in the conduct charged should the jury be instructed to acquit. "Voluntariness," within the meaning of Section 6.01(a) refers only to one's physical bodily movements. While the defense of accident is no longer present in the penal code, this Court has long held that homicide that is not the result of voluntary conduct is not to be criminally punished.

We hold that if the admitted evidence raises the issue of the conduct of the actor not being voluntary, then the jury shall be charged, when requested, on the issue of voluntariness. The trial court did not grant appellant's request and the court of appeals correctly reversed the trial court. We hereby affirm the decision of the court of appeals.

Prince, J. dissenting
I respectfully dissent to the majority's decision to affirm the court of appeals because I do not believe that article 6.01(a) constitutes a defense and, therefore, appellant was not entitled to an affirmative defensive jury instruction regarding the voluntariness of his act.

Because the Legislature expressed an intent to model our Code after the Model Penal Code, we may also look to the Model Code for guidance. The comparable American Law Institute Model Penal Code as well as its commentaries offer more guidance on this issue than the Texas Code. In relevant part, the Model Penal Code section explains:

The following are not voluntary acts within the meaning of this Section:
    (a) a reflex or convulsion;
    (b) a bodily movement during

unconsciousness or sleep;
(c) conduct during hypnosis or resulting from hypnotic suggestion;
(d) a bodily movement that otherwise is not a product of the effort or determination of the actor, either conscious or habitual.

Although a voluntary act is an absolute requirement for criminal liability, it does not follow that every act up to the moment that the harm is caused must be voluntary. This concept is best demonstrated by an example: *A* who is subject to frequent fainting spells voluntarily drives a car; while driving he faints, loses control of the vehicle and injures a pedestrian; *A* would be criminally responsible. Here, *A*'s voluntary act consists of driving the car, and if the necessary mental state can be established as of the time he entered the car, it is enough to find *A* guilty of a crime.

Section 6.01(a) functions as a statutory failsafe. Due process guarantees that criminal liability be predicated on at least one voluntary act. In all criminal prosecutions the State must prove that the defendant committed at least one voluntary act — voluntary conduct is an implied element of every crime. Because it is an implied element, the State is not required to allege it in the charging instrument. For most offenses, proof of a voluntary act, although a separate component, is achieved by proving the other elements of the offense.

In the present case, proof of the elements of the offense also establishes the necessary voluntary conduct. Proof of the culpable mental state for the offense of murder, intentionally or knowingly, and the fact that the defendant voluntarily aimed a loaded gun at another human being, insured that the jury found appellant's conduct to be sufficiently voluntary. Appellant, however, did request the inclusion of a voluntary conduct instruction in the jury charge. Under the facts of this case, appellant was not entitled to this instruction. The trial court properly denied his request.

PEOPLE v. MARTINO, 970 N.E.2d 123 (2012 Ill. App.)

PRESIDING JUSTICE JORGENSEN delivered the judgment of the court, with opinion.

On November 8, 2008, defendant, Thomas F. Martino, and his wife, Carmen Keenon, got into an argument, and, when police responded, they observed defendant on top of Keenon on the stair landing outside of the couple's apartment. The officers ordered defendant to get off Keenon, defendant refused to comply with the officers' orders, the officers tased defendant, and defendant fell on Keenon's arm, breaking it. . . . Subsequently, defendant was charged with, among other things, aggravated domestic battery and aggravated battery. In both of these counts defendant was charged with knowingly causing great bodily harm to Keenon when he broke her arm. The trial court found defendant guilty of aggravated domestic battery, aggravated battery, unlawful restraint and two counts of resisting or obstructing a police officer. . . . On appeal, defendant claims that he was not proved guilty beyond a reasonable doubt of aggravated domestic battery. . . . For the reasons that follow, we reverse defendant's conviction of and sentence for aggravated domestic battery. . . .

Defendant and Keenon, who lived in a second-floor apartment in downtown Wheaton, went out for drinks and dinner in downtown Wheaton. At around midnight, the couple was walking home when defendant fell into a pile of leaves. Keenon testified that defendant did not fall into the leaves because he was intoxicated. Rather, Keenon believed that defendant was playing around, enjoying the last nice fall day of the year.

When Keenon was unable to get defendant out of the pile of leaves, she threw her wedding ring at him and walked home. A neighbor saw defendant in the leaves and helped defendant walk back to the couple's apartment. After the neighbor left, Keenon asked defendant if he picked up her wedding ring before he came home. Defendant, who was angry at Keenon for throwing her ring, grabbed Keenon by the throat and shoved her down the stairs outside of the couple's apartment. Keenon landed on the first small landing of the stairs, with her head resting on the first stair leading up to the couple's apartment. As she lay in this position, defendant, who was on top of her, began using a great amount of force to choke her. Keenon, who believed that she was going to die, threw up as defendant was choking her.

The police were called, and, when they arrived, they ordered defendant to get off of Keenon, who was asking for help and crying. Defendant, who was no longer choking Keenon, explained to the police that Keenon was throwing up and that he was trying to help her. The police ordered defendant to get off of Keenon, telling him that they would help her. Defendant replied, in a combative tone, "[Y]ou ain't going to fucking do anything." The police again told defendant to get off of Keenon and come down the stairs and that, if he did not comply, he would be tased. After the police repeated these orders several more times and began moving up the stairs toward defendant, defendant stood up, moved to the front of the landing, and "squared off" against the police in a way that indicated that he wanted to fight. Defendant then took "an aggressive stance," clenching his fists and placing his hands down at his sides. While standing in this position, defendant yelled at the police, "Come on."

At this point, one of the officers tased defendant. Defendant dropped to the ground, having lost control of his muscles because of being tased. Defendant fell backward on top of Keenon, who had not moved since the police arrived. When defendant fell, Keenon heard a "crunch." Although Keenon did not initially feel any pain in her arm when defendant landed on her, she learned later that defendant broke her elbow when he fell on it.

At the close of the State's case, defendant moved for a directed finding, arguing, among other things, that he should not be found guilty of battering Keenon, because Keenon's arm was broken as a result of his involuntary act of collapsing on Keenon after the police tased him. The trial court denied the motion.

. . .

Every offense is comprised of both a voluntary act and a mental state. A defendant who commits a voluntary act is held accountable for his act, but a defendant is not criminally liable for an involuntary act. Involuntary acts are those that "occur as bodily movements which are not controlled by the conscious mind." Examples of involuntary acts include those acts performed while a defendant is convulsing, sleeping, unconscious, under hypnosis, or seizuring. Acts that result from a reflex or that "are not a product of the effort or determination of [the defendant], either conscious or habitual," are also considered involuntary acts for which the defendant cannot be held accountable. Here, defendant was convicted pursuant to section 12-3.3(a) of the Criminal Code of 1961 which provides, in pertinent part, that "[a] person who, in committing a domestic battery, intentionally or knowingly causes great bodily harm, or permanent disability or disfigurement commits aggravated domestic battery." Thus, a defendant can be guilty of aggravated domestic battery only if his voluntary act "causes great bodily harm, or permanent disability or disfigurement."

Given the circumstances of this case, we cannot conclude that the State proved beyond a reasonable doubt that defendant's voluntary act resulted in Keenon's broken arm. Specifically, although the evidence revealed that defendant defied the police and that, because of this defiance, the police tased him, the evidence also established that the tasing of defendant rendered defendant incapable of controlling his muscles. Because defendant was incapable of controlling his muscles, his act of falling on Keenon and breaking her arm was an involuntary act for which he cannot be held accountable. Accordingly, we determine that defendant was not proved guilty beyond a reasonable doubt of aggravated domestic battery

SLEEPWALKING

American courts have occasionally recognized that individuals who commit acts while asleep should not be convicted. Although these court decisions talk in terms of sleepwalking being a defense to crime, it is perhaps more accurate to say that these are not criminal acts because the actus reus element of the crime could not be established. In *State v. Deer* (2012), a woman was charged with having sex with a boy under the age of 16. She did not dispute that the sex acts occurred but asserted she was asleep during the sexual acts, and that thus the sexual acts were not volitional. The Washington Supreme Court agreed that if she had been asleep this would make her sexual acts non-volitional, but found that the state was not required to prove that she was not asleep. Although the state generally must prove all elements of a crime beyond a reasonable doubt, and one of those elements is actus reus, the Washington court held that the defendant's claim that she was asleep was an affirmative defense and that she would have to carry the burden of proof on that (meaning she would have to present evidence (the burden of production) and convince the jury (the burden of persuasion). This next case, *King v. Cogdon* is an oft-cited case from England.

KING v. COGDON,
(Morris 1951, 29)

FACTS

Mrs. Cogdon worried unduly about her daughter Pat. She told how, on the night before her daughter's death, she had dreamed that their house was full of spiders and that these spiders were crawling all over Pat. In her sleep, Mrs. Cogdon left the bed she shared with her husband, went into Pat's room, and awakened to find herself violently brushing at Pat's face, presumably to remove the spiders. This woke Pat. Mrs. Cogdon told her she was just tucking her in. At the trial, she testified that she still believed, as she had been told, that the occupants of a nearby house bred spiders as a hobby, preparing nests for them behind the pictures on their walls. It was these spiders which in her dreams had invaded their home and attacked Pat.

There had also been a previous dream in which ghosts had sat at the end of Mrs. Cogdon's bed and she had said to them, "Well, you have come to take Pattie." It does not seem fanciful to accept the psychological explanation of these spiders and ghosts as the projections of Mrs. Cogdon's subconscious hostility toward her daughter; a hostility which was itself rooted in Mrs. Cogdon's own early life and marital relationship.

The morning after the spider dream, she told her doctor of it. He gave her a sedative and, because of the dream and certain previous difficulties she had reported, discussed the possibility of psychiatric treatment.

That evening, while Pat was having a bath before going to bed, Mrs. Cogdon went into her room, put a hot water bottle in the bed, turned back the bedclothes, and placed a glass of hot milk beside the bed ready for Pat. She then went to bed herself. There was some desultory conversation between them about the war in Korea, and just before she put out her light, Pat called out to her mother, "Mum, don't be so silly worrying there about the war, it's not on our front doorstep yet."

Mrs. Cogdon went to sleep. She dreamed that "the war was all around the house," that soldiers were in Pat's room, and that one soldier was on the bed attacking Pat. This was all of the dream she could later recapture. Her first "waking" memory was of running from Pat's room, out of the house to the home of her sister who lived next door. When her sister opened the front door, Mrs. Cogdon fell into her arms, crying "I think I've hurt Pattie." In fact, Mrs. Cogdon had, in her somnambulistic state, left her bed, fetched an axe from the woodheap, entered Pat's room, and struck her two accurate forceful blows on the head with the blade of the axe, thus killing her.

At Mrs. Cogdon's trial for murder, Mr. Cogdon testified that, "I don't think a mother could have thought any more of her daughter. I think she absolutely adored her." On the conscious level, at least, there was no reason to doubt Mrs. Cogdon's deep attachment to her daughter. Mrs. Cogdon pleaded not guilty.

OPINION

Mrs. Cogdon's story was supported by the evidence of her physician, a psychiatrist, and a psychologist. The jury believed Mrs. Cogdon. The jury concluded that Mrs. Cogdon's account of her mental state at the time of the killing, and the unanimous support given to it by the medical and psychological evidence, completely rebutted the presumption that Mrs. Cogdon intended the natural consequences of her acts. [She didn't plead the insanity defense "because the experts agreed that Mrs. Cogdon was not psychotic."] The jury acquitted her because "the act of killing itself was not, in law, regarded as her act at all."

Other Cases—Voluntary Acts

People v. Stowell, 2002 WL 1068259 (Cal. Ct. App. 2002)

The victim, a four-year-old girl, and her mother were spending the night with the defendant and his girlfriend. Stowell claims that he has no recollection of how he got into bed with the girl, undressed her, and digitally penetrated her. He claims that he was asleep, and that the judge erred in not instructing the jury about an "involuntariness defense" of sleepwalking. The appellate court made several findings: 1) although there was testimony that he walked in his sleep on prior occasions, he hadn't claimed that he was sleep walking on the night of the molestation until the trial; 2) there was no evidence that he engaged in sexual behavior when sleep walking in the past; 3) there was no expert testimony at trial that a supports that a sleep walker could have undressed and sexually molested a child. The appellate court concluded there was no substantial evidence that supported giving the instruction.

Martin v. State, 17 So.2d 427 (1944)

Police took the drunk defendant from his home and placed him on the highway. He was then prosecuted for being drunk in public. The Court held he did not commit a voluntary act and that the statute presupposed a voluntary appearance in public. The defendant was involuntarily and forcibly carried to the public place by the officer, so there was no voluntary act.

State v Eaton, 229 P.3d 704 (2010)

Defendant had drugs on his person when he was stopped for a traffic crime, was arrested and was brought into jail. The state sought a sentencing enhancement based on the fact that the drugs were found in the jail. Eaton claimed he should not have been subject to the sentencing enhancement since he did not voluntarily bring the drugs into the jail. The Washington Supreme Court held that upon arrest, Eaton no longer had control over his location. The court stated,

"From the time of arrest, his movement from street to jail became involuntary: involuntary not because he did not wish to enter the jail, but because he was forcibly taken there by State authority. He no longer had the ability to choose his own course of action. Nor did he have the ability. . . to avoid entering the area that would have increased the penalty for the . . . crime."

State v. Alvarado, 200 P3d 1037 (Ariz. Ct. App. 2008).

Defendant was arrested, taken to jail, and at the jail drugs were found on his possession. Court held that defendant voluntarily possessed controlled substances in jail.

"[A]fter being advised of the consequences of bringing drugs into the jail, the Appellant consciously chose to ignore the officers' warnings, choosing instead to enter the jail in possession of cocaine."

State v. Field, 376 S.E.2d 749 (North Carolina, 1989)

Defendant was convicted of first degree murder after the trial court refused to instruct the jury on the defense of unconsciousness (also known as automatism—capable of action, but not conscious of what he is doing). His evidence showed that immediately preceding and during the killing of his victim he was unconscious. His family testified to a substantial history of defendant acting as if he were in his own world. Expert testimony established that he was prone to experiencing dissociative states, that he was acting like sort of a robot.

The appellate court held that the defendant's evidence merited the instruction, because if the jury believed that the defendant was unable to exercise conscious control of his physical actions when he shot the victim, they would find him not guilty.

OPINION
The court stated,

"the defense of unconsciousness does not apply to a case in which the mental state of the person in question is due to insanity, mental defect, or voluntary intoxication resulting from the use of drugs or intoxicating liquor, but applies only to cases of the unconsciousness of persons of sound mind, as for example, sleepwalkers or persons suffering from the delirium of fever, epilepsy, a blow on the head or the involuntary taking of drugs or intoxicating liquor, and other cases in which there is no functioning of the conscious mind and the person's acts are controlled solely by the subconscious mind."

State v. Jerrett, 307 S.E.2d 339 (1983)
Bruce Jerrett terrorized Dallas and Edith Parsons—he robbed them, killed Dallas, and kidnapped Edith. At trial, Jerrett testified that he could remember nothing of what happened until he was arrested, and that he had suffered previous blackouts following exposure to Agent Orange during military service in Vietnam. The trial judge refused to instruct the jury on the defense of automatism.

OPINION
[The North Carolina Supreme Court reversed and ordered a new trial, holding:}

"Where a person commits an act without being conscious thereof, the act is not a criminal act even though it would be a crime if it had been committed by a person who was conscious. . . .

In this case, there was corroborating evidence tending to support the defense of unconsciousness. Defendant's very peculiar actions in permitting the kidnapped victim to repeatedly ignore his commands and finally lead him docilely into the presence and custody of a police officer lends credence to his defense of unconsciousness. We therefore hold that the trial judge should have instructed the jury on the defense of unconsciousness."

Actus reus—Omission to Act When There Is A Legal Duty

The actus reus, voluntary act, requirement also may be satisfied by not acting. These omissions or failures to act are referred to as "acts of omission." By voluntarily failing to act an individual may commit the actus reus of a crime. For example, a person may be held liable for murder by poisoning another (an act of commission) or by withholding life-saving medicine from an ill person (an act of omission).

Although acts of commission and acts of omission can both be the basis of actus reus, the law treats them differently in one respect. All persons can be held liable for acts of commission, but only people who have a legal duty to act, but do not act, can be criminal liability for their acts of omission. A moral duty to intervene to provide aid/care for someone who is in need, does not give rise to a legal duty. Rather, a legal duty to act must be found either in statutes or common law. Legal duties to act arise from a person's status, a statute, a contract, an assumption of the duty to intervene/provide care, the creation of the peril, or positions of control.

> Why is it that an omission constitutes the actus reus for a crime only when the actor has a legal duty to act? The answer lies in the basic function of the criminal law to hold liable those who are most directly responsible for causing harm. A person who performs an affirmative act that directly causes harm (as, for example, the person who poisons another) clearly establishes his primary responsibility for the act. On the other hand, acts of omissions are commonly shared by many persons. When an individual who could have been saved by emergency medical care dies, it often is true that there are a number of persons who could have called for an ambulance or otherwise provided that care. It is only the person with the legal obligation to provide the care who can be said to be responsible for legally causing the death. He is the only person as to whom the law can say, "You should have acted and your failure to do so makes you as responsible as a person who caused the same harm by an affirmative act." Kerper, *supra* at 98.

The MPC (§2.01(3))[9] makes failures to act the basis of liability when the omission is expressly made sufficient by the law defining the offense (i.e., the statute spells out that an omission to act counts as the voluntary act) or when there is a duty to perform the act that is otherwise imposed by law. For example, there is a federal law that makes it criminal to not pay your income taxes owed.

---

[9] §2.01 Omission as Basis of Liability
(3) Liability for the commission of an offense may not be based on an omission unaccompanied by action unless:
(a) the omission is expressly made sufficient by the law defining the offense; or
(b) duty to perform the omitted act is otherwise imposed by law.

OMISSION ACTUS REUS: DUTY TO ACT CREATED BY STATUTES

Under the law in most American jurisdictions, liability is limited to situations where a statute explicitly makes it a crime to omit to do some act, or there are other factors that show a distinct duty to act. A number of statutes impose a duty to do an affirmative act (for example, pay taxes or register as a sex offender). Sometimes it is more difficult to prove liability in situations where the statute is phrased in a way that implies an affirmative act but the harm comes about because of a failure to act. For example, if the homicide statute states that it is a crime to kill someone unlawfully, then it is hard to apply that statute when the death comes about because of the defendant's failure to prevent someone's death--even where there was a clear duty to protect the individual victim.

Other Cases – Duties Created By Statute

Jones v. United States, 308 F.2d 307 (D.C. Cir 1972.
The Court held,

"There are at least four situations in which the failure to act may constitute breach of a legal duty. One can be held criminally liable: first, where a statute imposes a duty to care for another; second, where one stands in certain relationship to another; third, where one has assumed a contractual duty of care for another; and fourth, where one has voluntarily assumed the care of another and so secluded the helpless person as to prevent others from rendering aid."

Craig v. State, 155 A.2d 684 (Md. 1959).
Parents (the defendants) treated their child's fatal illness with prayer rather than medicine and were convicted of failing to obtain medical care for their deceased 6-year-old daughter.

The court ruled that the parents had breached their duty under a statute that provided that a father and mother are jointly and individually responsible for the "support, care, nurture, welfare, and education of their minor children." Although the statute failed to mention medical care, the court held that it was embraced within the broad scope of the language used in the statute.

The parents ultimately were held not to be grossly negligent in causing their daughter's death because they did not know how serious her illness was until two or three days before her death and at that point, medical assistance would not have saved her life.

OMISSION ACTUS REUS: DUTY CREATED BY A SPECIAL RELATIONSHIP

Legal duties arise when there is a special relationship between the defendant and the victim. For example, parents have a duty to care for their children, and failure to provide food, clothing, shelter that results in the child's harm may result in criminal charges. Similarly, a parent who fails to protect a child from harm from another person may be held criminal liable.

STATE v. MALLEY,
366 P.2d 868 (1961)

JAMES T. HARRISON Chief Justice.

The defendant, Michael R. Mally, was convicted of involuntary manslaughter following trial in Silver Bow County under an information charging manslaughter.

The defendant's conviction was based upon his failure to provide medical care for his wife, Kay Mally, after she had been found injured in their home.

Prior to her injury, Kay Mally was in poor physical condition suffering from chronic hepatitis, biliary cirrhosis, osteoarthritis, and obesity. She also had small areas of cystic degeneration in the brain and was an alcoholic. In 1956 her physician, Dr. Peterson, diagnosed the condition of the liver disease and the kidney disease as being terminal, i.e., fatal.

Kay Mally's injury which occurred Tuesday evening, May 26, 1959, evidently fractured both humeri (large bones of the upper arm). After the injury defendant picked up his wife and placed her in the bedroom where she remained without medical aid from Tuesday evening to Thursday morning, May 28, 1959. No help was sought or given, although at all times either the defendant or his brother, John Mally, remained in the house.

The reason that the defendant's brother did not seek medical aid during this period was brought out by his testimony, when he stated the reason Kay Mally was not brought to the hospital sooner was because he did what the defendant told him to do.

Thursday morning the defendant called Dr. Peterson, who after examining the patient informed the defendant's brother that her condition was critical. An ambulance was called and Kay Mally was taken to the hospital. The ambulance driver testified that upon his arrival he found Kay Mally unconscious. He stated she was badly bruised around the head and face, the right side of her face was swollen and the right eye was black. Her arms were bruised and swollen.

These statements were corroborated by the X-ray technician and a nurse who observed Kay Mally after she was admitted to the hospital. The nurse testified Kay had bruises on her arms and head with swelling and she was unconscious.

The efforts of Kay Mally's doctor to save her life were to no avail. She died June 3, 1959, without regaining consciousness. The cause of her death was diagnosed as degeneration of the kidneys. She had suffered severe shock as a result of the fracture of both arms, and such shock caused the degeneration of the kidneys which in turn caused her death.

At the beginning of the State's case in chief and at the close of the State's case, the defendant made a motion requesting the court to require the State to elect between involuntary manslaughter and voluntary manslaughter as the information charged only manslaughter. The motions were denied.

The jury, being charged that they could only find the defendant guilty of involuntary manslaughter and not voluntary, returned a verdict of guilty, and the defendant was

sentenced to a term of three years in the state prison.

Defendant on this appeal alleges the following specifications of error:

>   . . . .
>   4. That the verdict is contrary to the law, in that the evidence fails to show the commission of a crime, or a causal connection between the act of defendant and death.
>   5. That the verdict is not supported by the evidence.

. . .

Turning to the issue of whether the verdict was contrary to law.

". . . [I]n order to impose criminal liability for a homicide caused by negligence, there must be a higher degree of negligence than is required to establish negligent default on a mere civil issue. The negligence must be aggravated, culpable, gross, or reckless, that is, the conduct of the accused must be such a departure from what would be the conduct of an ordinarily prudent or careful man under the same circumstances as to be incompatible with a proper regard for human life, or, in other words, a disregard for human life or an indifference to consequences.'"

Other jurisdictions have held that the failure to obtain medical aid for one who is owed a duty is such criminal negligence as would constitute manslaughter.

In *People v. Beardsley*, the defendant, a married man, was prosecuted for failure to provide medical aid for a woman with whom he had an arrangement. During the course of the evening she took morphine and subsequently died. The court although reversing because there was no duty owing to the woman by the defendant . . . stated: "`If a person who sustains to another the legal relation of protector, as husband to wife, parent to child, master to seaman, etc., knowing such person to be in peril, willfully or negligently fails to make such reasonable and proper efforts to rescue him as he might have done, without jeopardizing his own life, or the lives of others, he is guilty of manslaughter at least, if by reason of his omission of duty the dependent person dies.'"

In *State v. Bischert*, 131 Mont. 152, 308 P.2d 969, the defendant was charged with manslaughter. The information charged the defendant and his wife with the killing of their child by neglecting and refusing to provide the necessary food to sustain the infant's life. Although the conviction was reversed because of prejudicial photographs, this court held that the failure to provide the necessities of life to one whom is owed a duty is a sufficient basis on which to predicate and sustain a conviction for a negligent homicide, i.e., involuntary manslaughter.

In *Territory v. Manton*, 8 Mont. 95, 19 P. 387, 393, the defendant and his wife after an evening of drinking walked home. The wife evidently passed out and the defendant left her, although she was poorly clad and he was within easy calling distance from the house. He was convicted of manslaughter. The court held that a legal duty exists between husband and wife, and if the husband withholds necessaries from his wife and she dies as a result; it is manslaughter. The court quoted

> "`If the act is one of negligence not clearly showing danger to life, yet, if death follows, the offense is only manslaughter; whereas, if the exposure or neglect is of a dangerous kind, it is murder. Ordinarily, if a husband should withhold necessaries from his wife, and she dies, it will be only manslaughter, since this act is not so immediately dangerous to life as the other. Whether death caused by neglect is murder or manslaughter is made to depend on the nature and character of the neglect'."

Therefore, from the authorities quoted . . . the conclusion is inescapable that the failure to obtain medical aid for one who is owed a duty is a sufficient degree of negligence as to constitute involuntary manslaughter provided death results from the failure to act.

However, the defendant strenuously asserts that as a prerequisite for a conviction of involuntary manslaughter based on a failure to provide medical aid, the state must prove the ability on the part of the defendant to furnish such aid.

In *Stehr v. State*, 92 Neb. 755, 139 N.W. 676, 678, 45 L.R.A., N.S., 559, the defendant was charged with negligently causing the death of his stepson because he failed to provide medical aid. The defendant was a man without means, he called two doctors who refused the case because of defendant's lack of funds. The court in affirming the conviction stated: "In such a case, where the party charged is unable to supply the necessary succor, he ceases to be responsible, but this responsibility is not divested in case where poor laws exist. In such case the person owing the duty should report the case to the public authorities for their relief." The court also quoted from 1 Wharton, Criminal Law (11th ed.) § 484, "`If the parent has not the means for the child's nurture, his duty is to apply to the public authorities for relief; and failure to do so is itself culpable neglect wherever there are public authorities capable of affording such relief.'"

There are provisions in our statutes under which the poor may obtain medical aid. See section 71-308, R.C.M. 1947.

Therefore, it is the opinion of this court that the State in prosecuting for manslaughter because of the failure to provide medical aid is not required as an element of their proof to show the ability on behalf of the defendant to furnish such aid. If a defendant could not obtain aid, either through normal procedure or the poor laws, this is a matter for his defense.

Finally, in order to convict a person for a homicide the negligent act must be the basis of the death. In *State v. Ramser*, 17 Wn.2d 581, 136 P.2d 1013, 1015, the court stated:

> "When a person is charged with manslaughter by reason of negligence on his part, whether it be the doing of some act, or his failure to do something he should have done, or whether the negligence is cast upon him as a matter of law by reason of his violation of some statute, there must be causal connection between the negligence and the death of the person involved, so that it can be said that the act done or omitted was a proximate cause of the resultant death." (Citing cases.)

Therefore, it must appear from the evidence that the defendant's failure to obtain medical aid was the proximate cause of the death of his wife.

It appearing that the verdict was not contrary to law, the question remains whether the verdict was supported by the evidence.

. . . .

We are aware that the large majority of homicide cases involving a failure to provide medical aid involve a parent-child relationship. This is undoubtedly due to the fact that a person of mature years is not generally in a helpless condition. However, fact situations do arise, such as the instant case, wherein it is apparent that an adult is as helpless as the newborn. The record is replete with evidence that Kay Mally could not have consciously or rationally denied medical aid.

The defendant's brother, the same man who testified that Kay Mally refused aid, stated that Kay Mally was in the same condition when Dr. Peterson arrived Thursday morning as she was in the interim. Dr. Peterson testified that upon his arrival he had found her in a semi-comatose condition. Also in answer to a question he stated:

> "Q. Doctor, when you were called to the Mally home, you were told that she had been in this comatose condition for two days. Who related that to you? A. Again, I believe it was her brother-in-law, (John) but I can't state with any degree of certainty."

This testimony, the previously discussed physical condition of Kay Mally, and her condition upon arrival at the hospital was sufficient for the jury to conclude that Kay Mally during the period she remained in the defendant's home after her accident was indeed a helpless woman and solely at the mercy of her husband.

Therefore, the remaining problem is whether the defendant's neglect in summoning medical aid was the proximate cause of his wife's death.

In the eyes of the criminal law, if a person hastens death, such person is considered the cause of the death. Though a person may be at the threshold of death, if the spark of life is extinguished by a wrongful act, it is sufficient for a conviction.

In State v. Smith, 73 Iowa 32, 41, 34 N.W. 597, 601, the court stated: "Life at best is but of short duration, and one who causes death ought not to be excused for his act because his victim was soon to die from other causes, whatever they may be."

Therefore, if Michael Mally's failure to provide medical aid for his wife hastened her death, then his failure to act was the proximate cause of the death.

It is conceded that Kay Mally, because of her previous physical condition, when her injury occurred and both arms were fractured, was at death's door. From the medical testimony, it is apparent that even with immediate medical aid Kay Mally in all probability would not have survived. However, the medical testimony does establish that the failure to summon medical aid did hasten Kay Mally's death.

The testimony given by Dr. Newman is as follows:

> "Q. Dr. Newman, in taking the postmortem and doing the autopsy on Kay S. Mally, did you have any professional opinion as to whether her neglect of treatment caused or contributed to her death?
>
> A. Well, I certainly think it hastened it; the shock must have become very difficult if not impossible to treat to bring her out of shock because she had been in it so long."

Therefore, it appearing that there is sufficient evidence in the record to support a conviction for involuntary manslaughter, and it further appearing that the verdict is not contrary to law, the conviction of Michael R. Mally for involuntary manslaughter is sustained.

STATE v. MIRANDA,
715 A.2d 680 (1998)

FACTS
Santos Miranda started living with his girlfriend and her two children in an apartment in September 1992. On January 27, 1993, Miranda was 21 years old, his girlfriend was 16, her son was 2, and her daughter, the victim in this case, born on September 21, 1992, was 4 months old. Although he was not the biological father of either child, Miranda took care of them and considered himself to be their stepfather.

He represented himself as such to the people at Meriden Veteran's Memorial Hospital where, on January 27, 1993, the victim was taken for treatment of her injuries following a 911 call by Miranda that the child was choking on milk. Upon examination at the hospital, it was determined that the victim had multiple rib fractures that were approximately two to three weeks old, two skull fractures that were approximately seven to ten days old, a brachial plexus injury to her left arm, a rectal tear that was actively "oozing blood," and nasal hemorrhages.

The court determined that anyone who saw the child would have had to notice these injuries, the consequent deformities, and her reactions. Indeed, the trial court found that Miranda had been aware of the various bruises on her right cheek and the nasal hemorrhages, as well as the swelling of the child's head; that he knew she had suffered a rectal tear, as well as rib fractures posteriorly on the left and right sides; and that he was aware that there existed a substantial and unjustifiable risk that the child was exposed to conduct that created a risk of death.

The trial court concluded that despite this knowledge, the defendant "failed to act to help or aid the child by promptly notifying authorities of her injuries, taking her for medical care, removing her from her circumstances and guarding her from future abuses. As a result of his failure to help her, the child was exposed to conduct which created a risk of death to her, and the child suffered subsequent serious physical injuries."

OPINION
We conclude that, based upon the trial court's findings that the defendant had established a familial relationship with the victim's mother and her two children, had assumed responsibility for the welfare of the children, and had taken care of them as though he were their father, the defendant had a legal duty to protect the victim from abuse.

PEOPLE v STEPHENS,
3 AD3d 57 (2003)

OPINION OF THE COURT
This appeal requires us to consider the nature and extent of the duty owed to a child by an unrelated adult when the child resides in the adult's household along with his own children and those of his paramour. In particular, we consider whether the prosecution in this case properly relied upon the application of the "in loco parentis" doctrine to convict defendant of murder based upon a failure to provide medical care to a child who was not his biological child.

This prosecution concerns the death of nine-year-old Sabrina Green, who was, at the time, the charge of her older sister, Yvette Green. Defendant Darryl Stephens and Yvette Green had lived together since 1985; defendant was the father of 8 of Yvette's 10 children. Sabrina came to live in their household in November of 1996. Defendant and Yvette were both convicted of murder in the second degree, under Penal Law § 125.25 (4), for Sabrina's death.

Sabrina Green was born on August 28, 1988 to a crack-addicted mother, with whom she lived until her mother died in 1991. Sabrina was then cared for by a family friend, Sylvia Simmons, until Simmons died in 1996. Sabrina then briefly lived with a relative, Denise Nelson, but

Nelson found Sabrina to be too "hyper" and therefore, in November 1996, she went to live in the household of her older sister Yvette. Yvette was awarded legal guardianship of Sabrina.

Sabrina had severe behavior problems. At age five she was diagnosed with attention deficit and hyperactivity disorder; the pediatric neurologist who testified at trial suggested she might also have been suffering from oppositional defiant disorder. While she had been treated with Ritalin for years with some success by the time she came to live with them, Yvette did not, or could not, continue to provide her with the medication.

Soon after she moved in, Sabrina began to regularly exhibit aggressive behavior, including throwing tantrums, hitting her head and arms against furniture when she did not get her way, and getting into fights with the other children in the apartment and at school; she also wet her bed. She had difficulty following household rules, and in this household, a breach of these rules resulted in punishment, imposed either by Yvette or by defendant, such as having to stand in the corner, being grounded in her room, and being whipped with a belt or stick. Sabrina was punished almost daily.

Tyrone Green, Yvette's son, then 19 years old, testified that he had observed Sabrina taking food out of the refrigerator one night, a serious breach of the household rules which he went to report to Yvette and defendant. Yvette was asleep, and defendant responded to Tyrone that he "would take care of it." The next day Tyrone saw a gauze wrapping on Sabrina's hand, and he later saw that it had been burned. Almost every night thereafter, either Yvette or defendant would tie Sabrina's arms and legs to the bed with a jump rope, for the entire night. In addition, Sabrina was required to spend most of her time sitting in the hallway where she could be watched by both Yvette and defendant. The condition of her hand grew worse, and she was no longer allowed to go to school or outside to play. Despite the older children's entreaties that Sabrina be taken to a doctor, neither Yvette nor defendant did so. Yvette told the children that she was afraid to do so because she might be blamed for the injuries and have her children taken away.

Despite the testimony of Yvette's sons Tyrone and Marcus, relating that in September 1997 defendant stated that he could no longer deal with Sabrina and that Yvette was going to have to take over being in charge of her, Tyrone also testified that one morning, perhaps about a week before Sabrina died, Tyrone saw defendant hitting Sabrina with a belt 10 or 12 times.

At the time of Sabrina's death, on November 8, 1997, she was suffering from multiple conditions, including subdural hemorrhage caused by numerous blunt impacts to the head, a third-degree burn to her hand which was left untreated until infection and gangrene set in, and pneumonia. Dr. Ozuah, the physician who examined Sabrina's body at the hospital, observed bruises, some fresh, which were consistent with being hit with a belt, scars that were consistent with her hands being tied with a rope, and bed sores indicating she had been immobilized for many days. There was a severe third-degree burn to her left hand through all layers of skin, which was consistent with being held to a surface such as an iron or stove, and there were fresh injuries on top of the burn. There were injuries to Sabrina's right hand consistent with being slammed repeatedly in a refrigerator door some time in September; the flesh was decaying and gangrenous. Dr. Ozuah also found an old injury to Sabrina's head as well as several that had been inflicted within 24 hours of her death. All the head injuries were serious, requiring a great deal of force, such as from a baseball bat, and could not have been self-inflicted by a nine-year-old banging her head on the floor.

An autopsy report revealed that Sabrina had died as the result of six recent severe blunt impact wounds to the head, as well as pneumonia caused by an infection which spread from her hands to her bloodstream and lungs. There were numerous scars, including scars to her back, thighs and legs consistent with a severe beating with a belt one week before her death.

The medical examiner who testified at trial based upon the autopsy report suggested that the cause of death was septic shock resulting from a bacterial infection in the bloodstream due to the untreated burn. It was the expressed opinion of both the examining physician and the medical examiner that Sabrina had been a victim of child abuse.

DISCUSSION
Sufficiency and Weight of Evidence

The provision of Penal Law § 125.25 under which defendant was charged with murder in the second degree requires that the defendant, under circumstances evincing a depraved indifference to human life, recklessly engaged in conduct which created a grave risk of serious physical injury or death to a person less than 11 years of age. The People's theory regarding defendant's guilt was that acting in concert with Yvette Green, with the requisite mental state, he had engaged in conduct which caused injuries that had resulted in Sabrina's death, and in addition, that he had failed to get her the medical care she needed or take any other steps to protect her, when he knew of her grave injuries.

Defendant's challenge to the sufficiency of the evidence is two-pronged: first, that the evidence failed to show that he was responsible for the injuries that caused Sabrina's death, and second, since he was neither the child's father nor her guardian, he had no legal duty toward Sabrina, and therefore was not legally chargeable with his mere failure to act to ensure she got medical treatment. We do not agree with his contentions.

First, there was sufficient evidence to permit the jury to find that defendant, acting in concert with Yvette, under circumstances evincing a depraved indifference to human life, had recklessly engaged in conduct which created a grave risk of serious physical injury or death to Sabrina, thereby causing her death.

Moreover, the evidence similarly supported the People's alternate theory, which was based upon the application of the doctrine of in loco parentis. We reject defendant's suggestion that he may not be held liable for his failure to ensure that Sabrina received necessary medical attention due to his lack of legal connection to the child.

Defendant correctly points out that since he was neither the child's parent nor her legal guardian, he may only be convicted based upon a failure to take action to protect the child from harm if a legal duty may be imposed upon him under the in loco parentis doctrine: "Criminal liability cannot be premised on a failure to act . . . unless the party so charged has a legal duty to act. A person who has no familial relationship to a child ordinarily has no legal duty to provide for it, unless it can be shown that he or she has assumed all of the responsibilities incident to parenthood. That a party has taken some part in meeting the child's daily needs is not enough; a 'full and complete . . . interest in the well-being and general welfare' of the child is necessary, as is the intent to fully assume a parental role, with the concomitant obligations to support, educate, and care for the child on an ongoing basis

However, the evidence fully supports the application of the doctrine here.

People v Myers presented circumstances in which the in loco parentis doctrine could not support criminal liability. There, the court dismissed the indictment of the defendant for manslaughter (and for endangering the welfare of a child) of a two-month-old child who had died of severe dehydration and malnutrition; although the defendant was the live-in boyfriend of the infant's mother, the evidence merely showed that he contributed to household finances, occasionally purchasing formula for the infant and acting as a babysitter, not that he had "intended to shoulder any responsibility for the child's welfare"

In contrast, the evidence here reflected that Darryl Stephens was far more than a live-in boyfriend who took no part in the raising of the child. Rather, it supported the conclusion that during his long-term live-in relationship with Yvette, he "assumed all of the responsibilities incident to parenthood"

The 11 children living in the household, including Sabrina, were all housed, clothed, fed and supervised jointly by Yvette and defendant. Defendant took the children, including Sabrina, to school, stayed with them when Yvette was out, set down rules for them and punished them for any infractions. The testimony supports a finding that defendant treated Sabrina with the same degree of responsibility as he did the other children, not as a mere babysitter or short-term helper, but as one of the two coequal adults functioning in the role of parent.

. . . [I]t is instructive to consider those cases in which live-in paramours have been held to be "person[s] legally responsible" for a child.

In *People v. Sheffield* (265 AD2d 258 [1999]), the defendant shared his apartment with the 11-year-old child and her mother, he called the child his "stepdaughter" and had sole custody of her on a daily basis. *In Matter of Heather U.* (220 AD2d 810 [1995]), respondent had been living with the subject child's mother in a family-like setting for approximately three years, had fathered her youngest child, and was a regular member of the subject child's household.

Similarly, in *People v. Carroll* (244 AD2d 104, 107 [1998], affd 93 NY2d 564 [1999]), this Court upheld a prosecution of a nonparent for endangering the welfare of a child under Penal Law § 260.10 (2), which applies to a "parent, guardian or other person legally charged with the care or custody of a child," because the evidence showed that the nonparent has assumed the role of stepparent during the period in question.

. . . [T]he in loco parentis doctrine requires consideration of whether the person charged actually undertook the fundamental responsibilities that are normally those of a parent. Its application here was entirely proper.

Defendant argues that, despite his serving in a parental capacity for all the other children living in his home, including the two who were not his natural children, he could relinquish that role for Yvette's young sister and ward by the simple expedient of making an announcement to that effect. However, even assuming that he could have successfully eradicated, through a pronouncement, the responsibility he had previously undertaken, so as to eliminate Sabrina from his sphere of responsibilities, the evidence makes it unnecessary for us to definitively decide that point. Even if defendant made such pronouncement, the testimony that he continued to take part in the ongoing punishments of Sabrina up until just days before her death, and the lack of evidence that he took any other steps to remove all responsibility for her from his life, permit the conclusion that any such pronouncement did not reflect any actual change in his previous parental posture toward her.

The evidence was legally sufficient to prove beyond a reasonable doubt that defendant was responsible for the victim's care at the time of her death, and that, acting in concert with Yvette, under circumstances evincing a depraved indifference to human life, he recklessly engaged in conduct which created a grave risk of serious physical injury or death to Sabrina. Moreover, the verdict was not against the weight of the evidence (see

Jury Charge

. . .

The court's acting-in-concert charge was proper. . . . The court did not say that mere recklessness was all that was required to convict defendant of murder in the second degree based upon his acting in concert with Yvette, but rather that the jury must find that he acted recklessly "under circumstances evincing a depraved indifference to human life" that created "a grave risk of serious physical injury or death to a person less than 11 years old, and thereby cause[d] the death of such person." The court specifically stated that it was essential that the People prove that both defendant and Yvette "acted with the mental culpability required for the commission of the crimes charged."

There was no error in the court's responses to the jury's notes.

Accordingly, the judgment . . . convicting defendant, after a jury trial, of murder in the second degree, and sentencing him to a term of 25 years to life, should be affirmed.

Actus Reus: Duty Created by a Contract

A legal duty to act may arise out of a contract. A contract is simply an agreement between two parties -- even ones that are not between the defendant and the victim. For example, if the city hires a lifeguard to guard a city pool, the lifeguard has a contractual duty to protect all the swimmers. When the lifeguard does nothing for a drowning victim, he has satisfied the actus reus requirement because he has failed to dow hat he contracted to do -- to make efforts to save drowning swimmers. When the duty arises because of a contract, the contract's terms govern whether a legal duty exists or not.

COMMONWEALTH. v. PESTINIKAS, 617 A.2d 1339 (421 Pa. Superior Ct. 371 (1992)

. . . .

WIEAND, Judge:

Joseph Kly met Walter and Helen Pestinikas in the latter part of 1981 when Kly consulted them about pre-arranging his funeral. In March, 1982, Kly, who had been living with a stepson, was hospitalized and diagnosed as suffering from Zenker's diverticulum, a weakness in the walls of the esophagus, which caused him to have trouble swallowing food. In the hospital, Kly was given food which he was able to swallow and, as a result, regained some of the weight which he had lost. When he was about to be discharged, he expressed a desire not to return to his stepson's home and sent word to appellants that he wanted to speak with them. As a consequence, arrangements were made for appellants to care for Kly in their home on Main Street in Scranton, Lackawanna County.

Kly was discharged from the hospital on April 12, 1982. When appellants came for him on that day they were instructed by medical personnel regarding the care which was required for Kly and were given a prescription to have filled for him. Arrangements were also made for a visiting nurse to come to appellants' home to administer vitamin B-12 supplements to Kly. Appellants agreed orally to follow the medical instructions and to supply Kly with food, shelter, care and the medicine which he required.

According to the evidence, the prescription was never filled, and the visiting nurse was told by appellants that Kly did not want the vitamin supplement shots and that her services, therefore, were not required. Instead of giving Kly a room in their home, appellants removed him to a rural part of Lackawanna County, where they placed him in the enclosed porch of a building, which they owned, known as the Stage Coach Inn. This porch was approximately nine feet by thirty feet, with no insulation, no refrigeration, no bathroom, no sink and no telephone. The walls contained cracks which exposed the room to outside weather conditions. Kly's predicament was compounded by appellants' affirmative efforts to conceal his whereabouts. Thus, they gave misleading information in response to inquiries, telling members of Kly's family that they did not know where he had gone and others that he was living in their home.

After Kly was discharged from the hospital, appellants took Kly to the bank and had their names added to his savings account. Later, Kly's money was transferred into an account in the names of Kly or Helen Pestinikas, pursuant to which moneys could be withdrawn without Kly's signature. Bank records reveal that from May, 1982, to July, 1983, appellants withdrew amounts roughly consistent with the three hundred ($300) dollars per month which Kly had agreed to pay for his care. Beginning in August, 1983 and continuing until Kly's death in November, 1984, however, appellants withdrew much larger sums so that when Kly died, a balance of only fifty-five ($55) dollars remained. In the interim, appellants had withdrawn in excess of thirty thousand ($30,000) dollars.

On the afternoon of November 15, 1984, when police and an ambulance crew arrived in response to a call by appellants, Kly's dead body appeared emaciated, with his ribs and sternum greatly pronounced. Mrs. Pestinikas told police that she and her husband had taken care of Kly for three hundred ($300) dollars per month and that she had given him cookies and orange juice at 11:30 a.m. on the morning of his death. A subsequent autopsy, however, revealed that Kly had been dead at that time and may have been dead for as many as thirty-nine (39) hours before his body was found. The cause of death was determined to be starvation and dehydration. Expert testimony opined that Kly would have experienced pain and suffering over a long period of time before he died.

At trial, the Commonwealth contended that after contracting orally to provide food, shelter, care and necessary medicine for Kly, appellants engaged in a course of conduct calculated to deprive Kly of those things necessary to maintain life and thereby cause his death. The trial court instructed the jury that appellants could not be found guilty of a malicious killing for failing to provide food, shelter and necessary medicines to Kly unless a duty to do so had been imposed upon them by contract. The court instructed the jury, inter alia, as follows:

> In order for you to convict the defendants on any of the homicide charges or the criminal conspiracy or recklessly endangering charges, you must first find beyond a reasonable doubt that the defendants had a legal duty of care to Joseph Kly. There are but two situations in which Pennsylvania law imposes criminal liability for the failure to perform an act. One of these is where the express language of the law defining the offense provides for criminal [liability] based upon such a failure. The other is where the law otherwise imposes a duty to act.

> Unless you find beyond a reasonable doubt that an oral contract imposed a duty to act upon Walter and Helen Pestinikas, you must acquit the defendants.

Appellants contend that this was error. The applicable law appears at 18 Pa.C.S. § 301(a) and (b) as follows:

> (a) General rule. A person is not guilty of an offense unless his liability is based on conduct which includes a voluntary act or the omission to perform an act of which he is physically capable.
> (b) Omission as basis of liability. Liability for the commission of an offense may not be based on an omission unaccompanied by action unless:
> (1) the omission is expressly made sufficient by the law defining the offense; or
> (2) a duty to perform the omitted act is otherwise imposed by law.

. . . .

As stated in A.R.S. Sec. 13-201 and demonstrated by the case law, the failure to perform a duty imposed by law may create criminal liability. In the case of negligent homicide or manslaughter, the duty must be found outside the definition of the crime itself, perhaps in another statute, or in the common law, or in a contract. The most commonly cited statement of the rule is found in *People v. Beardsley*, 150 Mich. 206, 113 N.W. 1128 (1907): "The law recognizes that under some circumstances the omission of a duty owed by one individual to another, where such omission results in the death of the one to whom the duty is owing, will make the other chargeable with manslaughter.... This rule of law is always based upon the proposition that the duty neglected must be a legal duty, and not a mere moral obligation. It must be a duty imposed by law or by contract, and the omission to perform the duty must be the immediate and direct cause of death.

In *Jones v. United States*, 308 F.2d 307 (C.A.D.C.1962), the court stated:

"There are at least four situations in which the failure to act may constitute breach of a legal duty. One can be held criminally liable: first, where a statute imposes a duty to care for another; second, where one stands in a certain status relationship to another; third, where one has assumed a contractual duty to care for another; and fourth, where one has voluntarily assumed the care of another and so secluded the helpless person as to prevent others from rendering aid.". . .

. . . .

As a general rule, where one person owes to another either a legal or a contractual duty, an omission to perform that duty resulting in the death of persons to whom the duty was owing renders the person charged with the performance of such duty guilty of a culpable homicide. If several enter into a joint undertaking imposing upon all alike a personal duty in respect of its performance, the death of a third party by reason of the neglect or omission of such duty renders them all jointly liable. The duty imposed, however, must be a plain duty. It must be one on which different minds must agree, or generally agree, and which does not admit of any discussion as to its obligatory force. Where doubt exists as to what conduct should be pursued in a particular case, and intelligent men differ as to the proper action to be taken, the law does not impute guilt to anyone, where, from the omission to adopt one course instead of another, fatal consequences follow to others. The law does not enter into the reasons governing the conduct of men in such cases to determine whether they are culpable. Again, the duty must be one which the party is bound to perform by law or by contract, and not one the performance of which depends simply upon his humanity, or his sense of justice or propriety. It has been said that a legal duty to assist another does not arise out of a mere moral duty. Furthermore, where a legal duty is shown to have existed, it must also appear as a condition to culpability that the death was the direct and immediate consequence of the omission.

Consistently with this legal thinking we hold that when . . . the statute provides that an omission to do an act can be the basis for criminal liability if a duty to perform the omitted act has been imposed by law, the legislature intended to distinguish between a legal duty to act and merely a moral duty to act. A duty to act imposed by contract is legally enforceable and, therefore, creates a legal duty. It follows that a failure to perform a duty imposed by contract may be the basis for a charge of criminal homicide if such failure causes the death of another person and all other elements of the offense are present. Because there was evidence in the instant case that Kly's death had been caused by appellants' failure to provide the food and medical care which they had agreed by oral contract to provide for him,

their omission to act was sufficient to support a conviction for criminal homicide, and the trial court was correct when it instructed the jury accordingly.

Our holding is not that every breach of contract can become the basis for a finding of homicide resulting from an omission to act. A criminal act involves both a physical and mental aspect. An omission to act can satisfy the physical aspect of criminal conduct only if there is a duty to act imposed by law. A failure to provide food and medicine, in this case, could not have been made the basis for prosecuting a stranger who learned of Kly's condition and failed to act. Even where there is a duty imposed by contract, moreover, the omission to act will not support a prosecution for homicide in the absence of the necessary mens rea. For murder, there must be malice. Without a malicious intent, an omission to perform duties having their foundation in contract cannot support a conviction for murder. In the instant case, therefore, the jury was required to find that appellants, by virtue of contract, had undertaken responsibility for providing necessary care for Kly to the exclusion of the members of Kly's family. This would impose upon them a legal duty to act to preserve Kly's life. If they maliciously set upon a course of withholding food and medicine and thereby caused Kly's death, appellants could be found guilty of murder.

. . . .

With respect to the alleged insufficiency of the evidence, it may also be observed that appellants' culpable conduct, according to the evidence, was not limited merely to an omission to act. It consisted, rather, of an affirmative course of conduct calculated to deprive Kly of the food and medical care which was otherwise available to him and which was essential to continued life. It included efforts to place Kly beyond the ability of others to provide such needs. Such a course of conduct, the jury could find, as it did, had been pursued by appellants willfully and maliciously, who thereby caused Kly's death.

Appellants argue that, in any event, the Commonwealth failed to prove an enforceable contract requiring them to provide Kly with food and medical attention. It is their position that their contract with Kly required them to provide only a place for Kly to live and a funeral upon his death. This obligation, they contend, was fulfilled. Although we have not been provided with a full and complete record of the trial, it seems readily apparent from the partial record before us, that the evidence was sufficient to create an issue of fact for the jury to resolve. The issue was submitted to the jury on careful instructions by the learned trial judge and does not present a basis entitling appellants to post-trial relief.

. . . .

AFFIRMED.

TAMILIA, J. **concurring:**

. . . The dissent errs in asserting that a contract may not create a legal duty which can lead to a homicide charge and conviction when the evidence establishes the breach of that duty was the direct cause of death, and secondly, in presuming that the evidence established a simple omission of the duty. It is clear that a contractual undertaking to feed, clothe and shelter an elderly dependent person establishes a legal duty to provide such reasonable care and that failure to do so, resulting in the death of the dependent person, may be the basis for a homicide charge. All that remains to be determined is the degree of the crime based upon whether the omission was negligent or intentional. As to the degree of the homicide, where the evidence establishes malice by reason of the prolonged denial of food, liquids and adequate care and shelter, the seclusion, isolation and concealment of the dependent person from professional caretakers, while withdrawing funds from the victim's bank account for the personal use of the caretaker, malice and implied intent were present and a jury properly could find beyond a reasonable doubt guilty of murder in the third degree.

. . .

Appellants were charged with first degree murder,[1] third degree murder,[2] voluntary manslaughter,[3] involuntary manslaughter,[4] criminal conspiracy to commit murder[5] and recklessly endangering another person.[6] Walter Pestinikis was also charged with two counts of intimidation of witnesses.

Following a jury trial lasting sixty (60) days, appellants were found guilty of murder in the third degree and recklessly endangering another person.

It should be considered first whether the court erred in instructing the jury that if the Commonwealth established beyond a reasonable doubt that the defendants owed Mr. Joseph Kly a legal duty of care by virtue of a contract clearly understood by defendants, who had the means, ability and opportunity to perform the duties of care, and the omission or failure to take care of Mr. Kly was the direct cause of his death, it could proceed to determine whether the Commonwealth proved each of the defendants guilty of any of the crimes.

Appellants contend and the dissent agrees the charge was in error because a civil contract cannot support a legal duty, the breach of which can result in criminal prosecution for homicide. Section 301(b)(2) of the Crimes Code provides in relevant part:

> Liability for the commission of any offense may not be based on an omission unaccompanied by action unless ... a duty to perform the omitted act is otherwise imposed by law.

…

The majority properly holds section 301 is broad enough to include a contractual undertaking. There is no Pennsylvania case which holds otherwise or requires the stringent interpretation adopted by the dissent. The listing of statutory provisions by the dissent, which includes the term "imposed by law," because they codify duties in many areas of the law, does not thereby limit the application of that term in this instance. Since the legislature has not spelled out its intent, we may look to the common law, the model penal code from which the section was drawn, and to the interpretation of such provisions by courts in other jurisdictions to guide us.

. . .

While Pennsylvania is silent on the precise

meaning to be given to the term "duty imposed by law," other states have made such determinations.

Duty imposed by law ... means either duty imposed by a valid statutory enactment of the legislature or a duty imposed by a recognized common law principle declared in reported decisions of the appellate courts of the State or jurisdiction involved.

. . . .

What makes the contract or assumption of care a duty imposed by law is assumption of a responsibility for the care of a dependent person who thereby loses the protection he would have for being cared for by others with more specific legal responsibility. The history of homicide by omission to provide care primarily is traced through English law and American cases that clearly followed English law. The majority of cases resulting in murder or manslaughter charges involved infants and children, spouses, prison inmates, poor house inmates and sailors. In each of those categories there was a duty of care owed by dominant persons to dependent persons who were subject to the control of the superior persons. These duties were fixed in common law long before any rights were established by statute or made punishable at criminal law. . . .

But it has never been doubted that if death is the directed consequence of the malicious omission of the performance of a duty (as a mother to nourish her infant child) this is a case of murder. If the omission was not malicious and arose from negligence only, it is a case of manslaughter.

. . .

The crime of murder in the third degree in its elements comprehends . . . culpability. In describing the element of malice which is necessary to a finding of third degree murder, supplying the specific intent required, our Court has stated: "Malice consists either of an express intent to kill or inflict great bodily harm, or of a wickedness of disposition, hardness of heart, cruelty, recklessness of consequences, and a mind regardless of social duty, indicating unjustified disregard for the probability of death or great bodily harm."

The irrationality of the dissent's position is the implication that by entering into a contract appellants are somehow insulated from all the acts and omissions which clearly establish their guilt of third degree murder because the Legislature did not specifically define a contract as creating a duty imposed by law. The only rational interpretation of duty is that the law will find the duty when the duty clearly exists by statute, contract or action of the parties. See Model Penal Code § 2.01, Comment 3, N. 30: "The duty imposed by law may be a statutory duty, a contractual duty, or duty arising from tort law." In construing the legislative intent we cannot fail to consider the comments of the Model Penal Code and the guidance provided by common law which it codifies.

The question as proposed by the dissent ignores the quintessential elements of this case which are the active and passive negligence and intentional denial of life-sustaining care to a dependent elderly person appellants undertook to maintain at the victim's expense. It is not the contract alone which measures the liability but also the callous mistreatment that went beyond the mere failure to fulfill the contract. This contractual failure was exacerbated and made more culpable by the appellants' actions in active concealment of the victim's condition from relatives and medical authorities, thereby preventing him from being saved from incredible suffering and death comparable only to that suffered by persons incarcerated in German, Russian and Japanese death camps during World War II. . . .

. . . The trial court gave a carefully, thought out and well-worded instruction on creation of a legal duty by means of an oral or implied contract. Coupled with the evidence of deliberate life-threatening abuse and neglect as we understand those terms today, the jury properly and without any other reasonable choice concluded the elements of third degree murder were established beyond a reasonable doubt by the Commonwealth.

OLSZEWSKI, J., joins **concurring** opinion by TAMILIA, J. Omitted.

McEWEN, J. **dissenting**:
The author of the majority opinion has, in his

customary fashion, provided so persuasive an expression of view upon this trying issue that one can hardly be resolute in dissent, particularly since I wholeheartedly concur with the conclusion of the majority that there is ample evidence upon which to sustain the homicide convictions of appellants. Nonetheless, I must respectfully depart the company of my eminent colleagues who find that the trial court properly instructed the jury that the failure to perform a civil contract, though simple omission alone, is sufficient to meet the voluntary act requirements of Section 301 of the Crimes Code.

. . . .

> Liability for the commission of any offense may not be based on an omission unaccompanied by action unless ... a duty to perform the omitted act is otherwise imposed by law.

The precise issue thus becomes whether the legislature intended that a "contractual duty" constitutes a "duty imposed by law" for purposes of ascertaining whether conduct is criminal. While I share the desire of the prosecutor and the jury that appellants must not escape responsibility for their horribly inhuman and criminally culpable conduct, I cling to the view that an appellate court is not free to reshape the intention or revise the language of the Crimes Code. Rather, our constitutional obligation is to implement the intent and comply with the direction of the legislature.

While the Attorney General argues that a finding of criminal responsibility based upon a breach of a contractual duty would be "consistent with principles established in common law," our legislature has, with the enactment of the Crimes Code, abolished common law crimes . . . and . . . evidenced as well a departure from reliance upon principles of common law in the Crimes Code.

Nor do I find support in Pennsylvania case law for this argument advanced by the Commonwealth. It is true that this Court has upheld convictions for endangering the welfare of children . . . in at least four instances based upon a knowing violation by omission of a parent's duty of care for a minor child. Similarly, this Court . . . upheld the involuntary manslaughter conviction of a mother who had failed to protect her child from physical abuse inflicted by the mother's paramour. However, all of the cases which our research has yielded involved, where liability is based upon a failure to act, the parent-child relationship and the statutory imposition of duties upon the parents of minors. . . . In the instant case, where there was no "status of relationship between the parties" except landlord/tenant, a failure to perform a civil contract cannot alone sustain a conviction for third degree murder.

While a minority of other jurisdictions have sustained convictions for involuntary manslaughter under similar circumstances, . . . the function of this Court is to interpret and apply the provisions of the criminal law in accordance with the intent of the legislature of Pennsylvania. . . . [T]he legislature, in employing the phrase "imposed by law", intended that the phrase denote duties specifically imposed by a statute, ordinance or administrative regulation, and not duties voluntarily assumed by private individuals.

Thus, it is that I dissent.

DEL SOLE, J. **dissenting**.

. . . . Resolution of the instant case is controlled by the definition of the phrase "a duty imposed by law." I believe that this phrase, encompasses only those duties which are imposed by statute or regulation and specifically does not include a contractual obligation.

. . . .

Generally to be convicted of a crime the performance of a voluntary act is necessary, but an omission may be a basis for criminal liability in certain situations.

. . . .

Since the crimes charged did not include in their definitions an omission as one of their basic elements, the trial court instructed the jury that guilt could be found based upon an omission as described in § 301(b)(2). The jury was charged that the duty to perform the omitted act may be imposed by law where it is based upon a contractual agreement. The court instructed the jury that "unless you find beyond a reasonable doubt that an oral contract imposed a duty to act upon Walter and Helen Pestinikas, you must acquit the defendants." I find that such an instruction was in error.

Duties which are "imposed by law" do not encompass those which arise out of a contract or agreement. A person who enters a contract does so freely. The duties contained in a contract are those which the person who is entering the contract agrees to undertake voluntarily in exchange for some other consideration. The duties themselves are not "imposed by law" they are assumed by the terms of the agreement. Although breach of the agreement may result in some legal recourse, the law will fashion a remedy only if the injured party seeks one. The Pestinikases' omissions which resulted in a breach of their agreement to care for Mr. Kly do not constitute an omission which could be the basis of liability. . . .

. . . .

I am concerned that the position argued by the Commonwealth in this case would subject those parties who breach a contract to criminal responsibility even though no specific crime involving their actions has been defined by the legislature. These concerns require us to remain mindful that a penal statute such as that found in the instant case should be strictly construed in favor of the defendant. The strict construction rule regarding penal statutes is based on the rationale that it would be unjust to convict a person without clear notice that the contemplated conduct is unlawful, as well as providing that individual with notice of the potential penalties. This rationale provides sound reasoning for the conclusion that the term "duties imposed by law" does not encompass those duties contained in a contract. . . .

Unfortunately at the time of Mr. Kly's death there were no statutes or regulations governing the Pestinikases' conduct. . . .

Because the statute we are asked to examine, which must be strictly construed, refers solely to "duties imposed by law," and because a contractual duty alone is not one "imposed by law," I join the dissent of Judge McEwen.

Omission Actus Reus: Duty Created by the Assumption of Care

Legal duties arise when a person "assumes a duty to care" for another. For example, if the defendant found a person lying unconscious and bleeding on the sidewalk, and instead of taking the injured person to the hospital, took him home and let him bleed to death, the defendant has assumed a duty of care and the failure to act is an unlawful omission to act.

PEOPLE v. OLIVER,
258 Cal. Rptr. 138 (1989)

OPINION
STRANKMAN, J.
The victim, Carlos Cornejo, became acquainted with appellant Carol Ann Oliver at a bar. He accompanied her to her home and injected himself with heroin in her bathroom. He then collapsed to the floor unconscious. Appellant had her daughter drag him outside the house. The next morning he was discovered dead in the yard. The cause of death was heroin overdose.

Appellant was charged with and, following a jury trial, convicted of involuntary manslaughter and receiving stolen property. A three-year, eight-month sentence was imposed. We affirm.

I FACTS
Appellant met Cornejo on the afternoon of July 6, 1986, when she was with her boyfriend at a bar in the City of Pleasant Hill. She and her boyfriend purchased jewelry from Cornejo. In the late afternoon, when appellant was leaving the bar to return home, Cornejo got into the car with her, and she drove home with him. At the time, he appeared to be extremely drunk. At her house, he asked her for a spoon and went into the bathroom. She went to the kitchen, got a spoon and brought it to him. She knew he wanted the spoon to take drugs. She remained in the living room while Cornejo "shot up" in the bathroom. He then came out and collapsed onto the floor in the living room. She tried but was unable to rouse him.

Appellant then called the bartender at the bar where she had met Cornejo. The bartender advised her to leave him and to come back to the bar, which appellant did.

Appellant's daughter returned home at about 5 p.m. that day with two girlfriends. They found Cornejo unconscious on the living room floor. When the girls were unable to wake him, they searched his pockets and found eight dollars. They did not find any wallet or identification. The daughter then called appellant on the telephone. Appellant told her to drag Cornejo outside in case he woke up and became violent. The girls dragged Cornejo outside and put him behind a shed so that he would not be in the view of the neighbors. He was snoring when the girls left him there.

About a half hour later, appellant returned home with her boyfriend. She, the boyfriend, and the girls went outside to look at Cornejo. Appellant told the girls that she had watched him "shoot up" with drugs and then pass out.

The girls went out to eat and then returned to check on Cornejo later that evening. He had a pulse and was snoring.

In the morning, one of the girls heard appellant tell her daughter that Cornejo might be dead. Cornejo was purple and had flies around him. Appellant called the bartender at about 6 a.m. and told her she thought Cornejo had died in her backyard. Appellant then told the girls to call the police and she left for work. The police were called.

Officer Mark Eggold arrived at appellant's house on July 7. After he found Cornejo's body outside, he searched the residence. In the bathroom, he found some tissue stained with blood. In the kitchen, he found a spoon with a blackish-gray residue on it, and a flat rubber strap in a kitchen drawer. He also found a travel case containing drug paraphernalia.

Later that day, appellant complied with a request to answer questions at the police station. After changing her version of events several times, she finally told the police that Cornejo was extremely drunk when she drove him to her home. He went into the bathroom and asked for a spoon, which she gave him. Cornejo "shot up" and then collapsed. She said she believed that he had collapsed from the injection of drugs, and that he had "hotshotted."

On July 8, appellant delivered some jewelry to a friend. She told her friend she had taken the jewelry off a man who had died of a drug overdose at her house. She asked her friend to keep the jewelry for her temporarily. The friend delivered the jewelry to the police.

An autopsy revealed that Cornejo died of morphine poisoning. The heroin (which shows up in the blood as morphine) was injected shortly before his death. Cornejo also had a .28 percent blood-alcohol level. The forensic pathologist who testified at trial was reasonably certain that Cornejo's death was not caused by the alcohol.

II Prosecution of Involuntary Manslaughter Charge

Section 192, subdivision (b), defines involuntary manslaughter as manslaughter (1) in the commission of an unlawful act not amounting to a felony (misdemeanor /manslaughter); or (2) in the commission of a lawful act which might produce death, in an unlawful manner, or without due caution and circumspection (criminal negligence). Here, the People prosecuted the charge of involuntary manslaughter under both theories…

As to the first theory, the prosecution contended appellant had aided and abetted Cornejo in the commission of a violation of Health and Safety Code section 11550 (use of controlled substance). As to the second theory, the prosecution contended that appellant was criminally negligent when she failed to summon medical aid for Cornejo and then abandoned him, when she must have known he needed medical attention.

[At a pretrial hearing the prosecutor tried to reserve the right to argue that Oliver sold or furnished drugs to Cornejo (another offense), but the trial court ruled the evidence would be inadmissible for the criminal negligence theory but could be used as evidence to support the aiding and abetting theory]

At trial, appellant did not testify. Evidence was introduced of appellant's statements to the police concerning her ex-husband's death caused by a drug overdose in 1978. Police Sergeant Harper testified that in 1978 appellant had told him that although she had not been with her ex-husband at the time of his death, she thought he had used heroin to counter the effects of crank, and that his system had overloaded. Appellant was upset that the people who were with him had delayed in seeking medical help.

At the close of the prosecution's case, defense counsel moved for a judgment of acquittal on the involuntary manslaughter charge. As to the misdemeanor/manslaughter theory, he argued there was no evidence of the criminal intent necessary to establish aiding and abetting. As to the criminal negligence theory, he argued that the evidence failed to establish a duty of care owed by appellant to Cornejo because there was no special relationship between them, and that absent a duty of care there was no negligence.

The trial court ruled that as to the misdemeanor/manslaughter theory, there was ample evidence to support the finding that appellant had intended to facilitate, and therefore had aided and abetted Cornejo's use of drugs; and that as to the criminal negligence theory, there was sufficient evidence of a duty owed. The trial court accordingly denied the motion for judgment of acquittal.

The jury was instructed on the two theories of involuntary manslaughter. [Footnote 4, see below]. The verdict finding appellant guilty of involuntary manslaughter did not specify the theory or theories upon which the jury based its verdict.

III
THE EVIDENCE SUPPORTS THE TRIAL COURT'S DENIAL OF THE SECTION 1118.1 MOTION AND THE CONVICTION OF INVOLUNTARY MANSLAUGHTER

As to the criminal negligence theory, the evidence supports the trial court's determination that appellant owed a duty to seek medical attention for Cornejo, and there was substantial evidence of criminal negligence. Criminal negligence is premised on conduct more reckless and culpable than that of "ordinary," or civil negligence. The conduct must be such a sharp departure from the conduct of an ordinarily prudent person that it evidences a disregard for human life, and raises a presumption of conscious indifference to the consequences.

A necessary element of negligence, whether criminal or civil, is a duty owed to the person injured and a breach of that duty. [1b] Appellant claims that, regardless of whether her conduct evidenced a disregard for Cornejo's life, she did not cause his condition and therefore as a matter of law did not owe him any duty to seek medical care. She contends the question of whether her conduct amounted to criminal negligence therefore should never have gone to the jury.

Generally, one has no legal duty to rescue or render aid to another in peril, even if the other is in danger of losing his or her life, absent a special relationship which gives rise to such duty. Further, "[t]he fact that the actor realizes or should realize that action on his part is necessary for another's aid or protection does not of itself impose upon him a duty to take such action."

In California civil cases, courts have found a special relationship giving rise to an affirmative duty to act where some act or omission on the part of the defendant either created or increased the risk of injury to the plaintiff, or created a dependency relationship inducing reliance or preventing assistance from others. Where, however, the defendant took no affirmative action which contributed to, increased, or changed the risk which would otherwise have existed, and did not voluntarily assume any responsibility to protect the person or induce a false sense of security, courts have refused to find a special relationship giving rise to a duty to act.

. . .

Neither appellant nor respondent cites any California decision involving a charge of criminal negligence which is helpful to our determination of the nature, if any, of the duty owed here. The cases cited by them in which the defendant was charged with criminal negligence involved relationships which undisputably gave rise to a duty of care.

We find, however, that the rules governing the imposition of a duty to render aid or assistance as an element of civil negligence, are applicable to the imposition of a duty in the context of criminal negligence. As stated by one leading commentator on criminal law: "[T]he 'measuring stick' [of duty] is the same in a criminal case as in the law of torts. It is the exercise of due care and caution as represented by the conduct of a reasonable person under like circumstances, and this in itself is intended to represent the same requirement whatever the case may be."

We conclude that the evidence of the combination of events which occurred between the time appellant left the bar with Cornejo through the time he fell to the floor unconscious, established as a matter of law a relationship which imposed upon appellant a duty to seek medical aid. At the time appellant left the bar with Cornejo, she observed that he was extremely drunk, and drove him to her home. In so doing, she took him from a public place where others might have taken care to prevent him from injuring himself, to a private place -- her home -- where she alone could provide such care. To a certain, if limited, extent, therefore, she took charge of a person unable to prevent harm to himself.   She then allowed Cornejo to use her bathroom, without any objection on her part, to inject himself with narcotics, an act involving the definite potential for fatal consequences. When Cornejo collapsed to the floor, appellant should have known that her conduct had contributed to creating an unreasonable risk of harm for Cornejo -- death. At that point, she owed Cornejo a duty to prevent that risk from occurring by summoning aid, even if she had not previously realized that her actions would lead to such risk. Her failure to summon any medical assistance whatsoever and to leave him abandoned outside her house warranted the jury finding a breach of that duty.

Appellant next contends that even if the evidence supports the trial court's finding of a duty and breach thereof, there is no substantial evidence which supports a finding of gross

negligence necessary to impose criminal liability. She points to the testimony of the prosecution's witness, Dr. Daugherty, that even he would not be able to tell, merely from the fact that Cornejo had injected himself with heroin and passed out, that he had overdosed on the drug. She also points to the evidence that Cornejo was snoring after he collapsed and continued to snore after he had been moved outside. She contends such evidence is inconsistent with a finding that her conduct had the "know[ing] and apparent potentialities for resulting in death."

We disagree. "The fundamental requirement fixing criminal responsibility is knowledge, actual or imputed, that the act of the accused tended to endanger life." Here, the evidence established that appellant knew that Cornejo wanted a spoon to administer drugs, that he then "shot up," i.e., injected himself with drugs, and then collapsed to the floor unconscious. There was also evidence that appellant believed that Cornejo had collapsed because he had "hotshotted," from which the jury could infer that she believed he had injected a dangerous dose, if not a fatal dose, of drugs. Such evidence constitutes substantial evidence that appellant either knew or should have known that Cornejo's condition was critical, that immediate medical aid was necessary, and that the failure to summon aid tended to endanger Cornejo's life. Such finding is particularly warranted by the evidence that appellant's ex-husband had died of a drug overdose, and that appellant believed that the persons who were with him at the time had delayed too long in seeking medical help.

Substantial evidence also supports a finding that appellant's negligence was a legal cause of Cornejo's death. Dr. Daugherty testified that prompt medical attention, including the use of Narcan, an antidote to morphine which is normally given in cases of morphine overdose, might save a person who collapses from a heroin overdose if that person remains alive for some period after injecting the overdose. Such evidence reasonably supports the inference that appellant's inaction constituted a substantial factor leading to Cornejo's death, and therefore was a proximate cause of his death.

Aiding and abetting.

Appellant contends there was insufficient evidence to support a finding that she aided and abetted Cornejo's use of heroin.

A person aids and abets the commission of a crime when he or she, with knowledge of the unlawful purpose of the perpetrator, and with the intent or purpose of committing, encouraging, or facilitating the commission of the offense, by act or advice aids, promotes, encourages or instigates the commission of the crime. (*People v. Beeman* (1984). Whether a person has aided and abetted the commission of a crime is ordinarily and primarily a question for the trier of fact.)

Here, the evidence establishes that appellant was aware of Cornejo's criminal purpose when he asked for a spoon. The evidence of appellant's act of giving Cornejo a spoon and allowing him to use her bathroom to inject drugs, with the evidence of the flat rubber strap and other drug paraphernalia found by the police at appellant's house, support the finding that appellant facilitated the commission of Cornejo's use of heroin.

The foregoing evidence, and all reasonable inferences drawn therefrom, also support the finding that appellant intended to facilitate Cornejo's use of drugs. The law presumes that an aider and abettor intends the natural and reasonable consequences of the acts he intentionally performs. …

People v. Hopkins (1951), though predating *Beeman*, supports our conclusion. There the decedent purchased heroin with the defendant's money. They then prepared the narcotic for injection in the defendant's car and injected themselves, the defendant helping to manipulate a handkerchief-tourniquet around the decedent's arm while he did so. When the decedent fell unconscious, the defendant rushed him to the hospital where he died. The court held there was sufficient evidence to hold the defendant to answer a charge of manslaughter based upon aiding and abetting the decedent's use of heroin. The court further

noted: "If [defendant] had not touched decedent's arm or otherwise physically aided him, but had merely stood by and kept a lookout for passers-by he could still be charged as a principal …."

We conclude the record supports the trial court's denial of the section 1118.1 motion, and the conviction of involuntary manslaughter on both theories presented to the jury.

[The court affirmed the defendant's conviction.}

FN 4. As to the theory of criminal negligence, the jury was instructed in part as follows: "The term 'without due caution and circumspection' as used in these instructions refers to negligent acts which are aggravated, reckless and gross and which are such a departure from what would be the conduct of an ordinarily prudent or careful man under the same circumstances as to be contrary to a proper regard for human life or, in other words, a disregard for human life or an indifference to consequences. …

"The act [constituting criminal negligence] must be one which has knowable and apparent potentialities for resulting in death. Mere inattention or mistake of judgment resulting even in death of another is not criminal unless the quality of the act makes it so. The fundamental requirement fixing criminal responsibility is knowledge, actual or imputed, that the act of the accused tended to endanger life. …

"In determining whether the defendant's failure to summon medical assistance rose to the level of criminal negligence, you should consider whether an ordinarily prudent person, put in the place of the defendant, and confronted with the same circumstances as the defendant, including but not limited to the intoxicated state of Carlos Cornejo due to his voluntary ingestion of alcohol, and his apparent state of sleep, would have reasonably known at that time that Carlos Cornejo was helpless and in danger of death or great bodily harm."

Omission Actus Reus: Duty Created by Creation of Peril

Legal duties arise when the defendant creates the peril that ultimately harms the victim. A person who intentionally or negligently places another in danger has a duty to rescue them. For example, in the oft-cited case of *Jones v. Indiana*, 220 Ind. 384, 387 (Ind. 1942) the defendant raped a twelve-year-old girl who then fell off a bridge (or maybe jumped off the bridge) into a stream. Jones went into the water, but did not rescue the girl. The court stated, "Can it be doubted that one who by his own overpowering criminal act has put another in danger of drowning has the duty to preserve her life." 220 Ind., at 387.

Other Cases—Duties Created by Creation of Peril

People v. Fowler, 178 Cal. 657 (1918). The court upheld defendant's conviction for murder when he committed battery on the victim and violated a duty to rescue the victim by leaving him unconscious on the side of the road where he was later run over by a car.	***Moreland v. State, 139 S.E.77 (Ga. 1927).*** A car owner had a duty to prevent his chauffeur from speeding. Court held that an employer may have a duty to prevent employees from committing crimes while the employees are performing their work duties.

Landowner's Duty

Property owners have a legal duty to others they invite onto their lands. For example in one case the defendant invited the victim over to barbeque out on his deck which hung out 100 feet above the canyon. The defendant knew the deck unstable and was held liable when the deck collapsed because he failed to take precautions to prevent the harm to the victim.

Other Cases—Duties Created By Being a Land Owner

Commonwealth v. Karetny, (Penn. Supr. Ct., August 2015).
The Pennsylvania Supreme Court allowed the case to proceed to a jury on the charge of risking a catastrophe. Rather than focusing on the omission to act despite a landlord's duty to act as the interim court of appeals did, the Supreme Court listed the many affirmative acts it did that upon which a jury could find criminal responsibility. One of those ways included an omission—"taking no measures to inform, warn, or protect" and for which the Court seems to assume, without saying, that there was an obligation to do so.

"For approximately five and one half years, appellees allowed the structural soundness of their pier to steadily decline in large part because of the cost to repair it satisfactorily. . . [N]ot only did appellees ignore or discount their own observations of the severity of the pier's decline, they also repeatedly and consistently disregarded assessments and warnings from their engineers that put appellees on notice of the increasing likelihood of the pier's collapse. Indeed, this evidence, if believed, shows that, on the morning of the very day that the pier collapsed, their engineer predicted the approximate tide-related time at which and the manner in which the pier would collapse. Appellees disregarded that warning. It would be one thing if appellees, faced with the prospect of the pier collapsing, simply allowed it to happen under circumstances where it would affect nothing but the continued existence of the pier. But, under the Commonwealth's evidence, appellees did not simply abandon the collapsing structure to the inexorable effect of "natural forces." Nor did appellees abandon the structure while posting warning signs to keep persons away from the danger, or alert them to what appellees knew. Instead, the evidence adduced at the hearing would support a finding that appellees persisted in promoting the nightclub, booking in advance events at their several facilities on the pier. Moreover, this evidence plainly advances the Commonwealth's position that, on the night of the collapse, appellees engaged in what amounted to a literal "cover-up": they ordered that the ever-growing crack in the floor of their banquet building-tell-tale evidence of the very real calamity awaiting any person who ventured onto the premises-be concealed.

[S]ubstantial evidence indicat[es] that appellees, after having been made specifically aware of the imminent danger that the pier posed to human life, took affirmative measures to keep that knowledge to themselves and, at the same time, took affirmative steps that exposed others to the risk. The evidence of appellees' conduct in this case was sufficient to warrant a jury in finding the reckless creation of a risk of catastrophe.

… Here, under the Commonwealth's evidence, appellees' persistence in promoting the nightclub; keeping it open to the public for business; taking no measures to inform, warn, or protect the public; and affirmatively concealing the very visible evidence of the pier's impending collapse had the potential to cause-and indeed, did cause-the catastrophic death of three young women and injuries to forty-three others.

[The court held] . . . that the evidence presented by the Commonwealth was sufficient to make a prima facie showing that appellees "recklessly created a risk of catastrophe in the employment" of "any other means of causing potentially widespread injury or damage."

People v. Nelson, 128 N.E.2d 391 (N.Y. 1955).
Landlord found liable when he failed to provide a fire escape from a multiple unit dwelling when tenants of a rented apartment died after they were unable to escape from the burning building.

Commonwealth v. Welansky, 55 N.E. 2d 902 (Mass 1944).
Owner of a nightclub who failed to supply proper fire escapes were found guilty when patrons died in a fire.

Duty to intervene: the Good Samaritan Rule and the American Bystander Rule.

Under the American Bystander Rule, an individual is not legally required to assist a person who is in peril. This general rule, followed across the United States, holds that even though it may be morally reprehensible not to render assistance, the law does not create a legal duty to intervene to help another person. Some of the reasons justifying the American Bystander Rule include:

➢ Individuals intervening may be placed in jeopardy.
➢ Bystanders also may misperceive a situation, unnecessarily interfere, and create needless complications.
➢ Individuals may lack the physical capacity and expertise to subdue an assailant or to rescue a hostage and place themselves in danger.
➢ The circumstances in which individuals should intervene and the acts required to satisfy the obligation to assist another would be difficult to clearly define.
➢ Criminal prosecutions for a failure to intervene would burden the criminal justice system.
➢ Individuals in a capitalistic society are responsible for their own welfare and should not expect assistance of others.
➢ Most people will assist others out of a sense of moral responsibility and there is no need for the law to require intervention. Lippman, *Criminal Law,* at 99

For example, on a subway platform near Times Square in New York City in December 2012, a drifter pushed a man onto the tracks of an oncoming subway train. Several people were on the platform at the time, but no one came to the pushed man's aid. The man was hit by the train and killed. Under the American Bystander Laws, none of them would be liable for failure to come to the aid of the stranger.

"Good Samaritan" statutes, common in Europe, require individuals to intervene to assist those who may be in peril. The Good Samaritan Rule is said to promote a sense of community and regard for others. Proponents of the Good Samaritan Rule argue that there is no difference between pushing a child on the railroad tracks and failing to intervene to ensure the child's safety. They contend that criminal liability should extend to both acts and omissions. Id.

Connaughty v. State, 1 Wis. 159 (1853)
Bystander was not guilty of murder even though it was committed in his presence and he made no

effort to prevent it. Court held that moral duty alone is not enough.

Actus Reus: Status

Actus reus does not include a person's status or condition (addict, alcoholic, felon, homeless). The word "status" as used in the context of criminal law, means a condition over which a person has no control. The Court held in *Robinson v. California*, 370 U.S. 660 (1962), that it is cruel and unusual punishment to convict a person for a "status offense." In *Robinson*, the statute criminalized the act of being addicted to narcotics. The Court, reversing Robinson's conviction stated,

> We deal with a statute which makes the "status" of narcotic addiction a criminal offense, for which the offender may be prosecuted "at any time before he reforms. ..." We hold that a state law which imprisons a person thus afflicted as a criminal, even though he has never touched any narcotic drug within the State or been guilty of any irregular behavior there, inflicts a cruel and unusual punishment in violation of the Fourteenth Amendment. Even one day in prison would be cruel and unusual punishment for the 'crime' of having a common cold. 370 U.S. at 666-667

Powell v. Texas, 392 U.S. 514 (1968), shows that it is not always easy to distinguish between what is a status and what is an action. Powell, an alcoholic, was arrested and charged with public intoxication after officers found him drunk and in a public place. He appealed his conviction, arguing that he had been unlawfully prosecuted for his status as an alcoholic--something over which he had no control. The Court upheld his conviction, finding that he was being punished, not for his status, but for his action in placing himself in a public place on a particular occasion while intoxicated.

One persistent concern in most communities today is how to deal with homeless, transient individuals--many of whom have substance abuse and mental health issues. These individuals often are caught up in the criminal justice system when they are charged with some form of criminal trespass after entering on public or businesses' property after being told not to come back ("trespassed"). Because they are homeless, these defendants are less likely to be conditionally released while awaiting resolution of their cases. Since many are poor, they are unlikely to be able to post security for their release and end up spending short, but frequent, stays in the local jail--repeatedly pleading guilty to the charges and hoping to get released before they do "dead time" (continued incarceration after the recommended, negotiated sentence for a guilty plea). Mental health and veteran's courts are trying to respond to mitigate the harshness of the criminal justice system which essentially criminalizes the status of homelessness. That said, several "quality of life" or "public order" cases you will read in this book involve the legislatures' attempts to deter "vagrancy" "loitering" "public inebriation" or "wandering about with no visible means of support." In distinguishing *Robinson* and *Powell,* the Court focused on whether the defendant had any control over the behavior. Robinson didn't have any ability to control his present state as an addict, but Powell had control over where he drank. The Court noted it was not deciding whether a homeless person who was an alcoholic and had no choice but to drink in public could permissibly be punished. This question was squarely before the court in the next case, *People v. Kellogg.*

PEOPLE v. KELLOGG,
14 Cal Rptr, 3d 507 (Cal. Ct. App. 2004)

FACTS (Summary)

At trial, Defendant was found to suffer from chronic alcohol dependence and a mental disorder. He was homeless at the time of his

arrest, and due to his alcohol dependence which was both physical and psychological and made him unable to stop drinking, he was unable to take advantage of any program targeting homeless individuals. The court sentenced him to 180 days' jail, and suspended the execution of sentence for three years on the condition that he complete an alcohol treatment program. He could not. His probation was revoked and he was ordered to serve the 180-day jail sentence. He claimed this was cruel and unusual punishment prohibited by the Eighth Amendment.

OPINION

We conclude that the California legislature's decision to allow misdemeanor culpability for public intoxication, even as applied to a homeless chronic alcoholic such as Kellogg, is neither disproportionate to the offense nor inhumane. In deciding whether punishment is unconstitutionally excessive, we consider the degree of the individual's personal culpability as compared to the amount of punishment imposed. To the extent Kellogg has no choice but to be drunk in public given the nature of his impairments, his culpability is low; however, the penal sanctions imposed on him . . . are correspondingly low. Given the state's interest in providing for the safety of its citizens, including Kellogg, imposition of low-level criminal sanctions for Kellogg's conduct does not tread on the federal or state constitutional proscriptions against cruel and/or unusual punishment.

JUDGE MCDONALD, **dissenting**,

A . . . public intoxication offense, both in the abstract and as committed by Kellogg, is a non-violent, fairly innocuous offense. . . . It is a nonviolent offense, does not require a victim, and poses little, if any danger to society in general. As committed by Kellogg, the offense was nonviolent, victimless, and posed no danger to society. Kellogg was found intoxicated sitting under a bush in a public area. He was rocking back and forth and talking to himself, and gesturing. The record does not show that Kellogg's public intoxication posed a danger to other persons or society in general. His motive in drinking presumably was merely to fulfill his physical and psychological compulsion as an alcoholic to become intoxicated. Because Kellogg is involuntarily homeless and did not have the alternative of being intoxicated in private, he did not have any specific purpose or motive to be intoxicated in a public place. Rather, it was his only option. . . . As an involuntarily homeless person, Kellogg cannot avoid appearing in public. As a chronic alcoholic, he cannot stop drinking and being intoxicated. Therefore, Kellogg cannot avoid being intoxicated in a public place.

Based on the nature of the offense and the offender, Kellogg's . . . public intoxication conviction "shocks the conscience and offends fundamental notions of human dignity," and therefore constitutes cruel and unusual punishment. . . .

Other Cases – Status and Actus Reus

Wheeler v. Goodman, 306 F. Supp 58 (W.D.N.C. 1969).
Defendants were arrested and punished because they were unemployed "hippies." Federal district court judge stated,

> "A man is free to be a hippie, a Methodist, a Jew, a Black Panther, a Kiwanian, or even a Communist so long as his conduct does not imperil others, or infringe upon their rights. In short, it is no crime to be a hippie . . .

Status—even that of a gambler or prostitute—may not be made criminal. . . . The acts of gambling, prostitution, and operating bawdy houses are criminally punishable, of course, but the states cannot create the special status of vagrant for person who commit those illegal acts and then punish the status instead of the act."

Actus reus: Possession

Although possessing something doesn't seem like an action, there are several crimes for which the actus reus is possessing some forbidden object. For example, statutes criminalize the possession of drugs, burglar tools, stolen credit cards, or other stolen property. See, e.g., MPC § 5.06[10] The overwhelming majority of states and the Model Penal Code hold that for possession to be criminal, it must be "knowing possession." MPC §2.01(4) provides that "[p]ossession is an act . . . if the possessor knowingly procured or received the thing possessed or was aware of his control thereof for a sufficient period to have been able to terminate his possession." The case of State v. Bash further explores the differences between *knowing possession*, *mere possession[11]*, *actual possession* and *constructive possession*.

Sometimes it is difficult to prove possession when several people have access to or joint possession of an object—for example, drugs on a table in the living room of a house shared by several people. Most courts hold that anyone in the room can be found to have been in possession of the drugs as long as there is some specific proof connecting each person to the object.   When analyzing possession ask: did defendant have knowledge of the presence of the object, did the defendant exercise dominion and control over the object, and whether the defendant had knowledge of the character of the object.

STATE v. BASH,
670 N.W.2d 135 (Iowa, 2003)

FACTS
On January 17, 2001, six Spirit Lake police officers executed a search warrant at an apartment shared by the defendant, her husband Kevin, and her three sons. The search warrant indicated that the officers were looking for, among other things, controlled substances and a safety deposit box. The defendant, her husband, and their son Ty were home at the time the officers entered the apartment. The officers immediately arrested Kevin on an outstanding warrant and removed him from the residence.

One of the officers read the search warrant to the defendant whereupon, according to the officer, the defendant said she could "show

[him] where the stuff is." The officer testified that he believed the defendant was referring to "any illegal drugs or contraband that may be in the residence." After reading the defendant her *Miranda* rights, the officer followed the defendant into the master bedroom and she told him, "it's on his nightstand in a cardboard box, that it's Kevin's stuff, that is his bong … sitting on the floor next to the bed."

The defendant's version was somewhat different from the officer's testimony. She testified she heard officers talking about a lock box they were looking for in the residence. When officers asked her if there was "anything in the house they should know about," she responded, "If there is anything here, it would be on Kevin's side of the bed." She pointed

---

[10] MPC § 5.06 Possessing Instruments of Crime; Weapons.
(1) Criminal Instruments Generally. A person commits a misdemeanor if he possesses any instrument of crime with purpose to employ it criminally. "Instrument of crime" means:
(a) anything specially made or specially adapted for criminal use; or
(b) anything commonly used for criminal purposes and possessed by the actor under circumstances that do not negative unlawful purpose.

(2) Presumption of Criminal Purpose from Possession of Weapon. If a person possesses a firearm or other weapon on or about his person, in a vehicle occupied by him, or otherwise readily available for use, it is presumed that he had the purpose to employ it criminally, unless:
(a) the weapon is possessed in the actor's home or place of business;
(b) the actor is licensed or otherwise authorized by law to possess such weapon; or
(c) the weapon is of a type commonly used in lawful sport.

"Weapon" means anything readily capable of lethal use and possessed under circumstances not manifestly appropriate for lawful uses it may have; the term includes a firearm that is not loaded or lacks a clip or other component to render it immediately operable, and components that can readily be assembled into a weapon.
[11] Only two states, Washington and North Dakota, criminalize mere possession, but in practice both states impose a knowing requirement to guarantee fair results.

towards his nightstand which was on the left side of the bed. The officer then arrested her and read her *Miranda* rights to her.

On Kevin's nightstand the officers found a cardboard box bearing the word "Friscos." Inside the box, they found a green plant material later identified as 1.37 grams of marijuana. The defendant testified she did not know what was in the box until after the officers opened it. However, she admitted that she knew there had been marijuana in the house, in the box, in the past.

The defendant also directed the officers to the lock box, which contained a marriage certificate, birth certificates, insurance papers, and the key to the box.

The state charged the defendant with possession of a controlled substance (marijuana), in violation of Iowa Code Section 124.401 (5)(Supp. 1999). Later, the defendant moved to dismiss, contending the State would be unable to prove she exercised dominion and control over the controlled substance. Following the State's resistance, the district court denied the defendant's motion. The district court sentenced the defendant to a thirty-day suspended sentence with credit for time served and imposed a $250 fine and a $75 surcharge.

Following the defendant's appeal, we transferred the case to the court of appeals, which affirmed. We granted the defendant's application for further review.

REASONING
Unlawful possession of a controlled substance requires proof that the defendant: (1) exercised dominion and control over the contraband, (2) had knowledge of its presence, and (3) had knowledge that the material was a controlled substance. Proof of opportunity of access to the place where contraband is found will not, without more, support a finding of unlawful possession.

In her motion for judgment of acquittal, the defendant argued:

> "We know from the *State v. Atkinson* case and other cases of a similar nature on

constructive possession that mere proximity to contraband is insufficient to meet the State's burden.

Here, the facts are very similar (to those in *Atkinson*). We have the premises shared by these two people, the married persons, and contraband found in that location. It is undisputed that it was Kevin Bash that was the target of their investigation, undisputed that these were Kevin Bash's effects, not the defendant's effects, wherein the contraband was found.

There is no evidence that the State has brought forward to show that my client had any dominion or control, any ownership or proprietary interest in the contraband that was found, and we cannot infer that dominion and control where the defendant is not in the exclusive possession of the premises. These were premises shared by her and her husband. And the State then has to come forward with some evidence that shows that she had that dominion and control. They have not provided any evidence of the dominion and control element as required."

As in the district court, the defendant's sufficiency-of-the-evidence challenge here is to the first element of the crime charged: dominion and control. Possession can be either actual or constructive. Actual possession occurs when the controlled substance is found on the defendant's person. Constructive possession occurs when the defendant has knowledge of the presence of the controlled substance and has the authority or right to maintain control of it. It is undisputed here that the defendant did not have actual possession of the marijuana because the officers did not find the controlled substance on her person. We are left with whether the defendant had constructive possession.

At the time of this incident, it is undisputed that the premises were shared by the defendant, her husband, and their children. Under these circumstances, knowledge of the presence of the marijuana and the authority or right to maintain control of it, that is, constructive possession, could not be inferred by the jury from the defendant's joint control of the premises, but had to be established by other proof. Such proof could include incriminating statements made by the defendant, incriminating actions of the defendant upon the police's discovery of the controlled substance among or near the defendant's personal belongings, the defendant's fingerprints on the packages containing the controlled substance, and any other circumstances linking the defendant to the controlled substance.

In her motion for judgment of acquittal, the defendant's sufficiency-of-the-evidence challenge did not include her lack of knowledge of the presence of the marijuana. Rather, as her argument on the motion indicates, such challenge only included the authority or right to maintain control of the marijuana. On this point, the State relies heavily on the following testimony from the defendant:

Q. Now, could you have—was there any legal reason that would prevent you from taking that box and disposing of it?
A. It wasn't mine.
Q. I understand that. But is there—it's proper that you generally regard it as your husband's?
A. Correct.
Q. But you shared that apartment with him?
A. Correct.
Q. Now, is there any legal reason why you could not have picked up that box and taken it and removed it from the house?
A. It was not mine.
Q. Could you have taken the contents of that box and flushed it down the toilet?
A. No. It was not mine.

Q. Okay. Physically, would you have been able to do that?
A. Physically, yes.

The State argues that the defendant's admission that she could physically have flushed the marijuana down the toilet is proof that she had the authority or right to maintain control of the marijuana. This position is at odds with what we said in *State v. Atkinson*: "While it seems anomalous to look at a defendant's 'right' to control illegal drugs in order to establish possession, that concept basically distinguishes a defendant's raw physical ability to exercise control over contraband simply because of the defendant's proximity to it and the type of rights that can be considered constructive possession."

Thus, the authority or right to maintain control includes something more than the "raw physical ability" to exercise control over the controlled substance. The defendant must have some proprietary interest or an immediate right to control or reduce the controlled substance to the defendant's possession. No such proof was produced here. The State seems to concede, as it must, that the box containing marijuana was located on the husband's side of the bed with his personal effects. Additionally, there was no evidence that the defendant shared any ownership of the box or the marijuana in it or had any right to control either item.

HOLDING
Accordingly, we conclude the State failed to prove the defendant had dominion and control over the marijuana and thus failed to prove constructive possession of it. We therefore vacate the court of appeals decision, reverse the judgment of the district court, and remand the case for dismissal.

STATE v. TOUPS, No. 2001-K-1875 (La. Supreme Ct, 2002)

FACTS
After receiving confidential information that a person named "Stan" was selling drugs from a residence at 633 North Scott Street and conducting a controlled purchase of drugs from that address on the afternoon of October 18, 1999, on that evening, New Orleans Police Department Officer Dennis Bush and five other officers executed a search warrant at that residence. Before executing the warrant, the officers conducted a surveillance of the residence for approximately thirty minutes. After receiving no response at the front door, Bush entered the shotgun residence. He observed defendant Mary Toups and Stanley Williams, the known resident of that address, seated on a sofa in the front living room, facing

one another and apparently engaged in conversation. Two pieces of crack cocaine, three clear glass crack pipes and a razor blade were found on a coffee table positioned directly in front of defendant and Williams. Defendant was approximately three feet from the drugs on the table, which were directly in front of her. Another 16 rocks of cocaine found at the home were located in a plastic container that was next to Williams. Police also seized $304.00 in cash from the same area. The officers did not see defendant or Williams smoking from the pipes. The officers did not see defendant enter the residence during their 30-minute surveillance, indicating she was in the residence for at least that long, but were unable to find any indication that defendant resided there. Defendant falsely gave her name as "Mary Billiot" at the time of her arrest. While defendant was not charged with any offense with regard to the cocaine in the container, the State filed a bill of information charging defendant with possession of the two pieces of cocaine found on the coffee table.

At trial . . . a criminologist with the New Orleans Police Department Crime Laboratory testified that the rocks in the container, the two additional rocks, and the pipes all tested positive for cocaine. None of the items were submitted for fingerprint analysis.

. . . .

DISCUSSION

. . . .

Toups was charged with possession of cocaine, a violation of La. R.S. 40:967, which makes it unlawful for any person to knowingly or intentionally possess a controlled dangerous substance. The State need not prove that the defendant was in physical possession of the narcotics found; constructive possession is sufficient to support a conviction. The law on constructive possession is as follows:

> A person may be in constructive possession of a drug even though it is not in his physical custody, if it is subject to his dominion and control. Also, a person may be deemed to be in joint possession of a drug which is in the physical custody of a companion, if he willfully and knowingly shares with the other the right to control it. Guilty knowledge is an essential ingredient of the crime of

unlawful possession of an illegal drug.

However, it is well settled that the mere presence in an area where drugs are located or the mere association with one possessing drugs does not constitute constructive possession.

A determination of whether there is "possession" sufficient to convict depends on the peculiar facts of each case. Factors to be considered in determining whether a defendant exercised dominion and control sufficient to constitute constructive possession include his knowledge that drugs were in the area, his relationship with the person found to be in actual possession, his access to the area where the drugs were found, evidence of recent drug use, and his physical proximity to the drugs. ...

Toups argued to the jury that the only evidence connecting her with the drugs was her mere presence in the area where the drugs were found. However, most, if not all, of the factors used to determine whether a defendant exercised dominion and control sufficient to constitute constructive possession have been met in this case: (1) Toups inevitably had knowledge that drugs were in the area in that they were in plain view directly in front of her; (2) Toups had access to the area where the drugs were found; (3) Toups was in very close physical proximity to the drugs; and (4) the area was frequented by drug users, as the police received confidential information on the morning of October 18, 1999 that Williams was conducting drug transactions and the police did a controlled purchase of drugs from Williams that afternoon, and another 16 rocks of cocaine were on the sofa next to Williams. While there was no evidence presented of any specific relationship between Toups and Stanley Williams, it is reasonable to conclude that they were not strangers given that she was with Williams for at least 30 minutes prior to their arrest and that Williams would not sit at his coffee table with crack cocaine in plain view ready to be smoked with someone he did know personally or someone who he did not know would be amenable to using the drugs. Further, although there was no evidence presented of recent drug use, the fact that the drugs and paraphernalia were on the table in front of them and that the paraphernalia contained drug residue suggests that they were preparing to use, or had already used, drugs. Finally, it is important to note that the jury was presented with evidence that Toups gave a false name, "Mary Billiot," to the police upon her arrest, indicating consciousness of guilt. ... The jury was presented with all this evidence and determined that Toups exercised dominion and control over the drugs sufficient to constitute constructive possession. We find that this evidence was sufficient to convince a rational trier of fact that all of the elements of the crime had been proved beyond a reasonable doubt.

We disagree with the court of appeal's view that "[c]onsidering the evidence adduced at trial, one can only speculate as to what the defendant was doing in the residence," suggesting that "[s]he could have been a non-drug using member of a neighborhood church proselytizing defendant." The jury rejected the "innocent" hypothesis that Toups was merely present at the sofa in front of illegal drugs, for the obvious reasons that there was no evidence presented to lead the jury to that conclusion and that any hypothesis other than possessing drugs was unreasonable. We agree.

. . . [C]ontrary to the facts in Bell where the drugs were wrapped in a package with no accompanying paraphernalia and therefore not susceptible of immediate use, in this case the drugs and necessary paraphernalia were placed directly in front of Toups ready for use.

This case is also distinguishable from . . . State v. Jackson. In Jackson, . . . the defendant was found standing in front of a homemade bar in a co-defendant's residence, on which were displayed a mirror with cocaine residue, two cocaine pipes (one of which was positive for cocaine residue), and one razor blade with cocaine residue. The court of appeal found that

although the defendant was standing next to drug paraphernalia, there was no evidence that the pipe with residue was warm or that the defendant was anything other than a guest in the house. In the instant case, Toups was not only near paraphernalia which had been used at some unknown time, she was seated in front of two rocks of cocaine, not mere residue, in plain view and within arm's length.

This case is more in line with State v. Harris. ... In Harris, the court of appeal found that where the defendant was sitting at his brother's kitchen table where cocaine was easily accessible and openly displayed along with drug paraphernalia, and the defendant's brother was nearby free basing cocaine, the evidence was sufficient to establish that the defendant knowingly possessed the drugs on the kitchen [table]. Although the defendant claimed he was only at his brother's house to eat a chicken dinner, the jury did not accept this hypothesis of innocence and the court of appeal confirmed the conviction.

CONCLUSION
We find that the evidence presented in this case, viewed in the light most favorable to the prosecution, was sufficient to convince a rational trier of fact that the State proved that defendant exercised dominion and control over the cocaine sufficient to constitute constructive possession beyond a reasonable doubt. Most, if not all, of the factors used to help make this determination were present in this case. In addition, defendant gave police a false name upon her arrest. While certainly one could speculate about other reasons for defendant's presence at the residence, given the facts presented, the jury correctly concluded that any other explanation was unreasonable.

Other Cases—Possession as Actus Reus

PEOPLE v. E.C., 761 N.Y.C.2d 443 (Supreme Court, Queens County, N.Y., 2003).
FACTS
E.C. (defendant) was employed by Primo Security to work a bouncer at a bar, was told to confiscate illegal contraband before anyone was allowed inside, and that their policy was that if anything was confiscated, he should contact Primo who would turn in the contraband to the police. On the night in question, the defendant confiscated 14

packets of cocaine from a patron on his way into the bar. Prior to his having an opportunity to contact Primo, the police responded to noise outside the bar at which time the defendant gave the police the 14 packets of cocaine. E.C. was charged with fourth-degree criminal possession of a controlled substance. sought jury instruction on defense of temporary and lawful possession.

OPINION

The People do not dispute the existence of this defense with respect to weapons, rather they argue against applying it to other possessory crimes such as criminal possession of a controlled substance. The People seem to be taking an absolutist position to the temporary and innocent possession of a controlled substance. This position makes little sense in real life and runs contrary to public policy considerations. It also allows for certain factual situations to be criminalized where it is clear that the state would not want to punish people doing the right thing. While many real life situations come to mind, three intriguing ones came up in oral argument.

First, if a parent discovers illegal drugs in their child's bedroom and decided to confront the child with these drugs-just like we see on the public service announcements on television-the parent would be guilty of a degree of criminal possession of a controlled substance under the People's absolutist position.

Second, if a teacher, dean, guidance counselor or principal in a school came into possession of a controlled substance by either taking it from a student or finding it in a desk, open locker, the hall or any other part of the school, the teacher, dean, guidance counselor or principal would be guilty of a degree of criminal possession of a controlled substance under the People's absolutist position.

The third example might be the most intriguing especially in drug cases. During the trial, like other drugs cases, after the People entered into evidence the 14 packets of cocaine, they published them to the jury. The jurors, one-by-one, took the cocaine into their hands and looked at it and then passed them to the next juror. The last juror returned the 14 packets to the court. Under this situation, each juror would be guilty of a degree of criminal possession of a controlled substance under the People's absolutist position.

The same policy consideration for weapons are equally valid for controlled substances. We want people, not just law enforcement, to confiscate illegal drugs from their children and students and turn them in to the proper authorities. We want people who find drugs on the street to pick them up and turn them in to the proper authorities. We want jurors to be able to examine evidence without fear of prosecution. It makes no sense whatsoever to criminalize this type of behavior. It runs contrary to public policy.

PORTER v. STATE, 2003 WL 1919477 (Ark. App.).

FACTS

Little Rock Police Officer Beth McNair testified that she stopped a vehicle with no license plate on the evening of May 23, 2002. Porter was a passenger in the vehicle and was sitting in the back seat on the passenger side. Porter's cousin was the driver of the vehicle, and his uncle was in the front passenger seat. As McNair approached the vehicle, she testified that she observed Porter reaching toward the floor with his left hand. McNair told Porter to keep his left hand where she could see it. As McNair shined her flashlight into the vehicle, she testified that she saw a handgun on Porter's left shoe and that the barrel of the gun was pointing toward her. McNair drew her weapon and alerted her assisting officer that there was a gun.

Officer Robert Ball testified that he assisted McNair with the traffic stop. Ball stated that he was standing near the trunk on the driver's side of the vehicle, when he heard McNair yell "Gun." Ball drew his weapon and came to the passenger side of the vehicle, where he saw that Porter had his hand near his shin and that there was a gun lying on top of Porter's foot. Porter was then taken into custody. McNair testified that the gun was a Ruger .357 revolver, which was loaded. Another weapon was found in plain view in the floorboard of the front passenger seat.

Porter testified that his cousin and his uncle had picked him up at a hotel and that they were taking him to his sister's house. Porter stated that he had only been in the car for approximately five minutes when it was stopped, that he did not know that there were any guns inside the vehicle, and that the gun found near his foot was not his. He also denied that he bent over and reached toward the floor, and he testified that there was nothing touching his foot. Porter admitted that the gun may have been found near his foot but explained that it probably "slid back there" from underneath the seat when they were driving up some steep hills.

OPINION

Porter contends that the State failed to prove that he possessed the gun because the vehicle was also occupied by two other persons. It is not necessary for the State to prove actual physical possession of a firearm; a showing of constructive possession is sufficient. To prove constructive possession, the State must establish beyond a reasonable doubt that the defendant exercised care, control, and management over the contraband and that the defendant knew the matter possessed was contraband.

Although constructive possession can be implied when the contraband is in the joint control of the accused and another, joint occupancy of a vehicle, standing alone, is not sufficient to establish possession. In a joint-occupancy situation, the State must prove some additional factor, which links the accused to the contraband and demonstrates the accused's knowledge and control of the contraband, such as:

(1) whether the contraband was in plain view;
(2) whether the contraband was found on the accused's person or with his personal effects;
(3) whether it was found on the same side of the car seat as the accused was sitting or in near proximity to it;
(4) whether the accused is the owner of the vehicle or exercises dominion or control over it;
(5) and whether the accused acted suspiciously before or during the arrest.

In making its finding that Porter had possession of the handgun found in the back seat of the vehicle, the trial court stated that almost all of the above factors were present except that Porter was not the owner or driver of the vehicle. Porter, however, contends that all of these factors must be shown to prove that he had constructive possession. Because the trial court did not find there to be any exercise of dominion and control over the vehicle, Porter argues that it was not proven that he exercised dominion and control over the handgun.

Contrary to Porter's argument, it is not necessary that all of the above stated factors be shown in order to find a person in constructive possession of contraband in a case of joint occupancy; rather, there must be "some additional factor linking the accused" to the contraband.

There is substantial evidence in this case supporting the trial court's finding that Porter had possession of the handgun. According to the police officers' testimonies, the handgun was found in plain view on the floorboard of the back seat of the vehicle, the gun was lying on Porter's left foot, it was on the same side of the vehicle as Porter was sitting, and Porter acted suspiciously prior to his arrest by reaching toward the floor with his left hand. The presence of these factors is sufficient to show Porter's knowledge and control of the handgun. Although Porter testified that the gun was not his, that he did not know that there were guns in the vehicle, and that the gun must have "slid back" near his foot when the vehicle went up a steep hill, the trial court specifically stated that it credited the testimony of the State's witnesses.

We defer to the trial court in matters of credibility of witnesses, and the trial court is not required to believe the testimony of the accused, as he is the person most interested in the outcome of the trial. Thus, we affirm.

Mens Rea

One of fundamental principles in criminal law is that we punish only blameworthy individuals. What a person was thinking at the time they committed an act plays a key role in deciding our response. As Oliver Wendell Holmes Jr. remarked, "Even a dog distinguishes between being stumbled over and being kicked."[12] If, while standing in a crowded subway, someone touched your leg, your response (say, pulling away) would be similar regardless of what the person intended, but how you view the act and the type of consequence you want would likely be different if the person touched you on accident from if they intended to grope you. In this manner, the criminal law differentiates punishment based upon an actor's intent.

The Latin, mens rea, means "guilty mind," of "evil intent" and another Latin phrase, *scienter*, means "guilty knowledge." The legal maxim *"actus non facit reum nisi mens sit rea* ("an act does not make a person guilty unless the mind is guilty") means that the state must prove that, in addition to a voluntary act or

---

[12] "Early Forms of Liability," Lecture I from *The Common Law.* (1909)

omission to act, the defendant acted with the criminal intent required by the statute. Both mens rea and *scienter* have been used to refer to the mental part of the crime.

Common Law Mens Rea

The common law spoke of two categories of mens rea: general intent and specific intent. The trend in modern statutes is to abandon these distinctions, but these terms continue to exist in some criminal statutes. General intent is the intent to commit the actus reus or to do the criminal act. So, if the crime is assault and battery, the state needs to prove that the defendant intended to strike the victim--the state need not prove that the defendant intended to violate the law, that the defendant knew that the act was a crime, nor that the defendant knew the act would result in any specific type of harm--just that the offender intended to strike the victim. Since defendants rarely announce their intentions, proof that the defendant intended to strike the victim must be inferred from the circumstances surrounding the behavior.

Specific intent is the intent to engage in the criminal act and cause the particular result. For example, murder is considered a specific intent crime. In order to convict a defendant of murder, the state must show not only that the defendant wished to take out a gun and shoot it (the act), but also that the defendant wished that the bullet would strike the victim and that the victim would die (the act and the result).

The common law also recognized "transferred intent." Transferred intent applies in situations where an individual intends to harm one victim, but instead injures another. When Kendall throws a rock at Barb but the rock misses Barb and strikes Dawn, then the law "transfers" Kendall's criminal intent from Barb (intended victim) to Dawn (actual victim). The common law doctrine of transferred intent states that Kendall's guilt is exactly what it would have been had she hit Barb with the rock. Some states limit the transferred intent doctrine to situations in which the type of harm done is similar to the type of harm intended. In those states, Kendall would be not be guilty of striking Dawn with the rock if she had intended to break a window with the rock but instead accidentally hit Dawn (since the intent to injure property is different than the intent to injure a person.)

The final type of common law intent was "constructive intent." Constructive intent is used in situations in which an offender is particularly reckless. Individuals who are grossly and wantonly reckless are said to intend the natural consequences of their actions (even if they really don't). The law infers their intent from the recklessness of their actions. For example, if James dropped a big cement block from a freeway overpass and it hit Kelly's car causing her to swerve and crash into the barrier killing her, the state could prove the mens rea requirement through his constructive intent.

Model Penal Code Mens Rea

Common law distinctions between *scienter*, general intent, and specific intent became confused and incorrectly applied over time. The Model Penal Code reflects an attempt to clarify the criminal intent by limiting it to four distinct mental states. Except in the rare case of a strict liability crime (discussed below), all crimes require a mental element. Under the MPC all crimes requiring a mental element must include one of these four mental states: purposely, knowingly, recklessly, and negligently.

MPC §2.02 General Requirements of Culpability.

(1) Minimum Requirements of Culpability. Except as provided in Section 2.05, a person is not guilty of an offense unless he acted purposely, knowingly, recklessly or negligently, as the law may require, with respect to each material element of the offense.

(2) Kinds of Culpability Defined
(a) Purposely. A person acts purposely with respect to a material element of an offense when:
(i) if the element involves the nature of his conduct or a result thereof, it is his conscious object to engage in conduct of that nature or to cause such a result; and

(ii) if the element involves the attendant circumstances, he is aware of the existence of such circumstances or he believes or hopes that they exist.

(b) Knowingly. A person acts knowingly with respect to a material element of an offense when:

(i) if the element involves the nature of his conduct or the attendant circumstances, he is aware that his conduct is of that nature or that such circumstances exist; and
(ii) if the element involves a result of his conduct, he is aware that it is practically certain that his conduct will cause such a result.

(c) Recklessly. A person acts recklessly with respect to a material element of an offense when he consciously disregards a substantial and unjustifiable risk that the material element exists or will result from his conduct. The risk must be of such a nature and degree that, considering the nature and purpose of the actor's conduct and the circumstances known to him, its disregard involves a gross deviation from the standard of conduct that a law-abiding person would observe in the actor's situation.

(d) Negligently. A person acts negligently with respect to a material element of an offense when he should be aware of a substantial and unjustifiable risk that the material element exists or will result from his conduct. The risk must be of such a nature and degree that the actor's failure to perceive it, considering the nature and purpose of his conduct and the circumstances known to him, involves a gross deviation from the standard of care that a reasonable person would observe in the actor's situation.

(3) Culpability Required Unless Otherwise Provided. When the culpability sufficient to establish a material element of an offense is not prescribed by law, such element is established if a person acts purposely, knowingly or recklessly with respect thereto. (Translation: when the statute or law is silent on the level of mens rea, requires culpability, culpability (defendant's guilt can be established if the defendant acted purposely, knowingly or recklessly. Note: this does not include negligently).

(7) Requirement of Knowledge Satisfied by Knowledge of High Probability. When knowledge of the existence of a particular fact is an element of an offense, such knowledge is established if a person is aware of a high probability of its existence, unless he actually believes that it does not exist.

(8) Requirement of Willfulness Satisfied by Acting Knowingly. A requirement that an offense be committed willfully is satisfied if a person acts knowingly with respect to the material elements of the offense, unless a purpose to impose further requirements appears.

(9) Culpability as to Illegality of Conduct. Neither knowledge nor recklessness or negligence as to whether conduct constitutes an offense or as to the existence, meaning or application of the law determining the elements of an offense is an element of such offense, unless the definition of the offense or the Code so provides. (Translation: knowing that the action constitutes a crime (the illegality of the conduct) isn't something the prosecution needs to prove unless the MPC says the defendant needs to know).

In *United States v. Baile,* 444 U.S. 394 (1980), the Court said that in a "general sense, 'purpose' corresponds loosely with the common-law concept of specific intent, while 'knowledge' corresponds loosely with the concept of 'general intent.'" In *United States v. Gypsum Co.*, the Court stated that in the case of most crimes, "the limited distinction between knowledge and purpose has not been considered important." In some states, and under MPC §2.02(5), if the state charges the defendant acted with reckless mental state, the prosecutor can prove its case if the jury finds that the defendant acted recklessly, knowingly, or intentionally/purposefully; similarly, if the state charges that the defendant acted knowingly, it can prove its case if the jury finds that the defendant acted knowingly or intentionally.

Material Elements Of A Crime--Applying The Levels Of Intent

The four basic mental states (purposefully, knowingly, recklessly, and negligently) may be applied to different "material elements of a crime." Criminal statutes can be tricky to interpret, and this is particularly so in deciding what criminal mindset the statute requires. One statute may have more than one level of mens rea depending on the material element. For example, if the statute stated, "a person commits the crime of criminal mischief when the person recklessly, knowingly or purposefully damages the property of another," there are several questions about criminal intent that the jury may need to answer. For example, is the state required to prove that the defendant recklessly, knowingly, or purposefully swung the bat at the victim's car (the act)? Or, is the state required to prove that the defendant recklessly, knowingly, or purposefully damaged the car (the result)? Or, is the state required to prove that the defendant recklessly, knowingly, or purposefully damaged the car _of another_ (the attendant circumstance)? The material elements include:

1. The actor's physical conduct. The mens rea required about the physical conduct relates to the actor's awareness of his physical conduct. In the example above, this would require that the defendant recklessly, knowingly, or purposefully swung the bat.

2. The result produced by the conduct. The mens rea required about the result relates to the actor's awareness of the harm that is or may be caused. Many crimes require that defendant cause a particular harm. In the example above, the crime of criminal mischief requires that the defendant damage (the result-harm) the victim's property. If the defendant knowingly swung the bat but had taken great precautions not to be anywhere near the car and there is no evidence that she intended to damage the car, the state may not be able to prove the mens rea required in the statute concerning the material element of result.

3. The surrounding or "attendant" circumstances that exist apart from the individual's conduct. Certain crimes specify particular circumstances that must exist for the crime to be committed. In our example, the attendant circumstance is that the property must be the property of another. If defendant thought she was damaging her own car, then she would not be guilty of the crime. Another example of a crime involving an attendance circumstance is that of providing alcohol to a minor. If the statute requires the defendant provide alcohol to a person knowing that person to be under age, then the defendant would not be convicted if he believed the person was not a minor. If, however, the statute required only that the state prove the defendant was negligent as to the recipient's age, the defendant may be convicted.

Purposefully/Intentionally

State v. Stark, below, explores the mens rea of purposefully or intentionally—it also revisits a concept from Chapter One: void for vagueness.

STATE V. STARK,
832 P. 2d 109 (Wash: Court of Appeals, 2nd Div. 1992)

PETRICH, C.J.

This is a consolidated appeal from a jury trial on one count and a bench trial on two counts of second degree assault. At both trials, Calvin Stark was found guilty of intentionally exposing his sexual partners to the human immunodeficiency virus (HIV). After the jury trial for which he was found guilty of one count, referred to as count 1, the trial court imposed an exceptional sentence. After the bench trial for which he was found guilty of two additional counts, referred to as counts 2 and 3, the trial court imposed concurrent standard range sentences. Stark contends that in both trials the State improperly used confidential information and presented insufficient evidence of intent to expose his sexual partners to HIV. He also challenges the constitutionality of the second degree assault statute as vague and contends that the exceptional sentence the court imposed for count 1 was unjustified. We affirm the convictions, but remand for resentencing on count 1.

On March 25, 1988, Calvin Stark tested positive for HIV, which was confirmed by further tests on June 25 and on June 30, 1988. From June 30, 1988, to October 3, 1989, the staff of the Clallam County Health Department had five meetings with Stark during which Stark went through extensive counseling about his infection. He was taught about "safe sex", the risk of spreading the infection, and the necessity of informing his partners before engaging in sexual activity with them. On October 3, 1989, Dr. Locke, the Clallam County Health Officer, after learning that Stark had disregarded this advice and was engaging in unprotected sexual activity, issued a cease and desist order as authorized by RCW 70.24.024(3)(b).

Stark did not cease and desist, and, consequently, on March 1, 1990, Dr. Locke went to the county prosecutor's office intending to seek the prosecutor's assistance, pursuant to RCW 70.24.034(1), in obtaining judicial enforcement of the cease and desist order. The prosecutor instead had Dr. Locke complete a police report. The State then charged Stark with three counts of assault in the second degree. Each count involved a different victim:

Count 1: The victim and Stark engaged in sexual intercourse on October 27 and October 29, 1989. On both occasions, Stark withdrew his penis from the victim prior to ejaculation. The victim, who could not become pregnant because she had previously had her fallopian tubes tied, asked Stark on the second occasion why he withdrew. He then told her that he was HIV positive.

Count 2: The victim and Stark had sexual relations on at least six occasions between October 1989, and February 1990. Stark wore a condom on two or three occasions, but on the others, he ejaculated outside of her body. On each occasion, they had vaginal intercourse. On one occasion Stark tried to force her to have anal intercourse. They also engaged in oral sex. When she told Stark that she had heard rumors that he was HIV positive, he admitted that he was and then gave the victim an AZT pill "to slow down the process of the AIDS."

Count 3: The victim and Stark had sexual relations throughout their brief relationship. It was "almost nonstop with him", "almost every night" during August 1989. Stark never wore a condom and never informed the victim he was HIV positive. When pressed, Stark denied rumors about his HIV status. The victim broke off the relationship because of Stark's drinking, after which Stark told her that he carried HIV and explained that if he had told her, she would not have had anything to do with him.

. . . In the bench trial, Dr. Locke testified. There the State also presented the testimony of one of Stark's neighborhood friends. She testified that one night Stark came to her apartment after drinking and told her and her daughter that he was HIV positive. When she asked him if he knew that he had to protect himself and everybody else, he replied, "I don't care. If I'm going to die, everybody's going to die."

The jury found Stark guilty on count 1. A second trial judge found Stark guilty of the second and third counts at a bench trial. On count 1, Stark was given an exceptional sentence of 120 months based on his future danger to the community. The standard range for that offense was 13 to 17 months. On counts 2 and 3, Stark was given the low end of the standard range, 43 months each, to be served concurrently, but consecutively to count 1.
. . . .

SUFFICIENCY OF THE EVIDENCE

Stark also contends that his convictions should be dismissed because the State failed to present sufficient evidence of an intent to inflict bodily harm. In determining whether sufficient evidence supports a conviction, "[t]he standard of review is whether, after viewing the evidence in a light most favorable to the State, any rational trier of fact could have found the essential elements of the charged crime beyond a reasonable doubt." Under this standard, we resolve all inferences in favor of the State.

Stark contends that there is insufficient evidence to prove that he "exposed" anyone to HIV or that he acted with intent to inflict bodily harm. Since Stark is undisputedly HIV positive, he necessarily exposed his sexual partners to the virus by engaging in unprotected sexual intercourse. The testimony of the three victims supports this conclusion.

The testimony supporting the element of intent to inflict bodily harm includes Dr. Locke's statements detailing his counseling sessions with Stark. With regard to the first victim, we know that Stark knew he was HIV positive, that he had been counseled to use "safe sex" methods, and that it had been explained to Stark that coitus interruptus will not prevent the spread of the virus. While there is evidence to support Stark's position, all the evidence viewed in a light most favorable to the State supports a finding of intent beyond a reasonable doubt. The existence of noncriminal explanations does not preclude a finding that a defendant intended to harm his sexual partners. With regard to the later victims, we have, in addition to this same evidence, Stark's neighbor's testimony that Stark, when confronted about his sexual practices, said, "I don't care. If I'm going to die, everybody's going to die." We also have the testimony of the victim in count 2 that Stark attempted to have anal intercourse with her and did have oral sex, both methods the counselors told Stark he needed to avoid. *See also Commonwealth v. Brown.* (Defendant threw his feces into face of prison guard. Court found that there was sufficient evidence to support finding of intent to inflict bodily harm when defendant had been counseled by both a physician and a nurse about being tested HIV positive and that he could transmit the virus through his bodily fluids.); *State v. Haines* (sufficient evidence to convict of attempted murder when defendant, knowing he was HIV positive, spit, bit, scratched, and threw blood at officer); *Scroggins v. State* (sufficient evidence to convict of aggravated assault with intent to murder when defendant, knowing he was HIV positive, sucked up excess sputum, bit an officer, and laughed about it later); *Zule v. State,* (sufficient evidence that defendant transmitted virus to victim).

UNCONSTITUTIONAL VAGUENESS

Stark contends that this court should dismiss his convictions because RCW 9A.36.021(1)(e) is unconstitutionally vague. He contends that the statute does not define the prohibited conduct with sufficient specificity to put an ordinary citizen on notice as to what conduct he or she must avoid. Statutes that are susceptible to arbitrary and discriminatory enforcement are invalid. Criminal statutes must contain ascertainable standards for consistent adjudication.

To succeed on his claim, Stark must prove beyond a reasonable doubt that the statute is unconstitutionally vague, thereby defeating the presumption of constitutionality. This same burden applies on appeal when the review is de novo. If persons of common intelligence must necessarily guess at a statute's meaning and differ as to its application, the statute is unconstitutionally vague.

When a defendant asserts that a statute is unconstitutionally vague on its face, as opposed to vague as applied, the reviewing court must still look to the facts of the case before looking for hypothetically constitutional situations. If the defendant's conduct fits within the proscribed conduct of the statute, the defendant cannot assert other hypothetical applications of the law. *Worrell,* at 541.

"[I]mpossible standards of specificity are not required." "[A] statute is not unconstitutionally vague merely because a person cannot predict with complete certainty the exact point at which his actions would be classified as prohibited conduct." "'[I]f men of ordinary intelligence can understand a penal statute, *notwithstanding some possible areas of disagreement,* it is not wanting in certainty.'"

Where, as here, the statute requires proof of specific criminal intent, the remaining terms are less vague or indefinite than they might otherwise be considered. Moreover, because the assault statute does not implicate any First Amendment rights, Stark cannot claim the statute is facially vague; he may only argue that it is vague as applied to him. It is therefore irrelevant whether the statute gives adequate notice that the hypothetical conduct he describes is prohibited.

Stark complains that the statute "nowhere defines the term expose, nor does it state that it is a crime to transmit the HIV virus to another human being." No reasonably intelligent person would think the statute criminalizes the transmission of HIV to nonhumans. Stark's argument regarding the term "expose" is also unpersuasive. Any reasonably intelligent person would understand from reading the statute that the term refers to engaging in conduct that can cause another person to become infected with the virus. Stark engaged . . . . in unprotected sexual intercourse with other human beings after being counseled on several occasions that such conduct would expose his partners to the virus he carries. He was not forced to guess at what conduct was criminal.

Other Cases – Purposefully

See, Forrest v. State (see, Chapter Six)

Knowingly

The Model Penal Code mens rea of knowledge or knowingly requires that the individual be aware that a circumstance exists or that a result is practically certain to follow from his or her conduct. For example, in a case of receiving stolen property, if the statute requires knowledge, it suffices for the state to prove that the defendant is aware that there is a high probability that the property is stolen (he or she needs not be certain). States have taken different positions on whether willful ignorance satisfies the knowledge mens rea. *State v. Jantzi* demonstrates how difficult it can be for legislators to define and for jurors to apply the requisite mens rea (even when the fact-finder is a judge). *Perez-Castillo v. State* explores whether willful ignorance constitutes knowledge under Georgia law.

STATE v. JANTZI, 641 P.2d 62 (1982 Or.App.)

HISTORY
Pete Jantzi was convicted in the Circuit Court, Klamath County, of assault in the second degree, and he appealed. The Court of Appeals held that where defendant knew he had a dangerous weapon and that a confrontation was going to occur but he did not intend to stab victim, defendant acted "recklessly," not "knowingly," and, thus, could be convicted of assault in the third degree rather than assault in the second degree. Affirmed as modified; remanded for resentencing.

GILLETTE, J.
FACTS
Pete Jantzi, the defendant, testified and the trial court judge believed that he was asked to accompany Diane Anderson, who shared a house with defendant and several other people, to the home of her estranged husband, Rex. While Diane was in the house talking with Rex, defendant was using the blade of his knife to let the air out of the tires on Rex's van. Another person put sugar in the gas tank of the van.

While the Andersons were arguing, Diane apparently threatened damage to Rex's van and indicated that someone might be tampering with the van at that moment. Rex's roommate ran out of the house and saw two men beside the van. He shouted and began to run toward

the men. Rex ran from the house and began to chase defendant, who ran down a bicycle path. Defendant, still holding his open knife, jumped into the bushes beside the path and landed in the weeds. He crouched there, hoping that Rex would not see him and would pass by. Rex, however, jumped on top of defendant and grabbed his shirt. They rolled over and Rex was stabbed in the abdomen by defendant's knife. Defendant could not remember making a thrusting or swinging motion with the knife; he did not intend to stab Rex.

OPINION
The indictment charged that defendant "did unlawfully and knowingly cause physical injury to Rex Anderson by means of a deadly weapon, to-wit: knife, by stabbing the said Rex Anderson with said knife." ORS 163.175 provides that:

(1) A person commits the crime of assault in the second degree if he:
(b) Intentionally or knowingly causes physical injury to another by means of a deadly or dangerous weapon;

"Knowingly" is defined in ORS 161.085(8):

"Knowingly" or "with knowledge" when used with respect to conduct or to a circumstance described by a statute defining an offense, means that a person acts with an awareness that [his] conduct is of a nature so described or that a circumstance so described exists."

[The trial court continued:] "Basically, the facts of this case are: that Defendant was letting air out of the tires and he has an open knife. He was aware of what his knife is like. He is aware that it is a dangerous weapon. He runs up the bicycle path. He has a very firm grip on the knife, by his own admission, and he knows the knife is dangerous. It is not necessary for the state to prove that he thrust it or anything else. Quite frankly, this could have all been avoided if he had gotten rid of the knife, so he 'knowingly caused physical injury to Rex Anderson.' And, therefore, I find him guilty of that particular charge."

Although the trial judge found defendant guilty of "knowingly" causing physical injury to Anderson, what he described in his findings is recklessness. The court found that defendant knew he had a dangerous weapon and that a confrontation was going to occur. The court believed that defendant did not intend to stab Anderson. The court's conclusion seems to be based on the reasoning that because defendant knew it was possible that an injury would occur, he acted "knowingly." However, a person who "is aware of and consciously disregards a substantial and unjustifiable risk" that an injury will occur acts "recklessly," not "knowingly."

We have authority, pursuant to . . . the Oregon Constitution, to enter the judgment that should have been entered in the court below. Assault in the third degree is a lesser included offense of the crime of assault in the second degree charged in the accusatory instrument in this case. We modify defendant's conviction to a conviction for the crime of assault in the third degree.

PEREZ-CASTILLO v. STATE, 572 S.E.2d 657 (Ga. Ct. App. 2002)

BLACKBURN, Chief Judge.

Following a jury trial, Edwin Perez Castillo appeals his conviction for trafficking in more than fifty pounds of marijuana, contending in two related enumerations of error that the jury should not have been instructed to consider the doctrine of "deliberate ignorance" and, in the absence of this doctrine, the evidence was insufficient to support the verdict. For the reasons set forth below, we affirm.

[The] . . . record shows that, on September 17, 1997, California police intercepted two boxes from the mail containing approximately eighty-two pounds of marijuana. The boxes were addressed to a Bob Cliff residing at 692 Sheffield Road in Norcross, Georgia. California police then informed their counterparts in Norcross, Georgia, about the marijuana, and, on September 18, 1997, Norcross police took custody of the packages.

On September 19, 1997, Gwinnett County police made a controlled delivery of the packages. At the address listed on the boxes, Castillo answered the door. The undercover police officer announced that he had a package for Mr. Cliff, and Castillo responded, "Bob Cliff." Castillo then signed the name "Bob Cliff" in the appropriate box indicating acceptance of delivery and printed the name "Jose Resimos" in another area. Shortly after the delivery of the packages, Castillo was arrested while trying to drive away from the premises. The home was then searched, and the marijuana was recovered from the living room and the bathroom.

After questioning, Castillo admitted that he accepted the boxes for Wilfrido Escutia, who previously pled guilty to a trafficking charge. Castillo recounted that Escutia told him to use an American name to sign for the boxes. In addition, both Castillo and Escutia tracked the boxes while they were in transit, and, after the delivery, Castillo would meet Escutia in a public restroom at a department store to deliver the boxes. Following delivery, Castillo would meet Escutia at yet another location to be paid approximately $200 per box for accepting delivery.

Although Castillo stated that he did not know that the boxes contained contraband, he gave varying accounts about the contents to different people. At trial, he maintained at one point that he had no idea what was in the boxes. Then, he changed his testimony and said that he believed they contained videotapes containing English lessons. Prior to trial, however, he had told his sister that the packages contained coffee and leather goods sent to him by his mother from Mexico.

When asked, Castillo opined that he did not find anything suspicious about his arrangements with Escutia. He stated that he did not find it at all odd that Escutia paid him such a large sum to collect the packages, and he was not concerned about the furtive nature of their transactions.

This evidence was sufficient to support Castillo's conviction. OCGA § 16-13-31(c) provides: "Any person who knowingly sells, manufactures, grows, delivers, brings into this state, or has possession of a quantity of marijuana exceeding 50 pounds commits the offense of trafficking in marijuana." Castillo contends that his conviction was unwarranted because there was no evidence that he had any knowledge about the contents of the packages he accepted.

There was, however, circumstantial evidence upon which the jury could conclude that Castillo knew that he was accepting illegal contraband and remained deliberately ignorant of the exact contents of the packages. As the Eleventh Circuit Court of Appeals has pointed out:

Under ... binding precedent in this Circuit, the knowledge element of a violation of a criminal statute can be proved by demonstrating either actual knowledge or deliberate ignorance. This Court has consistently recognized deliberate ignorance of criminal activity as the equivalent of knowledge. The deliberate ignorance instruction is based on the alternative to the actual knowledge requirement at common law that if a party has his suspicions aroused but then deliberately omits to make further enquiries, because he wishes to remain in ignorance, he is deemed to have knowledge. Although we recognize that the delivery of

such an instruction is proper only in those comparatively rare cases where there are facts that point in the direction of deliberate ignorance, we are satisfied that there was sufficient evidence in this case to warrant an instruction on deliberate ignorance.

Castillo contends, nonetheless, that the trial court erred in charging the jury regarding his deliberate ignorance of the contents of the packages he accepted. "A deliberate ignorance instruction is appropriate when the facts support the inference that the defendant was aware of a high probability of the existence of the fact in question and purposely contrived to avoid learning all of the facts in order to have a defense in the event of a subsequent prosecution."

The trial court charged the jury:

The element of knowledge, intent, may be satisfied by inferences drawn from proof that a defendant deliberately closed his eyes to what would otherwise have been obvious to him. A finding beyond a reasonable doubt of conscious purpose to avoid enlightenment would permit an inference of knowledge. Stated another way, a defendant's knowledge of a fact may be inferred from willful blindness to the existence of the fact. Again, whether or not you draw any such inference is a matter solely within your discretion.

Castillo maintains that this instruction is faulty because it obviates the State's burden of proving that he had actual knowledge of the contents of the packages. This argument, however, is myopic. If we were to accept Castillo's argument, we would be granting protection to trafficking middlemen like Castillo, allowing them to escape prosecution simply by stating that they did not know the specific contents of the packages they were accepting, despite the obvious conclusion that they were dealing in contraband.

In this case, Castillo accepted packages for which he would not sign his own name. Indeed, he used two aliases when accepting them. Then, pursuant to his plans with Escutia, he delivered the packages covertly in a department store bathroom, and he had to wait to be paid hundreds of dollars for his courier services at yet another location. This is exactly the sort of deliberate ignorance of

undeniably shady transactions that should not be tolerated.

State v. Nations, 676 SW2d 282 (Mo. Ct. App. 1984)

FACTS:

Defendant, Sandra Nations, owns and operates the Main Street Disco, in which police officers found a scantily clad sixteen year old girl "dancing" for "tips". Consequently, defendant was charged with endangering the welfare of a child "less than seventeen years old," Defendant was convicted and fined $1,000.00. Defendant appeals. We reverse.

[D]efendant argues the state failed to show she knew the child was under seventeen and, therefore, failed to show she had the requisite intent to endanger the welfare of a child "less than seventeen years old." We agree.

The pertinent part of § 568.050 provides:

"1. A person commits the crime of endangering the welfare of a child if:

....

(2) He knowingly encourages, aids or causes a child less than seventeen years old to engage in any conduct which causes or tends to cause the child to come within the provisions of subdivision (1)(c) .. of section 211.031, RSMo ...."

...

§ 568.050 requires the state to prove the defendant "knowingly" encouraged a child "less than seventeen years old" to engage in conduct tending to injure the child's welfare, and "knowing" the child to be less than seventeen is a material element of the crime.

"Knowingly" is a term of art, whose meaning is limited to the definition given to it by our present Criminal Code. Literally read, the Code defines "knowingly" as actual knowledge. "A person `acts knowingly', or with knowledge, (1) with respect ... to attendant circumstances when he is aware ... that those circumstances exist ...." § 562.016.3. So read, this definition of "knowingly" or "knowledge" excludes those cases in which "the fact [in issue] would have been known had not the person wilfully `shut his eyes' in order to avoid

knowing." The Model Penal Code, the source of our Criminal Code, does not exclude these cases from its definition of "knowingly". Instead, the Model Penal Code proposes that "[w]hen knowledge of the *existence of a particular fact* is an element of an offense, such knowledge is established if a person is aware of a high probability of its existence ...." Model Penal Code § 2.02(7) (Proposed Official Draft 1962). This definition sounds more like a restatement of the definition of "recklessly" than "knowingly". The similarity is intentional. The Model Penal Code simply proposes that wilful blindness to a fact "be viewed as one of acting knowingly when what is involved is a matter of existing fact, but not when what is involved is the result of the defendant's conduct, necessarily a matter of the future at the time of acting." Thus, as noted, the Model Penal Code proposes that "[w]hen knowledge of the existence of a particular fact is an element of an offense, such knowledge is established if a person is aware of a high probability of its existence."

Our legislature, however, did not enact this proposed definition of "knowingly". Although the definitions of "knowingly" and "recklessly" in our Criminal Code are almost identical to the primary definitions of these terms as proposed in the Model Penal Code, the Model Penal Code's proposed expanded definition of "knowingly", encompassing wilful blindness of a fact, is absent from our Criminal Code. The sensible, if not compelling, inference is that our legislature rejected the expansion of the definition of "knowingly" to include wilful blindness of a fact and chose to limit the definition of "knowingly" to actual knowledge of the fact. Thus, in the instant case, the state's burden was to show defendant actually was aware the child was under seventeen, a heavier burden than showing there was a "high probability" that defendant was aware the child was under seventeen. In short, the state's burden was to prove defendant acted "knowingly", not just "recklessly". The state proved, however, that defendant acted "recklessly", not "knowingly".

. . .

The record shows that, at the time of the incident, the child was sixteen years old. When the police arrived, the child was "dancing" on stage for "tips" with another female. The police watched her dance for some five to seven minutes before approaching defendant in the service area of the bar. Believing that one of the girls appeared to be "young," the police questioned defendant about the child's age. Defendant told them that both girls were of legal age and that she had checked the girls' identification when she hired them. When the police questioned the child, she initially stated that she was eighteen but later admitted that she was only sixteen. She had no identification.

Aside from the child's age, these facts were established by the testimony of a police officer. The state also called the child as a witness. Her testimony was no help to the state. She testified the defendant asked her for identification just prior to the police arriving, and she was merely crossing the stage to get her identification when the police took her into custody. Nor can the state secure help from the defendant's testimony. She simply corroborated the child's testimony; i.e., she asked the child for her identification; the child replied she would "show it to [her] in a minute"; the police then took the child into custody.

These facts simply show defendant was untruthful. Defendant could not have checked the child's identification, because the child had no identification with her that day, the first day defendant "hired" the child. This does not prove that defendant knew the child was less than seventeen years old. At best, it proves defendant did not know or refused to learn the child's age. The latter is the best case for the state. But defendant's refusal to learn the age of this "young" child who was "dancing" "scantily clad" in her disco bar simply proves that defendant was "aware of a high probability" that the child was under seventeen, or, stated otherwise, in the definitional language of our Criminal Code, proves that defendant was conscious of "a substantial and unjustifiable risk" that the child was under seventeen and that defendant's disregard of the risk was a "gross deviation" from the norm. *See* § 562.016.4. This, however, is not "knowledge" under our Criminal Code. It is "recklessness", nothing more. Having failed to prove defendant knew the child's age was less than seventeen, the state failed to make a submissible case.

Recklessly:

Most states follow the MPC and hold that recklessness involves consciously disregarding a known and substantial risk when doing so is a gross deviation of the standard of conduct of a law-abiding person under the same circumstances. The factfinder will have to consider whether the defendant knew of the risk, consciously disregarded the risk, and whether in doing so, really acted quite a bit differently than others would under those same circumstances.

PEOPLE v. BAKER,
NY Slip Op 00623 (2004)

ROSE, J.

After a three-year-old child died while defendant was babysitting in the child's home, she was charged with both intentional and depraved indifference murder. At trial, the evidence established that, on a warm summer night, the victim died of hyperthermia as a result of her prolonged exposure to excessive heat in a bedroom of her foster parents' apartment. The excessive heat was caused by the furnace having run constantly for many hours as the result of a short circuit in its wiring. The victim was unable to leave her bedroom because defendant engaged the hook and eye latch on its door after putting her to bed for the night. Defendant then remained in the apartment watching television while the furnace ran uncontrollably. The victim's foster parents and another tenant testified that when they returned in the early morning hours and found the victim lifeless in her bed, the living room of the apartment where defendant sat waiting for them felt extremely hot, like an oven or a sauna, and the victim's bedroom was even hotter. Temperature readings taken later that morning during a police investigation while the furnace was still running indicated that the apartment's living room was 102 degrees Fahrenheit, the victim's bedroom was 110 degrees Fahrenheit and the air coming from the vent in the bedroom was more than 130 degrees Fahrenheit.

In characterizing defendant's role in these events, the prosecutor argued that the key issue for the jury was whether or not defendant had intended to kill the victim. The prosecution's proof on this issue consisted primarily of the second of two written statements given by defendant to police during a four-hour interview conducted a few hours after the victim was found. In the first statement, defendant related that she had been aware of the oppressive heat in the victim's bedroom, kept the victim latched in because the foster parents had instructed her to do so, had not looked at or adjusted the thermostat even though the furnace was running on a hot day, heard the victim kicking and screaming to be let out and felt the adverse effects of the heat on herself. The second statement, which defendant disavowed at trial, described her intent to cause the victim's death by turning up the thermostat to its maximum setting, closing all heating vents except the one in the victim's bedroom and placing additional clothing on the victim which she then removed after the victim died. Because these actions differed from those described in the first statement and each reflects an intent to kill the victim, the jurors' initial task, as proposed by the prosecutor during summation, was to decide which statement they would accept.

After trial, the jury acquitted defendant of intentional murder . . . and instead convicted her of depraved indifference murder of a child. County Court sentenced her to a prison term of 15 years to life, and she now appeals.

Initially, we are unpersuaded that the prosecutor's summation improperly impugned defendant's credibility. Given the contradictions between defendant's testimony disavowing her second statement and the testimony of the officer who prepared that statement, the prosecutor's portrayal of the issue for the jury as being whether defendant or the police officer had lied represents a fair commentary on the evidence. … In any event, defendant demonstrated no resulting prejudice as the jury acquitted her of the intentional murder charge founded upon the second statement. …

We agree with defendant, however, that the evidence in the record is legally insufficient to prove the gross recklessness and additional aggravating circumstances necessary for a conviction of depraved indifference murder. In our view, the jury could not reasonably infer from the evidence a culpable mental state greater than criminal negligence due to the unique combination of events that led to the victim's death, as well as the lack of proof that defendant actually perceived and ignored an obvious and severe risk of serious injury or death.

A verdict is supported by legally sufficient evidence when the proof, viewed in the light most favorable to the prosecution, establishes the elements of the crime beyond a reasonable doubt. Here, County Court instructed the jury as to the elements of intentional murder in the second degree, depraved indifference murder in the second degree, as well as the lesser included offenses of manslaughter in the first degree with intent to cause physical injury, reckless manslaughter in the second degree and criminally negligent homicide. The jury's finding that defendant was not guilty of intentional murder clearly indicates that it rejected defendant's second statement. That statement contains an explicit admission of an intent to kill the victim and a description of a series of acts reflecting such an intent. Inasmuch as there is no other evidence, and no argument, that these acts were done for any other purpose, we must assume that the jury rejected the acts when it rejected the charge of intentional murder. Thus, we look elsewhere in the record to ascertain whether there is other evidence establishing first, that the circumstances surrounding defendant's conduct evince a depraved indifference to human life, and second, that defendant perceived and disregarded a substantial risk of serious injury or death.

To support defendant's conviction of depraved indifference murder of a child, there must be proof that, "based on an objective assessment of the risk defendant recklessly created and disregarded, the likelihood of causing [serious physical injury or] death from defendant's conduct was so obviously severe that it evinced a depraved indifference to human life" … . Although the excessive heat in the victim's bedroom ultimately proved fatal and defendant failed to provide relief from the heat by removing the victim from her bedroom or attempting to reduce the heat, the evidence does not establish that her acts and omissions were "committed under circumstances which evidenced a wanton indifference to human life or a depravity of mind"... . "Illustrative of such conduct is driving an automobile on a city sidewalk at an excessive speed and striking a pedestrian without applying the brakes, firing several bullets into a house, beating an infant over a five-day period, and placing a bomb in a public place. In each illustration the basic crime was aggravated by additional egregious conduct" ... . In cases where the victim is a child, there typically are one or more instances of direct harmful contact with the child, as well as other egregious conduct (*see People v Mills*, [adult struck 12-year-old victim from behind hard enough to cause him to hit his head on a concrete pier and slip off the pier into the water, and then abandoned the submerged victim without summoning help]; *People v Strawbridge* [mother dropped her newborn child into a toilet, placed her in a plastic bag causing death by asphyxiation and disposed of her body in a dumpster]; *People v Mitchell* [mother repeatedly struck infant daughter's head against a wall causing skull fractures and did not call for emergency aid until several hours later]; *People v Dexheimer*, [adult repeatedly struck young child and failed to summon emergency aid]; *People v Bryce*, [father violently shook infant son and inflicted multiple impacts causing severe head trauma]; *cf. People v Sika*, [mother's failure to provide adequate nourishment and seek medical assistance for infant son was held not to be "so brutal, callous or wanton that it evinced a depraved indifference to human life"]). Here, by contrast, there was neither obviously dangerous conduct by defendant nor harmful physical contact between defendant and the victim.

In addition to the lack of physical contact, there is no evidence that defendant knew the actual temperature in any portion of the apartment or subjectively perceived a degree of heat that would have made her aware that serious injury or death from hyperthermia would almost certainly result. Put another way, the risk of serious physical injury or death was not so obvious under the circumstances that it demonstrated defendant's actual awareness.

There was only circumstantial evidence on this point consisting of the subjective perceptions of other persons who later came into the apartment from cooler outside temperatures. Defendant, who had been in the apartment as the heat gradually intensified over many hours, and who was described by others as appearing flushed and acting dazed, could not reasonably be presumed to have had the same perception of oppressive and dangerous heat. Rather, defendant testified that she knew only that the heat made her feel dizzy and uncomfortable, and denied any awareness of a risk of death. Most significantly, there is no dispute that defendant remained in a room that was nearly as hot as the victim's bedroom for approximately nine hours and checked on the victim several times before the foster parents returned. This evidence of defendant's failure to perceive the risk of serious injury stands unrefuted by the prosecution.

Defendant's ability to appreciate such a risk was further brought into doubt by the prosecution's own expert witness, who described her as having borderline intellectual function, learning disabilities and a full-scale IQ of only 73. We also note that here, unlike where an unclothed child is shut outside in freezing temperatures, the circumstances are not of a type from which it can be inferred without a doubt that a person of even ordinary intelligence and experience would have perceived a severe risk of serious injury or death.

...[W]e find that defendant's conduct was not proven to have been "so wanton, so deficient in a moral sense of concern, so devoid of regard of the life or lives of others, and so blameworthy as to warrant the same criminal liability as that which the law imposes upon a person who intentionally causes the death of another". ... Accordingly, no valid line of reasoning and permissible inferences could have led the jury to the conclusion that it reached.

We turn next to the issue of whether the record evidence establishes, beyond a reasonable doubt, one or more lesser included offenses. As to manslaughter in the first degree, there is no proof, other than defendant's discredited second statement, that she intentionally caused "serious physical injury" or "physical injury".

As to the lesser included offenses of manslaughter in the second degree and criminally negligent homicide, we must compare the requisite culpable mental states. A person is guilty of manslaughter in the second degree when he or she recklessly causes the death of another person and of criminally negligent homicide when, with criminal negligence, he or she causes the death of another person. Reckless criminal conduct occurs when the actor is aware of and consciously disregards a substantial and unjustifiable risk, and criminal negligence is the failure to perceive such a risk.

As we have noted, there is no support for a finding that defendant perceived and consciously disregarded the risk of death which was created by the combination of the "runaway" furnace and her failure to release the victim from her bedroom. None of defendant's proven conduct reflects such an awareness and the fact that she subjected herself to the excessive heat is plainly inconsistent with a finding that she perceived a risk of death.

However, the evidence was sufficient to establish defendant's guilt beyond a reasonable doubt of criminally negligent homicide. A jury could reasonably conclude from the evidence that defendant *should* have perceived a substantial and unjustifiable risk that the excessive heat, in combination with her inaction, would be likely to lead to the victim's death. Since defendant was the victim's caretaker, this risk was of such a nature that her failure to perceive it constituted a gross deviation from the standard of care that a reasonable person in the same circumstances would observe in such a situation. Thus, defendant's conduct was shown to constitute criminal negligence and such a finding would not be against the weight of the evidence. Accordingly, we reduce the conviction from depraved indifference murder to criminally negligent homicide and remit the matter to County Court for sentencing on the reduced charge.

Hraniky v. State
12-00-431-CR (Tex Crim App, 2005)

Relevant Facts: A newspaper advertisement offering tiger cubs for sale caught the eye of eight-year-old Lauren Villafana. She decided she wanted one. She expressed her wish to her mother, Kelly Dean Hranicky, and to Hranicky, her stepfather.

Over the next year, the Hranickys investigated the idea by researching written materials on the subject and consulting with owners of exotic animals. They visited tiger owner and handler Mickey Sapp several times. They decided to buy two rare tiger cubs from him, a male and a female whose breed is endangered in the wild. They brought the female cub home first, then the male about a month later.

Sapp trained Hranicky in how to care for and handle the animals. In particular, he demonstrated the risk adult tigers pose for children. Sapp escorted Hranicky, Kelly Hranicky, and Lauren past Sapp's tiger cages. He told the family to watch the tigers' focus of attention. The tigers' eyes followed Lauren as she walked up and down beside the cages. The Hranickys raised the cubs inside their home until they were six or eight months old. Then they moved the cubs out of the house, at first to an enclosed porch in the back and ultimately to a cage Hranicky built in the yard.

The tigers matured into adolescence. The male reached 250 pounds, the female slightly less. Lauren actively helped Hranicky care for the animals. By June 6, 1999, the tigers were two years old. Lauren was ten. She stood 57 inches tall and weighed 80 pounds. At dusk that evening, Lauren joined Hranicky in the tiger cage. Suddenly, the male tiger attacked her. It mauled the child's throat, breaking her neck and severing her spinal cord. She died instantly.

The record reflects four different versions of the events that led to Lauren's death. Hranicky told the grand jury Lauren and he were sitting side-by-side in the cage about 8:00 p.m., petting the female tiger. A neighbor's billy goat cried out. The noise attracted the male tiger's attention. He turned toward the sound. The cry also caught Lauren's attention. She stood and looked at the male tiger. When Lauren turned her head toward the male tiger, "that was too much," Hranicky told the grand jury. The tiger attacked. Hranicky yelled. The tiger grabbed Lauren by the throat and dragged her across the cage into a water trough. Hranicky ran after them. He struck the tiger on the head and held him under the water. The tiger released the child.

Kelly Dean Hranicky testified she was asleep when the incident occurred. She called for emergency assistance. Through testimony developed at trial, she told the dispatcher her daughter had fallen from a fence. She testified she did not remember giving that information to the dispatcher. However, police officer Daniel Torres, who responded to the call, testified he was told that a little girl had cut her neck on a fence. Hranicky gave Torres a verbal statement that evening.

Torres testified Hranicky told him that he had been grooming the female tiger. He asked Lauren to come and get the brush from him. Lauren came into the cage and grabbed the brush. Hranicky thought she had left the cage because he heard the cage door close. Then, however, Hranicky saw Lauren's hand "come over and start grooming the female, start petting the female cat, and that's when the male cat jumped over." The tiger grabbed the child by the neck and started running through the cage. It dragged her into the water trough. Hranicky began punching the tiger in the head, trying to get the tiger to release Lauren.

Justice of the Peace James Dawson performed an inquest at the scene of the incident. Judge Dawson testified Hranicky gave him an oral statement also. Hranicky told him Lauren went to the cage on a regular basis and groomed only the female tiger. He then corrected himself to say she actually petted the animal. Hranicky was "very clear about the difference between grooming and petting." Hranicky maintained that Lauren never petted or groomed the male tiger. Hranicky told Dawson that Lauren asked permission to enter the cage that evening, saying "Daddy, can I come in?" Sapp, the exotic animal owner who sold the Hranickys the tigers, testified Hranicky told him yet another version of the events that night. When Sapp asked Hranicky how it happened, Hranicky

replied, "Well, Mickey, she just snuck in behind me."

On the day of Hranicky's grand jury testimony, Hranicky admitted to Sapp he had allowed Lauren to enter the cage. Hranicky told Sapp he had lied because he did not want Sapp to be angry with him. Hranicky told the grand jury that Sapp and other knowledgeable sources had said "there was no problem in taking a child in the cage." He did learn children were especially vulnerable because the tigers would view them as prey. However, Hranicky told the grand jury, he thought the tigers would view Lauren differently than they would an unfamiliar child. He believed the tigers would not attack her, he testified. They would see her as "one of the family." Hranicky also told the grand jury the tigers' veterinarian allowed his young son into the Hranickys' tiger cage.

Several witnesses at trial contradicted Hranicky's assessment of the level of risk the tigers presented, particularly to children. Sapp said he told the Hranickys it was safe for children to play with tiger cubs. However, once the animals reached forty to fifty pounds, they should be confined in a cage and segregated from any children. "[T]hat's enough with Lauren, any child, because they play rough, they just play rough." Sapp further testified he told the Hranickys to keep Lauren away from the tigers at that point because the animals would view the child as prey. He also said he told Lauren directly not to get in the cage with the tigers. Sapp did not distinguish between children who were strangers to the tigers and those who had helped raise the animals. He described any such distinction as "ludicrous." In fact, Sapp testified, his own two children had been around large cats all of their lives. Nonetheless, he did not allow them within six feet of the cages. The risk is too great, he told the jury. The Hranickys did not tell him that purchasing the tigers was Lauren's idea. Had he known, he testified, "that would have been the end of the conversation. This was not for children." He denied telling Hranicky that it was safe for Lauren to be in the cage with the tigers.

Charles Currer, an animal care inspector for the United States Department of Agriculture, met Hranicky when Hranicky applied for a USDA license to exhibit the tigers. Currer also denied telling Hranicky it was permissible to let a child enter a tiger's cage. He recalled giving his standard speech about the danger big cats pose to children, telling him that they "see children as prey, as things to play with." On his USDA application form, Hranicky listed several books he had read on animal handling. One book warned that working with exotic cats is very dangerous. It emphasized that adolescent males are particularly volatile as they mature and begin asserting their dominance. Big cat handlers should expect to get jumped, bit, and challenged at every juncture. Another of the listed books pointed out that tigers give little or no warning when they attack. The book cautioned against keeping large cats such as tigers as pets.

Veterinarian Dr. Hampton McAda testified he worked with the Hranickys' tigers from the time they were six weeks old until about a month before the incident. McAda denied ever allowing his son into the tigers' cage. All large animals present some risk, he testified. He recalled telling Hranicky that "wild animals and female menstrual periods . . . could cause a problem down the road" once both the animals and Lauren matured. Hranicky seemed more aware of the male tiger, the veterinarian observed, and was more careful with him than with the female.

Robert Evans, the Curator of Mammals at the San Antonio Zoo, testified that it is zoo policy to enter a tiger's cage only after anesthetizing the animal. Otherwise, entering the cage is too dangerous. However, Evans conceded on cross-examination, these zoo policies are not known to the general public.

James Boller, the Chief Cruelty Investigator for the Houston SPCA, testified that tigers, even those raised in captivity, are wild animals that act from instinct. Anyone who enters a cage with a conscious adult tiger should bring a prop to use as a deterrent. Never take one's eyes off the tiger, Evans told the jury. Never make oneself appear weak and vulnerable by diminishing one's size by crouching or sitting. Never bring a child into a tiger cage. The danger increases when the tigers are in adolescence, which begins as early as two years of age for captive tigers. Entering a cage with

more than one tiger increases the risk. Entering with more than one person increases the risk further. Entering with a child increases the risk even more. Tigers' activity level depends on the time of day, Boller told the jury. They tend to be more active during the early morning, twilight, and late evening. Thus, the time of day one enters a cage also can increase the risk factor. Boller identified eight o'clock on a summer evening as a high activity time. A child should never enter a tiger cage in the first place, Boller testified. Taking a child into a tiger cage "during a high activity time for the animal is going to increase your risk dramatically."

Dr. Richard Villafana, Lauren's biological father, told the jury he first learned of the tigers when his daughter told him over the phone she had a surprise to show him at their next visit. When he came to pick her up the following weekend, he testified, she took him into the house and showed him the female cub. Villafana described his reaction as "horror and generalized upset and dismay, any negative term you care to choose." He immediately decided to speak to Kelly Hranicky about the situation. He did not do so in front of Lauren, however, in an effort to avoid a "big argument." Villafana testified he later discussed the tigers with Kelly Hranicky, who assured him Lauren was safe. Villafana "always had lingering doubts," however. He did not learn of the second tiger until a month or two after he saw the first one. The jury heard that Villafana was not comfortable around either animal, but that he had a "little bit more fear" of the male than the female, as "the male tiger seemed much more aggressive or excitable." As the tigers matured, no one told Villafana the Hranickys allowed Lauren in the cage with them. Had he known, he "would have talked to Kelly again" and "would have told her that [he] was greatly opposed to it and would have begged and pleaded with her not to allow her in there." He spoke to his daughter about his concerns about the tigers "almost every time" he saw her. Kelly Hranicky told the jury Lauren was a very obedient child. Villafana agreed. Lauren would not have gone into the tiger cage that evening without Hranicky's permission.

An accused is entitled to notice of the acts or omissions the State alleges the accused committed. When recklessness is an element of an offense, the charging instrument must allege, with reasonable certainty, the acts relied on to constitute recklessness. Article 21.15 imposes two requirements on a charging instrument alleging reckless misconduct. First, the indictment must allege the act or acts relied on to constitute the forbidden conduct committed with recklessness. Second, the indictment must allege the acts or circumstances relied on to demonstrate that the forbidden conduct was committed in a reckless manner. "[I]n no event shall it be sufficient to allege merely that the accused, in committing the offense, acted recklessly or with criminal negligence." Here, the amended indictment alleged what acts constituted the forbidden conduct by alleging the acts of:

> asking and directing her to assist [him] in the cage, and by nodding his head in the affirmative when [she] requested to enter the cage, and by verbally giving [her] permission to enter the cage, and by walking towards [her] to make sure a tiger did not go into the containment area and closed the door after she entered the cage.

We find that the indictment, as amended, alleged acts the State relied on to constitute the forbidden conduct Hranicky committed with recklessness. Further, the amended indictment alleged not merely that Hranicky acted recklessly in causing serious bodily injury to the child, but that he did so by allowing her to "enter a cage occupied by two (2) tigers." We also find that the indictment, as amended, gave sufficient notice to Hranicky of the reckless manner in which he engaged in the prohibited conduct.

c. Act or Omission

An "act" is "a bodily movement, whether voluntary or involuntary and includes speech." An "omission" is a failure to act. For his proposition that the indictment charges an omission and not an act and is therefore fatally defective, Hranicky relies on *Herring v. State*. The State charged the accused in Herring with "allowing" another man to touch his genitals. The court of appeals found that the charging instrument charged the accused with not preventing the touching. Since not preventing the touching is not an offense, the allegations

did not charge a penal offense. *Herring v. State*. Here, the State did not charge Hranicky with failing to prevent Lauren's entry into the tiger cage. As amended, the indictment charged Hranicky with acts that granted Lauren access to the cage. The appellants in *Hill v. State* made an argument similar to Hranicky's. The State charged the Hills, parents of a 13-year-old boy, with intentional injury to a child by omission. At trial, the State proved they kept their son chained up and denied him food as punishment. The son eventually starved to death. On appeal, the Hills asserted that the State charged an omission but proved only their actions. The court of appeals disagreed, characterizing the "appellant's argument [as] simply a battle waged in semantics." Even though the evidence "may have been sufficient to support a conviction for injury to a child by actions," the *Hill* court concluded, "it does not prevent the State from establishing the offense of injury to a child by omission." The State proved that the Hills acted in restraining their child and also failed to act by not providing adequate nourishment. Applying the rationale of *Hill* to this case, the State had the option of choosing whether to charge Hranicky with injury to a child by act or omission. While there may be sufficient evidence to support a conviction of injury to a child by omission, it does not prevent the State from establishing the offense of injury to a child by action. Thus, while Hranicky might have failed to act by not preventing Lauren's entry into the tiger cage, he also acted by asking her to assist him in the cage, or by affirmatively giving her permission to enter the cage by either nodding his head, verbally granting entry, or by closing the gate after Lauren entered the cage. We conclude that the indictment, as amended, charged Hranicky with reckless acts, not an omission.

Accordingly, it was unnecessary for the State to allege Hranicky had a duty to act. . . . Finally, we note that the amended indictment substantially tracks the language of section 22.04 of the penal code. Alternate pleading of the differing methods of committing an offense may be charged in one indictment. We find that the amended indictment was sufficient to apprise Hranicky of the offense with which he was charged. We also find that the amended indictment set forth in plain and intelligible language sufficient information to enable

Hranicky to prepare his defense. …

…

III. SUFFICIENCY ANALYSES
… Hranicky challenges the legal and factual sufficiency of the evidence to support his conviction.

A. Legal-Sufficiency Analysis 1. Legal-Sufficiency Standard and Scope of Review A legal-sufficiency challenge calls for appellate review of the relevant evidence in the light most favorable to the prosecution. … Similarly, in reviewing the legal sufficiency of the evidence, we look to all of the evidence introduced during either stage of the trial. Legal sufficiency in this case is measured against the elements of the offense as defined by a hypothetically correct jury charge for the case. …

2. The Hypothetically Correct Jury Charge One of the ways a person commits injury to a child is by recklessly or with criminal negligence, by act, causing a child serious bodily injury. Therefore, the hypothetically correct jury charge for this case, as modified by the amended indictment, would ask the jury if Hranicky: (1) recklessly or with criminal negligence, (2) asked or directed Lauren to assist him in the cage, or (3) nodded his head in the affirmative when Lauren requested to enter the cage, or (4) verbally gave Lauren permission to enter the cage, (5) wherein one of the tigers did attack Lauren by biting her about the neck with its mouth; (6) causing serious bodily injury to Lauren. Injury to a child is a "result-oriented" or "result of conduct" offense. … Therefore, the culpable mental state relates to the result of the conduct and not to the nature or the circumstances surrounding the conduct. The definitions in the hypothetically correct jury charge in this case concerning the applicable culpable mental state should be limited to the result of the conduct, rather than the nature or the circumstances surrounding the conduct. A person acts recklessly with respect to the result of conduct when the person is "aware of but consciously disregards a substantial and unjustifiable risk" the result will occur. Further, "the risk must be of such a nature and degree that its disregard constitutes a gross deviation from the standard of care that an ordinary person would exercise under all

the circumstances as viewed from the actor's standpoint." Criminal responsibility arises if the result would not have occurred but for the conduct, "operating either alone or concurrently with another cause, unless the concurrent cause was clearly sufficient to produce the result and the conduct of the actor clearly insufficient." For a concurrent cause to excuse liability, the accused's conduct must be clearly insufficient, by itself, to produce the result. Further, the concurrent cause must be clearly sufficient, by itself, to produce the result. A fact finder may infer the accused's mental state from the acts, words, and conduct of the accused and from the circumstances surrounding the acts in which the accused engaged. An accused rarely facilitates conviction by admitting to the requisite intent or knowledge. It seldom is possible to prove by direct evidence what an accused intended or knew at the time of the incident. Thus, the fact finder usually must infer intent and knowledge from circumstantial evidence rather than direct proof. Further, the fact finder may draw an inference of guilt from the accused's acts, words, and conduct before, during, and after the incident … In his second issue, Hranicky challenges the sufficiency of the evidence on legal-sufficiency grounds. With a hypothetically correct jury charge in mind that reflects the correct instructions and elements of the offense as modified by the indictment, we turn to our legal-sufficiency analysis.

3. Measuring the Legal Sufficiency of the Evidence against the Hypothetically Correct Jury Charge

Hranicky focuses his legal-sufficiency argument on causation. He contends that the tiger's attack was a concurrent cause sufficient by itself to produce the result. Conviction of a result-oriented offense cannot be based solely on a finding that the accused intentionally or knowingly engaged in conduct that happened to cause the result. …
Instead, "what matters is that the conduct (whatever it may be) is done with the required culpability to effect the result the legislature has specified." With a result-oriented offense, a person is criminally responsible if the result would not have occurred "but for" the actor's conduct. "But for" causation can be established in two ways: (1) when the accused's conduct is clearly sufficient to produce the result; or (2)

when the accused's conduct plus another cause is sufficient to produce the result. Hranicky relies on Patterson, which states that convictions cannot stand merely because a defendant is associated with the actual perpetrator of a crime.

In Patterson, the defendant's boyfriend kidnapped her children and murdered one of them. The defendant delayed notifying authorities and withheld her suspicion that her boyfriend had taken them. She was convicted of knowingly causing injury to a child by omission for failing to aid and protect her children while they were being kidnapped, for failing to report to law enforcement authorities and summon aid immediately when she knew the children had been kidnapped, or for failing to report to the authorities that her boyfriend had kidnapped the children. The appellate court reduced her conviction to that of reckless injury to a child after finding there was no evidence that she knew "to a reasonable certainty that she could stop [the boyfriend] and thus prevent injury to the children." We first distinguish Patterson by noting that the State had charged the accused in that case with an omission. Further, the State charged her with intentional injury to a child, not recklessness. The facts of this case present a circumstance more like that in Traxler. There, the accused kept, at a home occupied by a child, a dog known to be vicious and dangerous to humans. The dog bit the child about the head and neck. The defendant was found guilty of reckless injury to a child. In one of his issues on appeal, he contended that his conduct was insufficient to produce the injuries. The court of appeals overruled his causation issue, holding that an animate object, such as a dog, could be the manner and means for accomplishing an assault. Applying Traxler to the facts of this case, a tiger, like a dog, is an animate creature that could be the manner and means for accomplishing injury to a child. As with the defendant in Traxler, Hranicky was aware of the risk. The dog was known to be dangerous to humans; the tiger was known to view children as prey. Accordingly, we find that Hranicky's actions, in conjunction with the tiger, were the "but for" causes of Lauren's death. Viewing the evidence in the light most favorable to the State, we conclude that any rational trier of fact could have found beyond a

reasonable doubt that Hranicky caused Lauren's death. Accordingly, we hold the evidence legally sufficient to support Hranicky's conviction for reckless injury to a child.

B. Factual-Sufficiency Analysis 1. Factual-Sufficiency Standard and Scope of Review

. . . When an appellant challenges the factual sufficiency of the elements of the offense, we ask whether "a neutral review of all the evidence . . . demonstrates that the proof of guilt is so obviously weak as to undermine confidence in the jury's determination, or the proof of guilt, although adequate if taken alone, is greatly outweighed by contrary proof." . . .

2. Measuring the Factual Sufficiency of the Evidence against the Hypothetically Correct Jury Charge a. The Main Factual-Sufficiency Arguments
Hranicky . . . raises the issue of intent, arguing that his conduct does not represent a gross deviation from the standard of care.

(1) Awareness of Risk

Viewing all the evidence neutrally, favoring neither the prosecution nor Hranicky, in addition to the evidence analyzed in our legal-sufficiency analysis, the record reflects that each of the witnesses who came into contact with Hranicky in connection with the tigers testified they told him that: (1) large cats, even those raised in captivity, are dangerous, unpredictable wild animals; and (2) children were particularly at risk from adolescent and adult tigers, especially males. Expert animal handlers whom Hranicky consulted and written materials he claimed to have read warned Hranicky that the risks increased with adolescent male tigers, with more than one person in the cage, with more than one tiger in the cage, at dusk during the animals' heightened activity period, and when diminishing one's size by sitting or crouching on the ground. They each cautioned that tigers attack swiftly, without warning, and are powerful predators. Further, Hranicky's initial story to Sapp that Lauren had sneaked into the cage evidences Hranicky's awareness of the risk. The jury also could have inferred his awareness of the risk when he concealed from

Sapp that the family was purchasing the tigers for Lauren. The jury also could have inferred Hranicky's consciousness of guilt when he gave several different versions of what happened. On the other hand, the record shows that before buying the tigers, Hranicky researched the subject and conferred with professionals. He received training in handling the animals. Further, Kelly Hranicky testified she also understood the warnings about not allowing children in the tiger cage to apply to strangers, not to Lauren. Hranicky told the grand jury he did not think the warnings applied to children, like Lauren, who had helped raise the animal. He said he had seen other handlers, including Sapp and McAda, permit Lauren and other children to go into tiger cages. He testified Currer told him it was safe to permit children in tiger cages. Further, while the State's witness described zoo policies for handling tigers, those policies were not known to the general public. Finally, none of the significant figures in Lauren's life fully appreciated the danger the tigers posed for Lauren. Hranicky was not alone in not perceiving the risk.

(2) Substantial and Unjustifiable Risk and Gross Deviation from the Standard of Care

Hranicky testified to the grand jury he did not view the risk to be substantial because he thought the tigers were domesticated and had bonded with the family. He claimed not to have any awareness of any risk. The tigers were acting normally. Lauren had entered the cage numerous times to pet the tigers with no incident. Further, he asserted, other than a minor scratch by the male as a cub, the tigers had never harmed anyone. Thus, he argues, he had no knowledge of any risk. Viewing all the evidence neutrally, favoring neither Hranicky nor the State, we find that proof of Hranicky's guilt of reckless injury to a child is not so obviously weak as to undermine confidence in the jury's determination.

Negligently

Negligence involves engaging in harmful behavior while being unaware of the risk that a reasonable person would have been aware of. It isn't always easy to prove that a person was aware of the risk. The case of *Koppersmith v. State*, explores the differences between reckless and negligent behavior. Both involve behavior that is a gross deviation from the standard of care of a reasonable person.

KOPPERSMITH v. STATE, 742 So.2d 206 (Ala. App. 1999)

HISTORY
Gregory Koppersmith, the appellant, was charged with the murder of his wife, Cynthia ("Cindy") Michel Koppersmith. He was convicted of reckless manslaughter, and the trial court sentenced him to 20 years in prison. The Alabama Court of Appeals reversed and remanded.

FACTS
Gregory Koppersmith (appellant) and his wife were arguing in the yard outside of their residence. Cindy tried to enter the house to end the argument, but Greg prevented her from going inside. A physical confrontation ensued, and Cindy fell off of a porch into the yard. She died as a result of a skull fracture to the back of her head.

In a statement he made to law enforcement officials after the incident, the appellant gave the following summary of the events leading up to Cindy's death. He and Cindy had been arguing and were on a porch outside of their residence. Cindy had wanted to go inside the house, but he had wanted to resolve the argument first. As she tried to go inside, he stepped in front of her and pushed her back. Cindy punched at him, and he grabbed her.

When Cindy tried to go inside again, he wrapped his arms around her from behind to stop her. Cindy bit him on the arm, and he "slung" her to the ground. He then jumped down and straddled her, stating that he "had her by the head" and indicating that he moved her head up and down, as if slamming it into the ground. When Cindy stopped struggling, he rolled her over and found a brick covered with blood under her head. The appellant stated that, although Cindy fell near a flowerbed, he did not know there were bricks in the grass.

At trial, Greg testified that Cindy had tried to go into the house two or three times, but he had stopped her from doing so. During that time, she punched at him and he pushed her away from him. At one point, he put his arms around her from behind to restrain her, and she turned her head and bit him. When she bit him, he pulled her by her sweater and she tripped. He then "slung" her off of him, and she tripped and fell three to four feet to the ground. He jumped off of the porch and straddled her, grabbing her by the shoulders and telling her to calm down. When he realized she was not moving, he lifted her head and noticed blood all over his hands.

Greg testified that, when he grabbed Cindy from behind, he did not intend to harm her. He also testified that, when he "slung" her away from him off of the porch, he was not trying to hurt her and did not intend to throw her onto a brick. Rather, he stated that he simply reacted after she bit his arm. He also testified that he did not know there were bricks in the yard, that he had not attempted to throw her in a particular direction, and that he was not aware of any risk or harm his actions might cause.

Greg further testified that, when he grabbed and shook her after she fell, he did not intend to harm her, he did not know there was a brick under her head, and he did not intend to hit her head on a brick or anything else. Instead, he testified that he was trying to get her to calm down.

The medical examiner, Dr. Gregory Wanger, testified that the pattern on the injury to the victim's skull matched the pattern on one of the bricks found at the scene. He stated that, based on the position of the skull fracture and the bruising to the victim's brain, the victim's head was moving when it sustained the injury. He testified that her injuries could have been caused by her falling off of the porch and hitting her head on a brick or from her head being slammed into a brick.

The indictment in this case alleged that the appellant "did, with the intent to cause the death of Cynthia Michel Koppersmith, cause the death of Cynthia Michel Koppersmith, by striking her head against a brick, in violation of § 13A-6-2 of the Code of Alabama. (C.R.11)." Koppersmith requested that the trial court instruct the jury on criminally negligent homicide as a lesser included offense of murder. However, the trial court denied that request, and it instructed the jury only on the offense of reckless manslaughter.

OPINION

[Alabama law]… provides that a person commits the crime of manslaughter if he recklessly causes the death of another person. A person acts recklessly with respect to a result or to a circumstance described by a statute defining an offense when he is aware of and consciously disregards a substantial and unjustifiable risk that the result will occur or that the circumstance exists. The risk must be of such nature and degree that disregard thereof constitutes a gross deviation from the standard of conduct that a reasonable person would observe in the situation.

"A person commits the crime of criminally negligent homicide if he causes the death of another person by criminal negligence." A person acts with criminal negligence with respect to a result or to a circumstance which is defined by statute as an offense when he fails to perceive a substantial and unjustifiable risk that the result will occur or that the circumstance exists. The risk must be of such nature and degree that the failure to perceive it constitutes a gross deviation from the standard of care that a reasonable person would observe in the situation. A court or jury may consider statutes or ordinances regulating the defendant's conduct as bearing upon the question of criminal negligence.

The only difference between manslaughter under Section 13A-6-3(a)(1) and criminally negligent homicide is the difference between recklessness and criminal negligence. The reckless offender is aware of the risk and "consciously disregards" it. On the other hand, the criminally negligent offender is not aware of the risk created ("fails to perceive") and, therefore, cannot be guilty of consciously disregarding it. The difference between the terms "recklessly" and "negligently" is one of kind, rather than degree. Each actor creates a risk or harm. The reckless actor is aware of the risk and disregards it; the negligent actor is not aware of the risk but should have been aware of it.

Thus, we must determine whether there was any evidence before the jury from which it could have concluded that the appellant did not perceive that his wife might die as a result of his actions. We conclude that there was evidence from which the jury could have reasonably believed that his conduct that caused her to fall was unintentional and that he was not aware he was creating a risk to his wife. He testified that, after she bit him, his reaction—which caused her to fall to the ground—was simply reflexive.

He also testified that he did not know there were bricks in the yard. Even in his statement to the police in which he said he was slamming her head against the ground, Koppersmith said he did not know at that time that there was a brick under her head.

Finally, he stated that he did not intend to throw her onto a brick or harm her in any way when he "slung" her, and that he did not intend to hit her head on a brick or otherwise harm her when he grabbed and shook her after she had fallen.

Because there was a reasonable theory from the evidence that would have supported giving a jury instruction on criminally negligent homicide, the trial court erred in refusing to instruct the jury on criminally negligent homicide. Thus, we must reverse the trial court's judgment and remand this case for a new trial.

Motive

The mens rea of a criminal statute is not the same thing as motive. Motive refers to a person's reasons or motivations for committing a crime. For example, a person may commit a theft or robbery in order to further buy drugs or pay off a gambling debt. Unless the crime is a strict liability crime (see below), the state must prove the defendant's mens rea, but it does not have to prove the defendant's motive. That said, it is much easier for the jury to convict the defendant if jurors can understand the defendant's motivations for committing the crime.

Transferred Intent

Ordinarily, for a defendant to be guilty of a crime, he or she must have intended the actual harm done (when the statute requires he act purposefully) or been practically certain that the harm would occur because of his conduct (when the statute requires that he act knowingly), or at least been aware that the harm could occurred but chosen to do the act anyway (when the statute requires that he act recklessly). But what happens when the defendant intends to harm one person but instead harms another? Or what happens when the defendant intends to damage one piece of property, but instead damages another? The doctrine of transferred intent tells us that if the defendant intends to harm one person or item of property and does greatly similar harm to a different person or item, he will be treated as if he had, in fact, intended the result that occurred (i.e., the intent is transferred) and he will be liable for the crime.

PEOPLE v. SCOTT,
927 P.2d 288 (Cal. 1996)

BROWN, J.
[Damien Scott and Derrick Brown's mother, Elaine Scott, was dating the victim, Calvin Hughes. Hughes broke up with Scott, and her sons, the defendants here, retaliated by shooting at Hughes. The bullet struck his shoe heel, but passed through and struck and killed an innocent teenager, Jack Gibson.]

A jury convicted defendants Damien Scott and Derrick Brown of various crimes for their part in a drive-by shooting which resulted in the death of one person and injury to several others. We must decide in this case whether the doctrine of transferred intent may be used to assign criminal liability to a defendant who kills an unintended victim when the defendant is also prosecuted for the attempted murder of an intended victim.

Under the classic formulation of California's common law doctrine of transferred intent, a defendant who shoots with the intent to kill a certain person and hits a bystander instead is subject to the same criminal liability that would have been imposed had " 'the fatal blow reached the person for whom intended.' " In such a factual setting, the defendant is deemed as culpable as if he had accomplished what he set out to do.

Here, it was established at trial that defendants fired an automatic weapon into a public park in an attempt to kill a certain individual, and fatally shot a bystander instead. The case presents the type of factual setting in which courts have uniformly approved reliance on the transferred intent doctrine as the basis of determining a defendant's criminal liability for the death of an unintended victim. Consistent with a line of decisions beginning with Suesser nearly a century ago, we conclude that the jury in this case was properly instructed on a transferred intent theory of liability for first degree murder.

Moreover, defendants' exposure to a murder conviction based on a transferred intent theory of liability was proper regardless of the fact they were also charged with attempted murder of the intended victim. Contrary to what its name implies, the transferred intent doctrine does not refer to any actual intent that is "used up" once it has been employed to convict a defendant of a specific intent crime against an intended victim. Rather, the doctrine of transferred intent connotes a policy. As applied here, the transferred intent doctrine is but another way of saying that a defendant who shoots with an intent to kill but misses and hits a bystander instead should be punished for a crime of the same seriousness as the one he tried to commit against his intended victim.

In this case, defendants shot at an intended victim, missed him, and killed another person instead. In doing so, defendants committed crimes against two persons. Defendants' criminal liability for causing the death of the unintended victim may be determined on a theory of transferred intent in accordance with the classic formulation of the doctrine under California common law. Their criminal liability for shooting at the intended victim with an intent to kill is that which the law assigns.

Other Cases – Transferred Intent

Regina v. Saunders & Archer, 75 Engl. Rep. 705 (1575)
Saunders gave his wife a poisoned apple. She took one bite of it, and handed it over to her daughter. The daughter finished off the apple, and died. Saunders was charged with intentionally killing his daughter, and the judge convicted him finding that his intent to kill his wife transferred to his daughter.

The Special Case of Strict Liability Crimes

When analyzing a statute, you might notice that it is silent with regard to mens rea (i.e., it does not have the words "purposely" or "knowingly" or "recklessly" or "negligently" listed). This can mean one of two things. First, the legislature intended to require mens rea but just forgot to write it in, or assumed that its citizenry would know what it meant; or second it was the legislature intent to not require the state to prove mens rea. Strict liability crimes represent the latter. For some reason, the legislature decided that the offender can be punished even without the state proving he or she had a guilty mind. This frequently happens with traffic violations and other regulatory offenses. Consider the case of a speeder, the state does not have to prove that the driver intended to violate the speed limit-- only that he or she drove too fast.

One fundamental and central tenant to criminal law, however, is the idea that only individuals who are personally blameworthy and responsible for a criminal act should be punished for the act. Inherent in this belief is the notion that only individuals who have a guilty mind while committing the prohibited act are blameworthy. Strict liability laws allow the state to prove a crime without proving the defendant's guilty intent. Because, strict liability crimes allow us to hold people guilty or blameworthy for criminal acts regardless of their mental state/intent, they are against public policy.

Strict liability crimes arose during the industrial revolution to support the health and welfare regulations required by the new, more dangerous, industries. The nature of these crimes differ from those crimes at common law, and often addressed neglect and inaction by an industry which created the danger of injury. Strict liability crimes were written to protect society against unsafe working conditions, defective drugs and impure food, pollution, unsafe trucks, and railroads. According to Lippman, the purpose of strict liability laws is to deter unqualified people from participating in potentially dangerous activities. *Criminal Law*, supra at 130. By requiring prosecutors to establish criminal intent for these relatively minor cases, time and energy would be diverted from other cases.

Although historically, strict liability crimes were restricted to *malum prohibitum* type offenses, the trend is toward expanding strict liability into non-public welfare crimes that carry relatively severe punishment. One example of this is the strict liability crime of driving while intoxicated (DWI) or driving under the influence of an intoxicant (DUII). The Supreme Court has, nevertheless, shown willingness to strike down putative (so called) strict liability statutes and require mens rea when the penalty is very severe and the nature of the crime is one that traditionally would require the defendant to possess criminal intent. Model Penal Code §1.04(5) adopts strict liability offenses but limits the crimes to "violations" that are not subject to imprisonment and are only punishable by a fine, forfeiture or other civil penalty.

As mentioned above, to create a strict liability crime, the legislature must write a statute that omits the mens rea requirement. Sometimes, however, legislatures do not intend to create a strict liability crime but through inattention or poor draftsmanship they inadvertently omit reference to criminal intent. The legislature's failure to identify the mens rea in a criminal statute does not necessarily make the crime a strict liability crime. How then, does the court decide whether the legislature intended to create a strict liability crime, or just enacted a poorly drafted crime? Courts will start by looking at any evidence of the legislative intent. In addition to the missing mens rea requirement, the courts will consider the following factors in deciding whether the legislature intended to create a strict liability crime:

➢ Was the offense a crime at common law? (If the crime has a common law counterpart, it is unlikely to be considered a strict liability offense)
➢ Would a single violation of the statute pose danger to a large number of people?
➢ Is the risk of conviction of an "innocent" individual (one without moral culpability) outweighed by the public interest in preventing harm to society?
➢ Is the penalty relatively minor? (the more severe the punishment, the less likely the court will consider the crime to be a strict liability one).
➢ Does a conviction harm the defendant's reputation? (if so, then it is less likely to be considered a strict liability crime).
➢ Does the law significantly impede the rights of individuals or impose a heavy burden.
➢ Are these acts ones that most people avoid?
➢ Do individuals who engage in such acts generally possess criminal intent?

Sometimes legislatures intend for strict liability to exist with regard to a specific material element of a crime, but not for another material element. And, as you can imagine, this is where it gets really tricky. For example, the crime of statutory rape prohibits even consensual sexual conduct with an individual under a certain age. In many jurisdictions, the state must prove that the defendant had the mens rea to commit the sexual act (i.e., he knowingly had intercourse), but it does not have to prove that the defendant had the mens rea regarding the victim's age (i.e, that he knew his partner was 15 years old). In this respect, the crime is strict liability with respect to the circumstance of age. The following cases demonstrate court's efforts to identify whether a statute creates a strict liability crime or not.

COMMONWEALTH. v. FLEMINGS,
652 A.2d 1282 (Pa. 1995)

PAPADAKOS, Justice.   The facts underlying Appellee's conviction by the jury in the instant case are as follows. On October 11, 1990, two members of the vice squad of the Erie Police Department were working undercover as drug purchasers. Appellee approached the vehicle in which the two officers were seated and essentially offered to sell them cocaine. Appellee left and returned a short time later accompanied by one Tisa Howard. Ms. Howard approached the passenger side of the vehicle where she conversed with Officer Yeaney. Meanwhile, Appellee approached the driver's side where he conversed with Officer Mioduszewski. As Officer Mioduszewski leaned toward the passenger window to consummate a drug transaction with Ms. Howard, his Smith and Wesson pistol was exposed to Appellee who then stole the pistol; and as Officer Mioduszewski turned around, Appellee had the gun pointed directly at him, as well as in the direction of Officer Yeaney and Ms. Howard. Appellee slowly backed off while pointing the gun at the officers. He then fled on foot. The officers gave chase and eventually caught Appellee exiting a nearby house. Prior to catching him, Appellee had stated, "Officers, I'll give you back your gun." Prior to that statement, the officers had not identified themselves as such. Appellee [Flemings] admitted that most of those events occurred, but testified that he did not know that Yeaney or Mioduszewski were police officers, but when he saw the firearm, he became frightened and took it so that no one would get injured. (N.T., 7/11/91, at 111.)

[T]he jury convicted Appellee of the numerous charges, including two counts of aggravated assault. At the completion of the trial, Appellee requested that the jury be instructed that Appellee must have known that the undercover officers were police officers when he pointed the gun at them in order to be found guilty of aggravated assault on a police officer. The trial court refused this requested instruction concluding that knowledge of the fact that the victims were police officers is not an element of the crime under 18 P.S. § 2702(a)(3). During the course of their deliberations, the jury asked the trial court whether Appellee had to know whether the victims were police officers at the time of the assault. The trial court answered that it was not necessary that Appellee know they were police.

On appeal, the Superior Court reversed and remanded for a new trial holding that knowledge by Appellee that the victims were police officers was an element of the crime and must be proven. The Superior Court reasoned as follows:

18 P.S. § 2702(a)(3) provides:
   (a) Offense defined. — A person is guilty of aggravated assault if he: . . .
   (3) attempts to cause or intentionally or knowingly causes bodily injury to a police officer . . . in the performance of duty; . . .
      . . .
. . . [T]his case raises an issue of first impression in Pennsylvania that as a matter of pure verbal logic could go either way. We are guided, however, by the United States Supreme Court's decision in *United States v. Feola*, 420 U.S. 671 (1975), where the court concluded, with respect to a comparable federal statute, that knowledge that a victim is a federal officer is not an element of the crime of assaulting a federal officer.
   . . .

In *Feola*, the United States Supreme Court specifically held . . . that criminal liability for the offense of assaulting a federal officer under 18 U.S.C. § 111 does not depend on whether or not the assailant harbored the specific intent to assault a federal officer. While conceding that either this conclusion, or its opposite, was "plausible" as a matter of determining legislative intent, the court concluded that Congress intended to protect federal officers, as well as federal functions, and that the rejection of a strict scienter requirement was consistent with both purposes.

Mr. Justice Blackmun went on to reason for the majority as follows:
   . . . All the statute requires is an intent to assault, not an intent to assault a federal officer. A contrary conclusion would give insufficient protection to the agent enforcing an unpopular law, and none to the agent active under cover.

This interpretation poses no risk of unfairness to defendants. It is no snare for the unsuspecting. Although the perpetrator of a narcotics "rip-off," such as the one involved here, may be surprised to find that his intended victim is a federal officer in civilian apparel, he nevertheless knows from the very outset that his planned course of conduct is wrongful. The situation is not one where legitimate conduct becomes unlawful solely because of the identity of the individual or agency affected. In a case of this kind the offender takes his victim as he finds him. . . . 420 U.S. at 684-685, 95 S.Ct. at 1264 (footnote omitted).

Mr. Justice Blackmun's reasoning is equally applicable to the case at bar and our aggravated assault statute.

The liability imposed by 18 Pa.C.S. § 2702(a)(3) is not absolute, since to be convicted of aggravated assault under that section, the defendant must be shown to have possessed a criminal mens rea, i.e., the intent to cause bodily injury. Thus, the defendant's ignorance of an officer's official status is relevant in those rare cases in which an officer fails to identify himself and then engages in a course of conduct which could reasonably be interpreted as the unlawful use of force directed either at the defendant or his property. Under such circumstances, a defendant would normally be justified in using reasonable force against his assailant. He could then be found to have exercised self defense, which would negate the existence of mens rea.

The same principle does not apply, however, where a defendant clearly intends to commit a crime and unwittingly chooses a police officer as his victim. Such a scenario scarcely argues the existence of an "honest mistake." Rather, under these circumstances the defendant's ignorance of the victim's official status is irrelevant since he knows from the outset that his planned course of conduct is unlawful. Once he chooses to engage in such conduct, he takes his victim as he finds him.

Similarly, the statute's requirement that the officer be "in the performance of duty" in no way implies that liability depends on whether the defendant is aware of his victim's official status. The duties of a police officer, like the officers in the instant case, frequently include undercover investigation in which the officer's official status is intentionally concealed. We do not interpret the language "in performance of duty" to require a defendant to have knowledge of the officer's official status since such a reading would all but strip the undercover officer of the protection the legislature intended to afford him. Rather, we hold that a defendant's lack of knowledge should only be considered in those cases in which a defendant acts with the *mistaken* belief that he is threatened with an intentional tort by a private citizen. That is not, however, quite the case here. Although appellant may in fact have believed that Officer Mioduszewski was a rival drug dealer, appellant's seizure of the officer's gun, which he then aimed at Mioduszewski, was a preemptive action, not one which is consistent with self-defense. His knowledge or otherwise of the officer's status is, thus, under the present facts, irrelevant — there is no honest mistake involved in the situation here.

In short, on the facts before us, the offender must take his victim as he finds him. Appellee here was clearly a wrongdoer. Knowledge that the victim is a police officer is not an element of the crime of aggravated assault under 18 P.S. § 2702(a)(3) and need not be proven. Proof of intent to assault is sufficient.

MORISETTE v. UNITED STATES, 342 U.S. 246 (1951)

FACTS
. . . The Government established a practice bombing range over which the Air Force dropped simulated bombs at ground targets. These bombs consisted of a metal cylinder about forty inches long and eight inches across, filled with sand and enough black powder to cause a smoke puff by which the strike could be located. At various places about the range, signs read "Danger -- Keep Out -- Bombing Range." Nevertheless, the range was known as good deer country, and was extensively hunted.

Spent bomb casings were cleared from the

targets and thrown into piles "so that they will be out of the way." They were not sacked or piled in any order, but were dumped in heaps, some of which had been accumulating for four years or upwards, were exposed to the weather and rusting away.

Morissette, in December of 1948, went hunting in this area but did not get a deer. He thought to meet expenses of the trip by salvaging some of these casings. He loaded three tons of them on his truck and took them to a nearby farm, where they were flattened by driving a tractor over them. After expending this labor and trucking them to market in Flint, he realized $84.

Morissette, by occupation, is a fruit stand operator in summer and a trucker and scrap iron collector in winter. An honorably discharged veteran of World War II, he enjoys a good name among his neighbors and has had no blemish on his record more disreputable than a conviction for reckless driving.

The loading, crushing and transporting of these casings were all in broad daylight, in full view of passers-by, without the slightest effort at concealment. When an investigation was started, Morissette voluntarily, promptly and candidly told the whole story to the authorities, saying that he had no intention of stealing. but thought the property was abandoned, unwanted and considered of no value to the Government. He was indicted, however, on the charge that he "did unlawfully, wilfully and knowingly steal and convert" property of the United States of the value of $84, in violation of 18 U.S.C. § 641, which provides that "whoever embezzles, steals, purloins, or knowingly converts" government property is punishable by fine and imprisonment. Morissette was convicted and sentenced to imprisonment for two months or to pay a fine of $200.

On his trial, Morissette, as he had at all times told investigating officers, testified that, from appearances, he believed the casings were cast-off and abandoned, that he did not intend to steal the property, and took it with no wrongful or criminal intent. The trial court, however, was unimpressed, and ruled:

"[H]e took it because he thought it was

abandoned and he knew he was on government property. . . . That is no defense. . . . I don't think anybody can have the defense they thought the property was abandoned on another man's piece of property."

The court stated: "I will not permit you to show this man thought it was abandoned. . . . I hold in this case that there is no question of abandoned property." The court refused to submit or to allow counsel to argue to the jury whether Morissette acted with innocent intention. It charged:

"And I instruct you that if you believe the testimony of the government in this case, he intended to take it. . . . He had no right to take this property. . . . [A]nd it is no defense to claim that it was abandoned because it was on private property. . . . And I instruct you to this effect: that if this young man took this property (and he says he did), without any permission (he says he did), that was on the property of the United States Government (he says it was), that it was of the value of one cent or more (and evidently it was), that he is guilty of the offense charged here. If you believe the government, he is guilty. . . . The question on intent is whether or not he intended to take the property. He says he did. Therefore, if you believe either side, he is guilty."

Petitioner's counsel contended, "But the taking must have been with a felonious intent." The [trial] court ruled, however: "That is presumed by his own act."

The Court of Appeals suggested that "greater restraint in expression should have been exercised," but affirmed the conviction because, "As we have interpreted the statute, appellant was guilty of its violation beyond a shadow of doubt, as evidenced even by his own admissions.". . . . The court ruled that this particular offense requires no element of criminal intent.

[The Court held that Congress's failure to require a mental element as part of the statute, although expedient and convenient for the government, would not necessarily govern whether the crime was a strict liability crime or a crime that required a mental element. The Court chose not to take the omission as clear indication that the statute imposed a strict liability crime. Instead, it looked at the nature of the crime (here common law larceny or theft) and found that historically these types of crime required that the government prove mens rea.] . . .

"Stealing, larceny, and its variants and equivalents were among the earliest offenses known to the law that existed before legislation; they are invasions of rights of property which stir a sense of insecurity in the whole community and arouse public demand for retribution, the penalty is high and, when a sufficient amount is involved, the infamy is that of a felony, which, says Maitland, is ". . . as bad a word as you can give to man or thing." State courts of last resort, on whom fall the heaviest burden of interpreting criminal law in this country, have consistently retained the requirement of intent in larceny-type offenses." …

"Congressional silence as to mental elements in an Act merely adopting into federal statutory law a concept of crime already so well defined in common law and statutory interpretation by the states may warrant quite contrary inferences than the same silence in creating an offense new to general law, for whose definition the courts have no guidance except the Act."

[Thus the Court indicated it would look to legislative history to see if, in fact, the legislature intended to make the offense one which is complete even without the offender possessing any ill-will, spite, malice, intent, knowledge, etc. But, when the legislative history is silent, the court will look to other factors to decide whether the statute is a strict liability one or just a law that is invalid for failing to require a mens rea element.]

"We hold that mere omission of any mention of intent will not be construed as eliminating that element from the crime denounced.
…
We find no grounds for inferring any affirmative instruction from Congress to eliminate intent from any offense with which

this defendant was charged

Where intent of the accused is an ingredient of the crime charged, its existence is a question of fact which must be submitted to the jury. State court authorities cited to the effect that intent is relevant in larcenous crimes are equally emphatic and uniform that it is a jury issue. …

It follows that the trial court may not withdraw or prejudge the issue by instruction that the law raises a presumption of intent from an act.

We think presumptive intent has no place in this case. [Both a conclusive presumption . . . [and a permissive presumption] . . . would conflict with the overriding presumption of innocence with which the law endows the accused and which extends to every element of the crime. Such incriminating presumptions are not to be improvised by the judiciary. …

Moreover, the conclusion supplied by presumption in this instance was one of intent to steal the casings, and it was based on the mere fact that defendant took them. The court thought the only question was, "Did he intend to take the property?" That the removal of them was a conscious and intentional act was admitted. But that isolated fact is not an adequate basis on which the jury should find the criminal intent to steal or knowingly convert, that is, wrongfully to deprive another of possession of property. Whether that intent existed, the jury must determine, nor only from the act of taking, but from that together with defendant's testimony and all of the surrounding circumstances.

Of course, the jury, considering Morissette's awareness that these casings were on government property, his failure to seek any permission for their removal, and his self-interest as a witness, might have disbelieved his profession of innocent intent and concluded that his assertion of a belief that the casings were abandoned was an afterthought. Had the jury convicted . . . [after receiving] . . . proper instructions it would be the end of the matter. But juries are not bound by what seems inescapable logic to judges. They might have concluded that the heaps of spent casings left in the hinterland to rust away presented an appearance of unwanted and abandoned junk, and that lack of any conscious deprivation of property or intentional injury was indicated by Morissette's good character, the openness of the taking, crushing and transporting of the casings, and the candor with which it was all

admitted. They might have refused to brand Morissette as a thief. Had they done so, that too would have been the end of the matter.

United States v. Osguthorpe, 13 F. Supp. 2d 1212 (D Utah 1988.)
Defendant allowed his sheep to graze on forest service land. Congress had done away with the word "willfully" within the statute, and the court first decided that the statute was not a strict liability one even though no mens rea requirement was provided in the statute. Because the Court held that the statute was NOT a strict liability crime and the state had to prove some level of criminal mens rea, the court then had to decide what level of mens rea the state had to prove. Guided by the Model Penal Code, the Court determined that recklessness was the best mens rea fit for the statute. The Court stated,

"While it is true there is no clear rationale in the regulation or legislative history which would indicate that recklessness, as opposed to negligence, should be the appropriate standard, this Court makes such ruling based, in part, upon the long held notion that "ambiguity concerning the ambit of statutes should be resolved in favor of lenity."
(Translation = when in doubt, err on the side of favoring the defendant. Requiring the state to prove the higher mens rea of recklessness favors the defendant over the lesser proof for negligence).

Concurrence of Actus reus and Mens Rea

To be a crime, the criminal act must be triggered by the criminal intent. Stated otherwise, the act or result must be attributable to the defendant's guilty state of mind. This is called the concurrence requirement of actus reus and mens rea. Generally, the defendant must have had the requisite intent at the moment he performed the act. It is not essential that the intent and the result concur in time. For example, assume that on day one Jack decides to run over Jill because he is angry that she tumbled down the hill and spilled the water. Assume also that Jack does nothing, cools off, and later decides he could never harm anyone-- even Jill. On day two, Jack runs Jill over as he backs out of his driveway. His criminal intent on day one does not trigger his running over Jill on day two, so Jack cannot be found guilty of a crime. (This example also illustrates the difficulty in proving intent. How would anyone know that Jack had decided to run Jill over when he did nothing to act upon it?)

There are very few cases illustrating this element, and the one generally cited involves more the question of in which jurisdiction did the mens rea and actus reus collide. See, Commonwealth v. Jackson, 38 SW 422 (Ky 1896) (Kentucky court rejected defendant claims that he could not be found guilty of murder in Kentucky because he administered drugs to his victim in Ohio (intending to kill her), but instead, the actual death of his victim occurred when he decapitated her to destroy her body (in Kentucky) (thus, the actus reus causing the death (the decapitation) did not concur with the mens rea (intending to kill her)).

Causation

In crimes that require the state to prove harm (see below), the state must prove beyond a reasonable doubt that defendant caused the harm. The causation element of the crime limits liability to people whose actions produce the prohibited harm. The government must prove both that the defendant is both the factual cause and the proximate cause of the victim's harm. When the defendant set into motion the chain of events that resulted in the victim's harm, he is said to be the "factual cause" of the harm. This is also referred to as "cause in fact." "actual cause," or "but/for cause." When circumstances are such that it is fair to hold the defendant responsible for the harm, the defendant is said to be the "legal cause" or the "proximate cause" of the harm.

"Actual Cause," "Cause In Fact," "But For" Causation

The defendant is actual cause of the harm when, but for the defendant's act, the victim would not have been harmed. Generally, actual causation is fairly easy to establish. If the defendant set into motion a chain of events that resulted in the victim's harm, then he or she is said to be the actual cause of the harm. If not for the defendant's shooting the victim, would the victim have died? If not for the fact that the defendant struck the victim, would the victim have a welt over his eye? If not for the fact that the defendant drove carelessly and ran into a tree, would the victim have sustained the injuries in the crash? If the answer is, "yes," then the defendant is the "actual cause" or "cause in fact" of the harm.

"Legal Cause" Or "Proximate Cause"

But/for causation is very broad, and it does not take much involvement for a defendant to be the cause-in-fact of the harm. Because of this, criminal liability will only be imposed when the defendant is also the proximate cause of the harm. Legal or proximate cause is about fairness. When people cause foreseeable harm, then it is fair for society to hold them responsible and blameworthy. When a person, does not, however, cause the harm, then it is not fair to hold him or her responsible. Fairness and foreseeability determinations are ones for the jury, and reasonable minds can disagree.

According to court decisions, the key to whether a person is the proximate or legal cause of the harm is whether the harm was a foreseeable result of defendant's conduct. In most cases, the defendant is clearly both the actual cause and legal cause of the harm. But sometimes circumstances exist which make the question of legal or proximate cause not so clear. Consider the following: Chris drank several beers before getting into his car and driving the wrong way down the highway. He swerved to miss an oncoming car, and instead hit a tree. Shawn his passenger, sustained a broken foot in the crash. So far, it should be pretty obvious that Chris is the cause in fact of the Shawn's harm. If charged with an assault or battery, Chris should be convicted. (But for his driving into a tree, Shawn would not have been injured). But, what if Shawn after being raced to the hospital was shot by a crazed gunman on a rampage at the hospital? Chris is still the cause in fact of the Shawn's death. (But for the fact that Chris ran into a tree, Shawn would not have been at the hospital and been killed, so it is clear that Chris "set into motion a chain of events that ultimately resulted in (the harm) Shawn's death. But, is it fair to charge Chris with Shawn's murder? Assault? Sure. But murder?

To find proximate cause, the jury must find that not only is the harm a foreseeable result of the defendant's actions, but also that the manner in which the harm occurred was foreseeable. For example, a jury may find that it is very foreseeable that a person who drives drunk will cause a crash in which someone will die. What is not foreseeable is the existence of the crazed gunman at the hospital. The crazed hospital gunman is considered an intervening cause. And, in this case the gunman is considered a "superseding intervening" cause. It is fair to hold the gunman liable for Shawn's death when the deadly shot is the cause of death, but what if the gunman's shot only grazed Shawn and the hospital doctors failed to properly treat Shawn, will Chris still "be off the hook" for Shawn's death? Probably not. Emanuel notes that a third party's failure to act, unlike an affirmative act, will never be considered a superseding cause that cuts off defendant's liability.

For the most part, a defendant who commits a crime is responsible for the natural and probable consequences of his or her actions. In most instances the defendant will be liable for the harm that occurs from the victim's response to the situation the defendant placed them in. The issue is whether the victim's response is foreseeable, not whether the victim's response is reasonable.

What if two different things happen independently and either could have caused the harm? Consider this example: Abe poisons Jocelyn--thus weakening her immune system. Jocelyn is later in a car crash and dies as a result of the accident and the pre-accident weakened condition. Is Abe the proximate cause of Jocelyn's death? According to Emanuel, Abe's chance of escaping liability is better if the intervening act is independent from the defendant's acts. Since the car crash is independent from the poisoning, Abe may be able to evade responsibility for Jocelyn's death. But, what if Abe poisoned Jocelyn--thus weakening Jocelyn's immune system, and Jocelyn subsequently catches a virus that a person with a healthy immune system would easily have survived. The virus is a "dependent intervening cause." As such, the virus will break off liability for Abe's actions only if it was both unforeseeable and abnormal that 1) poisoning a person results in a weakened immune system, 2) a person with a weakened immune system would get the virus, or 3) a person with a weakened immune system would die from the virus.

At least where the final result could have been anticipated from the dangerous nature of the defendant's conduct, the ultimate test may be whether the result was "too remote or accidental in its occurrence to have a just bearing on the actor's liability." Kerper, *supra* at 110-111.

The presence of intervening causes makes the determination of proximate cause more complicated. In addition, states have taken differing and opposing positions on the role of intervening causes and whether they cut off liability. To make matters worse, the terminology surrounding proximate cause is not consistent. That said, the jury's decision finding defendant to be the cause of harm will generally be upheld as it hangs upon a non-legal determination of fairness. Courts, in reviewing these decisions, will examine several factors, including:

> ➤ whether the actor intended to inflict serious harm,
> ➤ whether the actor did inflict serious harm,
> ➤ whether the intervening event was a product of "natural events" (e.g., the infection of the wound) or the action of a third person (e.g., the sloppy doctor),
> ➤ whether the final result was foreseeable.

Because causation is a factually specific determination, it is helpful to review what courts have done in a variety of settings in order to get a sense of when defendants will be found to be the factual and legal cause of harm.

PEOPLE v. ARMITAGE, *239 Cal. Rptr. 515 (1987)*

FACTS
On the evening of May 18, 1985, defendant and his friend, Peter Maskovich, were drinking in a bar in the riverside community of Freeport. They were observed leaving the bar around midnight. In the early morning hours defendant and Maskovich wound up racing defendant's boat on the Sacramento River while both of them were intoxicated. An autopsy revealed that at the time of his death Maskovich had a blood alcohol level of .25 percent. . . .

James Snook lives near the Sacramento River in Clarksburg. Some time around 3 a.m. defendant came to his door. Defendant was soaking wet and appeared quite intoxicated. He reported that he had flipped his boat over in the river and had lost his buddy. He said that at first he and his buddy had been hanging on to the overturned boat, but that his buddy swam for shore and he did not know whether he had made it. As it turned out, Maskovich did not

make it; he drowned in the river.

…

Deputy Snyder attempted to question defendant about the accident and defendant stated that he had been operating the boat at a high rate of speed and zig-zagging until it capsized. Defendant also stated that he told the victim to hang on to the boat but his friend ignored his warning and started swimming for the shore. …

OPINION
The evidence establishes that at about 3 a.m., and while he was drunk, defendant operated his boat without lights at a very high rate of speed in an erratic and zig-zagging manner until he capsized it. This evidence supports the finding that defendant not only operated his boat while intoxicated, but that he operated his boat at an unsafe speed and in a reckless or negligent manner so as to endanger the life,

limb or property of other persons. In doing so defendant did an act forbidden by law, or neglected a duty imposed by law, in the operation of his boat. This evidence supports defendant's conviction.

Defendant contends his actions were not the proximate cause of the death of the victim. In order to be guilty of felony drunk boating the defendant's act or omission must be the proximate cause of the ensuing injury or death. Defendant asserts that after his boat flipped over he and the victim were holding on to it and the victim, against his advice, decided to abandon the boat and try to swim to shore. According to defendant the victim's fatally reckless decision should exonerate him from criminal responsibility for his death.

We reject defendant's contention. The question whether defendant's acts or omissions criminally caused the victim's death is to be determined according to the ordinary principles governing proximate causation. Proximate cause of a death has traditionally been defined in criminal cases as "a cause which, in natural and continuous sequence, produces the death, and without which the death would not have occurred." Thus, proximate cause is clearly established where the act is directly connected with the resulting injury, with no intervening force operating.

Defendant claims that the victim's attempt to swim ashore, whether characterized as an intervening or a superseding cause, constituted a break in the natural and continuous sequence arising from the unlawful operation of the boat. The claim cannot hold water. It has long been the rule in criminal prosecutions that the contributory negligence of the victim is not a defense. In order to exonerate a defendant, the victim's conduct must not only be a cause of his injury, it must be a superseding cause. A defendant may be criminally liable for a result directly caused by his act even if there is another contributing cause. If an intervening cause is a normal and reasonably foreseeable result of defendant's original act the

intervening act is "dependent" and not a superseding cause, and will not relieve defendant of liability. An obvious illustration of a dependent cause is the victim's attempt to escape from a deadly attack or other danger in which he is placed by the defendant's wrongful act. Thus, it is only an unforeseeable intervening cause, an extraordinary and abnormal occurrence, which rises to the level of an exonerating, superseding cause.

Consequently, in criminal law a victim's predictable effort to escape a peril created by the defendant is not considered a superseding cause of the ensuing injury or death. As leading commentators have explained it, an unreflective act in response to a peril created by defendant will not break a causal connection. In such a case, the actor has a choice, but his act is nonetheless unconsidered. "When defendant's conduct causes panic an act done under the influence of panic or extreme fear will not negative causal connection unless the reaction is wholly abnormal." This rule is encapsulated in a standard jury instruction: "It is not a defense to a criminal charge that the deceased or some other person was guilty of negligence, which was a contributory cause of the death involved in the case."

Here defendant, through his misconduct, placed the intoxicated victim in the middle of a dangerous river in the early morning hours clinging to an overturned boat. The fact that the panic stricken victim recklessly abandoned the boat and tried to swim ashore was not a wholly abnormal reaction to the perceived peril of drowning. Just as "detached reflection cannot be demanded in the presence of an uplifted knife" neither can caution be required of a drowning man. Having placed the inebriated victim in peril, defendant cannot obtain exoneration by claiming the victim should have reacted differently or more prudently. In sum, the evidence establishes that defendant's acts and omissions were the proximate cause of the victim's death.

VELAZQUEZ v. STATE,
561 So.2d 347 (Fla. App. 1990)

FACTS

At about 2:30 a.m., Isaac Alejandro Velazquez

met the deceased Adalberto Alvarez at a Hardee's restaurant in Hialeah, Florida. The two had never previously met but in the course of their conversation agreed to "drag race" each other with their automobiles. They accordingly left the restaurant and proceeded to set up a quarter-mile drag race course on a nearby public road that ran perpendicular to a canal alongside the Palmetto Expressway in Hialeah; a guardrail and a visible stop sign stood between the end of this road and the canal.

The two men began their drag race at the end of this road and proceeded away from the canal in a westerly direction for a quarter mile. Upon completing the course without incident, the deceased Alvarez suddenly turned his automobile 180 degrees around and proceeded east toward the starting line and the canal; Velazquez did the same and followed. Alvarez led and attained an estimated speed of 123 mph; he was not wearing a seat belt and subsequent investigation revealed that he had a blood alcohol level between .11 and .12.

Velazquez, who had not been drinking, trailed Alvarez the entire distance back to the starting line and attained an estimated speed of 98 mph. As both drivers approached the end of the road,

they applied their brakes, but neither could stop. Alvarez, who was about a car length ahead of Velazquez, crashed through the guardrail first and was propelled over the entire canal, landing on its far bank; he was thrown from his car upon impact, was pinned under his vehicle when it landed on him, and died instantly from the resulting injuries.

Velazquez also crashed through the guardrail but landed in the canal where he was able to escape from his vehicle and swim to safety uninjured. Velazquez was charged with vehicular homicide.

OPINION
In unusual cases like this one, whether certain conduct is deemed the legal cause of a certain result is ultimately a policy question. The question of legal causation thus blends into the question of whether we are willing to hold a defendant responsible for a prohibited result. Or, stated differently, the issue is not causation; it is responsibility. In my opinion, policy considerations are against imposing responsibility for the death of a participant in a race on the surviving racer when his sole contribution to the death is the participation in the activity mutually agreed upon.

PEOPLE v. KIBBE, 362 N.Y.S.2d 848 (1974)

FACTS
Barry Kibbe and a companion, Roy Krall, met George Stafford in a bar on a cold winter night. They noticed Stafford had a lot of money and was drunk. When Stafford asked them for a ride, they agreed, having already decided to rob him. "The three men entered Kibbe's automobile and began the trip toward Canandaigua. Krall drove the car while Kibbe demanded that Stafford turn over any money he had. In the course of an exchange, Kibbe slapped Stafford several times, took his money, then compelled him to lower his trousers and to take off his shoes to be certain that Stafford had given up all his money. When they were satisfied that Stafford had no more money on his person, the defendants forced him to exit the Kibbe vehicle.

As he was thrust from the car, Stafford fell onto the shoulder of the rural two-lane highway on

which they had been traveling. His trousers were still down around his ankles, his shirt was rolled up toward his chest, he was shoeless, and he had also been stripped of any outer clothing. Before the defendants pulled away, Kibbe placed Stafford's shoes and jacket on the shoulder of the highway. Although Stafford's eyeglasses were in Kibbe's vehicle, the defendants, either through inadvertence or perhaps by specific design, did not give them to him before they drove away.

Michael W. Blake, a college student, was driving at a reasonable speed when he saw Stafford in the middle of the road with his hands in the air. Blake could not stop in time to avoid striking Stafford and killing him.

OPINION
To be a sufficiently direct cause of death so as to warrant the imposition of a criminal penalty, it will suffice if it can be said beyond a

reasonable doubt, as indeed it can be here said, that the ultimate harm is something which should have been foreseen as being reasonably related to the acts of the accused. We conclude that Kibbe and his companion's activities were a sufficiently proximate cause of the death of George Stafford so as to warrant the imposition of criminal sanctions. In engaging in what may properly be described as a despicable course of action, Kibbe and Krall left a helplessly intoxicated man without his eyeglasses in a position from which, because of these attending circumstances, he could not extricate himself and whose condition was such that he could not even protect himself from the elements.

Under the conditions surrounding Blake's operation of his truck (i.e., the fact that he had his low beams on as the two cars approached; that there was no artificial lighting on the highway; and that there was insufficient time in which to react to Stafford's presence in his lane), we do not think it may be said that any intervening wrongful act occurred to relieve the defendants from the directly foreseeable consequences of their actions.

Other Cases – Causation

Kusmider v. State, 688 P.2d 957 (Ala. App.1984).

BRYNER, Chief Judge.

Thomas Kusmider was convicted, after a jury trial, of murder in the second degree.

On November 15, 1982, Kusmider's girlfriend told Kusmider that an acquaintance, Arthur Villella, had sexually assaulted her. Kusmider went to Villella's home in Anchorage. A confrontation ensued, and Kusmider shot Villella. The bullet entered Villella's neck above the Adam's apple. Although the wound did not sever any major arteries, it damaged smaller vessels, causing blood to drain down Villella's windpipe.

Villella was unconscious by the time an ambulance arrived. He was attended by paramedics, who inserted a tube in his windpipe to help his breathing. En route to the hospital, however, Villella began flailing his arms and pulled the tube from his throat. Villella died approximately one hour after arriving at the hospital.

At Kusmider's trial, a pathologist testified that Villella's death was caused by the gunshot wound to his throat. However, the pathologist stated that the wound, while life-threatening, might have been survivable. Kusmider then asked the court for permission to present evidence on the issue of proximate cause. He argued that, if allowed to pursue the issue, he might be able to establish that Villella would have survived the gunshot wound if he had not been able to pull the tube from his windpipe. Kusmider maintained that the paramedics who transported Villella might have been negligent in failing to restrain Villella's arms. Kusmider insisted that he was entitled to have the jury consider whether possible negligence by the paramedics constituted an intervening or superseding cause of Villella's death, rendering the gunshot wound too remote to be considered the proximate cause of death.

Judge Johnstone precluded Kusmider from pursuing the issue of proximate cause before the jury. The judge ruled that negligent failure to provide appropriate medical assistance could not, under the circumstances, interrupt the chain of proximate causation and that, therefore, no jury issue of proximate cause had been raised by Kusmider's offer of proof.

On appeal, Kusmider renews his argument, contending that the jury should have been permitted to hear evidence on the issue of proximate cause. We believe that Kusmider's argument is flawed. Kusmider is correct in asserting that proximate cause is ordinarily an issue for the jury. Of course, in every criminal case the state must establish and the jury must find that the defendant's conduct was the actual cause, or cause-in-fact, of the crime charged in the indictment. Here, testimony that Villella actually died from the gunshot wound was undisputed, and the actual cause of death was not in issue. On appeal, Kusmider does not argue that the trial court's exclusion of evidence relating to proximate cause infringed in any way on the jury's ability to determine actual cause.

Case law and commentators agree that, when death is occasioned by negligent medical treatment of an assault victim, the original assailant ordinarily remains criminally liable for the death, even if it can be shown that the injuries inflicted in the assault were survivable; under such circumstances, proximate cause is not interrupted unless the medical treatment given to the injured person was grossly negligent and unforeseeable

In the present case, Kusmider offered to prove only that the paramedics who treated Villella might have been negligent in failing to restrain Villella's arms. Kusmider did not argue that he could demonstrate gross negligence or recklessness, nor did he contend that the circumstances surrounding Villella's death were unforeseeable.[2] Since, as a matter of law, only grossly negligent and unforeseeable mistreatment would have constituted an intervening cause of death and interrupted the chain of proximate causation, we conclude that Judge Johnstone did not err in excluding evidence relating solely to the issue of negligence by the paramedics who treated Villella.

Even assuming Kusmider had offered to prove that the conduct of the paramedics was both unforeseeable and grossly negligent, we would still conclude that the trial court correctly excluded the evidence relating to proximate cause. In cases involving death from injuries inflicted in an assault, courts have uniformly held that the person who inflicted the injury will be liable for the death despite the failure of third persons to save the victim. …

Here, Kusmider did not claim that the conduct of the paramedics inflicted any new injuries on Villella nor did he even assert that the paramedics aggravated the injuries inflicted by the gunshot wound. Rather, the gist of his claim was that negligence in failing to restrain Villella's arms enabled Villella to disrupt the apparently successful emergency treatment that he had begun to receive. Thus, in support of his argument that proximate cause had been interrupted, Kusmider attempted to rely exclusively on the proof of a negative act: that the paramedics negligently failed to take adequate precautions to restrain Villella. Since Kusmider never offered to prove that the paramedics engaged in any affirmative conduct that might have aggravated Villella's injuries and hastened his death, he could not, as a matter of law, have established a break in the chain of proximate cause, even if he could have shown that the paramedics committed gross and unforeseeable negligence by their failure to act. In short, no matter how negligent the paramedics may have been in failing to prevent Villella's death, it is manifest that the gunshot fired by Kusmider remained a substantial factor if not the only substantial factor in causing Villella's death. No more is required for purposes of establishing proximate cause. Because the evidence proffered by Kusmider could not, as a matter of law, have established a break in the chain of proximate causation, we hold that Judge Johnstone did not err in excluding this evidence from trial.

People v. Schmies, 51 Cal. Rptr. 2d 185 (Cal. Ct. App. 1996).
Schmies fled on his motorcycle from traffic stop at speeds of up to ninety miles an hour and disregarded all traffic regulations. During the chase, one of the pursuing patrol cars struck another vehicle, killing the driver and injuring an officer. Schmies was convicted of grossly negligent vehicular manslaughter and of reckless driving. The court upheld the conviction finding that the officer's response and the resulting injury were reasonably foreseeable. The officer's reaction, in other words was not so extraordinary that it was unforeseeable, unpredictable and statistically extremely improbable

People v. Saavedra-Rodriguez, 971 P.2d 223 (Colo 1998).
Defendant cut victim with a knife during an altercation and the victim died at the hospital. Defendant claimed that the negligence of the doctors was the proximate cause of death. The Colorado court ruled that medical negligence is "too frequent to be considered abnormal" and that the defendant's stabbing the victim started a chain of events, the natural and probable result of which was the defendant's death.

United States v. Hamilton, 182 F.Supp. 548 (D.D.C. 1960).
The defendant beat the victim who ended up in the hospital due to his injuries. The nurse who changed the victim's clothes failed to reattach the victim's arm restraints, and the victim pulled out the breathing tubes in his nose and died. The defendant claimed he should not be considered the cause of the victim's death, but the court held that regardless of whether the victim accidentally or intentionally pulled out the tubes, the victim's death was ordinary and foreseeable consequences of the attack.

Harm, Future Harm, and Inchoate Offenses

Some criminal statutes require the state prove beyond a reasonable doubt that the perpetrator caused some harm. Many statutes do not list a specific harm, and in prosecuting those crimes, the state need not prove that harm occurred. Crimes are frequently classified by the nature of their harm, and in subsequent chapters we will examine crimes against persons (murder, rape, assault, battery, mayhem, etc.) and crimes against property and habitation (theft, burglary, criminal trespass, arson, criminal mischief, etc.). These categories of crime have easily identifiable victims. Other categories of crimes, such as crimes against public order and morality (disorderly conduct, vagrancy, riot, prostitution, etc.), crimes against the government (treason, espionage, terrorism, etc.), and crimes against the administration of justice (obstruction of justice, misprision of a felony, perjury, etc.) do not have easily identifiable victims—sometimes the harm is a vague, intangible harm to society in general or to the perpetrator himself or herself.

Sometimes the law seeks to prevent harm that may happen in the future. When individuals present a threat, but the threat they pose has yet to take shape and cause the harm, society is justified in acting to protect itself from this future harm. Each state has passed laws dealing with "inchoate offenses"—attempt, conspiracy and solicitation which address the risk of future harm. These will be discussed in greater detail in Chapter Four.

Special Elements and Non-Elements of Crimes

Attendant Circumstances

Statutes sometimes require the state to prove certain facts which are not necessarily considered elements of the crime. These circumstances, called attendant circumstances, are aspects of the crime which may reflect legislatures specific concerns.

> [S]ome criminal statutes may specify additional elements or circumstances that must be present in order to constitute a crime. These additional items are called necessary attendant circumstances and generally refer to the facts surrounding an event, such as the time or place of the conduct or the instrument used to facilitate the harmful act. The term necessary suggest that the existence of such statutorily identified circumstances is required in order to sustain a conviction.
> . . .
> Sometimes the inclusion of attendance circumstances is used to increase the degree, or level of seriousness of an offense.
> . . .
> Attendant circumstances surrounding a crime are often discussed in terms of aggravating circumstances (heightening a person's culpability) or mitigating circumstances (reducing a person's culpability). The presence of such factors can be used to increase or lessen the penalty that can be imposed on a convicted offender. In some jurisdictions, necessary attendant circumstances that increase potential criminal punishment are referred to as specifications. A specification is a separate factual allegation made in a charging instrument that serves as a supplement to the base criminal charge. This specification, if proven beyond a reasonable doubt, enhances the possible penalties for the underlying crime. For example, in an indictment for murder (the purposeful killing of another), the grand jury may also include a gun specification . . . that alleges that the defendant used a gun to commit the offense. This specification is written in addition to the primary charge of murder contained in an indictment
> . . .
> Other types of specifications include circumstances arising out of gang activity, sexual motivation, and repeat offenses. The idea behind these specifications and others is to distinguish between crimes committed under aggravating circumstances . . . from those

committed under average circumstances, and to allow courts to punish aggravated activity accordingly. Feldmeier and Schmalleger, *supra* at 82-83.
act.

The Special Case of Vicarious Liability

Vicarious liability allows us to hold people guilty for the acts of others. In vicarious liability cases the state does not need to prove that the defendant personally committed a voluntary act (or omission), nor must it prove that the defendant personally had a guilty mind (mens rea). Rather, vicarious liability transfers the liability of one actor (generally an employee or child) to the person or entity charged (a boss or a parent—generally due to a special relationship. Like strict liability, vicarious liability crimes violate our deeply rooted belief that criminal liability should be based on personal responsibility; they therefore are generally disfavored and against public policy.

Occasionally, however, vicarious liability statutes sometimes survive the defendant's challenge when there is a clear legislative intent to create a vicarious liability crime. Connecticut, Louisiana, Oregon, and Wyoming have found that vicarious liability statutes are unconstitutional as they violate due process. Statutes that impose a jail sentence as well as a fine are frequently found to violate due process guarantees. See *Koczwara*, below. Vicarious liability may also violate the Eighth Amendment's Cruel and Unusual Punishment Clause if the defendant had no ability to control the actual perpetrator or if conviction would impose too severe a penalty. Dix, *Gilbert's Law Summaries*, p. xiv.

Vicarious liability is generally limited to employer-employee relationships or parent-child relationships. The most common form of vicarious liability is holding an employer liable for the acts of an employee. The justification for allowing vicarious liability in employee/employer situations is to encourage employers to control and monitor employees to ensure that the public is protected from potential dangers. States are divided whether to impose vicarious liability when a crime was committed against the express directions of the employer. Some courts compromise and allow defendant to prove lack of fault.

STATE v. TOMAINO,
733 N.E.2d 1191 (Ohio App. 1999)

HISTORY
Peter Tomaino, the owner of an adult video store, was convicted in the Court of Common Pleas, Butler County, of disseminating matter harmful to juveniles. He appealed. The Court of Appeals reversed and remanded.

WALSH, J.
FACTS
Peter Tomaino, Appellant, owns VIP Video, a video sales and rental store in Millville, Ohio. VIP Video's inventory includes only sexually oriented videotapes and materials. On October 13, 1997, Carl Frybarger, age thirty-seven, and his son Mark, age seventeen, decided that Mark should attempt to rent a video from VIP. Mark entered the store, selected a video, and presented it to the clerk along with his father's driver's license and credit card.

The purchase was completed and the Frybargers contacted the Butler County

Sheriff's Department. After interviewing Mark and his father, Sergeant Greg Blankenship, supervisor of the Drug and Vice Unit, determined that Mark should again attempt to purchase videos at VIP Video with marked money while wearing a radio transmitter wire.

On October 14, 1997, Mark again entered the store. A different clerk was on duty. Following Blankenship's instructions, Mark selected four videos and approached the clerk. He told her that he had been in the store the previous day and that he was thirty-seven. Mark told the clerk that he had used a credit card on that occasion and that he was using cash this time and thus did not have his identification with him. The clerk accepted the cash ($100) and did not require any identification or proof of Mark's age. It is this video transaction that constitutes the basis of the indictment.

The clerk, Billie Doan, was then informed by Blankenship that she had sold the videos to a juvenile and that she would be arrested. Doan said that she needed to call appellant and made several unsuccessful attempts to contact appellant at different locations.

The grand jury indicted appellant Tomaino and Doan on two counts. Count One charged the defendants with recklessly disseminating obscene material to juveniles and Count Two charged the defendants with disseminating matter that was harmful to juveniles.

OPINION

Billie Doan was tried separately from appellant. Appellant moved to dismiss the indictment against him. During pretrial proceedings, appellant argued that criminal liability could not be imputed to him based on the actions of the clerk. The state moved to amend the bill of particulars to provide that appellant "recklessly failed to supervise his employees and agents." The trial court denied appellant's motion to dismiss and the case against appellant proceeded to a jury trial on August 25, 1998. Mark and Carl Frybarger and Blankenship testified on behalf of the state; the defense presented no evidence. Counsel for appellant made a motion for acquittal pursuant to Crim.R. 29 at the close of the state's case. The trial court overruled the motion.

The state argued that appellant was reckless by not having a sign saying "no sales to juveniles." Appellant argued in part that he was not liable for the clerk's actions. The jury was instructed that in order to convict they must find beyond a reasonable doubt that appellant, recklessly and with knowledge of its character or content, sold to a juvenile any material that was obscene (Count One) and harmful to a juvenile (Count Two).

The jury was also instructed on the definitions of knowingly and recklessly and on the definitions of obscene material and of material harmful to juveniles. The jury found appellant not guilty on Count One (disseminating obscene material) and guilty on Count Two (disseminating matter harmful to juveniles).

Following the verdict, appellant moved for both a judgment of acquittal and a new trial. Appellant again argued that he could not be held criminally liable for the acts of another and

that there was no evidence that he had recklessly provided material harmful to a juvenile. The trial court denied both motions. . . . The court stated that the jury could find that appellant was the owner of the store and thus had knowledge of the character or content of the material being sold in his store. The court also stated that appellant "did not implement any policies, plans or procedures to prohibit entrance of juveniles into his store or the sale of material to juveniles."

Appellant argues that no statute imposed criminal liability for his actions or inactions. Having carefully reviewed the state's arguments, we must agree, although we hold that the court erred in its instructions to the jury rather than in denying the motion for acquittal.

Appellant was convicted of disseminating matter harmful to juveniles. R.C. 2907.31 provides in relevant part:

(A) No person, with knowledge of its character or content, shall recklessly do any of the following:
(1) Sell, deliver, furnish, disseminate, provide, exhibit, rent, present to a juvenile any material or performance that is obscene or harmful to juveniles."

Ohio has no common law offenses. Criminal liability is rigidly and precisely limited to those situations that the General Assembly has specifically delineated by statute. In R.C. 2901.21, the legislature has further provided that a person is not guilty of an offense unless both of the following apply:

(1) His liability is based on conduct which includes either a voluntary act, or an omission to perform an act or duty which he is capable of performing;
(2) He has the requisite degree of culpability for each element as to which a culpable mental state is specified by the section defining the offense.

Vicarious liability for another's criminal conduct or failure to prevent another's criminal conduct can be delineated by statute; it cannot be created by the courts. Statutes defining offenses are to be strictly construed against the state and liberally construed in favor of the accused. The elements of a crime must be gathered wholly from the statute. Liability based on ownership or operation of a business may be specifically imposed by statute. For instance, the owner of premises used for gambling—even if he is not present while gambling occurs—can be criminally liable under the statute prohibiting operating a gambling house. Such premises-oriented liability is specifically imposed by the statute, which provides in part that "no person being the owner of premises, shall recklessly permit such premises to be used or occupied for gambling." R.C. 2915.03.

It is undisputed that the clerk furnished the video to the minor and that appellant was not present. Because we find that a plain reading of the disseminating matter harmful to juveniles statute requires personal action by a defendant and does not by its terms impose vicarious or premises oriented liability, the jury was not correctly instructed in this case.

Judgment reversed and cause remanded.

Vicarious Corporate Liability

Corporate liability is a form of vicarious liability. Someone who works for the corporation did something or didn't do something, and the corporation, through its agents, is being held responsible. Corporations can certainly be held civilly liable for violations of laws, but at common law criminal liability did not extend to corporations and associations.

> [I]t is one thing to hold that the faultless employer ought to pay for the damage which his employee inflicts upon third persons in the course of furthering his employer's business; it is much more drastic to visit criminal punishment and moral condemnation upon the employer who is innocent of any personal fault. LaFave, p. 266.

Because a corporation had no mind, the common law reasoned it could not have criminal intent. Because a corporation had no body and could not be imprisoned, it could not be guilty of a crime. The modern rule, however, is to impose corporate liability subject to policy considerations. Now,

> [i]t is almost universally conceded that a corporation may be criminally liable for actions or omissions of its agents in its behalf. Liability is imposed on corporations for the acts and omissions of corporate employees if "consistent with the legislative intent and dependent on the nature of the crime involved." Dix, *Gilberts, Criminal Law*, XIV.

The public policy behind supporting vicarious criminal liability for corporations is to "encourage corporate executives to vigorously prevent and punish illegal activity." Lippman. Additionally, because corporate decision making is collaborative at times, it may not be feasible to identify the specific individuals who were responsible for causing the criminal harm.

According to LaFave, if the crime is a minor one, then corporations are generally held liable merely upon proof that employee was acting in course of his employment. If the crime is a serious one, states are divided. Some states require only that an employee in the course of his employment committed the offense. Other states have adopted the MPC approach and permit conviction only if the perpetration of the offense was authorized, performed, or recklessly tolerated by the board of directors or a high managerial agent. Some states require proof that the corporation gave the actual perpetrator enough authority to act for it in the specific activities related to criminal conduct.

> [C]orporation may be held criminally liable for conduct performed by an agent of the corporation acting in its behalf within the scope of his employment. Under the better view, called the superior agent rule, corporate criminal liability for other than strict-liability regulatory offenses is limited to situations in which the conduct is performed or participated in by the board of directors or a high managerial agent. LaFave, 272.

Lippman identified two tests used to determine whether a corporation should be criminally liable under a statute that encompasses corporations:

1) Respondeat Superior: Under this test, a corporation may be held liable for the conduct of an employee who commits a crime within the scope of his or her employment who possesses the intent to benefit the corporation. Thus, corporations may be criminally responsible even when employees do something contrary to corporate policy.

2) MPC § 2.07: Under the Model Penal Code approach, corporations may be criminally liable in those instances where "the criminal conduct is authorized, requested, commanded, performed, or recklessly tolerated by the board of directors or by a high managerial official acting on behalf of the corporation within the scope of his or her office or employment." Thus, corporations may be criminally responsible only when the employee's actions are approved by high managerial officers.

Corporate crime may result in the criminal conviction of both the employee committing the offense as well as the owner and the corporation. To determine whether corporation may be criminally liable, courts first decide whether the legislature intended the criminal statute to apply to corporations and, if so, does the statute allow the corporation (through its officers) to be liable under the respondeat superior test or the MPC test.

COMMONWEALTH v. KOCZWARA, 397 Pa. 575 (1959)

John Koczwara, the defendant, is the licensee and operator of an establishment on Jackson Street in the City of Scranton known as J.K.'s Tavern. At that place he had a restaurant liquor license issued by the Pennsylvania Liquor Control Board. The Lackawanna County Grand Jury indicted the defendant on five counts for violations of the Liquor Code. ...

. . . .

Upon the conclusion of the trial, defendant ... was sentenced ... to pay the costs of prosecution, a fine of five hundred dollars and to undergo imprisonment in the Lackawanna County Jail for three months.

The defendant took an appeal to the Superior Court. . . . Because of the importance of the issues raised, the petition was allowed and an appeal granted.

Defendant raises two contentions, both of which, in effect, question whether the undisputed facts of this case support the judgment and sentence imposed by the Quarter Sessions Court. Judge HOBAN found as fact that "in every instance the purchase [by minors] was made from a bartender, not identified by name, and service to the boys was made by the

bartender. There was no evidence that the defendant was present on any one of the occasions testified to by these witnesses, nor that he had any personal knowledge of the sales to them or to other persons on the premises." We, therefore, must determine the criminal responsibility of a licensee of the Liquor Control Board for acts committed by his employees upon his premises, without his personal knowledge, participation, or presence, which acts violate a valid regulatory statute passed under the Commonwealth's police power.

While an employer in almost all cases is not criminally responsible for the unlawful acts of his employees, unless he consents to, approves, or participates in such acts, courts all over the nation have struggled for years in applying this rule within the framework of "controlling the sale of intoxicating liquor." At common law, any attempt to invoke the doctrine of respondeat superior in a criminal case would have run afoul of our deeply ingrained notions of criminal jurisprudence that guilt must be personal and individual. [Footnote 1] In recent decades, however, many states have enacted detailed regulatory provisions in fields which are essentially non-criminal, e.g., pure food and drug acts, speeding ordinances, building regulations, and child labor, minimum wage and maximum hour legislation. Such statutes are generally enforceable by light penalties, and although violations are labelled crimes, the considerations applicable to them are totally different from those applicable to true crimes, which involve moral delinquency and which are punishable by imprisonment or another serious penalty. Such so-called statutory crimes are in reality an attempt to utilize the machinery of criminal administration as an enforcing arm for social regulations of a purely civil nature, with the punishment totally unrelated to questions of moral wrongdoing or guilt. It is here that the social interest in the general well-being and security of the populace has been held to outweigh the individual interest of the particular defendant. The penalty is imposed despite the defendant's lack of a criminal intent or mens rea.

Not the least of the legitimate police power areas of the legislature is the control of intoxicating liquor. "There is perhaps no other area of permissible state action within which the exercise of the police power of a state is more plenary than in the regulation and control of the use and sale of alcoholic beverages." It is abundantly clear that the conduct of the liquor business is lawful only to the extent and manner permitted by statute. Individuals who embark on such an enterprise do so with knowledge of considerable peril, since their actions are rigidly circumscribed by the Liquor Code.

Because of the peculiar nature of this business, one who applies for and receives permission from the Commonwealth to carry on the liquor trade assumes the highest degree of responsibility to his fellow citizens. As the licensee of the Board, he is under a duty not only to regulate his own personal conduct in a manner consistent with the permit he has received, but also to control the acts and conduct of any employee to whom he entrusts the sale of liquor. Such fealty is the quid pro quo which the Commonwealth demands in return for the privilege of entering the highly restricted and, what is more important, the highly dangerous business of selling intoxicating liquor.

… [T]he defendant has … argued that a statute imposing criminal responsibility should be construed strictly, with all doubts resolved in his favor. While the defendant's position is entirely correct, we must remember that we are dealing with a statutory crime within the state's plenary police power. In the field of liquor regulation, the legislature has enacted a comprehensive Code aimed at regulating and controlling the use and sale of alcoholic beverages. The question here raised is whether the legislature intended to impose vicarious criminal liability on the licensee-principal for acts committed on his premises without his presence, participation or knowledge.

. . . [T]he legislature has set forth twenty-five specific acts which are condemned as unlawful, and for which penalties are provided. Section 493 contain the two offenses charged here. In neither of these subsections is there any language which would require the prohibited acts to have been done either knowingly, wilfully or intentionally, there being a significant absence of such words as "knowingly, wilfully, etc." [In another section] … the legislature intended such a requirement [by making it]… unlawful to knowingly sell any malt beverages to a person engaged in the business of illegally selling such beverages. The omission of any such word in this subsections is highly significant. It indicates a legislative intent to eliminate both knowledge and criminal intent as necessary ingredients of such offenses. . . .

As the defendant has pointed out, there is a distinction between the requirement of a mens rea and the imposition of vicarious absolute liability for the acts of another. It may be that the courts below, in relying on prior authority, have failed to make such a distinction. In any case, we fully recognize it. Moreover, we find that the intent of the legislature in enacting this Code was not only to eliminate the common law requirement of a mens rea, but also to place a very high degree of responsibility upon the holder of a liquor license to make certain that neither he nor anyone in his employ commit any of the prohibited acts upon the licensed premises. Such a burden of care is imposed upon the licensee in order to protect the public from the potentially noxious effects of an inherently dangerous business. We, of course, express no opinion as to the wisdom of the legislature's imposing vicarious responsibility under certain sections of the Liquor Code. There may or may not be an economic-sociological justification for such liability on a theory of deterrence. Such determination is for the legislature to make, so long as the constitutional requirements are met.

Can the legislature, consistent with the requirements of due process, thus establish absolute criminal liability? Were this the defendant's first violation of the Code, and the penalty solely a minor fine of from $100-$300, we would have no hesitation in upholding such a judgment. Defendant, by accepting a liquor license, must bear this financial risk. Because of a prior conviction for violations of the Code, however, the trial judge felt compelled under the mandatory language of the statute to impose not only an increased fine of five hundred dollars, but also a three month sentence of imprisonment. Such sentence of imprisonment in a case where liability is imposed vicariously cannot be sanctioned by this Court consistently with the law of the land clause of Section 9, Article I of the Constitution of the Commonwealth of Pennsylvania.

The Courts of the Commonwealth have already strained to permit the legislature to carry over the civil doctrine of respondeat superior and to apply it as a means of enforcing the regulatory scheme that covers the liquor trade. We have done so on the theory that the Code established petty misdemeanors involving only light monetary fines. It would be unthinkable to impose vicarious criminal responsibility in cases involving true crimes. Although to hold a principal criminally liable might possibly be an effective means of enforcing law and order, it would do violence to our more sophisticated modern-day concepts of justice. Liability for all true crimes, wherein an offense carries with it a jail sentence, must be based exclusively upon personal causation. It can be readily imagined that even a licensee who is meticulously careful in the choice of his employees cannot supervise every single act of the subordinates. A man's liberty cannot rest on so frail a reed as whether his employee will commit a mistake in judgment.

This Court is ever mindful of its duty to maintain and establish the proper safeguards in a criminal trial. To sanction the imposition of imprisonment here would make a serious change in the substantive criminal law of the Commonwealth, one for which we find no justification. We have found no case in any jurisdiction which has permitted a prison term for a vicarious offense. The Supreme Court of the United States has had occasion only recently to impose due process limitations upon the actions of a state legislature in making unknowing conduct criminal. *Lambert v. California*, 355 U.S. 225, 78 S. Ct. 240 (1957). Our own courts have stepped in time and again to protect a defendant from being held criminally responsible for acts about which he had no knowledge and over which he had little control. We would be utterly remiss were we not to so act under these facts.

In holding that the punishment of imprisonment deprives the defendant of due process of law under these facts, we are not declaring that Koczwara must be treated as a first offender under the Code. He has clearly violated the law for a second time and must be punished accordingly. Therefore, we are only holding that so much of the judgment as calls for imprisonment is invalid, and we are leaving intact the five hundred dollar fine imposed by Judge HOBAN under the subsequent offense section.

DISSENTING OPINION BY MR. JUSTICE MUSMANNO:

The Court in this case is doing what it has absolutely no right to do.

. . . .

It sustains the conviction of a person for acts admittedly not committed by him, not performed in his presence, not accomplished at his direction, and not even done within his knowledge. It is stigmatizing him with a conviction for an act which, in point of personal responsibility, is as far removed from him as if it took place across the seas. The Majority's decision is so novel, so unique, and so bizarre that one must put on his spectacles, remove them to wipe the lenses, and then put them on again in order to assure himself that what he reads is a judicial decision proclaimed in Philadelphia, the home of the Liberty Bell, the locale of Independence Hall, and the place where the fathers of our country met to draft the Constitution of the United States, the Magna Charta of the liberties of Americans and the beacon of hope of mankind seeking justice everywhere.

The decision handed down in this case throws a shadow over that Constitution, applies an eraser to the Bill of Rights, and muffles the Liberty Bell which many decades ago sang its song of liberation from monarchical domination over man's inalienable right to life, liberty, and the pursuit of happiness. Our legal system is based on precedent. The decision of today will become a precedent on which future Dracos may feed to their absolutist and tyrannical content.

. . . .

The Majority introduces into its discussion a proposition which is shocking to contemplate. It speaks of "vicarious criminal liability". Such a concept is as alien to American soil as the upas tree. There was a time in China when a convicted felon sentenced to death could offer his brother or other close relative in his stead for decapitation. The Chinese law allowed such "vicarious criminal liability". I never thought that Pennsylvania would look with favor on anything approaching so revolting a barbarity.

. . .

The defendant John Koczwara had been previously convicted of a violation of the Liquor Code and, because of that conviction, the Trial Court imposed, in addition to a fine of $500, a sentence of three months' imprisonment. The Majority Opinion finds the imprisonment part of the sentence contrary to law. Thus, in addition to the other things I have had to say about the Majority Opinion, I find myself compelled to pin on it the bouquet of inconsistency. The Majority says that it cannot permit the sentencing of a man to jail "for acts about which he had no knowledge and over which he had little control."

. . . .

The Majority enlarges on its inconsistency when it says: "Our own courts have stepped in time and again to protect a defendant from being held criminally responsible for acts about

which he had no knowledge and over which he had little control." If it is wrong to send a person to jail for acts committed by another, is it not wrong to convict him at all? There are those who value their good names to the extent that they see as much harm in a degrading criminal conviction as in a jail sentence. The laceration of a man's reputation, the blemishing of his good name, the wrecking of his prestige by a criminal court conviction may blast a person's chances for honorable success in life to such an extent that a jail sentence can hardly add much to the ruin already wrought to him by the conviction alone.

The Majority extends a sympathetic hand to prevent the jail doors from clanging shut behind John Koczwara. It says: "We would be utterly remiss were we not to do so under these facts." But is it not remiss in refusing to save Koczwara's constitutional prerogatives? Is it not remiss in not striking down this conviction which engrafts upon the criminal code something which up until this time has been unheard of in the Commonwealth of Pennsylvania? Is it not remiss in not reversing a conviction which cannot be based on any written provision of the law? Is it not remiss in giving to a criminal statute a broad interpretation (against the accused) instead of a strict interpretation as our decisions have proclaimed hundreds of times?

I conclude by saying that the Majority has been so remiss in affirming the conviction in this case that I myself would be remiss if I did not dissent against a decision which flouts the Constitution, ignores the Bill of Rights and introduces into the temple of the law the Asiatic rite of "vicarious criminal liability."

DISSENTING OPINION BY MR. JUSTICE McBRIDE:

I would agree that a man who sells liquor to a minor may be punished even if he did not know that the person to whom he sold was a minor. But in my opinion, the statute does not and cannot validly create an indictable misdemeanor under which a liquor licensee is punished by a fine or imprisonment, or both, for the act of an employee in selling to a minor, where, as here, the act itself is done without the licensee's knowledge, consent, or acquiescence. I would reverse the judgment and discharge the defendant.

NOTES
[1] The distinction between respondeat superior in tort law and its application to the criminal law is obvious. In tort law, the doctrine is employed for the purpose of settling the incidence of loss upon the party who can best bear such loss. But the criminal law is supported by totally different concepts. We impose penal treatment upon those who injure or menace social interests, partly in order to reform, partly to prevent the continuation of the antisocial activity and partly to deter others. If a defendant has personally lived up to the social standards of the criminal law and has not menaced or injured anyone, why impose penal treatment?

STATE v. ZETA CHI FRATERNITY, 142 N.H. 16, 696 A.2d 530 (1997)

FACTS (Summary)
Defendant, a New Hampshire corporation and college fraternity at the University of New Hampshire in Durham, held a "rush" to attract new members. In order to encourage people to attend the rush, the defendant hired two female strippers to perform at the event. Fraternity brothers encouraged guests to give the strippers dollar bills so that they would continue to perform. The brothers also told guest that the more they were given, the more they would do. One of the members of the fraternity was providing change for larger bills. Two witnesses testified at trial that they saw guests being led to the mattress after they gave money, at which point the guest performed oral sex on the strippers.

One 19-year-old guest at the party testified that he had learned that beer was available from a soda machine. He went to apartment in the fraternity where the soda machine was located and waited in line and purchased three to five cans of beer. This guest testified that he also observed fraternity members making change for the vending machine. The fraternity secretary testified that the fraternity members voted not to provide alcohol at the rush, and that they moved the vending machine into a separate apartment in another part of the fraternity housing the rush. He also testified that the fraternity had control over the vending machine and its proceeds. The corporation was convicted of selling alcohol to a person under the age of 21 and of prostitution.

OPINION
The defendant [the corporation] asserts that because the fraternity voted not to provide beer at the rush and the soda machine was moved from the main area in the fraternity house to a separate apartment at the back of the house, the defendant did not have control over the machine, and, therefore, could not have caused the sale of alcohol from the machine. Essentially, the defendant is arguing that the individuals responsible for making the beer available for sale to Strachan were not acting on behalf of the corporation or within the scope of their authority. We begin by noting that the only defendant in this case is a corporate entity. "A corporation is a jural person, but not a person in fact. It is an artificial creature, acting only through agents." A corporation may be held criminally liable for criminal acts performed on its behalf by agents or employees acting within the scope of their authority or employment. The criminal conduct need not have been "performed, authorized, ratified, adopted or tolerated by the corporation['s] directors, officers or other 'high managerial agents'" in order to be chargeable to the corporation."

In fact, a corporation can be convicted for actions of its agents even if it expressly instructed the agents not to engage in the criminal conduct. The agents, however, must have been acting within the scope of their actual or apparent authority. Express authority exists when the principal explicitly manifests its authorization for the agent to act. Implied authority is the "reasonable incident or construction of the terms of express authority or results from acquiescence by the principal in a course of dealing by the agent." Apparent authority, on the other hand, "exists where the principal so conducts [itself] as to cause a third party to reasonably believe that the agent is authorized to act." It is the rare case in which the corporate leadership explicitly authorizes its agents to engage in criminal conduct. "Of necessity, the proof [of] authority to so act must rest on all the circumstances and conduct in a given situation and the reasonable inferences to be drawn therefrom."

Evidence at trial indicates that the defendant had control over the apartment in which the vending machine was located, even though it had voted to make the apartment separate from the fraternity house. More importantly, however, witnesses testified that the defendant had control over the soda machine; that only the defendant had an interest in the proceeds from the machine; that only fraternity members had keys to the apartment in which the machine was located; that someone was making change for the machine; and that no one would have an interest in making change except a member of the fraternity. We believe that from these facts the jury could reasonably have found that an agent of the defendant sold beer from the vending machine and that this agent was acting on behalf of the corporation and within the scope of his authority.

The defendant next argues that the evidence was insufficient for the jury to find that the defendant acted recklessly, the mens rea charged in the indictment. Because the defendant is a corporation, its mental state depends on the knowledge of its agents. "[T]he corporation is considered to have acquired the collective knowledge of its employees and is held responsible for their failure to act accordingly."

A person acts recklessly with respect to a material element of an offense when he is aware of and consciously disregards a substantial and unjustifiable risk that the material element exists or will result from his conduct. The risk must be of such a nature and degree that, considering the circumstances known to him, its disregard constitutes a gross deviation from the conduct that a law-abiding person would observe in the situation.

In this case, the jury could reasonably have found that the defendant acted recklessly from the facts that about 150 guests, many of them under the age of twenty-one, were at the rush party that had been widely publicized on campus; that it was the defendant's vending machine; that only fraternity members had keys to the apartment in which the machine was located; that party guests gained access to the machine; that someone was making change; and that a number of people were waiting in line to use the machine.
. . .

The defendant next argues that the evidence was insufficient for the jury to find that the defendant knowingly permitted a place under its control to be used for prostitution. Specifically, the defendant argues that there was no evidence that actual sexual penetration occurred. . . .

We recently held that sexual penetration does not require proof of actual penetration when the act of fellatio is involved.

There was ample evidence for the jury to find in this case that the act of cunnilingus occurred. . . . Since cunnilingus does not require physical penetration, it is irrelevant that no witness could specifically testify to such physical intrusion.

The defendant next argues that even if cunnilingus occurred, the evidence was insufficient for the jury to find that it occurred in exchange for consideration. To the contrary, the record shows that the jury could find that the dancer allowed guests to perform oral sex in exchange for money.

The defendant also contends that the State failed to prove that the defendant knowingly allowed the prostitution and that if prostitution occurred, the individuals who allowed it were not acting within the scope of their authority. We will first address the issue of agency.

As noted above, in the context of corporate criminal liability, the corporation acts through its agents and those agents must be acting within the scope of either their actual or apparent authority in order for the corporation to be liable for their actions. The defendant asserts that because the members of the fraternity announced that guests were not allowed to touch the dancers and that, if the dancer stayed too long with one guest, members of the fraternity would move her along, this indicated the lack of actual or apparent authority.

"[W]hether an agent has acted within his actual or apparent authority . is a question for the trier of fact." Apparent authority can result when the principal "fails to disapprove of the agent's act or course of action so as to lead the public to believe that his agent possesses authority to act in the name of the principal." In this case, there was testimony that the guests were told that if they paid more money the dancers would do more; that on more than one occasion guests were led to the mattress that was brought into the room by the brothers to perform oral sex in exchange for money; and that at least one guest performed oral sex on the dancer for "quite a while." From these facts the jury could reasonably have found that members of the fraternity acted within the scope of their authority and on behalf of the corporation in allowing oral sex to be performed in exchange for money.

The defendant argues that the State failed to prove the requisite mens rea with regard to the prostitution charge, that is, that the defendant knowingly permitted oral sex to occur at the party. A person acts knowingly with respect to conduct or to a circumstance that is a material element of an offense when he is aware that his conduct is of such nature or that such

circumstances exist." The defendant argues that the material element to which the "knowingly" mens rea applies is permission. The defendant contends that there was no opportunity for the defendant to manifest its lack of permission before the oral sex occurred because the dancer's actions were unexpected.

Based on the facts of this case, the defendant's argument is without merit. As noted above, because the defendant is a corporation, and a corporation acts through its agents, the knowledge obtained by the agents of the corporation acting within the scope of their agency is imputed to the corporation. There was testimony that several guests performed oral sex on the dancer and that on at least one occasion it occurred for several minutes. Moreover, the fraternity president testified that he "was very well in control" of the party. Therefore, even if the first act caught members of the fraternity by surprise, the jury could reasonably have inferred that the defendant knowingly permitted oral sex to occur from the defendant's failure to prevent the subsequent conduct. . . . "A corporation is not insulated from criminal liability merely because it published instructions and policies which are violated by its employee; the corporation must place the acts outside the scope of an employee's employment by adequately enforcing its rules.".

Vicarious Parental Liability

Parents are often found liable for the actions of their children. Civil law has long imposed penalties on parents when their children cause damage to other individuals or their property. More recently several states have enacted "duty to supervise" laws which hold parents responsible for *their failure* to supervise their children, for *their failure* to take reasonable steps to prevent their children from engaging in serious or persistent criminal behaviors, and for *their failure* to control their children by not exercising reasonable care, supervision, protection and control. These statutes target parents of incorrigible children who may be involved in a variety of public order offenses. Because these "duty to supervise" statutes require the state prove the parents' actus reus (an omission to act when there is a statutory duty to act) and mens rea— generally criminal negligence or recklessness-- they are not considered vicarious liability statutes. Courts have routinely upheld these statutes, finding them to promote public policy, and have not found them to be unconstitutional. See, e.g., *Williams v. Garmetti*. Samaha mentions that "in one case, a father was found guilty for "allowing his child to violate a curfew ordinance," and, in another, a mother was convicted for "knowingly" permitting her children "to go at large in violation of a valid quarantine order." One case involves the Detroit suburb of St. Clair Shores, which had an ordinance making it a crime to fail to "exercise reasonable control" to prevent children from committing delinquent acts. Alex Provenzino, 16, committed a string of seven burglaries. The local police ordered his parents to "take control" of Alex. When his father tried to discipline him, Alex "punched his father." When he tried to restrain him, Alex escaped by pressing his fingers into his father's eyes. When Alex tried to attack him with a golf club, his father called the police.

The parents were charged with, but acquitted of, both vicariously committing the seven burglaries and failing to supervise their son.[13]

Vicarious liability laws which hold parents responsible for the acts of their children are much different than parental responsibility laws which hold parents responsible for failing to care for their children. Vicarious liability statutes hold parents criminally liable even though *they did* nothing wrong and may not even have had any idea that their children were engaging in the prohibited behavior. Parent-child vicarious liability statutes grew out of public fear, frustration, and anger over juvenile violence and parents' failure to control their kids. However, there are few cases in which appellate courts find parental liability for the crimes of child solely on the basis of the parent-child relationship. Social host liability laws hold adults liable for providing liquor in their home to minors in the event than an accident or injury occurs and are not actual vicarious liability statutes because they require the state prove that the adult did some act (providing alcohol, providing a place for teenagers to consume alcohol) with some *mens rea* (generally, negligence or recklessness).

STATE V. AKERS,
119 N.H. 161, 400 A.2d 38 (1979)

GRIMES, J.

FACTS (Summary)
The defendants are fathers whose minor sons were found guilty of driving snowmobiles in violation of New Hampshire statutes (operating on public ways, reasonable speed) The fathers were convicted of a New Hampshire statute provided that "(t)he parents or guardians or persons assuming responsibility will be responsible for any damage incurred or for any violations of this chapter by any person under the age of 18." The defendants argued the statute under which they were convicted, was not intended by the legislature to impose criminal responsibility, and (2) if in fact the legislative intention was to impose criminal responsibility, then the statute would violate the New Hampshire Constitution.

OPINION
...The language of RSA 269-C:24 IV, "parents . . . will be responsible . . . for any violations of this chapter by any person under the age of 18," clearly indicates the legislature's intention to hold the parents criminally responsible for the OHRV violations of their minor children. It is a general principle of this State's Criminal Code that "(a) person is not guilty of an offense unless his criminal liability is based on conduct that includes a voluntary Act or the voluntary

omission to perform an act of which he is physically capable." RSA 269-C:24 IV seeks to impose criminal liability on parents for the acts of their children without basing liability on any voluntary act or omission on the part of the parent. Because the statute makes no reference at all to parental conduct or acts it seeks to impose criminal responsibility solely because of their parental status contrary to the provisions of RSA 626:1 I.

The legislature has not specified any voluntary acts or omissions for which parents are sought to be made criminally responsible and it is not a judicial function to supply them. It is fundamental to the rule of law and due process that acts or omissions which are to be the basis of criminal liability must be specified in advance and not Ex post facto.
…
Without passing upon the validity of statutes that might seek to impose vicarious criminal liability on the part of an employer for acts of his employees, we have no hesitancy in holding that any attempt to impose such liability on parents simply because they occupy the status of parents, without more, offends the due process clause of our State constitution.

. . . Considering the nature of parenthood, we are convinced that the status of parenthood

---

[13] See, https://www.nytimes.com/1996/05/10/us/parents-convicted-for-a-youth-s-misconduct.html

cannot be made a crime. This, however, is the effect of RSA 269-C:24 IV. Even if the parent has been as careful as anyone could be, even if the parent has forbidden the conduct, and even if the parent is justifiably unaware of the activities of the child, criminal liability is still imposed under the wording of the present statute. There is no other basis for criminal responsibility other than the fact that a person is the parent of one who violates the law.

Vicarious Liability--Parking Tickets

Vicarious liability laws have been used to hold car owners liable for parking violations by others when driving their cars. Because of the very minor nature of the punishment, courts have upheld parking violation statutes that hold the owner of the vehicle to be *prima facia* (on its face) responsible for paying parking tickets. Unless the owner can show he or she wasn't responsible, he is presumed liable for the ticket.

Comparing Vicarious Liability With Accomplice, Conspiracy, And Solicitation Liability.

Vicarious liability differs from accomplice liability which will be discussed in Chapter Five. With vicarious liability the defendant did not aid and assist or in any way participate in the criminal venture whereas accomplice liability requires that the defendant have intended to aid (*mens rea*) and provided some assistance or encouragement (actus reus) toward the completion of the crime. Vicarious liability also differs from conspiracy and solicitation liability discussed in Chapter Four because the vicariously liable defendant neither agreed to the commission of the crime nor did they request that the other commit a crime on their behalf.

Other Cases—Vicarious Liability

United States v. Dotterweich, 320 U.S. 277 (1943). A company introduced adulterated and misbranded drugs into interstate commerce. The Court held that corporations, along with corporate executives and employees, could be held criminally liable for violations of the Federal Food, Drug and Cosmetic Act of 1943. The president of the corporation and the corporations executives were found to be vicariously liable for the strict liability crimes of employees because the law was intended to ensure that company executives and managers closely monitor the distribution of potentially dangerous drugs to the public.

United States v. Park, 421 U.S. 658 (1975). The Court upheld conviction of large national food store chain along with the president of the company for shipping adulterated food in interstate commerce.

Commonwealth v. Penn Valley Resorts, Inc. 494 A.2d. 1139 (Pa. Super. Ct. 1985.) Clancy, the president of a resort permitted a group of underage students to engage in a drinking binge at the result. Frazier, a 20-year-old, drank excessively for five or six hours. Clancy personally served alcohol to Frazier and seized Frazier's car keys but later handed the keys back to Frazier encouraging the drunk and hostile student to leave the resort. Frazier was killed when he drove his car off the road and hit a bridge. His blood alcohol content was .23%. The Pennsylvania Superior Court concluded that the resort through its managerial agent, committed involuntary manslaughter and reckless endangerment. Clancy was president and his acts legally obligated and financially benefitted the corporation.

People v. Travers, 124 Cal. Rptr. 728 (Cal. Ct. App. 1975) Mitchell, a service station employee, misrepresented the quality of motor oil he sold to the public. The defendant Travers was the owner of the station and was prosecuted along with Mitchell under a statute that punished the sale of a misbranded product. Travers complained that he was completely unaware of Mitchell's actions. The court reasoned that the importance of smoothly running motor vehicles and the right of the public to receive what they paid for justified the imposition of vicarious liability on Travers without the necessity of demonstrating that he possessed a criminal intent. The court explained that it was reasonable to expect a station owner to supervise the sale of motor oil, and requiring the prosecution to prove criminal intent would permit owners to escape punishment by pleading they were unaware of the quality or contents of the motor oil sold. This case shows it is possible to have a statute that imposes both strict liability and vicarious liability—these statutes are intended to protect the public health, safety and welfare.

WRAP UP

Criminal statutes specify elements of a crime that the prosecution must prove beyond a reasonable doubt in order to convict a defendant of a crime. Some statutes include only the elements of actus reus (a voluntary act, voluntary commission to act where there is a legal duty to act, or possession), the mens rea, any attendant circumstances, and punishments. Other criminal statutes also specify a particular harm and require the state prove that defendant caused the harm.

Strict liability crimes are ones where the government does not have to prove criminal intent. Courts are disinclined to find that a statute imposes strict liability unless there is clear indication that the legislature intended to create strict liability. The courts will examine legislative history, the seriousness of crime, whether the crime is *male in se* or *mala prohibitum*, and the seriousness of the punishment in deciding whether the state should be relieved of its obligation to prove criminal intent of the defendant.

Statutes are generally silent on the other elements of a crime: legality and concurrence. The legality element is met when a law is validly enacted and puts people on notice that certain behavior is illegal. Laws are presumed to be valid, and state generally does not have to begin each case by proving that proper procedure was followed in the enactment of the law. Although not generally specified in statute, the state must also prove the concurrence element--that the criminal intent triggered the criminal act.

Vicarious liability statutes violate our belief in individual responsibility. Only people who do something wrong should be blamed for the crime, but vicarious liability imputes (transfers) both the criminal intent and the criminal act of one person to another. Courts generally invalidate these purported vicarious liability statutes, but have at times upheld liability based upon an employer/employee relationship or a parent/child relationship.

Chapter Four: Inchoate Offenses

Overview

Inchoate crimes are preparatory crimes (*inchoate* means underdeveloped, incomplete, or only partly begun). Inchoate crimes often involve preparation to commit some harm, and, by criminalizing inchoate offenses, police are able to intercept suspects before they can inflict the injury involved in the intended crimes. The three inchoate offenses are attempt (an unsuccessful effort to commit a crime), conspiracy (an agreement to commit a crime coupled with an overt act in furtherance of the agreement), and solicitation (an effort to persuade another individual to commit a crime). Attempt, solicitation, and conspiracy, are not crimes in themselves, and must be tied to an intended offense. That said, prosecutors file separate and distinct charges for inchoate offenses. With attempt the successful defendant is charged with the completed offense (murder), and the unsuccessful defendant is charged with attempt (attempted murder).

The mens rea element for inchoate offenses is purposefully or intentionally. Thus, to convict for an inchoate offense, the state must prove defendant had the specific intent or purpose to accomplish the intended crime. The actus reus element for each of the inchoate offenses varies among jurisdictions, but generally, the state must prove defendant engaged in some act to carry out the purpose of the intended crime. Inchoate offenses are generally punished less severely than the intended crime.

Attempt

Modern Approaches to Attempt

Attempt statutes punish unsuccessful efforts to commit a crime. An attempt is a failure. There are two types of failures-- a *complete* (but imperfect) *attempt* and an *incomplete attempt*. A complete attempt occurs when an individual takes every act required to commit the crime and yet fails to succeed. An example is an individual firing a weapon and missing the intended target. An incomplete attempt occurs when an individual abandons, or is prevented from completing, the act because of some factor (such as the arrival of the police) outside of his or her control. An example is an individual who is about to fire the weapon when the police show up and he runs away. Some states recognize a third type of attempt--*impossible attempt*—in which perpetrator makes a mistake, such as aiming and firing the gun only to realize it is not loaded.

Common Law Attempt

According to Lippman, early English common law did not recognize or punish attempts. In 1784 attempt was finally recognized in England in *Rex v. Scofield*. In which Scofield placed a lighted candle and combustible material in a house with the intent of burning down the structure. By 1801 law of attempt was fully accepted, and in *Rex v. Higgins*, defendant urged a servant to steal his master's goods, and the court stated "all offenses of a public nature, that is, all such acts *or attempts* as tend to prejudice the community are indictable." Early on states accepted attempt, generally holding that attempts to commit both felonies and misdemeanors are misdemeanors.

Model Penal Code Attempt

MPC §5.01 (1) (a) provides that a person is guilty of an attempt to commit a crime if he purposely engages in conduct that would constitute the crime if the attendant circumstances were as he believes them to be. Paragraph (b) also says the person is guilty of attempt when causing a particular result is an element of the crime, and he does or omits to do anything with the purpose of causing the harm or with the belief that it will cause the harm. Paragraph (c) indicates a person is guilty of attempt when he purposely does or omits to do anything that, under the circumstances as he believes them to be is an act or omission which constitutes a substantial step in the course of conduct which will result in his commission of the crime. MPC § 5.01 (2) states that in order to be a substantial step in furtherance of the crime, the action has to be strongly corroborative of the actor's criminal purpose. It then gives several examples of behavior that is strongly corroborative of the actor's criminal purpose which includes:

(a) lying in wait, searching for or following the contemplated victim of the crime;

(b) enticing or seeking to entice the contemplated victim of the crime to go to the place contemplated for its commission;

(c) reconnoitering the place contemplated for the commission of the crime;

(d) unlawful entry of a structure, vehicle or enclosure in which it is contemplated that the crime will be committed;

(e) possession of materials to be employed in the commission of the crime, that are specially designed for such unlawful use or that can serve no lawful purpose of the actor under the circumstances;

(f) possession, collection or fabrication of materials to be employed in the commission of the crime, at or near the place contemplated for its commission, if such possession, collection or fabrication serves no lawful purpose of the actor under the circumstances;

(g) soliciting an innocent agent to engage in conduct constituting an element of the crime.

MPC §5.01 (3) indicates that a person who wants to aid and assist another to commit a crime and does conduct that would establish "his complicity under Section 2.06 if the crime were committed by such other person, is guilty of an attempt to commit the crime, although the crime is not committed or attempted by such other person." Thus, the MPC indicates a person can be guilty of an attempted crime on an aiding and abetting theory if the person does something to aid and abet the crime even if the crime is not committed.

Elements of Attempt

Attempts have three elements: mens rea, actus reus, and failure to complete the crime. The mens rea for attempt is the specific intent to complete the intended crime. The individual must possess the specific purpose to achieve a criminal objective. If the charge is attempted theft, for example, the state must prove that the defendant intended to steal someone's property. The commentary to the MPC gives the following example: an individual detonates a bomb with the intent of destroying the building knowing that people are inside and the bomb doesn't detonate. The defendant likely would not be responsible for attempted murder, because his or her purpose was to destroy the building not to kill the individuals inside the structure. (A conviction for attempted arson would certainly be possible). MPC § 5.01(1)(b) adopts a broad approach, however, in that it would allow an attempted murder conviction if the defendant knew that death is likely to result from the destruction of the building ("with the belief that it will cause such a result").

The actus reus of attempt is complicated, and legislatures, judges, and lawyers have long disagreed how far individuals must progress toward completing the intended crime before the individual can be held liable for attempt. An individual must intentionally perform acts that are proximate (closely connected) to the completion of a crime. At one end of the spectrum is mere preparation -- all agree that mere preparation is not sufficient to constitute the actus reus of attempt. At the other end of the spectrum is the commission of the last act necessary, although most states don't require the defendant take the last step in order to be liable for attempt. All jurisdictions require that, at the very least, the defendant needs to have committed some act or acts toward the commission of the crime.

The last element of attempt is the failure to commit the crime. If the crime is completed, the attempt folds into (or, in legal terminology, "merges into") the intended, completed crime and only the intended crime is charged.

ATTEMPT MENS REA

The mens rea of attempt has two components: (1) the intent to commit the acts or cause the result constituting the target crime; and (ii) the intent necessary for the target crime. Because attempts always require intentional or purposeful behavior, even attempts to do a strict liability crime requires proof of intent.

PEOPLE v. KIMBALL,
311 N.W.2d 343 (1981 Mich.App.)

HISTORY
James Kimball, Defendant, was charged with
and convicted of attempted unarmed robbery,
at a bench trial conducted in early August of
1979. He was sentenced to a prison term of
from 3 to 5 years and appeals by leave granted.
Reversed and remanded.

MAHER, J.

There is really very little dispute as to what
happened on May 21, 1979, at the Alpine Party
Store near Suttons Bay, Michigan. Instead, the
dispute at trial centered on whether what took
place amounted to a criminal offense or merely
a bad joke.

FACTS
James Kimball (defendant) went to the home of
a friend, Sandra Storey, where he proceeded to
consume a large amount of vodka mixed with
orange juice. Defendant was still suffering from
insect stings acquired the previous day so he
also took a pill called "Eskaleth 300,"
containing 300 milligrams of Lithium, which
Storey had given him.

After about an hour, the pair each mixed a half-
gallon container of their favorite drinks (vodka
and orange juice, in the defendant's case), and
set off down the road in Storey's '74 MGB
roadster. At approximately 8:15 or 8:30 in the
evening, defendant (who was driving) pulled
into the parking lot of the Alpine Party Store.
Although he apparently did not tell Storey why
he pulled in, defendant testified that the reason
for the stop was to buy a pack of cigarettes.

Concerning events inside the store, testimony
was presented by Susan Stanchfield, the clerk
and sole employee present at the time. She
testified that defendant came in and began
talking to and whistling at the Doberman
Pinscher guard dog on duty at the time. She
gave him a "dirty look," because she didn't
want him playing with the dog. Defendant then
approached the cash register, where Stanchfield
was stationed, and demanded money.
Stanchfield testified that she thought the
defendant was joking, and told him so, until he
demanded money again in a "firmer tone."

STANCHFIELD: "By his tone I knew he meant
business; that he wanted the money."
PROSECUTION: "You felt he was serious?"
STANCHFIELD: "I knew he was serious."

Stanchfield then began fumbling with the one
dollar bills until defendant directed her to the
"big bills." Stanchfield testified that as she was
separating the checks from the twenty dollar
bills defendant said "I won't do it to you;
you're good looking and I won't do it to you
this time, but if you're here next time, it won't
matter."

A woman then came in (Storey) who put a
hand on defendant's shoulder and another on
his stomach and directed him out of the store.
Stanchfield testified that she called after the
defendant, saying that she would not call the
police if he would "swear never to show your
face around here again." To this defendant is
alleged to have responded: "You could only get
me on attempted anyway." Stanchfield then
directed a customer to get the license plate
number on defendant's car while she phoned
the owner of the store.

Defendant also testified concerning events
inside the store. He stated that the first thing he
noticed when he walked in the door was the
Doberman Pinscher. When he whistled the dog
came to him and started licking his hand.
Defendant testified that while he was petting
the dog Stanchfield said "watch out for the dog;
he's trained to protect the premises."

DEFENDANT: Well, as soon as she told me that
the dog was a watchdog and a guarddog (sic), I
just walked up in front of the cash register and
said to Sue (Stanchfield) I said, "I want your
money."

I was really loaded and it just seemed to me like
it was kind of a cliché because of the fact that
they've got this big bad watchdog there that's
supposed to watch the place and there I was
just petting it, and it was kind of an open door
to carry it a little further and say hey, I want all
your money because this dog isn't going to
protect you. It just kind of happened all at once.

She said, I can't quote it, but something to the effect that if this is just a joke, it's a bad joke, and I said, "Just give me your big bills."

Then she started fumbling in the drawer, and before she pulled any money out of the drawer I don't know whether she went to the ones or the twenties I said as soon as she went toward the drawer to actually give me the money, I said, "Hey, I'm just kidding," and something to the effect that you're too good-looking to take your money.

And she said, "Well, if you leave right now and don't ever come back, I won't call the police," and I said, "Okay, okay," and I started to back up.

And Sandy (Storey) I mean I don't know if I was stumbling back or stepping back, but I know she grabbed me, my arm, and said, "Let's go," and we turned around and left, and that was it.

Both Stanchfield and the defendant testified that there were other people in the store during the time that defendant was in the store, but the testimony of these people revealed that they did not hear what was said between Stanchfield and the defendant.

Storey testified that she remained in the car while defendant went into the store but that after waiting a reasonable time she went inside to see what was happening. As she approached the defendant she heard Stanchfield say "just promise you will never do that again and I won't take your license number." She then took defendant's arm, turned around, gave Stanchfield an "apologetic smile," and took defendant back to the car.

Once in the car, defendant told Storey what had happened in the store, saying "but I told her (Stanchfield) I was only kidding." Defendant

and Storey then drove to a shopping center where defendant was subsequently arrested.

OPINION

The general attempt statute, under which defendant was prosecuted, provides in part as follows:

> Any person who shall attempt to commit an offense prohibited by law, and in such attempt shall do any act towards the commission of such offense, but shall fail in the perpetration, or shall be intercepted or prevented in the execution of the same, when no express provision is made by law for the punishment of such attempt, shall be punished. M.C.L. ß 750.92; M.S.A. ß 28.287.

The elements of an attempt are

(1) the specific intent to commit the crime attempted and
(2) an overt act going beyond mere preparation towards the commission of the crime.

Considering the second element first, it is clear that in the instant case defendant committed sufficient overt acts. As the trial court noted, there was evidence on every element of an unarmed robbery except for the actual taking of money. From the evidence presented, including the evidence of defendant's intoxication, the question of whether defendant undertook these acts with the specific intent to commit an unarmed robbery is a much closer question. After hearing all the evidence, however, the trial court found that defendant possessed the requisite intent and we do not believe that finding was clearly erroneous.

REVERSED AND REMANDED.

[The court reversed and remanded because the trial court didn't allow the defendant to prove that he voluntarily abandoned his attempt to rob the store.

AIDS and the likelihood that AIDS will be invariably fatal. It talked about legal standards necessary to make inferences, and ultimately concluded,

> we find no additional evidence from which to infer an intent to kill. Smallwood's actions are wholly explained by an intent to commit rape and armed robbery, the crimes for which he has already pled guilty. For this reason, his actions fail to provide evidence that he also had an intent to kill. Smallwood's knowledge of his HIV infected status provides the only evidence in this case supporting a conclusion that he intended anything beyond the rapes and robbery.

*See also: **People v. Moreland**, WL 459026 (Cal. App. 2 Dist. 2002)* (defendant could not be guilty of attempted murder unless he had the specific intent to kill the victim); ***Thacker v. Commonwealth**, 114 S.E. 504 (1922)* (shooting through tent with an intent to put light out does not equal attempted murder); ***People v. Matthews**, 258 N.E.2d 378 (Ill. 1970)* (attempts require the intent to commit acts or cause result and intent necessary for target crime).

ATTEMPT ACTUS REUS

The common law adopted a very restrictive approach to attempt and required the government prove that the defendant committed the last act necessary but nevertheless failed to complete the intended crime. Under the common law approach, for example, to be guilty of attempted arson, the person must have actually lit or ignited the fire.

States statutes on attempt have taken two general approaches when determining what acts are sufficient to constitute attempt. The objective approach to criminal attempt requires an act that comes extremely close to the commission of the crime. This approach distinguishes preparation or the planning and purchasing of materials (getting matches and kerosene) from acts taken to perpetrate the crime (spreading the kerosene and lighting the match). It stresses the danger posed by a defendant's acts. The subjective approach to criminal attempt focuses on an individual's intent rather than his or her acts. This approach is based on the belief that society should intervene as soon as an individual who possesses the required intent takes an act toward the commission of a crime. It focuses on the danger to society presented by a defendant who possesses a criminal intent.

The MPC as noted above and discussed below requires that the actor take a substantial step in furtherance of the crime (one which is strongly corroborative of his criminal intent) in order to commit the actus reus of attempt.

Below are samples of cases demonstrating the various tests of attempt actus reus. *Young v. State* provides a discussion of various tests of attempt actus reus.

Actus Reus -- All-But-The-Last-Act

COMMONWEALTH v. PEASLEE, 59 N.E. 55 (Mass. 1901)

FACTS
Lincoln Peaslee had made and arranged combustibles in a building he owned so they were ready to be lighted and, if lighted, would have set fire to the building and its contents. He got within a quarter of a mile of the building, but his would-be accomplice refused to light the fire.

OPINION
"A mere collection and preparation of materials in a room, for the purpose of setting fire to them, unaccompanied by any present intent to set the fire, would be too remote and not all but 'the last act' necessary to complete the crime."

Actus Reus -- Physical Proximity To The Commission Of A Crime

Under this approach, the defendant's acts must come very close to completing the crime. This approach focuses on the remaining steps required to complete the crime. Attempt occurs when act is very near or dangerously close to the completion of a crime.

PEOPLE v. RIZZO,
158 N.E. 888 (N.Y.App. 1927)

FACTS (Summary)
Charles Rizzo, Anthony J. Dorio, Thomas Milo, and John Thomasello were driving through New York City looking for a payroll clerk they intended to rob. While they were still looking for their victim, the police apprehended and arrested them. They were tried and convicted of attempted robbery. Rizzo appealed.

OPINION:
The Penal Law, § 2, prescribes that:
An act, done with intent to commit a crime, and tending but failing to effect its commission, is "an attempt to commit that crime." The word "tending" is very indefinite. It is perfectly evident that there will arise differences of opinion as to whether an act in a given case is one tending to commit a crime. "Tending" means to exert activity in a particular direction. Any act in preparation to commit a crime may be said to have a tendency towards its accomplishment.

The procuring of the automobile, searching the streets looking for the desired victim, were in reality acts tending toward the commission of the proposed crime.

The law, however, had recognized that many acts in the way of preparation are too remote to constitute the crime of attempt. The line has been drawn between those acts which are remote and those which are proximate and near to the consummation. The law must be practical, and therefore considers those acts only as tending to the commission of the crime which are so near to its accomplishment that in all reasonable probability the crime itself would have been committed, but for timely interference. The cases which have been before the courts express this idea in different language, but the idea remains the same. The act or acts must come or advance very near to the accomplishment of the intended crime.

Actus Reus -- Unequivocality or Clarity of Purpose Test (Stop The Film Test)

This approach asks whether an ordinary person looking at the defendant's acts, without any other information, would conclude without a doubt that the defendant intends to commit the crime. This test is criticized for lacking clear guidelines and providing jurors with considerable discretion.

STATE v. STEWART,
736 P.2d 572 (1988))

FACTS (Summary)
Scott Kodanko was waiting for a bus on a Saturday afternoon after leaving work. He was alone in a three-sided plexiglas bus shelter open to the street in downtown Milwaukee. Two men, Mr. Moore and Walter Lee Stewart, the defendant, entered the bus shelter while a third man, Mr. Levy, remained outside.

Moore and the defendant stood one to two feet from Kodanko. Kodanko was in a corner of the shelter, his exit to the street blocked by the two men. Moore asked Kodanko if he wanted to

buy some cigarettes. Kodanko responded that he did not. Moore then said, "Give us some change." When Kodanko refused, the defendant said "Give us some change, man." The defendant repeated this demand in an increasingly loud voice three to four times. Kodanko still refused to give the two men change. The defendant then reached into his coat with his right hand at about the waist level, whereupon Moore stated something to the effect of "put that gun away." At that point Levy, who had been waiting outside the bus shelter, entered and said to the defendant and Moore "Come on, let's go." Levy showed

Kodanko some money, stating, "I don't want your money, I got lots of money."

OPINION

If the defendant had been filmed in this case and the film stopped just before Levy entered the bus stop and the three men departed, we conclude that a trier of fact could find beyond a reasonable doubt that the defendant's acts were directed toward robbery. The film would show the defendant demanding money and appearing to reach for a gun. This evidence is sufficient to prove that the defendant had taken sufficient steps for his conduct to constitute an attempted robbery.

Actus Reus – MPC/Substantial Step Approach

Under this approach the actus reus for attempt is satisfied if defendant's acts are sufficient to clearly indicate that he or she possesses an intent to commit the crime. This test provides an understandable and easily applied test for attempt. The MPC states that to constitute an attempt an act must be a clear step toward the commission of a crime and the act must be "strongly corroborative of the actor's criminal purpose." This step is not required to come close to the completion of the crime itself. The focus is on the acts already taken by the defendant toward the commission of the crime.

YOUNG v. STATE,
493 A.2d 352 (Md. 1985)

HISTORY

Raymond Alexander Young, Defendant, was convicted before the Circuit Court for Prince George's County, of attempted armed robbery. He was sentenced to 20 years, and he appealed. The Court of Special Appeals affirmed the conviction and sentence, and Young petitioned for certiorari. The Maryland Court of Appeals (Maryland's highest court) affirmed his conviction.

ORTH, J.

The offense of criminal attempt has long been accepted as a part of the criminal law of Maryland. . . . [The court defined elements of the offense as:]

1) a specific intent to do a criminal act and
2) some act in furtherance of that intent going beyond mere preparation.

The sentence of a person who is convicted of an attempt to commit a crime may not exceed the maximum sentence for the crime attempted.

Such was the posture of the law of Maryland regarding criminal attempts when Raymond Alexander Young, also known as Morris Prince Cunningham and Prince Alexander Love, was found guilty by a jury in the Circuit Court for Prince George's County. In imposing sentence the court said:

Young is 41 years old. He has been a crime wave up and down the East Coast from New York to Tennessee. Now he stopped in Maryland, and look what he did here.

He is a violent criminal. Now I am sorry he doesn't have this consciousness of right or wrong. And I don't understand why he can't learn it, because he has had a chance to reflect in prison. But I have to take him off the street for the safety of people.

It appears from the transcript of the sentencing proceedings that at the time Young was sentenced upon the convictions here reviewed he was also sentenced upon convictions rendered at a separate trial of armed robbery and the use of a handgun in a crime of violence to 20 years and 15 years respectively to run concurrently, but consecutively to the sentences imposed in this case.

FACTS

Several banks in the Oxon Hill–Fort Washington section of Prince George's County had been held up. The Special Operations Division of the Prince George's Police Department set up a surveillance of banks in the area. In the early afternoon of 26 November 1982 the police team observed Young driving an automobile in such a manner as to give rise to a reasonable belief that he was casing several banks. They followed him in his reconnoitering.

At one point when he left his car to enter a

store, he was seen to clip a scanner onto his belt. The scanner later proved to contain an operable crystal number frequency that would receive Prince George's County uniform patrol transmissions. At that time Young was dressed in a brown waist-length jacket and wore sunglasses.

Around 2:00 P.M. Young came to rest at the rear of the Fort Washington branch of the First National Bank of Southern Maryland. Shortly before, he had driven past the front of the Bank and parked in the rear of it for a brief time.

He got out of his car and walked hurriedly beside the Bank toward the front door. He was still wearing the brown waist-length jacket and sunglasses, but he had added a blue knit stocking cap pulled down to the top of the sunglasses, white gloves and a black eye patch. His jacket collar was turned up. His right hand was in his jacket pocket and his left hand was in front of his face. As one of the police officers observing him put it, he was "sort of duck[ing] his head."

It was shortly after 2:00 P.M. and the Bank had just closed. Through the windows of his office the Bank Manager saw Young walking on the "landscape" by the side of the Bank toward the front door. Young had his right hand in his jacket pocket and tried to open the front door with his left hand. When he realized that the door was locked and the Bank was closed, he retraced his steps, running past the windows with his left hand covering his face. The Bank Manager had an employee call the police.

Young ran back to his car, yanked open the door, got in, and put the car in drive "all in one movement almost," and drove away. The police stopped the car and ordered Young to get out. Young was in the process of removing his jacket; it fell over the car seat and partially onto the ground. The butt of what proved to be a loaded .22 caliber revolver was sticking out of the right pocket of the jacket. On the front seat of the car were a pair of white surgical gloves, a black eye patch, a blue knit stocking cap, and a pair of sunglasses. Young told the police that his name was Morris P. Cunningham. As Young was being taken from the scene, he asked "how much time you could get for attempted bank robbery."

OPINION

A criminal attempt requires specific intent; the specific intent must be to commit some other crime. [The court concluded that the] evidence is most compelling if it is is more than legally sufficient to establish beyond a reasonable doubt that Young had the specific intent to commit an armed robbery as charged.

The determination of the overt act which is beyond mere preparation in furtherance of the commission of the intended crime is a most significant aspect of criminal attempts. If an attempt is to be a culpable offense serving as the basis for the furtherance of the important societal interests of crime prevention and the correction of those persons who have sufficiently manifested their dangerousness, the police must be able to ascertain with reasonable assurance when it is proper for them to intervene.

It is not enough to say merely that there must be "some overt act beyond mere preparation in furtherance of the crime" as the general definition puts it.

The definition does, however, highlight the problem as to what "proximity to completion person must achieve before he can be deemed to have attempted to commit a crime." In solving this problem, the interest of society and the rights of the individual must be kept in balance. Thus, the importance of the determination of the point at which the police may properly intervene is readily apparent.

There is no dispute that there must be some overt act to trigger police action. Bad thoughts do not constitute a crime, and so it is not enough that a person merely have intended and prepared to commit a crime. There must also be an act, and not any act will suffice.

What act will suffice to show that an attempt itself has reached the stage of a completed crime has persistently troubled the courts. They have applied a number of approaches in order to determine when preparation for the commission of a crime has ceased and the actual attempt to commit it has begun.

It is at the point when preparation has been

completed and perpetration of the intended crime has started that a criminal attempt has been committed and culpability for that misdemeanor attaches. A number of text writers have discussed and evaluated the different approaches employed by the courts to resolve the problem. We find the exposition of these approaches by LaFave and Scott to be the clearest, and what follows is taken largely from their comments on "The Act" at pages 431-438 of their *Handbook on Criminal Law, supra.*

In the "Proximity Approach" the act must be sufficiently proximate to the intended crime. But how proximate? The strictest approach is that the accused must have engaged in the "last proximate act," that is, have done everything he believes necessary to bring about the intended result. Some courts follow a less rigid formula. They deem that the act is proximate when it is indispensable to the criminal scheme. Other courts believe that an act is "proximate" when it is physically proximate to the intended crime so that there is a dangerous proximity to success. The emphasis is not so much upon what the accused has done as upon what remains to be done. Thus the time and place at which the intended crime is supposed to occur take on considerable importance. This appears to be the approach that the Court of Special Appeals followed in *Frye v. State, supra,* in determining that the evidence was insufficient to support the conviction of attempted kidnapping.

"The Probable Desistance Approach" contemplates an act which in the ordinary course of events would result in the commission of the intended crime except for the intervention of some extraneous factor. Under this approach the accused's conduct must pass that point where most men, holding such an intention as the accused holds, would think better of their conduct and desist.

In "The Equivocality Approach" the act which transforms the accused's conduct from preparation to perpetration constitutes a step towards the commission of the intended crime, and

the doing of the act can have no other purpose than the commission of that crime. This approach is also known as the *res ipsa loquitur* test.

"The Model Penal Code Approach" looks to § 5.01 of the Model Penal Code (Proposed Official Draft 1962) to solve the problem. Under subsection (1)(c) a person is guilty of an attempt to commit a crime if, acting with the kind of culpability otherwise required for commission of the crime, he purposely does or omits to do anything which, under the circumstances as he believes them to be, is an act or omission constituting a *substantial step* in a course of conduct planned to culminate in his commission of the crime. (emphasis added).

Each of these approaches is not without advantages and disadvantages in theory and in application, as is readily apparent from a perusal of the comments of various text writers and of the courts. We believe that the preferable approach is one bottomed on the "substantial step" test as is that of Model Penal Code. We think that using a "substantial step" as the criterion in determining whether an overt act is more than mere preparation to commit a crime is clearer, sounder, more practical and easier to apply to the multitude of differing fact situations which may occur. Therefore, in formulating a test to fix the point in the development of events at which a person goes further than mere unindictable preparation and becomes guilty of attempt, we eliminate from consideration the "Proximity Approach," the "Probable Desistance Approach" and the "Equivocality Approach."

Convinced that an approach based on the "substantial step" test is the proper one to determine whether a person has attempted to commit a crime, and that ß 110.00 of the Md. Proposed Criminal Code best expressed it, we adopt the provisions of that section.

This language follows § 5.01(1)(c) of the Model Penal Code, but eliminates failure to consummate the intended crime as one of the essential elements of a criminal attempt. Thus, the State is not required to prove beyond a reasonable doubt that the crime was not in fact committed. Furthermore, the elimination of failure as a necessary element makes attempt available as a compromise verdict or a compromise charge.

When the facts and circumstances of [this] case are considered in the light of the overt act standard which we have adopted, it is perfectly clear that the evidence was sufficient to prove that Young attempted the crime of armed robbery as charged.

As we have seen, the police did not arrive on the scene after the fact. They had the advantage of having Young under observation for some time before his apprehension. They watched his preparations. They were with him when he reconnoitered or cased the banks.

His observations of the banks were in a manner not usual for law-abiding individuals and were under circumstances that warranted alarm for the safety of persons or property. Young manifestly endeavored to conceal his presence by parking behind the Bank which he had apparently selected to rob. He disguised himself with an eye patch and made an identification of him difficult by turning up his jacket collar and by donning sunglasses and a knit cap which he pulled down over his forehead. He put on rubber surgical gloves. Clipped on his belt was a scanner with a police band frequency. Except for the scanner, which he had placed on his belt while casing the Bank, all this was done immediately before he left his car and approached the door of the Bank.

As he walked towards the Bank he partially hid his face behind his left hand and ducked his head. He kept his right hand in the pocket of his jacket in which, as subsequent events established, he was carrying, concealed, a loaded handgun, for which he had no lawful use or right to transport. He walked to the front door of the Bank and tried to enter the premises.

When he discovered that the door was locked, he ran back to his car, again partially concealing his face with his left hand. He got in his car and immediately drove away. He removed the knit hat, sunglasses, eye patch and gloves, and placed the scanner over the sun visor of the car. When apprehended, he was trying to take off his jacket. His question as to how much time he could get for attempted bank robbery was not without significance.

It is clear that the evidence which showed Young's conduct leading to his apprehension established that he performed the necessary overt act toward the commission of armed robbery, which was more than mere preparation.

Even if we assume that all of Young's conduct before he approached the door of the Bank was mere preparation, on the evidence, the jury could properly find as a fact that when Young tried to open the bank door to enter the premises, that act constituted a "substantial step" toward the commission of the intended crime. It was strongly corroborative of his criminal intention.

One of the reasons why the substantial step approach has received such widespread favor is because it usually enables the police to intervene at an earlier stage than do the other approaches. In this case, however, the requisite overt act came near the end of the line. Indeed, it would qualify as the necessary act under any of the approaches—the proximity approach, the probable desistance approach or the equivocality approach. It clearly met the requirements of the substantial step approach. Since Young, as a matter of fact, could be found by the jury to have performed an overt act which was more than mere preparation, and was a substantial step towards the commission of the intended crime of armed robbery, it follows as a matter of law that he committed the offense of criminal attempt.

We think that the evidence adduced showed directly, or circumstantially, or supported a rational inference of, the facts to be proved from which the jury could fairly be convinced, beyond a reasonable doubt, of Young's guilt of attempted armed robbery as charged. Therefore, the evidence was sufficient in law to sustain the conviction. We so hold.

State v. Reeves, 916 S.W. 2d 909 (Tenn 1996).
Two twelve-year-old girls, Mollie and Tracie agreed to poison their teacher, Ms. Geiger and then steal her car. They shared their scheme with an older high school student the night before the planned murder and were unable to persuade him to drive them to the mountains in Geiger's automobile. Later Molly revealed the plan to Mary (another student) and showed her the packet of rat poison on the bus to school. Mary told Ms. Geiger of the plan. During homeroom Geiger observed the two girls lean over her desk, giggle, and run back to their seats. Geiger also noticed a purse lying next to her coffee cup on the desk and arranged for Molly to be called to the principal's office where rat poison was found in the purse.

Collier v. State, 846 N.E. 2d 340 (Ind. Ct. App. 2006).
Estranged husband who had made several threats to wife and indicated desire to kill her to his friends, gathered tools and waited outside hospital where she was working, but court found after analyzing MPC substantial steps approach that he did not commit attempt.

State v. Fielder, 109 S.W. 580 (Mo. 1908).
Court held that the defendant must go far enough to obtain control over all factors indispensable to commission of crime. Must obtain ballot in order to be guilty for attempt to vote illegally.

Commonwealth v. Kennedy 48 N.E. 770 (Mass 1897)
Physical proximity test

Boyles v. State, 175 N.W. 2d 277 (Wisc. 1970).
Probable desistance test

United States v. Jackson, 560 F.2d 112 (2d Cir. 1977).
Substantial steps test of MPC.

People v. Lehnert, 163 P.3d 1111 (Colo 2007)
Substantial step test.

Commonwealth v. Gilliam, 417 A.2d. 1203 (Pa Supp 1980)

Defenses To Attempt: Impossibility

When defendants attempt to commit an act, the completion of which is impossible, they may have a defense to criminal liability for a charge of attempt depending on whether it was factually impossible to commit the crime or legally impossible to commit the crime. A legal impossibility exists (and is a defense to attempt) when an individual mistakenly believes that he or she is acting illegally. A commonly cited example is that of a people who take a tax deduction, thinking they are not entitled to it and believing they are breaking the law, when in fact, the law allows the deduction. The defense exists because the principle of legality prohibits punishing individuals for non-existent crimes. One practical issue about the defense of legal impossibility is that it will practically never be raised because prosecutors will not spend valuable time and energy prosecuting someone for behavior that is not criminal—thus, there are appellate opinions on this topic.

Factual impossibilities occur when defendants do everything possible to complete the crime but, for some reason, are prevented from completing the event by some extraneous factor beyond their control. Consider the defendant, Frank, who goes to the hospital thinking it is a good time to shoot his enemy Victor. Frank sneaks into Victor's room and shoots into Victor's bed. Frank's bullet strikes Victor's heart which had stopped beating ten minutes ago. Frank has no defense to attempted murder. It is factually impossible to murder a corpse, but that doesn't make the Frank any less dangerous. He did everything he could to kill Victor, but because of the extraneous fact (that Victor had died minutes before), his attempt was impossible. Factual impossibility, involves a situation where the perpetrator would have successfully completed the offense had the facts been as the perpetrator believed them to be. Because Offender who possess a criminal intent and who takes steps to commit an offense should not be free from legal guilt, factual impossibility is not a defense to attempt.

STATE v. DAMMS,
100 N.W.2d 592 (Wis. 1960)

HISTORY
The defendant Ralph Damms was charged by

information with the offense of attempt to commit murder in the first degree. The jury found the defendant guilty as charged, and the defendant was sentenced to imprisonment in the state prison at Waupun for a term of not more than ten years. Damms appealed to the Wisconsin Supreme Court. The Supreme Court affirmed the conviction.

CURRIE, J.
FACTS
The alleged crime occurred on April 6, 1959, near Menomonee Falls in Waukesha county. Prior to that date Marjory Damms, wife of the defendant, had instituted an action for divorce against him and the parties lived apart. She was thirty-nine years and he thirty-three years of age. Marjory Damms was also estranged from her mother, Mrs. Laura Grant.

That morning, a little before eight o'clock, Damms drove his automobile to the vicinity in Milwaukee where he knew Mrs. Damms would take the bus to go to work. He saw her walking along the sidewalk, stopped, and induced her to enter the car by falsely stating that Mrs. Grant was ill and dying. They drove to Mrs. Grant's home. Mrs. Damms then discovered that her mother was up and about and not seriously ill. Nevertheless, the two Damms remained there nearly two hours conversing and drinking coffee. Apparently it was the intention of Damms to induce a reconciliation between mother and daughter, hoping it would result in one between himself and his wife, but not much progress was achieved in such direction.

At the conclusion of the conversation, Mrs. Damms expressed the wish to phone for a taxicab to take her to work. Damms insisted on her getting into his car, and said he would drive her to work. They again entered his car, but instead of driving south towards her place of employment, he drove in the opposite direction. Some conversation was had in which he stated that it was possible for a person to die quickly and not be able to make amends for anything done in the past, and referred to the possibility of "judgment day" occurring suddenly.

Mrs. Damms' testimony as to what then took place is as follows: "When he was telling me about this being judgment day, he pulled a cardboard box from under the seat of the car and brought it up to the seat and opened it up

and took a gun out of a paper bag. He aimed it at my side and he said, 'This is to show you I'm not kidding.' I tried to quiet him down. He said he wasn't fooling. I said if it was just a matter of my saying to my mother that everything was all right, we could go back and I would tell her that."

They did return to Mrs. Grant's home and Mrs. Damms went inside and Damms stayed outside. In a few minutes he went inside and asked Mrs. Damms to leave with him. Mrs. Grant requested that they leave quietly so as not to attract the attention of the neighbors. They again got into the car, and this time drove out on Highway 41 towards Menomonee Falls. Damms stated to Mrs. Damms that he was taking her "up North" for a few days, the apparent purpose of which was to effect a reconciliation between them.

As they approached a roadside restaurant, he asked her if she would like something to eat. She replied that she wasn't hungry but would drink some coffee. Damms then drove the car off the highway beside the restaurant and parked it with the front facing, and in close proximity to, the restaurant wall.

Damms then asked Mrs. Damms how much money she had with her and she said "a couple of dollars." He then requested to see her checkbook and she refused to give it to him. A quarrel ensued between them. Mrs. Damms opened the car door and started to run around the restaurant building screaming, "Help!" Damms pursued her with the pistol in his hand.

Mrs. Damms cries for help attracted the attention of the persons inside the restaurant, including two officers of the State Traffic Patrol who were eating their lunch. One officer rushed out of the front door and the other the rear door. In the meantime, Mrs. Damms had run nearly around three sides of the building. In seeking to avoid colliding with a child, who was in her path, she turned, slipped and fell. Damms crouched down, held the pistol at her head, and pulled the trigger, but nothing happened. He then exclaimed, "It won't fire. It won't fire."

Damms testified that at the time he pulled the trigger the gun was pointing down at the ground and not at Mrs. Damms' head. However, the two traffic patrol officers both testified that Damms had the gun pointed directly at her head when he pulled the trigger. The officers placed Damms under arrest. They found that the pistol was unloaded. The clip holding the cartridges, which is inserted in the butt of the gun to load it, they found in the cardboard box in Damms' car together with a box of cartridges.

That afternoon, Damms was questioned by a deputy sheriff at the Waukesha county jail, and a clerk in the sheriff's office typed out the questions and Damms' answers as they were given. Damms later read over such typed statement of questions and answers, but refused to sign it. In such statement Damms stated that he thought the gun was loaded at the time of the alleged attempt to murder. Both the deputy sheriff and the undersheriff testified that Damms had stated to them that he thought the gun was loaded. On the other hand, Damms testified at the trial that he knew at the time of the alleged attempt that the pistol was not loaded.

OPINION
The two questions raised on this appeal are: (1) Did the fact, that it was impossible for the accused to have committed the act of murder because the gun was unloaded, preclude his conviction of the offense of attempt to commit murder?
(2) Assuming that the foregoing question is answered in the negative, does the evidence establish the guilt of the accused beyond a reasonable doubt?

Sec. 939.32(2), Stats., provides as follows:

> An attempt to commit a crime requires that the actor have an intent to perform acts and attain a result which, if accomplished, would constitute such crime and that he does acts toward the commission of the crime which demonstrate unequivocally, under all the circumstances, that he formed that intent and would commit the crime except for the intervention of another person or some other extraneous factor. (emphasis added)

The issue with respect to the first of the afore stated two questions boils down to whether the impossibility of accomplishment due to the gun being unloaded falls within the statutory words, "except for the intervention of some other extraneous factor." We conclude that it does.

In an article in 1956 *Wisconsin Law Review*, by assistant attorney general Platz, points out that "attempt" [in the Wisconsin statute] in a more intelligible fashion than by using such tests as "beyond mere preparation," the place at which the actor may repent and withdraw, or "dangerous proximity to success." Quoting the author:

> Emphasis upon the dangerous propensities of the actor as shown by his conduct, rather than upon how close he came to succeeding, is more appropriate to the purposes of the criminal law to protect society and reform offenders or render them temporarily harmless.

Sound public policy would seem to support the majority view that impossibility not apparent to the actor should not absolve him from the offense of attempt to commit the crime he intended. An unequivocal act accompanied by intent should be sufficient to constitute a criminal attempt. Insofar as the actor knows, he has done everything necessary to insure the commission of the crime intended, and he should not escape punishment because of the fortuitous circumstance that by reason of some fact unknown to him it was impossible to effectuate the intended result.

It is our considered judgment that the fact, that the gun was unloaded when Damms pointed it at his wife's head and pulled the trigger, did not absolve him of the offense charged, if he actually thought at the time that it was loaded.

We do not believe that the further contention raised in behalf of the accused, that the evidence does not establish his guilt of the crime charged beyond a reasonable doubt, requires extensive consideration on our part.

The jury undoubtedly believed the testimony of the deputy sheriff and undersheriff that Damms told them on the day of the act that he thought the gun was loaded. This is also substantiated by the written statement constituting a transcript of his answers given in his interrogation at the county jail on the same day.

The gun itself, which is an exhibit in the record, is the strongest piece of evidence in favor of Damms' present contention that he at all times knew the gun was unloaded. Practically the entire bottom end of the butt of the pistol is open. Such opening is caused by the absence of the clip into which the cartridges must be inserted in order to load the pistol. This readily demonstrates to anyone looking at the gun that it could not be loaded. Because the unloaded gun with this large opening in the butt was an exhibit which went to the jury room, we must assume that the jury examined the gun and duly considered it in arriving at their verdict.

We are not prepared to hold that the jury could not come to the reasonable conclusion that, because of Damms' condition of excitement when he grabbed the gun and pursued his wife, he so grasped it as not to see the opening in the end of the butt which would have unmistakably informed him that the gun was unloaded. Having so concluded, they could rightfully disregard Damms' testimony given at the trial that he knew the pistol was unloaded.

Judgment affirmed.

DIETERICH, J. **dissenting**
I disagree with the majority opinion in respect to their interpretations and conclusions. …

The issue raised on this appeal: Could the defendant be convicted of murder … when it was impossible for the defendant to have caused the death of anyone because the gun or pistol involved was unloaded?

…

In view of the statute, the question … is whether the impossibility of accomplishment due to the pistol being unloaded falls within the statutory words *"except for the intervention of . . . or some other extraneous factor."* It does not.

In interpreting the statute we must look to the ordinary meaning of words. Webster's New International Dictionary defines "extraneous"

as not belonging to or dependent upon a thing, originated or coming from without. The plain distinct meaning of the statute is: A person must form an intent to commit a particular crime and this intent must be coupled with sufficient preparation on his part and with overt acts from which it can be determined clearly, surely and absolutely the crime would be committed except for the intervention of some independent thing or something originating or coming from someone or something over which the actor has no control.

As an example, if the defendant actor had formed an intent to kill someone, had in his possession a loaded pistol, pulled the trigger while his intended victim was within range and the pistol did not fire because the bullet or cartridge in the chamber was defective or because someone unknown to the actor had removed the cartridges or bullets or because of any other thing happening which happening or thing was beyond the control of the actor, the actor could be guilty under sec. 339.32(2), Stats.

But when as in the present case (as disclosed by the testimony) the defendant had never loaded the pistol, although having ample opportunity to do so, then he had never completed performance of the act essential to kill someone, through the means of pulling the trigger of the pistol. This act, of loading the pistol, or using a loaded pistol, was dependent on the defendant himself. It was in no way an extraneous factor since by definition an extraneous factor is one which originates or comes from without.

Under the majority opinion the interpretations of the statute are if a person points an unloaded gun (pistol) at someone, knowing it to be unloaded and pulls the trigger, he can be found guilty of an attempt to commit murder. This type of reasoning I cannot agree with.

He could be guilty of some offense, but not attempt to commit murder. If a person uses a pistol as a bludgeon and had struck someone, but was prevented from killing his victim because he (the actor) suffered a heart attack at that moment, the illness would be an extraneous factor within the statute and the actor could be found guilty of attempt to commit murder, provided the necessary intent was proved.

. . .
The law judges intent objectively. It is impossible to peer into a man's mind particularly long after the act has been committed. Viewing objectively the physical salient facts, it was the defendant who put the gun, clip and cartridges under the car seat. It was he, same defendant, who took the pistol out of the box without taking clip or cartridges. It is plain he told the truth—he knew the gun would not fire, nobody else knew that so well. In fact his exclamation was "It won't fire. It won't fire."

The real intent showed up objectively in those calm moments while driving around the county with his wife for two hours, making two visits with her at her mother's home, and drinking coffee at the home. He could have loaded the pistol while staying on the outside at his mother-in-law's home on his second trip, if he intended to use the pistol to kill, but he did not do this required act.

Objective evidence here raises reasonable doubt of intent to attempt murder. It negatives intent to kill. The defendant would have loaded the pistol had he intended to kill or murder or used it as a bludgeon.

STATE v. ROBINS, 646 N.W. 2d 287 (Wis. 2002)

FACTS

Beginning on January 31, 2000, Brian Robins, using the screen name "WI4kink," had a series of online conversations with "Benjm13," initially in an Internet chat room known as "Wisconsin M4M." ["M4M" meant either Male for Male or Men for Men.]

Unbeknown to Robins, "Benjm13" was Thomas Fassbender, a 42-year-old DOJ agent posing online as a 13-year-old boy named Benjamin living in Little Chute, Wisconsin. The subject of "Benjamin's" age came up within the first twelve minutes of the first online conversation between Robins and Benjm13. Benjamin told Robins that he was 13 years old.

The initial and subsequent online conversations and emails between Robins and Benjm13 centered on explicit sexual matters (including, among other things, oral sex, masturbation, ejaculation, and penis size) and were recorded by Fassbender. . . . [The court here included several of these communications.]

According to the Wisconsin criminal code:
> An attempt to commit a crime requires that the actor have an intent to perform acts and attain a result which, if accomplished, would constitute such crime and that the actor does acts toward the commission of the crime which demonstrate unequivocally, under all the circumstances, that the actor formed that intent and would commit the crime except for the intervention of another person or some other extraneous factor. Wis. Stat. § 939.32(3).

Robins moved to dismiss the charge because, he argued, he was being charged with a crime that didn't exist because of a legal impossibility—there was no child.

OPINION

We reject Robins' argument that the case should be overruled. . . . The extraneous factor that intervened to make the crime an attempted rather than completed child enticement is the fact that "Benjm13" was an adult government agent rather than a 13-year-old boy.

That there may be or could have been other intervening factors does not make this an impermissible prosecution for an "attempt to attempt a crime."

We conclude that the crime of attempted child enticement contrary to Wis. Stat. § 948.07 may be charged where the extraneous factor that intervenes to make the crime an attempted rather than completed child enticement is the fact that, unbeknownst to the defendant, the "child" is fictitious.

Other Cases—Impossibility Defense

People v. Dlugash, 41 NY2D 725 (1977).
Bush shot Geller three times killing Geller. Dlugash then approached Geller's body and, believing Geller to be alive, shot him five times in the head. Court sustained conviction for attempt.

State v. Glass, 87 P.3D 302 (Idaho Ct. App. 2003).
Defendant believed he is conversing with minor and making arrangements with sexual liaison with minor, and instead he was communicating with an undercover police officer.

The court held that Idaho law did not provide the defense of impossibility for charges of attempt, stating,

"In determining that Idaho's attempt statute. . . .does not allow for an impossibility defense, we stated that "the statute provides no exception for those who intend to commit a crime but fail because they were unaware of some fact that would have prevented them from completing the intended crime."

Defense to Attempt: Voluntary Abandonment/ Renunciation

Are defendants who intend to commit crimes and do some act towards committing them but change their minds and decide not to go through with it still liable for attempt? The answer is, "it depends." Individuals who abandon their attempts to commit crimes because of some outside or extraneous factor (say the unexpected presence of the police at the location where he intended to commit the crime) remain criminally liable. But, those who voluntarily renounce their criminal schemes and manifest changes of heart may have a defense to a charge of attempt.

The Model Penal Code allows abandonment as a defense (also known as voluntary renunciation) when the defendant manifests a complete and voluntary renunciation of criminal purpose. The renunciation is not voluntary when it is motivated by a desire to avoid apprehension, when defendant just decides to postpone the crime, or when defendant decides that the crime is too difficult to commit.

Abandonment is a defense to attempt when an individual freely and voluntarily undergoes a change of heart and abandons the criminal activity. The defense of abandonment recognizes that an individual who abandons a criminal enterprise lacks firm commitment to complete the crime and should be permitted to avoid punishment. The defense also provides incentive for individuals to renounce their criminal conduct before completing the crime. *See,* LaFave, *supra* at 612-614. Some courts hold that once the attempt is complete, the individual cannot avoid criminal liability….but most court decisions recognize the defense and its justifications.

An individual who abandons an attempt to commit a crime based on the intervention of outside or extraneous factors remains criminally liable. But if offender voluntarily abandons his/her criminal scheme there may be a defense. The two following, similar, cases explore whether defendant voluntarily renounced his attempt to rape the victim.

ROSS v. STATE,
601 So.2d 872 (Miss. 1992)

FACTS (Summary)
The victim, Henley, and 7-year-old daughter lived in a trailer on gravel road. Henley was home alone when Defendant knocked on her door, asked directions. Ross pointed handgun at her, ordered her into house and onto couch. He told her to undress in a threatening manner. She attempted to escape and told him that her daughter would be home soon. She started talking about her daughter. Ross said that if she had a little girl he wouldn't do anything to

her….told her to go outside and turn her back, Ross then left.

OPINION
…[T] the primary issue here is whether sufficient evidence presents a question of fact as to whether Ross abandoned his attack as a result of outside intervention. Ross claims that the case should have gone to the jury only on a simple assault determination. Ross asserts that "it was not ... Henley's resistance that prevented her rape nor any independent intervening

cause or third person, but the voluntary and independent decision by her assailant to abandon his attack." The state, on the other hand, claims that Ross "panicked" and "drove away hastily."

As recited above, Henley told Ross that her daughter would soon be home from school. She also testified that Ross stated if Henley had a little girl, he wouldn't do anything to her and to go outside [the house] and turn her back [to him]. Ross moved that the court direct a verdict in his favor on the charge of attempted rape, which motion the court denied.

The trial court instructed the jury that if it found that Ross did "any overt act with the intent to have unlawful sexual relations with [the complainant] without her consent and against her will" then the jury should find Ross guilty of attempted rape. The court further instructed the jury that:

> before you can return a verdict against the defendant for attempted rape, that you must be convinced from the evidence and beyond a reasonable doubt, that the defendant was prevented from completing the act of rape or failed to complete the act of rape by intervening, extraneous causes. If you find that the act of rape was not completed due to a voluntary stopping short of the act, then you must find the defendant not guilty.

The statutory definition of the crime of attempted rape lies in two statutes: rape, section 97-3-65(2)[2] and attempt[3], section 97-1-7. The Mississippi Code defines rape as "forcible ravish[ing]." In Harden v. State, this Court held that lewd suggestions coupled with physical force constituted sufficient evidence to establish intent to rape.

The crime of attempt to commit an offense occurs when a person shall design and endeavor to commit an offense, and shall do any overt act toward the commission thereof, but shall fail therein, or shall be prevented from committing the same... Put otherwise, attempt consists of "1) an intent to commit a particular crime; 2) a direct ineffectual act done toward its commission, and 3) failure to consummate its commission." Pruitt v. State (attempted rape was voluntarily abandoned by defendant when

he told victim she was free to leave).

The Mississippi attempt statute requires that the third element, failure to consummate, result from extraneous causes. Thus, a defendant's voluntary abandonment may negate a crime of attempt. Where a defendant, with no other impetus but the victim's urging, voluntarily ceases his assault, he has not committed attempted rape. In Pruitt, 528 So. 2d at 830-831, where the assailant released his throathold on the unresisting victim and told her she could go, after which a third party happened on the scene, the Court held that the jury could not have reasonably ruled out abandonment.

In comparison, this Court has held that where the appellant's rape attempt failed because of the victim's resistance and ability to sound the alarm, the appellant cannot establish an abandonment defense. Alexander v. State. In the Alexander case, the evidence sufficiently established a question of attempt for the jury. The defendant did not voluntarily abandon his attempt, but instead fled after the victim, a hospital patient, pressed the nurse's buzzer; a nurse responded and the victim spoke the word "help." The Court concluded, "[T]he appellant ceased his actions only after the victim managed to press the buzzer alerting the nurse." In another case, the court properly sent the issue of attempt to the jury where the attacker failed because the victim resisted and freed herself.

Thus, abandonment occurs where, through the verbal urging of the victim, but with no physical resistance or external intervention, the perpetrator changes his mind. At the other end of the scale, a perpetrator cannot claim that he abandoned his attempt when, in fact, he ceased his efforts because the victim or a third party intervened or prevented him from furthering the attempt. Somewhere in the middle lies a case such as Alexander, where the victim successfully sounded an alarm, presenting no immediate physical obstacle to the perpetrator's continuing the attack, but sufficiently intervening to cause the perpetrator to cease his attack.

In this case, Ross appeals the denial of his motion for directed verdict; thus, he challenges only the sufficiency of the evidence, that is, whether it raised a sufficient factual issue to warrant a jury determination. Even under this rigorous standard of review, Ross's appeal should succeed on this issue. The evidence does not sufficiently raise a fact question as to whether he attempted rape. The evidence uncontrovertibly shows that he did not, but instead abandoned the attempt.

The key inquiry is a subjective one: What made Ross leave? According to the undisputed evidence, he left because he responded sympathetically to the victim's statement that she had a little girl. He did not fail in his attack. No one prevented him from completing it. Henley did not sound an alarm. No evidence shows that Ross panicked and hastily drove away, but rather, the record shows that he walked the complainant out to the back of her trailer before he left. Thus, the trial court's failure to grant a directed verdict on the attempted rape charge constituted reversible error. As this Court stated in Pruitt, this is not to say that Ross committed no criminal act, but "our only inquiry is whether there was sufficient evidence to support a jury finding that [Ross] did not abandon his attempt to rape [Henley]." This Court holds that there was not."

Ross raises a legitimate issue of error in the sufficiency of the evidence supporting his conviction for attempted rape because he voluntarily abandoned the attempt.

LE BARRON v. STATE, 145 N.W.2d 79 (Wis. 1966)

HISTORY
David Le Barron was convicted of attempted rape and sentenced to not more than fifteen years in prison. He appealed. The Wisconsin Supreme Court affirmed the conviction.
CURRIE, J.

FACTS
On March 3, 1965 at 6:55 P.M., the complaining witness, Jodean Randen, a housewife, was walking home across a fairly well-traveled railroad bridge in Eau Claire, Wisconsin. She is a slight woman whose normal weight is 95 to 100 pounds. As she approached the opposite side of the bridge she passed a man who was walking in the opposite direction.
The man turned and followed her, grabbed her arm and demanded her purse. She surrendered her purse and at the command of the man began walking away as fast as she could. Upon discovering that the purse was empty, he caught up with her again, grabbed her arm and told her that if she did not scream he would not hurt her.
He then led her—willingly, she testified, so as to avoid being hurt by him—to the end of the bridge. While walking he shoved her head down and warned her not to look up or do anything and he would not hurt her.
On the other side of the bridge along the railroad tracks there is a coal shack. As they approached the coal shack he grabbed her, put one hand over her mouth, and an arm around her shoulder and told her not to scream or he would kill her. At this time Mrs. Randen thought he had a knife in his hand.

He then forced her into the shack and up against the wall. As she struggled for her breath he said, "You know what else I want," unzipped his pants and started pulling up her skirt. She finally succeeded in removing his hand from her mouth, and after reassuring him that she would not scream, told him she was pregnant and pleaded with him to desist or he would hurt her baby.

He then felt her stomach and took her over to the door of the shack, where in the better light he was able to ascertain that, under her coat, she was wearing maternity clothes. He thereafter let her alone and left after warning her not to scream or call the police, or he would kill her.

OPINION
The material portions of the controlling statutes provide:

> § 944.01(1), Stats. Any male who has sexual intercourse with a female he knows is not his wife, by force and against her will, may be imprisoned not more than 30 years.

> § 939.32(2), Stats. An attempt to commit a crime requires that the actor have an intent to perform acts and attain a result which, if accomplished, would constitute such crime and that he does

acts toward the commission of the crime which demonstrate unequivocally, under all the circumstances, that he formed that intent and would commit the crime except for the intervention of another person or some other extraneous factor.

The two statutory requirements of intent and overt acts which must concur in order to have attempt to rape are as follows:

> (1) The male must have the intent to act so as to have intercourse with the female by overcoming or preventing her utmost resistance by physical violence, or overcoming her will to resist by the use of threats of imminent physical violence likely to cause great bodily harm;
> (2) the male must act toward the commission of the rape by overt acts which demonstrate unequivocally, under all the circumstances, that he formed the intent to rape and would have committed the rape except for the intervention of another person or some other extraneous factor.

The thrust of defendant's argument, that the evidence was not sufficient to convict him of the crime of attempted rape, is two-fold: first, defendant desisted from his endeavor to have sexual intercourse with complainant before he had an opportunity to form an intent to accomplish such intercourse by force and against her will; and, second, the factor which caused him to desist, viz., the pregnancy of complainant, was intrinsic and not an 'extraneous factor' within the meaning of sec. 939.32(2), Stats.

It is difficult to consider the factor of intent apart from that of overt acts since the sole evidence of intent in attempted rape cases is almost always confined to the overt acts of the accused, and intent must be inferred therefrom. In fact, the express wording of sec. 939.32(2), Stats. recognizes that this is so.

We consider defendant's overt acts, which support a reasonable inference that he intended to have sexual intercourse with complainant by force and against her will, to be these:

> (1) He threatened complainant that he would kill her if she refused to cooperate with him;
> (2) he forced complainant into the shack and against the wall; and
> (3) he stated, 'You know what else I want,' unzipped his pants, and started pulling up her skirt.

The jury had the right to assume that defendant had the requisite physical strength and weapon (the supposed knife) to carry out the threat over any resistance of complainant.

We conclude that a jury could infer beyond a reasonable doubt from these overt acts of defendant that he intended to have sexual intercourse with defendant by force and against her will. The fact that he desisted from his attempt to have sexual intercourse as a result of the plea of complainant that she was pregnant, would permit of the opposite inference. However, such desistance did not compel the drawing of such inference nor compel, as a matter of law, the raising of a reasonable doubt to a finding that defendant had previously intended to carry through with having intercourse by force and against complainant's will.

The argument that the pregnancy which caused defendant's desistance does not qualify as an "extraneous factor" is in conflict with our holding in *State v. Damms.*

Other Cases – Attempt Voluntary Abandonment Defense

People v. Staples, 6 Cal. App. 3d 61 (1970).
Defendant rented office above bank, learned that no one was in building on Saturday and moved in that day. He drilled several holes partway through the floor, and then covered them with a rug. He placed drilling tools in the closet and left the key in the office. Later, the landlord discovered the holes and notified the police. He was arrested and confessed, explaining that he abandoned his criminal plan after realizing that he couldn't enjoy life while living off stolen money. The Court held that he had voluntarily abandoned his attempt and had a true change of heart.

People v. Johnson, 750 P.2d 72 (Colo.App. 1987).
Following a fight with a friend outside a bar where the two had been drinking, defendant,

Floyd Johnson, walked a mile to his house, retrieved his .22 rifle and ten cartridges, walked back to the bar, and crawled under a pickup truck across the street to wait for the friend. Defendant testified that he, at first, intended to shoot the friend to "pay him back" for the beating he had received in their earlier altercation.

When the owner of the pickup arrived, defendant obtained his keys, instructed him to sit in the pickup, and gave him one or more bottles of beer. Defendant then crawled back under the pickup to resume his wait for his friend. The police were alerted by a passerby and arrested defendant before his friend emerged from the bar. There was also testimony that while he was lying under the pickup truck, defendant sobered up somewhat and began to think through his predicament. He testified that he changed his mind and removed the shells from the rifle, placing them in his

pocket. By that time there were two persons in the pickup truck, and he began a discussion with them, telling them his name and address and inviting them to his residence to have a party. The three of them were still there drinking and conversing when the police arrived, at which time the rifle was found to be unloaded and the shells were still in the defendant's pocket.

The trial court refused Johnson's request for an instruction on the affirmative defense of abandonment or renunciation. The Court of Appeals reversed and sent the case back to the trial court for a new trial. It stated, "Under the circumstances in this case, there was sufficient evidence to warrant an instruction on the affirmative defense of abandonment or renunciation."

Conspiracy

Conspiracy statutes punish an agreement to commit a crime. Conspiracy is among the most commonly charged federal offenses. It is a charge construed broadly by courts and used by prosecutors to a variety of situations. Federal and state racketeering statutes extend conspiracy law and potential liability. Racketeer Influenced and Corrupt Organization Act (RICO) statutes essentially eliminate the need for prosecutors to prove that individuals are part of a single conspiracy, and instead hold defendants responsible for all acts of racketeering undertaken as part of an enterprise which can include a range of state and federal offenses including murder, kidnapping, gambling, arson, robbery, bribery, extortion. Prosecutors may join co-defendants (co-conspirators) cases together in a single trial which also may contribute to the idea of guilt by association. Prosecutions for conspiracy may be filed in any jurisdiction in which the defendants entered into the agreement or committed an overt act in furtherance of the conspiracy. Finally, conspiracies, unlike attempts, do not merge into the completed crime, so a defendant can be convicted and sentenced for both of the target crime and the conspiracy to commit the target crime.

States vary on punishment for conspiracy—some states punish all conspiracies as misdemeanors; some punish conspiracy charges as they punish the target offense; some punish conspiracies to commit a felonies more harshly than conspiracies to commit misdemeanors. Most typically, conspiracies to commit felonies are felonies, and all conspiracies to commit misdemeanors are misdemeanors.

The MPC §5.03(1) states, "A person is guilty of conspiracy with another person or persons to commit a crime if with the purpose of promoting or facilitating its commission he: (a) agrees with such other person or persons that they or one or more of them will engage in conduct that constitutes such crime or an attempt or solicitation to commit such crime; or (b) agrees to aid such other person or persons in the planning or commission of such crime or of an attempt or solicitation to commit such crime." The MPC punishes conspiracy to the same degree as the most serious offense that is attempted, solicited, or objective of the conspiracy.

Actus Reus Conspiracy—Agreements and Overt Acts

The heart of conspiracy is the agreement between two or more people to commit a crime. The agreement to commit the crime need not be in writing. A simple understanding is sufficient. Parties to conspiracy must have a meeting of the minds (the agreement), and there must be at least two persons for a conspiracy to exist. (The exception to this is the unilateral approach to conspiracy which will be discussed below).

At common law, conspiracy was an agreement by two or more persons to accomplish a criminal act or to use unlawful means to accomplish a non-criminal objective. Today all jurisdictions have statutes that generally define conspiracy as an agreement between two or more persons to commit a criminal act. At common law a conspiracy was complete when an agreement existed to complete the crime, but most modern state statutes and federal law now require at least one party commit some affirmative act in furtherance of the intended crime. This "overt act" is necessary to prove that the parties entered into an agreement.

The overt act need not be a substantial movement toward the target offense—just any overt act tending to implement the conspiracy. The overt act may also be far removed from commission of a crime. Even a single telephone conversation arranging a meeting has been found to be sufficient proof of an overt act. Other examples of over acts include: attending a meeting of the communist party as an overt act in furtherance of a communist conspiracy to overthrow the U.S. government; purchasing large quantities of dynamite as the overt act in a conspiracy to blow up a school building; observing the movements of an intended kidnapping victim in a conspiracy to commit kidnapping, and purchasing stamps to send poison through the mail.

The actus reus of MPC conspiracy is agreeing with another. An overt act is required other than in the case of serious felonies. MPC §5.03 (5) provides, "No person may be convicted of conspiracy to commit a crime, other than a felony of the first or second degree, unless an overt act in pursuance of such conspiracy is alleged and proved to have been done by him or by a person with whom he conspired."

Mens Rea Conspiracy

In all states, the mens rea of conspiracy is the intent and purpose to complete a crime. According to Scheb, statutes frequently fail to mention the intent requirement in the offense of conspiracy, or the courts fail to clearly define it. In general, "the prosecution must prove that a defendant intended to further the unlawful object of the conspiracy, and such intent must exist in the minds of at least two people." Scheb, _supra_ at 129. Intent may, however, be inferred from the conduct of the parties.

In federal prosecutions, there must at least be proof of the criminal intent for each of the requirements of the intended offense. Some states require that the state prove that the defendants had the purpose of causing the result as well (purposeful standard). In other states it is sufficient that person knows that a result will occur (knowledge standard).

The Model Penal Code represents the predominant view, that specific intent to further the object of the conspiracy is needed. §5.03 (1) requires the defendant "possess the purpose of promoting or facilitating the commission of a crime." Knowledge does not satisfy the MPC's intent requirement.

STATE v. SMITH,
65 Wn. App. 468 (1992), 828 P.2d 654 (1992)

KENNEDY, J.
Appellant Brian Smith appeals his conviction of conspiracy to deliver a controlled substance, lysergic acid diethylamide (LSD). Smith contends that the evidence was insufficient to support a finding that he conspired to deliver a controlled substance. We affirm.

I

On the evening of February 16, 1988, Corporal Corey Cook of the Snohomish Police Department, working undercover, agreed to purchase 50 doses of LSD from Bruce Erickson. They arranged to meet at a park and ride lot in the city of Snohomish.

On that same evening, Smith stopped by Erickson's residence in Everett. Erickson asked Smith for a ride to Snohomish, ostensibly to meet David Hensler. Smith agreed to give Erickson a ride as Smith also wanted to see Hensler. Hensler owed Smith $600 for rent and telephone bills. Smith and Erickson arrived at the Snohomish park and ride lot at 8:15 p.m., in Smith's Datsun pickup. Smith drove and Erickson was in the passenger seat.

Corporal Cook approached the passenger side and spoke to Erickson, asking Erickson if he had any LSD. Erickson produced a plastic bag containing LSD. Corporal Cook asked Smith if he had tried the LSD and if it was any good. Smith replied that "he was going to college at the time and he couldn't afford to get messed up, but that his wife had taken some of it, and ... `it really [messed] her up.'" Corporal Cook testified that he took this to refer to a beneficial quality of LSD. Corporal Cook then agreed to purchase the LSD, handed the money to Erickson, and arrested both Smith and Erickson.

At the police station, Corporal Cook questioned Smith. Corporal Cook recorded the following statement in his police report:

Smith told me that he was aware that Erickson was selling me acid at the Park and Ride and said that he was in Everett at the time and had to go to Snohomish anyway and that Erickson said that he needed a ride.

Smith was charged with conspiracy to deliver a controlled substance. Smith waived his right to a jury trial. At the bench trial, Corporal Cook testified that he interpreted Smith's statement that he recorded in the police report to mean that Smith was in Everett when he learned of the impending LSD sale.

At the close of the State's case, Smith moved to dismiss for lack of sufficient evidence. ... The trial court denied the motion, finding that there was sufficient evidence of conspiracy because Smith agreed to assist Erickson in delivering LSD by giving Erickson a ride to Snohomish, knowing that Erickson's purpose was to sell LSD.

Smith then testified on his own behalf and stated that he had not known in advance of the sale that Erickson was going to sell

LSD. Smith also denied telling Corporal Cook that his wife had used LSD.

At the conclusion of the bench trial, the court found Smith guilty of conspiracy to deliver a controlled substance because Smith "knew that Erickson's purpose was to go sell some LSD."

II

. . . [T]o affirm Smith's conviction for conspiracy to deliver a controlled substance, we must determine whether a rational trier of fact could have found beyond a reasonable doubt that Smith agreed with Erickson to deliver LSD to Corporal Cook and that Smith intended that LSD be delivered to Corporal Cook.

A formal agreement is not essential to the formation of a conspiracy. State v. Casarez-Gastelum, 738 P.2d 303 (1987). An agreement can be shown by a "concert of action, all the parties working together understandingly, with a single design for the accomplishment of a common purpose.'" Proof of a conspiracy may be established by overt acts and "much is left to the discretion of the trial court."

Here the trial court found Smith guilty of violating RCW 69.50.407, conspiracy to deliver a controlled substance, which provides:
> Any person who attempts or conspires to commit any offense defined in this chapter is punishable by imprisonment or fine or both which may not exceed the maximum punishment prescribed for the offense, the commission of which was the object of the attempt or conspiracy.

The trial court noted that, because conspiracy is not defined in the controlled substances act, it was applying the definition of conspiracy under the general conspiracy statute, RCW 9A.28.040(1), without the substantial step requirement. RCW 9A.28.040(1) provides:
> A person is guilty of criminal conspiracy when, with intent that conduct constituting a crime be performed, he agrees with one or more persons to engage in or cause the performance of such conduct, and any one of them takes a substantial step in the pursuance of such agreement.

The court stated that it was omitting the

substantial step requirement based on *State v. Hawthorne*, 737 P.2d 717 (1987), which held that substantial step is not an element of conspiracy under RCW 69.50.407. Thus, the court defined conspiracy as "A person commits the crime of criminal conspiracy when, with the intent that conduct constituting a crime be performed, he or she agrees with one or more persons to engage in or causes the performance of such conduct."

The evidence, although conflicting in some respects, convinced the trier of fact that, although Smith's primary purpose in giving Erickson a lift to the park and ride lot was to meet with Hensler, who owed Smith $600, his secondary purpose was to assist Erickson in delivering LSD. As conceded by Smith . . . the presence of a primary, legal, reason for the trip, does not in and of itself negate a secondary illegal reason. By agreeing to drive Erickson to Snohomish with prior knowledge that the purpose of Erickson's trip was to sell LSD, Smith agreed to engage in the delivery. That the trip also satisfied Smith's own primary purpose of meeting up with Hensler does not negate the agreement and concerted action.

Smith argues that the trial court confused "knowledge" of the sale with the "agreement and concerted action" requirement of conspiracy. We disagree. Here there was evidence not only of knowledge of Erickson's unlawful purpose, but an agreement to assist with the plan by providing the necessary transportation. The evidence was sufficient to prove an agreement. An agreement may be proved by overt acts. See *Casarez-Gastelum* . Here there were two overt acts: first, that Smith drove Erickson to Snohomish knowing, according to Corporal Cook, Erickson's purpose for the trip; and second, that Smith provided encouragement for the sale by assuring the officer of the potency of the drug.

We hold that there is sufficient evidence to convince a rational trier of fact beyond a reasonable doubt that Smith agreed to transport Erickson to Snohomish for the common purpose of delivering LSD.

The State also had to prove that Smith intended to deliver LSD to convict him of conspiracy to deliver a controlled substance. See RCW 9A.28.040(1). In *Casarez-Gastelum*, the court held that once a conspiracy has been established, the State must prove beyond a reasonable doubt that the defendant had at least a "slight" connection with the conspiracy. Evidence establishing a "slight" connection with the conspiracy, must be of the quality which will reasonably support a conclusion that the particular defendant in question wilfully participated in the unlawful plan with the intent to further some object or purpose of the conspiracy.

Intent is defined as action "with the objective or purpose to accomplish a result which constitutes a crime." RCW 9A.08.010(1)(a). Smith argues that his conviction must be reversed because the trial court failed to find that he intended to deliver LSD. Smith contends that the trial court's finding that he had knowledge of Erickson's illegal purpose is insufficient to support a finding of intent. We disagree with Smith's interpretation of the trial court's findings.

… Implicit in the trial court's finding is that Smith not only knew of Erickson's unlawful purpose, but that Smith agreed to assist with the plan by providing the necessary transportation to complete the sale and that Smith provided encouragement for the sale by assuring Corporal Cook that the LSD was potent. Such evidence is sufficient to show that Smith intended to assist Erickson in the delivery of LSD.

UNITED STATES. v. GARCIA, 151 F.3d 1243 (CA9 1998)

…

REINHARDT, J.
One evening, a confrontation broke out between rival gangs at a party on the Pasqua Yaqui Indian reservation. The resultant gunfire injured four young people, including appellant Cody Garcia. Two young men involved in the shooting, Garcia and Noah Humo, were charged with conspiracy to assault three named

individuals with dangerous weapons. A jury acquitted Humo but convicted Garcia. Because there is no direct evidence of an agreement to commit the criminal act which was the alleged object of the conspiracy, and because the circumstances of the shootings do not support the existence of an agreement, implicit or explicit, the government relied heavily on the gang affiliation of the participants to show the existence of such an agreement. We hold that gang membership itself cannot establish guilt of a crime, and a general agreement, implicit or explicit, to support one another in gang fights does not provide substantial proof of the specific agreement required for a conviction of conspiracy to commit assault. The defendant's conviction therefore rests on insufficient evidence, and we reverse.

FACTS

The party at which the shootings occurred was held in territory controlled by the Crips gang. The participants were apparently mainly young Native Americans. While many of the attendees were associated with the Crips, some members of the Bloods gang were also present. Appellant Cody Garcia arrived at the party in a truck driven by his uncle, waving a red bandanna (the Bloods claim the color red and the Crips the color blue) out the truck window and calling out his gang affiliation: "ESPB Blood!" Upon arrival, Garcia began "talking smack" to (insulting) several Crips members. Prosecution witnesses testified that Garcia's actions suggested that he was looking for trouble and issuing a challenge to fight to the Crips at the party.

Meanwhile, Garcia's fellow Bloods member Julio Baltazar was also "talking smack" to Crips members, and Blood Noah Humo bumped shoulders with one Crips member and called another by a derogatory Spanish term. Neither Baltazar nor Humo had arrived with Garcia, nor is there any indication that they had met before the party to discuss plans or that they were seen talking together during the party.

At some point, shooting broke out. Witnesses saw both Bloods and Crips, including Garcia and Humo, shooting at one another. Baltazar was seen waving a knife or trying to stab a Crip. The testimony at trial does not shed light on what took place immediately prior to the shooting, other than the fact that one witness heard Garcia ask, "Who has the gun?" There is some indication that members of the two gangs may have "squared off" before the shooting began. No testimony establishes whether the shooting followed a provocation or verbal or physical confrontation.

Four individuals were injured by the gunfire: the defendant, Stacy Romero, Gabriel Valenzuela, and Gilbert Baumea. Stacy Romero who at the time was twelve years old was the cousin both of Garcia's co-defendant Humo and his fellow Blood, Baltazar. No evidence presented at trial established that any of the injured persons was shot by Garcia, and he was charged only with conspiracy. The government charged both Garcia and Humo with conspiracy to assault Romero, Valenzuela, and Baumea with dangerous weapons under 18 U.S.C. ß ß 371, 113(a)(3) and 1153.

After a jury trial, Garcia was convicted of conspiracy to assault with a dangerous weapon and sentenced to 60 months in prison. He appeals on the ground that there was insufficient evidence to support his conviction.

OPINION:

In order to prove a conspiracy, the government must present sufficient evidence to demonstrate both an overt act and an agreement to engage in the specific criminal activity charged in the indictment. While an implicit agreement may be inferred from circumstantial evidence, proof that an individual engaged in illegal acts with others is not sufficient to demonstrate the existence of a conspiracy. Both the existence of and the individual's connection to the conspiracy must be proven beyond a reasonable doubt. Even though a defendant's connection to the conspiracy may be slight, the connection must nonetheless be proven beyond a reasonable doubt.

The government claims that it can establish the agreement to assault in two ways: first, that the concerted provocative and violent acts by Garcia, Humo and Baltazar are sufficient to show the existence of a prior agreement; and second, that by agreeing to become a member of the gang, Garcia implicitly agreed to support his fellow gang members in violent confrontations.

However, no inference of the existence of any agreement could reasonably be drawn from the actions of Garcia and other Bloods members on the night of the shooting. An inference of an agreement is permissible only when the nature of the acts would logically require coordination and planning.

The government presented no witnesses who could explain the series of events immediately preceding the shooting, so there is nothing to suggest that the violence began in accordance with some prearrangement. The facts establish only that perceived insults escalated tensions between members of rival gangs and that an ongoing gang-related dispute erupted into shooting. Testimony presented at trial suggests more chaos than concert. Such evidence does not establish that parties to a conspiracy worked together understandingly, with a single design for the accomplishment of a common purpose.

Given that this circumstantial evidence fails to suggest the existence of an agreement, we are left only with gang membership as proof that Garcia conspired with fellow Bloods to shoot the three named individuals. The government points to expert testimony at the trial by a local gang unit detective, who stated that generally gang members have a "basic agreement" to back one another up in fights, an agreement which requires no advance planning or coordination. This testimony, which at most establishes one of the characteristics of gangs but not a specific objective of a particular gang—let alone a specific agreement on the part of its members to accomplish an illegal objective—is insufficient to provide proof of a conspiracy to commit assault or other illegal acts.

Recent authority in this circuit establishes that "membership in a gang cannot serve as proof of intent, or of the facilitation, advice, aid, promotion, encouragement or instigation needed to establish aiding and abetting." In overturning the state conviction of a gang member that rested on the theory that the defendant aided and abetted a murder by "fanning the fires of gang warfare," . . . *Mitchell v. Prunty*, 107 F.3d. 1337, expressed concern that allowing a conviction on this basis would

"smack of guilt by association." The same concern is implicated when a conspiracy conviction is based on evidence that an individual is affiliated with a gang which has a general rivalry with other gangs, and that this rivalry sometimes escalates into violent confrontations.

Acts of provocation such as "talking smack" or bumping into rival gang members certainly does not prove a high level of planning or coordination. Rather, it may be fairly typical behavior in a situation in which individuals who belong to rival gangs attend the same events. At most, it indicates that members of a particular gang may be looking for trouble, or ready to fight. It does not demonstrate a coordinated effort with a specific illegal objective in mind.

Conspiracy requires proof of both an intention and agreement to accomplish a specific illegal objective. The fact that gang members attend a function armed with weapons may prove that they are prepared for violence, but without other evidence it does not establish that they have made plans to initiate it. And the fact that more than one member of the Bloods was shooting at rival gang members also does not prove a prearrangement—the Crips, too, were able to pull out their guns almost immediately, suggesting that readiness for a gunfight requires no prior agreement. Such readiness may be a sad commentary on the state of mind of many of the nation's youth, but it is not indicative of a criminal conspiracy.

Finally, allowing a general agreement among gang members to back each other up to serve as sufficient evidence of a conspiracy would mean that any time more than one gang member was involved in a fight it would constitute an act in furtherance of the conspiracy and all gang members could be held criminally responsible—whether they participated in or had knowledge of the particular criminal act, and whether or not they were present when the act occurred. Indeed, were we to accept fighting the enemy as an illegal objective, all gang members would probably be subject to felony prosecutions sooner rather than later, even though they had never personally committed an improper act. This is contrary to fundamental principles of our justice system.

There can be no conviction for guilt by association.

Because of these concerns, evidence of gang membership cannot itself prove that an individual has entered a criminal agreement to attack members of rival gangs. Moreover, here the conspiracy allegation was even more specific: the state charged Garcia with conspiracy to assault three specific individuals—Romero, Baumea and Valenzuela—with deadly weapons. Even if the testimony presented by the state had sufficed to establish a general conspiracy to assault Crips, it certainly did not even hint at a conspiracy to assault the three individuals listed in the indictment. Of course, a more general indictment would not have solved the state's problems in this case. In some cases, when evidence establishes that a particular gang has a specific illegal objective such as selling drugs, evidence of gang membership may help to link gang members to that objective. However, a general practice of supporting one another in fights, which is one of the ordinary characteristics of gangs, does not constitute the type of illegal objective that can form the predicate for a conspiracy charge.

Because the government introduced no evidence from which a jury could reasonably have found the existence of an agreement to engage in any unlawful conduct, the evidence of conspiracy was insufficient as a matter of law. A contrary result would allow courts to assume an ongoing conspiracy, universal among gangs and gang members, to commit any number of violent acts, rendering gang members automatically guilty of conspiracy for any improper conduct by any member. We therefore reverse Garcia's conviction and remand to the district court to order his immediate release. As a result of this decision, Garcia is not subject to retrial. He has already served over a year in prison.

PEOPLE v. QUINTEROS,
16 Cal. Rptr.2d 462 (Cal.Ct.App. 1993)

FACTS

On the evening of October 18, 1991, the murder victim, Jason Escobedo (Jason) went to Will Rogers State Beach with Billy Reyes (Billy), Zonia Petraza (Zonia) and Irene Melendez (Irene). Jason went into a restroom and became involved in an altercation with defendant. Billy ran into the restroom and intervened. Defendant, a member of the "Southside 13" gang, issued a standard gang challenge, asking Jason "where he was from," to which Jason replied that he was not a gang member. Defendant also told Billy that if Billy gave him $2 defendant would forget the whole thing. Thereupon, Billy punched defendant in the face and a fight ensued. Zonia arrived on the scene to find defendant on top of Billy. Jason then pulled the two combatants apart and apologized to defendant for "stepping into his territory." Defendant responded by punching Jason in the mouth. Immediately thereafter, defendant whistled toward the beach and made a beckoning motion with his hands.

Jason, Billy, Zonia, and Irene then ran for Billy's truck, the vehicle in which they had arrived at the beach, and tried to leave the parking lot. They found the exit locked and returned to where they had previously parked. Since it appeared at that point that no one was around, Jason and Billy went down to the beach to retrieve some of the belongings they had left behind.

While the two girls remained in the truck, another truck pulled up alongside of them and eight young males got out, among them defendant. Defendant and two others began bashing the truck with a trash can, a barbell and their fists. The rest of the males ran toward the beach just as Billy and Jason were returning. Despite the pleas of Zonia and Irene that they were "just girls," defendant and the other two who, with him, were bashing the truck were unmoved; one said he didn't care and then started smashing the truck windows. Another male, Jose Alvarez, who testified at the preliminary hearing, got into Billy's truck and wrestled the keys from Irene, who, by that time, had succeeded in starting the truck and had begun backing it up.

Billy managed to make it back to the truck, but Jason was surrounded and could not escape. Billy,

Zonia, and Irene drove to a gas station nearby and telephoned "911." The police arrived in "about 15 minutes." However, by that time Jason lay dead on the other side of the restroom, his head having been severely beaten.

Although there were about 15 Southside 13 gang members present at the scene, only 3 were charged with the crimes against Jason, Billy, Zonia, and Irene: defendant, known as "Dreamer," codefendant Enrique Pantaleon, known as "Snoopy," and Abel Santamaria, known as "Drifter."

At the preliminary hearing, Rigoberto Rojas, another Southside 13 gang member who was present at the crime scene, testified that he was one of approximately 15 gang members who went to the beach that night, arriving by car and truck. He testified that defendant went to the restroom, came back bleeding and said that he had been "jumped by two guys." After that, one of the gang members said, "Fuck it. Let's go get him." At that point, all the gang members went to the restroom area "looking for them," the victims. Defendant and the gang members with him drove around a bit until they noticed Billy's truck with the two girls inside. They decided to "trash" it because they could not see the two guys who had been in the confrontation with defendant. Subsequently, they saw the "two guys," described as a "skinny guy" (Billy) and a "fat guy" (Jason), as those two were coming back up from the beach. The gang members jumped the two, whereupon, according to Rojas, the "skinny guy" hit defendant with a metal pipe, knocking him unconscious. Zonia, however, testified that Billy never had a pipe or anything else in his hand. Billy then fled in the truck with the two girls. At that point, the gang members turned their attention to the "fat guy" and began beating him. Codefendant Santamaria picked up a metal pole (three feet long, three inches wide) which, according to Rojas, had been left by Billy, and with assistance from another younger gang member, hit Jason over the head with it, knocking him unconscious.

Another gang member, Jose Alvarez, also testified at the preliminary hearing. He stated that he had been the one who wrestled the truck keys away from Irene. He also saw defendant being struck with "a stick," rendering defendant unconscious. Alvarez also testified, as had Rojas, that the gang's intention was to beat up Jason and Billy.

. . . .

[T]he preliminary hearing magistrate made no adverse factual finding but expressly stated that he was holding the evidence as to the conspiracy charged in count 2 and as to defendant's involvement in counts 1, 3, 4, and 5 to be insufficient as a matter of law. A conspiracy is shown by evidence of an agreement between two or more persons with the specific intent to agree to commit a public offense and with the further specific intent to commit such offense, which agreement is followed by an overt act committed by one or more of the parties for the purpose of furthering the object of the agreement. The agreement or the unlawful design of conspiracy may be proved by circumstantial evidence without the necessity of showing that the conspirators met and actually agreed to commit the offense which was the object of the conspiracy.

While mere association does not prove a criminal conspiracy, . . . common gang membership may be part of circumstantial evidence supporting the inference of a conspiracy. The circumstances from which a conspiratorial agreement may be inferred include "the conduct of defendants in mutually carrying out a common illegal purpose, the nature of the act done, the relationship of the parties [and] the interests of the alleged conspirators. Here, evidence of a conspiratorial agreement was abundant. Defendant and the others who sought to act against the victims were members of a street gang known as the "Southside 13" gang. The presence of that gang's graffiti with gang-related monikers at the scene in the vicinity of the decedent's body graphically shows the gang had marked Will Rogers State Beach as part of its gang territory. Defendant's acts in issuing the gang challenge "Where are you from?" and attempting to extort money for the right to have intruded into Southside 13 gang territory evidence a relationship between the territory and defendant's and his fellow gang members' conduct toward the victims. Indeed, the murder victim tried to apologize to defendant for having trespassed into the "territory" of defendant's gang.

Zonia testified that after defendant had struck Jason, he whistled and beckoned for his fellow gang members. Defendant's fellow gang member Rojas testified that after defendant told him what had happened to him in the restroom, one of the other gang members said, "Fuck it. Let's go get him." Thereupon, the gang members proceeded to seek out the two intruders into their territory in order to beat them up. This evidence sufficiently shows the existence of an agreement coupled with the requisite specific intent (to find the two intruders and beat them up), along with overt acts (the assaults on Jason, Billy, Zonia, and Irene) in which defendant directly participated, whether or not he was conscious at the time that the fatal blows were struck to the head of Jason. (5) A conspirator is criminally liable for the acts of coconspirators which follow as a probable and natural consequence of a common design, even where those acts were not intended as part of the original design or common plan.

The question of what constitutes a probable and natural consequence is a question for the trier of fact.

Here, the evidence at the preliminary hearing sufficiently establishes that defendant, along with his fellow gang members, designed to go and at the very least beat up Jason and Billy, who had been involved in the previous confrontation with defendant. Whether or not at some point during the carrying out of that design defendant was rendered unconscious does not absolve him of responsibility for a natural and probable consequence of the illegal conspiracy in which he participated. The murder of Jason and the assaults upon the other victims reasonably constitute natural and probable consequences of the conspiracy which was shown at the preliminary hearing. Hence, the information should not have been set aside.

UNITED STATES v. BROWN, 776 F.2d 397 (1985)

FRIENDLY, CIRCUIT JUDGE

This is another case . . . where the federal narcotics laws have been invoked with respect to the New York City Police Department's Operation Pressure Point in Harlem. Here . . . Officer William Grimball, acting under cover as an addict, procured a "joint" of heroin, and a backup team promptly pounced on those thought to have been involved in the sale.

The indictment . . . contained two counts. Count One charged appellant Ronald Brown and a codefendant, Gregory Valentine, with conspiring to distribute and to possess with intent to distribute heroin.... Count Two charged them with distribution of heroin.... After a three day trial, the jury convicted Brown on Count One but was unable to reach a verdict on Count Two.[1] . . . [T]he judge suspended imposition of sentence on Count One and placed Brown on three years' probation. Count Two was dismissed with the Government's consent. This appeal followed.

Officer Grimball was the Government's principal witness. He testified that early in the evening of October 9, 1984, he approached Gregory Valentine on the corner of 115th Street and Eighth Avenue and asked him for a joint of "D".[2] Valentine asked Grimball whom he knew around the street. Grimball asked if Valentine knew Scott. He did not. Brown "came up" and Valentine said, "He wants a joint, but I don't know him." Brown looked at Grimball and said, "He looks okay to me." Valentine then said, "Okay. But I am going to leave it somewhere and you [meaning Officer Grimball] can pick it up." Brown interjected, "You don't have to do that. Just go and get it for him. He looks all right to me." After looking again at Grimball, Brown said, "He looks all right to me" and "I will wait right here."

Valentine then said, "Okay. Come on with me around to the hotel." Grimball followed him to 300 West 116th Street, where Valentine instructed him, "Sit on the black car and give me a few minutes to go up and get it." Valentine requested and received $40, which had been prerecorded, and then said, "You are going to take care of me for doing this for you, throw some dollars my way?," to which Grimball responded, "Yeah."

Valentine then entered the hotel and shortly returned. The two went back to 115th Street and Eighth Avenue, where Valentine placed a cigarette box on the hood of a blue car. Grimball picked up the cigarette box and found a glassine envelope containing white powder, stipulated to be heroin. Grimball placed $5 of prerecorded buy money in the cigarette box, which he replaced on the hood. Valentine picked up the box and removed the $5. Grimball returned to his car and made a radio transmission to the backup field team that "the buy had went down" and informed them of the locations of the persons involved. Brown and Valentine were arrested. Valentine was found to possess two glassine envelopes of heroin and the $5 of prerecorded money. Brown was in possession of $31 of his own money; no drugs or contraband were found on him. The $40 of marked buy money was not recovered, and no arrests were made at the hotel.

The Government sought to qualify Officer Grimball as an expert on the bases that he had made over 30 street buys of small quantities of cocaine in Harlem, had received two 8 1/2 hour seminars at the Organized Crime Control Bureau "in respect to street value of drugs, safety, integrity," had once been assigned to the Manhattan North Narcotics Division where he had informal seminars with undercover detectives experienced in making street buys in the Harlem target area, and had participated in "ghost operations," where he as undercover would be placed "on the set" and would observe an experienced undercover detective in an actual buy operation. The judge having ruled him to be qualified as an expert, he testified that the typical drug buy in the Harlem area involved two to five people. As a result of frequent police sweeps, Harlem drug dealers were becoming so cautious that they employed people who act as steerers and the steerer's responsibility is basically to determine whether or not you are actually an addict or a user of heroin and they are also used to screen you to see if there is any possibility of you being a cop looking for a bulge or some indication that would give them that you are not actually an addict. And a lot of the responsibility relies [sic] on them to determine whether or not the drug buy is going to go down or not.

Officer Grimball was then allowed, over a

general objection, to testify that based on his experience as an undercover agent he would describe the role that Ronald Brown played in the transaction as that of a steerer.

. . . .

. . . [S]ince the jury convicted on the conspiracy count alone, the evidence must permit a reasonable juror to be convinced beyond a reasonable doubt not simply that Brown had aided and abetted the drug sale but that he had agreed to do so. On the other hand, the jury's failure to agree on the aiding and abetting charge does not operate against the Government; even an acquittal on that count would not have done so.

A review of the evidence against Brown convinces us that it was sufficient, even without Grimball's characterization of Brown as a steerer, although barely so. Although Brown's mere presence at the scene of the crime and his knowledge that a crime was being committed would not have been sufficient to establish Brown's knowing participation in the conspiracy, . . . the proof went considerably beyond that. Brown was not simply standing around while the exchanges between Officer Grimball and Valentine occurred. He came on the scene shortly after these began and Valentine immediately explained the situation to him. Brown then conferred his seal of approval on Grimball, a most unlikely event unless there was an established relationship between Brown and Valentine. Finally, Brown took upon himself the serious responsibility of telling Valentine to desist from his plan to reduce the risks by not handing the heroin directly to Grimball. A rational mind could take this as bespeaking the existence of an agreement whereby Brown was to have the authority to command, or at least to persuade. Brown's remark, "Just go and get it for him," permits inferences that Brown knew where the heroin was to be gotten, that he knew that Valentine knew this, and that Brown and Valentine had engaged in such a transaction before.

The mere fact that these inferences were not ineluctable does not mean that they were insufficient to convince a reasonable juror beyond a reasonable doubt. … When we add to the inferences that can be reasonably drawn from the facts to which Grimball testified the portion of his expert testimony about the use of steerers in street sales of narcotics, which was clearly unobjectionable once Grimball's qualifications were established, we conclude that the Government offered sufficient evidence, apart from Grimball's opinion that Brown was a steerer, for a reasonable juror to be satisfied beyond a reasonable doubt not only that Brown had acted as a steerer but that he had agreed to do so.[10]

Affirmed.

OAKES, Circuit Judge, **dissenting**"

...

When, as the majority concedes, numerous other inferences could be drawn from the few words of conversation in which Brown is said to have engaged, I cannot believe that there is proof of conspiracy, or Brown's membership in it, beyond a reasonable doubt, unless one gives the Court's emphasis on the word "any"--"any rational trier of fact," --such weight that the word "rational" receives little or no significance at all. Until now, as we said in United States v. Cepeda, "the court has insisted on proof, whether or not by circumstantial evidence, ... of a specific agreement to deal."[1]

. . . . If today we uphold a conspiracy to sell narcotics on the street, on this kind and amount of evidence, what conspiracies might we approve tomorrow? The majority opinion will come back to haunt us, I fear.

. . . I point out that Officer Grimball's four months of undercover narcotics experience (during which he made some thirty to fifty street purchases, none involving more than $50), by his own admission, did not give him enough experience (1) to say whether or not before "Operation Pressure Point" only one person was involved in street sales; (2) to testify of his own knowledge that "in some drug transactions ... the dealer will act like he is going somewhere else to retrieve the narcotics

when, in fact, he already has the drugs on his person"; or (3) ever to have participated in an operation (A) using a Nagra or other small tape recorder on an officer's body or (B) where photographs of the individuals or sale were taken. At the very least, he should not have been permitted to testify that Brown was a "steerer." . . . [W]ithout . . . [Grimball's} . . . "expert" testimony as to Brown's role, I do not believe that the evidence was sufficient to sustain a conviction, and therefore its admission was not harmless error

. . . Here the only overt act attributed in the indictment to Brown was the same conversation with Valentine that grounded the substantive charge of aiding and abetting, a charge on which Brown was acquitted. It may be that, in a given case evidence may support a conviction on an aiding and abetting count without supporting a conviction on a conspiracy count. But it is hard to see how, in the case of a completed sale, there can be a conviction of conspiracy but not of aiding and abetting, especially when there is no evidence of a "stake in the outcome."

Although, according to the majority, the admission of "expert" testimony is "rather offensive," the evidence was "sufficient ... although barely so," and the verdict is both inconsistent and very probably a compromise, the court permits this conspiracy conviction to stand. I fear that it thereby promotes the crime of conspiracy--"that darling of the modern prosecutor's nursery," to a role beyond that contemplated . . . . Precisely because this is another $40 narcotics case, I would draw the line. This case effectively permits prosecution of everyone connected with a street sale of narcotics to be prosecuted on two counts--a conspiracy as well as a substantive charge. And evidence showing no more than that a defendant was probably aware that a narcotics deal was about to occur will support a conspiracy conviction, our previous cases to the contrary notwithstanding.
Accordingly, I dissent.

Other Cases – Conspiracy Actus Reus

Commonwealth v. Azim, 459 A.2d.1244 (Pa. Super.Ct. (1983).
Azim pulled his car over to the curb and one of his passengers called to a nearby student. Student

refused to respond, and the passenger and another passenger got out of Azim's car, beat and choked the student, and took his wallet. The three then drove away from the area. Azim was convicted for conspiracy and the court pointed to his association with the two assailants, his presence at the crime scene, his waiting in the car with the engine running and lights on as the student was beaten as evidence of his conspiracy.

U.S. v. Falcone, 311 U.S. 205 (1940).
The Court held that individuals who provided sugar, yeast and cans to individuals whom they knew were engaged in illegally manufacturing alcohol were not liable for conspiracy. Court held that the state must prove defendants intended to promote the illegal enterprise.

People v. Lauria, 251 Cal App.2d 471, 59 Cal. Rptr 628 (1967).
Lauria operated a telephone answering service which came under scrutiny of police investigating a call-girl service. Defendant knew that some of his customers were prostitutes. The defendant and three prostitutes were indicted for conspiracy to commit prostitution. The trial and appellate courts set aside the indictments finding that the element of knowledge of the illegal use of goods or services and the intent to further that use must be present in order to make the supplier of the services guilty of criminal conspiracy. The court found that Lauria took no direct action to further, encourage, or direct the activities of the prostitutes. He had no special interest in the activities and would get paid regardless of whether his customers had a successful business or not. There were not excessive phone charges and the service had a legitimate use. Accordingly, he was not part of the conspiracy.

Numbers and Types Of Conspiracies

The Court has generally analyzed conspiracies as falling into two typical forms: a chain conspiracy or a wheel conspiracy. A chain conspiracy exists when the conspirators are linked together in a vertical chain to achieve a criminal objective. If there is only one single agreement, there is one conspiracy, regardless of how many crimes the conspirators plan to commit. *Doolin v. State*, 650 S.2d 44 (Fla. 1995). The classic example is an illegal drug or alcohol distribution conspiracy. See, e.g., *Braverman v. United States*, 317 U.S. 49 (1942) (defendants who plotted the illegal manufacture, transportation, and distribution of liquor in violation of a number of tax laws could be punished for only one conspiracy, and that the plans to violate several laws were all party of a single agreement.) In *United States v. Bruno,* 105 F.2d 921 (1939), eighty-eight defendants were indicted for a conspiracy to import, sell, and possess narcotics. The case involved smugglers who brought the narcotics into New York and sold them to middlemen who, in turn, distributed the drugs to retailers who then sold them to operatives in Texas and Louisiana for distribution to addicts. Bruno and Iacono appealed their convictions claiming there were three conspiracies rather than one large conspiracy. The court ruled that this was a single chain conspiracy in which the smugglers knew "that middlemen must purchase the drugs from smugglers. Even though the distributors didn't have an agreement with the smugglers, the conspirators at one end of the chain knew that the unlawful business would not and could not, stop with their buyers; and those at the other end knew that it had not begun with their sellers." Each member of the conspiracy knew that the success of that part with which he was immediately concerned, was dependent upon the success of the whole. As seen in *Bruno,* if a series of overlapping transactions are shown, then courts may construe these as a single conspiracy with each of the parties an individual "link" in the "chain" if the parties know that other links are involved and have a general interest in the success of the transactions.

> If those involved in each link of the transaction are unaware that the other transactions are taking place, or know about other transactions but are indifferent as to whether they take place, the situation will be characterized as involving multiple and separate conspiracies. The participants in each link transaction are conspirators only with those involved in that particular link transaction. Dix, at 162.

A wheel conspiracy involves a single person or group that serves as a hub or common core, connecting various independent individuals or spokes. The spokes typically interact with the hub rather than with one another. If each of the spokes shares a common purpose to succeed, then a single conspiracy exists. If one of the spokes has no interest in the success of the other spokes, then courts are likely to find multiple conspiracies rather than a single conspiracy. *Kotteakos v. United States*, 328 U.S. 750 (1946) is a frequently cited case demonstrating both a "wheel conspiracy" and whether the court characterizes the arrangement of one conspiracy of many conspiracies can have a significant impact on the outcome of a case.

The MPC does not use terms wheel or chain conspiracy. MPC 5.03 (2) and (3) § set forth the scope of the conspiratorial relationship and specifies the number of conspiracies.[14]

Special Conspiracy Issues

UNILATERAL CONSPIRACY OR BILATERAL CONSPIRACY

What if one party does not truly intend to go through with the crime? For example, if Kelly and Julie are sitting around in a bar, drinking, and Kelly suggests, "Hey, let's kill Shorty," and Julie says, "Yea, I hate that guy...let's get him." Is there an agreement when Kelly is just joking, but Julie is serious? Under the common law plurality requirement (there must be at least two conspirators) --a conspiracy exists only if both Julie and Kelly intend that they kill Shorty. It does not appear that they have a meeting of the minds, so there is no conspiracy At common law, both Kelly and Julie would be acquitted although Julie was quite serious about killing Shorty.

The plurality requirement presents particular problems in situations involving undercover officers who agree to participate in a crime in order to gain trust of the members of a drug ring. In this situation, the other party is fully committed to the agreement and to committing the intended crime, so he or she presents danger of future harm even if the officer does not. Because of this, the Model Penal Code and some jurisdictions have adopted a "unilateral approach to conspiracy" which allows the prosecution of individuals who believed they were agreeing to commit a crime, even though their "co-conspirators" never intended to commit the crime. The unilateral approach examines whether a single individual agreed to enter into a conspiracy, and a person who agrees with an undercover police officer can be convicted for conspiracy, even though the police officer only intended to deceive the defendant and not commit the crime. This approach has been criticized for making it too easy to prosecute those who haven't even entered into an agreement and too easy to manufacture crime by enticing individuals into these unilateral conspiratorial agreements.

---

[14] (2) Scope of Conspiratorial Relationship. If a person guilty of conspiracy, as defined by Subsection (1) of this Section, knows that a person with whom he conspires to commit a crime has conspired with another person or persons to commit the same crime, he is guilty of conspiring with such other person or persons, whether or not he knows their identity, to commit such crime.
(3) Conspiracy with Multiple Criminal Objectives. If a person conspires to commit a number of crimes, he is guilty of only one conspiracy so long as such multiple crimes are the object of the same agreement or continuous conspiratorial relationship.
(4) Joinder and Venue in Conspiracy Prosecutions.
(a) Subject to the provisions of paragraph (b) of this Subsection, two or more persons charged with criminal conspiracy may be prosecuted jointly if:
(i) they are charged with conspiring with one another; or
(ii) the conspiracies alleged, whether they have the same or different parties, are so related that they constitute different aspects of a scheme of organized criminal conduct.
(b) In any joint prosecution under paragraph (a) of this Subsection:
(i) no defendant shall be charged with a conspiracy in any county [parish or district] other than one in which he entered into such conspiracy or in which an overt act pursuant to such conspiracy was done by him or by a person with whom he conspired; and
(ii) neither the liability of any defendant nor the admissibility against him of evidence of acts or declarations of another shall be enlarged by such joinder; and
(iii) the Court shall order a severance or take a special verdict as to any defendant who so requests, if it deems it necessary or appropriate to promote the fair determination of his guilt or innocence, and shall take any other proper measures to protect the fairness of the trial.

The bilateral approach, represents the common law approach, and conspiracy charges against one conspirator will fail in the event that the other party to the conspiracy lacked the mens rea (this could be the undercover cop in the example above, but also any person who may be incapable of entering an agreement). The bilateral approach has been criticized for undermining the enforcement of conspiracy laws and for allowing the person who poses a danger to society to go unpunished.

PINKERTON RULE: ACTS AND STATEMENTS MADE BY CO-CONSPIRATORS WHILE FURTHERING A CONSPIRACY

In *Pinkerton v. United States,* 328 U.S. 640 (1946) the Court held that one co-conspirator is liable for all the crimes committed by any other conspirator if it was committed in furtherance of the conspiracy-- regardless of whether the individual aided or abetted or was even aware of the offense at the time. In that case, the Court held that Daniel Pinkerton was criminally responsible for his brother's failure to pay taxes despite the fact that Daniel was in prison at the time that Walter submitted his fraudulent tax return. The Court reasoned that conspirators are each other's agents. The "Pinkerton Rule" has broad implications and has been rejected by some courts. In a wheel conspiracy, each of the spokes, may not even know of the existence of the others. If the court had finds there to be only one conspiracy, then any crime committed by any of the "spokes" to promote their conspiracy would be considered a criminal action by each of the 30 other co-conspirators. If the court finds multiple separate conspiracies, then only the hub and the individual spoke would be liable for the acts of the other co-conspirator. Indeed, in the trial of the "Chicago Eight," anti-Vietnam war activists during the 1960, eight activists, most of whom did not know on another were prosecuted for conspiracy to cross state lines to incite a riot at the 1968 Chicago Democratic Convention— ultimately they were exonerated and freed.

Under federal and states' rules of evidence, statements made by a co-conspirator during the course of a crime are viewed as the defendant's own statements or admissions. Defendant's admissions are admissible into evidence and not treated as hearsay and can therefore be used against them at trial. Thus, co-conspirators statements are similarly admissible against all other co-conspirators. "In the eyes of the law, conspirators are one man, they breathe one breath, they speak one voice, they wield one arm, and the law says the acts, words, and declarations of each, while in pursuit of the common design, are the words and declarations of all." *Territory v. Goto*, 27 Hawaii 65 (1923).

Once formed, a conspiracy continues to exist until consummated, abandoned, or otherwise terminated by some affirmative act. *Cline v. State,* 319 S.W.2d 227 (Tenn. 1958). If a person joins a conspiracy and does not withdraw, he or she is not insulated from the actions of his or her co-conspirators. The case of *State v. Stein*, 360 A.2d 347 N.J. 1976) suggests the *Pinkerton* rule is limited to crimes that were reasonably foreseeable results of the conspiracy and committed in furtherance of the conspiracy.

The MPC rejects the Pinkerton rule. Individuals are responsible only for crimes that they solicited, aided, agreed to aid, or attempted to aid.

STATE v. STEIN,
360 A. 2d 347 (N.J. 1976)

FACTS
[D]efendant , a Trenton lawyer, suggested to a certain underworld figure that the house of one Dr. Gordon in Trenton was a likely target for a successful breaking and entering or burglary, as large amounts of cash were kept there. Defendant expected to share in the gains. As a result, there was an armed robbery at that home about a year later. While attempting to evade the police, who had been alerted to the affair, the perpetrators abducted members of the family and injured two policemen. They were caught and arrested. Subsequently defendant was lured by the police into providing money for a purported but fictitious effort to release one of the arrestees on bail so that he might supposedly flee the country.

. . . [D]efendant was indicted on counts of (a) conspiracy to steal currency; (b) armed robbery, assaults with an offensive weapon, kidnapping,

kidnapping while armed and assaults upon a police officer; and (c) obstruction of justice and conspiracy to obstruct justice. Defendant was convicted on all counts and sentenced concurrently to terms of imprisonment aggregating 30 years to 30 years and one day.
. . . .

The question as to the criminal responsibility of a conspirator for the commission by others of substantive offenses having some causal connection with the conspiracy but not in the contemplation of the conspirator has been a matter of considerable debate and controversy. Here there is no question but that Stein did not actually contemplate any criminal consequence of his "tip" to Pontani beyond a burglary and theft of money from the Gordon home. The trial court applied the conventionally stated rule that each conspirator is responsible for "anything done by his confederates which follows incidentally in the execution of the common design as one of its probable and natural consequences, even though it was not intended as part of the original design". . . .

. . . [T]he generally held rule, exemplified by the leading *Pinkerton* case cited above, . . . [is] . . . that so long as a conspiracy is still in existence "'an overt act of one partner may be the act of all without any new agreement specifically directed to that act,'" provided the substantive act could "be reasonably foreseen as a necessary or natural consequence of the unlawful agreement". 328 U.S. at 646-647, 647-648, 66 S.Ct. at 1184.

We regard the rule as just stated to be sound and viable. . . . We hold it represents the law of this State.

It remains to apply the rule to the instant fact situation. . . . The robbery was a "natural" or "probable" consequence of the conspiracy. But the Appellate Division concluded that the assaults with an offensive weapon on the wife and daughter of Dr. Gordon were "not connected with the robbery as such" but "with the preliminary acts of taking the Gordons as hostages and the eventual kidnappings" and therefore "not fairly * * * part of the

conspiratorial agreement". The assault convictions were therefore set aside.
We are not in complete agreement with this last determination. The brandishing of handguns by the robbers when they first encountered Dr. and Mrs. Gordon in the house was clearly a foreseeable event in the course of an unlawful invasion of the house for criminal purposes by armed men. That assault on Mrs. Gordon did not merge with the armed robbery, as the Appellate Division suggested might be the case, since the robbery charged was of Dr. Gordon alone, not the members of his family assaulted. Thus the assault conviction as to Mrs. Gordon should not have been set aside as too remote from the conspiracy.

As to the charge of assault with an offensive weapon on Shelly Gordon (daughter of the Gordons), since the evidence indicates that offense occurred only at the time of the attempted escape from the police, its disposition depends on the determination as to the other associated charges, discussed next below.

Liability of the defendant for the kidnapping, kidnapping while armed and assaults on a police officer presents a much closer question. The Appellate Division held that these substantive acts were "offenses committed by the criminals effecting the conspiratorial specific crime after that crime had been committed, as part of a plan to flee when it became evident that they were about to be apprehended" and that defendant could not be charged therefor. On balance, we are satisfied that this is a correct result, particularly in relation to the kidnapping phases of the episode. However, we rest our concurrence with the Appellate Division not on the ground that the substantive offenses took place subsequent to the commission of the crime conspired or that the offenses were part of a plan to flee, but rather that it would be unreasonable for a fact-finder to find as a fact beyond a reasonable doubt that they were necessary, natural or probable consequences of the conspiracy, having in mind the unique fact-complex presented

The Wharton Rule and the Gebardi Rule

The *Wharton Rule* (named after a legal theorist not a case) holds that if crimes require two individuals to be completed (for example, adultery or dueling), need at least a third person to agree with the other two for a conspiracy to exist. The rationale behind Wharton's Rule is that, unlike the usual conspiracy, the offenses named do not endanger the public generally. The *Gebardi* Rule provides that an individual who is in a class of persons excluded from criminal liability under the statute may not be charged with a conspiracy to violate that statute. In *Gebardi v. United States,* 287 U.S. 112 (1932), the Mann Act, 18 U.S.C. Sections 2421-2424, was at issue. The Mann Act prohibited transportation of a woman from one state to another for immoral purposes. The Court reasoned that the statute was intended to protect women from exploitation and was designed to punish only the person transporting the woman and not the woman who agreed to be transported. If Stuart (19 years of age) and Sally (17 years of age) agree to cross over from Portland, Oregon to Vancouver, Washington to engage in sex to take advantage of Washington's younger age of consent, Sally cannot, under the *Gebardi* Rule, be charged with conspiracy to violate the Mann Act because she is among the individuals the Mann Act is intended to protect.

The Model Penal Code incorporates the Gebardi Rule in §2.06(6)(a-b) stating that "a person is not guilty as an accomplice in the commission of an offense if he was the victim of the prohibited conduct." It, however, rejects the Wharton Rule.

Conspiracy Defenses

Voluntary Renunciation

It is difficult, but not impossible for a conspirator to withdraw from a conspiracy, and protect themselves against liability for the future acts of former co-conspirators. The general rule is that withdrawal from a conspiracy is no defense to the crime of conspiracy no matter when the withdrawal took place or the nature of the defendant's motive. *United States v. Read*, 658 F.2d 1225 (7th Cir. 1981). Some states' statutes allow defendants to raise a "withdrawal" or "renunciation" defense when charged with conspiracy. However, in the absence of statutory authority, courts have been reluctant to allow withdrawal as a defense reasoning that even if one of the co-conspirators wants to withdraw, the conspiracy can still proceed. When the defendant raises renunciation as a defense, the courts have generally required the defendant to take steps necessary to stop the objective of the conspiracy. In every state that allows the renunciation defense, the defendant bears the burden of establishing his or her withdrawal from the conspiracy. Many states also require the defendant to notify law enforcement authorities about the pertinent details of the conspiracy (in a timely manner) in order they might prevent the crime Conspirators who withdraw from the conspiracy are still liable for any acts already completed which were in furtherance of the conspiracy. Some states require that the withdrawing co-conspirator unequivocally state to each other co-conspirator that he or she is withdrawing. Some states also require the withdrawing co-conspirator to take actions necessary to prevent the commission of the target crime.

The Model Penal Code's renunciation/abandonment defense to the crime of conspiracy requires the conspirator not only renounce his criminal purpose but also take steps to "thwart the success of the conspiracy" under circumstances demonstrating a complete and voluntary renunciation of his criminal intent.[15]

---

[15] MPC §5.03 (6) Renunciation of Criminal Purpose. It is an affirmative defense that the actor, after conspiring to commit a crime, thwarted the success of the conspiracy, under circumstances manifesting a complete and voluntary renunciation of his criminal purpose.
(7) Duration of Conspiracy. For purposes of Section 1.06(4):

IMPOSSIBILITY

Most courts take the view that co-conspirators who could not have accomplished their objective because it was impossible to commit the crime have no defense. But, some court decisions, analogizing to impossibility defenses in attempt law, have held that a legal but not factual impossibility is a defense. Dix, at 168. The MPC recognizes a factual impossibility defense.

GALAN v. STATE,
184 N.E. 40 (Ohio Ct. App. 1932)

Judges: WASHBURN, J.

. . . [T]the evidence of the defendant and others establishes that the defendant entered into a conspiracy with Russell Ewerth and Barney Crimi to commit a robbery in the store of the A. Polsky Company.

. . . But where the mere forming of a conspiracy is not a crime, the law affords a locus poenitentiæ, or a time of repentance, and, therefore, although several parties conspire to do a criminal act, either one or all of them may so abandon their design before the act is done as to avoid criminal liability for the act.

The defendant in this case claims that, more than thirty days before the robbery, he withdrew from such conspiracy and notified his coconspirators of that fact and that he took no part in the robbery.

The case turns upon the question of whether the undisputed and credible evidence establishes that, before the robbery was committed, the defendant abandoned his design and withdrew from the conspiracy so as to escape criminal liability for the robbery.

The record discloses that the defendant met Ewerth, who was employed in the A. Polsky Company store and learned from him how money was handled in the store at certain times, and that the circumstances were such that probably a large sum of money could be secured by a well planned and executed robbery.

Soon thereafter defendant called on Ewerth at the store and inspected the situation, and, after the two had had several conferences on the subject, the defendant agreed to and did interest Barney Crimi in the matter and later brought Crimi to the store to meet Ewerth and look over the various rooms, stairways, and entrances to the building, with a view of planning a robbery.

The three then met at Ewerth's home and agreed upon plans for the robbery and the division of the spoils, it being understood that Ewerth was not to take any part in the robbery and that Joe Mihally was to drive the get-away car; and the plan as then contemplated was to hold up an employee of the Polsky Company on one of the stairways in the store.

That was some six weeks before the robbery took place; and then about three or four weeks before the robbery the three met again at the store, and at that time, according to the testimony of Crimi, "Galan kind of got to thinking it over and decided he wanted to withdraw from it. He said he didn't like it. He had run into some girl, and he said `that woman knows me, and I don't care to participate in it.'"

According to the testimony of the defendant, his version of what transpired at that meeting is

---

(a) conspiracy is a continuing course of conduct that terminates when the crime or crimes that are its object are committed or the agreement that they be committed is abandoned by the defendant and by those with whom he conspired; and

(b) such abandonment is presumed if neither the defendant nor anyone with whom he conspired does any overt act in pursuance of the conspiracy during the applicable period of limitation; and

(c) if an individual abandons the agreement, the conspiracy is terminated as to him only if and when he advises those with whom he conspired of his abandonment or he informs the law enforcement authorities of the existence of the conspiracy and of his participation therein.

as follows: "We looked over the inside of the building where we were figuring on doing the robbery, and I suggested to Barney (Crimi), `no use doing it in here, we might as well wash out of the whole thing.' I told him there was no possible chance, and I says `as far as doing it we are going to get caught up on it, as far as we are both concerned and I am going to drop out,' and he agreed with me at that time and that was the last I ever said to him about the Polsky robbery."

Ewerth also testified that later he had a talk with Crimi as to a change in the split of the proceeds, but that he had no talk on that subject "with Galan (defendant) after he dropped out;" and, when Ewerth was arrested and made a full confession, he said that in a certain conversation with the defendant he did not say anything about a payroll "because Tony (defendant) and I had dropped the whole thing."

After the conversation in which the defendant says he withdrew from the conspiracy, Crimi secured the help of four men with criminal records from Cleveland, and the plan was slightly changed to a holdup of the employee of the company with the money for the pay roll while in the street in front of the store, and that plan was successfully carried out.

There is no evidence in the record that the defendant knew about the Cleveland men until after the robbery, and neither is there any evidence that, after said claimed withdrawal, he conferred with any of said parties about robbing said store, but there is evidence that, just before the robbery, he was on the street near said store, and that, after the robbery, he unsuccessfully tried to get in touch with Crimi, and that he did go to see Ewerth, but he did not claim or receive any part of the proceeds of the robbery or take any part in the actual robbery.

Thus it will be seen that the defendant entered into a conspiracy to commit a robbery, which, in and of itself, is not a crime in Ohio, and that before the robbery he notified both of his fellow conspirators that he had withdrawn from the conspiracy and that they recognized and respected his withdrawal and went forward with others and committed the robbery, and that the defendant had no part in the

conspiracy after his withdrawal and no part in the robbery.

However, he did not repent from any worthy motive, did not attempt to dissuade his coconspirators from going ahead with the project, and he did not attempt to prevent the robbery by notice to the Polsky Company or the public authorities.

The trial judge evidently concluded that the defendant was the chief instigator in the conspiracy, and that, to render his withdrawal effective to absolve him, he was required to do something more than announce his withdrawal to his coconspirators and thereafter do nothing in furtherance of the conspiracy; that he was called upon to do something to prevent the carrying out of the act which he had induced others to agree to do.

While we sympathize with that view, we can find no support for it in the cases in this country which relate to the right of a conspirator to withdraw from a conspiracy before the act involved in the conspiracy has been committed.

…

There are very, very few cases involving the question of what a conspirator must do to withdraw from the conspiracy and escape responsibility for what is thereafter done in furtherance of the conspiracy. The general rule is stated as follows: [Note: here the court confusingly talks about aiding and abetting liability not conspiracy]

> "A person is not guilty of a crime as accessory or principal in the second degree because of counseling or consenting, if he repented and countermanded the other party, or withdrew, to the knowledge of the other, before the crime was committed. To relieve him from liability under this rule, however, he must in some way inform his confederates of his change of purpose."

"The fact that one who has counseled the commission of a crime, or agreed to take part in it, repents, and withdraws his advice, and abandons the purpose, may or may not relieve him from liability. If he does so when it is too late to notify the principal of such withdrawal, he is nevertheless guilty as accessory, but if he does so before his advice is acted on in any way, or if he does all in his power to prevent it, and his efforts are unavailing because some new cause intervenes, he is not guilty. Such notification may be by words or by acts; and if the words or acts are such as would ordinarily convey his intention to withdraw to the principal, he is not liable for further acts of the principal, whether they actually produced on the mind of the principal the effect which he intended to convey or not. Mere disapproval, however, after having counseled a crime, without any effort to prevent its commission, or mere withdrawal without the knowledge of his confederate, will not relieve him."

…[W]here a conspirator bona fide withdraws and seasonably notifies his coconspirators of his withdrawal, we can find no warrant in any of the cases for requiring him to go further and try to dissuade his coconspirators, or to try, by notice to public authorities or others, to prevent the carrying out of the act involved in the conspiracy. The law seems to be that if, by entering a conspiracy, I authorize others to act for me, I may revoke that authority, so far as my criminal liability is concerned, by simply withdrawing from the conspiracy and seasonably notifying the other conspirators of that fact, and doing nothing thereafter in furtherance of the conspiracy; if the rule is to be changed so as to require me to also try to dissuade my former coconspirators and to do all in my power to prevent the carrying out of the conspiracy, it should be changed by the Legislature and not by the courts.

There being no real conflict in the evidence in this case, we are bound to conclude that the defendant withdrew from said conspiracy and notified the other conspirators in time to relieve him from criminal responsibility for said robbery, and that he thereafter took no part in the conspiracy or the robbery, and that therefore the trial court should have granted the motion of the defendant for his discharge at the close of all of the evidence.

The judgment will therefore be reversed. . . .

Other Cases – Impossibility Defense to Conspiracy

United States v. Jimenez Recio, 537 U.S. 270 (2003),
FACTS
Police stopped a truck which was carrying illegal drugs. With the help of the truck drivers, the police set up a sting operation. Defendants Recio and Lopez-Meza came for the truck and were arrested.

A federal trial jury convicted the two of conspiracy, but the trial judge ordered a new trial because of a Ninth Circuit Court of Appeals precedent. The court held that the federal government could not prosecute the drug conspiracy defendants unless they joined the conspiracy before the government seized the drugs.

The new jury convicted them again. The Supreme Court decided that a conspiracy did not automatically end when the object of the conspiracy became impossible to achieve.

The Court held that the essence of conspiracy is the agreement to commit a crime and the fact that the government has defeated the object of the conspiracy does not prevent individuals from agreeing to participate in criminal activity and being held liable.

Justice Breyer's opinion noted the general consensus is that impossibility of success is not a defense to a conspiracy charge and that an agreement to commit an unlawful act is a "distinct evil" which "may exist and be punished whether or not the substantive crime ensues."
Conspiracies pose a threat to the public over and above the threat of the crime because participants are likely to commit other crimes.

Solicitation

The crime of solicitation involves a written or spoken statement in which an individual intentionally advises, requests, counsels, commands, hires, encourages, or incites another person to commit a crime (actus reus) with the intent that the other individual commit the crime (mens rea). Solicitation is complete the moment the statement requesting another to commit a crime is made. Is it solicitation when a person makes a comment intended as a joke or uttered out of frustration? No, because the person lacks the specific intent or purpose that the other person commit the crime. Similarly, a statement hoping that the crime is committed is not enough to be liable for solicitation--some effort must be made to get another person to commit the crime

Many states do not have solicitation statutes and rely instead on the common law of solicitation. The states that have solicitation statutes have adopted various approaches. Some punish the solicitation of all crimes and others limit solicitation to felonies. Solicitation convictions, like attempt convictions, generally result in punishment that is slightly less severe or the equivalent punishment to the intended crime.

Solicitation can be a form of accomplice liability if the person solicited agrees to render aid in the completion of the crime. Solicitation, however, is complete, even when the person solicited refuses to help commit the target crime. A person can be charged and convicted of both the target crime and the solicitation to commit the target crime, and unlike attempt, a charge of solicitation does not merge or fold into the completed crime. So, for example if John asks Sue to commit murder, John can be convicted and sentenced for both solicitation to commit murder (by asking another to complete the crime) and murder (on an aiding and abetting theory) if Sue agrees and in fact kills the person. John can also be convicted of solicitation to commit murder if Sue refuses to do so.

MPC §5.02(3) sets forth the Code's approach to solicitation: "A person is guilty of solicitation to commit a crime if with the purpose of promoting or facilitating its commission he commands, encourages or requests another person to engage in specific conduct that would constitute such crime or an attempt to commit such crime or would establish his complicity in its commission or attempted commission."

Solicitation Defenses

Solicitation occurs when the words are uttered making the request, not when the intended crime is completed. In fact, solicitation occurs even if the defendant never could convince anyone to agree to commit the crime. Thus, it is difficult for a person to successfully claim a defense to solicitation. If someone does agree to do the solicited crime, it is not enough for the person making the request or solicitation to simply change his or her mind. The person must take every action necessary to prevent the recipient of the solicitation from completing the crime to have a defense to solicitation. As with attempt, it is not a defense to solicitation that the defendant abandoned the criminal purpose based on the intervention of outside or extraneous factors.

The Model Penal Code provides an affirmative defense of renunciation when a person is able to persuade the person solicited not to do the crime or otherwise prevents the commission of the crime "under circumstances manifesting a complete and voluntary renunciation of his criminal purpose." MPC §5.02(3) The Code also recognizes a factual impossibility defense, stating, "It is a defense to a charge of solicitation . . . that if the criminal object were achieved, the actor would not be guilty of a . . . or as an accomplice. MPC § 5.04(2).

UNRECEIVED SOLICITATIONS

Unreceived solicitations present and interesting question: What happens when someone requests another to commit a crime, but the other person does not hear the request—or as seen in the next cases, what if the person sends a letter requesting another to commit a crime, but the letter gets lost or intercepted and is therefore not received by the intended recipient. States have taken two approaches which are discussed at length in the following cases. Under the Model Penal Code, an individual is guilty of solicitation when he or she writes a letter asking another to commit a crime even if the letter is intercepted and does not reach its intended recipient ("It is immaterial that the actor fails to communicate with the person he solicits to commit a crime if his conduct was designed to affect such communication." MPC §5.02 (2).) California takes the opposite approach.

PEOPLE v. SAEPHANH,
94 Cal. Rptr. 2d 910 (Cal. Ct. App, 2000)

FACTS

[Defendant wrote a letter while incarcerated asking a fellow gang member to murder his girlfriend because she was pregnant and he did not want to support the child. The letter never reached its intended recipient because it was intercepted by a correctional officer who had, per institutional policy, opened and read the letter. The institution informed the district attorney's office which charged the defendant with solicitation to commit murder.]

DISCUSSION

I.

THE SOLICITATION CONVICTION

Appellant contends there is insufficient evidence to support his conviction for solicitation of murder because the evidence establishes that the soliciting communication was not received by the intended recipient and, in fact, establishes no one was solicited. He asserts that California's solicitation statute, section 653f, requires proof of a completed communication. He suggests a "completed communication" occurs only when the intended recipient of the communication receives it.

Appellant acknowledges no published California case has so held and notes the issue is one of first impression in California. According to appellant, however, "two other states which have considered the issue under solicitation statutes similar to [California's section 653f], Oregon and New Mexico," concluded solicitation requires a "completed communication," i.e. one which was received by the intended recipient. He contends these authorities should be applied in California.

In *State v. Cotton* (App.1990) 109 N.M. 769, the defendant was convicted of two counts of criminal solicitation. While he was incarcerated in New Mexico, he wrote two letters to his wife in Indiana suggesting that she warn their daughter not to testify against defendant on molestation charges and that she persuade their daughter to leave New Mexico and go to Indiana. Neither letter ever reached defendant's wife, both having landed in the hands of law enforcement. On appeal, the defendant claimed

insufficient evidence to support the solicitation convictions because the letters never reached the intended recipient, the defendant's wife. (*Id.* at p. 1051.)

The New Mexico Court of Appeal agreed. First, it noted that New Mexico's criminal solicitation statute "adopts in part, language defining the crime of solicitation as set out in the Model Penal Code promulgated by the American Law Institute." (790 P.2d at pp. 1052-1053.) The court distinguished New Mexico's statute from the Model Penal Code, noting that New Mexico's solicitation statute

> "specifically omits that portion of the Model Penal Code subsection declaring that an uncommunicated solicitation to commit a crime may constitute the offense of criminal solicitation. The latter omission, we conclude, indicates an implicit legislative intent that the offense of solicitation requires some form of actual communication from the defendant to either an intermediary or the person intended to be solicited, indicating the subject matter of the solicitation." (790 P.2d at p. 1053, fn. omitted.)

Thus, by adopting in part the Model Penal Code section defining solicitation but omitting language from that section criminalizing uncommunicated solicitations, the New Mexico Legislature intended that the New Mexico statute not criminalize uncommunicated solicitations.

The court observed that one scholar suggests uncommunicated solicitations may have to be prosecuted as attempted solicitation. The court rejected the state's argument that uncommunicated solicitations nonetheless constitute solicitations because New Mexico's criminal solicitation statute expressly provides that one is guilty of solicitation where he "`otherwise attempted to promote or facilitate another person to engage in conduct constituting a felony....'" The court declined to read that provision "so broadly." The court reversed the judgment.

In *State v. Lee* (1991) 105 Or.App. 329, the Oregon Court of Appeal reached a similar result. There, the defendant, while in jail, wrote letters to an acquaintance in a juvenile center outlining plans to rob a store and residence. Authorities in the juvenile center intercepted the letters, which never reached the intended recipient. The defendant was convicted of solicitation to commit robbery. On appeal, he argued lack of evidence to sustain the conviction because the letters were never received by the intended recipient.

Citing *Cotton* and apparently following its reasoning, the Oregon court noted Oregon's criminal solicitation statute "was based, in part, on the Model Penal Code." (*State v. Lee, supra*, 804 P.2d at p. 1210.)

As did the court in *Cotton,* the *Lee* court noted the omission of Model Penal Code language criminalizing uncommunicated solicitations in Oregon's criminal solicitation statute.

> "Significantly, the legislature did not adopt the provision of the Model Penal Code that specifically provides that solicitation may be based on an incomplete communication." (State v. Lee, supra, 804 P.2d at p. 1210.)

The court concluded a completed communication is required to prove the crime of solicitation. The court determined attempted solicitation is a necessarily included offense of solicitation and remanded for entry of judgment of conviction on that crime. (804 P.2d at pp. 1210-1211.)

Respondent agrees no California authority has directly addressed the issue of whether one may be found guilty of solicitation where the intended recipient of the soliciting communication never received the message. Respondent notes there is a split in authorities from other jurisdictions addressing the issue.

In *People v. Lubow* the New York court concluded that state's criminal solicitation statute included in the crime uncommunicated solicitations. The court noted the New York statute indicated one is guilty of solicitation if, with the intent another engage in criminal conduct, the defendant "'solicits, requests, commands, importunes or otherwise attempts to cause such other person to engage in such conduct.'" The court noted New York's statute stems from the Model Penal Code. The court pointed to that portion of the New York statute stating one is guilty of solicitation if he solicits another to engage in criminal conduct, "'or otherwise attempts to cause'" such conduct. The court found "[t]his has the same effect as the Model Penal Code...." The court held,

> "[A]n attempt at communication which fails to reach the other person may also constitute the offense for the concluding clause 'or otherwise attempts to cause such other person to engage in such conduct' would seem literally to embrace as an attempt an undelivered letter or message initiated with the necessary intent."

Thus, the New York court reached a different conclusion as to the meaning of the "otherwise attempts" language in the New York statute than did the *Cotton* court as to the meaning of identical language in the New Mexico statute.

Does California's section 653f include in its ambit solicitations not received by the intended recipient? *Cotton* and *Lee* concluded the New Mexico and Oregon Legislatures intended their solicitation statutes to require a solicitation be received by the intended recipient for criminal liability to attach on the basis of the omission from their statutes of language contained in the Model Penal Code on which those statutes are based. Section 653f, enacted in 1929, is not based on the Model Penal Code. Thus, we disagree with appellant that *Cotton* and *Lee* examined "solicitation statutes similar to California's Penal Code section 653f," at least in terms of legislative history and intent. We find *Cotton* and *Lee* unpersuasive on the issue of whether section 653f criminalizes the making of soliciting communications not received by the intended recipient.

Likewise, *Lubow* provides no guidance on the issue because in that case the court noted New York's solicitation statute stems from the Model Penal Code. The court found that the "or otherwise attempts" language in the statute was akin to subsection 2 of Model Penal Code section 5.02. Section 653f, not derived from the Model Penal Code, does not contain attempt language.

As have the parties, we have located no California case squarely addressing the question of whether the intended recipient of a solicitation must receive the solicitation for liability to attach under section 653f.

Interpretation of a statute is a question of law which we review de novo. In interpreting a statute we ascertain legislative intent to effectuate the purpose of the law. To determine intent, we look first to the language of the statute, giving effect to its plain meaning. . . .

As noted, section 653f, subdivision (b) provides:

> "Every person who, with the intent that the crime be committed, solicits another to commit or join in the commission of murder shall be punished by imprisonment...."

The plain language of section 653f, in particular the phrase "solicits another," demonstrates that proof the defendant's soliciting message was received by an intended recipient is required for liability to attach. The facts of this case are illustrative of the plain meaning of the statute. Here, appellant intended to ask Saechao and the "homies or home girls" to kill Cassandra's fetus. However, neither Saechao nor the "homies or home girls" ever received the soliciting message. Thus, appellant did not solicit Saechao or the specifically designated others.

Respondent nonetheless contends the harm is in the asking and suggests the crime of solicitation was complete when appellant "deposited the correspondence with the requisite criminal intent." According to respondent, solicitation has two elements, a request to do a crime and intent that it be completed. Thus, respondent asserts, "appellant's letter was the murder request and, when he dropped it off to be mailed, he possessed the requisite criminal intent, thus satisfying both the elements to criminal solicitation."

We disagree that the letter, never received by any person appellant intended to solicit, in itself constitutes a "request" as that term may be applied in interpreting section 653f. Evidence appellant wrote the letter to Saechao is insufficient to show appellant actually requested Saechao, or the "homies or home girls" commit murder, in the absence of evidence any one of them received the letter. This is so even though appellant posted the letter. The crime of solicitation defined by section 653f requires that two or more persons must be involved, at least one being necessarily a solicitor and the other necessarily being the person solicited.

We agree with appellant that solicitation requires a completed communication.

Respondent insists that even if solicitation requires a completed communication, Vicki Lawrence, the correctional officer, received the letter. In our view, this argument evades the issue of whether appellant "solicited another." Appellant did not ask Vicki Lawrence to kill anyone, or do anything for that matter. She was not a person solicited.

Section 653f has the twofold purpose of protecting the inhabitants of California from being exposed to inducement to commit or join in the commission of crimes and preventing solicitations from resulting in the commission of the crimes solicited. Uncommunicated soliciting messages do not expose others to inducements to commit crimes. Nor is there a likelihood that an uncommunicated message would result in the commission of crimes. Thus, letters posted but not delivered do not give rise to the dangers from which section 653f seeks to protect society.

However, messages urging commission of a crime which are received expose individuals to invitation to crime and create a risk of criminal activity. Criminalizing completed solicitations furthers the policies of protecting individuals from exposure to inducements to commit crimes and preventing commission of the crimes solicited. Thus, a conviction for a violation of section 653f requires proof that the person solicited received the soliciting communication. One cannot "solicit another" without a completed communication. The communication is only completed when it is received by its intended recipient.

Appellant did not ask Vicki Lawrence to kill Cassandra's fetus and appellant was unsuccessful in asking Saechao (or, for that matter, the "homies or home girls") to do so because his letter was intercepted. Appellant did not "solicit another" to commit murder within the meaning of section 653f, subdivision (b). Thus, his conviction for solicitation of murder cannot stand.

II

Appellant next contends he is guilty of no crime . . . [arguing that the] . . . language in section 653f is a clear manifestation of legislative intent attempted solicitation is not a crime.

We disagree.

"Every person who attempts to commit any crime, but fails, or is prevented or intercepted in its perpetration, shall be punished where no provision is made by law for the punishment of those attempts ..."

Solicitation is a crime, and thus falls within section 664, which applies to the attempted commission of any crime. The plain language of section 664 makes clear the Legislature is aware of specific provisions regarding attempt in the context of some crimes, and it expressly applies to those crimes which do not address attempt. Attempted solicitation of murder is a crime in California.

DISPOSITION
The judgment of conviction for solicitation of murder is vacated. The matter is remanded to the trial court with instructions to enter a judgment of conviction for attempted solicitation of murder and thereupon to resentence appellant.

WRAP UP

In order to prevent future harm, state and federal governments have enacted statutes that criminalize attempts to commit crimes, conspiracies to commit crimes, and solicitations to commit crimes. With each of the inchoate crimes, the state must prove that the defendant intended to commit some other target crime--the highest level of criminal intent. State laws vary in the approaches and tests of whether the defendant has taken enough steps to be charged with attempt, but all agree that mere preparation does not constitute an attempt. Conspiracies involve an agreement between the parties to commit some crime; agreements require a meeting of minds. Solicitations do not even require an agreement, and a defendant is guilty of solicitation by simply asking another to commit a crime. Defendants, in some jurisdictions, may raise defenses such as voluntary renunciation or impossibility when charged with attempt, conspiracy, and solicitation.

Chapter Five: Accomplice Liability

Overview:

Sometimes people can be held liable for crimes that they personally did not commit. The term "accomplice liability" is used when multiple individuals work in concert, in some manner, to commit a crime. Other terms used to describe accomplice liability include "parties to the crime," "aiders and abetters" or "accessories." The modern trend is that when dealing with individuals who work together to commit crimes, "the hand of one is the hand of them all." This means that all involved with committing the crime will be held liable for it, even if the individual was not "the trigger man" or the primary offender.

Common Law Classifications

Common law judges were aware that often people worked together to complete a crime. Some individuals take a more active role in the crime (considered "principals"), and others less so (considered "accessories"). Some planned and carried out the crime, others helped get the tools needed to commit the crime, and still others were involved with helping their friends evade arrest or dispose of the fruits of their crimes. At common law the parties to a felony were classified according to their role in the perpetration of the crime and whether they were present at the crime. There were four classifications of parties: principals in the first degree, principals in the second degree, accessories before the fact, and accessories after the fact.

Principals in the first degree were the perpetrators of the crime.[16] In the frequently used bank-robbing example, the principal in the first degree is the person who entered the bank, pointed the gun at the teller, and took the money. Principals in the second degree either incited or abetted the crime and were physically present or constructively present at the scene of the crime and aided the principal in the first degree. (Constructive presence occurs when a person is not physically present at the scene, but is nevertheless an eyewitness and watching the crime.) See, e.g., *State v. Hamilton* 13 Nev. 386 (1878) (Defendant was posted as a lookout in a scheme to rob a stage coach; although he was physically absent from the stagecoach, he was constructively present). A lookout or the get-away driver would be a principal in the second degree. Accessories before the fact were individuals who helped prepare for the crime but who were not present during the crime. See, e.g., *State v. Spillman*, 468 P.2d 376 (Ariz 1970) (defendant encouraged victim to come to a place where another raped the victim. Defendant was not present at the time of the rape, but did aid before the crime.)

Accessories before the fact in the bank robbery include individuals who bought the guns and masks, got the blueprints for the bank, or encouraged the robbers. Accessories after the fact were individuals who assisted the perpetrators, knowing that they had committed a crime in an effort to help them evade capture. In the bank-robbing example, the accessories after the fact were the people who helped the bank robbers "lie low" or helped them hide the stolen money. At common law, a wife could not be an accessory after the fact to a crime committed by her husband, because she was considered to be under her husband's control and thus presumed to have acted under his coercion. Dix, at 67. (We will see in *State v. Ulvinen* that states continued to exclude certain individuals from possible accessory after the fact liability.) At common law a person could be convicted as an accessory after the fact only if the defendant concealed or assisted an individual whom he or she knew had committed a felony for the purpose of hindering the perpetrator's arrest, prosecution or conviction.

---

[16] A person could also be a principal in the first degree if they used the acts of an innocent human being (say, for example, a child who was not old enough to be held liable for a crime) or an inanimate agency. See, e.g. *Commonwealth v. Hill*, 11 Mass 136 (1841 (defendant used child victim to pass a counterfeit note).

Almost all crimes at common law were capital offenses, so a complicated set of rules developed to prevent individuals who were less involved, less culpable, or less blameworthy from being prosecuted, convicted, and executed when the more involved, more culpable, more blameworthy individuals escaped such punishment. At common law, for example, principals in the second degree could not be tried until the principal in the first degree had been tried and convicted (see, e.g., *Bowen v. State*, 6 So. 459 (Fla. 1889)), and accessories before or after the fact could only be tried in the states where their actions took place. An accessory could not be convicted of a more serious offense than that for which the principal was convicted. See, e.g., *Tomlin v. State*, 233 S.W.2d 303 (Tex. 1950). If there was a variance between the pleading (the charges filed) and the proof (facts shown at trial), then a party could be acquitted as well. See, e.g., *Sheldon v. Commonwealth*, 86 S.W.2d 1054 (KY 1935). If, for example, a person was charged as an accessory, he could not be convicted if the state proved at trial he was a principal; similarly, if the defendant was charged as a principal, he could not be convicted if the state proved he was an accessory. These limitations applied when dealing with situations involving principals and accessories and did not apply when dealing only with principals in the first degree and second degree. Additionally, these limitations generally did not apply when the crime charged was a misdemeanor and not a felony. Common law did not recognize criminal liability for someone who aided, after the fact, the commission of a misdemeanor.

Modern View: Accomplice Liability—Aiders and Abettors

Individuals who at common law were classified as principals in the first degree, principals in the second degree, or accessories before the fact are now called "accomplices." Accomplices are all treated as if they were the primary actor. Federal law states that, "whoever commits an offense against the United States or aids, abets, counsel, commands, induces, or procures its commission, is punishable as a principal." (18 U.S.C.A. §2 (a).) All accomplices are held to the same level of liability as the primary perpetrator. The law presumes that the individuals who assist in committing a crime implicitly consent to be bound by the conduct of the principal in the first degree. Individuals who were accessories-after-the-fact at common law are referred to as simply "accessories" and are now charged with separate minor offenses such as hindering prosecution or obstruction of justice.

PEOPLE v. POPLAR,
173 NW2d 732 (1970)

FACTS (Summary)

Williams and Lorrick broke into a recreation building in Flint, Michigan while the defendant, Marathon Poplar, acted as a lookout. When the building manager discovered Williams and Lorrick in the building, Williams shot him in the face with a shotgun. Poplar was charged as an aider and abettor of breaking and entering and with assault with intent to commit murder. Lorrick testified at Poplar's trial that he had met Poplar and Williams in a bar the night before the breaking and entering and had left with them and two others. All five had driven around for a while before they stopped and picked up some tools. They unsuccessfully attempted to enter a bowling alley with the tools, continued driving around during which time the shotgun accidentally discharged.

Lorrick testified that Poplar went up to a house to see if anyone was watching while they went up to the bowling alley. Poplar testified that he was just going to see his friend that that house because he thought friend could help him find employment.

OPINION
A more difficult question is whether Poplar may be found guilty, as an aider and abettor, or assault with intent to commit murder. Where a crime requires the existence of a specific intent, an alleged aider and abettor cannot be held as a principal unless he himself possessed the required intent or unless he aided and abetted in the perpetration of the crime knowing that the actual perpetrator had the required intent. . . . It is the knowledge of the wrongful purpose of the actor plus the encouragement provided by the aider and abettor that makes the latter equally guilty. Although the guilt of the aider and abettor is dependent upon that actor's crime, the criminal intent of the aider and abettor is

presumed from his actions with knowledge of the actor's wrongful purpose.

There was no evidence that Poplar harbored any intent to commit murder. Therefore, knowledge of the intent of Williams to kill the deceased is a necessary element to constitute Poplar a principal. This, however, may be established either by direct or circumstantial evidence from which knowledge of the intent may be inferred.

A typical case of this kind is one where, as here, a crime not specifically within the common intent and purpose is committed during an escape. Convictions for aiding and abetting such crimes have been carefully scrutinized. . . . Whether the crime committed was fairly within the scope of the common enterprise is a question of fact for the jury.

. . . .

In our opinion the jury could reasonable infer from the defendant's knowledge of the fact that a shotgun was in the car that he was aware of the fact that his companions might use the gun if they were discovered committing the burglary or in making their escape. If the jury drew that inference, then it could properly conclude that the use of the gun was fairly within the scope of the common unlawful enterprise.

STATE v. GLADSTONE,
474 P.2d 274 (Wash 1970)

OPINION

Galdstone's guilt as an aider and abettor in this case rests solely on evidence of a conversation between him and . . . Thompson concerning the possible purchase of marijuana from . . . Robert Kent. There is no other evidence to connect the accused with Ken who ultimately sold the marijuana to Thomspon. . . .

. . . [There is a fatal gap in proof]. Neither on direct examination nor under cross-examination did Thompson testify that he knew of any prior conduct, arrangements, or communications between Gladstone and Kent from which it could be even remotely inferred that the defendant had any understanding, agreement, purpose, intention or design to participate or engage in or aid or abet any sale of marijuana by Kent. Other than to obtain a simple map from Gladstone and to say that Gladstone told him that Kent might have some marijuana available, Thompson did not even establish that Kent and the defendant were acquainted with each other. . . .

The vital element — a nexus between the accused and the party whom he is charged with aiding and abetting in the commission of a crime is missing.. . . . He was not charged with aiding and abetting Thompson in the purchase of marijuana, but with Kent's sale of it. . . .

It would be a dangerous precedent indeed to hold that mere communications to the effect that another might or probably would commit a criminal offense amount to the aiding and abetting of the offense should it ultimately be committed.

Actus Reus Accomplice Liability

Statutes and court opinions describe the actus reus of accomplice liability using many terms: aid, abet, encourage, and command. Whatever called, the actus reus is satisfied by one who gives even a relatively insignificant amount of aid or encouragement. The state must prove that the accomplice assisted in the commission of a crime, but that assistance does not have to be crucial to the outcome of the crime. Being present and watching the crime, however, is not sufficient to satisfy the actus reus requirement under the mere presence rule.

MERE PRESENCE RULE:

Mere presence is ambiguous; it doesn't necessarily support an inference that the person encourages or wishes to aid the criminal. Even when a person flees with the principal, it does not necessarily mean that they are accomplices. See, *Bailey v. United States*, 416 F.2d 1110 (D.C. Cir. 1969). The one exception to the general rule that people will not be found liable as accomplices if they are present and do nothing is when the person had a duty to intervene. See, *State v. Walden*, 293 S.E. 2d 780 (1982). In those cases, mere presence, without the required action, is sufficient to satisfy accomplice liability.

BAILEY v. UNITED STATES,
416 F.2d 1110 (1969)

FACTS (Summary)
Bailey spent most of the afternoon shooting craps with another man. Then, when a man carrying cash walked by, Bailey's craps partner pulled a gun and robbed the man with the cash. Both Bailey and the other man fled the scene. Bailey was caught; the other man never was. The court held that although flight from the scene of a crime can be taken into account, it's not enough to prove accomplice actus reus.

OPINION

"We no longer hold tenable the notion that "the wicked flee when no man pursueth, but the righteous are as bold as a lion." The proposition that "one flees shortly after a criminal act is committed or when he is accused of something does so because he feels some guilt concerning the act" is not absolute as a legal doctrine "since it is a matter of common knowledge that men who are entirely innocent do sometimes fly from the scene of a crime through fear of being apprehended as guilty parties or from an unwillingness to appear as witnesses.""

STATE v. WALDEN
293 S.E.2d 780 (1982)

FACTS (Summary)
George Hoskins beat Aleen Walden's one-year-old son Lamont "repeatedly over an extended period of time," with a leather belt, until he was bloody. Walden "looked on the entire time the beating took place but did not say anything or do anything to stop the 'Bishop' [Hoskins] from beating Lamont or to otherwise deter such conduct (783)." A jury found Walden guilty as an accomplice to assault.

OPINION
The trial court properly allowed the jury to consider a verdict of guilty of assault upon a theory of aiding and abetting, solely on the ground that the defendant was present when her child was brutally beaten. A person who so aids or abets under another in the commission of a crime is equally guilty with that other person as a principal.

STATE v. ULVINEN,
313 N.W.2d 425 (Minn. 1981)

Helen Ulvinen was convicted of first-degree murder pursuant to Minn. Stat. § 609.05, subd. 1 (1980), which imposes criminal liability on one who "intentionally aids, advises, hires, counsels, or conspires with or otherwise procures" another to commit a crime. The Minnesota Supreme Court reversed.

FACTS
Carol Hoffman, Helen Ulvinen's (appellant's) daughter-in-law, was murdered late on the evening of August 10th or the very early morning of August 11th by her husband, David Hoffman. She and David had spent an amicable evening together playing with their children, and when they went to bed David wanted to make love to his wife.

However, when she refused him he lost his temper and began choking her. While he was choking her, he began to believe he was "doing the right thing" and that to get "the evil out of her" he had to dismember her body.

After his wife was dead, David called down to the basement to wake his mother, asking her to come upstairs to sit on the living room couch. From there she would be able to see the kitchen, bathroom, and bedroom doors and could stop the older child if she awoke and tried to use the bathroom.

Mrs. Ulvinen didn't respond at first but after being called once, possibly twice more, she came upstairs to lie on the couch. In the meantime, David had moved the body to the bathtub. Mrs. Ulvinen was aware that while she was in the living room her son was dismembering the body but she turned her head away so that she could not see.

After dismembering the body and putting it in bags, Hoffman cleaned the bathroom, took the body to Weaver Lake, and disposed of it. On returning home, he told his mother to wash the cloth covers from the bathroom toilet and tank, which she did. David fabricated a story about Carol leaving the house the previous night after an argument, and Helen agreed to corroborate it. David phoned the police with a missing person report and during the ensuing searches and interviews with the police, he and his mother continued to tell the fabricated story.

On August 19, 1980, David confessed to the police that he had murdered his wife. In his statement, he indicated that not only had his mother helped him cover up the crime but she had known of his intent to kill his wife that night. After hearing Hoffman statement the police arrested Mrs. Ulvinen and questioned her with respect to her part in the cover up [sic]. Police typed up a two-page statement, which she read and signed. The following day a detective questioned her further regarding events surrounding the crime, including her knowledge that it was planned.

Mrs. Ulvinen's relationship with her daughter-in-law had been a strained one. She moved in with the Hoffmans on July 26, two weeks earlier to act as a live-in babysitter for their two children. Carol was unhappy about having her move in and told friends that she hated Helen, but she told both David and his mother that they could try the arrangement to see how it worked.

On the morning of the murder, Helen told her son that she was going to move out of the Hoffman residence because "Carol had been so nasty to me." In his statement to the police, David reported the conversation that morning as follows:

Sunday morning I went downstairs and my mom was in the bedroom reading the newspaper and she had tears in her eyes, and she said in a very frustrated voice, "I've got to find another house." She said, "Carol don't want me here," and she said, "I probably shouldn't have moved in here." And I said then, "Don't let what Carol said hurt you. It's going to take a little more period of readjustment for her." Then, I told mom that I've got to do it tonight so that there can be peace in this house.

Q: What did you tell your mom that you were going to have to do that night?

A: I told my mom I was going to have to put her to sleep.

Q: Dave, will you tell us exactly what you told your mother that morning, to the best of your recollection?

A: I said I'm going to have to choke her tonight, and I'll have to dispose of her body so that it will never be found. That's the best of my knowledge.

Q: What did your mother say when you told her that?

A: She just—she looked at me with very sad eyes and just started to weep. I think she said something like "it will be for the best." David spent the day fishing with a friend of his. When he got home that afternoon he had another conversation with his mother. She told him at that time about a phone conversation Carol had had in which she discussed taking the children and leaving home. David told the police that during the conversation with his mother that afternoon he told her "Mom, tonight's got to be the night."

Q: When you told your mother, "Tonight's got to be the night," did your mother understand that you were going to kill Carol later that evening?

A: She thought I was just kidding her about doing it. She didn't think I could.

Q: Why didn't your mother think that you could do it?

A: Because for some time I had been telling her I was going to take Carol scuba diving and make it look like an accident.

Q: And she said?

A: And she always said, "Oh, you're just kidding me."

Q: But your mother knew you were going to do it that night?

A: I think my mother sensed that I was really going to do it that night.

Q: Why do you think your mother sensed you were really going to do it that night?

A: Because when I came home and she told me what had happened at the house, and I told her, "Tonight's got to be the night," I think she said, again I'm not certain, that "it would be the best for the kids."

OPINION
It is well-settled in this state that presence, companionship, and conduct before and after the offense are circumstances from which a person's participation in the criminal intent may be inferred. The evidence is undisputed that appellant was asleep when her son choked his wife. She took no active part in the dismembering of the body but came upstairs to intercept the children, should they awake, and prevent them from going into the bathroom.

She cooperated with her son by cleaning some items from the bathroom and corroborating David's story to prevent anyone from finding out about the murder. *She is insulated by statute from guilt as an accomplice after-the-fact for such conduct because of her relation as a parent of the offender.* (emphasis added). (See Minn. Stat. § 609.495, subd. 2 (1980).)

The jury might well have considered appellant's conduct in sitting by while her son dismembered his wife so shocking that it deserved punishment. Nonetheless, these subsequent actions do not succeed in transforming her behavior prior to the crime to active instigation and encouragement. Minn.Stat. § 609.05, subd. 1 (1980) implies a high level of activity on the part of an aider and abettor in the form of conduct that encourages another to act. Use of terms such as "aids,"

"advises," and "conspires" requires something more of a person than mere inaction to impose liability as a principal.

The evidence presented to the jury at best supports a finding that appellant passively acquiesced in her son's plan to kill his wife. The jury might have believed that David told his mother of his intent to kill his wife that night and that she neither actively discouraged him nor told anyone in time to prevent the murder. Her response that "it would be the best for the kids" or "it will be the best" was not, however, active encouragement or instigation. There is no evidence that her remark had any influence on her son's decision to kill his wife.

Minn.Stat. § 609.05, subd. 1 (1980), imposes liability for actions which affect the principal, encouraging him to take a course of action which he might not otherwise have taken. The state has not proved beyond a reasonable doubt that appellant was guilty of anything but passive approval.

However morally reprehensible it may be to fail to warn someone of their impending death, our statutes do not make such an omission a criminal offense. We note that mere knowledge of a contemplated crime or failure to disclose such information without evidence of any further involvement in the crime does not make that person liable as a party to the crime under any state's statutes.

David told many people besides appellant of his intent to kill his wife but no one took him seriously. He told a co-worker, approximately three times a week that he was going to murder his wife, and confided two different plans for doing so. Another co-worker heard him tell his plan to cut Carol's air hose while she was scuba diving, making her death look accidental, but did not believe him. Two or three weeks before the murder, David told a friend of his that he and Carol were having problems and he expected Carol "to have an accident sometime." None of these people has a duty imposed by law, to warn the victim of impending danger, whatever their moral obligation may be. [Court reversed conviction]

State v. Pace, 224 N.E.2d 312 (Ind. 1967).
Defendant, his wife and two children were travelling in their family car with another passenger named Rootes. Defendant, the driver, stopped and picked up a hitchhiker whom Rootes subsequently robbed at knifepoint. The Indiana Supreme Court reversed the defendant's conviction as an accomplice to the robbery reasoning that there was no evidence establishing that defendant aided and abetted in the crime. Defendant said nothing nor did he act in any way to show approval of the robbery.

State ex. Rel Attorney General v. Talley, 15 So. 722 (Alabama 1894).
[This case dealt with how significant or essential the aid must have been to the success of the crime.]

OPINION
The assistance given. . . need not contribute to the criminal result in the sense that but for it the result would have ensued. It is quite sufficient if it facilitated a result that would have transpired without it. It is quite enough if the aid merely renders it easier for the principal actor to accomplish the end intended by him and the aider and abettor, though in all human possibility the end would have been attained without it."

Commonwealth v. Raposo, 595 N.E.2d 773 (Mass 1992).
The trial judge's found: The defendant is the mother of a mildly retarded daughter, who was seventeen years old at the time of the incidents described below. The defendant's boyfriend, Manuel F. Matos, Jr., lived with the defendant and her daughter for about two months before May 22, 1988. Matos told the defendant that he intended to have sexual intercourse with her daughter. In response, the defendant expressed neither encouragement nor discouragement. On one occasion, Matos told the defendant that he was going to have intercourse with her daughter, stating that "she needs a man." The defendant did not respond, although she knew that her daughter did not want to have intercourse with Matos. Matos had intercourse with the daughter from two to four times by force and against her will. At least once, after Matos had entered the daughter's bedroom, the defendant pounded on the closed, unlocked door and told Matos to stop. On May 22, 1988, the defendant took her daughter to a New Bedford police station, where they gave statements about the sexual activity between Matos and the daughter. Prior to this visit at the police station, the defendant made no effort to enlist outside assistance to prevent Matos from engaging in sexual intercourse with her daughter.

[T]he basic question that prompted the report is whether a person may be found guilty of being an accessory before the fact to rape and to indecent assault and battery on a mentally retarded person where the victim is a minor, the defendant is the minor's parent, and the defendant failed to take reasonable steps to prevent, the sexual attacks by a third person.

The Commonwealth argues that . . . as the mother of the victim, the defendant had a common law duty to protect her child from harm, and that her failure to take reasonable steps to fulfil this duty is an omission sufficient to make her liable as an accessory--in allowing Matos access to her daughter and failing to take reasonable steps to stop his wrongful actions, the defendant "aided" Matos in committing the crimes and thus became a participant in the criminal activity. The defendant's intent that the underlying crimes be committed, the Commonwealth contends, can be inferred from her knowledge of the crimes and her intentional acts of omission.

. . .

While it is clear in this and other jurisdictions that a parent's failure to fulfil his or her duty to provide for the safety and welfare of a child may rise to the level of wanton or reckless conduct sufficient to support a manslaughter conviction, we decline to . . . read into our accessory before the fact law the principle that a mere omission by a parent to take action to protect a child, without more, is the equivalent of intentionally aiding in the commission of a felony against that child. By its very terms, [the relevant statute] requires more than an omission to act. As our case law makes clear, in order to be punished as an accessory before the fact, the defendant must have actually aided in the commission of the felony or counselled, hired, or otherwise procured someone to commit it.
[T]he Commonwealth has failed to show beyond a reasonable doubt that the defendant aided, counselled, hired, or procured Matos to commit rape and indecent assault and battery, or that she took any other action which would constitute participation in the commission of these crimes against her daughter. The fact that she knew ahead

of time of Matos's intent to commit the criminal acts, and did not report the subsequent crimes to the police immediately, does not make her guilty as an accessory before the fact.

Powell v. United States, 2 F.2d 47 (4th Cir. 1924)
Defendant was a train conductor who failed to report plainly visible, poorly hidden liquor being transported on train during Prohibition. He was found guilty on aiding and abetting grounds.

Middleton v. State 217 S.W. 1046 (Tex. 1919).
Removing daughter so she wouldn't see her mom be killed constituted aiding.

State v. Lord, 84 P.2d 80) NM 1938).
Perpetrator need not be aware of aid.

Mens Rea Accomplice Liability—Aiding And Abetting

There is a disagreement over the necessary mens rea for accomplice liability. The majority of the jurisdictions, as well as the Model Penal Code, use the standard adopted in *People v. Beeman*, 674 P.2d 1318 (Cal. 1984):

> Sound law require[s] that an aider and abettor act with knowledge of the criminal purpose of the perpetrator and with an intent or purpose either in committing, or encouraging or facilitating the commission of the offense. . . . When the definition of the offense includes the intent to do some act or achieve some consequence beyond the actus reus of the crime, the aider and abettor must share the specific intent of the perpetrator. An aider and abettor will "share" the perpetrator's specific intent when he or she knows the full extent of the perpetrator's criminal purpose and gives aid or encouragement with the intent or purpose of facilitating the perpetrator's commission of the crime. The liability of an aider and abettor extends also to the natural and reasonable consequences of the acts he knowingly and intentionally aids and encourages.

Similarly, in the oft-cited case of *United States v. Peoni*, 100 F.2d 401, 403 (2d Cir. 1938) the court summed up the mens rea requirement, stating that in order to have accomplice liability the aider and abettor must "in some sort associate himself with the venture, that he participate in it as something he wishes to bring about, that he seek by his action to make it succeed." Other courts have adopted a less stringent standard used by Fourth Circuit in *Backun v. United States*, 112 F.2d 635 (4th Cir. 1940). Under this standard, if an accomplice has knowledge of a person's criminal plans and acts to encourage or assist the commission of the offense even if there is no evidence he intended for the crime to actually occur, the mens rea for the requirement for accomplice liability is met. A conviction for accomplice liability requires that the defendant both assist and intend to assist the commission of a crime. States have not all agreed on whether the accomplice needs to simply intend to assist the primary party or whether the accomplice needs to intend that the primary party commit the offense charged (the difference is between wishing to help Joe generally, or wishing to help Joe steal the can specifically). Some states require the government to prove purposeful or intentional aiding and assisting, but others have held that knowingly aiding and assisting is enough.

> An accomplice, regardless of whether a "purposive" or "knowledge" standard is employed, is subject to the natural and probable consequences doctrine. This provides that a person encouraging or facilitating the commission of a crime will be liable as an accomplice for the crime he or she aided and abetted as well as for crimes that are the natural and probable outcome of the criminal conduct. Lippman, *Criminal Law, supra* at 162.

Other Cases—Accomplice Mens Rea

State v. Foster, 522 A2d 277 (Conn 1987).
Foster, believing Middleton had raped and robbed his girlfriend, hit him with his fist and a blunt instrument and knocked him to the ground. Foster then handed a knife to his friend, Otha Cannon, and told him to guard Middleton until he could get back and confirm he was the attacker. During Foster's absence, Cannon fatally stabbed Middleton. The state successfully prosecuted Foster for recklessly aiding and abetting Cannon

in causing the victim's death. The court, in deciding that Foster was an accomplice to negligent homicide, held that Foster was negligent and should have foreseen that Cannon might have stabbed Middleton.

Modern and Model Penal Code Approach to "Accessories After the Fact"

The modern view is that accessories after the fact get involved after the completion of the crime, and they should not be treated as harshly as the perpetrator of the crime or accomplices. Accessories are now prosecuted for "hindering prosecution" or "obstruction of justice." They are punished for frustrating the arrest, prosecution, or conviction of others who have committed felonies or misdemeanors. A spouse no longer is immune from prosecution in most states for accessory liability. Most states follow MPC §242.3 which provides:

A person commits an offense if, with purpose to hinder the apprehension, prosecution, conviction or punishment of another for crime, he:

➤ harbors or conceals the other
➤ provides or aides in providing a weapon, transportation, disguise or other means of avoiding apprehension or effecting escape; or
➤ conceals or destroys evidence of the crime, or tampers with a witness, informant, document or other source of information, regardless of its admissibility in evidence; or
➤ warns the others of impending discovery or apprehension.
➤ volunteers false information to a law enforcement officer.

STATE v. CHISM,
436 So.2d 464 (La. 1983)
…
FACTS

On the evening of August 26, 1981 in Shreveport, Tony Duke gave the defendant, Brian Chism, a ride in his automobile. Brian Chism was impersonating a female, and Duke was apparently unaware of Chism's disguise. After a brief visit at a friend's house the two stopped to pick up some beer at the residence of Chism's grandmother.

Chism's one-legged uncle, Ira Lloyd, joined them, and the three continued on their way, drinking as Duke drove the automobile. When Duke expressed a desire to have sexual relations with Chism, Lloyd announced that he wanted to find his ex-wife Gloria for the same purpose. Shortly after midnight, the trio arrived at the St. Vincent Avenue Church of Christ and persuaded Gloria Lloyd to come outside. As Ira Lloyd stood outside the car attempting to persuade Gloria to come with them, Chism and Duke hugged and kissed on the front seat as Duke sat behind the steering wheel.

Gloria and Ira Lloyd got into an argument, and Ira stabbed Gloria with a knife several times in the stomach and once in the neck. Gloria's shouts attracted the attention of two neighbors, who unsuccessfully tried to prevent Ira from pushing Gloria into the front seat of the car alongside Chism and Duke. Ira Lloyd climbed into the front seat also, and Duke drove off. One of the bystanders testified that she could not be sure but she thought she saw Brian's foot on the accelerator as the car left.

Lloyd ordered Duke to drive to Willow Point, near Cross Lake. When they arrived, Chism and Duke, under Lloyd's direction, removed Gloria from the vehicle and placed her on some high grass on the side of the roadway, near a wood line. Ira was unable to help the two because his wooden leg had come off. Afterwards, as Lloyd requested, the two drove off, leaving Gloria with him.

There was no evidence that Chism or Duke protested, resisted, or attempted to avoid the actions which Lloyd ordered them to take. Although Lloyd was armed with a knife, there was no evidence that he threatened either of his companions with harm.

Duke proceeded to drop Chism off at a friend's house, where he changed to male clothing. He placed the bloodstained women's clothes in a trash bin. Afterward, Chism went with his mother to the police station at 1:15 A.M. He gave the police a complete statement, and took the officers to the place where Gloria had been left with Ira Lloyd. The police found Gloria's body in some tall grass several feet from that spot.

An autopsy indicated that stab wounds had caused her death. Chism's discarded clothing disappeared before the police arrived at the trash bin.

OPINION:

According to Louisiana statute 14:25:

An accessory after the fact is any person who, after the commission of a felony, shall harbor, conceal, or aid the offender, knowing or having reasonable ground to believe that he has committed the felony, and with the intent that he may avoid or escape from arrest, trial, conviction, or punishment. . . .

Whoever becomes an accessory after the fact shall be fined not more than five hundred dollars, or imprisoned, with or without hard labor, for not more than five years, or both; provided that in no case shall his punishment be greater than one-half of the maximum provided by law for a principal offender. La.R.S. 14:25

Chism appealed from his conviction and sentence and argues that the evidence was not sufficient to support the judgment. Consequently, in reviewing the defendant's assigned error, we must determine whether, after viewing the evidence in the light most favorable to the prosecution, any rational trier of fact could have found beyond a reasonable doubt that:

(a) a completed felony had been committed by Ira Lloyd before Brian Chism rendered him the assistance described below; *and*
(b) Chism knew or had reasonable grounds to know of the commission of the felony by Lloyd;

and
(c) Chism gave aid to Lloyd personally under circumstances that indicate either that he actively desired that the felon avoid or escape arrest, trial conviction, or punishment or that he believed that one of these consequences was substantially certain to result from his assistance.

There was clearly enough evidence to justify the finding that a felony had been completed before any assistance was rendered to Lloyd by the defendant. The record vividly demonstrates that Lloyd fatally stabbed his ex-wife before she was transported to Willow Point and left in the high grass near a wood line. Thus, Lloyd committed the felonies of attempted murder, aggravated battery, and simple kidnapping, before Chism aided him in any way. A person cannot be convicted as an accessory after the fact to a murder because of aid given after the murderer's acts but before the victim's death, but under these circumstances the aider may be found to be an accessory after the fact to the felonious assault.

The evidence overwhelmingly indicates that Chism had reasonable grounds to believe that Lloyd had committed a felony before any assistance was rendered. In his confessions and his testimony Chism indicates that the victim was bleeding profusely when Lloyd pushed her into the vehicle, that she was limp and moaned as they drove to Willow Point, and that he knew Lloyd had inflicted her wounds with a knife.

The Louisiana offense of accessory after the fact deviates somewhat from the original common-law offense in that it does not require that the defendant actually know that a completed felony has occurred. Rather, it incorporates an objective standard by requiring only that the defendant render aid "knowing or having reasonable grounds to believe" that a felony has been committed.

The closest question presented is whether any reasonable trier of fact could have found beyond a reasonable doubt that Chism assisted Lloyd under circumstances that indicate that either Chism actively desired that Lloyd would avoid or escape arrest, trial, conviction, or punishment, or that Chism believed that one of these consequences was substantially certain to result from his assistance.

In this case we conclude that a trier of fact reasonably could have found that Chism acted with at least a general intent to help Lloyd avoid arrest because:

(1) Chism did not protest or attempt to leave the car when his uncle, Lloyd, shoved the mortally wounded victim inside;

(2) he did not attempt to persuade Duke, his would-be lover, to exit out the driver's side of the car and flee from his uncle, whom he knew to be one-legged and armed only with a knife;

(3) he did not take any of these actions at any point during the considerable ride to Willow Point;

(4) at their destination, he docilely complied with Lloyd's directions to remove the victim from the car and leave Lloyd with her, despite the fact that Lloyd made no threats and that his wooden leg had become detached;

(5) after leaving Lloyd with the dying victim, he made no immediate effort to report the victim's whereabouts or to obtain emergency medical treatment for her;

(6) before going home or reporting the victim's dire condition he went to a friend's house, changed clothing and discarded his own in a trash bin from which the police were unable to recover them as evidence;

(7) he went home without reporting the victim's condition or location;

(8) and he went to the police station to report the crime only after arriving home and discussing the matter with his mother.

The defendant asserted that he helped to remove the victim from the car and to carry her to the edge of the bushes because he feared that his uncle would use the knife on him. However, fear as a motivation to help his uncle is inconsistent with some of Chism's actions after he left his uncle. Consequently, we conclude that despite Chism's testimony, the trier of fact could have reasonably found that he acted voluntarily and not out of fear when he aided Lloyd and that he did so under circumstances indicating that he believed that it was substantially certain to follow from his assistance that Lloyd would avoid arrest, trial, conviction, or punishment.

For the foregoing reasons, it is also clear that the judge's verdict was warranted. There is evidence in this record from which a reasonable trier of fact could find a defendant guilty beyond a reasonable doubt. Therefore, we affirm the defendant's convictio

DUNN v. COMMONWEALTH, WL 147448 (Va.App. 1997)

FACTS

On two separate occasions, Charles Lee Dunn was a passenger in a car when two grand larcenies occurred. He claimed he didn't know the others in the car planned to break into cars and didn't participate in the thefts of stereo equipment and CDs. He admitted that, after the first theft on September 4, he voluntarily went with the others when they sold the equipment, and he received a small piece of crack cocaine from the proceeds. Regarding one of the offenses, he testified that he took no active part in the theft and was taken home immediately thereafter.

The Commonwealth's evidence included testimony from the investigating officer, Detective Ramsey, that appellant (Dunn) told him that he knew the purpose of going to the location of the first offense was "to take equipment belonging to Mr. Roberts. It was known there was equipment in his car."

As to the September 7, 1995 offense, Ramsey testified that Dunn said:

> The three of them went to a location near Mr. Jackson's house. Mr. Dunn waited in the car, and Mr. Walker and Mr. Kraegers approached Mr. Jackson's vehicle. They entered the vehicle through an unlocked door and took stereo equipment from the vehicle, brought it back to the car. [Appellant] states that they put the speaker box in the trunk, put the amp and a CD player in the car, and he says, I think they got some CDs. That equipment was also taken to the city and traded for crack cocaine which they all used, and that property has not been recovered.

Ramsey stated that Dunn admitted to participating and taking the property to the city in exchange for crack cocaine.

OPINION

While Dunn contends that the evidence failed to establish he did anything other than ride in a car with friends, the trial court was not required to accept his explanation.

Dunn admitted to Ramsey that he knew the others intended to steal on both occasions; he smoked crack cocaine purchased with the money received from disposing of the goods; and he went out with the codefendants three days after the first larceny occurred.

Under the facts of this case, the Commonwealth's evidence was sufficient to prove beyond a reasonable doubt that appellant was an accessory after the fact to the two grand larcenies.

Other Cases—Accessories After the Fact, Modern View

United States v. Graves, 143 F3d 1185 (9th Cir. 1998).

Defendant, Graves, accompanied Prince to a party on Treasure Island Naval Base in San Francisco, California. Immediately upon their arrival, Prince began yelling at his girlfriend to convince her to go home with him. During their argument, Prince displays a weapon. Graves attempted to persuade Prince to leave, but, unsuccessful, he went and waited in his truck. Naval security officers arrived, arrested Prince, and placed Prince in their police cruiser. They searched Prince, but did not find the gun. Graves got out of his truck, opened the door of the cruiser, and helped Prince escape. Prince and Graves ran down the street, into a nearby cul-de-sac where Graves threw an object into a trash can. Neighbors reported this to naval security officers who retrieved a revolver. Later that night Prince and Graves returned to the apartment and were arrested, taken to the naval security station house and received citations for carrying a loaded weapon in a public place and other charges. Prince used an alias, and it was not discovered until later that he had a felony conviction. He later was charged with being a felon in possession of a firearm. Ultimately, Graves was charged with being an accessory after the fact to Prince's charge of being a felon in possession of a firearm. At jury deliberations at

Grave's trial, the jury asked whether they needed to find that Graves knew that Prince had a prior felony conviction. The trial court said, "no." Graves appealed the accessory after the fact count claiming the jury instruction was unlawful. The appellate court stated,

"There is no dispute that the government had to prove that Graves knew that Prince possessed a gun.... .

Indeed, as we have previously recognized, a defendant who is accused of being an accessory after the fact must be shown to have had actual knowledge of each element of the underlying offense. ...

The evidence at trial did not, of course, support a finding that Graves knew Prince was a felon in possession. The only evidence that suggested that Graves knew Prince's possession was even "unlawful" was the fact that Graves had disposed of the gun in the trash can and that he tried to help Prince escape. Because Graves had observed Prince brandishing the gun at the party, an obviously unlawful act and knew that Prince had been arrested for *that* conduct, the only reasonable inference is that Graves acted in order to help Prince avoid prosecution for the offense he witnessed. As noted earlier, the judge specifically told the jury that they did not need to find that Graves knew of Prince's prior felony and that they could convict him as an accessory after the fact as long as they found he knew Prince possessed the gun "unlawfully".... . Graves conviction must be reversed. ...."

State v. Jordan, 590 S.S.E.2d 424 (N.C. Ct. App. 2004).
Defendant falsely stated that the victim was shot by husband because the victim was trying to rape her. Her conviction for being an accessory after the fact was affirmed.

State v. Newton 129 So. 3d 20 (La. 2013)
Defendants (parents) lied to police to get their sons out of criminal trouble held to have hindered prosecution.

Nebraska v. Anderson, 10 Neb App. 163 (2001).
Defendant lied to police and said that two guys were involved with killing who had nothing to do with it. Defendant got them in trouble, but also had the result of assisting the real perpetrator (who knew nothing about any of this!) Court affirmed her conviction.

Sherron v. State, 959 So.2d 30 Miss. Ct. App. 2006).
Court held that a mother who lied to protect her husband who had raped her daughter hindered prosecution.

Enmund v. Florida, 458 U.S. 782 (1987).
U.S. Supreme Court held it was unconstitutional to impose death penalty on driver of getaway car who did not participate in robbery and murder.

Tison v. Arizona, 481 U.S. 137 (1987).
U.S. Supreme Court says substantial participation in violent felony may warrant the death penalty even by defendant who lacked intent to kill.

People v. Hardin, 207 Cal. App. 2d 336 (1962).
At common law, the person assisted by the accessory after the fact must have actually completed the crime. Scope of Accomplice Liability: Natural and Probable Consequences

Accomplice Liability for Natural and Probable Consequences

The traditional rule is that an accomplice should be liable for all probable consequences (foreseeable consequences) of his conduct. Thus liability may be imposed not only for the offense incited or abetted but also for other crimes committed by the perpetrator that were reasonably foreseeable result of the contemplated crime. An aiders and abettor's intent to encourage or facilitate the primary crime is sufficient to impose liability for other reasonably foreseeable crimes committed by the perpetrator. On the other hand, accomplice liability does not extend to those crimes that were not reasonably foreseeable.

STATE v. ROBINSON,
715 N.W. 2d 44 (Mich. 2006)

... Defendant and a codefendant, Samuel Pannell, committed an aggravated assault, and Pannell shot and killed the victim, Bernard Thomas. After a bench trial, the trial court convicted defendant of second-degree murder under an aiding and abetting theory. The Court of Appeals reversed the trial court's judgment, because it concluded that there was insufficient evidence that defendant shared or was aware of

Pannell's intent to kill.

We hold that under Michigan law, a defendant who intends to aid, abet, counsel, or procure the commission of a crime, is liable for that crime as well as the natural and probable consequences of that crime. In this case, defendant committed and aided the commission of an aggravated assault. One of the natural and probable consequences of such a crime is death. Therefore, the trial court properly convicted defendant of second-degree murder. We reverse the judgment of the Court of Appeals and reinstate defendant's conviction of second-degree murder.

FACTS

According to the evidence adduced at trial, defendant and Pannell went to the house of the victim, Bernard Thomas, with the stated intent to "f*** him up." Under Pannell's direction, defendant drove himself and Pannell to the victim's house. Pannell knocked on the victim's door. When the victim opened the door, defendant struck him. As the victim fell to the ground, defendant struck the victim again. Pannell began to kick the victim. Defendant told Pannell that "that was enough," and walked back to the car. When defendant reached his car, he heard a single gunshot.

Following a bench trial, the trial court found defendant guilty of second-degree murder "on the prong of great bodily harm only." Specifically, the court found that defendant drove Pannell to the victim's house with the intent to physically attack the victim. The court also found that once at the victim's home, defendant initiated the attack on the victim, and that defendant's attack enabled Pannell to "get the upper-hand" on the victim. The court sentenced defendant to a term of 71 months to 15 years.

The Court of Appeals reversed defendant's murder conviction, holding . . . that the trial court improperly convicted defendant of second-degree murder because there was no evidence establishing that defendant was aware of or shared Pannell's intent to kill the victim.

ANALYSIS
This case involves liability under our aiding and abetting statute, MCL 767.39, which provides:

Every person concerned in the commission of an offense, whether he directly commits the act constituting the offense or procures, counsels, aids, or abets in its commission may hereafter be prosecuted, indicted, tried and on conviction shall be punished as if he had directly committed such offense.

Unlike conspiracy and felony murder, which also allow the state to punish a person for the acts of another, aiding and abetting is not a separate substantive offense. Rather, "being an aider and abettor is simply a theory of prosecution" that permits the imposition of liability for accomplices.

This Court recently described the three elements necessary for a conviction under an aiding and abetting theory:

"(1) the crime charged was committed by the defendant or some other person; (2) the defendant performed acts or gave encouragement that assisted the commission of the crime; and (3) the defendant intended the commission of the crime or had knowledge that the principal intended its commission at the time that [the defendant] gave aid and encouragement."

The primary dispute in this case involves the third element. Under the Court of Appeals analysis, the third element would require the prosecutor to prove beyond a reasonable doubt that a defendant intended to commit the identical offense, here homicide, as the accomplice or, alternatively, that a defendant knew that the accomplice intended to commit the homicide. We reaffirm that evidence of defendant's specific intent to commit a crime or knowledge of the accomplice's intent constitutes sufficient mens rea to convict under our aiding and abetting statute. However, as will be discussed later in this opinion, we disagree that evidence of a shared specific intent to commit the crime of an accomplice is the exclusive way to establish liability under our aiding and abetting statute.

AIDING AND ABETTING STATUTE
The theory that a defendant could be liable for another's criminal actions as an "aider and abettor" goes back to the common law. At

common law, there were four categories of offenders to a felony:

(1) principal in the first degree-he actually engaged in the felonious conduct; (2) principal in the second degree-he was present when the felony was committed and aid and abetted its commission; (3) accessory before the fact-he was not present when the felony was committed but aided and abetted prior to its commission; (4) accessory after the fact-he was not present when the felony was committed but rendered aid thereafter in order to protect the felon or to facilitate his escape.

Principals in the second degree had to intend to commit the crime charged or else be aware of the intent of the principal in the first degree to commit that crime. But accessories before the fact were "guilty of all incidental consequences which might reasonably be expected to result from the intended wrong." Thus, at common law, one could be guilty of the natural and probable consequences of the intended crime or the intended crime itself, depending on whether the actor was a principal in the second degree or an "accessory before the fact." Michigan's aiding and abetting statute has been in force and substantively unchanged since the mid-1800s. The 1855 statute, 1855 PA 77, §19, which is nearly identical to the current statute, stated:

> The distinction between an accessory before the fact, and a principal, and between principals in the first and second degree in cases of felony, is abrogated; and all persons concerned in the commission of a felony, whether they directly commit the act constituting the offence, or aid and abet in its commission, though not present, may hereafter be indicted, tried and punished, as principals, as in the case of a misdemeanor.
> . . . [W]e note that there is no language in the statute that demonstrates a legislative intent to abrogate the common-law theory that a defendant can be held criminally liable as an accomplice if: (1) the defendant intends or is aware that the principal is going to commit a specific criminal act; or (2) the criminal act committed by the principal is an "incidental consequence[ ] which might reasonably be expected to result from the

intended wrong."

Accordingly, we hold that when the Legislature abolished the distinction between principals and accessories, it intended for all offenders to be convicted of the intended offense, in this case aggravated assault, as well as the natural and probable consequences of that offense, in this case death. The case law that has developed since the Legislature codified these common-law principles provides examples of accomplice liability under both theories.

NATURAL AND PROBABLE CONSEQUENCES
Under the natural and probable consequences theory, "[t]here can be no criminal responsibility for any thing not fairly within the common enterprise, and which might be expected to happen if the occasion should arise for any one to do it." In *Knapp*, the defendant and several other men engaged in sexual intercourse with the victim. After the defendant left, one of the men threw the woman from a second-story window. A jury convicted the defendant of manslaughter. This Court reasoned that because there was no evidence that the defendant threw the victim out the window, the jury must have held him accountable for the actions of the other men.

The *Knapp* Court reversed the defendant's conviction for manslaughter because there was no proof that the woman's death was a part of the "common enterprise" of prostitution because one would not expect it "to happen if the occasion should arise to do it." Therefore, the defendant could not be held to be an accomplice to the manslaughter.

Similarly, in *People v. Chapman*, this Court held that a defendant was " 'responsible criminally for what of wrong flows directly from his corrupt intentions .' "Chapman involved a defendant who paid another man $25 to commit adultery with the defendant's wife so the defendant could divorce her. The defendant watched through a hole in the wall as the other man raped his wife. This Court held that the jury properly convicted the defendant of rape under an accomplice theory of liability because that crime directly flowed from the original corrupt intention to aid adultery.

In view of the framework established by these early cases, the propriety of the trial court's verdict is clear. The victim's death is clearly within the common enterprise the defendant aided because a homicide "might be expected to happen if the occasion should arise" within the common enterprise of committing an aggravated assault. The evidence establishes that the victim threatened his children in Pannell's presence, enraging Pannell. When defendant woke up at 10:00 that evening, Pannell was still "ranting and raving" in the house. Despite knowing that Pannell was in an agitated state, defendant agreed to drive to the victim's house with the understanding that he and Pannell would "f* * * him up." When the pair arrived at the victim's home, defendant initiated the assault by hitting the victim once in the face and once in the neck with the back of his hand. After the victim fell to the ground, Pannell punched him twice and began kicking him. In our judgment, a natural and probable consequence of a plan to assault someone is that one of the actors may well escalate the assault into a murder. Just as the planned seduction of the defendant's wife in Chapman escalated into a rape, Pannell's anger toward the victim escalated during the assault into a murderous rage. Defendant argues that he should not be held liable for the murder because he left the scene of the assault after telling Pannell, "That's enough." We disagree. Defendant was aware that Pannell was angry with the victim even before the assault. Defendant escalated the situation by driving Pannell to the victim's house, agreeing to join Pannell in assaulting the victim, and initiating the attack. He did nothing to protect Thomas and he did nothing to defuse the situation in which Thomas was ultimately killed by Pannell. A "natural and probable consequence" of leaving the enraged Pannell alone with the victim is that Pannell would ultimately murder the victim. That defendant serendipitously left the scene of the crime moments before Thomas's murder does not under these circumstances exonerate him from responsibility for the crime.

The fact that Pannell shot the victim, rather than beat him to death, does not alter this conclusion. It cannot be that a defendant can initiate an assault, leave an already infuriated principal alone with the victim, and then escape liability for the murder of that victim simply because the principal shot the victim to death, instead of kicking the victim to death. Like the defendant in Chapman, whose accomplice used rape, as

opposed to seduction, to accomplish their common criminal purpose, the defendant is criminally liable as long as the crime is within the natural and probable consequences of the intended assaultive crime.

…

CONCLUSION

We hold that a defendant must possess the criminal intent to aid, abet, procure, or counsel the commission of an offense. A defendant is criminally liable for the offenses the defendant specifically intends to aid or abet, or has knowledge of, as well as those crimes that are the natural and probable consequences of the offense he intends to aid or abet. Therefore, the prosecutor must prove beyond a reasonable doubt that the defendant aided or abetted the commission of an offense and that the defendant intended to aid the charged offense, knew the principal intended to commit the charged offense, or, alternatively, that the charged offense was a natural and probable consequence of the commission of the intended offense.

Under either prong of the aiding and abetting analysis, defendant was properly convicted. …

Cavanagh J., **dissenting**.
… I must respectfully dissent.

In sum, because this death was not the natural and probable consequence of this beating and defendant's intent and actions did not criminally cause this death, defendant cannot be convicted of second-degree murder under an aiding and abetting theory.

Kelly, J., **dissenting.**
With this decision, the majority improperly extends the reach of Michigan's aiding and abetting statute. . . . It will now include a rationale for finding criminal liability without the requisite element of intent.
. . .

A defendant cannot be convicted of second-degree murder under an aiding and abetting theory where the defendant did not intend the act that causes the death. In this case, defendant Robinson intended only to beat the victim, and the beating was not the cause of death. In order to convict Robinson of aiding and abetting murder, the majority must append language to the statute.

It currently states:

> Every person concerned in the commission of an offense, whether he directly commits the act constituting the offense or procures, counsels, aids, or abets in its commission may hereafter be prosecuted, indicted, tried and on conviction shall be punished as if he had directly committed such offense. [MCL 767.39.]

The majority effectively adds to it the phrase "as well as the natural and probable consequences of any such crime." Reading language into a statute to reach a result not intended by the Legislature is an abuse of this Court's power.

. . . [T]he trial judge's findings actually preclude Robinson's conviction of second-degree murder. One of the judge's most pertinent determinations was that Robinson did not share or know of Pannell's intent to kill.

This Court, like the Court of Appeals, should defer to the trial court's findings of fact, setting them aside only if they are clearly erroneous. . .
. . .
In the case at hand, the trial court found that the common enterprise was to beat the victim. There was no common enterprise to kill the victim. Robinson went along "only to beat up" the victim.

. . . In Robinson's words, "it was understood between us that we were going to f*** him up." As a practical matter, f***ing up someone necessarily entails leaving them alive. In the context of this case, it most likely means to "put

[the victim] in an extremely difficult or impossible situation." Offensive as the word is, it is not used to mean "to kill." We have many other slang words that mean "to kill," such as "bump off" "ice," "Knock off," "waste," "rub out," and "whack." . . . It is clear that Robinson agreed to harm the fvictim, not to kill him.

In this case, the trial court specifically found that Robinson did not intend or contemplate the result, Pannell's fatal shooting of the victim. Because Robinson did not share Pannell's intent to kill, he cannot be held answerable under the law for the fact that Pannell fatally shot the victim. The common enterprise was a beating. The fact that Pannell shot the victim, rather than beat him to death, is dispositive.

The victim's death here was not within Robinson and Pannell's common enterprise; a homicide by gun is not a natural and probable consequence of an intended assault and battery. The majority is mistaken in concluding otherwise. It errs by determining that the unintended result of an intentional act was a "natural and probable consequence" for which a defendant may be held criminally liable.

CONCLUSION

I agree with and completely support the Court of Appeals opinion in this matter. I would affirm the panel's decision to reverse Robinson's conviction of second-degree murder. I would reduce the charge of which Robinson was convicted to assault with intent to do great bodily harm less than murder and remand for resentencing on that reduced charge.

STATE v. BELLAMY,
7617 S.E. 2d 81 (N.C. Ct. App 2005)

FACTS (Summarized)

McCoy conspired with the defendant to rob the McDonald's store where McCoy worked. McCoy was working when the defendant entered the store, put a gun to the side of McCoy's co-worker's head, seized the deposit money as well as the co-worker's personal money. After taking the money, defendant told the co-worker to undress, and began to rape her when he discovered she had a tampon inserted her vagina. Defendant then fled. McCoy hit the silent alarm. The court had to decide whether the

attempted rape was the natural and probable consequences of the robbery. The court concluded it was not.

OPINION

In McCoy's first argument, he contends that the trial court erred in denying his motion to dismiss the charge of first-degree sexual offense. …The State's theory at trial was that Bellamy was the masked gunman who actually robbed the McDonald's, and who perpetrated the sexual assault on C.B., but that McCoy was his inside help, and that they planned the robbery together. As a party to the robbery, the State contends that

McCoy is liable as a principal under the theory of acting in concert for Bellamy's sexual assault on C.B..

The law of acting in concert in North Carolina is as follows: If

"two persons join in a purpose to commit a crime, each of them, if actually or constructively present, is not only guilty as a principal if the other commits that particular crime, but he is also guilty of any other crime committed by the other in pursuance of the common purpose . . . or as a natural or probable consequence thereof."

In the instant case, the State did not argue at trial, and does not argue on appeal, that the sexual assault was done "in pursuance of the common purpose" of the robbery with a dangerous weapon. The record is completely devoid of evidence that the defendants discussed any potential sexual assault prior to the robbery. The State argues that the sexual assault was "a natural or probable consequence thereof." Whether a sexual assault is a natural or probable consequence of a robbery with a dangerous weapon of a fast food restaurant is a question of first impression in North Carolina.

The State asserts that any sexual assault perpetrated in the course of any robbery with a dangerous weapon is a natural or probable consequence thereof. Clearly, a murder committed during the course of a robbery with a dangerous weapon is normally a natural or probable consequence of that robbery with a dangerous weapon. Conversely, a murder to conceal a previous arson might not be such a consequence. The question is one of foreseeability: if one takes the property of another at the point of a loaded gun, the violent use of that gun is a foreseeable consequence. Some jurisdictions have determined that whether a consequence of a robbery with a dangerous weapon was natural or probable is judged by an objective standard. *See People v. Nguyen*, 21 Cal. App. 4th 518, 531, 26 Cal.Rptr.2d 323, 331 (1993) ("the issue does not turn on the defendant's subjective state of mind, but depends upon whether, under all of the circumstances presented, a reasonable person in the defendant's position would have or should have known that the charged offense was a reasonably foreseeable

consequence of the" principal crime).

We decline to adopt a *per se* rule that any sexual assault committed during the course of a robbery is a natural or probable consequence of a planned crime. Rather, this determination must be made on a case by case basis, upon the specific facts and circumstances presented. The issue in the instant case is whether the sex offense Bellamy committed was a natural or probable consequence of the robbery with a dangerous weapon of the McDonald's.

Concerning the foreseeability of robbery turning into a sexual offense, the California Court of Appeals has stated:

Robbery is a crime that can be committed in widely varying circumstances. It can be committed in a public place, such as on a street or in a market, or it can be committed in a place of isolation, such as in the victim's home. It can be committed in an instant, such as in a forcible purse snatching, or it can be committed over a prolonged period of time in which the victim is held hostage. During hostage-type robberies in isolated locations, sexual abuse of victims is all too common. . . . "

When robbers enter the home, the scene is all too often set for other and more dreadful crimes such as that committed on [the victim] in this case. In the home, the victims are particularly weak and vulnerable and the robber is correspondingly secure. The result is all too often the infliction of other crimes on the helpless victim. Rapes consummated during the robbery of a bank or supermarket appear to be a rarity, but rapes in the course of a residential robbery occur with depressing frequency."

. . .

. . . We agree that in certain factual circumstances a sexual assault in the course of a robbery of a business may be a natural or probable circumstance, but that it is less likely to be so than in the context of a robbery taking place in a home.

In the instant case, Bellamy entered McDonald's at around 11:30 at night. Though that particular McDonald's was closed (the interior closed at 10:00 p.m. and the drive-thru closed at 11:00 p.m.), in light of the fact that many McDonald's stay open later than 11:30 p.m., it would not be unusual for prospective customers to arrive at or after 11:30. The very public nature of a fast food restaurant creates a significant risk that the masked gunman or the employees lying on the floor inside might be noticed by someone outside. This is a fact of which McCoy, as an employee, would have been well aware. McCoy was also aware that there were security cameras in the store recording events during the robbery, and that there were silent alarms which other employees might have activated before Bellamy obtained control of the employees. In light of these facts, a reasonable person in McCoy's position would expect Bellamy to get in and out of the restaurant as quickly as possible to avoid capture or recognition.

.

HOLDING

On these facts, and in this kind of a public business, we cannot find that a reasonable person in McCoy's position would have foreseen that Bellamy would take the time to deviate from the planned robbery to commit this type of bizarre sexual assault on C.B. It was the State's burden to prove beyond a reasonable doubt that this sexual assault was a natural and probable result of the robbery with a dangerous weapon, and it has failed to meet this burden. The trial court erred in failing to dismiss the first-degree sexual offense charge against McCoy. We reverse judgment on the conviction and remand McCoy's case to the trial court for resentencing on a single count of robbery with a dangerous weapon.

Other Cases—Natural and Probable Consequences

State v. Linscott

Fuller and Linscott decide to do a household robbery of Grenier. They planned to enter from the back door to prevent Grenier from accessing a shotgun that they knew he kept in the bedroom. Linscott was armed with a knife and a switchblade, and Fuller was armed with a shotgun. When they arrived at Grenier's home they saw that snow was blocking the backdoor, so they changed their plans. Linscott was to break the living room picture window, and Fuller would hold Grenier at gunpoint with the shotgun while Linscott took the money. Instead, Linscott broke through the window, and Fuller shot through the open window and killed Grenier. Fuller entered the house, took $1300 from Grenier's pocket, $500 of which he gave to Linscott.

Linscott was later arrested. At trial he testified that it was not unusual for Fuller to carry a shotgun, that

he was unaware that Fuller had a reputation for violence, and that he had no intention of killing Grenier during the robbery. Linscott was convicted of intentionally or knowingly killing Grenier. The court acknowledged that Linscott did not intent to kill Grenier and probably would not have agreed to participate in the robbery had he thought Grenier would be killed during the robbery. Nevertheless, the court held he had the requisite intent to commit the robbery and that murder was a reasonably foreseeable consequence of his participation in the robbery with Fuller.

"A person may be guilty of murder actually perpetrated by another, if he combines with such other party to commit a felony, engages in its commission, and death ensues in the execution of felonious intent."

Defenses to Accomplice Liability

Courts have allowed some defendants to escape liability as an accomplice when they withdraw from the joint endeavor if they announce in a timely fashion their withdrawal to the others. Some courts require the defendant to have thwarted the crime. Model Penal Code §2.06(6)(c) provides a defense to when the alleged accomplice "terminates his complicity prior to the commission of the offense and (i) wholly deprives it of effectiveness in the commission of the offense; or (ii) gives timely warning to the law enforcement authorities or otherwise makes proper effort to prevent the commission of the offense.

STATE v. BROWN,
26 Ill. 2d 308, 186 N.E.2d 321 (1962)

Mr. JUSTICE DAILY delivered the opinion of the   court:

Fred Brown, Leonard McGarry, James Washington and Charles Gunn. . . [were jointly charged] . . . with the murder of Richard Hunter, who was shot to death in the course of an attempted robbery. Washington and McGarry pleaded guilty to the crime, whereas Brown and Gunn, who waived a jury, were found guilty after a bench trial and each was sentenced to the penitentiary for a term of 14 years. . . . Brown. . . contends that . . . he had withdrawn from the robbery plan in such a manner as to avoid liability for its consequences . . . .

The victim of the homicide was among those present on July 12, 1959, at a party being held in a basement apartment of a building located at 4601 S. Michigan Avenue in Chicago. Gambling seems to have been the principal activity at the "party," while the "apartment" appears to have been in the nature of an unlicensed tavern. Around 3:30 A.M. four men, later identified as defendant and those indicted with him, entered the premises. Washington and McGarry produced guns, . . . announced that it was a stickup and ordered those present to lie on the floor. Decedent, however, jumped on McGarry's back and was shot by Washington, the fatal bullet first passing through McGarry's body. In the confusion the robbers were able to flee from the premises.

Defendant and Washington were apprehended in Nashville, Tennessee, and were delivered into the custody of Chicago police on August 17, 1959. At this time defendant made several oral statements and signed a written statement wherein he consistently acknowledged that he and his co-defendants had first met in a tavern in South Chicago on the night in question and that they had driven to the Michigan Avenue address in furtherance of an express plan to rob those at the party. In addition, he consistently stated at all times prior to trial that he had looked through a window when they arrived at the apartment, that he then advised his companions he was not going in because there were too many people, and that he then took a taxi back to South Chicago. In his written statement he said he next saw his co-defendants an hour later in South Chicago, that McGarry was then suffering from a gun shot wound in the back, and that McGarry had been taken to defendant's room and ministered to.

At the trial, however, defendant deviated materially from his prior statements and testified there had been no plan or conversation relating to a robbery and that he had gotten into the car with the others merely for the purpose of going to the party. He stated that just as they reached the entrance of the building McGarry announced he was "going to make him some money," whereupon defendant said he didn't want any part of it and took a taxi back to South Chicago.

The chief witness for the prosecution was defendant's co-conspirator, Leonard McGarry. Although completely irreconcilable with his subsequent testimony, McGarry also testified there had been no preconceived plan or intention of committing a robbery and stated he and his companions had set out for the apartment solely for the purpose of gambling. Gunn, it was stated, had lost money at the party earlier and wanted to win it back. According to McGarry, he and his three companions went into the apartment and found about 25 persons present. He said that Gunn walked in first and went to the bar, that Washington remained behind at the door, and that he and the defendant walked to the middle of the room at a point four to five feet equidistant from Gunn and Washington. One Jimmy Jones, who had driven the men to the apartment, remained outside in the car.

McGarry said that after looking around for a moment he remarked there were "too many people," and that defendant thereupon replied: "Yes, forget it, let's go." At this, to use McGarry's words, "most of us turned to go," but defendant asked him to wait and walked across the floor to a washroom. Immediately after defendant went into the other room, still according to McGarry, Washington pulled his gun, shouting as he did so, and when people started running about McGarry drew his pistol, fired a shot into the ceiling and announced that it was a "stickup." The witness said he then vaulted over the bar and demanded the money there and that defendant, "looking surprised," came out of the rest room at this time. Several patrons attempted to seize defendant but, McGarry testified, defendant fought them off and ran out the front door shouting that "one had got away." It was following this that Hunter was fatally shot as he grappled with McGarry. Concluding his testimony, McGarry stated that he staggered to the car, that he lost consciousness, and that his next recollection was being taken to defendant's house.

Fletcher Henderson, who was present at the party, appeared as a witness for the prosecution and pointed out defendant as one of the robbers. However, it appears he had been unable to identify defendant when called upon to do so on two occasions before the trial. Another prosecution witness, Helen Wilson, who was tending bar in the apartment, testified that defendant had had a drink at the bar, prior to the shooting, and that she had not seen him after the melee occurred. Gunn, who was jointly tried with defendant, testified on cross-examination that he was the last to arrive at the apartment where the murder took place, that defendant, Washington and McGarry were already present in the front room, and that he, the witness, had protested when Washington pulled a gun.

Defendant's initial contention that he is not guilty of murder because he had abandoned and withdrawn from the criminal enterprise of his companions must fail in two respects. We held in *People* v. *Rybka* that it is "the communication of intent to withdraw and not the naked fact of withdrawal that determines whether one who advised, encouraged or incited another to commit a crime is to be released from liability as an accessory before the fact." To this need may be added the further requirement that the withdrawal must be timely, that is to say it must be "such as to give his co-conspirators a reasonable opportunity, if they desire, to follow his example and refrain from further action before the act is committed," and it must be possible for the trier of fact "to say that the accused had wholly and effectively detached himself from the criminal enterprise before the act with which he is charged is in the process of consummation or has become so inevitable that it cannot reasonably be stayed." Stated otherwise,

withdrawal may not be effectively made from a felony murder when the "transaction which begets it has actually been commenced."

In the instant case, while there may have been "communication" by defendant to McGarry, the evidence in the record does not satisfactorily show communication to Washington and Gunn who were admittedly four to five feet away in a noisy, crowded room. Indeed, Washington was standing behind defendant and McGarry and his conduct in drawing a gun when he did strongly militates against the argument that he had been apprised of the alleged abandonment by defendant. However, even if it could be said that communication to Washington and Gunn is a matter in which reasonable doubt should be resolved for defendant, we are of the opinion the attempt at withdrawal came too late. Not only was there insufficient time given to provide the co-conspirators a reasonable opportunity to withdraw, but the criminal enterprise which begot the murder had already commenced. When defendant and his companions, at least two of whom were armed, entered the apartment they passed beyond mere preparation in their common plan to rob those present, and defendant, by his presence, was efficiently encouraging and aiding the others.

Nor is it of any consequence that defendant had fled the premises before the murder of Hunter took place. Defendant knew his companions were armed and is deemed to have known they would use their weapons if resistance was met. Where conspirators contemplate that violence may be necessary to enable them to carry out their conspiracy or common purpose, all are liable for the acts done in furtherance of the common object, and where death results from the prosecution of the common object, all are equally guilty of murder, whether or not each is actually present.

People v. Cooper, 332 N.E.2d 453 (Ill. App. 1975).
Defendant and two robber broke into a woman's house to carry out a robbery. The defendant helped tie up the victim, but then changed his mind and left the house without taking any valuables. The victim was killed by the other two robbers after defendant had left the house, and the defendant was thereafter prosecuted for murder. The court rejected the defendant's abandonment defense noting he had done nothing to free the victim.

Commonwealth v. Huber, 15 Pa. D & C 2d 726 (1958).
Defendant, Huber, loaned his gun to be used in a robbery. When invited to join the robbery, he

declined, saying "No, I ain't going to get involved in anything like that." The court stated,

"The fact that this defendant was asked to participate in the robbery as a principal, and that he refused, does not constitute such a withdrawal as would relieve him of criminal liability as an accessory before the fact. Had this defendant demanded and received back his rifle, or had he reported the principals to the police in time to thwart the robbery, then he could have been said to have withdrawn successfully. Having placed the rifle in the hands of John Goodwin who, according to defendant's own testimony told defendant "he was going to rob somebody", the defendant committed himself to a sequence of events from which he could only extricate himself by getting his rifle out of the hands of John Goodwin before the robbery, or by thwarting the robbery in some other way. The "aid" in this case was the rifle. Therefore, to effectively withdraw made it incumbent upon the defendant to get the rifle out of the hands of John Goodwin, or the equivalent thereof. He did neither of these things. He did, however, go to the police station where he learned of the perpetration of the robbery. He then rushed posthaste to get his rifle, not to withdraw from the crime, but to get incriminating evidence out of the possession of a principal who was then the object of a police investigation."

United States v. Southard, 700 F.2d 1 (1st Cir. 1983). When the victim of a blackmail pays the demand, this assists the person making the demand (the person committing extortion. But, the victim is not considered an aider and abettor to the crime because they are a protected person.

Accomplice Liability, Conspiracy, and Solicitation

Because accomplices associate with others in participating in crimes, the law of accomplice liability is frequently confused with the law of solicitation and conspiracy. These crimes differ, however.

With conspiracy, an agreement to commit a crime must be proven by the government: with accomplice liability, aid itself—not an express agreement—suffices. Furthermore, with accomplice liability the target crime must of course be committed: conspiracy liability can arise even if the target crime is not ultimately committed.

Solicitation is more closely related because it targets for liability those who instigate others to commit criminal acts. Once again, however, accomplice liability requires that the perpetrator actually commit the target crime. With solicitation, the crime solicited does not actually need to be committed: it is only necessary "that the actor with intent that another person commit a crime, have enticed, advised, incited, ordered or otherwise encouraged that person to commit a crime. Brody, D. and Acker, J. Criminal Law, 3d edition, Jones and Bartlett, 2015, p. 389.

WRAP UP

People who commit crimes frequently do so with assistance. Common law recognized four parties to a crime: principal in the first degree, principal in the second degree, accessory before the fact, and accessory after the fact. Many complicated legal rules developed to offset the harsh common law treatment of most crimes as capital offenses. The modern trend has been to recognize accomplices--people who render assistance before and during the crime--and accessories after the fact. Accomplices are held to be equally liable as the main perpetrator, but under the modern trend, those who provide assistance after the crime are generally charged with lesser crimes of hindering prosecution or obstructing justice.

Chapter Six: Criminal Homicide Overview

The next two chapter examine the common law and statutory approaches to crimes committed against other people. Six of the nine "common law felonies" were crimes against persons: murder, manslaughter, rape, sodomy, mayhem, and robbery (a hybrid person/property offense). (The other three were larceny, burglary, and arson). Assault and battery were both considered misdemeanors at common law, but today most states have enacted statutes treating the most serious forms of physical attacks or threats as felonies. In addition, since the 1930s states have enacted kidnapping and false imprisonment statutes—crimes not recognized as felonies at common law.

Criminal Homicide—Murder and Manslaughter

A criminal homicide occurs if the defendant causes the death of another person without justification or excuse. Many of the cases in the first seven chapters of this text involve defendants being charged with some form of criminal homicide. At common law there were two grades of criminal homicide: murder and manslaughter. State statutory schemes vary greatly in their treatment of criminal homicide but essentially all examine and grade the taking of a human life based on the perceived culpability of the offender. These statutes treat intentional killings more harshly than reckless or negligent killings; thus, they evaluate the offender's mens rea. They treat heinous and atrocious methods of killing more seriously than less heinous methods; thus, they evaluate the offender's actus reus. And states frequently treat the killing of some classifications of victims, such as police officers or judges, more seriously than other victims. The majority of states authorize capital punishment (the death penalty) for certain types of killings, but many do not. States vary in their decision about who is a person and when life begins and when life ends. Some states include the killing of a fetus in their criminal homicide statutes; some states do not. Some states consider the removal of a life-sustaining respirator as criminal homicide and others do not.

Criminal Homicide at Common Law

At common law, *homicide* was justifiable, excusable or criminal. *Justifiable homicides* are those authorized by law (see, Chapter 10); *excusable homicides* were those in which the killer was at fault but where circumstances did not justify infliction of full criminal penalty (see, Chapter 11). *Criminal* homicide was all killings which were neither justifiable or excusable. Initially, common law treated all types of criminal homicide as murder. By the 1550s, common law started distinguishing between criminal homicide that was *murder* and criminal homicide that was *manslaughter*.

Criminal Homicide Under Modern Statutes

Most states distinguish between criminal homicide and excusable or justifiable homicide. Criminal homicide is generally classified under modern statutes as murder, manslaughter, and criminally negligent homicide or vehicular homicide. Many states further distinguish between capital or aggravated murder, first-degree murder, second-degree murder, or depraved indifference murder. Many states further distinguish their manslaughter charges as voluntary or involuntary or by degrees.

Criminal Homicide Under The MPC

The Model Penal Code (§ 210.1 (2)) defines criminal homicide as either murder, manslaughter or negligent homicide. § 210.1 stated that "A person is guilty of criminal homicide if he purposely, knowingly, recklessly or negligently causes the death of another human being." MPC § 210.5 indicates that a person may also be convicted of criminal homicide for causing another to commit suicide only if he purposely causes such suicide by force, duress or deception.

Common Law Murder

Common law recognized no degrees of murder. At common law murder occurred "When a man of sound memory and of the age of discretion unlawfully killeth any reasonable creature in being, and under the King's peace, with malice aforethought, either express or implied by the law, the death taking place within a year and a day." (Sir Edward Coke, early 1600s.)

When dissecting this definition, we find that common law limited murder convictions to killings done by people who were not lunatics ("sound memory") or infants ("the age of discretion"—which at common law meant anyone over seven years old. Common law limited murder to killings of people born alive and breathing at the time of the killing ("reasonable creature in being"). Common law murder included only killings done without justification or excuse ("unlawfully") Murder could be committed in hundreds of different ways as long as the act caused the death of the person ("killeth"). "Under the King's peace" meant that common law murder extended protections not only to Englishmen but also to aliens and outlaws. The terms malice aforethought represented the mens rea that needed to be proven in order to successfully prosecute a person for murder. Finally, there was the "year and a day rule" which ensured that the government was able to prove causation—that the acts committed by the defendant were the cause of the victim's death.

Malice Aforethought

Malice aforethought at common law included the intent to kill, the intent to do serious bodily harm, the intent to commit a dangerous felony[17], the intent to create a greater than reckless risk of death or serious bodily harm, acting with such disregard for human life that the action evidences "abandoned and depraved heart", and the intent to resist arrest by force. The intent to kill was considered "express malice aforethought," and the intent to do serious bodily injury, commit a felony, create greater than reckless risk, and resist arrest were all considered "implied malice aforethought." (Today modern statutes distinguish between first and second degree murders, and the differences will be discussed below, but generally killing with express malice aforethought is considered first degree murder and those killings with implied malice aforethought are considered second degree murders.) At common law express malice aforethought killings and implied malice aforethought killings both constituted "murder."

According to the "deadly weapon" doctrine (seen in *Bantam v. State*, 85 A.2d 741 (Del. 1952)) one who intentionally uses a deadly weapon on another human being, and thereby kills him, is presumed to have intended the killing and thus would be guilty of murder.

People v. Geiger, 159 N.W.2d 383 (Mich. 1968) illustrates the intent to inflict serious bodily injury form of malice aforethought. In that case the defendant hit the victim several times, causing her to strike her head on the ground. When he discovered that she was unconscious, he simply placed her in his car where she died from the injuries. Although the defendant did not intend to kill the victim, he did intend to cause her serious bodily injury, and thus he had malice aforethought, the necessary mens rea and was rightfully found guilty of murder.

Implied malice aforethought also included situations where the defendant acted with unusually high risk that his conduct would cause death or serious bodily injury. The risk must have been so great that ignoring it demonstrated an "abandoned and malignant heart" or a "depraved mind." This was seen in *Commonwealth v. Malone*, 47 A.2d 445 (Pa. 1946) where the defendant killed the victim while playing a game of "Russian Roulette." She loaded a revolver with one bullet, and after spinning the chamber, placed the gun to victim's head and pulled the trigger--killing her.

---

[17] Note that early English common law did not recognize felony murder.

Malice aforethought may be proven by circumstantial evidence. Some courts have held that the proof that the defendant killed the victim creates a presumption that he or she acted with malice aforethought. But, *State v. Cuevas*, 488 P.2d. 322 (Hawaii 1971) indicates that the better view is that the trier of fact may infer, but need not presume, from the fact of the killing that the defendant had one of the states of mind necessary for murder.

Other Cases—Malice Aforethought

Errington & Others' Case, 168 Eng. Rep. 1133 (1838)

Errington and others (the defendants) were intoxicated and found the victim asleep on a chest. As a joke, they piled straw all around him and then threw a shovel of hot cinders on his belly. The straw ignited and the victim was burned to death. The evidence was that they were reckless and acted without the intent to kill or seriously injur the victim. The court found that because there was no evidence of express malice, they could not be convicted of murder. The jury found that the defendants only intended to frighten the victim in sport, so they had committed manslaughter, not murder.

Commonwealth v. McLaughlin, 142 A.213 (Pa. 1928)

McLaughlin was driving between 20 and 25 miles an hour one night. He struck and killed two persons walking near the center of the road. The evidence conflicted whether defendant was drunk and whether his lights were on. He claimed that the victims changed direction and darted in front of him at the last second. The evidence indicated that he had applied his brakes before striking the victims. He stopped after the crash, returned to assist the injured parties. He was convicted of murder and appealed. The court held that defendant's malice must be proved beyond a reasonable doubt and reversed the conviction. The state must prove malice for a second degree murder conviction and rarely will it be found in a motor vehicle accident. Malice cannot be found unless the defendant intended to strike the victims or was conscious of the peril to human life or his conduct was wanton and reckless. The majority found that the evidence did not establish malice and McLaughlin's attempt to help the victims showed his concern. The dissent said the court should have deferred to the jury's finding since they were best qualified to determine whether element was present.

Year And A Day

The year and a day rule dates back to 1278 and the original rationale for the rule was most likely tied to the limits of 13th century medicine to prove cause of death beyond a reasonable doubt after any longer period of time.

STATE v. MINSTER,
302 Md. 240; 486 A.2d 1197 (1985)

The issue here is whether we should abrogate[18] the common law rule of "a year and a day", which bars a prosecution for murder when the victim dies more than a year and a day after being injured. Inasmuch as we believe this issue is more appropriately addressed by the legislature, we shall not abrogate the common law rule. Accordingly, we affirm the trial court's dismissal of the indictment filed against the appellee, Larry Edmund Minster.

The facts in this case are undisputed. On July 8, 1982, Minster shot the victim, Cheryl Dodgson, in the neck. As a result of the shooting, Ms. Dodgson became a quadriplegic. Minster was charged in Prince George's County Circuit Court with attempted first degree murder, assault with

---

[18] Gardner and Anderson (Criminal Law, 13th edition, 2018) notes that, at our founding, common law rules became part of a new state's criminal law because virtually all states included in their constitution a clause that adopted the "common law of England" in place when the United States was formed. Subsequent changes to that common law, usually by state legislatures, were called 'abrogation' of the common law. Courts also possess the power to abrogate a common law rule.

intent to murder, assault and battery and use of a handgun in a crime of violence. He was brought to trial in April of 1983.

Minster was convicted of attempted first degree murder and the use of a handgun in a crime of violence. He was sentenced to 20 years imprisonment for attempted murder and received a 10 year concurrent sentence for the handgun violation. The Court of Special Appeals affirmed his conviction.

On October 3, 1983, Ms. Dodgson died from injuries the State contends resulted directly from Minster's actions on July 8, 1982 one year and eighty-seven days before the victim's death. One month after Ms. Dodgson's death, Minster was indicted for first degree murder. The Circuit Court for Prince George's County dismissed the indictment because the death of Ms. Dodgson occurred more than a year and a day after the shooting. Judge Johnson [the trial judge] noted that *State v. Brown* which held that the year and a day rule was valid in Maryland, barred the indictment. The State appealed the dismissal to the Court of Special Appeals. We granted certiorari prior to consideration by the Court of Special Appeals in order to address an issue of public importance.

The State's issue is simply stated: should the prosecution of Minster for the murder of Cheryl Dodgson be barred by the year and a day rule. It argues that the common law rule is now archaic and, in light of medical advances in life-saving techniques, there is no sound reason for retaining the rule today. Minster argues that there are legitimate justifications for the rule's continued application; moreover, because of the number of alternatives available to replace the year and a day rule, a change in the rule should be left to the legislature.

In *Brown*, . . . [t]he Court held that the rule was part of our common law and, although no Maryland case had previously addressed the issue, the rule was "in full force and effect in Maryland." In addition, "if change is to be made in the rule it should be by the General Assembly because expression and weighing of divergent views, consideration of potential effect, and suggestion of adequate safeguards, are better suited to the legislative forum." We are in accordance with this view.

We agree with Minster that there are a number of sound justifications for retaining this rule. As Chief Judge Orth stated in Brown, "[a]bolition of the rule may well result in imbalance between the adequate protection of society and justice for the individual accused, and there would remain a need for some form of limitation on causation."

Justice Musmanno, stated this concern more fully:
> "Dorothy Pierce, the alleged victim, died of pneumonia. It is possible, of course, that her weakened condition, due to the alleged hurt received thirteen months before, made her more susceptible to the attack of pneumonia. On the other hand, there is the likely possibility that the pneumonia had no possible connection with the injury allegedly inflicted by the defendant.

Suppose that the pneumonia occurred two years after the physical injury, would it still be proper to charge the defendant with murder? If a murder charge can be brought two years after a blow has been struck, will there ever be a time when the Court may declare that the bridge between the blow and death has now been irreparably broken? May the Commonwealth indict a man for murder when the death occurs ten years after the blow has fallen? Twenty years? Thirty years? One may search the majority opinion through every paragraph, sentence, clause, phrase and comma, and find no answer to this very serious question. The majority is content to open a Pandora's box of interrogation and let it remain unclosed, to the torment and possible persecution of every person who may have at one time or another injured another. I don't doubt that an "expert" of some kind can be found to testify that a slap in the face was the cause of a death fifteen years later.

If there is one thing which the criminal law must be, if it is to be recognized as just, it must be specific and definitive. We are reminded of the oft-cited explanation for the rule's existence: "[I]f he die[d] after that time [of a year and a day], it cannot be discerned, as the law presumes, whether he died of the stroke or poison, etc. or of a natural death; and in the case of life, the rule of law ought to be certain." 3 Coke Institutes of the Laws of England at 52 (1797).

In addition, a person charged with attempted first degree murder (as was the case here) can be sentenced to life imprisonment. Moreover, a sentencing judge may always consider the seriousness of the injury to, or the subsequent death of, the victim. The only additional conceivable punishment a first degree murder conviction entails is the death penalty. We do not believe this distinction is a sufficient reason to rescind a common law rule which has existed for over seven hundred years.

Assuming, arguendo, that we abrogate this rule, with what do we replace it?

In *People v. Stevenson*, the court addressed the identical issue we address today. Five alternatives to the rule were offered to that court: (1) The Court could retain the year and a day rule. (2) The Court could modify the rule by extending the span of time, for example, to three years and a day. (3) The Court could extend the rule to any length of time it chooses, perhaps two years, five years, or ten years. (4) The Court could change the rule from an irrebuttable presumption to a rebuttable one, but with a higher burden of proof. (5) Finally, the Court could simply abolish the rule entirely, leaving the issue of causation to the jury in light of the facts and arguments in each particular case. Similarly, in *State v. Young*, the justices were split between three alternatives: four justices favoring abrogation, two justices favoring retention, and one justice favoring a compromise "three years, and a day" rule. In fact, two jurisdictions, California and Washington, have enacted a three year and a day rule.

Thus we find there is a great difference of opinion surrounding the appropriate length of the period after which prosecution is barred and some doubt whether the rule should exist at all. Consequently, we believe it is the legislature which should mandate any change in the rule, if indeed any change is appropriate in Maryland. The legislature may hold hearings on this matter; they can listen to the testimony of medical experts; and they may determine the viability of this rule in modern times.

We also observe that if there is any discernible trend towards abrogation of the year and a day rule, the trend is towards abrogation by act of the legislature, not the judiciary. Of the thirteen jurisdictions which had enacted the year and a day rule by statute in 1941, only four jurisdictions retain the rule today. In addition, in two jurisdictions (New York and Oregon) the judiciary has held that the legislature abrogated the rule by failing to include it in the comprehensive revision of the state's Criminal Code. Thus, in eleven jurisdictions the rule has been abrogated by legislative action or omission. In contrast, judicial abrogation has occurred in only five jurisdictions.

We recognize the cogency of the State's argument concerning medical advances in life-saving techniques, and we are aware that other courts have been persuaded by this argument. Yet recent decisions have affirmed the viability of the year and a day rule, and, by our count, the rule remains extant in twenty six states. Two of these jurisdictions, however, have recently expressed doubt as to the rule's viability. In addition, in five jurisdictions the rule has been codified by the legislature and subsequently enforced by the courts. Current legislative research indicates that the statutes in these five jurisdictions have been repealed and therefore the status of the rule in those five states is questionable.

In sum, we uphold the application of the year and a day rule in Maryland. Accordingly, we affirm the trial court's dismissal of the indictment.

Other Cases-Year and a Day Rule

Rogers v. Tennessee, 532 U.S. 451 (2001).
The Tennessee Supreme Court held that the year and a day rule was part of the common law of the State, but that its rationale was outmoded. It abolished the rule, and retroactively applied the abolition to a conviction of second degree murder where the victim died 15 months after the fatal event. The U.S. Supreme Court upheld the conviction. It held that the common law "presupposes a measure of evolution" that can fairly be applied to criminal defendants so long as the new rules are not "unexpected and indefensible." There was nothing in the Tennessee Court's decision that represented an exercise of the sort of unfair and arbitrary judicial action against which the due Process Clause aims to protect." The

Tennessee Court's decision was a "routine exercise of common law decisionmaking in which the court brought the law into conformity with reason and common sense."

State v. Fairbanks, 842 N.W.2d 297 (Minn. 2014)
Fairbanks shot a police officer who died 18 months afterwards. Fairbanks raised the "year and a day" rule. The Minnesota Supreme Court rejected the year and a day argument indicating that even if the rule was ever a part of the common law of Minnesota, the criminal code adopted by the legislature clearly rejected the rule.

State v. Picotte, 661 N.W.2d 381 (Wis. 2003).
The Wisconsin Supreme Court abrogated the common law year and a day rule but made the abrogation prospective [only applicable in the future]. The defendant's conviction for reckless homicide of a victim who died more than one year after the crime occurred was reversed.

Ex Parte Keys, 890 So.2d 1056 (Ala. 2003).
Alabama Supreme Court reversed the conviction of the defendant for murder of a victim who died 18 months after the injury holding that the year-and-a-day rule was still part of the common law in Alabama.

People v. Moncada, 149 Cal. Rptr. 3d 1 (Cal. App. 2012).
The court affirmed an involuntary manslaughter and child abuse homicide where the defendant caused injury to a child that resulted in brain damage. The child died 8 years later. The court said that although he child died from a ruptured stomach, evidence showed children suffering brain damage often develop complications and the child's ruptured stomach was the proximate result of the original injury.

John Hinckley
NO MURDER CHARGE FOR HINCKLEY IN BRADY DEATH
By Peter Hermann WASHINGTON POST, JANUARY 03, 2015

WASHINGTON — Federal prosecutors said they will not charge John Hinckley with murder in the shooting of President Ronald Reagan's press secretary in a 1981 assassination attempt, even though a medical examiner concluded his August death was caused by the old wounds.

The decision, announced Friday by the US attorney for the District, comes four months after the coroner decided that James Brady's death at the age of 73 was caused by bullets fired 34 years ago outside the Washington Hilton.

Reagan, just 69 days into his presidency, was severely wounded. Brady was struck first, above the left eye, and the bullet broke into fragments in his head.

''The decision was made after a review of applicable law, the history of the case, and the circumstances of Mr. Brady's death, including recently finalized autopsy findings,'' the US attorney's office said.

Reasonable Creature In Being: When Life Begins

Murder, at common law, required that the victim be a reasonable creature in being. Reasonable creatures in being were persons born alive (i.e., not an unborn fetus). There have been some court opinions which depart from this rule. Low states,

> For example, a California court held . . . that a healthy baby in the process of being born was a "person" who could be the victim of a criminal homicide. And when in Keeler v. Superior Court of Amador County. . . the California Supreme Court refused to extend . . .[that] . . . principle to an unborn but viable fetus, the California legislature amended the law to provide that a killing of a fetus without the consent of the mother could be murder. New York has also modified the common law rule by statute to include "an unborn child with which a female has been pregnant for more than twenty-four weeks."… In most States, however, the common law "born alive" requirement still obtains." See, Peter Low, *Criminal Law: Black Letter Outlines*, 3rd ed, 2007, at 488.)

Samaha notes that fetal death statutes and abortion differ fundamentally.

Whatever personal values concern abortion, the procedure involves the medical termination of a pregnancy with the mother's consent. Fetal death statutes address killing a fetus without the mother's consent outside normal medical practice. For this reason many who oppose making abortion a form of criminal homicide at the same time support fetal death statutes because such statutes are directed toward third persons who, without the consent of the mothers and without medical skill, injure or kill fetuses.

Defining the beginning of life . . . is neither a purely medical nor a purely legal problem. The definition must ultimately rest more upon religious, moral, and ethical values than upon technical legal rules and medical science. . . . Public policy requires that legislators determine when life in its earliest—and latest—stages is sufficiently valuable that taking it amounts to criminal homicide. No amount of medical knowledge or skill in the techniques of law can answer this question. See, Joel Samaha, *Criminal* Law, 5th ed., at 297.

PEOPLE v. KURR,
654 N.W. 2d 651 (Mich. Ct. App. 2002)

Defendant, killed her boyfriend, Antonio Pena, with a knife. Pena had been abusive and assaultive to her, had hit her on other occasions, had caused her to seek hospital treatment and stay in a domestic violence shelter. She told police that Pena had punched her twice in the stomach on the day she stabbed him. She had warned him not to hit her because she was carrying his babies, and that when Pena came toward her again she stabbed him in the chest. He died as the result of his stab would. At trial, she requested the judge give the jury a "defense of others" instruction, originally the trial court had agreed to do so, but after the testimony the judge disallowed the defense because the fetus or fetuses would have only been sixteen or seventeen weeks in gestation at the time of the stabbing and thus they were nonviable. The jury found her guilty of voluntary manslaughter and the trial court sentenced her to five to twenty years' imprisonment. Defendant argued that she was improperly denied a jury instruction on defense of others—in this case her unborn child. The court agreed.

"[W]e must initially decide the purely legal question whether a nonviable fetus constitutes an "other" in the context of this defense. With certain restrictions, we conclude that it does.

"In Michigan, the killing of another person in self-defense is justifiable homicide if the defendant honestly and reasonably believes that his life is in imminent danger or that there is a threat of serious bodily harm." Deadly force may also be used "to repel an imminent forcible sexual penetration." Case law in Michigan also allows a person to use deadly force in defense of another. Traditionally, the "defense of others" concept applied solely to those persons with whom the defendant had a special relationship, such as a wife or brother. As recognized by CJI2d 7.21, however, the defense now makes no distinction between strangers and relatives with regard to its application.

We conclude that in this state, the defense should also extend to the protection of a fetus, viable or nonviable, from an assault against the mother,

. . . [T]he Legislature . . . [has concluded] that fetuses are worthy of protection as living entities as a matter of public policy . . . . Indeed, we note that a violation of M.C.L. § 750.90a is punishable by up to life imprisonment, nearly the harshest punishment available in our state.] Moreover, in enacting the fetal protection act, the Legislature did not distinguish between fetuses that are viable, or capable of surviving outside the womb, and those that are nonviable. In fact, the Legislature used the term "embryo" as well as the term "fetus" in describing the prohibited conduct . . . Moreover, the legislative analysis of the act indicates that, in passing the act, the Legislature was clearly determined to provide criminal penalties for harm caused to nonviable fetuses during assaults or negligent acts against pregnant women.

Because the act reflects a public policy to protect even an embryo from unlawful assaultive or negligent conduct, we conclude that the defense of others concept does extend to the protection of a nonviable fetus from an assault against the mother. We emphasize, however, that the defense is available solely in the context of an assault against the mother. Indeed, the Legislature has not extended the protection of the criminal laws to embryos existing outside a woman's body, i.e., frozen embryos stored for future use, and we therefore do not extend the applicability of the defense of others theory to situations involving these embryos.

Reasonable Creature In Being: When Life Ends

Courts have had similar difficulty in determining when a person ceases to be a reasonable creature in being. Scholars have noted the complexity of deciding what constitutes death in the context of proving murder. According to Samaha,

> Historically, *alive* meant breathing and having a heartbeat. The concept of brain death has gained prominence over the past several years, with implications not only for medicine and morals but also for criminal law. If artificial support alone maintains breathing and heartbeat while brain waves remain minimal or flat, brain death has occurred. . . More difficult are cases involving individuals with brain functions sufficient to sustain breathing and heartbeat but nothing more, such as patients in a deep coma who have suffered serious injury. They may breathe and their hearts may beat, even without artificial support, but they are not alive for criminal law purposes. Troubling cases arise where medical specialists have described deep coma patients as "vegetables," but the patients regain consciousness and live for a considerable time afterwards. 5th ed., at 301.

Low noted,

> The killing of any person who is still alive can be a criminal homicide. Thus, pulling the plug on a life-sustaining respirator or premature removal of a vital organ for transplantation can be a criminal homicide, even though it is perfectly clear that the victim would soon die anyway. There is no generally accepted definition of when death occurs for this purpose. There are cases that talk about brain death or about the cessation of heartbeat and respiration, but there are problems with both tests. The area is difficult and unresolved, and subject to constant change in any event because of medical advances. *Supra*, at 489.

Other Cases – Reasonable Creature in Being

[Note: the following cases show the process of adopting or abrogating the common law requirements that the victim be born alive]

Keeler v. Superior Court of Amador County, 87 Cal. Rptr. 481, 470 P.2d 617 (1970).
Keeler divorced his wife, not knowing that she was pregnant by another at the time. Later Keeler saw his ex-wife on the road and, after noticing that she was pregnant, said he would "stomp it out of you." Keeler beat his ex-wife causing her to miscarry, and the baby, who had reached the stage of viability, was born dead. At a preliminary hearing Keeler moved that the charges be dismissed arguing that the California murder statute did not cover the death of a fetus, but only of a human being or of a baby born alive. The trial court denied this request, but the California appellate court reversed finding that Keeler could not be charged with murder under the present statute (which followed the common law).

Under the common law, a human being did not exist until it was born alive. The killing of a fetus that was born dead would not subject the actor to a homicide charge. If the baby had been born alive and died shortly thereafter, a murder charged could be filed. In response to this holding, the California legislature modified the statute to include the killing of a fetus as a subject of a murder charge (except for legal abortions).

State v. Merrill, 450 N.W.2d 318 (Minn. 1990).
Defendant shot and killed Gail Anderson, who was pregnant with a 27 or 28-day-old embryo. The coroner's testimony was that there was no abnormality which would have caused a miscarriage and that the death of the embryo was the result of the death of Ms. Anderson. An embryo at that age of development is completely dependent upon its mother (thus, "not viable"). "Up to eighth week of development an "unborn child" is referred

to as an embryo; thereafter it is called a fetus. Medical science generally considers a fetus viable at 28 weeks following the conception although some fetuses as young as 20 or 21 weeks have survived." This case examined whether defendant was guilty of either the Minnesota statute, "Murder of an Unborn Child in the First Degree" and "Murder of an unborn child in the Second Degree." The first degree statute required the state to prove the defendant caused the death with "premeditation and with intent to effect the death of the unborn child or another." The second-degree statute also involved the intent to effect the death of the unborn child or another, but without the premeditation. The defendant argued that the statutes violated the equal protection clause because *Roe v. Wade* holds that a non-viable fetus is not a person, but that this statute adopts a classification equating viable fetuses and nonviable embryos with a person.

The court stated,

"The state's interest in protecting the "potentiality of human life" includes protection of the unborn child, whether an embryo or a nonviable or viable fetus, and it protects, too, the women's interest in her unborn child and her right to decide whether it shall be carried in utero.. The interest of a criminal assailant in terminating a woman's pregnancy does not outweigh the woman's right to continue the pregnancy. In this context, the viability of the fetus is "simply immaterial" to an equal protection challenge to the feticide statute."

The defendant also argued that the feticide statutes were impermissibly vague and failed to give notice to potential violator. "In short, defendant argues that causing the death of a 27-day-old embryo raises the perplexing question of when "life" begins, as well as the question of when "death" occurs.

The court responded,
"The state must prove only that the implanted embryo or the fetus in the mother's womb was living, that it had life and that it has life no longer. To have life, as that term is commonly understood, means to have the property of all living things to grow, to become. It is not necessary to prove, nor does the statute require, that the living organism in the womb in its embryonic or fetal state be considered a person or a human being. . . . Criminal liability here requires only that the genetically human embryo be a living organism that is growing into a human being. Death occurs when the embryo

is no longer living, when it ceases to have the properties of life."

People v. Davis, 872 P.2d 591 (Cal. 1994)
FACTS
Maria Flores, who was between 23 and 25 weeks pregnant went to a check-cashing store with her twenty-month-old son, Hector, to cash her check. As she left the store, the defendant pulled a gun from the waistband of his pants and demanded the money. She refused to hand over the purse and the defendant shot her in the chest. Flores fell to the ground and defendant fled. Flores underwent surgery to save her life, but the fetus was stillborn as a direct result of the Flores' blood loss, low blood pressure and state of shock. Flores survived.

OPINION
Defendant was charged with violating California Penal Code section 187 which provides that "murder is the unlawful killing of a human being, or a fetus, with malice aforethought." At issue was whether the statute required the state to prove the viability of the fetus as an element to the fetal murder statute. The California Supreme Court concluded that viability was not an element of the statute. But, it also found that, "because every prior decision that addressed the viability issue had determined that viability of the fetus was a pre-requisite to a murder conviction under section 187, that application of our construction of the statute to the defendant would violate due process and ex post facto principles."

The California Supreme Court noted that the Court of Appeals had construed fetus as a viable fetus as defined by *Roe v. Wade*.

"But *Roe v. Wade* does not hold that the state has no legitimate interest in protecting the fetus until viability. . . . The Roe decision, therefore forbids the state's protection of the unborn's interest only when these interests conflict with the constitutional rights of the prospective parent. The Court did not rule that the unborn's interests could not be recognized in situations where there was no conflict. Thus when the state's interest in protecting the life of a developing fetus is not counterbalanced against a mother's privacy right to an abortion or other equivalent interest, the state's interest should prevail."

The court found that as long as the state could show that the fetus has progressed beyond the embryonic state of seven to eight weeks, the murder statute applied. [The holding was not applied to this particular defendant though, and the trial court committed prejudicial error in a trial instruction.]

State v. Deborah Z, 596 N.W.2d (Wis. Ct. App. 1999).
FACTS
Defendant was drinking in a bar one week prior to her delivery date. She believed that she was about to give birth and called her mother who took her to the hospital. At the hospital she was uncooperative, belligerent at times and very intoxicated. Her blood alcohol level was more than .30%. She told the nurse that if they didn't keep her in the hospital she was just going to go home and keep drinking and drink herself to death and "I'm going to kill this thing because I don't want it anyways." She consented to a cesarean section, and the baby was born with a .119% BAC and presented fetal alcohol effects.

The baby recovered, and defendant was charged with attempted first degree murder and first degree reckless injury.

The state had argued that the Wisconsin murder statute which punished individuals who cause the death of a human being applied to individuals who cause injury to a fetus.

The Wisconsin court disagreed, noting that Wisconsin law defined a human being as one "who had been born alive." It concluded that the decision whether to extend protection to an unborn child" was a matter to be decided by the state legislature."

Whitner v. State, 492 S.E.2d 777 (S.C. 1997).
The South Carolina court held that a woman was properly convicted of child neglect who had caused her baby to be born with cocaine metabolites in its system because she had ingested cocaine during her third trimester of pregnancy.

Kilmon v. State, 905 A.2d 306 (Md 2006).
Maryland Court of Appeals held that a pregnant woman may not be held criminally liable for negligent endangerment of a fetus. Holdng a woman responsible, the court reasoned, would potentially subject her to prosecution for a range of activities, including drinking alcohol or smoking in moderation as well as skiing or riding horses.

Modern Statutory Approaches to Murder

Murder is the unlawful killing of an individual with malice aforethought. There are several classifications of murder including: capital and aggravated first-degree murder, first-degree murder, second-degree murder, and depraved heart murder.

Capital And Aggravated Murder.

The majority of states and the federal government have death penalty statutes that make "aggravated murder" or first-degree murder, committed under certain conditions, punishable by death. Other states have aggravated murder or first-degree murder statutes that punish these most serious and heinous killings with life imprisonment. Capital murder statutes typically require states to prove a premeditated killing, committed with the presence of various aggravating factors or special circumstances. Some circumstances focus on the manner of killing (heinous, atrocious, and cruel); some circumstances focus on the offender's mental state (cold, calculated, and premeditated). Some state statutes consider who the victim is—such that killing a police officer, a judge, a corrections worker, a juvenile or more than one victim is a capital offense; some states make offenders who have escaped prison or have prior aggravated murder conviction eligible for the death penalty; some states make terrorism, murder for hire, or killing during a prison escape or to prevent a person from testifying a capital offense; and finally some states designate felony murder (discussed later) as an aggravating factor leading to the death penalty.

First Degree Murder—Mens Rea

The mens rea of first-degree murder requires deliberation and premeditation as well as malice. Premeditation means the act was thought out prior to being committed. Deliberation entails an intent to kill that is carried out in a cool state of mind in furtherance of the design to kill. (Killings done with an intent to kill but without deliberation and premeditation are second-degree murders.) The courts are not necessarily consistent in their definition of premeditation. A few courts have interpreted premeditation to require substantial time to formulate a well-laid plan to kill. Many courts virtually eliminated the element of meaningful advanced planning by holding that it includes killings that take place even instantly after forming the intent to kill (see, e.g., the Snowden decision). Justice Daughtrey's opinion in *Brown* does an excellent job discussing the evolution of first degree murder; the *Forrest* case examines the premeditation requirement.

STATE v. BROWN,
836 S.W.2d 530 (1992)

DAUGHTREY, Justice.
This capital case arose from the death of four-year-old Eddie Eugene Brown and the subsequent conviction of his father for first-degree murder, as well as for child neglect. After careful review, we have reached the conclusion that the evidence introduced at trial is not sufficient to support a conviction for first-degree murder. We therefore hold that the defendant's conviction must be reduced to second-degree murder.

FACTS
[Mack Brown was convicted of first-degree murder of his 4-year-old son, Eddie Eugene Brown. Evidence introduced at trial was that Eddie's autopsy revealed he had been severely beaten over the course of his life: (he had) multiple skull fractures, injuries to internal organs, bruises all about his body of varying ages, lacerations, burn marks, evidence of being struck, recent and older head injuries, a broken arm, not treated, three to five weeks before his death.

Mack and his wife, Evajean Bell Brown (also charged) called for an ambulance, claiming that Eddie had fallen down some steps and had stopped breathing.

Expert testimony showed that Mack was borderline mentally retarded, was diagnosed with recurrent major depression and was a dependent personality, a condition characterized by inadequacy in decision making and a tendency to allow another person to accept the major responsibilities for his life.]

SUFFICIENCY OF THE EVIDENCE
We are asked first to decide whether the evidence was sufficient to support the verdict of first-degree murder. The defendant argues principally that premeditation was not shown. He also contends that adequate weight was not given to the fact that another adult (Eddie's mother) was in the home and that Eddie had sustained injuries in the past while she had sole custody of him.

. . . But even though the defendant failed to establish insanity as an absolute defense to homicide in this case, his mental state was nevertheless relevant to the charge of first-degree murder, to the extent that it related to the necessary elements of that offense. The statute in effect at the time of the homicide in this case defined first-degree murder as follows:

> Every murder perpetrated by means of poison, lying in wait, or by other kind of willful, deliberate, malicious, and premeditated killing, or committed in the perpetration of, or attempt to perpetrate, any murder in the first degree. . . is murder in the first degree.

Based upon our review of the record, we conclude that the evidence in this case is insufficient to establish deliberation and premeditation. Hence, the defendant's conviction for first-degree murder cannot stand. However, we do find the evidence sufficient to sustain a conviction of second-degree murder.

At common law, there were no degrees of murder, but the tendency to establish a subdivision by statute took root relatively early in the development of American law. The pattern was set by a 1794 Pennsylvania statute that identified the more heinous kinds of murder as murder in the first degree, with all other murders deemed to be murder in the second degree. Some states have subdivided the offense into three or even four degrees of murder, but since the enactment of the first such statute in 1829, Tennessee has maintained the distinction at two. It is one which this Court has found to be "not only founded in mercy and humanity, but ... well fortified by reason."

From the beginning, the statutory definition of first-degree murder required the state to prove that "the killing [was] done willfully, that is, of purpose, with intent that the act by which the life of a party is taken should have that effect; deliberately, that is, with cool purpose; maliciously, that is, with malice aforethought; and with premeditation, that is, a design must be formed to kill, before the act, by which the death is produced, is performed." Because conviction of second-degree murder also requires proof of intent and malice, the two distinctive elements of first-degree murder are deliberation and premeditation.

Intent to kill had long been the hallmark of common-law murder, and in distinguishing manslaughter from murder on the basis of intent, the courts recognized, in the words of an early Tennessee Supreme Court decision, that

> "[t]he law knows of no specific time within which an intent to kill must be formed so as to make it murder [rather than manslaughter]. If the will accompanies the act, a moment antecedent to the act itself which causes death, it seems to be as completely sufficient to make the offence murder, as if it were a day or any other time."

. . . . Premeditation involves a previously formed design, or actual intention to kill. But such design, or intention, may be conceived, and deliberately formed, in an instant. It is not necessary that it should have been conceived, or have pre-existed in the mind, any definite period of time anterior to its execution. It is sufficient that it preceded the assault, however short the interval. The length of time is not of the essence of this constituent of the offense. The purpose to kill is no less premeditated, in the legal sense of the term, if it were deliberately formed but a moment preceding the act by which the death is produced, than if it had been formed an hour before.

The mental state of the assailant at the moment, rather than the length of time the act may have been premeditated, is the material point to be considered. The mental process, in the formation of the purpose to kill, may have been instantaneous, and the question of vital importance is was the mind, at that moment, so far free from the influence of excitement, or passion, as to be capable of reflecting and acting with a sufficient degree of coolness and deliberation of purpose; and was the death of the person assaulted, the object to be accomplished the end determined upon.

Hence, perhaps the two most oft-repeated propositions with regard to the law of first-degree murder, that the essential ingredient of first-degree murder is premeditation and that premeditation may be formed in an instant, are only partially accurate, because they are rarely quoted in context. In order to establish first-degree murder, the premeditated killing must also have been done deliberately, that is, with coolness and reflection.

. . .

The obvious point to be drawn from this discussion is that even if intent (or "purpose to kill") and premeditation ("design") may be formed in an instant, deliberation requires some period of reflection, during which the mind is "free from the influence of excitement, or passion."

. . . Another weakness in our more recent opinions is the tendency to overemphasize the speed with which premeditation may be formed. The cases convert the proposition that no specific amount of time between the formation of the design to kill and its execution is required to prove first-degree murder, into one that requires virtually no time lapse at all, overlooking the fact that while intent (and perhaps even premeditation) may indeed arise instantaneously, the very nature of deliberation requires time to reflect, a lack of impulse, and, as the older cases had held at least since 1837, a "cool purpose."

This trend toward a confusion of premeditation and deliberation has not been unique to Tennessee. It was for a time reflected by the commentators. In *Clarke v. State*, the Court quoted from the 1957 edition of Wharton's Criminal Law and Procedure as follows:

"Deliberation and premeditation involve a prior intention or design to do the act in question. It is not necessary, however, that this intention should have been conceived at any particular period of time, and it is sufficient that only a moment elapsed between the plan and its execution... ."

A more recent version of Wharton's Criminal Law, however, returns the discussion of premeditation and deliberation to its roots:

Although an intent to kill, without more, may support a prosecution for common law murder, such a murder ordinarily constitutes murder in the first degree only if the intent to kill is accompanied by premeditation and deliberation. `Premeditation' is the process simply of thinking about a proposed killing before engaging in the homicidal conduct; and `deliberation' is the process of carefully weighing such matters as the wisdom of going ahead with the proposed killing, the manner in which the killing will be accomplished, and the consequences which may be visited upon the killer if and when apprehended. `Deliberation' is present if the thinking, i.e., the `premeditation,' is being done in such a cool mental state, under such circumstances, and for such a period of time as to permit a `careful weighing' of the proposed decision.

To the same effect is this analysis of the distinction between first- and second-degree murder

Almost all American jurisdictions which divide murder into degrees include the following two murder situations in the category of first-degree murder: (1) intent-to-kill murder where there exists (in addition to the intent to kill) the elements of premeditation and deliberation, and (2) felony murder where the felony in question is one of five or six listed felonies, generally including rape, robbery, kidnapping, arson and burglary. Some states instead or in addition have other kinds of first-degree murder.

(a) Premeditated, Deliberate, Intentional Killing. To be guilty of this form of first-degree murder the defendant must not only intend to kill but in addition he must premeditate the killing and deliberate about it. It is not easy to give a meaningful definition of the words `premeditate' and `deliberate' as they are used in connection with first-degree murder. Perhaps the best that can be said of `deliberation' is that it requires a cool mind that is capable of reflection, and of

`premeditation' that it requires that the one with the cool mind did in fact reflect, at least for a short period of time before his act of killing.

It is often said that premeditation and deliberation require only a `brief moment of thought' or a `matter of seconds,' and convictions for first-degree murder have frequently been affirmed where such short periods of time were involved. The better view, however, is that to `speak of premeditation and deliberation which are instantaneous, or which take no appreciable time, ... destroys the statutory distinction between first and second-degree murder,' and (in much the same fashion that the felony-murder rule is being increasingly limited) this view is growing in popularity. This is not to say, however, that premeditation and deliberation cannot exist when the act of killing follows immediately after the formation of the intent. The intention may be finally formed only as a conclusion of prior premeditation and deliberation, while in other cases the intention may be formed without prior thought so that premeditation and deliberation occurs only with the passage of additional time for `further thought, and a turning over in the mind.'

One further development in Tennessee law has tended to blur the distinction between the essential elements of first- and second-degree murder, and that is the matter of evidence of "repeated blows" being used as circumstantial evidence of premeditation. Obviously, there may be legitimate first-degree murder cases in which there is no direct evidence of the perpetrator's state of mind. Since that state of mind is crucial to the establishment of the elements of the offense, the cases have long recognized that the necessary elements of first-degree murder may be shown by circumstantial evidence. Relevant circumstances recognized by other courts around the country have included the fact "that a deadly weapon was used upon an unarmed victim; that the homicidal act was part of a conspiracy to kill persons of a particular class; that the killing was particularly cruel; that weapons with which to commit the homicide were procured; that the defendant made declarations of his intent to kill the victim; or that preparations were made before the homicide for concealment of the crime, as by the digging of a grave." Wharton's Criminal Law, supra, at § 140. This list, although obviously not intended to be exclusive, is notable for the omission of "repeated blows" as circumstantial evidence of premeditation or deliberation.

In Tennessee, the use of repeated blows to establish the premeditation necessary to first-degree murder apparently traces to Bass v. State. There the Court, after noting that "[b]oth premeditation and deliberation may be inferred from the circumstances of a homicide," went on to list a series of facts from which the Court concluded that the victim's death constituted first-degree murder. The first (but not the only) such circumstance mentioned was that "the deceased was not only struck and killed by a blow from an iron poker but apparently from the number and nature of his wounds, was beaten to death by a whole series of blows." While the Bass court did not interpret the fact of repeated blows to be sufficient, in and of itself, to constitute premeditation and deliberation, subsequent cases have done so. In Houston v. State, for example, the only circumstance relied upon by the majority to establish premeditation and deliberation was the fact that the victim had sustained "repeated shots or blows."

The culmination of this development is probably best represented by the analysis in *State v. Martin* where the Court said:

Repeated blows or shots may support an inference of premeditation. It is also possible that the jury could have found that during the struggle [with the victim] appellant decided to kill the victim, only a moment of time being required between the plan to kill and its execution.

Logically, of course, the fact that repeated blows (or shots) were inflicted on the victim is not sufficient, by itself, to establish first-degree murder. Repeated blows can be delivered in the heat of passion, with no design or reflection. Only if such blows are inflicted as the result of premeditation and deliberation can they be said to prove first-degree murder.
. . .

It is consistent with the murder statute and with case law in Tennessee to instruct the jury in a first-degree murder case that no specific period of time need elapse between the defendant's formulation of the design to kill and the execution of that plan, but we conclude that it is prudent to abandon an instruction that tells the jury that "premeditation may be formed in an instant." Such an instruction can only result in confusion, given the fact that the jury must also be charged on the law of deliberation. If it was not clear from the opinions emanating from this Court within the last half-century, it is now abundantly clear that the deliberation necessary to establish first-degree murder cannot be formed in an instant. It requires proof . . . that the homicide was "committed with `a cool purpose' and without passion or provocation," which would reduce the offense either to second-degree murder or to manslaughter, respectively.

This discussion leads us inevitably to the conclusion that Mack Brown's conviction for first-degree murder in this case cannot be sustained. The law in Tennessee has long recognized that once the homicide has been established, it is presumed to be murder in the second degree. The state bears the burden of proof on the issue of premeditation and deliberation sufficient to elevate the offense to first-degree murder.

Here, there simply is no evidence in the record that in causing his son's death, Mack Brown acted with the premeditation and deliberation required to establish first-degree murder. There is proof, circumstantial in nature, that the defendant acted maliciously toward the child, in the heat of passion or anger, and without adequate provocation all of which would make him guilty of second-degree murder. The only possible legal basis upon which the state might argue that a first-degree conviction can be upheld in this case is the proof in the record that the victim had sustained "repeated blows."

[The court discussed why its earlier precedent allowing first degree murder convictions on the basis of repeated blows could no longer be followed.]

The evidence in this case supports only the conclusion that the appellant intended not to kill his son but to further abuse him or that his intent, if it was to kill the child, was developed in a drunken, heated, rage while disciplining the child. Neither of those supports a finding of premeditation or deliberation.

The Arkansas court, in strengthening the

requirements for proof of premeditation and deliberation in a first-degree murder case involving a victim of child abuse, found it necessary to overrule prior case law to the extent that it was inconsistent with the opinion in *Midgett*. We do the same here. Like the *Midgett* court, we do not condone the homicide in this case, or the sustained abuse of the defenseless victim, Eddie Brown. We simply hold that in order to sustain the defendant's conviction, the proof must conform to the statute. Because the state has failed to establish sufficient evidence of first-degree murder, we reduce the defendant's conviction to second-degree murder and remand the case for resentencing.

STATE v. FORREST,
362 S.E.2d 252, 321 N.C. 186 (1987)

MEYER, Justice.

Defendant was convicted of the first-degree murder of his father, Clyde Forrest. …

The facts of this case are essentially uncontested, and the evidence presented at trial tended to show the following series of events. On 22 December 1985, defendant John Forrest admitted his critically ill father, Clyde Forrest, Sr., to Moore Memorial Hospital. Defendant's father, who had previously been hospitalized, was suffering from numerous serious ailments, including severe heart disease, hypertension, a thoracic aneurysm, numerous pulmonary emboli, and a peptic ulcer. By the morning of 23 December 1985, his medical condition was determined to be untreatable and terminal. Accordingly, he was classified as "No Code," meaning that no extraordinary measures would be used to save his life, and he was moved to a more comfortable room.

On 24 December 1985, defendant went to the hospital to visit his ailing father. No other family members were present in his father's room when he arrived. While one of the nurse's assistants was tending to his father, defendant told her, "There is no need in doing that. He's dying." She responded, *254 "Well, I think he's better." The nurse's assistant noticed that defendant was sniffing as though crying and that he kept his hand in his pocket during their conversation. She subsequently went to get the nurse.

When the nurse's assistant returned with the nurse, defendant once again stated his belief that his father was dying. The nurse tried to comfort defendant, telling him, "I don't think your father is as sick as you think he is." Defendant, very upset, responded, "Go to hell. I've been taking care of him for years. I'll take care of him."

Defendant was then left alone in the room with his father.

Alone at his father's bedside, defendant began to cry and to tell his father how much he loved him. His father began to cough, emitting a gurgling and rattling noise. Extremely upset, defendant pulled a small pistol from his pants pocket, put it to his father's temple, and fired. He subsequently fired three more times and walked out into the hospital corridor, dropping the gun to the floor just outside his father's room.

Following the shooting, defendant, who was crying and upset, neither ran nor threatened anyone. Moreover, he never denied shooting his father and talked openly with law enforcement officials. Specifically, defendant made the following oral statements: "You can't do anything to him now. He's out of his suffering." "I killed my daddy." "He won't have to suffer anymore." "I know they can burn me for it, but my dad will not have to suffer anymore." "I know the doctors couldn't do it, but I could." "I promised my dad I wouldn't let him suffer."

Defendant's father was found in his hospital bed, with several raised spots and blood on the right side of his head. Blood and brain tissue were found on the bed, the floor, and the wall. Though defendant's father had been near death as a result of his medical condition, the exact cause of the deceased's death was determined to be the four point-blank bullet wounds to his head. Defendant's pistol was a single-action .22-calibre five-shot revolver. The weapon, which had to be cocked each time it was fired, contained four empty shells and one live round.

At the close of the evidence, defendant's case was submitted to the jury for one of four possible verdicts: first-degree murder, second-degree murder, voluntary manslaughter, or not guilty. After a lengthy deliberation, the jury found defendant guilty of first-degree murder. Judge Cornelius accordingly sentenced defendant to the mandatory life term.

Defendant assigns three specific errors relative to his conviction at trial: first, that the trial court committed reversible error in its instruction to the jury concerning the issue of malice; second, that the trial court committed reversible error in its submission of the first-degree murder charge to the jury because there was insufficient evidence of premeditation and deliberation; third and finally, that the trial court committed reversible error when, during jury deliberation, it inquired into the jury's numerical division and subsequently instructed the jury about deliberating toward a verdict. We deal with each assignment of error in turn.

. . .

In his second assignment of error, . . . defendant argues that the trial court's submission of the first-degree murder charge was improper because there was insufficient evidence of premeditation and deliberation presented at trial. We do not agree, and we therefore overrule defendant's assignment of error.

. . . First-degree murder is the intentional and unlawful killing of a human being with malice and with premeditation and deliberation. Premeditation means that the act was thought out beforehand for some length of time, however short, but no particular amount of time is necessary for the mental process of premeditation. Deliberation means an intent to kill, carried out in a cool state of blood, in furtherance of a fixed design for revenge or to accomplish an unlawful purpose and not under the influence of a violent passion, suddenly aroused by lawful or just cause or legal provocation. The phrase "cool state of blood" means that the defendant's anger or emotion must not have been such as to overcome his reason.

Premeditation and deliberation relate to mental processes and ordinarily are not readily susceptible to proof by direct evidence. Instead, they usually must be proved by circumstantial evidence. Among other circumstances to be considered in determining whether a killing was with premeditation and deliberation are: (1) want of provocation on the part of the deceased; (2) the conduct and statements of the defendant before and after the killing; (3) threats and declarations of the defendant before and during the course of the occurrence giving rise to the death of the deceased; (4) ill-will or previous difficulty between the parties; (5) the dealing of lethal blows after the deceased has been felled and rendered helpless; and (6) evidence that the killing was done in a brutal manner. We have also held that the nature and number of the victim's wounds is a circumstance from which premeditation and deliberation can be inferred.

. . . [W]e hold in the present case that there was substantial evidence that the killing was premeditated and deliberate and that the trial court did not err in submitting to the jury the question of defendant's guilt of first-degree murder based upon premeditation and deliberation. Here, many of the circumstances that we have held to establish a factual basis for a finding of premeditation and deliberation are present. It is clear, for example, that the seriously ill deceased did nothing to provoke defendant's action. Moreover, the deceased was lying helpless in a hospital bed when defendant shot him four separate times. In addition, defendant's revolver was a five-shot single-action gun which had to be cocked each time before it could be fired. Interestingly, although defendant testified that he always carried the gun in his job as a truck driver, he was not working on the day in question but carried the gun to the hospital nonetheless.

Most persuasive of all on the issue of premeditation and deliberation, however, are defendant's own statements following the incident. Among other things, defendant stated that he had thought about putting his father out of his misery because he knew he was suffering. He stated further that he had promised his father that he would not let him suffer and that, though he did not think he could do it, he just could not stand to see his father suffer any more. These statements, together with the other circumstances mentioned above, make it clear that the trial court did not err in submitting to the jury the issue of first-degree murder based upon premeditation and deliberation. Accordingly, defendant's second assignment of error is overruled.

. . .

In conclusion, having reviewed the record and each of defendant's assignments of error, we find that defendant had a fair trial, free of prejudicial error. Accordingly, we leave undisturbed defendant's conviction of the first-degree murder of Clyde Forrest and his sentence of life imprisonment.

EXUM, Chief Justice, dissenting.

Almost all would agree that someone who kills because of a desire to end a loved one's physical suffering caused by an illness which is both terminal and incurable should not be deemed in law as culpable and deserving of the same punishment as one who kills because of unmitigated spite, hatred or ill will. Yet the Court's decision in this case essentially says there is no legal distinction between the two kinds of killing. Our law of homicide should not be so roughly hewn as to be incapable of recognizing the difference. I believe there are legal principles which, when properly applied, draw the desirable distinction and that both the trial court and this Court have failed to recognize and apply them.

Other Cases – Murder Mens Rea

State v. Snowden, 79 Idaho 266, 313 P.2d 706 (1957).

The court found that Snowden had premeditated the killing of Cora Dean and had formed the malice aforethought in the time it took for him to pull out his pocket knife and cut her throat. It quoted two earlier case,

"The unlawful killing must be accompanied with deliberate and clear intent to take life, in order to constitute murder of the first degree. The intent to kill must be the result of deliberate premeditation. It must be formed upon the pre-existing reflection, and not upon a sudden heat of passion sufficient to preclude the idea of deliberation . . . . There need be no appreciable space of time between the intention to kill and the act of killing. They may be as instantaneous as successive thoughts of the mind. It is only necessary that the act of killing be preceded by a concurrence of will, deliberation, and premeditation on the part of the slayer, and, if such is the case, the killing is murder in the first degree."

The court then stated,
"In the present case, the trial court had no other alternative than to find the defendant guilty of willful, deliberate, and premeditated killing with malice aforethought in view of the defendant's acts in deliberately opening up a pocket knife, next cutting the victim's throat, and then hacking and cutting until he had killed Cora Lucyle Dean and expended himself. The full purpose and design of the defendant's conduct was to take the life of the deceased."

State v. Bingham, 105 Wash.2d 820 (1986).

Defendant admitted to raping a victim, a retarded woman whose body was found three days after being last seen with the defendant. The victim had been raped and strangled, and the defendant agreed that a murder conviction was appropriate but argued on appeal that he should have been convicted of second-degree murder, not first-degree murder with rape the aggravating circumstance. Washington Supreme Court reversed Bingham's aggravated first-degree murder conviction, holding that the fact that Bingham choked his female victim for three to five minutes during sexual intercourse did not constitute sufficient evidence that the defendant premeditated and deliberated the victim's death. Manual strangulation alone, the court held, is not sufficient to support a finding of premeditation. The court stated,

"Premeditation is a separate and distinct element of first-degree murder. It involves the mental process of thinking over beforehand, deliberation, reflection, weighing or reasoning for a period of time, however short, after which the intent to kill is formed. The time required for manual strangulation [3 to 5 minutes in this case] is sufficient to permit deliberation. However, time alone is not enough. The evidence must be sufficient to support the inference that the defendant not only had the time to deliberate, but that he actually did so. . . . Premeditation cannot be inferred from intent. . . .

We agree with the Court of Appeals majority that to allow a finding of premeditation only because the act takes an appreciable amount of time obliterates the distinction between first and second degree murder. Having the opportunity to deliberate is not evidence the defendant did deliberate, which is necessary for a finding of premeditation. Otherwise, any form of killing which took more than a moment could result in a finding of premeditation, without some additional evidence showing reflection. Holding a hand over someone's mouth or windpipe does not necessarily reflect a decision to kill the person, but possibly only to quiet him or her. Furthermore, here a question of the ability to deliberate or reflect while engaged in sexual activity exists.

Here, no evidence was presented of deliberation or reflection before or during the strangulation, only the strangulation. The opportunity to deliberate is not sufficient."

[The court held that the defendant could be sentenced for second-degree murder as a lesser-included offense.]

People v. Wolff, 61 Cal. 2d 795 (1964).
(See Chapter Eleven). The court stated that the child was too young to have maturely and meaningfully reflected on the gravity of killing (his mom) before he continued to beat her to death. It provided a defense of immaturity. [In 1981, the California homicide statutes were amended to provide that there was no need to prove a defendant maturely and meaningfully reflected on the gravity of the killing to convict the defendant of first-degree murder.]

First-Degree Murder-Actus Reus

Generally, the actus reus of murder can be any act which results in the death of another. It includes shooting, strangling, drowning, garroting, poisoning, stabbing, etc. One type of first-degree murder, "heinous atrocious and cruel murder", focuses on the brutality in which the act was committed. Whereas premeditated and deliberate describe the offender's mens rea, "heinous atrocious and cruel" describes the offender's actus reus. In states that have an atrocious murder designation, the statute generally requires that the killer not only mean to kill but does the killing in an especially brutal murder. "Especially heinous, atrocious and cruel" is generally an aggravating factor that is used to support a death sentence or a sentence of life imprisonment.

SMITH v. STATE,
727 P.2d 1366 (1986)

BUSSEY, Judge:
The appellant, Lois Nadean Smith, was convicted . . . of Murder in the First Degree for which she received a sentence of death.

[Smith] . . . her son Greg, and Teresa Baker picked up Cindy Baillee at a Tahlequah motel early on the morning of July 4, 1982. Baillee had been Greg's girlfriend, but allegedly had made threats to have him killed.

As the group drove away from the motel, appellant confronted Ms. Baillee with rumors that she had arranged for Greg's murder. When Ms. Baillee denied making any threats or arrangements, appellant choked the victim and stabbed her in the throat with a knife found in the victim's purse. The car traveled to the home of Jim Smith, the appellant's ex-husband and Greg's father in Gans, Oklahoma. Present at the house were Smith and his wife Robyn. She left shortly after the group arrived.

While at the Smith house, appellant forced Ms. Baillee to sit in a recliner chair. She then

threatened to kill Ms. Baillee, and taunted her with a pistol. Finally, appellant fired a shot into the recliner, near Ms. Baillee's head. She then fired a series of shots at Ms. Baillee, and the wounded victim fell to the floor. As Greg Smith reloaded the pistol, appellant laughed while jumping on the victim's neck. Appellant took the pistol from Greg and fired four more bullets into the body. A subsequent autopsy showed Ms. Baillee had been shot five times in the chest, twice in the head, and once in the back. Five of these gunshot wounds were fatal. The knife wound was also potentially fatal.

An expert in blood splatter analysis testified blood stains on the blouse worn by appellant proved circumstantially that she had fired the fatal shots. Evidence also was presented by the State that appellant directed her companions to dispose of some evidence and arranged an alibi story for them.

Appellant testified on her own behalf that Teresa Baker actually shot and killed Ms. Baillee. She claimed Ms. Baker killed the victim because of jealousy over Greg.

. . .

The appellant next argues that the aggravating circumstance that the murder was especially heinous, atrocious, or cruel is being evaluated in an arbitrary manner. . . . [T]he death penalty convictions affirmed by this Court in which this aggravating circumstance has been found to be present have consistently passed constitutional challenge. The facts in this case overwhelmingly support this aggravating circumstance.

. . . We find that the aggravating circumstance of "heinous, atrocious, or cruel" is likewise supported. The victim was first choked, then stabbed in the throat, then taken to a house where she continued to beg for her life while the appellant tormented her with a revolver by shooting it into the chair in which the victim sat, and by alternately pointing it at her head and stomach until the first bullet wounds were inflicted. When the victim fell to the floor, the appellant jumped on her neck until the reloaded pistol was handed back to the appellant who discharged all six rounds into the helpless victim.

The judgment and sentence is AFFIRMED.

Other Cases—Murder Actus Reus

Commonwealth v. Golston, 373 Mass. 249, 366 N.E.2d 744 (1977).
On Sunday, August 24, 1975, a 34-year-old man came out of a store and walked toward his car. Golston, 19, tiptoed up behind the victim and hit him on the head with a baseball bat. Golston went into a building, changed his clothes and crossed the street to the store where he worked. When asked why he hit the man, Golston replied, "For kicks." The victim died and Golston was charged with a capital murder. The court had to decide whether it was an "atrocious murder" which qualified under the first degree murder statute. The court concluded it was:

"There was evidence of great and unusual violence in the blow which caused a four-inch cut on the side of the skull. . . . [T]here was also evidence that after he was struck the victim fell to the street, and that five minutes later he tried to get up, staggered to his feet and fell again to the ground. He was breathing very hard and a neighbor wiped vomit from his nose and mouth. Late, according to the testimony, the defendant said he did it, 'For kicks.'

There is no requirement that the defendant know that his act was extremely atrocious or cruel, and no requirement of deliberate premeditation. A murder may be committed with extreme atrocity or cruelty even though death results from a single blow. Indifference to the victim's pain, as well as actual knowledge of it and taking pleasure in it, is cruelty; and extreme cruelty is only a higher degree of cruelty."

Duest v. State, 462 So.2d 446 (Fla. 1985)
Defendant boasted that he was going to a gay bar to "roll a fag." He was later seen at a predominantly gay bar with John Pope. Pope and Duest left the bar and drove off in Pope's gold Camaro. Several hours later, Pope's roommate returned home and found the lights on, the stereo on loud, the house unlocked, and blood on the bed. He contacted the sheriff, and when the sheriff arrived he found Pope on the bathroom floor in a pool of blood with multiple stab wounds. Duest was found, arrested two months later. He was tried and found guilty of first-degree murder. The jury imposed the death sentence. Duest appealed alleging that this was not a particularly heinous or atrocious killing (findings necessary to support a death sentence). The Court of Appeals, upholding the death sentence, disagreed.

"The evidence presented at trial shows that the victim received eleven stab wounds, some of which were inflicted in the bedroom and some inflicted in the bathroom. The medical examiner's testimony revealed that the victim lived some minutes before dying."

Owen v. State, 862 So.2d 687 (Fla. 2003)
Karen Slattery, 14, was babysitting for a married couple one evening in March, 1984. She called home several times and spoke with her mother that evening, the last call at approximately 10:00 p.m. When the couple returned just after midnight, the lights and the television were off and Karen did not meet them at the door as was her practice. They called the police and the victim's body was found with multiple stab wounds. Evidence showed that the intruder entered by cutting the screen to the master bedroom window and then sexually assaulted the victim. He was convicted of first degree murder and was sentenced to death upon recommendation of the trial jury. At issue was whether the killing was especially heinous, atrocious or cruel (HAC), and whether the crime

was committed in a cold and calculated and premeditated (CCP) manner. The appellate court upheld the trial court's finding that the state had proven those aggravating factors justifying Owen's death sentence for the Slattery killing.

Owens was also found guilty and sentenced to death for killing Georgianna Worden in May 1984. The killing of Worden was similar to that of Ms. Slattery (intruder forcibly entered Boca Raton home of Ms. Worden at night, bludgeoned her with a hammer as she slept and then sexually assaulted her.

"This Court has consistently upheld the HAC aggravator where the victim has been repeatedly stabbed. Furthermore, we have reasoned that the HAC aggravator is applicable to murders that "evince extreme and outrageous depravity as exemplified either by the desire to inflict a high degree of pain or utter indifference to or enjoyment of the suffering of another. The HAC aggravator focuses on the means and manner in which the death is inflicted."

The court noted that Slattery suffered eighteen stab wounds, "air hunger" (the feeling of needing to breathe but not being able to do so," severe blood loss resulting in shock which causes high anxiety and terror, substantial pain because of the damage to the nerve receptors in the skin being injured, and that she would have survived and been conscious between twenty seconds and two minutes.

With regard to the findings of CCP, the court stated that the CCP aggravating factor is justified if (1) the killing was the product of cool and calm reflection and not an act prompted by emotional frenzy , panic or a fit of rage (cold) (the court indicated all the facts that demonstrated that Owen's killing met this condition); (2) the defendant must have had a careful plan or prearranged design to commit murder before the fatal incident (calculated) (the court indicated all the facts that demonstrated that Owen's killing met this condition); and (3) that defendant must have exhibited heightened premeditation and (4) the defendant must have had no pretense of moral or legal justification. The court found the third and fourth criteria were supported by substantial evidence.

The court also found that Owen's claim that his mental illness negated the CCP aggravator was unpersuasive. "We have held, 'A defendant can be emotionally and mentally disturbed or suffer from a mental illness but still have the ability to experience cool and calm reflection, make a careful plan or prearranged design to commit murder and exhibit heightened premeditation.

Henyard v. State, 689 So.2d 239 (Fla. 1996)

Defendant, 18-year-old Henyard, stole a gun from a family friend, and on January 29, 1993 he told a friend that he planned to go to a nightclub in Orlando and then visit his father in South Florida. He displayed the gun to his friend and told the friend that he planned to steal a car and kill the owner. Henyard convinced a 14-year-old friend, Smalls, to participate in a robbery, and they both followed Ms. Lewis as she left a grocery store. They watched her put her daughters, age three and seven in her car. Showing the gun to Lewis, Smalls ordered her and her daughters into the front seat. Henyard later stopped the car, ordered Lewis out, and raped her on the trunk of the car while her daughters remained in the back seat. Smalls also raped Lewis on the trunk of the car. Henyard then directed her to sit on the edge of the road and when she hesitated he pushed her to the ground and shot her in the leg. He then shot her three more times, wounding her in the neck, the mouth, and the middle of the forehead between her eyes. Henyard and Smalls pushed her unconscious body off to the side of the road. (Lewis subsequently regained consciousness and alerted police.) Henyard and Smalls reentered the auto and drove away as the girls cried and pleaded for their mother. Henyard stopped the car and led the two young girls to a grassy area where they each were killed by a single bullet fired into the head. They threw the girls' bodies over into some underbrush. Autopsies revealed that both girls died of gunshot wounds to the head at a very close range.

Henyard claimed that the heinous, atrocious, and cruel aggravating circumstance was not applicable since he killed the girls with a single shot and that they had not been physically harmed prior to their murder. The court held the fact that they had watched their mother shot, and at least one girl saw her sister murdered was heinous, atrocious and cruel.

Model Penal Code -- First-Degree Murder

Under the Model Penal Code, criminal homicide is murder, a first-degree felony, when (1) it is committed purposely or knowingly; or (2) it is committed recklessly under circumstances manifesting extreme indifference to the value of human life. Such recklessness and indifference are presumed if the actor is engaged or is an accomplice in the commission of, or an attempt to commit, or flight after committing or attempting to commit robbery, rape or deviate sexual intercourse by force or threat of force, arson, burglary, kidnapping or felonious escape. The Model Penal Code, thus, somewhat follows the common law distinction of recognizing only murder and manslaughter.

Felony Murder

The felony murder rule states that a killing--even one which is accidental--will be murder if it was caused with the intent to commit a felony. No intent to kill or other mental state regarding the occurrence of death is required (in a sense, felony murder is a strict liability crime.) The felony upon which a felony murder prosecution is based is often called the predicate felony. The felony murder rule seeks to deter felonies in general by increasing the threat of conviction if death results (even if they were unintentional). The rule is also believed to discourage the use of violence during the commission of felonies.

Early English common law did not recognize the felony murder rule. But later common law did and individuals who committed felonies that resulted in death were said to have acted with implied malice aforethought. Since all common law felonies in England were subject to the death penalty, a conviction for murder done with intent to kill was no different than a conviction for murder done during the course of a felony where death was unintended. *Regina v. Searne*, 16 Cox. Crim.Cas 311 (1887) is generally the first case cited for the felony-murder doctrine. In *Searne*, the defendant was charged with the murder of his son. The evidence suggested that the defendant set fire to his home in order to collect the insurance on his property and on the life of his imbecile son. The court instructed the jury that the defendant was guilty of murder if he acted with either knowledge that his actions would kill a person (malice) or an intent to commit a felony (felony murder). The jury returned a not guilty verdict, however, after the trial judge in his summation (an English tradition unknown in the American trial) expressed his doubts about the scope of the felony murder rule. Felony murder has been increasingly controversial, particularly as use of capital punishment has waned. The English abandoned the felony murder rule in 1957.

Even in the United States, the felony murder rule is controversial. Some argue that a person cannot be deterred from committing an accidental act and that a harsher punishment levied against a defendant who accidentally causes a death is capricious and an unfair imposition of increased liability on the unlucky felon. They further argue that the felony murder rule does not reflect the defendant's actual culpability since the defendant had no intent to cause the death. Finally, they argue that prosecutors do not need assistance in homicide prosecutions, especially since statistical evidence shows that homicides occur in felonies at a much lower rate than expected and, when a death occurs, there is usually evidence of the defendant's reckless intent.

As seen above, the MPC takes the position that death that results from the commission, attempted commission, or flight from the commission of robbery, rape, arson, burglary, kidnapping or escape is presumed to have been the product of recklessness manifesting extreme indifference to the value of human life. It, accordingly, treats felony murder as first degree murder.

States have taken a variety of approaches: some states enumerate the list of felonies which can trigger the felony murder doctrine; some states say that all felonies can trigger the felony murder rule; some states say inherently dangerous felonies trigger the doctrine and look at whether the felony was dangerous in the abstract (i.e., is there any way that the felony can be committed without posing a danger to human life); some states limit felony murder to inherently dangerous felonies but look at the facts of the case to determine whether it was committed in a dangerous fashion. Some states classify felony murder as a first-degree murder; some states classify felony murder as a second-degree murder. Some states hold that the felony murder rule is limited to foreseeable deaths. All states hold that felony murder rule is applicable to the acts of the felon, and most states include liability for the acts of any co-felon. Some states extend the felony murder rule to deaths caused by a non-co-felon such as a police officer or innocent third party.

Special problems arise when the victim's death was not caused directly by the defendant or co-felon, but rather someone else. States have adopted two approaches. The first is the agency analysis which finds no felony murder liability under those circumstances. In these jurisdictions, felony murder applies only when the death is caused by the defendant or someone acting as the defendant's agent. Since neither the victim of the felony nor intervening police officers are in any sense agents of the felons, a death directly caused by them cannot give rise to felony murder.

The alternate view is that felony murder liability does exist when a non-felon causes the death, reasoning that these situations present all that is necessary--a showing that "but for the commission of the felony, the victim would not have died.

STATE v. WESSON,
247 Kan. 63, 802 P.2d 574 (1990)

This is a direct appeal by the defendant, Kurt Donnell Wesson, from his convictions of felony murder and of attempted sale of crack cocaine (K.S.A. 1989 Supp. 65-4127a).

Wesson contends that the sale, or attempted sale, of crack cocaine cannot be the underlying felony to support a charge of felony murder . . . .

Early in the morning of June 11, 1989, a Kansas City, Kansas, police officer noticed a vehicle on a sidewalk that had run into a light pole. The tires were spinning and smoking, the windshield was cracked, and the left window was broken out. Inside the vehicle the officer found Cletis Crowley slumped against the steering wheel. The officer tore open Crowley's shirt and found stab wounds on Crowley's upper chest and arms. Crowley died a short time later from one of the stab wounds, which had penetrated his heart. An autopsy revealed that Crowley had been stabbed eight times by a single-edged instrument.

Crowley had in his possession a pipe with traces of cocaine in it. Because there was little broken glass on the ground where the car had come to the rest, the officers surmised that a altercation had taken place elsewhere. They backtracked to 13th and Wood, and area where drug sales are common, and discovered newly broken auto glass on the ground and two wooden knife handle halves. Lab tests showed that the glass found at 13th and Wood was consistent with the glass from Crowley's car.

Officers arrested Kurt Wesson at 13th and Wood later that day. A lock-blade knife was recovered from his pocket with the wooden handles missing. A subsequent analysis showed that the knife handles found at the scene were originally attached to Wesson's knife.

After arrest, Wesson told the police that he was trying to sell cocaine to Crowley. He told police that there were two people in the car and that the driver reached out and grabbed the cocaine and drove away. He told the officers that as the car turned the corner, it looked like the driver was fighting with the passenger. He said he chased the car, it stopped and the passenger jumped out, and he noticed the driver had blood on his chest. He said he broke the half open window, reached in, and retrieved his cocaine. The car then drove away.

At trial, Wesson denied making the preceding statement to officers. Wesson testified that he was selling fake crack made out of soap, wax, and baking soda. He testified that when he showed a sample to Crowley, Crowley took the sample, rolled up the car window trapping Wesson's arm and the sample inside and started driving. He testified that he eventually broke the window and escaped. He testified that an acquaintance, Philip White, had given him the knife to dispose of and that he did not know who stabbed Crowley.

Officers questioned two witnesses, Phillips White

and Kenneth Williams, both acquaintances of Wesson. At the preliminary hearing, they testified that they were at 13th and Wood early on the 11th. They saw Wesson with the upper half of his body inside the driver's side of Crowley's car, being dragged along. They both testified they ran after the car to try and help Wesson. Both witnesses saw Wesson hitting Crowley. White testified he saw a knife in Wesson's hand.

Both witnesses testified the car drove off after Wesson was freed. After Wesson was freed from the vehicle, White, Williams, and Wesson went to White's apartment. Both observed a knife and cuts on Wesson's hand. Both testified that Wesson admitted he stabbed Crowley. At trial, the State was unable to procure White's and Williams' attendance, and the court ultimately found them unavailable and allowed their testimony at the preliminary hearing to be introduced.

The jury found Wesson guilty and he appeals.

I. FELONY MURDER

In addition to an instruction on first-degree murder in the alternative, the jury was also instructed on the lesser included offenses of second-degree murder and voluntary manslaughter. The only instruction given concerning drug violations was on attempted sale of crack cocaine.

Prior to trial, Wesson moved to have Count I dismissed, and, at the close of the State's evidence, Wesson moved for acquittal. The trial court denied the motion, finding, in part:

"Mere possession of crack is not an inherently dangerous crime, but I am of the opinion ... that the sale or attempted sale of crack is an inherently dangerous felony. I don't care if we view the crime in the abstract or if we view it in reality. In reality, we know that the sale or attempted sale of dangerous drugs, narcotics is a dangerous occupation.

"We see — as courts, we see every day where people are injured and killed during the sale or attempted sale of narcotic drugs....

"We know that people who sell and who buy drugs are dangerous and sometimes violent individuals, that considerable money can be present during drug transactions.... So whether we view it in reality or in the abstract, I am of the opinion that the sale or attempted sale of a controlled substance, and especially cocaine or hard drugs, is an inherently dangerous crime."

On appeal, Wesson renews this argument that attempted sale of narcotics (or sale of narcotics) is not inherently dangerous.

In Kansas, unlike most states, felony murder is classified as first-degree murder. Most states set out specific felonies (for example, rape, robbery, burglary, and aggravated arson) as underlying felonies sufficient for first-degree murder and then make all other felony murders second degree. The purpose of the felony-murder rule is to supply the elements of premeditation and intent that are otherwise required to establish first-degree murder. Consequently, only felonies which are inherently dangerous are held to support felony murder. That the crime must be inherently dangerous has been the rule in Kansas for many years.

In *State v. Hoang*, the court said:
> "To support a conviction for felony murder, all that is required is to prove that a felony was being committed, which felony was inherently dangerous to human life, and that the homicide which followed was a direct result of the commission of that felony....
>
> "[T]he underlying felony in a felony-murder case must be a forcible felony, one inherently dangerous to human life." Hoang, 243 Kan. at 42.

K.S.A. 21-3110(8) provides that forcible felonies include "treason, murder, voluntary manslaughter, rape, robbery, burglary, arson, kidnapping, aggravated battery, aggravated sodomy and any other felony which involves the use or threat of physical force or violence against any person." (Obviously, this list contains some crimes which could not support felony murder as they are lesser included offenses of felony murder.)

In determining whether a crime is inherently dangerous, the majority of states examine the circumstances of the particular incident and determine whether the way that the particular crime was committed was inherently dangerous. This previously was the law in Kansas.

In *State v. Goodseal*, the court considered and expressly rejected the minority/California rule that the underlying felony is viewed only in the abstract in determining whether it is inherently dangerous. However, in *State v. Underwood*, 228 Kan. at 306, this court, in a 4 to 3 vote, held that the circumstances of the commission of the felony are not to be examined — the underlying felony is to be analyzed only in the abstract. *Goodseal* and *Moffitt* were overruled.

This rule--that the underlying felony is examined in the abstract--has been stated in subsequent cases, but not always strictly followed. In *State v. Lashley* (1983), the court held that felony theft, by obtaining or exerting unauthorized control over property, is an inherently dangerous felony. This court added: "[W]e wish to emphasize that theft may be the underlying felony in a charge of felony murder only in cases where the discovery of the thief during the course of the theft results in the death of a person."

Other cases, which apply the abstract analysis, are instructive in this case. In Underwood, this court held that unlawful possession of a firearm by a felon could not support felony murder, reasoning:

> "The possession of the firearm when viewed in the abstract is not inherently dangerous to human life. This is true because it seems unlikely that mere possession, which has been defined as dominion and control over an object, and not its use, could be undertaken in so dangerous a manner that the prohibited possession would result in murder in the first degree.... It appears quite impossible to find an intent in this collateral felony encompassing malice, deliberation and premeditation so as to transfer these elements to the homicide and relieve the prosecution from proof of the same."

... The possession or sale (attempted or actual) of cocaine is like the unlawful possession of a weapon. There is nothing inherently violent or forcible in the sale of crack cocaine. The State

attempts to distinguish *Brantley* and *Underwood* on the basis that they involved status crimes — it is the status of the person and mere possession which determine the illegality. The State argues that drug sales, on the other hand, are active crimes and that the nature of the "seedy" locations where the sales take place and the fact that most sales are for cash and large amounts of money may be present, and combine to "create a reckless disregard of consequences and fuel that opportunity for confrontation that the Court requires."

The State's argument fails for several reasons. The intent being transferred or presumed is not recklessness--it is premeditation, malice, etc. The determinative factor of *Brantley* and *Underwood* was not that the crimes therein were status crimes, but that there was no active violence as a part of the crimes; no threat of violence against the persons present. The violence accompanying drug sales is coincidental rather than necessarily inherent.

Cases from other states are of little benefit in that many states classify most felony murder as second-degree murder. Many states look at the circumstances of each crime. In *People v. Patterson*, the California Supreme Court instructed the trial court that "a felony is inherently dangerous to life when there is a high probability that its commission will result in death." In California, a homicide that is a direct result of furnishing a narcotic, if that furnishing is found to be inherently dangerous, is at least second-degree felony murder.

The cases from other states cited by the State are not persuasive either, because of the differences in felony-murder law. In *State v. Norwood*, 721 S.W.2d 175 (Mo. App. 1986), cited by the State for the proposition that drug crimes are inherently dangerous, a police officer was shot by a codefendant during a drug raid on a residence and the Court of Appeals affirmed the second-degree felony-murder conviction based on felony possession of marijuana. It was never argued in the case that possession is not an inherently dangerous felony. At issue was only whether one codefendant was responsible for the other's acts. Missouri, unlike Kansas, has a second-degree felony-murder statute that eliminates the transferred intent problem and, thus, whether a crime is inherently dangerous is of no consequence in Missouri in a second-degree felony-murder case.

Many other states never reach the issue. They hold that there is no causal connection between the drug-related felony and the death. For instance, in *King v. Commonwealth* [Va., 1988], the court held that when an aircraft carrying drugs crashed, killing the co-pilot, the connection between the felony and the death was too remote to support a felony-murder charge.

...[T]his state has a history of requiring that the question of whether a felony is inherently dangerous to human life must be determined when considered in the abstract only. We are not urged in this case that the rule be changed.

The legislature has been aware of this rule for many years and has not seen fit to change either the felony-murder statute or the definition of a "forcible felony." We invite the legislature to consider adopting a more specific first-degree felony-murder statute and a second-degree felony-murder statute.

Viewing a "sale" of a narcotic in the abstract does not mean we use the definition of a sale contained in the Uniform Commercial Code or consider sales of legitimate items by legitimate merchants in the ordinary course of their business. What it does mean is that we consider all sales of crack cocaine and not confine ourselves to the facts of this particular sale. A sale under the Uniform Controlled Substances Act has a broader meaning than "sale" usually has. In addition to "sale's" usual meaning, it includes a gift or any offer to make a gift, a barter, or an exchange, and it is not necessary that the prohibited substance be the property of the defendant or be in his or her physical possession. Simply put, we consider only the question whether the sale of crack cocaine, when viewed in the abstract, is inherently dangerous.

The record in this case is devoid of any evidence concerning whether the sale of crack cocaine is inherently dangerous. We are not unmindful of the cost to society of the use of illicit drugs and the cost in human tragedy. The legislature has recognized this problem and has consistently sought to control the problem with stiffer penalties and mandatory sentences. That, however, does not make the sale, when viewed

in the abstract, inherently dangerous. The sale, when viewed in the abstract, takes place literally everywhere in our society and with alarming frequency. On occasions isolated sales turn violent. We can only surmise from limited knowledge of the total number of sales alleged to take place in our society that violence is only involved in an extremely small percentage of the sales of illicit drugs. We cannot say that a sale of crack cocaine, when viewed in the abstract, is inherently dangerous. Thus, the conviction for felony murder must be reversed and remanded to the trial court for retrial as more fully set forth hereinafter.

II. FIRST-DEGREE MURDER

In Wesson's pretrial motion to dismiss, and in the motion for acquittal, he argued that the alternative charge against defendant for premeditated murder should be dismissed for lack of evidence. By virtue of our holding that sale of cocaine cannot be the underlying felony for first-degree felony murder, a question arises as to whether the defendant can be retried for first degree murder and any applicable lesser included offense.

....Premeditated murder and felony murder are both alternate theories to prove first-degree murder. The jury was instructed that it could convict Wesson on either theory and if the jury had a "reasonable doubt as to the guilt of the defendant as to the crime of murder in the first degree on either theory, then [it] must consider whether the defendant is guilty of murder in the second degree or voluntary manslaughter."

Finding Wesson guilty of felony murder did not adjudicate him not guilty of premeditated murder. Felony murder and premeditated murder, as instructed in this case, are not mutually exclusive. The theory behind felony murder is that the premeditation, malice, etc., is transferred from the underlying felony, so the State does not have to prove premeditation. Perhaps the jury just felt that the felony murder was a slightly stronger case than premeditated murder, but that there was proof beyond a reasonable doubt for both. We simply do not know. All that can be said is that it is not implicit in the verdict that Wesson was found not guilty of premeditated murder. A subsequent prosecution for premeditated murder and appropriate lesser included offenses is not precluded by double jeopardy in this case.

Wesson used a deadly weapon. Although premeditation is not presumed from use of a deadly weapon, the use of a deadly weapon may be considered along with other evidence to support a conviction for premeditated murder. The evidence could also be interpreted to show that Wesson chased after Crowley's car, giving Wesson time to think about his actions. There was a valid jury question on premeditation.

STATE v. STEWART, 663 A.2d 912 (1995)

WEISBERGER, Chief Justice.

This case comes before us on the appeal of the defendant, Tracy Stewart, from a judgment of conviction entered in the Superior Court on one count of second-degree murder in violation of G.L. 1956 (1981 Reenactment) § 11-23-1. We affirm the judgment of conviction. The facts insofar as pertinent to this appeal are as follows.

On August 31, 1988 twenty-year-old Tracy Stewart (Stewart or defendant) gave birth to a son, Travis Young (Travis). Travis's father was Edward Young, Sr. (Young). Stewart and Young, who had two other children together, were not married at the time of Travis's birth. Travis lived for only fifty-two days, dying on October 21, 1988, from dehydration.

During the week prior to Travis's death, Stewart, Young, and a friend, Patricia McMasters (McMasters), continually and repeatedly ingested cocaine over a two- to three-consecutive-day period at the apartment shared by Stewart and Young. The baby, Travis, was also present at the apartment while Stewart, Young, and McMasters engaged in this cocaine marathon. Young and McMasters injected cocaine intravenously and also smoked it while Stewart ingested the cocaine only by smoking it. The smoked cocaine was in its strongest or base form, commonly referred to as "crack." When the three exhausted an existing supply of cocaine, they would pool their money and Young and McMasters would go out and buy more with the accumulated funds. The primary source of funds from which the three obtained money for this cocaine spree was Stewart's and McMasters's Aid to Families with Dependent Children (AFDC) checks. Stewart and McMasters had each just received the second of their semimonthly AFDC checks. They both cashed their AFDC checks and gave money to Young, which he then used to purchase more cocaine. After all the AFDC funds had been spent on cocaine and the group had run out of money, McMasters and Young committed a robbery to obtain additional money to purchase more cocaine.

The cocaine binge continued uninterrupted for two to three days. McMasters testified that during this time neither McMasters nor Stewart slept at all. McMasters testified that defendant was never far from her during this entire two- to three-day period except for the occasions when McMasters left the apartment to buy more cocaine. During this entire time, McMasters saw defendant feed Travis only once. Travis was in a walker, and defendant propped a bottle of formula up on the walker, using a blanket, for the baby to feed himself. McMasters testified that she did not see defendant hold the baby to feed him nor did she see defendant change Travis's diaper or clothes during this period.

Ten months after Travis's death defendant was indicted on charges of second-degree murder, wrongfully causing or permitting a child under the age of eighteen to be a habitual sufferer for want of food and proper care (hereinafter sometimes referred to as "wrongfully permitting a child to be a habitual sufferer"), and manslaughter. The second-degree-murder charge was based on a theory of felony murder. The prosecution did not allege that defendant intentionally killed her son but rather that he had been killed during the commission of an inherently dangerous felony, specifically, wrongfully permitting a child to be a habitual sufferer. Moreover, the prosecution did not allege that defendant intentionally withheld food or care from her son. Rather the state alleged that because of defendant's chronic state of cocaine intoxication, she may have realized what her responsibilities were but simply could not remember whether she had fed her son, when in fact she had not.

The defendant was found guilty of both second-degree murder and wrongfully permitting a child to be a habitual sufferer. A subsequent motion for new trial was denied. This appeal followed.

I.
THE DENIAL OF THE MOTION TO DISMISS

. . . [Defendant} claimed that the charge should have been no greater than involuntary manslaughter. The basis of defendant's claim is that the predicate felony underlying the felony-murder charge, wrongfully permitting a child to be a habitual sufferer, is not an inherently dangerous felony as charged in the indictment.

II
. . .

A
Whether Wrongfully Permitting a Child to Be a Habitual Sufferer is an Inherently Dangerously Felony

Rhode Island's murder statute, § 11-23-1, enumerates certain crimes that may serve as predicate felonies to a charge of first-degree murder. A felony that is not enumerated in § 11-23-1 can, however, serve as a predicate felony to a charge of second-degree murder. Thus the fact that the crime of wrongfully permitting a child to be a habitual sufferer is not specified in § 11-23-1 as a predicate felony to support a charge of first-degree murder does not preclude such crime from serving as a predicate to support a charge of second-degree murder.

In Rhode Island second-degree murder has been equated with common-law murder. At common law, where the rule is unchanged by statute, "[h]omicide is murder if the death results from the perpetration or attempted perpetration of an inherently dangerous felony." To serve as a predicate felony to a charge of second-degree murder, a felony that is not specifically enumerated in § 11-23-1 must therefore be an inherently dangerous felony.

The defendant contends that wrongfully permitting a child to be a habitual sufferer is not an inherently dangerous felony and cannot therefore serve as the predicate felony to a charge of second-degree murder. In advancing her argument, defendant urges this court to adopt

the approach used by California courts to determine if a felony is inherently dangerous. This approach requires that the court consider the elements of the felony "in the abstract" rather than look at the particular facts of the case under consideration. With such an approach, if a statute can be violated in a manner that does not endanger human life, then the felony is not inherently dangerous to human life. Moreover, the California Supreme Court has defined an act as "inherently dangerous to human life when there is `a high probability that it will result in death.'"

In *Caffero* a two-and-one-half-week-old baby died of a massive bacterial infection caused by lack of proper hygiene that was due to parental neglect. The parents were charged with second-degree felony murder and felony-child abuse, with the felony-child-abuse charge serving as the predicate felony to the second-degree-murder charge. Examining California's felony-child abuse statute in the abstract, instead of looking at the particular facts of the case, the court held that because the statute could be violated in ways that did not endanger human life, felony-child abuse was not inherently dangerous to human life. By way of example, the court noted that a fractured limb, which comes within the ambit of the felony-child-abuse statute, is unlikely to endanger the life of an infant, much less of a seventeen-year-old. (the statute applied to all minors below the age of eighteen years, not only to young children. Because felony-child abuse was not inherently dangerous to human life, it could not properly serve as a predicate felony to a charge of second-degree felony murder.

The defendant urges this court to adopt the method of analysis employed by California courts to determine if a felony is inherently dangerous to life. Aside from California, it appears that Kansas is the only other state which looks at the elements of a felony in the abstract to determine if such felony is inherently dangerous to life. The case of *Ford v. State,* cited in defendant's brief for the proposition that possession of a firearm by an ex-felon is not an inherently dangerous felony which can support a felony-murder conviction, actually holds that the attendant circumstances of the particular case should be considered in determining whether the underlying felony "create[d] a foreseeable risk of death." In *Ford* the defendant (Ford) had previously been convicted of the felony of possession of cocaine with intent to distribute. Ford was visiting the home of his girlfriend's mother and had brought with him a semiautomatic pistol. While there he attempted to unload the pistol, but in so doing, he discharged the weapon, sending a bullet both through the floor and through the ceiling of a basement apartment located in the house. The bullet struck and killed the occupant of the basement apartment. There was no evidence that at the time of the shooting the defendant was aware of the existence of the apartment or of the victim's presence in it. Ford was charged with and convicted of felony murder, with the underlying felony being the possession of a firearm by a convicted felon.

The Georgia Supreme Court reversed the conviction for felony murder holding that a status felony, including the possession of a firearm by a previously-convicted felon, is not inherently dangerous. The court explained that there could indeed be circumstances in which such a felony could be considered dangerous (for example when the possession of the firearm was coupled with an aggravated assault or other dangerous felony) but that such circumstances were absent in that case. It held that in that particular case, which did not involve an assault or other criminal conduct, the underlying felony of possession of a firearm by a previously convicted felon was not inherently dangerous and thus could not serve as a predicate to the charge of felony murder.

We decline defendant's invitation to adopt the California approach in determining whether a felony is inherently dangerous to life and thus capable of serving as a predicate to a charge of second-degree felony murder. We believe that the better approach is for the trier of fact to consider the facts and circumstances of the particular case to determine if such felony was inherently dangerous in the manner and the circumstances in which it was committed, rather than have a court make the determination by viewing the elements of a felony in the abstract. We now join a number of states that have adopted this approach.

A number of felonies at first glance would not appear to present an inherent danger to human life but may in fact be committed in such a manner as to be inherently dangerous to life. The crime of escape from a penal facility is an example of such a crime. On its face, the crime of escape is not inherently dangerous to human life. But escape may be committed or attempted to be committed in a manner wherein human life is put in danger. Indeed in *State v. Miller* this court upheld the defendant's conviction of second-degree murder on the basis of the underlying felony of escape when a prison guard was killed by an accomplice of the defendant during an attempted escape from the Rhode Island State prison. By way of contrast, the California Supreme Court has held that the crime of escape, viewed in the abstract, is an offense that is not inherently dangerous to human life and thus cannot support a second-degree felony-murder conviction.

The amendment of our murder statute to include any unlawful killing "committed during the course of the perpetration, or attempted perpetration, of felony manufacture, sale, delivery, or other distribution of a controlled substance otherwise prohibited by the provisions of chapter 28 of title 21" lends further support for not following California's approach to determining the inherent dangerousness of a felony. According to the statute a person who delivers phencyclidine (PCP), a controlled substance ... to another person who then dies either as a result of an overdose or as a result of behavior precipitated by the drug use (such as jumping off a building because of the loss of spacial perception) could be charged with first-degree murder under § 11-23-1. Conversely, the California Court of Appeal has held that when viewed in the abstract, the standard used by California courts to determine whether a felony is inherently dangerous, the furnishing or selling of PCP is not a felony that carries a high probability that death will result. People v. Taylor (1992). Consequently, the California Court of Appeal held that the felony of furnishing PCP could not serve as a predicate to a charge of second-degree felony murder. It is clear that there is a profound ideological difference in the approach of the Rhode Island Legislature from the holdings of the courts of the State of California concerning appropriate criminal charges to be preferred against one who furnishes PCP (and presumably a host of other controlled substances) to another person with death resulting therefrom. The lawmakers of the

State of Rhode Island have deemed it appropriate to charge such a person with the most serious felony in our criminal statutes—first-degree murder. It appears that the appellate court of California, however, would hold that the most serious charge against one who furnishes PCP to another person with death resulting therefrom would be involuntary manslaughter.

The Legislature's recent amendment to our murder statute as well as this court's prior jurisprudence concerning second-degree felony murder reinforces our belief that we should not adopt the California approach to determine whether a felony is inherently dangerous. The proper procedure for making, such a determination is to present the facts and circumstances of the particular case to the trier of fact and for the trier of fact to determine if a felony is inherently dangerous in the manner and the circumstances in which it was committed. This is exactly what happened in the case at bar. The trial justice instructed the jury that before it could find defendant guilty of second-degree murder, it must first find that wrongfully causing or permitting a child to be a habitual sufferer for want of food or proper care was inherently dangerous to human life "in its manner of commission." This was a proper charge. By its guilty verdict on the charge of second-degree murder, the jury obviously found that wrongfully permitting a child to be a habitual sufferer for want of food or proper care was indeed a felony inherently dangerous to human life in the circumstances of this particular case.

...

Applying this standard, we are of the opinion that the evidence offered by the state was sufficient to prove beyond a reasonable doubt each of the elements of second-degree felony murder, including that the crime of wrongfully permitting a child to be a habitual sufferer was an inherently dangerous felony in its manner of commission. The defendant's motions for judgment of acquittal on the felony-murder charge on the ground that wrongfully permitting a child to be a habitual sufferer is not an inherently dangerous felony were properly denied.

STATE v. HEARRON,
228 Kan. 693, 619 P.2d 1157 (1980)

. . .

The facts in the case are undisputed and are essentially as follows: On the evening of January 22, 1979, Ann Terry, who resided on North 70th Street in Kansas City, Kansas, was looking out a window of her home and saw three . . . youths walk up the driveway. She saw and heard them try to open the garage doors. She advised her husband, Delmer Terry, who immediately turned on an outside light over the garage. The three youths then fled. After notifying the police, the Terrys decided to look for the youths. They got into their automobile and followed a white van which was driving slowly in front of their house. After two or three blocks, the van turned left. The Terrys turned right, spotting the youths who had attempted to break into their garage. Delmer Terry stopped the car, got out, and accused them of attempting to break into his house. The boys pulled firearms. Three shots were fired, wounding Terry. Terry fell back into the car and collapsed. A nearby resident came to the scene and then called an ambulance and the police. While Mrs. Terry remained with her husband, the white van again appeared. The van stopped across from the Terry vehicle. Ann Terry was able to see defendant, William Hearron, looking at their car, before slowly driving on. Defendant was the driver and sole occupant of the van. The whole episode lasted approximately five minutes. Delmer Terry later died from his wounds.

On February 1, 1979, Kansas City police officers obtained a search warrant and searched defendant's house. The police found two . . . youths hiding in the attic. One of the boys, James Scaife, was identified as the person who shot and killed Mr. Terry. The police also found goods stolen in other January 22, 1979, burglaries. Scaife and defendant were tried together. Scaife was convicted of felony murder. Defendant was also convicted of felony murder as an aider and abettor.

On appeal, the defendant challenges the sufficiency of the evidence to establish felony murder. The defendant maintains, in substance, that the attempted burglary had been completed at the time the shooting occurred and, hence, the felony-murder rule should not be applied. ...

K.S.A. 21-3401 includes as murder the killing of a human being "committed in the perpetration or attempt to perpetrate any felony." Although that statute does not specifically include, within the felony-murder rule, the killing of another during flight from the scene of the crime, it is the established law of this state that flight from the scene of the crime may be considered as a part of the res gestae of the crime and a killing during flight may constitute felony murder. In *State v. Boone*, 124 Kan. 208, 257 P. 739 (1927), the defendant was a member of a conspiracy to burglarize a railroad station. The defendant positioned herself in the getaway vehicle several blocks away, while two of her cohorts proceeded to the railroad station to commit the crime. Her two associates attempted to break into the station but were discovered and had to flee the scene with the police in close pursuit. The defendant's associates and the police exchanged gunfire, during which one police officer was killed. The defendant, Boone, was convicted of first-degree felony murder. She appealed, contending that the burglary had been abandoned prior to the killing, so that an instruction to the jury on felony murder was improper. The court upheld the conviction, holding that the evidence was sufficient to support the conviction of felony murder. The court pointed out that the evidence was clear that the defendant's associates had been previously armed and that the killing occurred in their attempt to avoid arrest and to escape from the scene of the crime.

Other jurisdictions, likewise, hold flight from the scene of the crime to be a part of the res gestae and that a killing during the escape or flight may justify application of the felony-murder rule. Some jurisdictions hold the killing to be within the res gestae of the underlying felony if committed during escape or attempt to escape and the accused has not yet reached a point of temporary safety. Other jurisdictions hold a killing to be within the felony-murder rule if the killing and felony are so "inextricably woven" that they may be considered as "one continuous transaction" or so connected that there is no break in the chain of events.

Time, distance, and the causal relationship between the underlying felony and the killing are factors to be considered in determining whether the killing is a part of the felony and, therefore, subject to the felony-murder rule. Whether the underlying felony had been abandoned or completed prior to the killing so as to remove it from the ambit of the felony-murder rule is ordinarily a question of fact for the jury to decide. When we apply the factors of time, distance, and causal relationship to the facts of this case, we have no hesitancy in holding that it was a factual issue for the jury to determine whether the killing of Delmer Terry occurred during the commission of the attempted burglary.

The judgment of the district court is affirmed.

Other Cases--Felony Murder

People v. Stamp, 2 Cal. App. 3d 203, 82 Cal. Rptr. 598 (1979).
Koory and Stamp robbed a store while armed with a gun and a blackjack. The defendants ordered the employees along with the owner, Honeyman, to lie down on the floor so that no one would get hurt" while they removed the money from the cash register. Honeyman collapsed on the floor15-20 minutes after the robbery and was pronounced dead on arrival at the hospital. He suffered from an advanced and dangerous hardening of the arteries, but doctors concluded that the fright from the robbery had caused the fatal seizure. Stamp was charged and convicted of felony murder and sentenced to life imprisonment. Even though there was no evidence that he intended to cause the victim's death, Stamp was still held responsible and his conviction and sentence were upheld by the California Court of Appeals. (Forseeability of the death was not required).

Enmund v. Florida, 458 U.S. 782 (1982)
Defendant was. convicted of felony murder and sentenced to death. He was the getaway car driver and remained outside of the home entered by his two codefendants as the cofelons robbed and killed the couple residing in the home. The U.S. Supreme Court upheld the felony murder conviction, but ruled that the Eighth Amendment's cruel and unusual punishments clause prohibited his execution.

Tison v. Arizona, 481 U.S. 137 (1987).

Defendants, brothers Ricky and Raymond, helped their father and his cellmate escape from prison. The four hijacked a car occupied by a family, and the defendants actively participated in that event. While defendants went for water for the family whose car had been commandeered, their father and his cellmate shot and killed the family members. The father was subsequently killed and Ricky and Raymond were apprehended and convicted of felony murder and sentenced to death. The U.S. Supreme Court in a 5-4 opinion upheld their sentence.

People v. Hernandez, 624 N.E.2d 661 (N.Y. 1993).
This case raised the question whether a conviction of felony murder could be sustained where the homicide victim, a police officer was shot not by one of the defendants but by a fellow officer during a gun battle following defendant's attempted robbery. The court found that it should. The defendants argued that an earlier case following the common law approach also followed by a significant number of jurisdictions was controlling.

The court stated,

"The rationale for requiring that one of the cofelons be the shooter (or more broadly, the person who commits the final, fatal act) has been framed in several ways. Some courts have held that when the victim or a police officer or a bystander shoots and kills, it cannot be said that the killing was in furtherance of a common criminal objective. Others have concluded that under such circumstances the necessary malice or intent is missing. Under the traditional felony murder doctrine the malice necessary to make the killing murder was constructively imputed from the mens rea incidental to the perpetration of the underlying felony. . . . Still other courts have expressed policy concerns about extending felony murder liability. They have asserted that no deterrence value attaches when the felon is not the person immediately responsible for the death or have contended that an expansive felony murder rule might unreasonably hold the felons responsible for the acts of others--for instance when an unarmed felon is fleeing the scene and a bystander is hit by the bad aim of the armed victim. . .

The causal language used in our felony murder provision and elsewhere in the homicide statutes has consistently been construed by this Court by the rule in *People v. Kibbe*, where we held that the

accused need not commit the final, fatal act to be culpable for causing death. ...

Unlike defendants and those courts adopting the so-called agency theory, we believe New York's view of causality, based on a proximate cause theory, to be consistent with fundamental principles of criminal law. Advocates of the agency theory suggest that no culpable party has the requisite mens rea when a nonparticipant is the shooter. We disagree. The basic tenet of felony murders liability is that the mens rea of the underlying felony is imputed to the participant responsible for the killing. By operation of that legal fiction, the transferred intent allows the law to characterize a homicide, though unintended and not in the common design of the felons, as an intentional killing. Thus the presence or absence of the requisite mens rea is an issue turning on whether the felon is acting in furtherance of the underlying crime at the time of the homicide, not on the proximity or attenuation of the death resulting from the felon's acts. Whether the death is an immediate result or an attenuated one, the necessary mens rea is present if the causal act is part of the felonious conduct."

People v. Burroughs, 35 Cal.3d 824, 201 Cal. Rptr. 319, 678 P.2d. 894 (1984).
The defendant treated Lee Swatsenbarg, a 24-year-old who was suffering from terminal leukemia with a special blend of lemonade, colored lights and a massage. Burroughs claimed that he had successfully treated thousands of people including physicians. Borroughs instructed Lee to buy his book, "Healing for the Age of Enlightenment, and then if he wished to continue treatment with him, Lee would need to avoid having contact with his prior physician, consume only the lemonade, salt water, and herbal tea. Lee read the book and subjected himself to Burroughs' care. Not surprisingly, within two weeks, he got worse. In fact, after a month of the treatment, he suffered a hemorrhage and died. Evidence strongly suggested that the hemorrhage may have been the result of the periodic massages Burroughs performed for an additional fee. [Victim suffered a pretty painful and horrific death.]

The California Supreme court ruled that the defendant's felonious unlicensed practice of medicine did not constitute an "inherently dangerous felony" because an unlicensed practitioner may be treating a common cold, sprained finger or an individual who may suffers from the delusion that he or she is President of the United States. The prosecutor in Burroughs could have avoided the "dangerous felony" issue by charging the defendant with implied malice, second-degree murder rather than felony murder.

The court stated, "The few times we have found an underlying felony inherently dangerous (so that it would support a conviction of felony murder), the offense has been tinged with malevolence totally absent from the facts of this case."

People v. Cline, 75 Cal. Rptr 459 (1969).

Cline illegally obtained the phenobarbital and Cline, Smith, and Bragg consumed drugs together. Bragg wasn't feeling the high, so he asked for some more, and Cline obliged. After taking 52 tablets, Bragg lapsed into unconsciousness and a few days later died from a central nervous system depression caused by barbiturate intoxication. California prosecuted Cline for felony murder and he was convicted. Cline argued that the underlying felony--illegal use of narcotics--was not inherently dangerous to human life. The California Supreme Court held:

"A homicide that is a direct causal result of the commission of a felony inherently dangerous to human life, . . . constitutes at least second-degree murder. However, there can be no deterrent where the felony is not inherently dangerous, since the potential felon will not anticipate that any injury or death might arise solely from the fact that he will commit the felony. . . . The crucial issue that must be resolved in this appeal is. . . . whether the felony of furnishing a restricted dangerous drug . . . is inherently dangerous to human life."

The trial judge found the defendant's act in furnishing a restricted dangerous drug to the deceased in violation of law was inherently dangerous to human life. His finding in this respect is amply supported by the evidence. It was the uncontroverted testimony of the pathologist that the consumption of phenobarbital in unknown strength was dangerous to human life. There was clear evidence that within a period of one half hour this drug was consumed in considerable quantity by Bragg in defendant's presence and with his knowledge. Even defendant admitted that the deceased consumed 15 of these pills within one-half hour. It is also significant that the Legislature has defined this type of drug as "dangerous."

Ultimately, the appellate court held that the forseeability of the death was not required.

State v. Hoang, 755 P.2d 7 (Kan. 1988).

Two participants in arson were accidentally killed in the fire, and remaining arsonists were found guilty of felony murder.
was required for felony murder conviction.

State v. Leech, 790 P.2d 160 (Wash. 1990).

Defendant set a building on fire, and firefighters arrived to fight the fire. One firefighter ignored the alarm on his breathing apparatus that signaled his air was about out and remained in the building. He died of carbon dioxide poisoning after his air ran out. Even though the firefighter was considered negligent, the defendant was found guilty of felony murder. A reasonable person would foresee dangerous firefighting as a result of setting fire to a building, and even some negligence on the part of the firefighters is a foreseeable result of arson.

People v. Phillips, 64 Cal.2d 574 (1966).

Linda Epping, an 8-year-old died from a rare and fast growing form of eye cancer. Her mother first observed a swelling over the girl's left eye in June of 1961. They consulted with a doctor who recommended that she be taken to an ophthalmologist. They did so, and Linda was admitted on July 17th to the U.C.L.A Medical Center. Dr. Straatsma performed exploratory observation and then advised that her only hope for survival lay in immediate surgical removal of the affected eye. The Eppings did not want to do so, but ultimately on July 21st Linda's dad called the hospital and gave oral consent. They arrived at the hospital to consult with the surgeon, and while they waited they encountered Mrs. Eaton who told them that defendant (Phillips) had cured her son of a brain tumor without surgery.

The Eppings called on the defendant at his office and he assured them he could cure Linda without surgery. He urged the Eppings to take Linda out of the hospital, claiming that the doctors there would use Linda as a "human guinea pig." And would relieve the Eppings of their money as well.

Relying on defendant's statements, the Eppings took Linda out of the hospital and placed her under defendant's care. They testified that if the defendant had not represented to them that he could cure the child without surgery, they would have proceeded with the scheduled operation. The prosecution introduced medical testimony which tended to prove that if Linda had undergone surgery on July 21st her life would have been prolonged or she would have been completely cured.

Defendant treated Linda from July 22 through August 12, 1961 and charged more than 700 for three months' care, pills, and medicine. On August 13th, Linda had not improved; the Eppings dismissed the defendant.

The Eppings then sought to cure Linda by means of a Mexican herbal drug and by September placed her under the care of the Christian Science movement. They did not take her back to the hospital for treatment.

Phillips was charged and a jury convicted him of felony murder. But, the California Supreme Court stated,

> "Only such felonies as are in themselves 'inherently dangerous to human life' can support the application of the felony murder rule. We have ruled that in assessing such peril to human life inherent in any given felony 'we look to the elements of the felony in the abstract, not the particular 'facts' of the case.
>
> We have thus recognized that the felony murder doctrine expresses a highly artificial concept that deserves no extension beyond its required application. . . . No case to our knowledge in any jurisdiction has held that because death results from a course of conduct involving a felonious perpetration of a fraud the felony murder doctrine can be invoked."

People v. Hansen, 9 Cal. 4th 300 (1994).
Defendant went to the victim's apartment after victim had ripped him off in a drug deal. Defendant fired several shots at the apartment and a young girl inside was killed. Defendant was guilty of the felony of willful discharge of a firearm at an inhabited dwelling and was convicted of felony murder because that felony was deemed inherently dangerous. Although the felony does not require that persons be in the dwelling when the firearm was discharged, people are generally in or around inhabited dwellings and thus the offense inherently involves a significant risk of death.

Ford v. State, 423 S.E. 2d 255 (Ga.1992).
Defendant was a convicted felon who should not have, but did have, a pistol. He went to a friend's house and while attempting to unload the pistol it accidentally discharged, killing the victim who lived in a basement apartment of the house. Defendant's possession of the pistol was the felony offense of possession of a firearm by a convicted felon. The court held that under those facts defendant could not be convicted of felony murder because his felony was no committed in a dangerous way.

People v. Ireland, 70 Cal. 2d 522 (1969).
This case illustrates that the killing needs to be somewhat separate and independent from the felony. So if the defendant intended to assault the victim, assaulted the victim, and the victim dies, the death, although the natural and probable consequence of the assault, is not sufficiently independent to justify a felony murder conviction. Instead the court would examine defendant's mens rea as to the underlying predicate felony. (Otherwise this would expand felony murder rule to cover far more situations than intended by the legislature. The assault or battery merges into the killing and "does not retain sufficient independence to be a predicate felony."

People v. Henderson, 19 Cal. 3d 86, 560 P.2d 1180 (1977).
The felony of false imprisonment. . . effected by violence, menace, fraud or deceit." did not trigger the felony murder doctrine. The definition of the crime stipulates alternative ways to commit the crime which do not involve force or violence.

Second Degree Murder

Second-degree murder is a catchall offense, including all criminal homicides that are neither first-degree murder nor manslaughter. One good way to think of murder is to consider "typical" murders as second-degree murder. Some special circumstances, outline under first-degree murder aggravate second-degree murder to first degree. Other special circumstances, outlined under the section on manslaughter . . . reduce second-degree murder to manslaughter. Ordinarily, second degree murders include murders that are committed without premeditation; with the intent to inflict serious bodily injury but not death; with depraved heart, "that is without the intent to kill but with extreme recklessness that shows a wanton disregard for human life; or without any intent to kill or injury but where death occurs during the commission of some felonies." Samaha, *Criminal Law*, 5th ed., at 314

PEOPLE v. THOMAS,
85 Mich. App. 618, 272 N.W.2d 157 (1978)

D.E. HOLBROOK, JR., P.J.
Charged with second-degree murder, defendant was convicted by a jury of involuntary manslaughter. Thereafter, sentenced to a prison term of 5 to 15 years, defendant appeals as of right.

FACTS
The victim, a 19-year-old male "catatonic schizophrenic", was at the time of his death a resident of Oak Haven, a religious practical training school. When it appeared he was not properly responding to ordinary treatment, defendant, the work coordinator at Oak Haven, obtained permission from the victim's parents to discipline him if such seemed necessary. Thereafter defendant, together with another supervisor at Oak Haven, took decedent to the edge of the campus, whereupon decedent's pants were taken down, following which he was spanked with a rubber hose. Such disciplinary session lasted approximately 15 to 30 minutes. During a portion thereof decedent's hands were tied behind his back for failure to cooperate.

Following the disciplinary session aforesaid, defendant testified that the young man improved for awhile but then commenced to backslide. Defendant again received permission from decedent's parents to subject him to further discipline. On September 30, 1976, defendant again took decedent to the approximate same location, removed his pants, bound his hands behind him with a rope looped over a tree limb and proceeded to beat him with a doubled-over rubber hose. This beating lasted approximately 45 minutes to an hour. While the evidence conflicted, it appears that the victim was struck between 30 to 100 times. The beating resulted in severe bruises ranging from the victim's waist to his feet. Decedent's roommate testified that decedent had open bleeding sores on his thighs. On the date of death, which was nine days after the beating, decedent's legs were immobile. At no time did defendant obtain medical attention for the victim.

Defendant admitted he had exercised poor judgment, after seeing the bruises, in continuing the discipline. He further testified that in the two days following the discipline, decedent seemed to be suffering from the flu, but by Sunday was up and walking and was in apparent good health until one week following the beating, when decedent became sick with nausea and an upset stomach. These symptoms continued for two days, when decedent died.

As a result of the autopsy, one Dr. Clark testified that the bruises were the result of a trauma and that decedent was in a state of continuous traumatization because he was trying to walk on his injured legs. Dr. Clark testified that decedent's legs were swollen to possibly twice their normal size. He further testified that the actual cause of death was acute pulmonary edema, resulting from the aspiration of stomach contents. Said aspiration caused a laryngeal spasm, causing decedent to suffocate on his own vomit. Although pulmonary edema was the direct cause of death, Dr. Clark testified that said condition usually had some underlying cause and that, while there were literally hundreds of potential underlying causes, it was his opinion that in the instant case the underlying cause was the trauma to decedent's legs. In explaining how the trauma ultimately led to the pulmonary edema, Dr. Clark testified that the trauma to the legs produced "crush syndrome" or "blast trauma", also known as "tubular necrosis".

"Crush syndrome" is a condition caused when a part of the body has been compressed for a long period of time and then released. In such cases, there is a tremendous amount of tissue damage to the body part that has been crushed. When the compression is relieved, the tissues begin to return to their normal position, but due to the compression, gaps appear between the layers of tissues, and these areas fill up with blood and other body fluids, causing swelling. In the present case, Dr. Clark estimated that about 10-15% of decedent's entire body fluids were contained in the legs, adding an additional ten pounds in weight to the normal weight of the legs and swelling them to twice their normal size. This extra blood and body fluid decreased the amount of blood available for circulation in the rest of the body and would cause the person to become weak, faint and pass out if he attempted to sit up or do other activities. Decedent was sitting up when he died. It was Dr. Clark's opinion that the causal connection between the trauma and death was more than medically probable and that it was "medically likely". He further testified he could say with a reasonable degree of medical certainty that the trauma to the legs was the cause of death.

Appellant claims that the prosecution failed to establish the malice element of second-degree murder. We disagree. Malice or intent to kill may be inferred from the acts of the defendant. In People v Morrin, Justice LEVIN, stated that the intent to kill may be implied where the actor actually intends to inflict great bodily harm or the natural tendency of his behavior is to cause death or great bodily harm. In the instant case defendant's savage and brutal beating of the decedent is amply sufficient to establish malice. He clearly intended to beat the victim and the natural tendency of defendant's behavior was to cause great bodily harm.

Appellant also claims that the prosecution failed to establish the elements of involuntary manslaughter. Again we disagree. Involuntary manslaughter may be based on the failure to perform a legal duty. Defendant was a supervisor of Oak Haven, stood in a position of authority over the victim and, by talking with the victim's parents and obtaining their permission to discipline the decedent, he directly and voluntarily assumed a parental function, and stood in a position of loco parentis to the decedent. Under such circumstances, defendant's beating of the victim coupled with his failure to provide medical attention, when decedent was unable to obtain same himself, violated defendant's legal duty to care for the victim. The elements of involuntary manslaughter were adequately established.

Lastly, defendant claims that the prosecution failed to present sufficient evidence of the causal connection between defendant's acts and the victim's death. Again we disagree.

In *People v Geiger*, defendant had struck his wife two or three times with his open hand and pushed her to the ground in such a manner that she bumped her head against the car. Defendant picked her up and put her in his car. While a need for immediate medical attention existed, defendant obtained none until after waiting 6 to 8 hours, during which time he drove over 180 miles. In *Geiger* the medical cause of death was "`aspiration of the gastric contents into the air passages with resultant shock, asphyxia, collapse and pulmonary edema.'" In short, sometime after the beating decedent choked to death on her own vomit. The pathologist who performed the autopsy testified he thought that the blows to the head or side of the face caused the minor brain damage which contributed to diminution of laryngeal reflexes, allowing the asphyxiation, and had it not been for the blows, the victim would have been able to vomit and remove her stomach contents in a normal fashion.

In *People v McFee*, where defendant, over a period of several hours, inflicted a severe beating upon a 12-year-old boy resulting in particles of partially digested food to become stuck in the vocal cord causing a cardiac arrest from the coughing reflex, the pathologist testified that in his best medical judgment there was a definite relationship between the bruising and the boy's death.

In both *Geiger* and *McFee* the Court found the prosecution to have established a sufficient causal relationship. The case at bar is closely analogous to the chain of events that led to the victim's death and that causation was not only medically probable but medically likely. In *People v Geiger*, the Court quoted with approval from 26 Am Jur, Homicide, § 52, p 195, wherein it states:

> "It is not indispensable to a conviction that the wounds be necessarily fatal and the direct cause of death. It is sufficient that they cause death indirectly through a chain of natural effects and causes unchanged by human action."

Depraved Heart Murder

Depraved heart murders are killings resulting from extremely reckless conduct of the defendant. The common law referred to "depraved heart or wanton murder, because they were the result of a depraved mind, an abandoned and malignant heart or wickedness." Acting with a depraved heart was considered as acting with implied malice aforethought.

Today it is more common to use the term reckless murder, and most states treat depraved heart murder as second-degree murder. Depraved heart murder occurs when a person kills another as a result of the deliberate perpetration of a knowingly dangerous act with reckless and wanton unconcern and indifference as to whether anyone is harmed or not. Defendants must create the risk, but courts differ whether the defendant must be aware of the risk or whether it is sufficient that a reasonable person would have been aware of the risk. The risk must be greater than that required in negligence cases, but it is difficult at times (and a jury decision) to draw the line between greater that reckless risk sufficient for murder and one negligence sufficient for manslaughter.

The Model Penal Code categorizes this as a killing that is committed recklessly under circumstances manifesting extreme indifference to the value of human life. One example cited in the MPC is shooting a loaded gun into an occupied car.

Other Cases-Depraved Heart Murder

Berry v. Superior Court, 256 Cal Rptr. 344 Cal. Ct. App. 1989).
The defendant purchased a bit bull from a breeder of fighting dogs. He trained the dog for professional dog fighting fights but tied the dog to the inside of a six-foot unenclosed fence to guard marijuana plants that he was illegally growing behind his house. Berry's next-door neighbor momentarily left her two-year-old child, James, playing on her patio. James wandered onto Berry's yard and was mauled to death by the dog. The court upheld his conviction for "killing with an abandoned and malignant heart."

State v. Doub, 95 P3d 116 (Kan. Ct. App. 2004).
Defendant drank six beers, struck two parked vehicles with his truck. Drove off because he didn't want to get caught for drinking and driving. He then drank more liquor, smoked crack cocaine, and two hours later drove into the rear of a car and killed a nine-year-old passenger. Expert testimony was that he drove at a rapid rate, drove up on top of the car, and drove down into the pavement propelling the car off the car and into a tree. Defendant again left the scene. He later denied driving and claimed his truck had been stolen. The nine-year old died 15 hours later as a result of traumatic injuries. Defendant confessed to his girlfriend six months later that he had been drinking, smoking crack, and had an argument with his ex-wife prior to the collision. The court of appeals upheld his second-degree depraved heart murder defined in Kansas as "the killing of a human being committed unintentionally but recklessly under circumstances manifesting extreme indifference to the value of human life.

MANSLAUGHTER

Manslaughter comprises a second category of homicide and is defined as an unlawful killing of another human being without malice aforethought. The common law distinguished between voluntary manslaughter and the less severe offense of involuntary manslaughter. The common law distinction continues to appear in many state statutes. Other state statutes distinguish between degrees of manslaughter, and a third approach provides for a single offense of manslaughter.

Voluntary manslaughter involves the killing of another human being in a sudden heat of passion in response to adequate provocation. (Adequate provocation is considered a provocation that would cause a person to lose self-control.) Involuntary manslaughter is the killing of another human being as a result of criminal negligence. Criminal negligence involves a gross deviation from the standard of care that a reasonable person would practice under similar circumstances." See, Lippman, *Contemporary Criminal Law*, 4th ed., at 327.

Voluntary Manslaughter

A killing that would otherwise be murder committed in response to certain provocation has traditionally been regarded as being without malice aforethought and therefore voluntary manslaughter. The defendant acts with the state of mind necessary for malice aforethought (i.e., intent to kill, intent to cause serious physical injury, depraved heart), but the provocation reduces the killing from murder to manslaughter. (See Dix, *Gilberts Law Summaries, Criminal Law*, at 200-201)

Whether provocation is reasonable under the circumstances is traditionally judged by an objective standard (would a reasonable person have been provoked.) Generally, the provocation must be such as might render ordinary persons of average disposition liable to ace rashly without deliberation, and from passion rather than judgment.

According to Dix, courts struggle with the extent to which the reasonable person should be regarded as having the peculiar characteristics that may have made the defendant unusually susceptible to provocation. Should the reasonable person step into the shoes of the defendant? Should all of the defendant's characteristics be taken into account? Should some of them? At some point, giving the reasonable person the defendant's characteristics destroys the objective nature of the standard. Some courts hold that the reasonable person should not be regarded as having any of the defendant's characteristic. See *Bedder v. Director of Public Prosecutions*, below. Other courts adopt a compromise position that lets them consider some of the defendant's personal characteristics. Under this approach, the reasonable person is not to be regarded as having any unusual reduced capacity for self-control that the defendant may have had. See, e.g., *State v. Ott*, 686 P.2d 1001 (Or. 1984). The MPC provides that the reasonableness of the disturbance that reduced a killing to manslaughter is to be determined from the viewpoint of a person in the defendant's position under the circumstances as the defendant believed them to be.

There has been some tendency to treat some situations as insufficient to constitute adequate provocation as a matter of law. For example, the traditional view is that words alone, no matter how insulting are not adequate provocation. See, e.g., *Lang v. State*, 250 A.2d 276 (Md. 1969). But, a few jurisdictions have rejected this rigid rule, particularly if the words are informational--i.e., conveying information of a fact that would constitute reasonable provocation if observed rather than simply insulting or abusive. See, e.g., *State v. Flory*, 276 P.458 (Wyo. 1929) (confession of rape). Similarly, many courts hold that a minor blow does not constitute adequate provocation, because it would not provoke a reasonable person to a killing passion. However, a violent and painful blow can be sufficient provocation. See *People v. Harris*, 134 N.E.2d 315 (Ill. 1956) (victim severely beat defendant with a nightstick). If the defendant provoked the blow, and then kills in response to a vigorous blow, *State v. Ferguson*, 20 S.C.L. (2 Hill), 619 (S.C. 1835) indicates that the homicide should not be reduced to voluntary manslaughter since the defendant was at fault and the initial aggressor. Discovery of one's spouse in the act of committing adultery has been held as a matter of law sufficient for a jury to find provocation. This "paramour rule," a common law presumption, was limited to husbands catching their wives in adultery and did not extend to wives catching their husbands. The modern trend is to extend the rule beyond situations where one spouse (either husband or wife) actually catches the other in the act, and some courts find sufficient provocation where the defendant is told of the spouse's adultery or even simply sees a person known to be having an affair with the spouse. See, e.g., *People v. Bridgehouse*, 47 Cal.2d 406 (1956). Mutual assault and battery was recognized as adequate provocation. Thus, if two persons voluntarily engage in a fight, which resulted in one killing the other, the homicide is only manslaughter. In this case it is not controlling which person struck the first blow because the intent to fight was mutual. Note however, that killing may not be reduced to manslaughter if at the beginning of the fight the defendant took an unfair advantage. See, e.g., *Whitehead v. State*, 262 A.2d 316 (Md. 1970).

If the defendant was mistaken in his belief that the situation constituted adequate provocation, the killing should be reduced to manslaughter if defendant's erroneous belief was a reasonable one. But, case law may vary on this.

What happens when the person killed is not the one who provoked? If the defendant intends to kill the provoking party, but killed someone else, either by accident or because he was mistaken about who had provoked him, the killing is still only voluntary manslaughter. See, e.g., *State v. Griego*, 294 P.2d 282 (N.M. 1956). If, however, the defendant intended to kill someone he knew was not the person who provoked him, the killing is not reduced to manslaughter--even if there was adequate provocation. (If defendant is so enraged that he simply strikes out and kills an innocent third party, this killing should not be reduced to voluntary manslaughter. See, e.g., *White v. State*, 72 S.W. 173 (Tex. 1902).)

No matter how reasonable the provocation, a killing will not be reduced to manslaughter unless the defendant was actually provoked. This is the subjective requirement of the sudden heat of passion rule. So, if a reasonable person would have suddenly lost control due to adequate provocation but the defendant was in fact not so bothered by the provocation, there will be no reduction to manslaughter.

The sudden heat of passion rule places emphasis on the time between the provocation and the killing. The majority position is than an objective standard is applied. Would a reasonable person's passions have cooled? See, e.g., *Sheppard v. State*, 10 So.2d 822 (Ala. 1942). The minority position is that the rule applies when the defendant's own passions have not subsided. Under this approach, it is immaterial that other's passions would have cooled during that period of time. See, e.g., *State v. Hazlett*, 113 .W. 374 (N.D. 1907). Although an adequate cooling period may have passed, intervening events can remind the defendant of the provoking event and "reinflame" his passions. Courts have varied on whether the cooling period should begin anew with reinflaming occurrence. See, e.g., *State v. Gounagias*, 153 P.9 (Wash. 1915), below. Some common law courts limited the impact of provocation to twenty-four hours, but the modern approach is to view the facts and circumstances of a case and determined whether a reasonable persons blood would have cooled. In *State v. Flory*, above, the court held that when the defendant who had been informed that his father-in-law had raped his wife and had walked all night long (more than 24 hours) to get to his home and kill him, he was still acting under the heat of passion.

GIROUARD v. STATE,
321 Md. 532 583 A.2d 718 (1991)

COLE, Judge.

In this case we are asked to reconsider whether the types of provocation sufficient to mitigate the crime of murder to manslaughter should be limited to the categories we have heretofore recognized, or whether the sufficiency of the provocation should be decided by the factfinder on a case-by-case basis. Specifically, we must determine whether words alone are provocation adequate to justify a conviction of manslaughter rather than one of second degree murder.

The Petitioner, Steven S. Girouard, and the deceased, Joyce M. Girouard, had been married for about two months on October 28, 1987, the night of Joyce's death. Both parties, who met while working in the same building, were in the army. They married after having known each other for approximately three months. The evidence at trial indicated that the marriage was often tense and strained, and there was some evidence that after marrying Steven, Joyce had resumed a relationship with her old boyfriend, Wayne.

On the night of Joyce's death, Steven overheard her talking on the telephone to her friend, whereupon she told the friend that she had asked her first sergeant for a hardship discharge because her husband did not love her anymore. Steven went into the living room where Joyce was on the phone and asked her what she meant by her comments; she responded, "nothing." Angered by her lack of response, Steven kicked away the plate of food Joyce had in front of her. He then went to lie down in the bedroom.

Joyce followed him into the bedroom, stepped up onto the bed and onto Steven's back, pulled his hair and said, "What are you going to do, hit me?" She continued to taunt him by saying, "I never did want to marry you and you are a lousy fuck and you remind me of my dad."[1] The barrage of insults continued with her telling Steven that she wanted a divorce, that the marriage had been a mistake and that she had never wanted to marry him. She also told him she had seen his commanding officer and filed charges against him for abuse. She then asked Steven, "What are you going to do?" Receiving no response, she continued her verbal attack. She added that she had filed charges against him in the Judge Advocate General's Office (JAG) and that he would probably be court martialed.[2]

When she was through, Steven asked her if she had really done all those things, and she responded in the affirmative. He left the bedroom with his pillow in his arms and proceeded to the kitchen where he procured a long handled kitchen knife. He returned to Joyce in the bedroom with the knife behind the pillow. He testified that he was enraged and that he kept waiting for Joyce to say she was kidding, but Joyce continued talking. She said she had learned a lot from the marriage and that it had been a mistake. She also told him she would remain in their apartment after he moved out. When he questioned how she would afford it, she told him she would claim her brain-damaged sister as a dependent and have the sister move in. Joyce reiterated that the marriage was a big mistake, that she did not love him and that the divorce would be better for her.

After pausing for a moment, Joyce asked what Steven was going to do. What he did was lunge at her with the kitchen knife he had hidden behind the pillow and stab her 19 times. Realizing what he had done, he dropped the knife and went to the bathroom to shower off Joyce's blood. Feeling like he wanted to die, Steven went back to the kitchen and found two steak knives with which he slit his own wrists. He lay down on the bed waiting to die, but when he realized that he would not die from his self-inflicted wounds, he got up and called the police, telling the dispatcher that he had just murdered his wife.

When the police arrived they found Steven wandering around outside his apartment building. Steven was despondent and tearful and seemed detached, according to police officers who had been at the scene. He was unconcerned about his own wounds, talking only about how much he loved his wife and how he could not believe what he had done. Joyce Girouard was pronounced dead at the scene.

At trial, defense witness, psychologist, Dr.

William Stejskal, testified that Steven was out of touch with his own capacity to experience anger or express hostility. He stated that the events of October 28, 1987, were entirely consistent with Steven's personality, that Steven had "basically reach[ed] the limit of his ability to swallow his anger, to rationalize his wife's behavior, to tolerate, or actually to remain in a passive mode with that. He essentially went over the limit of his ability to bottle up those strong emotions. What ensued was a very extreme explosion of rage that was intermingled with a great deal of panic." Another defense witness, psychiatrist, Thomas Goldman, testified that Joyce had a "compulsive need to provoke jealousy so that she's always asking for love and at the same time destroying and undermining any chance that she really might have to establish any kind of mature love with anybody."

Steven Girouard was convicted, at a court trial in the Circuit Court for Montgomery County, of second degree murder and was sentenced to 22 years incarceration, 10 of which were suspended. Upon his release, Petitioner is to be on probation for five years, two years supervised and three years unsupervised. The Court of Special Appeals affirmed the judgment of the circuit court in an unreported opinion. We granted certiorari to determine whether the circumstances of the case presented provocation adequate to mitigate the second degree murder charge to manslaughter.

Petitioner relies primarily on out of state cases to provide support for his argument that the provocation to mitigate murder to manslaughter should not be limited only to the traditional circumstances of: extreme assault or battery upon the defendant; mutual combat; defendant's illegal arrest; injury or serious abuse of a close relative of the defendant's; or the sudden discovery of a spouse's adultery. Petitioner argues that manslaughter is a catchall for homicides which are criminal but that lack the malice essential for a conviction of murder. Steven argues that the trial judge did find provocation (although he held it inadequate to mitigate murder) and that the categories of provocation adequate to mitigate should be broadened to include factual situations such as this one.

The State counters by stating that although there is no finite list of legally adequate provocations, the common law has developed to a point at which it may be said there are some concededly provocative acts that society is not prepared to recognize as reasonable. Words spoken by the victim, no matter how abusive or taunting, fall into a category society should not accept as adequate provocation. According to the State, if abusive words alone could mitigate murder to manslaughter, nearly every domestic argument ending in the death of one party could be mitigated to manslaughter. This, the State avers, is not an acceptable outcome. Thus, the State argues that the courts below were correct in holding that the taunting words by Joyce Girouard were not provocation adequate to reduce Steven's second degree murder charge to voluntary manslaughter.

Initially, we note that the difference between murder and manslaughter is the presence or absence of malice. Voluntary manslaughter has been defined as "an *intentional* homicide, done in a sudden heat of passion, caused by adequate provocation, before there has been a reasonable opportunity for the passion to cool" There are certain facts that may mitigate what would normally be murder to manslaughter. For example, we have recognized as falling into that group: (1) discovering one's spouse in the act of sexual intercourse with another; (2) mutual combat; (3) assault and battery. There is also authority recognizing injury to one of the defendant's relatives or to a third party, and death resulting from resistance of an illegal arrest as adequate provocation for mitigation to manslaughter. Those acts mitigate homicide to manslaughter because they create passion in the defendant and are not considered the product of free will.

In order to determine whether murder should be mitigated to manslaughter we look to the circumstances surrounding the homicide and try to discover if it was provoked by the victim. Over the facts of the case we lay the template of the so-called "Rule of Provocation." The courts of this State have repeatedly set forth the requirements of the Rule of Provocation:

1. There must have been adequate provocation;
2. The killing must have been in the heat of passion;
3. It must have been a sudden heat of passion — that is, the killing must have followed the

provocation before there had been a reasonable opportunity for the passion to cool;
4. There must have been a causal connection between the provocation, the passion, and the fatal act.

We shall assume without deciding that the second, third, and fourth of the criteria listed above were met in this case. We focus our attention on an examination of the ultimate issue in this case, that is, whether the provocation of Steven by Joyce was enough in the eyes of the law so that the murder charge against Steven should have been mitigated to voluntary manslaughter. For provocation to be "adequate," it must be "`calculated to inflame the passion of a reasonable man and tend to cause him to act for the moment from passion rather than reason.'" The issue we must resolve, then, is whether the taunting words uttered by Joyce were enough to inflame the passion of a *reasonable* man so that that man would be sufficiently infuriated so as to strike out in hot-blooded blind passion to kill her. Although we agree with the trial judge that there was needless provocation by Joyce, we also agree with him that the provocation was not adequate to mitigate second degree murder to voluntary manslaughter.

Although there are few Maryland cases discussing the issue at bar, those that do hold that words alone are not adequate provocation. Most recently, in *Sims v. State,* we held that "[i]nsulting words or gestures, no matter how opprobrious, do not amount to an affray, and standing alone, do not constitute adequate provocation." That case involved the flinging of racial slurs and derogatory comments by the victim at the defendant. That conduct did not constitute adequate provocation.

In *Lang v. State* the Court of Special Appeals stated that it is "generally held that mere words, threats, menaces or gestures, however offensive and insulting, do not constitute adequate provocation." Before the shooting, the victim had called the appellant "a chump" and "a chicken," dared the appellant to fight, shouted obscenities at him and shook his fist at him. The provocation, again, was not enough to mitigate murder.

The court in *Lang* did note, however, that words can constitute adequate provocation if they are accompanied by conduct indicating a present intention and ability to cause the defendant bodily harm. Clearly, no such conduct was exhibited by Joyce in this case. While Joyce did step on Steven's back and pull his hair, he could not reasonably have feared bodily harm at her hands. This, to us, is certain based on Steven's testimony at trial that Joyce was about 5'1" tall and weighed 115 pounds, while he was 6'2" tall, weighing over 200 pounds. Joyce simply did not have the size or strength to cause Steven to fear for his bodily safety. Thus, since there was no ability on the part of Joyce to cause Steven harm, the words she hurled at him could not, under the analysis in *Lang*, constitute legally sufficient provocation.

Other jurisdictions overwhelmingly agree with our cases and hold that words alone are not adequate provocation. One jurisdiction that does allow provocation brought about by prolonged stress, anger and hostility caused by marital problems to provide grounds for a verdict of voluntary manslaughter rather than murder is Pennsylvania. The Pennsylvania court left the determination of the weight and credibility of the testimony regarding the marital stress and arguments to the trier of fact.

We are unpersuaded by that one case awash in a sea of opposite holdings. ... *Perkins on Criminal Law*, at p. 62, states that it is "with remarkable uniformity that even words generally regarded as `fighting words' in the community have no recognition as adequate provocation in the eyes of the law." It is noted that mere words or gestures, however offensive, insulting, or abusive they may be, are not, according to the great weight of authority, adequate to reduce a homicide, although committed in a passion provoked by them, from murder to manslaughter, especially when the homicide was intentionally committed with a deadly weapon.

Thus, with no reservation, we hold that the provocation in this case was not enough to cause a reasonable man to stab his provoker 19 times. Although a psychologist testified to Steven's mental problems and his need for acceptance and love, we agree with the Court of Special Appeals speaking through Judge Moylan that "there must be not simply provocation in psychological fact, but one of certain fairly well-defined classes of provocation recognized as being adequate as a matter of law." The standard is one of reasonableness; it does not and should not focus on the peculiar frailties of mind of the Petitioner. That standard of reasonableness has not been met here. We cannot in good conscience countenance holding that a verbal domestic argument ending in the death of one spouse can result in a conviction of manslaughter. We agree with the trial judge that social necessity dictates our holding. Domestic arguments easily escalate into furious fights. We perceive no reason for a holding in favor of those who find the easiest way to end a domestic dispute is by killing the offending spouse.

COMMONWEALTH V. GEORGE A. SCHNOPPS, 383 Mass. 178 (1981)

At the trial of a defendant charged with the murder of his estranged wife, the judge erred in refusing to instruct the jury on voluntary manslaughter where there was evidence from which the jury could have found that the defendant shot his wife in the heat of passion after her sudden admission of adultery.

ABRAMS, J.

On October 13, 1979, Marilyn R. Schnopps was fatally shot by her estranged husband George A. Schnopps. A jury convicted Schnopps of murder in the first degree. . . . Schnopps claims that the trial judge erred by refusing to instruct the jury on voluntary manslaughter. We agree.

Schnopps does not claim that there was insufficient evidence to warrant the jury's verdict of murder in the first degree. He claims, however, that there is evidence which required the judge to instruct the jury on voluntary manslaughter. In deciding whether the judge should have charged on manslaughter, we assume the version of the facts most favorable to the defendant.

[The court summarized the facts of the case,...and you can read them in detail in Schnopps II (case follows). . . .]

The issue raised by Schnopps' appeal is whether

in these circumstances the judge was required to instruct the jury on voluntary manslaughter. Instructions on voluntary manslaughter must be given if there is evidence of provocation deemed adequate in law to cause the accused to lose his self-control in the heat of passion, and if the killing followed the provocation before sufficient time had elapsed for the accused's temper to cool. A verdict of voluntary manslaughter requires the trier of fact to conclude that there is a causal connection between the provocation, the heat of passion, and the killing.

Schnopps argues that "[t]he existence of sufficient provocation is not foreclosed absolutely because a defendant learns of a fact from oral statements rather than from personal observation," and that a sudden admission of adultery is equivalent to a discovery of the act itself, and is sufficient evidence of provocation, Schnopps asserts that his wife's statements constituted a "peculiarly immediate and intense offense to a spouse's sensitivities." He concedes that the words at issue are indicative of past as well as present adultery. Schnopps claims, however, that his wife's admission of adultery was made for the first time on the day of the killing, and hence the evidence

of provocation was sufficient to trigger jury consideration of voluntary manslaughter as a possible verdict.

The Commonwealth quarrels with the defendant's claim, asserting that the defendant knew of his wife's infidelity for some months, and hence the killing did not follow immediately upon the provocation. Therefore, the Commonwealth concludes, a manslaughter instruction would have been improper. The flaw in the Commonwealth's argument is that conflicting testimony and inferences from the evidence are to be resolved by the trier of fact, not the judge.

. . .

We do not question the propriety of the verdict returned by the jury. However, based on the defendant's testimony, voluntary manslaughter was a possible verdict. Therefore, it was error to withhold "from the consideration of the jury another verdict which, although they might not have reached it, was nevertheless open to them upon the evidence."

COMMONWEALTH v. SCHNOPPS, 390 Mass. 722 (1984) (After retrial...the rest of the story)

ABRAMS, J.

At a retrial, the defendant, George A. Schnopps, again was convicted of murder in the first degree. On appeal, Schnopps's sole argument is that we should exercise our power . . . to grant him a new trial or to direct the entry of a verdict of a lesser degree of guilt. We conclude that we should not exercise our power in favor of the defendant. We affirm.

We summarize the facts. On October 13, 1979, the defendant fatally shot his wife of fourteen years. The victim and the defendant began having marital problems approximately six months earlier when Schnopps became suspicious that his wife was seeing another man. Schnopps and his wife argued during this period over his suspicion that she had a relationship with a particular man, whom the defendant regarded as a "bum." On a few occasions the defendant threatened to harm his wife with scissors, with a knife, with a shotgun, and with a plastic pistol. A

few days prior to the slaying, Schnopps threatened to make his wife suffer as "she had never suffered before." However, there is no evidence that Schnopps physically harmed the victim prior to October 13.

Three weeks before the slaying, Schnopps telephoned his home using the signal he believed the other man had been using to call the victim. His wife answered the telephone and said, "Hello, Lover." When Schnopps identified himself, his wife hung up the telephone. On that day she moved to her mother's home and took their three children with her.
On October 12, 1979, while at work, the defendant asked a coworker to buy him a gun. He told the coworker he had been receiving threatening telephone calls. After work, Schnopps and the coworker went to Pownal, Vermont, where the coworker purchased a .22 caliber pistol and a box of ammunition for the defendant. The defendant purchased a starter pistol to scare the caller if there was an attempted break-in. The defendant stated he wanted to

protect himself and his son, who had moved back with him.

The defendant and his coworker had some drinks at a Vermont bar. The coworker instructed the defendant in the use of the .22 caliber pistol. The defendant paid his coworker for the gun and the ammunition. While at the bar the defendant told the coworker that he was "mad enough to kill." The coworker asked the defendant "if he was going to get in any trouble with the gun." Schnopps replied that "a bullet was too good for her, he would choke her to death."

On the day of the slaying, the defendant told a neighbor he was going to call his wife and have her come down to pick up some things. He said he was thinking of letting his wife have the apartment. This was the first time the defendant indicated he might leave the apartment. He asked the neighbor to keep the youngest child with her if his wife brought her so he could talk with his wife.

Shortly before 3 P.M., the defendant called a neighbor and said he had shot his wife and also had tried to kill himself. The defendant told the first person to arrive at his apartment that he shot his wife "because of what she had done to him."

Neighbors notified the police of the slaying. On their arrival, the defendant asked an officer to check to see if his wife had died. The officer told him that she had, and he replied, "[G]ood." A police officer took the defendant to a hospital for treatment of his wounds. The officer had known the defendant for twenty-nine years. The defendant said to the officer that he would not hurt a fly. The officer advised Schnopps not to say anything until he spoke with a lawyer. The defendant then said, "The devil made me do it." The officer repeated his warning at least three times. The defendant said that he "loved [his] wife and [his] children." He added, "Just between you and I, . . . I did it because she was cheating on me."

The defendant gave a statement to the police. He said that, when he spoke to his wife, he wanted to keep the family together. His wife replied, "I've got something bigger and better than you'll ever be." Pointing to her crotch, she said, "You'll never get into this again . . . . [You] are never going to touch me again." The defendant said

that these words "cracked" him. He explained that everything went "around" in his head, that he saw "stars." He went "toward the guns in the dining room." He asked his wife, "[Why] don't you try" (to salvage the marriage). He told her, "I have nothing more to live for," but she replied, "Never, I am never coming back to you." The victim jumped up to leave and the defendant shot her. He was seated at that time. He told her she would never love anyone else. After shooting the victim, the defendant said, "I want to go with you," and he shot himself.

The victim died of three gunshot wounds, to the heart and lungs. Ballistic evidence indicated that the gun was fired within two to four feet of the victim. The evidence also indicated that one shot had been fired while the victim was on the floor.

The defense offered evidence from friends and coworkers who noticed a deterioration in the defendant's physical and emotional health after the victim had left the defendant. The defendant wept at work and at home; he did not eat or sleep well; he was distracted and agitated. On two occasions, he was taken home early by supervisors because of emotional upset and agitation. He was drinking. The defendant was diagnosed at a local hospital as suffering from a "severe anxiety state." He was given Valium. The defendant claimed he was receiving threatening telephone calls.

The defendant and the Commonwealth each offered expert testimony on the issue of criminal responsibility. The defendant's expert claimed the defendant was suffering from a "major affective disorder, a major depression," a "psychotic condition," at the time of the slaying. The expert was of the opinion the defendant was not criminally responsible. The Commonwealth's expert claimed that the defendant's depression was a grief reaction, a reaction generally associated with death. The expert was of the opinion the defendant was grieving, over the breakup of his marriage, but that he was criminally responsible.

The judge instructed the jurors on every possible verdict available on the evidence. (remember this was the problem with the first trial—See Schnopps I). On appeal, the defendant "does not now quarrel with that range of possible verdicts nor with the instruction which the trial court gave to the jury . . . . [Nor] does . . . [the defendant] now dispute that there may be some view of . . . some of the evidence which might support the verdict returned in this matter." Rather, the defendant claims that his case is "not of the nature that judges and juries, in weighing evidence, ordinarily equate with murder in the first degree."

The defendant argues that the evidence as a whole demonstrates that his wife was the emotional aggressor, and that her conduct shattered him and destroyed him as a husband and a father. The defendant points to the fact that he was not a hoodlum or gangster, that he had no prior criminal record, and that he had a "good relationship" with his wife prior to the last six months of their marriage. The defendant concludes these factors should be sufficient to entitle him to a new trial or the entry of a verdict of a lesser degree of guilt.

The Commonwealth argues that the evidence is more than ample to sustain the verdict. The Commonwealth points out that at the time of the killing there was not a good relationship between the parties; that the defendant had threatened to harm his wife physically on several occasions; and that he had threatened to kill his wife. The defendant obtained a gun and ammunition the day before the killing. The defendant arranged to have his younger child cared for by a neighbor when his wife came to see him. The jury could have found that Schnopps lured his wife to the apartment by suggesting that he might leave and let her live in it with the children. The evidence permits a finding that the killing occurred within a few minutes of the victim's arrival at the defendant's apartment and before she had time to take off her jacket. From the facts, the jury could infer that the defendant had planned to kill his wife on October 13, and that the killing was not the spontaneous result of the quarrel but was the result of a deliberately premeditated plan to murder his wife almost as soon as she arrived.

Ballistic evidence indicated that as the victim was lying on the floor, a third bullet was fired into her. From the number of wounds, the type of weapon used, as well as the effort made to procure the weapon, the jurors could find that the defendant had "a conscious and fixed purpose to kill continuing for a length of time."

If conflicting inferences are possible, "it is for the jury to determine where the truth lies." There was ample evidence which suggested the jurors' conclusion that the defendant acted with deliberately premeditated malice aforethought. The defendant's domestic difficulties were fully explored before the jury. The jurors rejected the defendant's claim that his domestic difficulties were an adequate ground to return a verdict of a lesser degree of guilt. The degree of guilt, of course, is a jury determination. The evidence supports a conclusion that the defendant, angered by his wife's conduct, shot her with deliberately premeditated malice aforethought. The jurors were in the best position to determine whether the domestic difficulties were so egregious as to require a verdict of a lesser degree of guilt. We conclude, on review of the record as a whole, that there is no reason for us to order a new trial or direct the entry of a lesser verdict..

Other Cases--Heat of Passion

Mullaney v. Wilbur, 321 U.S. 684(1975).
[The question before the Court was which party bears the burden of proving (or disproving) the sudden heat of passion: the defendant or the state.]

Wilbur beat another man to death in a Maine hotel room after the victim made an unwanted homosexual advance on Wilbur. The trial court instructed that "if the prosecution established that the homicide was both intentional and unlawful, malice aforethought was to be conclusively implied unless the defendant proved by a fair preponderance of the evidence that he acted in the heat of passion on sudden provocation." The U.S. Supreme Court held that the jury instruction was unconstitutional because it shifted the burden to the defendant to disprove an element of the crime. (Under Maine law, malice was an element of the crime of murder.)

Bedder v. Director of Public Prosecutions, 2 ALL E.R. 801 (H.L.1954)
In this case an 18-year-old impotent man tried to have sex with a prostitute. The prostitute jeered at him, so he grabbed her. She slapped him and punched him in the stomach to get away. He grabbed her shoulders and pushed her back, and then as the defendant stated "she kicked me in the privates." He took his knife from his pocket and stabbed her twice.

Defendant claimed that the provocation by the prostitute should allow him to decrease the crime from murder to manslaughter. The court gave the instruction that "Provocation would arise if the conduct of the deceased woman, to the person was such as would cause a reasonable person, and actually caused the person to lose his self-control suddenly and to drive him into such a passion and lack of self-control that he might use violence of the degree and nature which the prisoner used here. The provocation must be such as would reasonably justify the violence used, the use of a knife. . . . The reasonable person, the ordinary person, is the person you must consider when you are considering the effect which any acts, any conduct, any words, might have to justify the steps which were taken in response . . . so that an unusually excitable or pugnacious individual, or a drunken one or a man who is sexually impotent is not entitled to rely on provocation which would not have led an ordinary person to have acted in the way which was in fact carried out."

The defendant argued that the jury should get to hear a provocation instruction that required them to decide what would the reaction be of a reasonably impotent man under the circumstances. The court disagreed. "But this makes nonsense of the test. Its purpose is to invite the jury to consider the act of the accused by reference to a certain standard or norm of conduct and with this object the "reasonable" or the "average" or the "normal" man is invoked. If the reasonable man is then deprived in whole or in part of his reason, or the normal man endowed with abnormal characteristics, the test ceases to have any value. . . . "

State v. Gounagias, 153 P.9 (Wash. 1915).
The victim sodomized the defendant, his co-worker, on April 19, 1914, after defendant had become helplessly intoxicated. The next day, defendant confronted the victim, and the victim dismissed the incident saying "You're all right, it did not hurt you." The defendant implored the victim not to tell the coworkers about the assault. Word of the incident nevertheless circulated, and his co-workers taunted the defendant. Over two weeks later, the defendant went to a coffeehouse where his co-workers again taunted him. He became highly agitated and "rushed from the coffeehouse, ran to his own house, made a necessary visit to the toilet, went to his mattress, took out the revolver and loaded it, went rapidly up the hill to the house where George lived, entered the house, and by the light of a match found George asleep in his bed, did not awaken him, but immediately shot him through the head, firing five shots, all that he had in the revolver."

The trial judge refused to allow the jury to hear about George's prior act of sodomizing the defendant ruling that the event was sufficiently removed in time from the homicide that it could not reasonably have been offered as provocation. The court held that a reasonable cooling time had passed between the provoking incident and the killing making the testimony about the sodomy irrelevant. Defendant appealed and the Washington Supreme Court discussed the "cooling time"

"There can be no doubt that the original outrage committed by the deceased would have been a sufficient provocation to take the case to the jury, if the appellant immediately upon realizing its perpetration, had sought out and slain the deceased. There can be little doubt that, had the appellant slain the deceased when, on meeting him the next day, the deceased impudently treated the outrage as inconsequential, the question of provocation would have been for the jury. No court would be warranted in saying that such callous conduct while the original wrong was but a day old, would have no reasonable tendency to produce immediate, uncontrollable anger, destroying the capacity for cool reflection in the average man.

"According to the offered evidence the appellant let these things pass repeatedly for many days without molesting the deceased, even to the extent of a remonstrance. The offered evidence makes it clear that the appellant knew and appreciated for days before the killing the full meaning of the words, signs, and vulgar gestures of his countrymen, which as the offer shows, he had encountered from day to day for about three weeks following the original outrage, wherever he went. The final demonstration in the coffeehouse was nothing new. It was exactly what the appellant, from his experience for the prior three weeks, must have anticipated. To say that it alone tended to create the sudden passion and heat of blood essential to mitigation is to ignore the admitted fact that the same thing created no such condition on its repeated occurrence during the prior three weeks. To say that these repeated demonstrations, coupled with the original outrage, culminated in a sudden passion and heat of blood when he encountered the same character of demonstration . . . is to say that sudden passion and heat of blood in the mitigative sense may be a cumulative result of repeated reminders of a single act of provocation. ... In the nature of the thing sudden anger cannot be cumulative. A provocation which does not cause instant resentment, but which is only resented after being thought upon and brooded over, is not a provocation sufficient in law to reduce intentional killing from murder to manslaughter, or under our statute to second degree murder, which includes every inexcusable, unjustifiable, unpremeditated, intentional killing. "

People v. Bridgehouse, 47 Cal.2d 406 (1956)
The victim, Marylou Bridgehouse, told her husband, the defendant, Bridgehouse, that she had been having an affair with William Bahr for the past six or seven months. (The defendant had been working two jobs to support his wife and their two sons). The defendant later found out that his wife and her lover had a joint bank account and that his wife had been using her credit cards (which he was paying for) to buy gifts for Bahr. The defendant later found that Bahr's clothes were hanging in his closet.. On the morning that the defendant killed Bahr, defendant invited Marylou to go skiing, but she told him that she was going fishing with her mother and Bahr. The defendant, a former sheriff, placed his service revolver in his belt and went over to his mother-in-law's house to allegedly get a pair of socks for his young son. At trial, Bridgehouse testified that he did not realize that Bahr was living there and, when he came upon Bahr at his mother-in-law's home, he lost control and only regained consciousness when he realized that his revolver was clicking on empty and Bahr was dead on the ground. A police officer testified that Bridgehouse was emotionally overwhelmed following the killing and told the officer that he wanted to "tell off" Bahr and that he "didn't want him around y children."

There was testimony that Bridgehouse was a peaceful guy and a good dad, and he claimed he was in shock. The court held there was insufficient evidence to prove second-degree murder but enough to show voluntary manslaughter.

Imperfect Defense Situations as Voluntary Manslaughter

Some courts have created an additional category of voluntary manslaughter consisting of imperfect defense cases. For example, when defendant argues that he is acting in self-defense, but the evidence presented falls short of proving that his actions were in self-defense because his conduct was not reasonable. See, e.g., *Sanchez v. People*, 470 P.2d 857 (Colo. 1970) (Sanchez killed the victim believing he needed to defend himself, but he used more force than was reasonably necessary. Sanchez was held guilty only of manslaughter though charged with murder.)

Model Penal Code Approach To Manslaughter

Under Model Penal Code §210.3, a killing that would otherwise be murder is reduced to manslaughter if it was committed "under the influence of extreme mental or emotional disturbance for which there is reasonable explanation or excuse." Merely showing a defendant was made angry or embarrassed by the victim's provoking conduct will not be sufficient to reduce murder to manslaughter even under the more liberal MPC approach.

The official commentary accompanying the MPC explains that

One major departure concerns the statement of the rule of provocation in Subsection (1)(b). The formulation in Subsection (1)(b) represents a substantial enlargement of the class of cases which would otherwise be murder but which could be reduced to manslaughter under then existing law because the homicidal act occurred in the "heat of passion" upon "adequate provocation." The decisive question is reframed to ask whether the homicide was committed "under the influence of extreme mental or emotional disturbance for which there is a reasonable explanation or excuse." The Model Code further provides that the "reasonableness of such explanation or excuse shall be determined from the viewpoint of a person in the actor's situation under the circumstances as he believes them to be.

This formulation treats on a parity with classic provocation cases situations where the provocative circumstance is something other than an injury inflicted by the deceased on the actor but nonetheless is an event that arouses extreme mental or emotional disturbance. There is a larger element of subjectivity in the standard than there was under prevailing law, though it is only the actor's "situation" and the "circumstances as he believed them to be," not his scheme of moral values, that are thus to be considered. The ultimate test, however, is objective; there must be a "reasonable" explanation or excuse for the actor's disturbance. This is to state in fair and realistic terms the criteria by which the mitigating import of mental or emotional distress should be appraised when it is a factor so grave a crime as homicide.

STATE v. DUMLAO,
715 P.2d 822 (1986)

HEEN, Judge.

Defendant Vidado B. Dumlao (Dumlao) appeals from his conviction of murder. He argues on appeal that the trial court erred in refusing to give his requested manslaughter instruction. [H]e contends there was sufficient evidence that he shot his mother-in-law, Pacita M. Reyes (Pacita), while "under the influence of extreme mental or emotional disturbance for which there [was] a reasonable explanation" to support an instruction. We agree and reverse.

The trial court instructed the jury that they could find Dumlao guilty of manslaughter if they concluded that he had recklessly shot Pacita to death but refused to give the instruction Dumlao had requested.

After a jury trial, Dumlao was convicted of murder for shooting Pacita, and of reckless endangering in the first degree for shooting and injuring his brother-in-law, Pedrito Reyes (Pedrito). He does not appeal the reckless endangering conviction.

The questions presented are: (I) what is the meaning of the language of HRS § 707-702(2); and (II) was there evidence to support the giving of Dumlao's requested instruction?

I.
HISTORY OF THE MITIGATING FACTOR IN MANSLAUGHTER

The principle that the presence of an extreme mental or emotional disturbance will reduce the offense of murder to manslaughter is a modification of the ancient distinction between slaying in cold blood and slaying in the heat of passion existing in Anglo-Saxon criminal law prior to the Norman conquest of 1066. The "Doctrine of Provocation" became firmly established in the common law in 1628 and the distinction between murder and manslaughter turned on the presence of heat of passion caused by adequate provocation.

In the United States mutual combat, assault and adultery were gradually recognized as having been legally adequate provocation at common law to reduce murder to manslaughter. In some jurisdictions illegal arrest, injuries to third parties, and even words tending to give rise to heat of passion are sufficient provocation.

The determination of the adequacy of the provocation gradually became a jury prerogative in marginal cases, and the reasonable person test was devised to assist the jury. Today the test has four elements: (1) provocation that would rouse a reasonable person to the heat of passion; (2) actual provocation of the defendant; (3) a reasonable person would not have cooled off in the time between the provocation and the offense; and (4) the defendant did not cool off. The reasonable person yardstick is strictly objective; neither the mental nor physical peculiarities of the accused are evaluated in determining whether the loss of self-control was "reasonable."

CRITICISM OF THE "REASONABLE PERSON" TEST

As originally developed the provocation defense focused on the mental state of the accused as the test for moral culpability; however, under the objective or "reasonable person" test the individual's mental state is not the determinative factor.

Some commentators have remarked on the inconsistency of the reasonable person test.

The reasonable man test, being objective in nature, is antithetical to the concept of mens rea. Like all objective standards, it is an external standard of general application that does not focus on an individual accused's mental state. Thus, from the point of view of traditional Anglo-American jurisprudence, a paradox is inherent in the use of the reasonable man standard to test criminal responsibility: the presence or absence of criminal intent is determined by a standard which ignores the mental state of the individual accused. (Citation omitted).

The objective test placed the jury in the conceptually awkward, almost impossible, position of having to determine when it is reasonable for a reasonable person to act unreasonably.

In the law of contract and tort, and elsewhere in the criminal law, the test of the reasonable man indicates an ethical standard; but it seems absurd to say that the reasonable man will commit a felony the possible punishment for which is imprisonment for life. To say that the "ordinary" man will commit this felony is hardly less absurd. The reason why provoked homicide is punished is to deter people from committing the offence; and it is a curious confession of failure on the part of the law to suppose that, notwithstanding the possibility of heavy punishment, an ordinary person will commit it. If the assertion were correct, it would raise serious doubts whether the offence should continue to be punished.

Surely the true view of provocation is that it is a concession to "the frailty of human nature" in those exceptional cases where the legal prohibition fails of effect. It is a compromise, neither conceding the propriety of the act nor exacting the full penalty for it. This being so, how can it be that that paragon of virtue, the reasonable man, gives way to provocation (Citation omitted.)

The MPC's response to this criticism is discussed below.

Since HRS § 707-702(2) is derived from MPC § 210.3,[9] we may look to the commentaries and cases from other jurisdictions explaining and construing that section for insight into the meaning of the language of our statute. ...

A.

"Extreme mental or emotional disturbance" sometimes is, but should not be, confused with the "insanity" defense. The point of the extreme emotional disturbance defense is to provide a basis for mitigation that differs from a finding of mental defect or disease precluding criminal responsibility. *State v. Ott,* 297 Or. at 391, 686 P.2d at 1011. The disturbance was meant to be understood in relative terms as referring to a loss of self-control due to intense feelings.

The extreme mental or emotional disturbance concept of the MPC must also be distinguished from the so-called "diminished capacity" defense.

The doctrine of diminished capacity provides that evidence of an abnormal mental condition not amounting to legal insanity but tending to prove that the defendant could not or did not entertain the specific intent or state of mind essential to the offense should be considered for the purpose of determining whether the crime charged or a lesser degree thereof was in fact committed. (Citation omitted).

Although the MPC does *not* recognize diminished capacity as a distinct category of mitigation, by placing more emphasis than does the common law on the actor's subjective mental state, it also may allow inquiry into areas which have traditionally been treated as part of the law of diminished responsibility or the insanity defense.

Thus, the MPC is said to have in fact adopted an expanded concept of diminished capacity to reduce murder to manslaughter.

The MPC merges the two concepts of heat of passion and diminished capacity.

It is enough if the killing occurs while the defendant's capacity to form an intent to murder is diminished by an extreme mental or emotional *disturbance* deemed to have a reasonable explanation or excuse from the defendant's standpoint.

An explanation of the term "extreme emotional disturbance" which reflects the situational or relative character of the concept was given in *People v. Shelton,* as follows:

> [T]hat extreme emotional disturbance is the emotional state of an individual, who: (a) has no mental disease or defect that rises to the level established by Section 30.05 of the Penal Law;[11] and (b) is exposed to an extremely unusual and overwhelming stress; and (c) has an extreme emotional reaction to it, as a result of which there is a loss of self-control and reason is overborne by intense feelings, such as passion, anger, distress, grief, excessive agitation or other similar emotions.

It is clear that in adopting the "extreme mental or emotional disturbance" concept, the MPC intended to define the provocation element of manslaughter in broader terms than had previously been done. It is equally clear that our legislature also intended the same result when it adopted the language of the MPC.

We turn then to the second prong of our analysis, the test to determine the reasonableness of the explanation for the mental or emotional disturbance. It is here that the most significant change has been made in the law of manslaughter.

B.

The anomaly of the reasonable person test was corrected by the drafters of the MPC through the development of an objective/subjective test of reasonableness. [The]. . . 1980 MPC Commentary explains that, it makes the test more, although not entirely, subjective, by requiring the jury to test the reasonableness of the actor's conduct, "from the viewpoint of a person in the actor's situation." Thus, the actor's sex, sexual preference, pregnancy, physical deformities, and similar characteristics are apt to be taken into consideration in evaluating the reasonableness of the defendant's behavior.

This more subjective version of the provocation defense goes substantially beyond the common law by abandoning preconceptions of what constitutes adequate provocation, and giving the jury wider scope.

Under the prior law of provocation, personal characteristics of the defendant were not to be considered. Under the MPC a change from the old provocation law and the reasonable person standard has been effected by requiring the factfinder to focus on a person in the defendant's situation. Thus, the MPC, while requiring that the explanation for the disturbance must be reasonable, provides that the reasonableness is determined from the defendant's viewpoint. The phrase "actor's situation," as used in § 210.3(b) of the MPC, is designedly ambiguous and is plainly flexible enough to allow the law to grow in the direction of taking account of mental abnormalities that have been recognized in the developing law of diminished responsibility.

Moreover, the MPC does not require the provocation to emanate from the victim as was argued by the State here.

In light of the foregoing discussion and the necessity of articulating the defense in comprehensible terms, we adopt the test enunciated by the New York Court of Appeals in *People v. Casassa,*

> [W]e conclude that the determination whether there was reasonable explanation or excuse for a particular emotional disturbance should be made by viewing the subjective, internal situation in which the defendant found himself and the external circumstances as he perceived them at the time, however inaccurate that perception may have been, and assessing from that standpoint whether the explanation ... for his emotional disturbance was reasonable, so as to entitle him to a reduction of the crime charged from murder ... to manslaughter... . [Footnote omitted.]

The language of HRS § 707-702(2) indicates that the legislature intended to effect the same change in the test for manslaughter in Hawaii's law as was made by the MPC. Therefore, we hold that under HRS § 707-702(2) the broader sweep of the emotional disturbance defense applies when considering whether an offense should be reduced from murder to manslaughter. . . .

Thus, we hold in the instant case that the trial court was required to instruct the jury as requested by Dumlao, if there was any evidence to support a finding that at the time of the offense he suffered an "extreme mental or emotional disturbance" for which there was a "reasonable explanation" when the totality of circumstances was judged from his personal viewpoint.

We turn now to the question of whether there was evidence to support the proffered instruction.

. . .

CONCLUSION

Reviewing the evidence within the context of the meaning of HRS § 707-702(2), we conclude that it was sufficient to require the trial court to give Dumlao's requested instruction on manslaughter. There was evidence, "no matter how weak, inconclusive or unsatisfactory," that Dumlao

killed Pacita while under the influence of "extreme emotional disturbance." Whether a jury will agree that there was such a disturbance or that the explanation for it was reasonable we cannot say. However, Dumlao was entitled to have the jury make that decision using the objective/subjective test.

The fact that the other witnesses contradicted his testimony concerning an attack by Pedrito, and that his testimony that he was only trying to scare Pedrito does not comport with the manslaughter defense, does not detract from Dumlao's right to the instruction based on the above evidence. Dumlao was entitled to an instruction on every theory of defense shown by the evidence. It was the jury's province to determine the weight and credibility of that evidence.

Reversed and remanded for new trial.

Other Cases—Extreme Emotional Disturbance

State v. Raguseo, 622 A.2d 519 (1990).
This case highlights the application of a modern statute based on the MPC and indicates the trial judge was required to submit to the jury whether the killing was under the influence of extreme disturbance. In this case, the defendant returned to his apartment to find that someone had parked in his assigned lot. The police refused to tow the car away. Around two hours later, the car owner returned and there was a confrontation between Raguseo and the car owner in which Raguseo stabbed the victim to death. Some evidence at trial indicated that Raguseo was extremely upset, but there was also testimony that he was calm.
The court found that the issue was close enough to warrant the instruction, but that the jury's verdict rejecting Raguseo's theory was supported by the evidence. The dissent noted that the jury should determine whether the explanation for the disturbance would be reasonable from defendant's point of view given his subjective characteristics (Raguseo was paranoid and unusually sensitive about his car, and the dissent thought that the jury should be able to consider than when determining whether the car owner's improper parking was a reasonable excuse for the emotional disturbance.

Involuntary Manslaughter

Involuntary manslaughter may take many forms. State statutes may refer to: unlawful act manslaughter (or the misdemeanor manslaughter rule), criminally negligent homicide, or vehicular homicide. Involuntary manslaughter is the appropriate charge when an unintentional homicide is committed without due caution and circumspection which involves negligence (criminal negligence). Gross negligence is that which causes an unreasonable risk to human life. The difference between second-degree murder (depraved heart murder) and involuntary manslaughter is that second-degree murder involves gross recklessness whereas involuntary manslaughter only involves no malice--mere recklessness or gross (criminal) negligence. The dividing line between gross recklessness and mere recklessness is vague and is ultimately a jury question. If the defendant consciously takes a risk that demonstrates a wanton disregard for human life, then gross recklessness or malice exists and the defendant is guilty of second-degree murder. If the defendant does not realize the risk or does not appreciate its seriousness, or shows there was some social utility (usefulness) in taking it, then the defendant is only guilty of involuntary manslaughter. Recall the involuntary manslaughter cases of *Baker v. State*, and *Koppersmith v. State* in Chapter Two. The difference between gross recklessness and gross negligence depends on whether the defendant was consciously aware of the serious and unwarranted risk to human life.

In drunk driving cases, courts frequently will find defendants guilty of second-degree murder rather than involuntary manslaughter, despite the defendants claiming they were too intoxicated to realize the risk they posed to human life. Courts note that these defendants are conscious of the risk when they decided to drink and drive, or must have known the risk because of the extremely careless manner in which they drove.

Some jurisdictions recognize a "misdemeanor manslaughter rule" or "unlawful act doctrine." The principle supporting this type of involuntary manslaughters is similar to the felony murder rule. When in the course of committing a misdemeanor or an unlawful act someone dies, the person committing the misdemeanor can be tried and convicted of this type of involuntary manslaughter even when they had no intention whatsoever to cause the death of the victim.

Most jurisdictions punish, as involuntary manslaughter, death-causing conduct in the commission or attempted commission of an unlawful act (generally a misdemeanor), especially if that act is *malum in se* or if that act involves a danger of death or serious bodily injury to another person or to others. If the unlawful act is *malum prohibitum* the defendant generally is held not guilty of manslaughter unless the death is the foreseeable consequence of his conduct in committing the act. The modern trend is toward the abolition of unlawful-act manslaughter. LaFave and Scott, *Criminal Law, at 594.*

The Model Penal Code in §210.4 treats criminal homicide as negligent homicide when "it is committed negligently" and punishes it as a third degree felony.

Some jurisdictions have enacted a separate offense known as "vehicular murder" or "vehicular manslaughter" to avoid the fiction of asserting the defendant must have had actual awareness of the risk of fatal harm at the time of the accident. The MPC approach to drunk driving deaths is to treat vehicular homicides as murder. See, *State v. Dugifeld*, 549 A.2d 1205 (N.H. 1988).

Other Cases—Involuntary Manslaughter

Walker v. Superior Court, 47 Cal.3d112, 763 P.2d 852 (1988).
Members of Church of Christ Scientists used prayer rather than medicine to cure illness, and their child died. Defendants were convicted of involuntary manslaughter.

State v. Williams, 4 Wash. App. 908, 484 P.2d 1167 (1971).
Defendants were convicted of involuntary manslaughter for the death of their 17-moth child. The defendants failed to seek medical attention for their child who had a serious tooth infection because they did not realize how ill the child was and were afraid that authorities might try to take the child from them. When the child died, defendants were charged with manslaughter. The court upheld the conviction because it found that a reasonable person in the defendant's situation would have taken the child to the doctor. Even though the defendants loved their child and did not knowingly risk his life, they still acted negligently and were therefore guilty of manslaughter.

People v. Schmies, 51 Cal. Rptr. 2d 185 (Cal. Ct. App. 1996)
Schmies fled on his motorcycle from traffic stop at speeds of up to ninety miles an hour and disregarded all traffic regulations. During the chase, one of the pursuing patrol cars struck another vehicle, killing the driver and injuring an officer. Schmies was convicted of grossly negligent vehicular manslaughter and of reckless driving. The court upheld the conviction finding that the officer's response and the resulting injury were reasonably foreseeable. The officer's reaction, in other words was not so extraordinary that it was unforeseeable, unpredictable and statistically extremely improbable.

State v. Mays (Ohio App. Dist. 1, 2000).
Facts
On August 19, 1999, nineteen-year-old Nicholas Mays was operating an automobile in which his cousin was a passenger. At approximately 1:45 a.m., they saw a pedestrian, later identified as Michael Boumer, in a grocery-store parking lot. According to Mays, Boumer appeared to be

intoxicated, and the two young men decided that they would "mess with" Boumer by appearing to offer him a ride. Mays intended to nudge Boumer with the vehicle and then drive away.

Investigating officers confirmed that Boumer had consumed some alcohol. However, the record also indicates that Boumer was mentally handicapped. Mays did drive the vehicle in the direction of Boumer, but instead of merely nudging him, he inadvertently ran over him, causing him fatal injuries. Upon seeing that Boumer was injured, Mays drove to another location and called for emergency aid. He then went to a car wash, where he cleaned the vehicle to remove evidence of the fatal collision.

On the day after the incident, Mays took a planned trip to Florida, during which his mother convinced him that he should report his involvement in the crime. Mays did so, returning to Cincinnati and giving a full confession to the police. . .
[Mays entered pleas to aggravated vehicular homicide and tampering with evidence.]

OPINION

. . . The sole issue posed . . . is whether the record supports the trial court's findings [imposing the maximum sentence for the offense] . . . We hold that the trial court's findings with respect to the seriousness of the offenses is supported by the record. . . .

[T]he [trial] court found that Mays had committed the worst form of aggravated vehicular homicide. We disagree.
. . . Though the evidence certainly indicates that Mays exercised extremely poor judgment in carrying out his wish to "mess with" Boumer, there is no indication that he harbored any malice toward the victim. Instead, the record indicates that Mays's conduct started as a reckless, poorly conceived prank and ended in tragedy. And while we in no way wish to minimize the loss of a human life or to condone Mays's actions, this is not the type of conduct for which the legislature has reserved the maximum sentence.

Furthermore, although he admittedly thought of his own interests before seeking help for Boumer, Mays did take steps to ensure that emergency personnel were notified promptly. His actions therefore did not reflect an utter lack of concern for

Boumer or otherwise demonstrate a perversity of character that would justify the imposition of the maximum sentence. Further, there is no indication that the victim suffered for a prolonged period of time before he died or suffered to a greater degree than any other victim of a vehicular homicide. Finally, Mays surrendered to authorities and confessed to the crimes. Under these circumstances, we cannot say that Mays committed the worst form of the offense . . . We therefore hold that the tiral court erred in imposing the maximum term for that offense.

People v. Datema, 533 N.W.2d 272 (Mich. 1995). Defendant, his wife and two friends were socializing in the early hours of December 22, 1988. They were all smoking marijuana and defendant and his wife had been drinking throughout the evening. Defendant and his wife began to argue and as she arose from her chair he slapped her once across the face with an open hand. Mrs. Datema slumped back onto her chair, screamed that she hoped defendant would "got to Florida and stay there," then slipped from the chair onto the floor.
Initially, defendant and the two others . . . thought the wife had passed out from drinking too much but, after five to ten minutes, they became concerned and tried to wake her. When they were unable to do so, they called an ambulance. Mrs. Datema never regained consciousness and died soon after.
Victim's blood alcohol level wasn't that high, but with the combination of the marijuana, when she was struck, she did not reflexively stiffen as would normally happen. She suffered a tear in an artery in her head.

The jury convicted defendant of involuntary manslaughter. Defendant was convicted as a second-felony offender (Defendant's prior felony conviction was for malicious destruction of property in a building.) and sentenced to 7 to 22 ½ years in prison.

Defendant argued on appeal that if the death is not committed in recklessly or with gross negligence, the crime should no longer be recognized as a form of common-law involuntary manslaughter. The Michigan Supreme Court stated,

> Involuntary manslaughter is a catch-all concept including all manslaughter not characterized as voluntary. Every unintentional killing of a human being is

involuntary manslaughter if it is neither murder nor voluntary manslaughter nor within the scope of some recognized justification or excuse. . . . At common law, if an unlawful act was malum in se, inherently wrong, the only mens rea required was the mens rea of the underlying act. . . We conclude that if an assault and battery is committed with a specific intent to inflict injury and causes unintended death, the actor may be found guilty of (at least) involuntary manslaughter.. . .

Dissent:

"In *State v. Aaron*, we recognized that it is inherently unjust to presume the existence of the mens rea for murder merely on a showing of the mens rea required for an underlying felony. Specifically, our holdings in Aaron were premised on the following principle of criminal jurisprudence: 'If one had to choose the most basic principle of criminal law . . . it would be that criminal liability for causing a particular result is not justified in the absence of some culpable mental state in respect to that result.'

The unlawful-act misdemeanor manslaughter rule violates the principle set forth in Aaron, and it too should be abrogated. Pursuant to the unlawful-act misdemeanor manslaughter rule, a defendant may be convicted of involuntary manslaughter where it has been shown that the defendant committed the unlawful act that proximately caused death. Proof of the mens rea for manslaughter is presumed to exist on the basis of a showing of the mens rea required for the underlying misdemeanor.

Contrary to the principle that we endorsed in Aaron, liability for a homicide is imposed without an independent showing of a mens rea with regard to the homicide. To eliminate the perpetuation of such an injustice, this Court should abolish the unlawful-act misdemeanor-manslaughter rule. . . .

The instant case is another example of a situation in which it could be shown that the defendant had a specific intent to injure, but perhaps it could not be shown that the defendant willfully disregarded a high risk of death or serious bodily injury. . . . [The medical examiner's testimony] . . . strongly suggests that a high risk of death or serious bodily injury was not created when the 'defendant slapped [his wife] once across the face with an open hand." Notably, the prosecutor characterizes the victim's death in this case as "entirely unexpected."

See above: Velazquez v. State, 561 So.2d 347 (Fla. App. 1990)

WRAP UP

Taking another's life is serious business. When no excuse or justification defense can be raised, then taking another's life is criminal homicide. The common law, modern statutes, and the Model Penal Code all recognize different levels of killing and generally distinguish between murder and manslaughter and between degrees of murder or manslaughter based on the circumstances surrounding the killing. State homicide laws vary tremendously, but generally, levels of criminal homicide are determined by looking at: the offender's mens rea (did the offender act with premeditation and deliberation, or with recklessness (gross and simple) or gross negligence (criminal negligence)); the offender's actus reus (did the offender act in a particularly brutal fashion); or who was killed (did the offender kill a particular type of victim). Murder under modern statutes is generally divided into degrees, and manslaughter is generally divided into voluntary and involuntary manslaughter. Some of the attendant circumstances at common law, such as the year and a day rule or the requirement that the victim be born alive, are no longer part of the law of criminal homicide followed under state statutes.

Chapter Seven: Other Crimes Against Persons

Rape and other sexual assaults

Common Law Approach to Rape

Early on, common law recognized the felony of rape. The traditional definition of rape is the "carnal knowledge of a woman forcibly and against her will." Carnal knowledge meant penile-vaginal intercourse between a man and a woman. At common law there needed to be penetration, however slight. At common law, a husband could not rape his wife. To prosecute a rape at common law, the state needed to prove force by the man (meaning either force or threat of severe bodily harm) and lack of consent by the woman.

"At common law, the sex act out of wedlock was a criminal offense (fornication or adultery). A woman who engaged in consensual sex with a man who was not her husband was committing a crime. A claim of rape was therefore one way for the woman to escape from criminality, which may explain why . . . there are analogies between the coercion that was required by early rape law and the duress that will serve as an excuse for crime. Rape victims were, in effect, pleading for an excuse for their own crimes." Low, at 62.

According to Lippman,

"The common law of rape reflects a distrust of women, and various requirements were imposed to ensure that the prosecutrix (victim) was not engaged in blackmail or in an attempt to conceal a consensual affair or was not suffering from a psychological illness. The fear of an unjust conviction was reflected in Lord Matthew Hale's comment that rape 'is an accusation easy to be made, hard to be proved, but harder to be defended by the party accused though innocent.' Lord Hale stressed that there was a danger that a judge and jury would be emotionally carried away by the seriousness of the charge and convict a defendant based on false testimony."

In order to successfully prosecute a rapist at common law the prosecutor had to convince the jury that the victim reported the rape promptly, that the allegation of rape was corroborated by other witnesses or physical evidence, and that the victim had a reputation for chastity. Additionally, judges were required to issue jury instructions in rape cases admonishing the jury that the victim's testimony should be carefully scrutinized because rape is easily charged and difficult to prove. Common law required that the prosecution prove that the victim did not consent to the sexual intercourse. Although this did not mean that the prosecution had to show physical injury or assault, women had to prove their lack of consent through outward resistance. Samaha notes that proof of nonconsent by resistance is "peculiar to the law of rape. In no other crime where lack of consent is an element of the crime does the law treat passive acceptance as consent." *Criminal Law,* 8th ed., at 336.

The degree to which the woman had to resist has changed over time. From the 1800s through the mid-1950s, courts employed the "utmost resistance standard." The case frequently cited that demonstrates the high bar this standard set is *Brown v. State*, 106 N.W. 536 (1906). In that case a 16-year-old virgin testified that she tried as

"hard as I could to get away. I was trying all the time to get away just as hard as I could. I was trying to get up; I pulled at the grass; I screamed as hard as I could, and he told me to shut up, and I didn't, and then he held his hand on my mouth until I was almost strangled.

The jury convicted the neighbor (the defendant) of rape. Nevertheless, the Wisconsin Supreme Court ruled

"Not only must there be entire absence of mental consent or assent, but there must be the most vehement exercise of every physical means or faculty within the woman's power to resist the penetration of her person, and this must be shown to persist until the offense is consummated."

The Wisconsin Court noted that the alleged victim also failed to corroborate her complaint by "bruises, scratches and ripped clothing."

The resistance to the utmost" standard was not followed when the victim reasonably believed that she confronted a threat of "great and immediate bodily harm that would impair a reasonable person's will to resist." Furthermore, no resistance was required to prove lack of consent if victims were incapacitated by intoxication, mental deficiency, or insanity. Sexual intercourse with a minor who consented was defined as rape at common law because the common law did not recognize the consent of minors. By the 1950s, courts began relaxing the utmost resistance standard and adopted the reasonable resistance standard which focused on the individual circumstances of each case.

Model Penal Code Approach to Rape

The Model Penal Code, if you recall, was the draft code of the American Law Institute that was formulated in the 1950s and adopted in 1962. The MPC's provisions on rape probably represent the thinking at the time and may have even been seen as progressive for the times. But, still the MPC retained many of the features of common law rape. For example, it retains the provision that a man cannot rape his own wife. It also retains the male against female aspect of common law, but it does include a lesser offense in sex neutral terms. The MPC requires prompt complaint and requires that the victim's testimony be corroborated. It also requires an instruction that the testimony of the complaining witness must be considered with special care. These MPC provisions are much criticized and are not followed today in most jurisdictions.[19]

---

[19] MPC § 213.0 Definitions.
(2) "Sexual intercourse" includes intercourse per os or per anum, with some penetration however slight; emission is not required.
(3) "Deviate sexual intercourse" means sexual intercourse per os or per anum between human beings who are not husband and wife, and any form of sexual intercourse with an animal.

MPC § 213.1 Rape and Related Offenses
(1) Rape. A man who has sexual intercourse with a female not his wife is guilty of rape if:
(a) he compels her to submit by force or by threat of imminent death, serious bodily injury, extreme pain or kidnapping, to be inflicted on anyone; or
(b) he has substantially impaired her power to appraise or control her conduct by administering or employing without her knowledge drugs, intoxicants or other means for the purpose of preventing resistance; or
(c) the female is unconscious; or
(d) the female is less than 10 years old.

Rape is a felony of the second degree unless:
(i) in the course thereof the actor inflicts serious bodily injury upon anyone, or
(ii) the victim was not a voluntary social companion of the actor upon the occasion of the crime and had not previously permitted him sexual liberties, in which case the offense is a felony of the first degree.

(2) Gross Sexual Imposition. A male who has sexual intercourse with a female not his wife commits a felony of the third degree if:
(a) he compels her to submit by any threat that would prevent resistance by a woman of ordinary resolution; or
(b) he knows that she suffers from a mental disease or defect which renders her incapable of appraising the nature of her conduct; or
(c) he knows that she is unaware that a sexual act is being committed upon her or that she submits because she mistakenly supposes that he is her husband.

MPC § 213.2 Deviate Sexual Intercourse by Force or Imposition
(1) By Force or Its Equivalent. A person who engages in deviate sexual intercourse with another person, or who causes another to engage in deviate sexual intercourse, commits a felony of the second degree if:
(a) he compels the other person to participate by force or by threat of imminent death, serious bodily injury, extreme pain or kidnapping, to be inflicted on anyone; or
(b) he has substantially impaired the other person's power to appraise or control his conduct, by administering or employing without the knowledge of the other person drugs, intoxicants or other means for the purpose of preventing resistance; or
(c) the person is unconscious; or
(d) the other person is less than 10 years old.

(2) By Other Imposition. A person who engages in deviate sexual intercourse with another person, or who causes another to engage in sexual intercourse, commits a felony of the third degree if:
(a) he compels the other person to participate by any threat that would prevent resistance by a person of ordinary resolution; or
(b) he knows that the other person suffers from a mental disease or defect which renders him incapable of appraising the nature of his conduct; or
(c) he knows that the other person submits because he is unaware that a sexual act is being committed upon him.

MPC §213.3 Corruption of Minors and Seduction
(1) Offense Defined. A male who has sexual intercourse with a female not his wife, or any person who engages in deviate sexual intercourse, is guilty of an offense if:
(a) the other person is less than [16] years old and the actor is at least [four] years older than the other person; or
(b) the other person is less than 21 years old and the actor is his guardian or otherwise responsible for general supervision of his welfare; or
(c) the other person is in custody of law or detained in a hospital or other institution and the actor has supervisory or disciplinary authority over him; or
(d) the other person is a female who is induced to participate by a promise of marriage which the actor does not mean to perform.

(2) Grading. An offense under paragraph (a) of Subsection (1) is a felony of the third degree. Otherwise an offense under this section is a misdemeanor.

MPC §213.4 Sexual Assault
A person who has sexual contact with another not his spouse, or causes such other to have sexual conduct with him, is guilty of sexual assault, a misdemeanor, if:
(1) he knows that the contact is offensive to the other person; or
(2) he knows that the other person suffers from a mental disease or defect which renders him or her incapable of appraising the nature of his or her conduct; or
(3) he knows that the other person is unaware that a sexual act is being committed; or
(4) the other person is less than 10 years old; or
(5) he has substantially impaired the other person's power to appraise or control his or her conduct, by administering or employing without the other's knowledge drugs, intoxicants, or other means for the purpose of preventing resistance; or
(6) the other person is less than [16] years old and the actor is at least [four] years older than the other person; or
(7) the other person is less than 21 years old and the actor is his guardian or otherwise responsible for general supervision of his welfare; or
(8) the other person is in custody of law or detained in a hospital or other institution and the actor has supervisory or disciplinary authority over him.

Sexual conduct includes "any touching of the sexual or other intimate parts of the person for the purpose of arousing or gratifying sexual desire."

MPC §213.6 Provisions Generally Applicable to Article 213
(1) Mistake as to Age. Whenever in this Article the criminality of conduct depends on a child's being below the age of 10, it is not defense that the actor did not know the child's age, or reasonably believed the child to be older than 10.

Modern Approaches to Rape

From 1970 on, most states drastically modified their approach to rape. States abolished the corroboration requirement, passed rape shield laws which prevent examination into the victim's past sexual conduct, and relaxed the prompt reporting requirement. Many states have abolished the marital rape exception. Rape statutory reform also included consolidating sexual assault statutes and expanding the definition of rape. Most states now include all sexual penetration: vaginal, anal, and oral. States also created sexual contact statutes which criminalizes offensive touching of breasts and buttocks. Sex offenses are now gender-neutral and men can sexually assault men or women and women can sexually assault women or men. Generally, the seriousness of sex offenses is based on several criterial: whether the contact involved penetration or contact with penetration being more serious and forcible penetration being more serious than simple nonconsensual penetration and contact. Additionally, physical injury to the victim aggravates the offense.

The elements of modern rape laws include the actus reus of sexual penetration between the perpetrator and victim; the actus reus of force, or threat of force, to accomplish sexual penetration; the mens rea of intentional sexual penetration; and the circumstance of the victim's non-consent.

Rape Actus Reus

Rape actus reus consists of sexual penetration by force or threat of force. Courts have adopted two standards to determine whether penetration was accomplished by an act of force: the extrinsic force standard and the intrinsic force standard. The following two cases demonstrate how the standards differ. The first of the following two cases traces the history of rape law from common law to the modern reform efforts. I have included it mostly in its entirety because the opinion is well written and well researched (though most of the citations have been omitted) and highlights most of what you have read in the previous pages). The actual use of force is not required if there is a threat of force. To satisfy the threat of force requirement the prosecution must prove that the victim honestly feared imminent and serious bodily harm and that the fear was reasonable under the circumstances. Brandishing a weapon satisfies the requirement. So do verbal

---

When criminality depends on the child's being below a critical age other than 10, it is a defense for the actor to prove by a preponderance of the evidence that he reasonably believed the child to be above the critical age.

(2) Spouse Relationships. Whenever in this Article the definition of an offense excludes conduct with a spouse, the exclusion shall be deemed to extent to persons living as man and wife, regardless of the legal status of their relationship. The exclusion shall be inoperative as respects spouses living apart under a decree of judicial separation. Where the definition of an offense excludes conduct with a spouse or conduct by a woman, this shall not preclude conviction of a spouse or woman as an accomplice in a sexual act which he or she causes another person, not within the exclusion to perform.

(3) Sexually Promiscuous Complainants. It is a defense to prosecution under Section 213.3 and paragraphs (6), (7) and (8) of Section 213.4 for the actor to prove by a preponderance of the evidence that the alleged victim had, prior to the time of the offense charged, engaged promiscuously in sexual relations with others.

(4) Prompt Complaint. No prosecution may be instituted or maintained under this Article unless the alleged offense was brought to the notice of public authority within [3] months of its occurrence or, where the alleged victim was less than [16] years old or otherwise incompetent to make complaint, within [3] months after a parent, guardian or other competent person specially interested in the victim learns of the offense.

(5) Testimony of Complainants. No person shall be convicted of any felony under this Article upon the uncorroborated testimony of the alleged victim. Corroboration may be circumstantial. In any prosecution before a jury for an offense under this Article, the jury shall be instructed to evaluate the testimony of a victim or complaining witness with special care in view of the emotional involvement of the witness and the difficulty of determining the truth with respect to alleged sexual activities carried out in private.

threats—like threats to kill, seriously injure, or kidnap. But the threat doesn't have to include showing weapons or specifically threatening words. Courts can consider all the following in deciding whether the victim's fear was reasonable:

➤ Respective ages of the perpetrator and the victim
➤ Physical sizes of the perpetrator and the victim
➤ Mental condition of the perpetrator and the victim
➤ Physical setting of the assault
➤ Position of authority, domination, or custodial control of the perpetrator over the victim.

Samaha, notes that "Not even the threat of force is required in cases where the perpetrators obtain consent fraudulently, or when a minor, a mentally deficient person, or an insane person consents. In these cases, penetration alone is enough." 8th ed., at 345.

STATE OF NEW JERSEY IN THE INTEREST OF M.T.S., 609 A.2d 1266 (N.J. 1992)

… HANDLER, J.

Under New Jersey law a person who commits an act of sexual penetration using physical force or coercion is guilty of second-degree sexual assault. The sexual assault statute does not define the words "physical force." The question posed by this appeal is whether the element of "physical force" is met simply by an act of non-consensual penetration involving no more force than necessary to accomplish that result.

That issue is presented in the context of what is often referred to as "acquaintance rape." The record in the case discloses that the juvenile, a seventeen-year-old boy, engaged in consensual kissing and heavy petting with a fifteen-year-old girl and thereafter engaged in actual sexual penetration of the girl to which she had not consented. There was no evidence or suggestion that the juvenile used any unusual or extra force or threats to accomplish the act of penetration.

The trial court determined that the juvenile was delinquent for committing a sexual assault. The Appellate Division reversed the disposition of delinquency, concluding that non-consensual penetration does not constitute sexual assault unless it is accompanied by some level of force more than that necessary to accomplish the penetration. We granted the State's petition for certification.

I.

The issues in this case are perplexing and controversial. We must explain the role of force in the contemporary crime of sexual assault and then define its essential features. We then must consider what evidence is probative to establish the commission of a sexual assault. The factual circumstances of this case expose the complexity and sensitivity of those issues and underscore the analytic difficulty of those seemingly-straightforward legal questions.

On Monday, May 21, 1990, fifteen-year-old C.G. was living with her mother, her three siblings, and several other people, including M.T.S. and his girlfriend. A total of ten people resided in the three-bedroom town-home at the time of the incident. M.T.S., then age seventeen, was temporarily residing at the home with the permission of the C.G.'s mother; he slept downstairs on a couch. C.G. had her own room on the second floor. At approximately 11:30 p.m. on May 21, C.G. went upstairs to sleep after having watched television with her mother, M.T.S., and his girlfriend. When C.G. went to bed, she was wearing underpants, a bra, shorts, and a shirt. At trial, C.G. and M.T.S. offered very different accounts concerning the nature of their relationship and the events that occurred after C.G. had gone upstairs. The trial court did not credit fully either teenager's testimony.

C.G. stated that earlier in the day, M.T.S. had told her three or four times that he "was going to make a surprise visit up in [her] bedroom." She said that she had not taken M.T.S. seriously and considered his comments a joke because he frequently teased her. She testified that M.T.S. had attempted to kiss her on numerous other occasions and at least once had attempted to put his hands inside of her pants, but that she had rejected all of his previous advances.

C.G. testified that on May 22, at approximately 1:30 a.m., she awoke to use the bathroom. As she was getting out of bed, she said, she saw M.T.S., fully clothed, standing in her doorway. According to C.G., M.T.S. then said that "he was going to tease [her] a little bit." C.G. testified that she "didn't think anything of it"; she walked past him, used the bathroom, and then returned to bed, falling into a "heavy" sleep within fifteen minutes. The next event C.G. claimed to recall of that morning was waking up with M.T.S. on top of her, her underpants and shorts removed. She said "his penis was into [her] vagina." As soon as C.G. realized what had happened, she said, she immediately slapped M.T.S. once in the face, then "told him to get off [her], and get out." She did not scream or cry out. She testified that M.T.S. complied in less than one minute after being struck; according to C.G., "he jumped right off of [her]." She said she did not know how long M.T.S. had been inside of her before she awoke.

C.G. said that after M.T.S. left the room, she "fell asleep crying" because "[she] couldn't believe that he did what he did to [her]." She explained that she did not immediately tell her mother or anyone else in the house of the events of that morning because she was "scared and in shock." According to C.G., M.T.S. engaged in intercourse with her "without [her] wanting it or telling him to come up [to her bedroom]." By her own account, C.G. was not otherwise harmed by M.T.S.

At about 7:00 a.m., C.G. went downstairs and told her mother about her encounter with M.T.S. earlier in the morning and said that they would have to "get [him] out of the house." While M.T.S. was out on an errand, C.G.'s mother gathered his clothes and put them outside in his car; when he returned, he was told that "[he] better not even get near the house." C.G. and her mother then filed a complaint with the police.

According to M.T.S., he and C.G. had been good friends for a long time, and their relationship "kept leading on to more and more." He had been living at C.G.'s home for

about five days before the incident occurred; he testified that during the three days preceding the incident they had been "kissing and necking" and had discussed having sexual intercourse. The first time M.T.S. kissed C.G., he said, she "didn't want him to, but she did after that." He said C.G. repeatedly had encouraged him to "make a surprise visit up in her room."

M.T.S. testified that at exactly 1:15 a.m. on May 22, he entered C.G.'s bedroom as she was walking to the bathroom. He said C.G. soon returned from the bathroom, and the two began "kissing and all," eventually moving to the bed. Once they were in bed, he said, they undressed each other and continued to kiss and touch for about five minutes. M.T.S. and C.G. proceeded to engage in sexual intercourse. According to M.T.S., who was on top of C.G., he "stuck it in" and "did it [thrust] three times, and then the fourth time [he] stuck it in, that's when [she] pulled [him] off of her." M.T.S. said that as [428] C.G. pushed him off, she said "stop, get off," and he "hopped off right away."

According to M.T.S., after about one minute, he asked C.G. what was wrong; she replied with a back-hand to his face. He recalled asking C.G. what was wrong a second time, and her replying, "how can you take advantage of me or something like that." M.T.S. said that he proceeded to get dressed and told C.G. to calm down, but that she then told him to get away from her and began to cry. Before leaving the room, he told C.G., "I'm leaving ... I'm going with my real girlfriend, don't talk to me ... I don't want nothing to do with you or anything, stay out of my life ... don't tell anybody about this ... it would just screw everything up." He then walked downstairs and went to sleep.

On May 23, 1990, M.T.S. was charged with conduct that if engaged in by an adult would constitute second-degree sexual assault of the victim. …

Following a two-day trial on the sexual assault charge, M.T.S. was adjudicated delinquent. After reviewing the testimony, the court concluded that the victim had consented to a session of kissing and heavy petting with M.T.S. The trial court did not find that C.G. had been sleeping at the time of penetration, but nevertheless found that she had not consented to the actual sexual act. Accordingly, the court concluded that the State had proven second-degree sexual assault beyond a reasonable doubt. On appeal, following the imposition of suspended sentences on the sexual assault and the other remaining charges, the Appellate Division determined that the absence of force beyond that involved in the act of sexual penetration precluded a finding of second-degree sexual assault. It therefore reversed the juvenile's adjudication of delinquency for that offense.

II.

The New Jersey Code of Criminal Justice . . . defines "sexual assault" as the commission "of sexual penetration" "with another person" with the use of "physical force or coercion." An unconstrained reading of the statutory language indicates that both the act of "sexual penetration" and the use of "physical force or coercion" are separate and distinct elements of the offense. . . [These words are not defined in the Code]. . . The initial inquiry is, therefore, whether the statutory words are unambiguous on their face and can be understood and applied in accordance with their plain meaning. The answer to that inquiry is revealed by the conflicting decisions of the lower courts and the arguments of the opposing parties. The trial court held that "physical force" had been established by the sexual penetration of the victim without her consent. The Appellate Division believed that the statute requires some amount of force more than that necessary to accomplish penetration.

The parties offer two alternative understandings of the concept of "physical force" as it is used in the statute. The State would read "physical force" to entail any amount of sexual touching brought about involuntarily. A showing of sexual penetration coupled with a lack of consent would satisfy the elements of the statute. The Public Defender urges an interpretation of "physical force" to mean force "used to overcome lack of consent." That definition equates force with violence and leads to the conclusion that sexual assault requires the application of some amount of force in addition to the act of penetration.

Current judicial practice suggests an

understanding of "physical force" to mean "any degree of physical power or strength used against the victim, even though it entails no injury and leaves no mark." Resort to common experience or understanding does not yield a conclusive meaning. The dictionary provides several definitions of "force," among which are the following: (1) "power, violence, compulsion, or constraint exerted upon or against a person or thing," (2) "a general term for exercise of strength or power, esp. physical, to overcome resistance," or (3) "strength or power of any degree that is exercised without justification or contrary to law upon a person or thing."

Thus, as evidenced by the disagreements among the lower courts and the parties, and the variety of possible usages, the statutory words "physical force" do not evoke a single meaning that is obvious and plain. Hence, we must pursue avenues of construction in order to ascertain the meaning of that statutory language. Those avenues are well charted. When a statute is open to conflicting interpretations, the court seeks the underlying intent of the legislature, relying on legislative history and the contemporary context of the statute. With respect to a law, like the sexual assault statute, that "alters or amends the previous law or creates or abolishes types of actions, it is important, in discovering the legislative intent, to ascertain the old law, the mischief and the proposed remedy." We also remain mindful of the basic tenet of statutory construction that penal statutes are to be strictly construed in favor of the accused. Nevertheless, the construction must conform to the intent of the Legislature.

The provisions proscribing sexual offenses found in the Code of Criminal Justice, became effective in 1979, and were written against almost two hundred years of rape law in New Jersey. The origin of the rape statute that the current statutory offense of sexual assault replaced can be traced to the English common law. Under the common law, rape was defined as "carnal knowledge of a woman against her will." . . . Those three elements of rape — carnal knowledge, forcibly, and against her will — remained the essential elements of the crime until 1979.

Under traditional rape law, in order to prove

that a rape had occurred, the state had to show both that force had been used and that the penetration had been against the woman's will. Force was identified and determined not as an independent factor but in relation to the response of the victim, which in turn implicated the victim's own state of mind. "Thus, the perpetrator's use of force became criminal only if the victim's state of mind met the statutory requirement. The perpetrator could use all the force imaginable and no crime would be committed if the state could not prove additionally that the victim did not consent." Although the terms "non-consent" and "against her will" were often treated as equivalent, under the traditional definition of rape, both formulations squarely placed on the victim the burden of proof and of action. Effectively, a woman who was above the age of consent had actively and affirmatively to withdraw that consent for the intercourse to be against her will. . . .

The presence or absence of consent often turned on credibility. To demonstrate that the victim had not consented to the intercourse, and also that sufficient force had been used to accomplish the rape, the state had to prove that the victim had resisted. According to the oft-quoted Lord Hale, to be deemed a credible witness, a woman had to be of good fame, disclose the injury immediately, suffer signs of injury, and cry out for help. Courts and commentators historically distrusted the testimony of victims, "assuming that women lie about their lack of consent for various reasons: to blackmail men, to explain the discovery of a consensual affair, or because of psychological illness." Evidence of resistance was viewed as a solution to the credibility problem; it was the "outward manifestation of nonconsent, [a] device for determining whether a woman actually gave consent." The resistance requirement had a profound effect on the kind of conduct that could be deemed criminal and on the type of evidence needed to establish the crime. *See, e.g., State v. Brown,* 127 Wis. 193, 106 *N.W.* 536 (1906) (overturning forcible rape conviction based on inadequate resistance by the victim). . . Courts assumed that any woman who was forced to have intercourse against her will necessarily would resist to the extent of her ability. *People v. Barnes,* 42 *Cal.*3d 284, 228 *Cal. Rptr.* 228, 721 *P.*2d 110, 117 (1986) (observing

that "[h]istorically, it was considered inconceivable that a woman who truly did not consent to sexual intercourse would not meet force with force"). In many jurisdictions the requirement was that the woman have resisted to the utmost. "Rape is not committed unless the woman oppose the man to the utmost limit of her power." *People v. Carey,* 223 *N.Y.* 519, 119 *N.E.* 83 (N.Y. 1918). "[A] mere tactical surrender in the face of an assumed superior physical force is not enough. Where the penalty for the defendant may be supreme, so must resistance be unto the uttermost." *Moss v. State,* 208 Miss. 531, 45 *So.*2d 125, 126 (1950). Other states followed a "reasonableness" standard, while some required only sufficient resistance to make non-consent reasonably manifest.

At least by the 1960s courts in New Jersey followed a standard for establishing resistance that was somewhat less drastic than the traditional rule. . . . *State v. Harris* . . . recognized that the "to the uttermost" test was obsolete. *Id.* at 16, 174 *A.*2d 645. "The fact that a victim finally submits does not necessarily imply that she consented. Submission to a compelling force, or as a result of being put in fear, is not consent." Nonetheless, the "resistance" requirement remained an essential feature of New Jersey rape law. Thus, in 1965 the Appellate Division stated: "[W]e have rejected the former test that a woman must resist `to the uttermost.' We only require that she resist as much as she possibly can under the circumstances."

The judicial interpretation of the pre-reform rape law in New Jersey, with its insistence on resistance by the victim, greatly minimized the importance of the forcible and assaultive aspect of the defendant's conduct. Rape prosecutions turned then not so much on the forcible or assaultive character of the defendant's actions as on the nature of the victim's response. "[I]f a woman assaulted is physically and mentally able to resist, is not terrified by threats, and is not in a place and position that resistance would have been useless, it must be shown that she did, in fact, resist the assault." Under the pre-reform law, the resistance offered had to be "in good faith and without pretense, with an active determination to prevent the violation of her person, and must not be merely passive and perfunctory." That the law put the rape victim on trial was clear.

The resistance requirement had another untoward influence on traditional rape law. Resistance was necessary not only to prove non-consent but also to demonstrate that the force used by the defendant had been sufficient to overcome the victim's will. The amount of force used by the defendant was assessed in relation to the resistance of the victim. In New Jersey the amount of force necessary to establish rape was characterized as "`the degree of force sufficient to overcome any resistance that had been put up by the female.'" Resistance, often demonstrated by torn clothing and blood, was a sign that the defendant had used significant force to accomplish the sexual intercourse. Thus, if the defendant forced himself on a woman, it was her responsibility to fight back, because force was measured in relation to the resistance she put forward. Only if she resisted, causing him to use more force than was necessary to achieve penetration, would his conduct be criminalized. Indeed, the significance of resistance as the proxy for force is illustrated by cases in which victims were unable to resist; in such cases the force incident to penetration was deemed sufficient to establish the "force" element of the offense.

The importance of resistance as an evidentiary requirement set the law of rape apart from other common-law crimes, particularly in the eyes of those who advocated reform of rape law in the 1970s. However, the resistance requirement was not the only special rule applied in the rape context. A host of evidentiary rules and standards of proof distinguished the legal treatment of rape from the treatment of other crimes. Many jurisdictions held that a rape conviction could not be sustained if based solely on the uncorroborated testimony of the victim. Often judges added cautionary instructions to jury charges warning jurors that rape was a particularly difficult charge to prove. Courts in New Jersey allowed greater latitude in cross-examining rape victims and in delving into their backgrounds than in ordinary cases. Rape victims were required to make a prompt complaint or have their allegations rejected or viewed with great skepticism. Some commentators suggested that there be mandatory psychological testing of rape victims.

During the 1970s feminists and others criticized the stereotype that rape victims were inherently more untrustworthy than other victims of criminal attack. Reformers condemned such suspicion as discrimination against victims of rape. They argued that "[d]istrust of the complainant's credibility [had] led to an exaggerated insistence on evidence of resistance," resulting in the victim rather than the defendant being put on trial. Reformers also challenged the assumption that a woman would seduce a man and then, in order to protect her virtue, claim to have been raped. If women are no less trustworthy than other purported victims of criminal attack, the reformers argued, then women should face no additional burdens of proving that they had not consented to or had actively resisted the assault.

To refute the misguided belief that rape was not real unless the victim fought back, reformers emphasized empirical research indicating that women who resisted forcible intercourse often suffered far more serious injury as a result. That research discredited the assumption that resistance to the utmost or to the best of a woman's ability was the most reasonable or rational response to a rape.

The research also helped demonstrate the underlying point of the reformers that the crime of rape rested not in the overcoming of a woman's will or the insult to her chastity but in the forcible attack itself — the assault on her person. Reformers criticized the conception of rape as a distinctly sexual crime rather than a crime of violence. They emphasized that rape had its legal origins in laws designed to protect the property rights of men to their wives and daughters. Although the crime had evolved into an offense against women, reformers argued that vestiges of the old law remained, particularly in the understanding of rape as a crime against the purity or chastity of a woman. The burden of protecting that chastity fell on the woman, with the state offering its protection only after the woman demonstrated that she had resisted sufficiently.

That rape under the traditional approach constituted a sexual rather than an assaultive crime is underscored by the spousal exemption. According to the traditional reasoning, a man could not rape his wife because consent to sexual intercourse was implied by the marriage contract. Therefore, sexual intercourse between spouses was lawful regardless of the force or violence used to accomplish it.

Critics of rape law agreed that the focus of the crime should be shifted from the victim's behavior to the defendant's conduct, and particularly to its forceful and assaultive, rather than sexual, character. Reformers also shared the goals of facilitating rape prosecutions and of sparing victims much of the degradation involved in bringing and trying a charge of rape. There were, however, differences over the best way to redefine the crime. Some reformers advocated a standard that defined rape as unconsented-to sexual intercourse, others urged the elimination of any reference to consent from the definition of rape. Nonetheless, all proponents of reform shared a central premise: that the burden of showing non-consent should not fall on the victim of the crime. In dealing with the problem of consent the reform goal was not so much to purge the entire concept of consent from the law as to eliminate the burden that had been placed on victims to prove they had not consented.

Similarly, with regard to force, rape law reform sought to give independent significance to the forceful or assaultive conduct of the defendant and to avoid a definition of force that depended on the reaction of the victim. Traditional interpretations of force were strongly criticized for failing to acknowledge that force may be understood simply as the invasion of "bodily integrity." In urging that the "resistance" requirement be abandoned, reformers sought to break the connection between force and resistance.

III

The history of traditional rape law sheds clearer light on the factors that became most influential in the enactment of current law dealing with sexual offenses. The circumstances surrounding the actual passage of the current law reveal that it was conceived as a reform measure reconstituting the law to address a widely-sensed evil and to effectuate an important public policy. Those circumstances are highly relevant in understanding legislative intent and in determining the objectives of the current law.

In October 1971, the New Jersey Criminal Law Revision Commission promulgated a Final Report and Commentary on its proposed New Jersey Penal Code. The proposed Code substantially followed the American Law Institute's Model Penal Code (MPC) with respect to sexual offenses. . . .

The Legislature did not endorse the Model Penal Code approach to rape. Rather, it passed a fundamentally different proposal in 1978 when it adopted the Code of Criminal Justice. The new statutory provisions covering rape were formulated by a coalition of feminist groups assisted by the National Organization of Women (NOW) National Task Force on Rape. Both houses of the Legislature adopted the NOW bill, as it was called, without major changes and Governor Byrne signed it into law on August 10, 1978. The NOW bill had been modeled after the 1976 Philadelphia Center for Rape Concern Model Sex Offense Statute. The Model Sex Offense Statute in turn had been based on selected provisions of the Michigan Criminal Sexual Conduct Statute and on the reform statutes in New Mexico, Minnesota, and Wisconsin. The stated intent of the drafters of the Philadelphia Center's Model Statute had been to remove all features found to be contrary to the interests of rape victims. According to its proponents the statute would "`normalize the law. We are no longer saying rape victims are likely to lie. What we are saying is that rape is just like other violent crimes.'"

Since the 1978 reform, the Code has referred to the crime that was once known as "rape" as "sexual assault." The crime now requires "penetration," not "sexual intercourse." It requires "force" or "coercion," not "submission" or "resistance." It makes no reference to the victim's state of mind or attitude, or conduct in response to the assault. It eliminates the spousal exception based on implied consent. It emphasizes the assaultive character of the offense by defining sexual penetration to encompass a wide range of sexual contacts, going well beyond traditional "carnal knowledge. Consistent with the assaultive character, as opposed to the traditional sexual character, of the offense, the statute also renders the crime gender-neutral: both males and females can be actors or victims.

The reform statute defines sexual assault as penetration accomplished by the use of "physical force" or "coercion," but it does not define either "physical force" or "coercion" or enumerate examples of evidence that would establish those elements. Some reformers had argued that defining "physical force" too specifically in the sexual offense statute might have the effect of limiting force to the enumerated examples. The task of defining "physical force" therefore was left to the courts.

. . . [T]he New Jersey Code of Criminal Justice does not refer to force in relation to "overcoming the will" of the victim, or to the "physical overpowering" of the victim, or the "submission" of the victim. It does not require the demonstrated non-consent of the victim. As we have noted, in reforming the rape laws, the Legislature placed primary emphasis on the assaultive nature of the crime, altering its constituent elements so that they focus exclusively on the forceful or assaultive conduct of the defendant.

The Legislature's concept of sexual assault and the role of force was significantly colored by its understanding of the law of assault and battery. As a general matter, criminal battery is defined as "the unlawful application of force to the person of another." The application of force is criminal when it results in either (a) a physical injury or (b) an offensive touching. Any "unauthorized touching of another [is] a battery." Thus, by eliminating all references to the victim's state of mind and conduct, and by broadening the definition of penetration to cover not only sexual intercourse between a man and a woman but a range of acts that invade another's body or compel intimate contact, the Legislature emphasized the affinity between sexual assault and other forms of assault and battery.

The intent of the Legislature to redefine rape consistent with the law of assault and battery is further evidenced by the legislative treatment of other sexual crimes less serious than and derivative of traditional rape. The Code

redefined the offense of criminal sexual contact to emphasize the involuntary and personally-offensive nature of the touching. Sexual contact is criminal under the same circumstances that render an act of sexual penetration a sexual assault, namely, when "physical force" or "coercion" demonstrates that it is unauthorized and offensive. Thus, just as any unauthorized touching is a crime under traditional laws of assault and battery, so is any unauthorized sexual contact a crime under the reformed law of criminal sexual contact, and so is any unauthorized sexual penetration a crime under the reformed law of sexual assault.

The understanding of sexual assault as a criminal battery, albeit one with especially serious consequences, follows necessarily from the Legislature's decision to eliminate non-consent and resistance from the substantive definition of the offense. Under the new law, the victim no longer is required to resist and therefore need not have said or done anything in order for the sexual penetration to be unlawful. The alleged victim is not put on trial, and his or her responsive or defensive behavior is rendered immaterial. We are thus satisfied that an interpretation of the statutory crime of sexual assault to require physical force in addition to that entailed in an act of involuntary or unwanted sexual penetration would be fundamentally inconsistent with the legislative purpose to eliminate any consideration of whether the victim resisted or expressed non-consent.

We note that the contrary interpretation of force — that the element of force need be extrinsic to the sexual act — would not only reintroduce a resistance requirement into the sexual assault law, but also would immunize many acts of criminal sexual *contact* short of penetration. The characteristics that make a sexual contact unlawful are the same as those that make a sexual penetration unlawful. An actor is guilty of criminal sexual contact if he or she commits an act of sexual contact with another using "physical force" or "coercion." That the Legislature would have wanted to decriminalize unauthorized sexual intrusions on the bodily integrity of a victim by requiring a showing of force in addition to that entailed in the sexual contact itself is hardly possible.

Because the statute eschews any reference to the victim's will or resistance, the standard defining the role of force in sexual penetration must prevent the possibility that the establishment of the crime will turn on the alleged victim's state of mind or responsive behavior. We conclude, therefore, that any act of sexual penetration engaged in by the defendant without the affirmative and freely-given permission of the victim to the specific act of penetration constitutes the offense of sexual assault. Therefore, physical force in excess of that inherent in the act of sexual penetration is not required for such penetration to be unlawful. The definition of "physical force" is satisfied under *N.J.S.A.* 2C:14-2c(1) if the defendant applies any amount of force against another person in the absence of what a reasonable person would believe to be affirmative and freely-given permission to the act of sexual penetration.

Under the reformed statute, permission to engage in sexual penetration must be affirmative and it must be given freely, but that permission may be inferred either from acts or statements reasonably viewed in light of the surrounding circumstances. Persons need not, of course, expressly announce their consent to engage in intercourse for there to be affirmative permission. Permission to engage in an act of sexual penetration can be and indeed often is indicated through physical actions rather than words. Permission is demonstrated when the evidence, in whatever form, is sufficient to demonstrate that a reasonable person would have believed that the alleged victim had affirmatively and freely given authorization to the act.

Our understanding of the meaning and application of "physical force" under the sexual assault statute indicates that the term's inclusion was neither inadvertent nor redundant. The term "physical force," like its companion term "coercion," acts to qualify the nature and character of the "sexual penetration." Sexual penetration accomplished through the use of force is unauthorized sexual penetration. That functional understanding of "physical force" encompasses the notion of "unpermitted touching" derived from the Legislature's decision to redefine rape as a sexual assault. As already noted, under assault

and battery doctrine, any amount of force that results in either physical injury or offensive touching is sufficient to establish a battery. Hence, as a description of the method of achieving "sexual penetration," the term "physical force" serves to define and explain the acts that are offensive, unauthorized, and unlawful.

That understanding of the crime of sexual assault fully comports with the public policy sought to be effectuated by the Legislature. In redefining rape law as sexual assault, the Legislature adopted the concept of sexual assault as a crime against the bodily integrity of the victim. Although it is possible to imagine a set of rules in which persons must demonstrate affirmatively that sexual contact is unwanted or not permitted, such a regime would be inconsistent with modern principles of personal autonomy. The Legislature recast the law of rape as sexual assault to bring that area of law in line with the expectation of privacy and bodily control that long has characterized most of our private and public law. In interpreting "physical force" to include any touching that occurs without permission we seek to respect that goal.

Today the law of sexual assault is indispensable to the system of legal rules that assures each of us the right to decide who may touch our bodies, when, and under what circumstances. The decision to engage in sexual relations with another person is one of the most private and intimate decisions a person can make. Each person has the right not only to decide whether to engage in sexual contact with another, but also to control the circumstances and character of that contact. No one, neither a spouse, nor a friend, nor an acquaintance, nor a stranger, has the right or the privilege to force sexual contact. *See Definition of Forcible Rape, supra,* 61 *Va.L.Rev.* at 1529 (arguing that "forcible rape is viewed as a heinous crime primarily because it is a violent assault on a person's bodily security, particularly degrading because that person is forced to submit to an act of the most intimate nature").

We emphasize as well that what is now referred to as "acquaintance rape" is not a new phenomenon. Nor was it a "futuristic" concept in 1978 when the sexual assault law was enacted. Current concern over the prevalence of forced sexual intercourse between persons who know one another reflects both greater awareness of the extent of such behavior and a growing appreciation of its gravity. Notwithstanding the stereotype of rape as a violent attack by a stranger, the vast majority of sexual assaults are perpetrated by someone known to the victim. One respected study indicates that more than half of all rapes are committed by male relatives, current or former husbands, boyfriends or lovers. Similarly, contrary to common myths, perpetrators generally do not use guns or knives and victims generally do not suffer external bruises or cuts. Although this more realistic and accurate view of rape only recently has achieved widespread public circulation, it was a central concern of the proponents of reform in the 1970s.

The insight into rape as an assaultive crime is consistent with our evolving understanding of the wrong inherent in forced sexual intimacy. It is one that was appreciated by the Legislature when it reformed the rape laws, reflecting an emerging awareness that the definition of rape should correspond fully with the experiences and perspectives of rape victims. Although reformers focused primarily on the problems associated with convicting defendants accused of violent rape, the recognition that forced sexual intercourse often takes place between persons who know each other and often involves little or no violence comports with the understanding of the sexual assault law that was embraced by the Legislature. Any other interpretation of the law, particularly one that defined force in relation to the resistance or protest of the victim, would directly undermine the goals sought to be achieved by its reform.

IV

In a case such as this one, in which the State does not allege violence or force extrinsic to the act of penetration, the factfinder must decide whether the defendant's act of penetration was undertaken in circumstances that led the defendant reasonably to believe that the alleged victim had freely given affirmative permission to the specific act of sexual penetration. Such permission can be indicated either through words or through actions that, when viewed in the light of all the surrounding circumstances,

would demonstrate to a reasonable person affirmative and freely-given authorization for the specific act of sexual penetration.

In applying that standard to the facts in these cases, the focus of attention must be on the nature of the defendant's actions. The role of the factfinder is not to decide whether reasonable people may engage in acts of penetration without the permission of others. The Legislature answered that question when it enacted the reformed sexual assault statute: reasonable people do not engage in acts of penetration without permission, and it is unlawful to do so. The role of the factfinder is to decide not whether engaging in an act of penetration without permission of another person is reasonable, but only whether the defendant's belief that the alleged victim had freely given affirmative permission was reasonable.

In these cases neither the alleged victim's subjective state of mind nor the reasonableness of the alleged victim's actions can be deemed relevant to the offense. The alleged victim may be questioned about what he or she did or said only to determine whether the defendant was reasonable in believing that affirmative permission had been freely given. To repeat, the law places no burden on the alleged victim to have expressed non-consent or to have denied permission, and no inquiry is made into what he or she thought or desired or why he or she did not resist or protest.

In short, in order to convict under the sexual assault statute in cases such as these, the State must prove beyond a reasonable doubt that there was sexual penetration and that it was accomplished without the affirmative and freely-given permission of the alleged victim. As we have indicated, such proof can be based on evidence of conduct or words in light of surrounding circumstances and must demonstrate beyond a reasonable doubt that a reasonable person would not have believed that there was affirmative and freely-given permission. If there is evidence to suggest that the defendant reasonably believed that such permission had been given, the State must demonstrate either that defendant did not actually believe that affirmative permission had been freely-given or that such a belief was unreasonable under all of the circumstances. Thus, the State bears the burden of proof throughout the case.

In the context of a sexual penetration not involving unusual or added "physical force," the inclusion of "permission" as an aspect of "physical force" effectively subsumes and obviates any defense based on consent. *See N.J.S.A.*2C:2-10c(3). The definition of "permission" serves to define the "consent" that otherwise might allow a defendant to avoid criminal liability. Because "physical force" as an element of sexual assault in this context requires the *absence* of affirmative and freely-given permission, the "consent" necessary to negate such "physical force" under a defense based on consent would require the *presence* of such affirmative and freely-given permission. Any lesser form of consent would render the sexual penetration unlawful and cannot constitute a defense.

In this case, the Appellate Division concluded that non-consensual penetration accomplished with no additional physical force or coercion is not criminalized under the sexual assault statute. It acknowledged that its conclusion was "anomalous" because it recognized that "a woman has every right to end [physically intimate] activity without sexual penetration." Thus, it added to its holding that "[e]ven the force of penetration might... be sufficient if it is shown to be employed to overcome the victim's unequivocal expressed desire to limit the encounter."

The Appellate Division was correct in recognizing that a woman's right to end intimate activity without penetration is a protectable right the violation of which can be a criminal offense. However, it misperceived the purpose of the statute in believing that the only way that right can be protected is by the woman's unequivocally-expressed desire to end the activity. The effect of that requirement would be to import into the sexual assault statute the notion that an assault occurs only if the victim's will is overcome, and thus to reintroduce the requirement of non-consent and victim-resistance as a constituent material element of the crime. Under the reformed statute, a person's failure to protest or resist cannot be considered or used as justification for bodily invasion.

We acknowledge that cases such as this are inherently fact sensitive and depend on the reasoned judgment and common sense of judges and juries. The trial court concluded that the victim had not expressed consent to the act of intercourse, either through her words or actions. We conclude that the record provides reasonable support for the trial court's disposition.

Accordingly, we reverse the judgment of the Appellate Division and reinstate the disposition of juvenile delinquency for the commission of second-degree sexual assault.

COMMONWEALTH v. BERKOWITZ, 537 Pa. 143 (1994)

[In this case we address the] . . . question of the precise degree of force necessary to prove the "forcible compulsion" element of the crime of rape. . . .

The relevant facts of this case are as follows. The complainant, a female college student, left her class, went to her dormitory room where she drank a martini, and then went to a lounge to await her boyfriend. When her boyfriend failed to appear, she went to another dormitory to find a friend, Earl Hassel. She knocked on the door, but received no answer. She tried the doorknob and, finding it unlocked, entered the room and discovered a man sleeping on the bed. The complainant originally believed the man to be Hassel, but it turned out to be Hassel's roommate, Appellee. Appellee asked her to stay for a while and she agreed. He requested a back-rub and she declined. He suggested that she sit on the bed, but she declined and sat on the floor.

Appellee [Berkowitz] then moved to the floor beside her, lifted up her shirt and bra and massaged her breasts. He then unfastened his pants and unsuccessfully attempted to put his penis in her mouth. They both stood up, and he locked the door. He returned to push her onto the bed, and removed her undergarments from one leg. He then penetrated her vagina with his penis. After withdrawing and ejaculating on her stomach, he stated, "Wow, I guess we just got carried away," to which she responded, "No, we didn't get carried away, you got carried away."

In reviewing the sufficiency of the evidence, this Court must view the evidence in the light most favorable to the Commonwealth as verdict winner, and accept as true all evidence and reasonable inferences that may be reasonably drawn therefrom, upon which, if believed, the jury could have relied in reaching its verdict. If, upon such review, the Court concludes that the jury could not have determined from the evidence adduced that all of the necessary elements of the crime were established, then the evidence will be deemed insufficient to support the verdict.

The crime of rape is defined as follows:

§ 3121. Rape A person commits a felony of the first degree when he engages in sexual intercourse with another person not one's spouse: (1) by forcible compulsion; (2) by threat of forcible compulsion that would prevent resistance by a person of reasonable resolution; (3) who is unconscious; or (4) who is so mentally deranged or deficient that such person is incapable of consent.

The victim of a rape need not resist. "The force necessary to support a conviction of rape . . . need only be such as to establish lack of consent and to induce the [victim] to submit without additional resistance. . . . The degree of force required to constitute rape is relative and depends on the facts and particular circumstance of the case."
In regard to the critical issue of forcible compulsion, the complainant's testimony is devoid of any statement which clearly or adequately describes the use of force or the threat of force against her. In response to defense counsel's question, "Is it possible that [when Appellee lifted your bra and shirt] you took no physical action to discourage him," the complainant replied, "It's possible." When asked, "Is it possible that [Appellee] was not making any physical contact with you . . . aside

from attempting to untie the knot [in the drawstrings of complainant's sweatpants]," she answered, "It's possible." She testified that "He put me down on the bed. It was kind of like He didn't throw me on the bed. It's hard to explain. It was kind of like a push but not I can't explain what I'm trying to say." She concluded that "it wasn't much" in reference to whether she bounced on the bed, and further detailed that their movement to the bed "wasn't slow like a romantic kind of thing, but it wasn't a fast shove either. It was kind of in the middle." She agreed that Appellee's hands were not restraining her in any manner during the actual penetration, and that the weight of his body on top of her was the only force applied. She testified that at no time did Appellee verbally threaten her. The complainant did testify that she sought to leave the room, and said "no" throughout the encounter. As to the complainant's desire to leave the room, the record clearly demonstrates that the door could be unlocked easily from the inside, that she was aware of this fact, but that she never attempted to go to the door or unlock it.

As to the complainant's testimony that she stated "no" throughout the encounter with Appellee [Berkowitz], we point out that, while such an allegation of fact would be relevant to the issue of consent, it is not relevant to the issue of force. In Commonwealth v. Mlinarich, this Court sustained the reversal of a defendant's conviction of rape where the alleged victim, a minor, repeatedly stated that she did not want to engage in sexual intercourse, but offered no physical resistance and was compelled to engage in sexual intercourse under threat of being recommitted to a juvenile detention center. The Opinion in Support of Affirmance acknowledged that physical force, a threat of force, or psychological coercion may be sufficient to support the element of "forcible compulsion", if found to be enough to "prevent resistance by a person of reasonable resolution." However, under the facts of Mlinarich, neither physical force, the threat of physical force, nor psychological coercion were found to have been proven, and this Court held that the conviction was properly reversed by the Superior Court. Accordingly, the ruling in Mlinarich implicitly dictates that where there is a lack of consent, but no showing of either physical force, a threat of physical force, or psychological coercion, the "forcible compulsion" requirement under 18 Pa.C.S. § 3121 is not met.

Moreover, we find it instructive that in defining the related but distinct crime of "indecent assault" under 18 Pa.C.S. § 3126, the Legislature did not employ the phrase "forcible compulsion" but rather chose to define indecent assault as "indecent contact with another . . . without the consent of the other person." The phrase "forcible compulsion" is explicitly set forth in the definition of rape under 18 Pa.C.S. § 3121, but the phrase "without the consent of the other person," is conspicuously absent. The choice by the Legislature to define the crime of indecent assault utilizing the phrase "without the consent of the other" and to not so define

the crime of rape indicates a legislative intent that the term "forcible compulsion" under 18 Pa.C.S. § 3121, be interpreted as something more than a lack of consent. Moreover, we note that penal statutes must be strictly construed to provide fair warning to the defendant of the nature of the proscribed conduct.

Reviewed in light of the above described standard, the complainant's testimony simply fails to establish that the Appellee forcibly compelled her to engage in sexual intercourse as required under 18 Pa.C.S. § 3121. Thus, even if all of the complainant's testimony was believed, the jury, as a matter of law, could not have found Appellee guilty of rape. Accordingly, we hold that the Superior Court did not err in reversing Appellee's conviction of rape.

Rape Mens Rea

Although at common law the government had to prove lack of consent, it was unclear whether the defendant had to be aware that the sexual intercourse was without the female's consent. There are three approaches that states follow. The first approach (the subjective approach) holds that the defendant is not liable for rape if he believed that the woman consented to sex—regardless of whether that belief was reasonable. This is the approach used in England, but rejected by most American courts. In *Director of Public Prosecutions v. Morgan*, [1976] AC 182, [1975]UKHL3, a married man invited three of his drinking buddies to come over to have sex with his wife. He assured his friends that, although his wife would protest, his wife enjoyed "kinky sex" and this was the only way she could get aroused. The defendants took him up on his offer. The three men held the woman down while they took turns having sex with his wife. The English House of Lords acquitted the defendants holding that rape required the specific intent to have sex against the will and without the consent of the victim. Since these men had an honest belief the woman did consent, they lacked the requisite mens rea for rape.

The second approach is the objective approach which recognizes a defense to rape if the defendant reasonably and honestly believed that the rape victim consented. This approach was first espoused in the California case of *People v. Mayberry, 15 Cal. 3d* 143 (1975). In that case, the victim claimed that she had been kidnapped while shopping and had involuntarily accompanied the kidnapper to an apartment where she was raped by the defendant and another male. The California Supreme Court held that the defendant was entitled to have a jury instruction about a reasonable mistake of fact. The Court held that legislators must have intended the defense be available given the seriousness of the charge. A defendant who "entertains a reasonable and bona fide belief that a prosecutrix voluntarily consented to accompany him and to engage in sexual intercourse . . . does not possess the wrongful intent that is a prerequisite to a conviction of rape by means of force or threat." The majority of American states follow this objective approach. Lippman notes that this approach requires "equivocal conduct" "meaning that the victim's nonconsensual reactions were capable of being reasonably, but mistakenly interpreted by the assailant as indicating consent."

The third approach is the strict liability approach. Several states do not recognize the mistake of fact defense and maintain that a defendant's belief as to whether the victim consented should not be considered in determining guilt. If the state can prove that the victim did not consent, then the defendant's belief about her consent is irrelevant. For example, in *State v. Reed*, 479 A.2d 129 (1984) the Court ruled that rape is a strict liability crime. The Maine Supreme Judicial Court held,

> Certain crimes are defined to expressly include a culpable state of mind and others are not.
> The more forceful or egregious sexual conduct, including rape compelled by force, is

defined without reference to the actor's state of mind. The legislature, by carefully defining the sex offenses in the criminal code, and by making no reference to a culpable mental state for rape, clearly indicate that rape compelled by force or threat requires no culpable state of mind.

Other Cases—Rape Mens Rea

State v. Bonds, 477 N.W.2d 265 (Wisc. 1991). Victim contacted Bonds in a boarding house where she resided. Bonds had previously lived in the building but had been evicted. When the victim saw Bonds, she told him that a guard was waiting for him downstairs. She then returned to her room. Bonds yelled profanities and followed the victim back to her room. She considered his words threatening, and when she turned aroud to confront defendant, he reached out his hand, grabbed the nipple of her left breast, squeezed and pulled it, causing pain. She responded by knocking his hand away. Bonds then attempted to bring his fist toward her face, and she grabbed his hand and bit it.

Bonds entered a plea and was sentenced to six years in prison. At his plea hearing, Bonds claimed that he squeezed and pulled the victim's nipple to hurt her, but not to violate her sexually.

On appeal, the court of appeals held that the defendant's actions did not constitute sexual contact by use or threatened use of force. Thus, if determined that his actions did not constitute second-degree sexual assault and so it reversed defendant's conviction. The state appealed.

OPINION:
"The issue in this case is whether a defendant's use of force in making sexual contact with his victim by forcibly grabbing her nipple and then squeezing and pulling it, constitutes the crime of second-degree sexual assault. Under [the pertinent law] one is guilty of second degree sexual assault when an individual has 'sexual contact or sexual intercourse with another person without consent of that person by use or threat of force or violence.'"

[Bonds asserts that he should be charged with battery or fourth degree sexual assault which did not require a showing of force, violence or injury.]

The defendant argues that the statutory element "by use or threat of force or violence " . . . requires that a causal relationship exists between the "use or threat of force or violence" and the sexual contact or intercourse. . . .

By its very terms, [the statute' prohibits nonconsensual sexual contact "by use or threat of force or violence." Sexual contact under this section includes "actual or attempted battery." "Sexual contact is defined as . . . any intentional touching by the complainant or defendant, either directly or through clothing by the use of any body part or object, of the complainant's or defendant's intimate parts if that intentional touching is either for the purpose of sexually degrading or for the purpose of sexually humiliating the complainant or sexually arousing or gratifying the defendant or if the touching contains the elements of actual or attempted battery. . . .

> "Intimate parts" is defined. . . and includes any of the following: "breast, buttock, anus, groin, scrotum, penis, vagina or pubic mound of a human being."

> "Battery occurs when one "causes bodily harm to another by an act done with intent to cause bodily harm to that person or another without the consent of the person so harmed." . . .

The defendant admitted using force and conceded that he had intended to hurt his victim . . . . We conclude that based on the plain language of the statute, the defendant falls within second-degree sexual assault because he made sexual contact of a complainant's intimate part through the means of actual or attempted battery.

Statutory Rape

Modern day "statutory rape" comprises having sex with minors. Statutes spell out how young the minor must be for the sex to be criminal regardless of the victim's consent and the presence of force. Statutory rape does not require the use of force or threat of force; instead the victim's immaturity takes the place of the force. Lack of consent is not an element with statutory rape because minors are not able to legally consent to sex. (Although statutory rape is a modern classification, the premise was the same at common law—youth cannot *legally* give consent to have sex even though they may have agreed to, in fact, have sex). Statutory rape is a strict liability crime (see *Garnett v. State*, below), but some states do allow the defendant to raise a defense of reasonable mistake of age. Recently, states have enacted "Romeo and Juliet" laws which treat sex between minors as not rape as long as the partner's ages are within typically within two, three, or four years.

GARNETT v. STATE,
632 A. 2d 797, 332 Md. 571 (1993)

[In this case] . . . we consider whether under the present statute, the State must prove that a defendant knew the complaining witness was younger than 14 and, in a related question, whether it was error at trial to exclude evidence that he had been told, and believed, that she was 16 years old.

I

Raymond Lennard Garnett is a young retarded man. At the time of the incident in question he was 20 years old. He has an I.Q. of 52. His guidance counselor from the Montgomery County public school system, Cynthia Parker, described him as a mildly retarded person who read on the third-grade level, did arithmetic on the 5th-grade level, and interacted with others socially at school at the level of someone 11 or 12 years of age. Ms. Parker added that Raymond attended special education classes and for at least one period of time was educated at home when he was afraid to return to school due to his classmates' taunting. Because he could not understand the duties of the jobs given him, he failed to complete vocational assignments; he sometimes lost his way to work. As Raymond was unable to pass any of the State's functional tests required for graduation, he received only a certificate of attendance rather than a high-school diploma.

In November or December 1990, a friend introduced Raymond to Erica Frazier, then aged 13; the two subsequently talked occasionally by telephone. On February 28, 1991, Raymond, apparently wishing to call for a ride home, approached the girl's house at about nine o'clock in the evening. Erica opened her bedroom window, through which Raymond entered; he testified that "she just told me to get a ladder and climb up her window." The two talked, and later engaged in sexual intercourse. Raymond left at about 4:30 a.m. the following morning. On November 19, 1991, Erica gave birth to a baby, of which Raymond is the biological father.

Raymond was tried before the Circuit Court for Montgomery County (Miller, J.) on one count of second degree rape under § 463(a)(3) proscribing sexual intercourse between a person under 14 and another at least four years older than the complainant. At trial, the defense twice proffered evidence to the effect that Erica herself and her friends had previously told Raymond that she was 16 years old, and that he had acted with that belief. The trial court excluded such evidence as immaterial, explaining:

> "Under 463, the only two requirements as relate to this case are that there was vaginal intercourse, [and] that ... Ms. Frazier was under 14 years of age and that ... Mr. Garnett was at least four years older than she.

> "In the Court's opinion, consent is no defense to this charge. The victim's representation as to her age and the defendant's belief, if it existed, that she was not under age, what amounts to what otherwise might be termed a good faith defense, is in fact no defense to what

amount[s] to statutory rape.

> "It is in the Court's opinion a strict liability offense."

The court found Raymond guilty. It sentenced him to a term of five years in prison, suspended the sentence and imposed five years of probation, and ordered that he pay restitution to Erica and the Frazier family. Raymond noted an appeal; we granted certiorari prior to intermediate appellate review by the Court of Special Appeals to consider the important issue presented in the case.

Section 463(a)(3) does not expressly set forth a requirement that the accused have acted with a criminal state of mind, or mens rea. The State insists that the statute, by design, defines a strict liability offense, and that its essential elements were met in the instant case when Raymond, age 20, engaged in vaginal intercourse with Erica, a girl under 14 and more than 4 years his junior. Raymond replies that the criminal law exists to assess and punish morally culpable behavior. He says such culpability was absent here. He asks us either to engraft onto subsection (a)(3) an implicit mens rea requirement, or to recognize an affirmative defense of reasonable mistake as to the complainant's age. Raymond argues that it is unjust, under the circumstances of this case which led him to think his conduct lawful, to brand him a felon and rapist.

III

Raymond asserts that the events of this case were inconsistent with the criminal sexual exploitation of a minor by an adult. As earlier observed, Raymond entered Erica's bedroom at the girl's invitation; she directed him to use a ladder to reach her window. They engaged voluntarily in sexual intercourse. They remained together in the room for more than seven hours before Raymond departed at dawn. With an I.Q. of 52, Raymond functioned at approximately the same level as the 13-year-old Erica; he was mentally an adolescent in an adult's body. Arguably, had Raymond's chronological age, 20, matched his socio-intellectual age, about 12, he and Erica would have fallen well within the four-year age difference obviating a violation of the statute, and Raymond would not have been charged

with any crime at all.

The precise legal issue here rests on Raymond's unsuccessful efforts to introduce into evidence testimony that Erica and her friends had told him she was 16 years old, the age of consent to sexual relations, and that he believed them. Thus the trial court did not permit him to raise a defense of reasonable mistake of Erica's age, by which defense Raymond would have asserted that he acted innocently without a criminal design. At common law, a crime occurred only upon the concurrence of an individual's act and his guilty state of mind. In this regard, it is well understood that generally there are two components of every crime, the *actus reus* or guilty act and the mens rea or the guilty mind or mental state accompanying a forbidden act. . . . .

To be sure, legislative bodies since the mid-19th century have created strict liability criminal offenses requiring no mens rea. Almost all such statutes responded to the demands of public health and welfare arising from the complexities of society after the Industrial Revolution. Typically misdemeanors involving only fines or other light penalties, these strict liability laws regulated food, milk, liquor, medicines and drugs, securities, motor vehicles and traffic, the labeling of goods for sale, and the like. … Statutory rape, carrying the stigma of felony as well as a potential sentence of 20 years in prison, contrasts markedly with the other strict liability regulatory offenses and their light penalties.

Modern scholars generally reject the concept of strict criminal liability. Professors LaFave and Scott summarize the consensus that punishing conduct without reference to the actor's state of mind fails to reach the desired end and is unjust:

> "`It is inefficacious because conduct unaccompanied by an awareness of the factors making it criminal does not mark the actor as one who needs to be subjected to punishment in order to deter him or others from behaving similarly in the future, nor does it single him out as a socially dangerous individual who needs to be incapacitated or reformed. It is unjust because the actor is subjected to

the stigma of a criminal conviction without being morally blameworthy. Consequently, on either a preventive or retributive theory of criminal punishment, the criminal sanction is inappropriate in the absence of mens rea.'"

Conscious of the disfavor in which strict criminal liability resides, the Model Penal Code states generally as a minimum requirement of culpability that a person is not guilty of a criminal offense unless he acts purposely, knowingly, recklessly, or negligently, *i.e.*, with some degree of mens rea. The Code allows generally for a defense of ignorance or mistake of fact negating mens rea. The Model Penal Code generally recognizes strict liability for offenses deemed "violations," defined as wrongs subject only to a fine, forfeiture, or other civil penalty upon conviction, and not giving rise to any legal disability.

The commentators similarly disapprove of statutory rape as a strict liability crime. In addition to the arguments discussed above, they observe that statutory rape prosecutions often proceed even when the defendant's judgment as to the age of the complainant is warranted by her appearance, her sexual sophistication, her verbal misrepresentations, and the defendant's careful attempts to ascertain her true age. Voluntary intercourse with a sexually mature teen-ager lacks the features of psychic abnormality, exploitation, or physical danger that accompanies such conduct with children.

. . . The drafters of the Model Penal Code remarked:

"[T]he actor who reasonably believes that his partner is above that age [of consent] lacks culpability with respect to the factor deemed critical to liability. Punishing him anyway simply because his intended conduct would have been immoral under the facts as he supposed them to be postulates a relation between criminality and immorality that is inaccurate on both descriptive and normative grounds. The penal law does not try to enforce all aspects of community morality, and any thoroughgoing attempt to do so would

extend the prospect of criminal sanctions far into the sphere of individual liberty and create a regime too demanding for all save the best among us."

Id., Comment to § 213.6, at 415. We acknowledge here that it is uncertain to what extent Raymond's intellectual and social retardation may have impaired his ability to comprehend imperatives of sexual morality in any case.

IV

The legislatures of 17 states have enacted laws permitting a mistake of age defense in some form in cases of sexual offenses with underage persons. In Kentucky, the accused may prove in exculpation that he did not know the facts or conditions relevant to the complainant's age. In Washington, the defendant may assert that he reasonably believed the complainant to be of a certain age based on the alleged victim's own declarations. In some states, the defense is available in instances where the complainant's age rises above a statutorily prescribed level, but is not available when the complainant falls below the defining age. In other states, the availability of the defense depends on the severity of the sex offense charged to the accused.

In addition, the highest appellate courts of four states have determined that statutory rape laws by implication required an element of mens rea as to the complainant's age. In the landmark case of *People v. Hernandez*, the California Supreme Court held that, absent a legislative directive to the contrary, a charge of statutory rape was defensible wherein a criminal intent was lacking; it reversed the trial court's refusal to permit the defendant to present evidence of his good faith, reasonable belief that the complaining witness had reached the age of consent. In so doing, the court first questioned the assumption that age alone confers a sophistication sufficient to create legitimate consent to sexual relations: "the sexually experienced 15-year-old may be far more acutely aware of the implications of sexual intercourse than her sheltered cousin who is beyond the age of consent." The court then rejected the traditional view that those who engage in sex with young persons do so at their peril, assuming the risk that their partners are underage:

"[I]f [the perpetrator] participates in a mutual act of sexual intercourse, believing his partner to be beyond the age of consent, with reasonable grounds for such belief, where is his criminal intent? In such circumstances he has not consciously taken any risk. Instead he has subjectively eliminated the risk by satisfying himself on reasonable evidence that the crime cannot be committed. If it occurs that he has been mislead, we cannot realistically conclude for such reason alone the intent with which he undertook the act suddenly becomes more heinous.... [T]he courts have uniformly failed to satisfactorily explain the nature of the criminal intent present in the mind of one who in good faith believes he has obtained a lawful consent before engaging in the prohibited act."

The Supreme Court of Alaska has held that a charge of statutory rape is legally unsupportable unless a defense of reasonable mistake of age is allowed. The Supreme Court of Utah construed the applicable unlawful sexual intercourse statute to mean that a conviction could not result unless the state proved a criminal state of mind as to each element of the offense, including the victim's age. The Supreme Court of New Mexico determined that a defendant should have been permitted at trial to present a defense that his partner in consensual sex told him she was 17, not 15, that this had been confirmed to him by others, and that he had acted under that mistaken belief. Two-fifths of the states, therefore, now recognize the defense in cases of statutory sexual offenses.

V

We think it sufficiently clear, however, that Maryland's second degree rape statute defines a strict liability offense that does not require the State to prove mens rea; it makes no allowance for a mistake-of-age defense. The plain language of § 463, viewed in its entirety, and the legislative history of its creation lead to this conclusion.

It is well settled that in interpreting a statute to ascertain and effectuate its goal, our first recourse is to the words of the statute, giving them their ordinary and natural import. While penal statutes are to be strictly construed in favor of the defendant, the construction must ultimately depend upon discerning the intention of the Legislature when it drafted and enacted the law in question. To that end, the Court may appropriately look at the larger context, including external manifestations of the legislative purpose, within which statutory language appears.

Section 463(a)(3) prohibiting sexual intercourse with underage persons makes no reference to the actor's knowledge, belief, or other state of mind. As we see it, this silence as to mens rea results from legislative design. First, subsection (a)(3) stands in stark contrast to the provision immediately before it, subsection (a)(2) prohibiting vaginal intercourse with incapacitated or helpless persons. In subsection (a)(2), the Legislature expressly provided as an element of the offense that "the person performing the act *knows or should reasonably know* the other person is mentally defective, mentally incapacitated, or physically helpless." Code, § 463(a)(2) (emphasis added). In drafting this subsection, the Legislature showed itself perfectly capable of recognizing and allowing for a defense that obviates criminal intent; if the defendant objectively did not understand that the sex partner was impaired, there is no crime. That it chose not to include similar language in subsection (a)(3) indicates that the Legislature aimed to make statutory rape with underage persons a more severe prohibition based on strict criminal liability.

Second, an examination of the drafting history of § 463 during the 1976 revision of Maryland's sexual offense laws reveals that the statute was viewed as one of strict liability from its inception and throughout the amendment process.

. . . [T]he Legislature explicitly raised, considered, and then explicitly jettisoned any notion of a mens rea element with respect to the complainant's age in enacting the law that formed the basis of current § 463(a)(3). In the light of such legislative action, we must inevitably conclude that the current law imposes strict liability on its violators. This interpretation is consistent with the traditional view of statutory rape as a strict liability crime designed to protect young persons from the dangers of sexual exploitation by adults, loss of chastity, physical injury, and, in the case of girls, pregnancy. The majority of states retain statutes which impose strict liability for sexual acts with underage complainants. We observe again, as earlier, that even among those states providing for a mistake-of-age defense in some instances, the defense often is not available where the sex partner is 14 years old or less; the complaining witness in the instant case was only 13. The majority of appellate courts, including the Court of Special Appeals, have held statutory rape to be a strict liability crime

VI

Maryland's second degree rape statute is by nature a creature of legislation. Any new provision introducing an element of mens rea, or permitting a defense of reasonable mistake of age, with respect to the offense of sexual intercourse with a person less than 14, should properly result from an act of the Legislature itself, rather than judicial fiat. Until then, defendants in extraordinary cases, like Raymond, will rely upon the tempering discretion of the trial court at sentencing.

ELDRIDGE, Judge, **dissenting**:
Both the majority opinion and Judge Bell's dissenting opinion view the question in this case to be whether, on the one hand, Maryland Code (1957, 1992 Repl.Vol.), Art. 27, § 463(a)(3), is entirely a strict liability statute without any mens rea requirement or, on the other hand, contains the requirement that the defendant knew that the person with whom he or she was having sexual relations was under 14 years of age.

The majority takes the position that the statute defines an entirely strict liability offense and has no mens rea requirement whatsoever. The majority indicates that the defendant's "knowledge, belief, or other state of mind" is wholly immaterial. The majority opinion at one point states: "We acknowledge here that it is uncertain to what extent Raymond's intellectual and social retardation may have impaired his ability to comprehend imperatives of sexual morality in any case." Nevertheless, according to the majority, it was permissible for the trial judge to have precluded exploration into

Raymond's knowledge and comprehension because the offense is entirely one of strict liability.

Judge Bell's dissent, however, argues that, under the due process clauses of the Fourteenth Amendment and the Maryland Declaration of Rights, any "defendant may defend on the basis that he was mistaken as to the age of the prosecutrix."

In my view, the issue concerning a mens rea requirement in § 463(a)(3) is not limited to a choice between one of the extremes set forth in the majority's and Judge Bell's opinions. I agree with the majority that an ordinary defendant's mistake about the age of his or her sexual partner is not a defense to a prosecution under § 463(a)(3). Furthermore, I am not persuaded, at least at the present time, that either the federal or state constitutions require that a defendant's honest belief that the other person was above the age of consent be a defense. This does not mean, however, that the statute contains no mens rea requirement at all.

Neither the statutory language nor the legislative history of § 463(a)(3), or of the other provisions of the 1976 and 1977 sexual offense statutes, indicate that the General Assembly intended § 463(a)(3) to define a pure strict liability offense where criminal liability is imposed regardless of the defendant's mental state. The penalty provision for a violation of § 463(a)(3), namely making the offense a felony punishable by a maximum of 20 years imprisonment (§ 463(b)), is strong evidence that the General Assembly did not intend to create a pure strict liability offense.
…
It is unreasonable to assume that the Legislature intended for one to be convicted under § 463(a)(3), or under any of the other statutes proscribing sexual activity with underage persons, regardless of his or her mental state. …

An impaired mental condition may show the absence of mens rea, depending upon the circumstances. . . . As previously mentioned, the majority opinion itself acknowledges that it is uncertain to what extent Raymond's intellectual and social retardation may have impaired his ability to comprehend standards of sexual morality. The problem in this case is that the trial judge's view of the statute, which the majority adopts, precluded an exploration into the matter.

The majority points out that the trial court would not allow testimony that Erica and her friends had told the defendant that she was 16 years old. The trial court, however, went further. The court would not allow the defendant to testify concerning his knowledge. More importantly, the trial judge took the position that the offense proscribed by § 463(a)(3) is "a strict liability offense" and that the only requirements for conviction were that "the defendant had sexual intercourse with Erica Frazier, that at that time she was 13 years of age, [and] at that time the defendant was more than 4 years older than she. These are the only requirements that the State need prove beyond a reasonable doubt." The trial court's position that the offense lacked any mens rea requirement, and that the defendant's mental state was wholly immaterial, was, in my view, erroneous.
I would reverse and remand for a new trial.

BELL, Judge, **dissenting**.
…
I do not dispute that the legislative history of Maryland Code (1957, 1992 Repl.Vol.), Art. 27, section 463 may be read to support the majority's interpretation that subsection (a)(3) was intended to be a strict liability statute. Nor do I disagree that it is in the public interest to protect the sexually naive child from the adverse physical, emotional, or psychological effects of sexual relations. I do not believe, however, that the General Assembly, in every case, whatever the nature of the crime and no matter how harsh the potential penalty, can subject a defendant to strict criminal liability. To hold, *as a matter of law,* that section 463(a)(3) does not require the State to prove that a defendant possessed the necessary mental state to commit the crime, *i.e.* knowingly engaged in sexual relations with a female under 14, or that the defendant may not litigate that issue in defense, "offends a principle of justice so rooted in the traditions of conscience of our people as to be ranked as fundamental" and is, therefore, inconsistent with due process.

… [A]ccording to the defendant, he intended to have sex with a 16, not a 13, year old girl. This mistake of fact was prompted, he said, by the prosecutrix herself; she and her friends told him that she was 16 years old. Because he was mistaken as to the prosecutrix's age, he submits, he is certainly less culpable than the person who knows that the minor is 13 years old, but nonetheless engages in sexual relations with her. Notwithstanding, the majority has construed section 463(a)(3) to exclude any proof of knowledge or intent. But for that construction, the proffered defense would be viable. I would hold that the State is not relieved of its burden to prove the defendant's intent or knowledge in a statutory rape case and, therefore, that the defendant may defend on the basis that he was mistaken as to the age of the prosecutrix

Generally, a culpable mental state, often referred to as mens rea, or intent, is, and long has been, an essential element of a criminal offense. A crime ordinarily consists of prohibited conduct *and* a culpable mental state; a wrongful act and a wrongful intent must concur to constitute what the law deems a crime, the purpose being to avoid criminal liability for innocent or inadvertent conduct. Historically, therefore, unless the actor also harbored an evil, or otherwise culpable.

A man who engages in consensual intercourse in the reasonable belief that his partner has reached [the age of consent evidences no abnormality, no willingness to take advantage of immaturity, no propensity to corruption of minors. In short, he has demonstrated neither intent nor inclination to violate any of the interests that the law of statutory rape seeks to protect. At most, he has disregarded religious precept or social convention. In terms of mental culpability, his conduct is indistinguishable from that of any other person who engages in fornication. Whether he should be punished at all depends on a judgment about continuing fornication as a criminal offense, but at least he should not be subject to felony sanctions for statutory rape. Model Penal Code § 213.6, Comment at 415.
. . .
When the Legislature enacts a strict liability crime, *i.e.,* promulgates a statute which excludes as an element, the defendant's mental

state, it essentially creates an irrebuttable presumption that the defendant's mental state, *i.e.,* knowledge or intent, is irrelevant. That is the case with regard to statutory rape. Notwithstanding that it chooses to accomplish that result by defining the crime, rather than by means of an express presumption, which relieves the State of its burden of proof, the fact remains that the result is exactly the same: anyone who has sexual relations with a female under the age of 14 is treated as if he knew that she was under 14 and so intended to have such relations with a 14 year old female. It thus relieves the State of any duty to produce relevant evidence to prove the defendant's mental state, that he knew the prosecutrix's age, and prevents the defendant from proving the contrary. Because the irrebuttably presumed fact does not follow inextricably from the fact of sexual relations with a 14 year old, its use to relieve the State of its burden of proof to prove the defendant's intent in that regard runs afoul of the due process clause of the Fourteenth Amendment.

Irrebuttable, mandatory, presumptions have long been disfavored and held to be violative of due process. One of the bases for the disfavor is that they may conflict with the overriding presumption of innocence which the law accords to the accused and invade the fact finding process, which, in a criminal case, is the exclusive province of the jury. The more usual reason for disfavoring irrebuttable presumptions, however, is that the fact conclusively presumed "is not necessarily or universally true in fact," and, so, excusing the proponent of that fact from having to establish it renders the statute "arbitrary, illegal, capricious and hence unconstitutional." This is especially so when the presumed fact bears little or no relation to the statute's expressed objective.

In the case *sub judice,* by consciously and intentionally excluding from section 463(a)(3) any requirement that the defendant's knowledge of the victim's age be proven, the Legislature has relieved the State of that obligation; without that legislation, of course, the State's burden would have included proving, at the very least, that the defendant knew the prosecutrix's age. On the issue of the defendant's intent, section 463(a)(3) only

requires proof of the victim's age and its differential with that of the defendant. As such, once those facts have been proven, it is conclusively established that the defendant's intent was to have sexual relations with a girl of the proscribed age. As we have seen, not requiring proof of the defendant's intent has been accomplished by so defining the crime, not by means of an express presumption. Again, that is of no real consequence, however. By defining the crime, the Legislature prescribes what must be proven. In other words, by that process, it has determined what the rule of substantive law will be — by defining the crime so as to exclude proof of knowledge or intent, the Legislature naturally precludes the admission of any evidence bearing on the element, the proof of which it has excused. In so doing, it has made that element — intent or knowledge of the victim's age — irrelevant to the definition of the crime and, hence, irrebuttable. It follows, therefore, that, once the other elements are proven, the defendant's knowledge or intent is necessarily established as well. It does not necessarily follow, however, that simply because the victim is 13 years old, the defendant had knowledge of her age or intended to have sexual relations with a 13 year old girl. He may have had knowledge or intent, to be sure, but, by the same token, he may not have. The defendant should have been permitted to present evidence on the issue.

. . . In the case of statutory rape all aspects of the defendant's knowledge, save proof of the intercourse itself, has been rendered, by definition, irrelevant and, so, off limits for the trial. That is, I repeat, by no means comparable.

The critical issue in a statutory rape case is "the age of the rape victim." That is true because the victim's age serves two related, but distinct purposes: (1) it establishes the victim's capacity to consent and (2) it represents notice to a defendant of proscribed conduct. The Maryland statute seeks irrebuttably to presume not only that the victim could not consent by virtue of age, but also that, when a defendant engages in sexual relations with a minor under the age of 14, he has notice of that fact. Assuming that, based on the victim's age, the Legislature could legitimately exclude consent as an element of the crime, it absolutely should not be able to excuse the State from its obligation to prove the defendant's knowledge of the victim's age or prevent the defendant from producing evidence on that issue. No matter how forcefully it may be argued that there is a rational relationship between the capacity to consent and the age the Legislature selected, given the tremendous difference between individuals, both in appearance and in mental capacity, there can be no such rational relationship between the proof of the victim's age and the defendant's knowledge of that fact.

[T]here is precedent that a felony statute which prescribes substantial penalties and conviction of which will subject the defendant to significant social stigma, violates due process unless it requires the State to prove intent or knowledge,

… I believe that due process both under the Fourteenth Amendment and under the Declaration of Rights, precludes strict criminal liability for statutory rape. Interpreting section 463(a)(3) as the majority does has the effect of

largely relieving the State of its burden of proof and burden of persuasion. By making the defendant's intent, and, hence, blameworthiness, irrelevant, the Legislature has made inevitable, the petitioner's conviction. Moreover, upon conviction of the felony offense of statutory rape under section 463(a)(3), in addition to a substantial penalty of up to 20 years imprisonment, a defendant's reputation will be gravely besmirched. Where there is no issue as to sexual contact, which is more likely than not to be the case in statutory rape prosecutions, proof of the prosecutrix's age is not only proof of the defendant's guilt, it is absolutely dispositive of it and, at the same time, it is fatal to the only defense the defendant would otherwise have. So interpreted, section 463(a)(3) not only destroys absolutely the concept of fault, but it renders meaningless, in the statutory rape context, the presumption of innocence and the right to due process.

Fornication, Adultery, And Seduction

Fornication is sexual intercourse between unmarried persons. Adultery is generally defined as sexual intercourse between a male and female, at least one of whom is married to someone else. At common law, neither was considered a common law crime unless committed openly. Rather they were regarded as offenses against morality and punished in the ecclesiastical courts in England (i.e., the church courts rather than the king's courts). Similarly, seduction (when a male obtains sexual intercourse with a virtuous female (i.e., a virgin), by promises to marry her) was not a common law crime, and it exists only by statute. A threatened prosecution for seduction was to induce the male to actual marry the woman he seduced. Most states have repealed their seduction statutes.

Sodomy

Sodomy was defined by Blackstone as a "infamous crime against nature" which had "deeper malignity" than rape. Sodomy is oral or anal sex between humans and sexual intercourse between humans and animals (also referred to as bestiality). Sodomy can be consensual or nonconsensual. Nonconsensual sodomy is considered a crime against a person and is often charged along with rape in states with older, narrower statutory definitions of rape. … Consensual sodomy, on the other hand, was viewed traditionally as an offense against public morality. Prior to the United States Supreme Court opinion in *Lawrence v. Texas* in 2003 (see, Chapter One) many states had already abolished the offense of consensual sodomy either through legislative or judicial action.

Incest

Incest is sexual intercourse within or outside the bonds of marriage between persons related within certain prohibited degrees. Incest was not a common law crime, but was punished as a crime against morality in the English ecclesiastical courts.

There are strong religious and moral taboos against incest. Furthermore, it has been almost universally believed that incest not only disrupts family relationships but also leads to genetically defective offspring. For these reasons, all states prohibit marriage or sexual relationships between certain close relatives. . . .

Statutes that prohibit intermarriage or sexual relations between persons within certain degrees of kinship usually refer to relationship by consanguinity (that is blood relationships). But historically some went further and classified as incestuous close relationships between persons related by affinity (that is, marriage) as well as relationships by the bloodline. Scheb and Scheb, at 250.

Bigamy and Polygamy

Bigamy is marriage between two persons when one is already legally married to another. Bigamy statutes usually require the prosecution prove that the defendant had knowledge of the prior marital status of the person whom he or she married. Polygamy is the practice of one person being married to several spouses at the same time. In *Reynolds v. United States*, 98 U.S. 145 (1878), the U.S. Supreme Court rejected the argument that polygamy was protected under the First Amendment's Free Exercise of Religion Clause. That case involved a Mormon polygamist who challenged the constitutionality of a federal statute prohibiting polygamy in the federal territories. Subsequently, the Church of Latter-Day Saints officially disavowed the practice of polygamy. Nevertheless, polygamy is still practiced in some fundamentalist Mormon communities. In *State v. Green*, 99 P.3d 820 (2004) the Utah Supreme Court upheld Thomas Green's conviction on four counts of bigamy and one count of child rape from 2001. Green, a fundamentalist Mormon, had five wives and thirty children. He was sentenced to five years' imprisonment, and appealed. The court found that the state statute prohibiting bigamy neither violated the Free Exercise Clause nor was it unconstitutionally vague as applied.

Prostitution

Prostitution, considered a crime against public morality, was not a common law offense, but it was proscribed by statutes in all states. Today, it is illegal in all states except Nevada, where it exists, strictly regulated, by local option in some counties. Prostitution statutes target persons who indulge in sexual activity for hire. Today statutes frequently include both the payer (customer) as well as the payee (prostitute) in their definitions of prostitution, however, historically laws prohibiting prostitution were directed almost exclusively at the prostitute (payee). Most statutes make it an offense to solicit for a prostitute or to live off the earnings of persons engaged in prostitution. Statutes also declare brothels and houses of prostitution as public nuisances.

Other Sex-Related Statutory Crimes

There are numerous other sex-related statutory crimes that states have adopted including: pimping; indecent exposure; voyeurism; "lewd and lascivious conduct;" child pornography; obscenity (if challenged it is likely that obscenity statutes would be struck down as protected speech); human trafficking, etc. These are all modern statutory offenses not recognized at common law.

Assault and Battery

Common Law Assault And Battery

The common law crimes of assault and battery were considered misdemeanors, but there were more serious forms of battery that were felonies: mayhem (a felony requiring not only bodily injury but also dismemberment-type of injury, discussed below), rape (discussed above), and robbery (a felony involving the unlawful taking of another's property by violence amounting to a battery or by threat amounting to an assault). These crimes were, however, not referred to as "battery."

Modern Statutory Approaches To Assault And Battery

Today assault and battery are statutory crimes in all American jurisdictions. Simple assault and simple battery are generally punishable as misdemeanors under criminal codes, but some statutes do not define these crimes, but rather leave the matter to be determined by reference to the common law.

> Although the word 'assault' is sometimes used loosely to include a battery, and the whole expression "assault and battery" to mean battery, it is more accurate to distinguish between the two separate crimes, assault and battery, on the basis of the existence or non-existence of physical injury or offensive touching. Battery requires such an injury or touching. Assault on the other hand, needs no such physical contact; it might almost be said that it affirmatively requires an absence of contact. Battery like murder and manslaughter, malicious mischief and arson, thus is a crime defined in terms of conduct which produces a specified harmful result (injury or offensive touching). Assault . . . may in some jurisdictions be committed in either of one of two ways—attempted battery or intentional frightening— the former requiring no harmful physical result but the latter requiring the result, not of physical contact as with battery, but rather of mental apprehension in the mind of the victim. LaFave, Criminal Law, 2000, 736-737.

Legislatures have added the more serious crimes of aggravated assaults and aggravated batteries, which generally involve more serious injuries or the use of weapons during the assault and or battery.

Battery

Criminal battery is defined as the unlawful application of force to the person of another.[20] It can be divided into three elements: defendant's conduct (either an act or omission); defendant's mental state (which includes an intent to kill or injure, criminal negligence or recklessnes, or perhaps the doing of an unlawful act); and the harmful result to the victim (which may be either a bodily injury or an offensive touching). Bodily injury includes wounding caused by weapons or hands and even a temporarily painful blow will suffice for bodily injury even though there is no wound or bruise afterward to show for it. Battery also includes offensive physical touching such as where a man puts his hands upon another's body or kisses a woman against her will, or where one person spits into another's face. See, LaFave, at 737-738..

The modern approach to battery is found in the MPC which limits battery to instances of physical injury and covers unwanted sexual advances. Some terms used in modern statutes to describe the harm include: "physical injury", "bodily injury," "bodily harm," "physical harm," "force or violence upon the person, or "serious bodily injury." Some statutes are broader and include "offensive physical contact" or "insulting or provoking contact" or done in "a rude, insolent, or angry manner." The federal statute defines battery as merely "striking" the victim has been construed to require no injury at all. See, *United States v. Gan*, 636 F.2d 28 (2 Cir. 1980).

Mens Rea--Battery

According to LaFave, there are three distinct ways of committing a battery. These forms differ based on the defendant's mens rea. The first type is where the defendant acts (or omits to act) with intent to injure; the second is where the defendant acts with criminal negligence but has no intent to injure; and the third type is where defendant's mens rea, though it does not amount to criminal negligence, is nevertheless

---

[20] The force used in battery need not be direct force. If one shoots at another, or strikes him with a knife, club or fist, this is direct force and qualifies as the wrongful conduct. However, force may also be indirectly applied to the victim, as where one whips the horse on which the victim is riding, causing the horse to bolt and throw the rider.

unlawful, but he has no intent to injure. "When his conduct, under these conditions, actually causes injury to another person, he is clearly guilty of battery under the first circumstance and (in most jurisdictions) under the second; his guilt is not so clear under the third." LaFave, at 739.

Aggravated Battery

Some battery is considered aggravated based on the victim. Statutes generally define battery against police officers as aggravated battery Some statutes aggravate batteries against jailers, teachers, bus drivers, state officers in general, participants in court proceedings, youthful, elderly or pregnant. Another common aggravating factor has to do with the amount of harm inflicted. Most statutes consider it aggravated battery if the defendant inflicts serious bodily injury with intent or knowledge, but some statutes do not require the higher mental states. A few states also aggravate intentional or knowing batteries even without the additional serious harm.

Assault

The crime of assault is defined in statutes in a variety of ways: for example, "unlawful attempt, coupled with a present ability, to commit a battery;" "attempted battery;" or "placing another in reasonable apprehension of a battery." A few assault-type statutes do not define the offense at all, and a few others have no assault statutes whatsoever. Some, like Oregon, attach name "assault" to conduct which has traditionally been called "battery." In these states, the assault of the attempted battery is covered by the general law of attempt, and the intent-to-frighten type of assault is labeled as threatening or menacing.

At common law there were two types of "assaults" and these are discussed in the following cases of *Harrod v. State* and *Carter v. Commonwealth*.

HARROD v. STATE,
65 Md. App. 128499, A.2d 959 (1985)

ALPERT, Judge.
We are called upon in this appeal to decide, *inter alia*, whether a person can be convicted of assaulting another who has suffered no harm and was never aware of the alleged assault. Appellant John G. Harrod was charged with two counts of assault and two counts of carrying a deadly weapon openly with intent to injure. He was convicted of these offenses on December 11, 1984, following a trial without a jury in the Circuit Court for Carroll County (Lerner, J., presiding), and sentenced on January 21, 1985, to two terms of two years' imprisonment for the assault convictions and two terms of one year's imprisonment for the weapons convictions, all sentences to run concurrently.

I.

The common law crime of assault encompasses two definitions: (1) an attempt to commit a battery or (2) an unlawful intentional act which places another in reasonable apprehension of receiving an immediate battery. The facts in the instant case present this court with an excellent

opportunity to explain the distinctions between these two different types of assault.

The assault charges arose out of a confrontation among appellant, his wife Cheryl, and her friend Calvin Crigger. The only two witnesses at trial were appellant and Cheryl Harrod.

Cheryl testified that on September 15, 1983, Calvin Crigger came over to visit when she thought appellant had gone to work; that "all of a sudden [appellant] came out of the bedroom with a hammer in his hand, swinging it around, coming after me and my friend [Calvin]"; that Calvin ran out of the house and down the steps; that appellant "had thrown the hammer over top of [Christopher's] port-a-crib in the living room, and it went into the wall"; that appellant then reentered the bedroom and returned with a five-inch blade hunting knife; that appellant told Cheryl that he was going to kill her and that, if she took his daughter away from him, he was going to kill Christopher; that appellant put the knife into the bannister near Cheryl's arm; that appellant followed Cheryl out to Calvin's car and "went after Calvin, going around and around the car."

Appellant testified that he missed his ride to work that day; that he came back home around 10:00 a.m. and went to sleep in a back room; that he was awakened by Calvin's deep voice; that appellant picked up his hammer and, walking into the living room, told Calvin to leave; that Cheryl told Calvin he didn't have to leave; that he then told Calvin, "Buddy, if you want your head busted in, stand here; if you want to be healthy and leave, go." Appellant said that Calvin just stood there, so he swung the hammer, Calvin moved his head back, and the hammer struck the wall over Christopher's crib, which was near the door.

In rendering its verdict, the court stated:
    And, the Court finds beyond a reasonable doubt and to a moral certainty that Mr. Harrod ... came after [Cheryl] and ... Calvin; and that Mr. Harrod came out of his room swinging a ... hammer, and ultimately threw it, not too far from the child, Christopher, and that he went after both Cheryl and Calvin, down the steps with a knife, with a blade of about four to five inches. The Court finds that he is guilty of two counts of Carrying a Deadly Weapon; that is the knife and the hammer; and, also two counts of Assault; one against Cheryl and one against the minor child.
    .....
Defense counsel inquired of the court: "On the second count of the Information, is the Court finding specific intent on behalf of the Defendant to injure his child?" The court responded, "Yes. Threw that hammer within a very short distance--sticking it--it was still sticking in the wall."

A. Two Types of Assault

Appellant (Harrod) contends that there was insufficient evidence to demonstrate that he harbored a specific intent to injure Christopher when he threw the hammer. Further, he notes that there was no evidence that Christopher was injured by the hammer or that he was even aware that a hammer was thrown. Therefore, appellant claims that the trial court's finding that he committed a criminal assault upon Christopher was clearly erroneous. We agree

for the reasons set forth below.

[A]n assault "is committed when there is *either* an attempt to commit a battery *or* when, by an unlawful act, a person is placed in reasonable apprehension of receiving an immediate battery." These two types of assaults--*attempted battery* and *putting another in fear* --are indeed two distinct crimes that have been inadvertently overlapped and confused. One commentator explained this confusion:

In the early law the word "assault" represented an entirely different concept in criminal law than it did in the law of torts. As an offense it was an attempt to commit a battery; as a basis for a civil action for damages it was an intentional act wrongfully placing another in apprehension of receiving an immediate battery. The distinction has frequently passed unnoticed because a misdeed involving either usually involves both. If, with the intention of hitting X, D wrongfully threw a stone that X barely managed to dodge, then D would have been guilty of a criminal assault because he had attempted to commit a battery, and he would also have been liable in a civil action of trespass for assault because he had wrongfully placed X in apprehension of physical harm.

B. Attempted Battery

[I]n an attempted battery-type assault, the victim need not be aware of the perpetrator's intent or threat.

If a person be struck from behind, or by stealth or surprise, or while asleep, he is certainly the victim of a battery. But if we accept the oft-repeated statement that every battery included or is preceded by an assault, and if there could be no assault without premonitory apprehension in the victim, then it could be argued that there was no battery. That is not the law. In other words, because there may be committed a battery without the victim first being aware of the attack, an attempted battery-type assault cannot include a requirement that the victim be aware.

1. Specific Intent
The facts in [this case] do not support a finding that appellant committed an attempted battery towards the infant, Christopher. An attempt to

commit any crime requires a specific intent to commit that crime. An attempted battery-type assault thus requires that the accused harbor a specific intent to cause physical injury to the victim and take a substantial step towards causing that injury.

Nowhere does the record indicate that appellant threw the hammer with the specific intent to injure Christopher. The court expressly stated that it found specific intent on behalf of appellant because he "[t]hrew that hammer within a very short distance" of the child. The court here is merely inferring a criminal intent from reckless or negligent acts of the appellant. This is not sufficient, . . . especially where all of the evidence tends to the contrary: that appellant's intent was to injure Calvin.

2. Transferred Intent

An additional question raised by the parties in the briefs is whether the necessary specific intent as against Christopher could derive from the specific intent toward Calvin; in other words, did the intent to injure Calvin *transfer* to Christopher? This doctrine of "transferred intent" was explained by the Court of Appeals in *Gladden v. State*:

> "[I]f one intends injury to the person of another under circumstances in which such a mental element constitutes mens rea, and in the effort to accomplish this end he inflicts harm upon a person other than the one intended, he is guilty of the same kind of crime as if his aim had been more accurate." In such cases all the components of the crime are present. The psychical element which consists of a certain general mental pattern is not varied by the particular person who may be actually harmed.

Id. at 404, 303 A.2d 176.

Gladden, as well as all of the cases cited in that opinion, involved an attempt to kill one person, but resulted in the death or injury of another, unintended victim. In every case cited in *Gladden,* the third party to whom the intent was "transferred" was in fact injured. The Court of Appeals expressly held that, under the doctrine, "the mens rea of a defendant as to his intended victim will carry over and affix his

culpability *when such criminal conduct causes the death of an unintended victim.*"

By illustration, Professor Perkins explains the logic underlying the limited application of this doctrine:

> If, without justification, excuse or mitigation D with intent to kill A fires a shot which misses A but unexpectedly inflicts a non-fatal injury upon B, D is guilty of an attempt to commit murder — but the attempt was to murder A whom D was trying to kill and not B who was hit quite accidentally. And so far as the criminal law is concerned there is no transfer of this intent from one to the other so as to make D guilty of an attempt to murder B. Hence, an indictment or information charging an attempt to murder B, or (under statute) an assault with intent to murder B, will not support a conviction if the evidence shows that the injury to B was accidental and the only intent was to murder A.

Perkins, *Criminal Law* 826 (2d ed. 1969) (footnote omitted).

The closest case we have found to support the rule that the doctrine does not apply absent actual injury is *State v. Martin.* In *Martin,* the defendants were charged with assault upon Lloyd DeCasnett, with the intent to maim. The evidence in that case showed that the defendants threw a sulphuric acid-filled light bulb at a vehicle in which DeCasnett was a passenger. However, there was no evidence that the defendants knew that DeCasnett was in fact there, while there was ample evidence that they were aware of other persons in the target vehicle. The Missouri court considered the common law notion in homicide cases "that a constructive intent follows the bullet," but stated, "it cannot be the law in a case like this *where no one was hurt,* and the State's case rests solely on the overt act of throwing the acid-filled bulb and the felonious intent to be deduced therefrom." The court went on to reverse the conviction for assault with intent to maim DeCasnett, because, although the record evidence demonstrated a felonious intent to injure a passenger in the car, it did not appear that DeCasnett was the object of that intent.

To extend the doctrine of transferred intent to

cases where the intended victim is not harmed would be untenable. The absurd result would be to make one criminally culpable for each unintended victim who, although in harm's way, was in fact not harmed by a missed attempt towards a specific person. We refuse, therefore, to extend the doctrine of transferred intent to cases where a third person is not in fact harmed.

This is the situation before us in the instant case. The record indicates that appellant swung a hammer which struck the wall "not too far from" Christopher. Significantly, there is no evidence that Christopher was harmed. Further, the weight of the evidence shows that appellant's specific intent, if any, was to injure Calvin, not Christopher. Why the State charged appellant with assaulting Christopher, rather than Calvin, we will not speculate. There is clearly insufficient evidence to find that appellant committed an attempted battery-type

.

assault upon Christopher.

C. Assault by Placing One in Fear

There is likewise insufficient evidence that appellant, by an unlawful intentional act, placed Christopher in reasonable apprehension of receiving an immediate battery. By definition the victim must be aware of the impending contact.

There is no evidence in the record before us that Christopher was in fact aware of the occurrences in his home on the morning in question. Therefore, there was insufficient evidence to find appellant guilty of the putting victim in fear-type assault.

Because the trial court was clearly erroneous in finding appellant guilty of an assault on Christopher, we must reverse that conviction

---

CARTER v. COMMONWEALTH, 42 Va. App. 681, 594 S.E.2d 284 (2004)

CLEMENTS, J.

Michael Anthony Carter was convicted in a bench trial of assaulting a police officer, in violation of Code § 18.2-57(C). On appeal, he contends the evidence presented at trial was insufficient to support his conviction because the Commonwealth did not prove he had the present ability to inflict actual violence upon the officer. On September 9, 2003, a divided panel of this Court affirmed Carter's conviction, holding the evidence was sufficient to convict Carter of assaulting a police officer because Carter's conduct "reasonably and unequivocally" indicated to the officer that Carter had "an intention and the present ability to harm the officer." On October 14, 2003, we granted Carter's petition for a rehearing en banc, stayed the mandate of the panel decision, and reinstated the appeal. Upon rehearing en banc, we affirm Carter's conviction.

I. BACKGROUND

. . . [O]n December 29, 1998, around 11:00 p.m., Officer-B.N. O'Donnell of the City of

Charlottesville Police Department observed a speeding car and, activating his vehicle's overhead flashing blue emergency lights, initiated a traffic stop. O'Donnell, who was on routine patrol at the time in a high crime area of the city, was driving a marked police vehicle and wearing his police uniform and badge. After the car pulled over, O'Donnell shone his vehicle's "take down" lights and spotlight onto the car and approached it on foot.

Two people were inside the car, the driver and Carter, who was seated in the front passenger seat. O'Donnell initiated a conversation with the driver, asking for his driver's license and registration and informing him why he had been stopped. The driver responded to O'Donnell in a "hostile" tone of voice. "While conversing with the driver, O'Donnell used his flashlight to conduct a "plain view search" of the car to make sure there were no visible weapons or drugs in it. O'Donnell noticed that Carter had his right hand out of sight "down by his right leg." Carter then suddenly brought his right hand up and across his body. Extending the index finger on his right hand straight out and the thumb straight up, he pointed his index finger at the officer and said, "Pow." Thinking Carter "had a weapon and was going to shoot" him, O'Donnell "began to move backwards" and went for his weapon. A "split second" later, O'Donnell realized "it was only [Carter's] finger." O'Donnell testified: "The first thing I thought was that I was going to get shot. I it's a terrifying experience, and if I could have gotten my weapon, I would have shot him." Immediately after the incident, O'Donnell, who was "visibly shaken," asked Carter "if he thought it was funny," and Carter responded, "Yes, I think it is funny."

At the conclusion of the Commonwealth's evidence at trial and at the close of all the evidence, Carter moved to strike the evidence, arguing the Commonwealth's evidence was insufficient to prove assault because it failed to prove Carter had the present ability to inflict actual violence upon the officer. The Commonwealth responded that proof of such ability was unnecessary as long as the evidence proved the officer reasonably believed Carter had the present ability to inflict actual bodily harm upon him.

The trial court agreed with the Commonwealth. Finding Carter's "act of pointing what the officer believed at the time to be a weapon at him" did, "in fact, place Officer O'Donnell in reasonable apprehension or fear," the trial court found the evidence sufficient to prove beyond a reasonable doubt that Carter was guilty of assault. Thus, the trial court denied Carter's motion to strike the evidence and subsequently convicted him of assaulting a police officer, in violation of Code § 18.2-57(C). At sentencing, the court imposed a sentence of three years, suspending two years and six months.

This appeal followed.

II. ANALYSIS

Code § 18.2-57(C) provides, in pertinent part, that "any person [who] commits an assault . . . against . . . a law-enforcement officer . . . engaged in the performance of his public duties as such . . . shall be guilty of a Class 6 felony."

On appeal, Carter asserts the Commonwealth failed to prove his conduct constituted an assault of a law-enforcement officer because, in pointing his finger at the officer and saying "pow," he did not have the present ability to inflict harm upon the officer, as required under the common law definition of assault. Thus, he contends, the trial court erred, as a matter of law, in finding the evidence sufficient to sustain a conviction for assault.

In response, the Commonwealth contends that, under long-established Virginia case law, a defendant need not have had the present ability to inflict harm at the time of the offense to be guilty of assault. It is enough, the Commonwealth argues, that, as in this case, the defendant's conduct created in the mind of the victim a reasonable fear or apprehension of bodily harm. Accordingly, the Commonwealth concludes, the trial court properly found the evidence sufficient to convict Carter of assaulting a police officer.

[While statutorily proscribed and regulated, the offense of assault is defined by common law in Virginia] . . . Assault has, thus, long been defined at common law "as being (1) an attempt to commit a battery or (2) an intentional placing of another in [reasonable] apprehension of receiving an immediate battery." Today, most jurisdictions include both of these separate types of assault, attempted battery and putting the victim in reasonable apprehension, within the scope of criminal assault. In Virginia, our Supreme Court has long recognized the existence of both concepts of assault in the criminal law context. . . .

Faced with the specific issue of whether, under the common law, the crime of assault included the put-in-apprehension type of tortious assault or was limited to the attempted-battery type of assault, the Court sustained the jury instruction stating: The instruction under consideration, therefore, presents the question on which there is a sharp and irreconcilable conflict in the authorities on the subject; diametrically opposed positions being taken by the authorities, namely [it is sufficient to constitute assault that the person is put in well founded fear or apprehension of bodily harm although the victim is not put in actual peril or if it is essential that the act done must be with the intent to place the person in fear of harm and regardless of whether he is in action peril.] We think that, both in reason and in accordance with the great weight of modern authority. . . a present ability to inflict bodily harm upon the victim is not an essential element of criminal assault in all cases. Indeed those cases, to be guilty of . . . criminal assault, a defendant need have only an apparent present ability to inflict harm.

Moreover, as previously discussed, the two types of criminal assault recognized at common law attempted assault and putting the victim in reasonable apprehension of bodily harm are separate and distinct forms of the same offense. They have different elements and are, thus, defined differently and applied under different circumstances.

[W]e hold that, under the common law definition of assault, one need not, in cases such as this, have a present ability to inflict imminent bodily harm at the time of the alleged offense to be guilty of assault. It is enough that one's conduct created at the time of the alleged offense a reasonable apprehension of bodily harm in the mind of the victim. Thus, an apparent present ability to inflict imminent bodily harm is sufficient to support a conviction for assault.

In this case, the trial court found that Carter's "act of pointing what the officer believed at the time to be a weapon at him" did, "in fact, place Officer O'Donnell in reasonable apprehension

or fear." The evidence in the record abundantly supports this finding, and the finding is not plainly wrong.

. . . O'Donnell testified that he thought he was "going to get shot." It was, he said, "a terrifying experience, and if I could have gotten my weapon, I would have shot him."

The trial court could reasonably conclude from these facts that the officer was terrified and thought he was about to be shot. That the officer's terror was brief does not alter the fact, as found by the trial court, that the officer believed for a moment that Carter had the intention and present ability to kill him. Moreover, under the circumstances surrounding the incident, we cannot say, as a matter of law, that such a belief was unreasonable. Thus, although Carter did not have a weapon, the trial court could properly conclude from the evidence presented that Carter had an apparent present ability to inflict imminent bodily harm and that his conduct placed Officer O'Donnell in reasonable apprehension of such harm.

Hence, the trial court did not err, as a matter of law, in finding the evidence sufficient to convict Carter of assault under the common law tort definition of assault that has long been recognized as a part of the definition of criminal assault in Virginia. Accordingly, we affirm Carter's conviction for assault under Code § 18.2-57(C).

Model Penal Code Approach To Assault And Battery

The Model Penal Code does not grade of batteries based upon the status of the victim. It distinguishes between simple assault and aggravated assault, but merges batter into the crime of assault. The threatened battery type of assault is "reckless endangerment" or in its more serious form, "terroristic threats."[21]

---

[21] MPC § 211.1 Assault
(1) Simple Assault. A person is guilty of assault if he:
(a) attempts to cause or purposely, knowingly or recklessly causes bodily injury to another; or
(b) negligently causes bodily injury to another with a deadly weapon; or
(c) attempts by physical menace to put another in fear of imminent serious bodily harm.

Simple assault is a misdemeanor unless committed in a fight or scuffle entered into by mutual consent, in which case it is a petty misdemeanor.

(2) Aggravated Assault. A person is guilty of aggravated assault if he:
(a) attempts to cause serious bodily injury to another, or causes such injury purposely, knowingly, or recklessly under circumstances manifesting extreme indifference to the value of human life; or

Mayhem

Common Law Approach To Mayhem

Mayhem was a common law felony in which the offender caused physical injury to the victim in such a way that caused the victim unable to defend themselves at war. Generally, this required some form of dismemberment or permanent disfigurement. Blackstone defined mayhem as an ancient common law crime as "the violently depriving another of the use of such of his members as may render him the less able in fighting either to defend himself, or to annoy his adversary." Blackstone included the following as forms of mayhem: cutting off or permanently disabling a hand or finger, striking out an eye, striking out a front tooth, castration. Blackstone recognized cutting off an ear of the nose as conduct which disfigures but did not impair the victim's fighting. At common law permanently disabling a leg or cutting off a leg constituted mayhem. Originally mayhem was punished by the loss of the same member of which the defendant deprived the victim (literally, an eye for an eye). Later, imprisonment or death was used. Gradually, under English statutes, mayhem was broadened to include cutting out or disabling the tongue, severing the ear, or slitting the nose or lip.

Modern Approach To Mayhem

Mayhem under American law is frequently referred to as "maiming" was generally a felony under early American statutes in all states. Under modern American statutes, only a few states have codes that contain mayhem. Instead these crimes are included in statutes on aggravated battery. Although statutes vary, all abolish the military significance of the injury. Mayhem (like murder, manslaughter, and battery) is a cause and result crime, which means it is not committed unless the defendant's conduct causes the bad result (dismemberment, disablement, or disfigurement.) Modern statutes now vary with regard to the extent and permanency of the injury needed for mayhem or maiming.

The mens rea for mayhem varies among mayhem statutes, and certainly includes the intent to cause a specific injury covered by the mayhem statute. It is unclear whether mayhem mens rea includes intending to injury someone but not having the intent to cause a mayhem-type injury when the crime results in that injury.

> The mental element required for mayhem cannot be quite so exactly stated. (1) Of course, one who (without justification) intends a specific injury of the mayhem type, and who accomplishes that exact injury, is guilty as where A with a knife intentionally cuts off B's left ear. However, (2) one may intend one sort of mayhem-injury and achieve another sort, as where A, swinging his axe at B's right hand with intent to sever it, misses that hand but cuts off B's left hand or leg or puts out an eye. Or (3) one may intend bodily injury but not have in mind any mayhem type of injury; thus A intentionally knocks down B who, to A's surprise, falls against a root and loses and ear. Progressing further down the road leading

---

(b) attempts to cause or purposely or knowingly causes bodily injury to another with a deadly weapon.

Aggravated assault under paragraph (a) is a felony of the second degree; aggravated assault under paragraph (b) is a felony of the third degree.

MPC § 211.2 Reckless Endangerment
A person commits a misdemeanor if he recklessly engages in conduct which places or may place another person in danger of death or serious bodily injury. Recklessness and danger shall be presumed where a person knowingly points a firearm at or in the direction of another, whether or not the actor believed the firearm to be loaded.

MPC §211.3 Terroristic Threats
A person is guilty of a felony of the third degree if he threatens to commit any crime of violence with the purpose to terrorize another or to cause evacuation of a building, place of assembly or facility of public transportation, or otherwise to cause serious public inconvenience, or in reckless disregard of the risk of causing such terror or inconvenience.

from greater fault to lesser fault, one who encounters the situation of the person who (4)recklessly or negligently or (5) in the commission(or attempted commission) of an unlawful act causes another to suffer an unintended injury of the mayhem type—as where A, by reckless driving or by driving on the wrong side of the road in violation of statute or ordinance, runs his car against motorist B, inflicting injuries so severe that B requires the amputation of his leg or suffers the loss of his eyesight.

The answer in these situations depends to a great extent upon the wording of the mayhem statute. If the statute punishes one who unlawfully or maliciously dismembers or disfigures then one is guilty in situation (3) above, where he intentionally injures another thereby unintentionally causing an injury of the mayhem type. On the other hand, a statute of the modern type punishing one who "with intent to disable or disfigure antoehr," successfully disables or disfigures him is not violated by one with such an indefinite state of mind; this statute would require the mental element involved in situation (2) above—i.e., the intent to maim, though not necessarily to cause the specific maiming injury, actually inflicted. As to the states of mind referred to in (4) and (5) above – involving reckless or unlawful conduct by the defendant—it seems quite clear that mayhem is not committed under these circumstances, in the absence of some special wording in the mayhem statute. LaFave, at 751-752.

PEOPLE V. ROBINSON,
CAL. SUP. CT. (CERTIFIED FOR PUBLICATION 12/8/14)

Defendant Renee Robinson was charged with both aggravated mayhem, in violation of Penal Code section 205, and mayhem, in violation of Penal Code section 203 (sometimes hereafter called "simple mayhem"). Both charges were based on a single incident in which defendant poured scalding water over her husband's head, resulting in serious burns to his face and various parts of his body, with residual scarring. She contends that she could not be convicted of both offenses based on the same act because simple mayhem is a lesser included offense of aggravated mayhem.

PROCEDURAL HISTORY

Defendant was charged with. . . [and convicted of] . . . aggravated mayhem, torture; mayhem, assault with a deadly weapon, to wit, boiling water, and by force likely to cause great bodily injury , and domestic battery with corporal injury. ...

FACTS
Because of the nature of the issues raised on appeal, a brief summary of the facts suffices.

Defendant and the victim, Sam Wright, were married in 1999. During the marriage, Wright had an affair which resulted in the birth of a child in 2009. On September 15, 2011, defendant had been drinking rum and possibly smoking crack cocaine and haranguing Wright for about an hour about the child, saying that he took better care of the child than he did of her. She put two pots of water on the stove and heated them. She walked up behind Wright, who was seated in the living room, and poured the contents of a three- to four-quart pot of scalding water onto his head, shoulders, stomach and back. Wright said the pain was "the worst pain [he'd] ever felt," about nine and a half out of 10.

Wright went outside and rolled on the wet grass. A neighbor called the paramedics. Deputy Sheriff Butcher, who was among the responders, observed that Wright's skin was starting to bubble and looked like it was melting off.

Wright suffered second degree burns of varying depth on his face, shoulders, back, stomach, thigh and neck. He was hospitalized for about two weeks in the burn unit at Arrowhead Regional Hospital. By the time of the trial, Wright still had some scarring on his left thigh and on his shoulders, back and abdomen. The director of the burn unit testified that he could not say whether Wright would be permanently disfigured.

DISCUSSION

1.

Section 203 provides: "Every person who unlawfully and maliciously deprives a human being of a member of his body, or disables, disfigures, or renders it useless, or cuts or disables the tongue, or puts out an eye, or slits the nose, ear, or lip, is guilty of mayhem."

Section 205 provides, in pertinent part: "A person is guilty of aggravated mayhem when he or she unlawfully, under circumstances manifesting extreme indifference to the physical or psychological well-being of another person, intentionally causes permanent disability or disfigurement of another human being or deprives a human being of a limb, organ, or member of his or her body."

In her opening brief, defendant contends that section 203 is a lesser included offense of section 205 because serious bodily injury is an element of both offenses, even though it is not explicitly an element of section 205. She contends that permanent disfigurement or disability or the deprivation of a limb, organ or bodily member is necessarily a serious bodily injury, and because case law has held that serious bodily injury is an element of section 203, a violation of section 205 necessarily also constitutes a violation of section 203.

. . . .

…[W]e now conclude that simple mayhem is a necessarily included lesser offense of aggravated mayhem.

…

Our role in interpreting a statute is to determine and effectuate the intent of the Legislature. If the statutory language is unambiguous, its plain meaning controls. "Where, however, the statutory language is ambiguous on its face or is shown to have a latent ambiguity such that it does not provide a definitive answer, we may resort to extrinsic sources to determine legislative intent. [Citations.] Under this circumstance, 'the court may examine the context in which the language appears, adopting the construction that best harmonizes the statute internally and with related statutes.' [Citation.] 'In such cases, a court may consider both the legislative history of the statute and the wider historical circumstances of its enactment to ascertain the legislative intent.'" … Because of the ambiguity in section 203, we may look to extrinsic aids to attempt to harmonize it with section 205.

In *People v. Keenan* (1991) 227 Cal.App.3d 26 (*Keenan*), the court affirmed a conviction for simple mayhem based on the infliction of cigarette burns on the victim's breasts. In response to the defendant's argument that the resulting scarring was too minor to amount to mayhem, the court stated:

"Mayhem, an older form of the word 'maim,' was at common law restricted to injuries that 'substantially reduced the victim's formidability in combat' [citation]; the rationale being to preserve the king's right to the military services of his subjects.

Gradually, the crime evolved to include injuries that did not affect the victim's fighting ability. Our current mayhem statute is based upon the Coventry Act of 1670, which first broadened mayhem to include mere disfigurement. That statute imposed a sentence of death on any person who, with malice aforethought, 'cut out or disable[d] the tongue, put out an eye, slit the nose, cut off a nose or lip, or cut off or disable[d] any limb or member of any other person.' [Citation.] [¶] While many contemporary mayhem cases involve conduct that squarely fits the traditional understanding of the offense [citations], courts recently have expanded mayhem to include acts not within the original definition of the crime. Thus, in *People v. Newble* (1981) the court upheld a conviction for mayhem based upon the infliction of a three-inch long facial wound and observed, '"the modern rationale of the crime [of mayhem] may be said to be the preservation of the *natural completeness and normal appearance* of the human face and body."' Similarly, in *People v. Page,* . . . the court reasoned that '[t]he law of mayhem as it has developed protects the integrity of the victim's person,' and affirmed a mayhem conviction based on the application of permanent tattoos to the victim's breast and abdomen." *Keenan* recognized these cases as "practical and proper applications of an old statute to modern- day reality."

…

In *Santana*, . . . the court stated: ". . . the modern rationale of the crime [of simple mayhem] may be said to be the preservation of the natural completeness and normal appearance of the human face and body, and not, as originally, the preservation of the sovereign's right to the effective military assistance of his subjects."' In other words, section 203 'protects the integrity of the victim's person.' " Under that rationale, scarring of the torso, which damages the natural appearance of the body, constitutes simple mayhem even though the torso is arguably not a bodily member. Further, under

the rationale espoused by the court in *Santana*, an act which "deprives a human being of a member of his body, or disables, disfigures, or renders it useless" (§ 203) cannot be distinguished from "causes permanent disability or disfigurement of another human being or deprives a human being of a limb, organ, or member of his or her body" (§ 205), except by the intent and mental state with which the act is committed. Consequently, we conclude that under the statutory elements test, simple mayhem in violation of section 203 is a necessarily included lesser offense of aggravated mayhem in violation of section 205. Accordingly, defendant's conviction on count 3 [simple mayhem] must be reversed

Kidnapping

Common Law Approach to Kidnapping

Kidnapping is an "ancient offense that originally involved holding the kings' relatives for ransom. It was a serious offense (but not a felony) because it involved interfering with the personal liberty of members of the royal families. At common law, kidnapping was the forcible abduction or stealing away of a person from his or her own country and sending him into another country. The elements of kidnapping at common law were 1) seizing; 2) carrying away ("asportation"); 3) confining; 4) another person; 5) by force, threat of force, or deception; and 6) with the intent to deprive the other person of his or her liberty.

Modern Approach to Kidnapping

During the early 1900s, kidnapping became a serious felony offense in the United States—some states even made it a capital offense. During Prohibition (1919-1933) kidnapping was prevalent among organized crime figures. Rivaling gang members abducted another gang's member, took him for a ride and killed him, or commonly captured them and held them hostage for ransom. Soon, the kidnapping and holding for hostage of prominent wealthy citizens became common. *State v. Hauptmann*, 115 NJL 412 (N.J. 1935) involved the prosecution for the kidnapping and murder of Charles Lindburg Jr, the young son of the popular aviator who flew solo across the Atlantic Ocean in the Spirit of St. Louis. Lindberg had paid $50,000 ransom, but his son was found dead in the woods five miles from the Lindbergh home. Hauptmann was prosecuted, convicted and then later executed for the kidnapping and murder. After this case, "the Lindbergh Law," a federal kidnapping act, was enacted which prohibits the kidnapping and carrying of an individual across state lines for the purpose of obtaining a ransom or reward. By the 1950s most states increased their classification of kidnapping making it a felony punishable by death or life imprisonment.

In 1981 Congress enacted the Parental Kidnapping Prevention Act which gives the FBI jurisdiction when a child is abducted by the non-custodial parent and transported across state lines. In 2000 Congress enacted the Victims of Trafficking and Violence Protection Act of 2000 and, in 2003, the PROTECT Act of 2003 which target the crime of international sexual trafficking. Lippman notes that roughly one million children have been either forcibly abducted or have been persuaded to leave their mostly rural village homes in poor countries and have been forced into sexual slavery or low-wage industrial labor.

State statutes on kidnapping vary widely, but in common they have as their actus reus the act of detention and moving or detaining and hiding through the use of force or threat of force. The mens rea of kidnapping is the specific intent to take, detain, restrain or hold another person in secret beyond the aid of family, friends, and the law. The attendant circumstance is generally that the movement (asportation) must be a substantial distance. In early days, the victim had to be carried at least as far as another county and usually across state borders. Although there was a period where case law suggested that the distance and asportation requirement was almost meaningless (see, People v. Chessman, 35 Cal.2d 455 (1950), in which the defendant, a serial rapist, forced a young woman to leave her car and get into his car 22 feet away, was found guilty of kidnapping --there the court held that the mere fact of moving the victim, not how far she was moved, satisfied the asportation requirement), more recent cases suggest that the movement involved needs to be something more than incidental to some other crime. Courts recognized that often the crimes of robbery, rape, murder involve some degree of moving the victim.

Although frequently thought of involving requests for ransom, the crime of kidnapping does not need to be financially motivated. Kidnapping is usually divided into simple kidnapping and aggravated kidnapping. Aggravated kidnapping involves kidnapping for the purpose of sexual invasion (sexual assault or rape), obtaining a hostage, obtaining ransom, robbery, murder, blackmail, terrorizing the victim, or achieving political aims.

Model Penal Code Approach To Kidnapping

The Model Penal Code on Kidnapping §212.1 indicates that

"A person is guilty of kidnapping if he unlawfully removes another from his place of residence or business, or a substantial distance from the vicinity where he is found, or if he unlawfully confines another for a substantial period in a place of isolation with any of the following purposes:
(a) to hold for ransom or reward, or as a shield or hostage; or
(b) to facilitate commission of any felony or flight thereafter; or
(c) to inflict bodily injury on or to terrorize the victim or another; or
(d) to interfere with the performance of any governmental or political function.

The Code also establishes a crime of felonious restraint (§212.2) which involves knowingly restraining another unlawfully in circumstances exposing him to risk of serious bodily injury or holding another in a condition of involuntary servitude.

STATE v. BEATTY,
347 N.C. 555, 495 S.E.2d 367 (1998)

WHICHARD, J.

On 23 May 1994 a Mecklenburg County grand jury indicted defendant Edward Ronald Beatty for robbery with a dangerous weapon, assault with a deadly weapon with intent to kill inflicting serious injury, felonious breaking and entering, safecracking, first-degree kidnapping, two counts of second-degree kidnapping, and possession of a firearm by a convicted felon.

The jury found defendant guilty as charged . . . . The trial court arrested judgment on the conviction for first-degree kidnapping and sentenced defendant to imprisonment of thirty years for the robbery with a dangerous weapon, ten years for felonious assault, ten

years for entering, and fifteen years for each of the second-degree kidnappings, all sentences to be served consecutively.

Defendant appealed to the Court of Appeals asserting, *inter alia*, that his kidnapping convictions should be vacated because there was insufficient evidence of restraint separate and apart from that inherent in the crime of robbery with a dangerous weapon to support those convictions. The Court of Appeals majority disagreed. Judge Wynn dissented in part on the ground that "the restraint in this case was an inherent and inevitable feature of the commission of the armed robbery" and thus could not support a conviction for second-degree kidnapping. Defendant appeals based upon Judge Wynn's dissent. For reasons that follow, we affirm with regard to defendant's conviction for the second-degree kidnapping of victim Koufaloitis, and we reverse with regard to defendant's conviction for the second-degree kidnapping of victim Poulos.

The State's evidence tended to show that on 19 March 1994 defendant met a group of men at a party. They decided to rob South 21, a drive-in restaurant in Charlotte, North Carolina. When they approached the restaurant, the owner, Nicholas Copsis, stood just outside near an open door. The robbers approached this door, put a gun to Copsis' head, and told him to go inside and open the safe.

Once inside, the robbers saw restaurant employees Hristos Poulos and Tom Koufaloitis. Poulos was on his knees washing the floor at the front, and Koufaloitis stood three to four feet from the safe cleaning the floor in the back. One robber put a gun to Poulos' head and stood beside him during the robbery. An unarmed robber put duct tape around Koufaloitis' wrists and told him to lie on the floor.

Copsis did not open the safe on his first attempt. One robber said, "Let's go. We're taking too long. Hurry up." Another shot Copsis twice in the legs. Copsis then opened the safe. The robbers took more than $2,000 and fled. The robbery took approximately three to four minutes.

Defendant contends that his convictions for second-degree kidnapping must be vacated because the State presented insufficient evidence of restraint separate from that inherent in the robbery. He asserts that such evidence is necessary to satisfy the requirements …of the kidnapping statute.

N.C.G.S. § 14-39(a) provides in pertinent part that a person is guilty of kidnapping if he or she
shall unlawfully confine, restrain, or remove from one place to another, any other person 16 years of age or over without the consent of such person … if such confinement, restraint or removal is for the purpose of:
….
(2) Facilitating the commission of any felony or facilitating flight of any person following the commission of a felony….

N.C.G.S. § 14-39(a) (1993) (amended 1994). In *Fulcher* this Court recognized that certain felonies, such as robbery with a dangerous weapon, cannot be committed without some restraint of the victim; and it held that "restraint, which is an inherent, inevitable feature of such other felony," could not form the basis of a kidnapping conviction. *Fulcher*, 294 N.C. at 523, 243 S.E.2d at 351. The Court stated that the legislature did not intend N.C.G.S. § 14-39 "to permit the conviction and punishment of the defendant for both crimes."

As noted, under N.C.G.S. § 14-39 as construed and applied in *Fulcher*, a person cannot be convicted of kidnapping when the only evidence of restraint is that "which is an inherent, inevitable feature" of another felony such as armed robbery. "The key question … is whether the kidnapping charge is supported by evidence from which a jury could reasonably find that the necessary restraint for kidnapping `exposed [the victim] to greater danger than that inherent in the armed robbery itself.'" Here, the robbers, including defendant, restrained two victims, Koufaloitis and Poulos, and defendant was convicted of one count of second-degree kidnapping for each restraint. We address each in turn.

The evidence of defendant's restraint of victim Koufaloitis supports a finding that the robbers, including defendant, put duct tape around the victim's wrists, forced him to lie on the floor, and kicked him in the back twice. Because the binding and kicking were not inherent, inevitable parts of the robbery, these forms of restraint "exposed [the victim to a] greater danger than that inherent in the armed robbery itself." *Irwin; see also Pigott* (holding that when the defendant bound the victim's hands and feet, he exposed the victim to a greater danger than that inherent in the armed robbery and therefore upholding the defendant's kidnapping conviction); *Fulcher* (holding that binding of victims' hands was *not* an inherent and inevitable feature of rape and therefore upholding the defendant's kidnapping convictions based upon that restraint). When defendant bound this victim's wrists and kicked him in the back, he increased the victim's helplessness and vulnerability beyond what was necessary to enable him and his comrades to rob the restaurant. Such actions constituted sufficient additional restraint to satisfy the restraint element of kidnapping under N.C.G.S. § 14-39, and the Court of Appeals properly found no error in defendant's conviction for the second-degree kidnapping of victim Koufaloitis.

With regard to victim Poulos, the evidence shows only that one of the robbers approached the victim, pointed a gun at him, and stood guarding him during the robbery. The victim did not move during the robbery, and the robbers did not injure him in any way. In order to commit a robbery with a dangerous weapon under N.C.G.S. § 14-87(a), defendant had to possess, use, or threaten to use a firearm while taking personal property from a place of business where persons were in attendance. The only evidence of restraint of this victim was the threatened use of a firearm. This restraint is an essential element of robbery with a dangerous weapon under N.C.G.S. § 14-87, and defendant's use of this restraint exposed the

victim to no greater danger than that required to complete the robbery with a dangerous weapon. We thus hold that threatening victim Poulos with a gun was an inherent, inevitable feature of the robbery and is insufficient to support a conviction for kidnapping under N.C.G.S. § 14-39. The Court of Appeals therefore erred in finding no error in defendant's conviction for the second-degree kidnapping of victim Poulos.

For the reasons stated, we affirm the Court of Appeals with regard to defendant's conviction for the second-degree kidnapping of victim Koufaloitis, and we reverse the Court of Appeals with regard to defendant's conviction for the second-degree kidnapping of victim Poulos. We remand the case to the Court of Appeals for further remand to the Superior Court, Mecklenburg County, for entry of an order arresting judgment on defendant's conviction for the second-degree kidnapping of victim Poulos.

PEOPLE v. ALLEN, 64 Cal. Rptr. 2d 497 (1997)

Appellant appeals from criminal convictions for carjacking, kidnapping of a person under the age of 14, first degree burglary, second degree robbery, receiving stolen property, and auto theft following a bifurcated jury trial of two consolidated cases.

[W]e conclude the jury could properly consider the nature, character, and purpose of the victim's asportation, in addition to actual measured distance, when determining whether the movement was significant . . . .

On August 7, 1995, May Sun-Young and her family lived at 2951 Treat Street in San Francisco. That morning, Ms. Sun-Young was on her way to take her 7-year old daughter, Kirstie, to summer camp and stopped her automobile briefly in the driveway to close her garage door manually as she was backing out onto the street.

As Ms. Sun-Young closed her garage door, a man approached her from behind and said,

"Excuse me, can you do me a favor?" While turning around she saw the man later identified as appellant 2 getting into her vehicle, whose engine was still running. He then locked the car doors. Kirstie was still in the vehicle with her seatbelt on and began crying. Because the driver's side window was rolled down about seven inches, Ms. Sun-Young put her arms through the window and struggled with appellant in an attempt to reach the ignition key and turn off the engine.

Appellant (Allen) then released the parking brake, put the vehicle in reverse, and backed out of the driveway with Kirstie inside and Ms. Sun-Young running alongside the vehicle still attempting to reach the ignition key. The vehicle backed across Treat Street, which was a two-lane road with two parking lanes, until it hit the opposite curb and came to a stop. Appellant estimated the vehicle movement was 30-40 feet. While respondent now claims this estimate to be "speculation," below both sides at different times suggested that the distance moved was approximately 5 car lengths, or 50 feet. Appellant exited the vehicle, threw the car keys onto the ground, shoved Ms. Sun-Young against a fence, and ran down the street carrying her purse which had been left in the vehicle. Shortly thereafter, a neighbor on Treat Street several blocks away saw a man run by. In response to the neighbor's attempts to stop the man, the fleeing suspect stated, "Stay back, I got a gun." After a brief struggle, the man ran off but was later apprehended by San Francisco police officers and identified as appellant.

The jury instruction given regarding the simple kidnapping count was CALJIC No. 9.52, which sets forth the elements of kidnapping of a person under 14 years of age as follows: "Every person who unlawfully and with physical force or by any other means of instilling fear moves any other person under 14 years of age without her consent for a substantial distance, that is, a distance more than slight or trivial, is guilty of the crime of kidnapping ." The only element of the crime for which appellant asserts there was insufficient evidence and inadequate jury instructions is asportation. For "simple" kidnapping, that is, a kidnapping not elevated to a statutory form of "aggravated" kidnapping, the movement needed must be "substantial," or a distance that is more than "trivial, slight, or insignificant."

Appellant first argues that his conviction for simple kidnapping must be reversed because the minimum distance requirement for asportation is not met. He asserts the movement of Ms. Sun-Young's vehicle 30-50 feet down her driveway and across Treat Street with Kirstie inside as a matter of law cannot be "substantial," or a distance that is more than "trivial, slight or insignificant."

Appellant is correct that under most cases decided pre-1981 which have examined only the actual distance involved, the movement here would not meet the legal test of substantiality. In *People v. Brown* (1974) after breaking into the victim's residence, the defendant forced the victim to accompany him through a search of her house for her husband. When the victim's husband was not found, the defendant moved the victim outside and along a passageway next to the house until a neighbor's intervention caused the defendant to abandon the victim and flee alone. The total distance the victim was moved was unascertained. The Supreme Court held the asportation of the victim was insufficient to satisfy the "substantial" requirement and was no more than trivial.

In the case of *Caudillo*, the defendant accosted the victim in an apartment building elevator and led her away to a storage room and then to her apartment. Once again the record was silent as to the actual distance traveled between the elevator and storage room or between the storage room and the victim's apartment. The court reversed the simple kidnapping conviction concluding the record did not support a finding of "substantial" movement. The People argued distance alone was not determinative, and the jury could consider other factors such as the character of the movement and its purpose to find "substantiality." While stating such factors might be relevant to aggravated kidnapping, the court stated

> "Most of our decisions holding forcible movements of a victim to be 'substantial' within the meaning of the law of kidnap[p]ing involved distances far in excess of that here shown. . . . The shortest distance this court has ever held to be 'substantial' for this purpose was a full city block."

Despite persistent pronouncements that there is no mathematical "bright line" test for the asportation element of simple kidnapping, the decisions exemplified by those discussed above exhibit an apparent juridical thirst for just such a test. To the contrary, with one exception, another line of more contemporary cases, including others authored by the Supreme Court, have resisted setting forth a specific minimum distance below which the asportation requirement could not be satisfied, or have considered the nature and character of the movement in addition to the absolute distance measured in inches, feet, yards, or miles.

For more than 90 years California has recognized kidnapping committed during the commission of certain crimes to be "aggravated" forms of kidnapping meriting increased penalties. (Although kidnapping during the commission of robbery was the first form of aggravated kidnapping, in recent years kidnapping in the commission of rape and kidnapping in the commission of a carjacking have been added.

Where a form of aggravated kidnapping is charged, in addition to the movement meeting the "substantiality" test, it also must be of such a nature as to substantially increase the risk of harm to the victim beyond the danger posed by the associated crime and not be merely incidental to its commission. In Rayford, the defendant was charged, among other crimes, with kidnapping with intent to commit rape. The victim had been forcibly moved 105 feet after being accosted while walking home from a bus stop. The path of movement was from a parking lot to a nearby wall where the defendant and victim would be better obscured from view by passersby. After ordering the victim to remove her clothes, the defendant robbed her but apparently was dissuaded by the victim from committing rape. The entire incident took 15-20 minutes.

The trial court had instructed the jury in accordance with the asportation requirement believed necessary for an "aggravated" kidnapping, that is, movement for a substantial distance, more than that incident to the commission of the intended crime of rape, and of such a nature that there was a substantial risk of harm from the movement beyond the risk attendant to the intended crime.

The Supreme Court [held] the asportation requirement for kidnapping a victim with intent to commit rape is derived from another "aggravated" kidnapping, and thus the trial court was correct in the manner in which the jury was instructed. The Supreme Court noted the two-pronged test [:] . . . the asportation must first be "substantial," and more than "trivial" or "slight," as is required for simple kidnapping. [and] . . . the movement must also be beyond that which is incidental to commission of the underlying crime and involve exposing the victim to risk of harm over and above that associated with the commission of the underlying crime.

In commenting upon the asportation requirement common to all forms of kidnapping, the Supreme Court in Rayford revealed a dissatisfaction with those cases which have refused to consider factors beyond simple mathematical distance when evaluating the "substantiality" of movement.

Therefore, those cases which have considered the quality and character of the movement in addition to its absolute distance have weighed the purpose for the movement, whether it posed an increased risk of harm to the victim, and the "context of the environment in which the movement occurred. Purposes for movement found to be relevant have been those undertaken to facilitate the commission of a further crime, to aid in flight, or to prevent detection. We believe these factors are appropriate considerations. "Substantiality" implies something more than only measured distance. While "slight" is consistent with a quantitative analysis, the term "trivial" is a qualitative term suggestive of the conclusion that more is envisioned in determining whether a kidnapping occurs than simply how far the victim is moved. The legal requirement for asportation is satisfied by a finding of either. (CALJIC No. 9.52.)

In so holding, we conclude that while in absolute footage the distance moved here may have been empirically short, it was of a character sufficient to justify a finding of "substantiality" by the jury. The movement, in part, was plainly made to prevent Ms. Sun-Young from regaining possession of her vehicle and to facilitate appellant's flight from the area with Kirstie. In addition to evasion of capture, the vehicle was moved from a position of relative safety onto a thoroughfare. The boundary crossed was significant because it placed Kirstie at greater risk of injury. We confirm these factors, coupled with the distance traveled, are sufficient to satisfy the "substantial movement" requirement for the crime of simple kidnapping.

False Imprisonment

False imprisonment is kidnapping without the asportation (moving the victim). Like kidnapping, the crux of the crime is depriving another of their personal liberty. *McKendree v. Christy*, 29 Ill. App.2d 195 (1961), (McKendree sued police officers for false imprisonment arising from an unlawful arrest) defined false imprisonment as compelling a person "to remain where he does not wish to remain or to go where he does not wish to go. The actus reus of false imprisonment is restraining another person's liberty—forcible detention or confinement suffice. Force includes physical force and threats of force. False imprisonment can also include confinement without physical restraint or force for example by locking a door. Restraints authorized by law (for example, a parent restricting their child to their room) are not false imprisonment. The mens rea of false imprisonment is the specific intent to restrain the liberty of the person ("intentionally confining or restraining another person without his consent").

The Model Penal Code recognizes two types of false imprisonment. §212.3 states that a person commits the misdemeanor of false imprisonment if he "knowingly restrains another unlawfully so as to interfere substantially with his liberty. §212.5 states that a person is guilty of the crime of criminal coercion when, with purpose to unlawfully restrict another's freedom of action to his detriment, he threatens to commit any criminal offense, accuse anyone of a criminal offense; expose any secret tending to subject ay person to hatred, contempt or ridicule, or to impair his credit or business repute; or take or withhold action as an official or cause an official to take or withhold an action."

PEOPLE v. ISLAS,
210 Cal.App.4th 116, 147 Cal. Rptr. 3d 872 (2012)

KLEIN, P. J. —
Erasto Islas and Pablo Alexander Giron appeal the judgments entered following their conviction by jury of first degree burglary with a person present and five counts of false imprisonment by violence or menace, a felony. The jury found each offense had been committed for the benefit of a criminal street gang The trial court sentenced Islas and Giron to state prison for burglary and imposed concurrent terms on the false imprisonment counts.

Islas and Giron contend the convictions of felony false imprisonment must be reduced to misdemeanors because the evidence does not establish violence or menace. As a result, the burglary convictions, which were based on entry with the intent to commit felony false imprisonment, must be reversed or reduced to trespass.

We reject the attack on the sufficiency of the evidence to support the convictions of felony false imprisonment. The evidence indicated Islas, Giron and numerous other gang members were congregating in front of an apartment building in downtown Los Angeles that was a

gang "stronghold." When police officers arrived, the gang members ran into the building. Islas and Giron climbed up a ventilation shaft and entered the bathroom of a studio apartment occupied by Teresa Salado, an 11 year resident of the building, and her four daughters, ages 13 to four years. Islas and Giron were shirtless with their gang tattoos exposed; their heads were shaved and they wore baggy pants. One put his finger to his mouth and told Salado to hide them from the police. Giron turned off the lights in the apartment. Salado and her daughters huddled together while Islas stood and Giron sat on a couch six feet from them. When Salado said she was scared, Islas and Giron told her they were not going to harm her. After 15 minutes, police officers knocked on the door. Islas told Salado to pretend she was Giron's aunt. Giron answered the door and was pulled from the apartment by the officers. Islas was found hiding under a pile of clothes.

Although Islas and Giron used no weapons, did not touch Salado or her children and issued no express threat of harm, the evidence was sufficient to support the jury's finding the false imprisonment was effected by menace, i.e., an express or implied threat of harm. Thus, we affirm the convictions of felony false imprisonment and burglary.

DISCUSSION

1. Substantial evidence supports the convictions of felony false imprisonment and burglary.

a. The law of false imprisonment.

(1) "False imprisonment is the unlawful violation of the personal liberty of another." "False imprisonment is a misdemeanor unless it is `effected by violence, menace, fraud, or deceit,' in which case it is a felony." "All that is necessary to make out a charge of false imprisonment, a misdemeanor, is that `the individual be restrained of his liberty without any sufficient complaint or authority therefor, and it may be accomplished by words or acts [together with the requisite intent to confine] which such individual fears to disregard.' To raise the offense to a felony, violence or menace, which may or may not be life endangering, or fraud or deceit, which presents no present significant danger to the victim, must be established. "Menace is a threat of harm express or implied by words or act. "An express threat or use of a deadly weapon is not necessary."

b. Islas's and Giron's contentions.

Islas and Giron contend their conduct in asking Salado to hide them from the police constituted only misdemeanor false imprisonment, that is, an exercise of express or implied force which compelled Salado and her daughters to stay where they did not wish to stay. They assert the evidence did not demonstrate menace, i.e., an express or implied threat to do harm. They note there was no use of a weapon.

Also, they did not touch the victims.

They issued no verbal threats to harm the victims. They did not act in a hostile manner and they told Salado they were *not* going to harm her or her children.

Islas and Giron conclude there was insufficient evidence of menace to support the jury's finding Islas and Giron committed felony false imprisonment. Thus, the false imprisonment convictions must be reduced to misdemeanors

and the burglary convictions, which were based on entry with the intent to commit felony false imprisonment, must be set aside.

…

d. The evidence supports the convictions of felony false imprisonment.

We find evidentiary support for the convictions of felony false imprisonment in the repeated criticism of *People v. Matian* (1995) a case that reduced a conviction of felony false imprisonment to a misdemeanor. In *Matian*, the defendant was convicted of sexual battery by restraint, felony false imprisonment and genital penetration with a foreign object. …
Matian stated: "The evidence supporting the conviction for felony false imprisonment consists of the just completed sexual assaults during which appellant squeezed [the victim's] breast sufficiently hard to cause her pain, and possibly even bruising." When the victim prepared to leave, "[a]ppellant then grabbed her arm and yelled at her not to go. He yelled at her, `nothing happened' and told her to go wash her face. She then retreated to a chair and appellant went into an office nearby within view of [the victim]. Each time she got up from her chair, appellant glared at her and got up out of his chair to approach her. She testified she was afraid, did not want him to touch her again and sat back down."

Although *Matian* defined menace as an express or implied threat of harm, it found reported decisions that had upheld convictions of felony false imprisonment by menace generally involved the use of a deadly weapon or verbal threats of harm. Based thereon, *Matian* held:

"The only evidence of `menace' or `implied threat of harm' in this case would have to be based on appellant's earlier sexual assaults causing pain and possible injury and later glaring at her while getting out of his chair and approaching her each time she tried to leave. Based on the foregoing authorities however, this evidence is inadequate to establish an express or implied threat of harm. There was no evidence of a deadly weapon. Nor is there anything in the record to indicate the defendant ever verbally threatened [the victim] with additional physical harm. Similarly, there was no evidence to suggest appellant raised his fist or otherwise made any threatening movements suggesting harm each time [the victim] got out of the chair to leave. Based on the lack of evidence of either violence or menace in restraining [the victim] against her will, we must reverse appellant's conviction for felony false imprisonment." (*Id.* at pp. 486-487.)

The result in *Matian* has been criticized for suggesting menace requires either a weapon or a direct threat to sustain a conviction of felony false imprisonment. *People v. Castro* stated it had "no problem" concluding the evidence in *Matian* "supported the conviction for felony false imprisonment by menace, if not violence."
…
People v. Aispuro found the conduct of the defendant in *Matian* "constituted a threat of harm to his victim, even though he did not specifically say to the victim, `If you leave I'm going to physically harm you,' and even though he did not raise his fist or display a deadly weapon…*People v. Wardell* . . . similarly held "[a]n express threat or use of a deadly weapon is not necessary" to sustain a conviction for false imprisonment by menace. Rather, a jury may reasonably find a defendant committed false imprisonment by menace if the "defendant's acts or words expressly or impliedly threatened harm...."

(2) Based on the criticism of *Matian* in *Castro, Aispuro* and *Wardell*, it is clear the absence of an express threat, weapons or physical contact with the victim is not determinative. As noted in *Aispuro,* "An express or implied threat of harm does not require the use of a deadly weapon or an express verbal threat to do additional harm. Threats can be exhibited in a myriad number of ways, verbally and by conduct."

Here, Salado and her 13-year-old daughter heard noises indicating police activity outside the apartment building about an hour before Islas and Giron entered the apartment. Salado told her daughter to lie on the floor to avoid being struck by flying bullets, thereby indicating the dangerousness of the neighborhood and the situation. When Salado

heard noises at the back wall of her apartment, she turned the apartment light on and saw Islas and Giron in her bathroom. Upon seeing the intruders, Salado and her daughters were terrified. Salado testified Islas and Giron looked like "gang members," Salado's 13-year-old daughter repeatedly referred to Islas and Giron as "gangsters," and Salado's nine-year-old daughter called them "criminals."

Islas put a finger to his mouth and "told" Salado to hide them from the police. Giron then turned off the lights in the apartment. Islas remained standing while Giron sat on the couch, both about six feet from Salado and her children in the 14-by-14-foot apartment. This conduct, which occurred in an apartment building that was one of the gang's few remaining strongholds, coupled with the display of gang tattoos, constituted menace. As the prosecutor argued to the jury, the exposed tattoos implied, "you better do as we tell you to do or else."

The prosecutor's argument in this regard was supported by the testimony of the gang expert who indicated the gang intimidated law-abiding citizens by tagging buildings and causing residents to fear retaliation if a crime were reported. The expert indicated members of the gang believed they could commit crime with impunity at the apartment building. The expert testified the exposure of gang tattoos told the victims "I'm a gang member," instilled fear and advised the victims to cooperate or be harmed.

Islas argues there is no evidence indicating Salado and her daughters recognized his tattoos as gang tattoos or interpreted the tattoos as an implicit threat of harm. However, Salado had been a resident of the apartment building for 11 years. It reasonably can be inferred she was aware of the gang activity in the building and the neighborhood, which included sale of heroin, robbery and murder. Further, Islas and Giron each had "4" and "2" tattooed prominently on their exposed upper bodies, immediately identifying them as members of the gang that controlled the building.

The statement Islas and Giron would not harm Salado must be evaluated in context. As the prosecutor argued at trial, there was no reason for Islas and Giron to say they were not going to harm Salado or her daughters "unless the message was, if you don't comply, you will get hurt." Salado testified she did not believe Islas and Giron when they said they were not going to harm her and she repeatedly testified she feared the intruders would harm her or her children if she did not comply. Officer Ibarra testified Salado was shaking with fear and was unable to make eye contact when he spoke to her shortly after the incident.

Additional evidence of Salado's fear can be found in her recantation of her initial statement to Officer Ibarra that Islas and Giron were shirtless with exposed gang tattoos on the night of the incident. Also, Salado testified she continued to fear Islas and Giron might be released and harm her or her daughters. This fear derived, at least in part, from the display of tattoos indicating Islas and Giron were members of the gang that considered the apartment building its stronghold. To suggest Salado, an 11-year resident of the building, and her children did not recognize the gang tattoos as threatening disregards the evidence.

Giron suggests the subjective fear experienced by the victims is not relevant in determining the sufficiency of the evidence because menace must be established by the words and acts of the defendant. [But neither case cited by defendant] . . . states a victim's fear is an irrelevant consideration in determining whether menace has been shown.

Indeed, the victim's fear frequently is mentioned in cases that address whether an express or implied threat of harm has been proven in a felony false imprisonment case. Thus, contrary to Giron's assertion, a jury properly may consider a victim's fear in determining whether the defendant expressly or impliedly threatened harm.

Finally, Islas asserts the record shows the jury struggled with the issue of menace. . . . The fact the jury struggled with the evidence and did not reach a verdict quickly does not mean the evidence was insufficient to support the convictions.

In sum, the evidence permitted the jury to find Islas and Giron controlled the situation, made themselves comfortable in Salado's home, created a climate of fear and intimidation and coerced the victims into cooperating with their demands through an implied threat of harm. Given the gang evidence, the jury properly could conclude Islas and Giron would take whatever action was necessary to avoid capture. Thus, the evidence supports the reasonable conclusion Islas and Giron falsely imprisoned the victims by menace, i.e., an express or implied threat of harm.

e. Sufficiency of the evidence of burglary. Because the evidence supports the convictions of felony false imprisonment, the assertion the burglary lacked an underlying felony must be rejected.

"Child Snatching" and Custodial Interference

Many states have enacted custodial interference statutes which target illegal taking or confinement of a child by a non-custodial parent. These statutes allow the prosecution of the non-custodial parent who if, "knowing or having reason to know that the person has no legal right to do so, the person takes, entices or keeps another person from the other person's lawful custodian or in violation of a valid joint custody order with intent to hold the other person permanently or for a protracted period."

Some states include not only children but any person who is subject to a custodial order. (See, e.g., Tennessee statute — "takes, entices or keeps from lawful custody any mentally disabled or other person entrusted by authority of law to the custody of another person or to an institution." Some states adopt a knowing mens rea where others require specific intent. (See, e.g., Louisiana, require an intentional "taking, enticing, or decoying away of a minor child by a parent not having a right of custody, with intent to detain or conceal such child from a parent having a right of custody…")

Most states make "child snatching" a felony which subjects offenders to extradition to the state where the offense occurs. In addition, many trial judges require in divorce decrees court approval before one parent can take a child from the state where the divorce is granted, and violations of this decree are subject to contempt of court. Further, all states follow the Uniform Child Custody Jurisdiction and Enforcement Act in which the court in which the child resides has jurisdiction over the matter. This Act promotes cooperation amongst the courts and prevents judge and venue shopping. Additionally, Congress passed the Parental Kidnapping Prevention Act in 1980 which is designed to prevent jurisdictional conflicts over child custody and takes precedence over state law (including the UCCJA). Its goal is to reduce any incentive for parental child snatching.

The Model Penal Code recognizes custodial interference. MPC §212.4 states that "a person commits an offense if he knowingly or recklessly takes or entices any child under the age of 18 from the custody of its parent, guardian or other lawful custodian, when he has no privilege to do so. (It is an affirmative defense that: (a) the actor believed that his action was necessary to preserve the child from danger to its welfare; or (b) the child, being at the time not less than 14 years old, was taken away at its own instigation without enticement and without purpose to commit a criminal offense with or against the child.

Other Cases—Kidnapping, False Imprisonment

Shue v. State, 553 S.E. 2d 348 (Ga. Ct. App. 2001).
James Shue attacked and threatened to kill the victim unless she got into her car. Victim testified that as the defendant pushed her into the car, she tightly grabbed the steering wheel and honked the horn. Defendant then left. Victim testified that she voluntarily entered her car after Shue fled. Shue was convicted of false imprisonment but acquitted of kidnapping.

Georgia statutes stated that false imprisonment is committed by an "arrest, confinement or detention of the person without legal authority, which violates the person's personal liberty." Kidnapping is when an individual "abducts or steals away any person without lawful authority or warrant and holds such person against his will." The court held that the only difference between kidnap and false imprisonment is the asportation requirement.

State v. Overton, N.C. Ct. App. 4-327, LEXIS 915 (2005).
North Carolina appellate court affirmed conviction of Overton for second –degree kidnapping his girlfriend, Elsie Fennell, for purpose of terrorizing her when she threatened to kick him out if he refused to start paying the bills. Overton "caught and restrained" Fennell from leaving the house and only gave her the car keys once she agreed to not call the police. Overton appealed on the grounds that he should have been convicted of false imprisonment not kidnapping because he confined and restrained her for the purpose of avoiding detection rather than for the purpose of terrorizing her. The North Carolina court recognized that "if the purpose of the restraint was to accomplish one of the purposes in the kidnapping statute. . . . the offense is kidnapping. In the absence of one of the statutorily specified purposes, the unlawful restraint is false imprisonment. The court affirmed Overton's conviction stating it was irrelevant if he changed his purpose during the course of the restraint.

United State v. Bradley, 390 F.3d 145 (1ˢᵗ Cir. 2004).
Two New Hampshire defendants were convicted under the United States Victims of Trafficking and Violence Protection Act of 2000 which punishes acts of slavery and forced labor when they misrepresented the working conditions of their tree removal company to workers recruited from Jamaica who were threatened, forcibly detained, and abused when they attempted to return home.

WRAP UP

This chapter has explored a variety of crimes against persons at common law, under modern statutes, and under the MPC. At common law, rape and mayhem were considered felonies, and assault, battery, kidnapping, and false imprisonment were considered misdemeanors. Now, the seriousness of the crime generally depends on the harm or injury inflicted. The laws covering sexual assaults have seen significant change over time, and now most modern statutes are written in gender neutral terms with the requirements of resistance, prompt reporting, and victim chastity have been removed. Many of the common law crimes involving sexual relationships (adultery, sodomy, and fornication for example) no longer are prosecuted even when they remain "on the books." At common law assault meant either attempting to cause physical injury to someone or threatening to cause physical injury to someone; battery meant actually causing physical injury. Many modern statutes merge these into "assault and battery" charges or, like Oregon, use different names such as "menacing" or "harassment." Kidnapping and false imprisonment are crimes against a person's liberty—the main difference between the two is that kidnapping involves moving the victim whereas false imprisonment does not. Newer custodial interference crimes are based on concern for the rights of the custodial parent and the respect for judicial custody orders, in addition to addressing the child's liberty interests.

Chapter Eight: Crimes Against Habitation

Overview

Common law emphasized the "sanctity of one's dwelling." Two common law felonies burglary and arson, and two common law misdemeanors, trespass and malicious mischief, arose which protected an individual's dwelling. These common law crimes been codified and modified by state statutes to reflect societal changes.

Burglary

Common Law Burglary

At common law, burglary was the "breaking and entering of the dwelling of another at night with the intent to commit a felony therein." According to Blackstone burglary was a "heinous offense" that caused "abundant terror" which constitutes a violation of the right of habitation and provides the "inhabitant of a dwelling with the natural right of killing the aggressor." Common law felonies included: murder, manslaughter, rape, robbery, larceny, arson, and sodomy (and burglary), and each were punished by the death penalty.

BREAKING

Common law burglary required a breach or a creation of an opening; a mere trespass at law was insufficient. 3 Coke, Institutes of the Laws of England 63 (1644). The point of the breaking requirement was to verify that the occupants had not invited entry. If the occupant of the dwelling had created the opening, it was felt that he had not entitled himself to the protection of the law, as he had not properly secured his dwelling. Entry through pre-existing opening, such as an open door or window did not constitute a breaking. Further opening an already partially opened door or window also was not a breaking. (Except for the thief who came down a chimney). Breaking did not require force or violence, so opening a door or window which was closed but not locked was sufficient breaking. The purpose of the crime of burglary was to keep out unauthorized intruders, so anyone given authority to enter had not committed a breaking. When authority was restricted to certain portions of the dwelling or times of the day, there was a breaking when the structure was opened in violation of the restrictions. So, servants who entered parts of a dwelling which was closed off to him was considered a breaking. Similarly, if the servant opened the dwelling to a co-conspirator, that was considered a breaking. Constructive breaking occurred when entry was gained by fraud or threat of force. It was disputed whether one who gained entry without a breaking but committed a breaking in order to leave was guilty of burglary. In England that question was settled by a statute making the breaking to leave sufficient for commission of burglary. See, LaFave and Scott, at 708-709.

ENTERING

Entry at common law occurred when any part of the intruder's person intruded albeit momentarily into the structure—it was not good enough that the person had put a stick or tool through the opening. Even just part of a hand entering was held sufficient as was part of a foot kicking out a window. If the intruder used some instrument which protruded into the structure no entry occurred unless he was simultaneously using the instrument to achieve the felonious purchase Constructive entry occurred when a person sent one incapable of committing an offense (say, for example, a child) in to the dwelling to achieve the felonious purpose. The person being sent in was deemed only a tool being used by the actor. A causal connection between the breaking and entering was reqired. If an intruder gained admittance without a breaking but committed a breaking once inside, there was no burglary. However, if there was a breaking on one night, and an entry the next night through the breach previously created, then there would be sufficient breaking and entering connection for burglary. See, LaFave and Scott, at 710-711.

DWELLING

The third element of burglary at common law was that the intruder break and enter a dwelling. Dwellings were simply places where people slept and originally it included all dwellings--regardless of their size—even though the burglary definition used the words "mansion house." Occupancy and not ownership was the controlling factor. That said, the resident or dweller did not need to be at be home during the offense. If residents were away, be it for a short period or even for an extended portion of the year, it was nevertheless considered a dwelling. If, however, the home was unfinished, or not resided in (even if by a workman who constantly slept there for the purpose of protection) it was not considered a dwelling and no burglary could be proven. A business resided in by a proprietor or employee could be burglarized, but a business used only during the day could not. A hotel room or an apartment could be burglarized because they were places of residence. Barns, stables, were not places which could be burglarized unless they were part of the home's curtilage (i.e., those that were generally surrounded by the residence.) The courts examined whether they were spacially close enough to the dwelling to be part of the curtilage (fenced in area).

OF ANOTHER

Another attendant circumstance included in common law burglary was that the dwelling be that of another. One could not burglarize one's own residence at common law. When several people occupied the same dwelling, none could commit burglary of the residence unless a portion of the structure had been set aside for one residence (for example, someone renting a room or apartment), Some commentators said that a separate entry was required, but generally the common law view was that rooms could have been set aside regardless of the exits or entrances. Transient guests or lodgers could not have an interest in a dwelling so that they could be the victims of burglary (for example, an "Airbnb" renter could not claim to have been burglarized), and at common law, landlord would be considered the victim rather than the paying guest.

AT NIGHT

Another attendant circumstance required the burglary occur at night. Night was considered the time when honest men might fall prey to criminals. 4 Blackstone, Commentaries on the Laws of England (1769), at 224. The difference between day and night at common law was whether a man's face could be discerned by natural light even though the sun may have set. Id. The presence of artificial light or intense moonlight did not convert the night into day, however. Finally, while the acts had to take place during the night, there was no requirement that they be done during the same night, and if the breaking occurred one night and the entry the next night, this still constuituted burglary. See, LaFave and Scott, at 714.

INTENT TO COMMIT A FELONY

Common law burglary was a specific intent crime. It requires not only the intent to commit the actus reus of breaking and entering but also the intent to commit a crime once inside. The key element that distinguishes burglary from criminal trespass at common law was that the intruder, at the time he entered, must have intended to commit a felony. If the actor only broke and entered to commit a trespass (enter unlawfully) then there was no burglary … even if he subsequently committed a felony while in the dwelling. If the intruder broke and entered with only the intent to assault or batter the resident (both of which were common law misdemeanors), then there would be no burglary, even if the victim subsequently died from the battery. But, if the intruder entered with the intent to commit a felony it did not matter whether he actually accomplished his goal. The intent had to be to commit a felony while in the house. At early common law, the crime had to be a serious "heinous" felony); but it expanded to include other, non-violent felonies. Most commonly the breaking and entering involved the intent to steal something which was the common law felony of larceny.

Modern Statutory Burglary

Modern burglary statutes drastically differ from common law burglary. Modern codes commonly define different levels of burglary based on seriousness of crime contemplated, or the type of building entered, or the time of day entered. One factor upon which statutes aggravate a burglary is when the offender entered the building while armed or that he injured or threatened to injure a person in the premises.

The breaking requirement has been significantly relaxed. Most statutes now say "unlawfully" or "unauthorized" or "by trespass" or "without authority" "without consent." The statutes generally require that the entry be unprivileged. Additionally, under modern statutes, surreptitious remaining (i.e., entering a business which is open to the public, and then staying beyond the permission or license to enter) also meets the former breaking requirement. The requirement of entry still exists in modern statutes, but generally the requirement is now either "enter" or unlawfully remain on the premises. Relaxing the entry to remaining means that a person who enters without the intent to commit a crime, but then unlawfully remains and forms the intent while unlawfully remaining is guilty of burglary under modern statutes in a way not fathomed under the common law.

> This common statutory expansion in the definition of burglary makes great sense. A lawful entry does not foreclose the kind of intrusion burglary is designed to reach, as is illustrated by the case of a bank customer who hides in the bank until it closes and then takes the bank's money. Moreover, this expansion forecloses any argument by a defendant found in premises then closed that he had entered earlier when they were open. But for this expansion not also to cover certain situations in which the unlawful remaining ought ot be treated as burglary it is best to limit the remaining within alternative to where that conduct is done surreptitiously. LaFave, at 887.

Modern statutes have rejected the requirement that the building be a dwelling. All states now take the position that a variety of buildings or structures can be burglarized. Statutes tend to aggravate or have higher degrees for burglary committed in a dwelling. Some statutes include vehicles (cars, boats, etc.) as places that can be burglarized. Statutes no longer require that the building be "of another." As long as the entry is unprivileged or unauthorized then the offender can be held guilty of burglary. See, _State v. Altamirano_, 803 P.2d 425 (Ariz. App. 1990) (Though burglary statutes cover any "residential structure" court holds defendant not guilty of burglary where he sexually assaulted his daughter in his own home as the defendant was not unlawfully present.). The nighttime requirement has been abolished under all statutes. Some states aggravate the burglary if it is committed at night. For those statutes which retain it for some degrees of burglary, one defines it as the period between sunset and sunrise, while others define it as thirty minutes past sunset to thirty minutes before sunrise.

States have adopted a variety of approaches with regard to the common law requirement of intent to commit a felony. Modern statutes commonly require that the actor have an intent to commit a felony or some form of theft within the structure. The prevailing view in the modern codes is that an intent to commit any offense will do. "This is a sound position as "an intrusion for any criminal purpose creates elements of alarm and danger to persons who may be present in a place where they should be entitled to freedom from intrusion." LaFave, at 892. One state provides that the actual commission of the offense within is an alternative basis for the conviction (i.e., that it may be presumed from the actual commission of the act that the offender intended to commit the act upon unlawfully entering or remaining). Most states also prohibit possession of burglar tools. Burglary is a distinct offense and does not merge into the underlying offense.

Some critics of modern burglary statutes claim that they no longer redress the harm initially contemplated by common law burglary. According to LaFave,

> The modern law of burglary has little in common with its common law ancestor except for the title of burglary. The modern offense cannot be justified from its history. It cannot be

rationalized as giving a recognized protection to citizens who have secured themselves in their homes. . . for the requirements of a breaking and entering of a dwelling house have been eroded. It cannot be justified any longer as protecting helpless citizens from brigands who roam in the night as the requirement that acts occur in the nighttime is also vanishing. Nor is protection from serious crime a justification for the offense, for the intent requirement itself is beginning to be eroded. LaFave, at 892.

Here are some recent burglary "facts" according to Kasey Tross, freelance writer and CERT member: 1) A 2016 burglary victimization survey revealed that most burglaries now occur between the hours of noon and 4:00 p.m. Nighttime burglaries make up only 17% of all modern burglaries. 2) The number of burglaries increase 10 percent in summer months. 3) More burglaries occur in rural areas than in metropolitan areas (New Mexico is the most "burglarized" state in the U.S. followed by Mississippi, Louisiana, Oklahoma, and Arkansas). 4) The 2017 FBI crime statistics show that there are 23 burglaries across the nation every minute, making it the most frequent crime behind larceny/theft. 5) A 2017 study of professional burglars revealed that they bypass living rooms and downstairs areas and head straight to the bedrooms for cash and jewelry; they grab small stuff they can put in their pockets rather than just large electronics/televisions. 6) The average burglary loss is $2416.00. 7) Since 2008 until 2017, burglaries have decreased by about 37 percent. (Overall, property crime has decreased by over 65% since 1993). See, https://www.safewise.com/blog/8-surprising-home-burglary-statistics/

Burglary Under Model Penal Code

Model Penal Code §221.1 provides, "A person is guilty of burglary if he enters a building or occupied structure, or separately secured or occupied portions thereof, with purpose to commit a crime therein, unless the premises are at the time open to the public or the actor is licensed or privileged to enter. It is an affirmative defense to prosecution for burglary that the building or structure was abandoned." It aggravates burglaries done while armed, in a dwelling, or at night—treating them as second degree felonies; otherwise, burglary is considered a felony in the third degree. The MPC does not require that the intruder enter with the intent to commit a felony; any crime will do. Under the MPC, burglary merges into the completed crime unless the underlying offense is a serious felony (such as rape, violent robbery, or murder).

JEWELL v. STATE, 672 N.E.2d 419 (1996)

ROBERTSON, Judge.

Barry L. Jewell broke into his estranged wife's house, beat her lover in the head with a board until he was unconscious, amputated the lover's penis with a knife, and fed the severed penis to the dog. Jewell appeals his convictions, after a jury trial, of Burglary with a deadly weapon resulting in serious bodily injury, a class A felony, and Battery resulting in serious bodily injury, a class C felony. Jewell was sentenced to an aggregate term of 48 years imprisonment. Jewell raises seven issues, which we restate and consolidate into six, none of which constitute reversible error.

FACTS
The facts in the light most favorable to the verdict reveal that, in 1989, Bridget Fisher, who

later married Jewell and changed her name to Bridget Jewell, purchased a home on contract in her maiden name from her relatives. Bridget and Jewell lived in the house together on and off before and after they married in 1990. Jewell helped fix the house up, and therefore, had some "sweat equity" in the house.

Jewell and Bridget experienced marital difficulties and dissolution proceedings were initiated. Jewell moved out of the house and Bridget changed the locks so that Jewell could not reenter. At a preliminary hearing in the dissolution proceedings, Bridget's attorney informed Jewell that Bridget wanted a divorce and wanted Jewell to stop coming by the house. Jewell moved into a friend's house, agreeing to pay him $100.00 per month in rent and to split the utility expenses.

Bridget resumed a romantic relationship with her former boyfriend, Chris Jones. Jewell told a friend that he wanted to get Jones in a dark place, hit him over the head with a 2x4 (a board), and cut his "dick" off. Jewell confronted Jones at his place of employment and threatened to kill him if he were to continue to see Bridget. Jewell was observed on numerous occasions watching Bridget's house. Jewell used a shortwave radio to intercept and listen to the phone conversations on Bridget's cordless phone.

At approximately 4:00 a.m. on the morning of June 13, 1991, Jewell gained entry to Bridget's house through the kitchen window after having removed a window screen. Bridget and Jones were inside sleeping. Jewell struck Jones over the head with a 2x4 until he was unconscious, amputated Jones' penis with a knife, and fed the severed penis to the dog. Bridget awoke and witnessed the attack, but she thought she was having a bad dream and went back to sleep. Bridget described the intruder as the same size and build as Jewell and as wearing a dark ski mask similar to one she had given Jewell. She observed the assailant hit Jones on the head with a board, and stab him in the lower part of his body.

A bloody 2x4 was found at the scene. The sheets on the bed where Bridget and Jones had been sleeping were covered in blood. Bridget discovered that one of her kitchen knives was missing. However, the police did not preserve the sheets or take blood samples and permitted Bridget to dispose of the sheets. A police officer involved explained that the possibility that any of the blood at the crime scene could have come from anyone other than Jones had not been considered.

Jones' severed penis was never found and he underwent reconstructive surgery. His physicians fashioned him a new penis made from tissue and bone taken from his leg. Jones experienced complications and the result was not entirely satisfactory.

At the crime scene, Bridget gave a statement to police in which she identified Jewell as the assailant. Later that morning, however, she waffled on the certainty of her identification, explaining that the assailant had worn a mask

and that she had thought that she had been having a dream. However, in the written statement she gave later that morning, she repeatedly stated that she was certain that Jewell had been the assailant.

The police visited the house where Jewell had been staying at approximately 6:00 that morning. One roommate stated that Jewell had not been home when the roommate went to bed at 1:30 a.m. Another roommate stated that he saw Jewell asleep on the couch at 5:30 a.m. The police observed that the hood of Jewell's car was warm and there was no dew on the car, in contrast to the other car parked there. The police told Jewell that they were investigating a complaint that Jones had been hit on the head at Bridget's house. Jewell denied involvement and stated that he had been out cruising around with his buddies the night before. Jewell later told his roommate that the police had accused him of hitting Jones with a board. (The police had not mentioned that Jones had been hit with a board.) Later that day, Jewell went to a house where he had been working. There, he again stated that the police had been at his house investigating a report that a man had been hit on the head with a board.

Jewell admitted to a good friend of his that he had committed the crime. Jewell asked the friend to lie to the police and tell them that he and Jewell had been out drinking beer and riding around the night of the attack. Initially, this friend corroborated Jewell's false alibi with the police, but later recanted and told police that Jewell had told him that he had committed the crime and had enlisted his aid to falsely corroborate his alibi.

The police obtained an arrest warrant and arrested Jewell. At the jail, a detective enlisted the aid of an inmate to collect evidence against Jewell. The detective told the inmate that someone was going to be put in his cell, and that the inmate should report anything he learned from this person. The inmate had not been given any information about the instant crime, and had been instructed not to question Jewell, but only to report what he heard. The inmate overheard Jewell's conversation with another inmate in which Jewell stated that he had committed the crime and described it in detail. In this conversation, Jewell mentioned that there were rubber gloves in a coat pocket. Jewell threatened the inmate not to tell the police what he had heard. The police obtained and executed a search warrant upon the house where Jewell had been staying and found the rubber gloves in the coat pocket. The inmate who reported Jewell's conversation received a favorable disposition of the charges against him.

DECISION

IV.

B.

Jewell argues the trial court erred by refusing his tendered instruction on the offense of burglary regarding the "concurrence of conduct and intent," that is, that the jury need find that when Jewell broke in and entered the house, he did so with the intent of committing the crime of battery with a deadly weapon therein. Jewell's instruction informed the jury that the State could not meet its burden by proving that he had formed the intent to commit a felony after he had entered the house. The State concedes that Jewell's instruction correctly stated the law.

However, the trial court gave the following instruction:

> To convict the defendant of burglary as alleged in Count 1 of the relevant Information the State must have approved [sic] each of the following elements: The defendant 1; knowingly or intentionally, 2; did break and enter, 3; the dwelling of Bridget Jewell, 4; with the intent to commit a felony in it, to-wit: Battery with a deadly weapon, and 5; and the burglary resulted in serious bodily injury to Christopher K. Jones. To convict the defendant of burglary as charged in Count 1 of the relevant Information you also must find that at the time of the alleged breaking and entering of the dwelling of Bridget Jewell the defendant had an intent to commit a felony in the dwelling of Bridget Jewell. If the State failed to prove each of these elements beyond a reasonable doubt you should find the defendant not guilty. If the State did prove each of these elements beyond a reasonable doubt, you should find the defendant guilty of Burglary, a Class A felony.

(Emphasis added). This instruction adequately informed the jury regarding the requirement that they find a "concurrence of conduct and intent." Therefore, the substance of Jewell's tendered instruction was covered by the trial court's instruction, and we find no error.

V.

Sufficiency

A.

Jewell attacks the sufficiency of evidence supporting his conviction of Burglary, which is defined as:

> A person who breaks and enters the building or structure *of another person,* with intent to commit a felony in it, commits burglary.
> Ind.Code 35-43-2-1 (Emphasis added).
> Jewell argues he was improperly convicted of breaking into his own house.

…

The Burglary statute's requirement that the dwelling be that "of another person" is satisfied if the evidence demonstrates that the entry was unauthorized. In *Ellyson,* we held a husband was properly convicted of burglary for breaking into the house in which he and his estranged wife had lived previously with the intent of raping his wife. We noted that dissolution proceedings had been initiated and that wife alone controlled access to the home. We upheld the husband's burglary conviction even though he may have had a right to possession of the house co-equal with his wife at the time of the breaking and entering.

In the present case, Bridget had purchased the house in her own name before the marriage. When she and Jewell experienced marital difficulties, Jewell moved out and Bridget changed the locks to prevent Jewell from reentering the house. Bridget alone controlled access to the house. Jewell entered the house at 4:00 a.m. through the kitchen window after having removed the screen. The evidence supports the conclusion that the entry was unauthorized; and, therefore, we find no error.

B.

Next, Jewell argues there was insufficient evidence that he had entered the house with the intent to commit a felony battery therein. That a burglary defendant entered the structure with the intent to commit the felony charged therein is a matter that the jury can infer from the surrounding circumstances. Although the fact of breaking and entering is not itself sufficient to prove the entry was made with the intent to commit the felony, such intent may be inferred from the subsequent conduct of the defendant inside the premises.

In the present case, before the date of the crime,

Jewell had expressed his intention to get Jones in a dark place, hit him with a 2x4, and cut off his penis. Jewell did precisely that after breaking into his estranged wife's house. The jury could properly infer that Jewell broke into the house with the intent to commit the felony battery therein as charged. Therefore, we find no error.

Judgment affirmed.

BRUCE v. COMMONWEALTH, 469 S.E.2d 64 (Va. 1996)

ELDER, Judge.

Donnie Lee Bruce (appellant) appeals his conviction for breaking and entering his estranged wife's residence armed with a deadly weapon, with the intent to commit assault, in violation of Code § 18.2-91. Appellant contends that the evidence was insufficient to prove the elements of the charge. Disagreeing with appellant, we affirm his conviction.

I.

FACTS

Appellant and Deborah Bruce (Deborah), although married, lived in separate residences during late 1993. Deborah lived with the couple's son, Donnie Bruce, Jr. (Donnie) and Donnie's girlfriend at Greenfield Trailer Park in Albemarle County, Virginia. Although appellant stayed with Deborah at the residence during a period of time in September or October of 1993, his name was not on the lease, he was not given a key to the residence, and he did not have permission to enter the residence at the time of the alleged offense.

On December 5, 1993, at approximately 2:00 p.m., Deborah, Donnie, and Donnie's girlfriend left their residence. Earlier that morning, Donnie told appellant that Deborah would not be home that afternoon. Upon departing, Donnie and Deborah left the front door and front screen door closed but unlocked. The front door lacked a knob but had a handle which allowed the door to be pulled shut or pushed open.

After Deborah, Donnie, and Donnie's girlfriend left their residence, a witness observed appellant drive his truck into the front yard of the residence and enter through the front door

without knocking. Appellant testified, however, that he parked his truck in the lot of a nearby supermarket and never parked in front of the residence. Appellant stated that the front screen door was open and that the front door was open three to four inches when he arrived. Appellant testified that he gently pushed the front door open to gain access and entered the residence to look for Donnie.

While preparing to leave the residence, appellant answered a telephone call from a man with whom Deborah was having an affair. The conversation angered appellant, and he threw Deborah's telephone to the floor, breaking it. Appellant stated that he then exited through the residence's back door, leaving the door "standing open," and retrieved a .32 automatic gun from his truck, which was parked in the nearby supermarket parking lot. Appellant returned to the residence through the open back door. Appellant, who testified that he intended to shoot himself with the gun, went to Deborah's bedroom, lay on her bed, and drank liquor.

When Deborah, Donnie, and Donnie's girlfriend returned to their residence, appellant's truck was not parked in the front yard. Upon entering the residence, Donnie saw that someone was in the bathroom, with the door closed and the light on. When police arrived soon thereafter, they found appellant passed out on Deborah's bed and arrested him.

On May 24, 1994, a jury in the Circuit Court of Albemarle County convicted appellant of breaking and entering a residence, while armed with a deadly weapon, with the intent to commit assault. Appellant appealed to this

Court.

II.
PROOF OF REQUISITE ELEMENTS

In order to convict appellant of the crime charged, the Commonwealth had to prove that appellant broke and entered into his wife's residence with the intent to assault her with a deadly weapon. Under the facts of this case, the Commonwealth satisfied this burden.

Breaking, as an element of the crime of burglary, may be either actual or constructive.... *Actual breaking* involves the application of some force, slight though it may be, whereby the entrance is effected. Merely pushing open a door, turning the key, lifting the latch, or resort to other slight physical force is sufficient to constitute this element of the crime. "Where entry is gained by threats, fraud or conspiracy, a *constructive breaking* is deemed to have occurred." "[A] breaking, either actual or constructive, to support a conviction of burglary, must have resulted in an *entrance* contrary to the will of the occupier of the house."

Appellant's *initial entry* into Deborah's residence constituted an actual breaking and entering. Sufficient credible evidence proved that appellant applied at least slight force to push open the front door and that he did so contrary to his wife's will. However, as the Commonwealth concedes on brief, appellant did *not* possess the intent to assault his wife with a deadly weapon at this time. The Commonwealth bears the burden of "proving beyond a reasonable doubt each and every constituent element of a crime before an accused may stand convicted of that particular offense." The Commonwealth therefore had to prove appellant intended to assault his wife when he reentered the residence with his gun.

We hold that the Commonwealth presented sufficient credible evidence to prove the crime charged. On the issue of intent, the jury reasonably could have inferred that the phone call from Deborah's boyfriend angered appellant, resulting in his destruction of the telephone and the formation of an intent to commit an assault with a deadly weapon upon Deborah. Viewed in the light most favorable to the Commonwealth, credible evidence proved that appellant exited the back door of the residence, leaving the door open, moved his truck to a nearby parking lot, and re-entered the residence carrying a gun with the intent to assault Deborah.

Well-established principles guide our analysis of whether appellant's exit and re-entry into the residence constituted an actual or constructive breaking. As we stated above, an "[a]ctual breaking involves the application of some force, slight though it may be, *whereby the entrance is effected.*" "In the criminal law as to housebreaking and burglary, [breaking] means the tearing away or removal of any part of a house or of the locks, latches, or other fastenings intended to secure it, or otherwise exerting force to gain an entrance, with criminal intent...." *Black's Law Dictionary* 189 (6th ed. 1990). Virginia, like most of our sister states, follows the view that "breaking out of a building after the commission of a crime therein is not burglary in the absence of a statute so declaring." In this case, appellant *exited* the back door of the residence on his way to retrieve the gun from his truck. In doing so, the appellant did not break for the purpose of escaping or leaving. Rather, by opening the closed door, he broke in order to facilitate his re-entry. At the time he committed the breaking, he did so with the intention of re-entering after retrieving his firearm. Although appellant used no force to effect his re-entry into the residence, he used the force necessary to constitute a breaking by opening the closed door on his way out. Even though no prior case involves facts similar to the instant case, the breaking and the entry need not be concomitant, so long as the intent to commit the substantive crime therein is concomitant with the breaking and entering.

Sound reasoning supports the conclusion that a breaking from within in order to facilitate an entry for the purpose of committing a crime is sufficient to prove the breaking element of burglary. The gravamen of the offense is breaking the close or the sanctity of the residence, which can be accomplished from within or without. A breaking occurs when an accomplice opens a locked door from within to enable his cohorts to enter to commit a theft or by leaving a door or window open from within to facilitate a later entry to commit a crime.

Accordingly, a breaking occurred when appellant opened the back door of the victim's residence, even though the breaking was accomplished from within. Thus, because the evidence was sufficient to prove an intent to commit assault at the time of the breaking and the entering, the Commonwealth proved the elements of the offense. Thus, we affirm appellant's conviction.

State v. Sandoval, 94 P.3d 323 (Wash. Ct. App. 2004)

John Sandoval, an alcoholic consumed a 12-pack of beer while watching a football game, he then walked to a bar and drank more beer. He left the bar, walked into Christensen's home after kicking the door in. Christensen, a police reserve deputy, demanded to know who Sandoval was and what he was doing in his home. Sandoval asked Christensen, "who are you?" and pushed Christensen back a few feet. Christensen then subdued Sandoval (punched him in the head, wrestled him to the ground, held him down). Sandoval, did not remember leaving the bar or any other location until he woke up in jail facing first-degree burglary charges. Washington's burglary law states that it is burglary in the first degree if, "with the intent to commit a crime against a person or property therein, an individual "enters or remains unlawfully in a building" and if while entering "the actor . . . assaults any person." No property was taken by Sandoval, and he did not know Christensen. The Washington appellate court reversed Sandoval's conviction.

State v. Holt, 352 P.3d 702 (NMCA, 2015)

OPINION

Anthony Holt (Defendant) was trying to remove a window screen from Carolyn Stamper's (Stamper) home when he noticed her through the window. Although he turned and left the premises without breaching the window, he was convicted of one count of breaking and entering and now appeals on two grounds. First, he argues that the Legislature did not intend to punish as breaking and entering an intrusion into the space between the screen and the window. Second, he maintains that the evidence was insufficient for the jury to conclude that he in fact entered that space. We affirm.

BACKGROUND

Stamper, a resident of Las Cruces, New Mexico, was relaxing on her sofa one December afternoon when she heard the doorbell ring and a rustling sound at the front door. She did not see anyone through the peephole in the door. She then heard a "metal on metal" sound at the window, which was approximately seven feet from the front door. The window was open approximately four inches because Stamper's "smelly old dog" was in the room with her. The curtains over the window were drawn except for a gap of about four inches. Through the gap, Stamper could see a man at the window who was working to remove the aluminum window screen. The screen was halfway removed from the window and the man was trying to get the screen free of the track at the bottom of the window frame. At trial, Stamper agreed with the State that while holding the screen, the man's "fingers were ... in that area between the window and the screen[.]"

After a few seconds, the man looked up and noticed Stamper. He said, "Oh, I'm sorry," then turned and left. As he was leaving, Stamper told him, "You better be sorry, you thief[.]" Stamper testified that the screen "was pretty well destroyed" and had to be replaced. She also testified that she was frightened by the incident and that it "was the first time [she] had been confronted with this in [her] own home."

DISCUSSION

{5} Defendant makes two arguments on appeal. First, he argues that the facts of this case do not fit within a breaking and entering charge, because entering the space between a screen and a window is not the same as entering the interior of a home or structure. Second, he argues that the evidence was not sufficient to support a conclusion that Defendant entered the space between the screen and window.

The Breaking and Entering Statute Encompasses Entry Into the Space Between the Screen and Window

Defendant argues that, even if his fingers were between the screen and the window, he cannot be convicted of breaking and entering. Defendant makes two contentions: (1) the plain language of the breaking and entering statute requires entry into the interior of a structure, i.e., entry beyond the last barrier to the structure's interior; and (2) the breaking and entering statute is ambiguous because it does not define the boundaries of a structure, and thus, under the rule of lenity, must be construed against the State. . . . Based on our construction of the statute, we conclude that it is not ambiguous such that the rule of lenity applies. Hence, we need not address Defendant's second argument.

Section 30–14–8(A) defines "breaking and entering" as

> the unauthorized entry of any ... dwelling or other structure, movable or immovable, where entry is obtained by fraud or deception, or by the breaking or dismantling of any part of the ... dwelling or other structure, or by the breaking or dismantling of any device used to secure the ... dwelling or other structure.

As it relates to the facts here, UJI 14–1410 NMRA requires the jury to find that (1) "[t]he defendant entered [the structure] without permission" and (2) "[t]he entry was obtained by" breaking or dismantling a part of the structure. Unlike in some other states' statutes, neither the breaking and entering statute nor the burglary statute states what delimits a structure. We conclude that the plain language of the breaking and entering statute sheds little light on the Legislature's intent as to the issue before us: whether the space between a window screen and an open window is protected space under the statute.

We next examine the purposes of the breaking and entering statute to determine whether the conduct here falls within the harm the Legislature sought to prevent. Because "New Mexico's breaking-and-entering statute is itself grounded in common law burglary[,]" cases interpreting the burglary statute inform our analysis. ... Like burglary, "the purpose of New Mexico's breaking-and-entering statute is ... to protect possessory rights.". ... Those possessory rights, however, "go beyond the mere right to physical possession of an object" and include the right to exclude, privacy interests, and "security of habitation." "It is the invasion of privacy and the victim's feeling of being

personally violated that is the harm caused by the modern burglar, and the evil that our society is attempting to deter through modern burglary statutes."

"[I]n order for an area to be considered prohibited space under [the burglary statute], it must have some sort of enclosure." ... "[I]t is this enclosed space that the Legislature intended to protect." The burglary statute defines prohibited space as "any vehicle, watercraft, aircraft, dwelling or other structure, movable or immovable [.]" Section 30–16–3. The breaking and entering statute includes the same list. Section 30–14–8(A). In both statutes, the spaces in which possessory, privacy, and security interests are implicated are delineated by an enclosure.

Our question thus becomes whether a window screen forms an enclosure such that penetration beyond the screen is sufficient for entry of a structure. "[I]n general, the roof, walls, doors, and windows constitute parts of a building's outer boundary, the penetration of which is sufficient for entry." But other types of boundaries might also suffice because "[i]t is the nature of the enclosure that creates [prohibited space]." "'[T]he proper question is whether the nature of a structure's composition is such that a reasonable person would expect some protection from unauthorized intrusions.' "

Relying in part on this test, the *Muqqddin* Court concluded that "a vehicle's gas tank and wheel wells do not constitute protected space under [the burglary statute]." No New Mexico court since *Muqqddin* has used this test to address the legal question here. However, in *Nible,* the case from which the test was derived, the California Court of Appeals stated that "the focus of the question whether the penetration of a [partially open] window screen constitutes a burglarious entry must be on whether a reasonable person would believe a window screen provides some protection against unauthorized intrusions." It found that the answer to this question "is unequivocally in the affirmative." It went on to state that the screen door [or window] is not to be considered as a mere protection against flies, but rather as a permanent part of the dwelling. The holdings [in case law] proceed, it would seem, on the grounds that the screen door [or window] is a part of the house on which the occupants rely for protection and that to open such a door [or window] is a violation of the security of the dwelling house which is the peculiar gravamen of a burglarious breaking. It concluded that "when a screen which forms the outer barrier of a protected structure is penetrated, an entry has been made for purposes of the burglary statute." We note that the *Nible* court found this analysis "especially apposite to the [facts in that] case, where the window screen was affixed in a slot in the frame with no handle or other device to facilitate its removal from the exterior of the apartment." *Id.* Here, Stamper testified that removal of the screen required use of a screwdriver or knife and that it was "not ... a snap" to remove. In addition, in *Nible,* like here, the window behind the screen was partially open and the residence's occupants were inside.

[The court goes on to list a long litany of cases from other states where the court had to decide this same issue].

. . . To the extent that Defendant argues that our holding will produce absurd results because "[t]his interpretation would convict of [b]reaking and [e]ntering any person who opens a screen door to knock on the door itself [,]" we disagree because under the "reasonable belief test" it would be unreasonable to believe that an unlocked screen door was a barrier "a member of the general public could not pass without authorization." *Valencia,*

[W]e conclude that ...Defendant's placement of his hands behind the window screen was an intrusion into the structure's enclosure and infringed on Stamper's possessory rights. Such conduct is associated with the "feeling of violation and vulnerability" that the Legislature sought to prevent with the breaking and entering statute.

There is Sufficient Evidence to Support the Jury's Conclusion That Defendant "Entered" the Structure

We turn next to Defendant's second argument that there was insufficient evidence that Defendant intruded into the structure at all.

To convict Defendant, the jury had to find that (1) "the defendant entered [Stamper's residence] without permission; the least intrusion constitutes an entry;" and (2) "the entry was obtained by the dismantling of a window screen[.]" As we have discussed, because the window screen was part of the enclosure around the home, any intrusion into the space between the screen and window constitutes an "entry" for purposes of the breaking and entering statute. Stamper testified that "[she] saw this man, and he had the screen halfway off the window, and he had his hand on each side of the screen, and he was twisting it and turning it and looking down.... He was trying to get the screen off." She described Defendant's fingers as being "over the screen." On redirect, she agreed with the State that Defendant's fingers "were then in that area between the window and the screen[.]" Viewed in the light most favorable to the verdict, this testimony is sufficient to permit the jury to conclude that Defendant had intruded into the protected space between the screen and window.

Kennedy Dissent: The expansion of the nature of structures that could be burgled resulted in our Court's having "gone astray" from the intent of both the common law and statutory roots of burglary according to our Supreme Court. Burglary traditionally entailed a home invasion, and the crime has evolved to "protect occupants against the terror and violence that can occur as a result of such an entry." The privacy interest protected by burglary statutes is related to the terror of having an intruder inside of one's home, into which the entry is fully accomplished. This Opinion recognizes this privacy interest and that Stamper's reaction to Defendant's actions is squarely within these senses of invasion, terror, and concern for possible personal violence that the burglary statute is designed to address. It is there the degree of "entry" falls short. Certainly, Defendant *attempted* an entry. But, the California Supreme Court stated, more specifically, "[t]he laws are primarily designed, then, not to deter the trespass and the intended crime, which are prohibited by other laws, so much as to forestall the germination of a situation dangerous to personal safety."*Magness,* This case falls short of that standard. Breaking and entering differs from burglary because it protects a lesser interest than burglary. ... Attempt is the taking an act in furtherance of an intention to commit a crime. Defendant did not complete the act of entry and, given his likely intent and location of his crime, it is attempted burglary, not breaking and entering, that accounts for what the Majority says protects a heightened interest against "invasion of privacy" and security to justify their new boundary. If the Majority follows the conservative approach given us by *Muqqddin,* then Defendant here should be criminally responsible for attempted residential burglary or, perhaps, attempted breaking and entering, criminal trespass, and criminal damage. The distinction is notable, and the existing criminal statutes are fully adequate as written

Trespass

Common law trespass was recognized as a misdemeanor crime against habitation. It involved the uninvited, unprivileged, unauthorized intrusion onto an individual's property and dwelling. It comprised all the common law elements of burglary except "with the intent to commit a felony"-- the crime of trespass does not require the intruder to intend to commit a crime at the point of entry onto the property of another.

Today, much like the modern law of burglary, the elements of trespass have been relaxed. Trespass now includes defiant trespass. "A defiant trespass occurs when an individual knowingly enters or remains on a premise after receiving a clear notice that he or she is trespassing," Lippman, *supra,* at 397. Modern statutes typically divide trespass into various degrees. First degree criminal trespass typically entails entering or remaining in the dwelling of another and is punished as a minor felony. Second degree criminal trespass involves entering or remaining in enclosed buildings or fenced-in property and is typically punished as a misdemeanor. Third degree criminal trespass is usually categorized as a petty misdemeanor and entails entering in or remaining on unenclosed land and is punished with a fine. Some states punish all criminal trespass as a misdemeanor. Id.

Under the Model Penal Code, "A person commits an offense if, knowing that he is not licensed or privileged to do so, he enters or surreptitiously remains in any building or occupied structure, or separately secured or occupied portion thereof." MPC § 221.2(1). The offender knows he is not licensed or privileged to enter when the owner gives him actual notice, posts a notice, or fences the property or constructs an "enclosure manifestly designed to exclude intruders." See MPC §221.2(2). The Code punishes trespass as a misdemeanor if it is committed in a dwelling at night, otherwise it is treated as a petty misdemeanor. The Code also makes clear that a person commits criminal trespass when he defies an order to leave personally communicated to him by the owner of the premises or other authorized person. MPC §221.2(3) provides an affirmative defense when the building or occupied structure was abandoned, when the premise was open to members of the public and the offender had complied with all the lawful conditions imposed on that open access, or when the "actor reasonably believed that the owner of the premises or other persons empowered to license access thereto, would have licensed him to enter or remain."

Arson

Common Law Arson

Arson was a common law felony designed to protect the security of a residence. Common law arson consisted of the willful and malicious (the mens rea requirement) burning (the actus reus requirement) of a dwelling of another. The common law elements that arson shares with burglary were defined in the same manner as they were with burglary, so refer to that discussion above. The elements which are particular to arson include the willful and malicious burning. This meant that the person had to set the dwelling on fire. Merely setting a fire would not be enough; the fire had to reach the structure and burn it. The did not mean, however that the burned dwelling had to be destroyed or damaged—mere charring was sufficient. But, it did need to be more than scorching or smoke damage. Burning was commonly defined as the consuming of the material of the house or the burning of any part of the house. Even a spot on the floor was sufficient. The common law did not consider an explosion to be arson unless it resulted in a fire.

Common law regarded arson as a general intent crime (willful and malicious) meaning that the offender had the intent to burn and not necessarily the intent to destroy or cause the harm. It also included knowledge that the structure would burn. "A negligent or involuntary burning does not satisfy the requirement for common law arson." Lippman, 4th ed., at 400. Malice was presumed when an individual intentionally set fire to another's dwelling. LaFave. At common law, one could not commit arson by setting one's own home on fire.

Modern Arson Statutes

Modern statutes have extended the offense of arson to include the intentional burning of buildings, structures, and vehicles of all types. Thus, it is no longer strictly a crime against habitation. Arson statutes continue to be seen as "general intent" statutes. They do not require that the arsonist intent to burn down a structure; it suffices that the arsonist intend to start a fire (i.e., arson is not a crime of result). "In other words, the purpose requirement refers to the act in arson (burning or setting fire to buildings) and not to the harm (burning down or destroying buildings)." Samaha, 5th ed,, at 408. Most statutes do not exclude burning one's own property. Several states have enacted arson statutes that include using explosives to damage a structure. These statutes include explosions based on the idea that explosions threaten equally the lives property and security that arson was designed to protect. Most statutes grade arson by degrees based on the type of building that was burned. Commonly, arson is divided into three degrees in which first degree arson is the most serious and includes burning homes or other occupied structures where there is a possibility of danger to human life; second degree arson includes setting fire to, or burning, unoccupied structures and perhaps vehicles; and third degree arson includes setting fire to or burning personal property. Most states have statutes which make it a crime to burn property with the intent to defraud insurance companies.

Model Penal Code And Arson

The MPC revises the common law and provides that "starting a fire" even if the fire never touches the structure aimed at, satisfies the burning requirement. The drafters justify expanding the common law rule on the ground that no meaningful difference separates a fire that has already started but has not yet reached the basic structure and a fire that has reached the structure but has not yet done any real damage to it. Burning also includes explosions. The MPC divides arson into two degrees. First degree arson includes those individuals who intend to destroy buildings and not merely set fire to or burn them. Second-degree arson includes those who set buildings on fire for other purposes.

LYNCH v. STATE,
370 N.E.2d 401 (1977)

FACTS
[I]n the early morning hours of June 18, 1975, a man identified as Lynch was seen throwing a burning object at the residence of Mr. and Mrs. Estel Barnett (Barnett). Immediately after the object struck the house flames engulfed the side of the residence. The flames lasted for several minutes and then died out. The fire department was not called.

The Barnetts, who were awakened by a passing neighbor, investigated and discovered a bottle containing flammable liquid with a cotton or cloth wick protruding from the opening. A "burn trail" extended from the lawn approximately ten feet to the house. Damage to the building's aluminum siding consisted of blistering and discoloration of the paint. The amount of the damage was Ninety-one and

29/100 ($91.29) Dollars. No other part of the house was damaged.

Lynch was subsequently charged by information with the crime of First Degree Arson.

ISSUE
Is the phrase "sets fire to" synonymous with "burn", so that an actual consumption of a residence by fire is required before the "burning" element of the statute is satisfied?

Lynch . . . argues that the verdict is not sustained by sufficient evidence of a "burning" of the house as no part of the house was actually consumed by fire.

The gist of Lynch's position is that he is not guilty of arson because "sets fire to" and "burns" as used in the First Degree Arson statute are synonymous, and no "burning" took place, i.e., the house was not consumed. . . .

The phrase "sets fire to" in the First Degree Arson statute means something less than an actual burning and therefore is not synonymous with the word "burn".

The statute, Ind. Code § 35-16-1-1 [10-301], provides:
> Arson in the First Degree. Any person who willfully and maliciously sets fire to or burns, or causes the setting of fire to or the burning, or who aids, counsels or procures the setting of fire to or the burning of any dwelling house, rooming house, apartment house or hotel, finished or unfinished, occupied or unoccupied; or any kitchen, shop, barn, stable, garage or other outhouse, or other building that is part or parcel of any dwelling house, rooming house, apartment house or hotel, or belonging to or adjoining thereto, finished or unfinished, occupied or unoccupied, such being the property of another; . . . shall be guilty of arson in the first degree... .

Observe that the drafter used the disjunctive word "or" in separating the phrase "sets fire to" from the word "burns".

If we construe "or" in its "plain, or ordinary and usual, sense" as we are bound to do, Ind. Code § 1-1-4-1. . . separates two different things. "Sets fire to" and "burns" are not synonymous in this context. Thus the legislative intent is trumpeted in the first lines of the statute as heralding the assertion of different concepts strung out by a series of "ors" describing alternative (different) acts ("causes", "who aids", etc.).

Our search discloses no Indiana cases defining the two terms. Other jurisdictions have reached differing conclusions.

Traditionally the common law rigidly required an actual burning. The fire must be actually communicated to the object to such an extent as to have taken effect upon it.

Other jurisdictions have recognized the distinction between "sets fire to" and "burns" as two different concepts. To "set fire to" a structure is to "place fire upon", or "against" or to "put fire in connection with" it. It is possible to set fire to a structure which, by reason of the sudden extinction of the fire, will fail to change the characteristics of the structure. Nevertheless, it has been "set fire to".

In *Borza v. State*, supra, the distinction was emphasized. ...
> We are not satisfied that setting fire to and burning, have been established by any legal authority to be synonymes . . and that it was not necessary the stack should be burned, the words of the act being `set fire to'. This authority seems clearly to decide that setting fire to and burning are not legal synonymes. If they were, there would be no reason for that redundancy of language ...

Unlike Lynch, then, we cannot conclude that he is not guilty of first degree arson because there was no burning of the house. He set fire to the house by causing a flammable substance to burn thereon causing a scorching or blistering of the paint which was an integral part of the structure. The composition of the structure was changed. No more was necessary.

Thus the modern construction of statutory terms we are interpreting is that they are not synonymous, each having a separate, independent meaning, thereby eliminating any ambiguity.

The judgment is affirmed.

Other Cases – Arson

In re Jesse L., 270 Cal. Rptr. 389 (Cal. Ct. App. 1990.
Defendant set a fire at his high school early in the morning of 1980. Firefighters arrived and put out the fire. A fire investigator testified that someone entered the administration building by breaking a window next to a door, reaching around, and pressing the panic bar on the locked door allowing it to open. Jesse L's fingerprints were found in three different places on the window. Investigator Salveson determined that three fires had been ignited, two on the tops of desks and one on the

floor, by heaping files and papers, dousing them with a flammable liquid and igniting them. The cost of the damage to the equipment and supplies and to the structure itself was approximately $250.000. Ultimately the defendant admitted being involved in setting the fire, and several students testified against him.

The relevant statute stated that "A person is guilty of arson when he or she willfully and maliciously sets fire to or burns or causes to be burned or who aids, counsels, or procures the burning of any structure, forest land or property.

Jesse L claimed there was insufficient evidence presented to establish that a structure was burned. The court cited the earlier case of *People v. Haggerty* (1873) in which the California Supreme Court stated, "Upon the question of what is a sufficient burning to constitute the crime, Mr. Bishop states the rule thus:
The word "burn" . . . means to consume by fire. If the wood is blackened, but no fibers are wasted, there is no burning; et the wood need not be in a blaze. And the burning of any part, however small, completes the offense, the same as of the whole. Thus, if the floor of the house is charred in a single place, so as to destroy any of the fibers of the wood, this is a sufficient burning in a case of arson."

The Court noted that in *Haggerty*, the court found that the defendant was guilty of arson even though there was conflicting testimony whether the fibers were blackened and not charred. "But we cannot say that the verdict was so contrary to the evidence as to justify us in reversing the judgement. . ."

The court also sited *People v. Simpson* (1875) in which the court held that evidence of a wooden partition inside the building and annexed to it, charred by fire and burned through in one place was sufficient evidence of burning to constitute arson."
The court here held that
"Salveson's uncontradicted testimony of burn patterns on the floor of the building and the bottom edge of the counter and on the face of the doors was sufficient to establish that an area on the floor and a door were charred so as to destroy the fibers of the wood by the fire set by the appellant. Mr. Salveson's testimony clearly distinguished between smoke damage and these so-called "burn patterns." To illustrate, he used the term "burn pattern" to describe the burning of both the desks and the counter which he specifically testified were charred as opposed to smoke stains around the entrance door. Moreover, Salveson also testified the "plastic covers for the lights had melted and some of them had fallen on the ground, others were hanging from the metal framework that they were originally positioned in." Thus, a further question is presented whether the destruction by fire of a light fixture is sufficient evidence of structural fire damage to support a conviction. . . . [A] fixture is a thing, originally personal property, but later affixed or annexed to realty, so that it is considered real property.. ". "Our Civil code. . . supports the conclusion that a fixture . . . becomes part of the structure to the extent that a burning or charring or destruction by fire is all that is required to constitute a burning sufficient to support a conviction of arson . . . Thus we conclude that the evidence of "burn patterns" which indicates at least minor charring of the structure together with the damage to the light fixture is ample evidence of the . . . [arson statute.]

BUCKLEY v. STATE, 875 So.2d 1110 (2004)

SOUTHWICK, P.J., for the Court.

A circuit court jury found Arbie Jo Buckley guilty of capital murder. We find her argument that the indictment was fatally flawed to be valid.

There was evidence from George House that his wife, the defendant Arbie Jo Buckley, poured kerosene onto him as he lay on a sofa. The kerosene soaked into his clothes and also onto the sofa and floor of the trailer home in which he lay. She then threw a match onto him. He awoke to find himself on fire. His injuries were mortal ones, but before he died he gave an explanation of what happened.

George House died and the trailer in which he was located was destroyed.

Buckley's testimony was that House had been angry and intoxicated, which caused her and their children to leave the trailer home. She then went to the sheriff's department for help. Upon returning to the trailer, she found it on fire. She said that she awoke her husband. Seeing the fire, House grabbed a nearby jug of kerosene, perhaps thinking it was water. Buckley took the jug from him, but the kerosene spilled onto House. She tried but was unable to put out the fire.

Buckley was indicted, tried and convicted for capital murder with the underlying felony of arson. She received a life sentence after a jury trial and appeals.

Buckley asserts . . . that the facts set forth in the indictment do not fall within the scope of arson. The indictment charged Buckley in this way: That, Arbie Jo Buckley, ... did wilfully, unlawfully and feloniously kill George House without authority of law. Arbie Jo Buckley was engaged in the commission of arson. Arbie Jo Buckley put a flammable liquid on George House and set him afire with or without any design to effect the death of George House, in direct violation of Section 97-3-19(2)(e).

The statute that is cited in the indictment is the one for capital murder. It requires that a person have been killed while the perpetrator was in the act of committing one of several felonies other than a homicide. It is not necessary that the accused have intended that the victim be killed; it is necessary that there exist an intent to commit the felony during which the death occurred:

The killing of a human being without the authority of law by any means or in any manner shall be capital murder in the following cases:...(e) When done with or without any design to effect death, by any person engaged in the commission of the crime of rape, burglary, kidnapping, arson, robbery, sexual battery, unnatural intercourse with any child under the age of twelve (12), or nonconsensual unnatural intercourse with mankind, or in any

attempt to commit such felonies.

According to the indictment, the arson that Buckley was committing and during the course of which George House was killed, was the setting of the victim himself on fire. The issue that this raises is whether intentionally putting a flammable liquid on a person and then causing it to ignite on the person constitutes the crime of arson. Is that instead initially the crime of aggravated assault using fire as the deadly weapon, and then a murder either by deliberate design or with a depraved heart if the person dies?

To answer this, we examine the statutory elements of arson. There are several arson crimes. The indictment did not list which one allegedly was being committed by Buckley when she set her husband on fire. Some clearly are inapplicable, such as the setting of woods or other lands on fire. ... We find the following to be the only ones worth analyzing on the charges against Buckley.

Arson in the first degree has these elements:

(1) Any person who willfully and maliciously sets fire to or burns or causes to be burned or who aids, counsels or procures the burning of any dwelling house, whether occupied, unoccupied or vacant, or any kitchen, shop, barn, stable or other outhouse that is parcel thereof, or belonging to or adjoining thereto, or any state-supported school building in this state whether the property of himself or of another, shall be guilty of arson in the first degree, and upon conviction thereof, be sentenced to the penitentiary for not less than five (5) nor more than twenty (20) years and shall pay restitution for any damage caused.

Arson in the third degree is defined in this manner:
Any person who wilfully and maliciously sets fire to or burns or causes to be burned, or who aids, counsels or procures the burning of any personal property of whatsoever class or character; (such property being of the value of twenty-five dollars and the property of another person), shall be guilty of arson

in the third degree and upon conviction thereof, be sentenced to the penitentiary for not less than one nor more than three years.

Obviously, neither statute supports the charging of arson for someone who deliberately and directly sets a person on fire. A person is not a building nor personal property. The different forms of the crime of arson are all in a section of the Code for "Crimes Against Property. Arson has been called both a crime against property and one against persons, as the primary protection being provided by criminalizing the burning of structures was to protect those occupying the building. Still, regardless of the interests being protected, the crime traditionally required the burning of a structure, starting with dwellings at common law and then expanding to other kinds of buildings. Here a structure did burn, namely the house trailer, but the indictment did not charge Buckley with killing her husband while burning down the trailer.

The legislature has the authority to redefine crimes from those in the common law. We must find that there is a statute which by reasonable interpretation permits the crime of arson to be charged based on the facts of setting a person on fire. We have found none. The two we quoted are the closest, but they are not anywhere near close enough.

The capital murder that this indictment charged was the form that requires that the death occur while a different, underlying felony was being committed. Miss.Code Ann. § 97-3-19(2)(e). Felony murder as a capital crime requires by definition two felonies to be involved, the homicide being the intentional or unintentional product of the other felony. The elements set out in the indictment against Buckley only charged one felony—that Buckley killed House by setting *him* on fire. That act is not a capital offense. It is a gruesome and terrible act . . . . Under current law, the indictment needed to set out a valid charge of two felonies, one the arson and the other a homicide that occurred during the commission of the arson.

The crime charged here was murder, the instrument used directly against the victim to cause death being fire. In order for Buckley to be charged with capital murder, she must be charged with arson by setting the house trailer or sofa on fire and that she killed her husband as a result. Though that would have been consistent with the statutes on capital murder, it may not have been supported by the evidence on this record. The State's evidence was that House declared as he was dying from his wounds that Buckley had poured the kerosene on him and set him on fire, which then set the trailer ablaze. The indictment as written in this case did not charge capital murder.

Malicious Mischief

At common law, the crime of malicious mischief was a misdemeanor committed when a person destroyed or damaged personal property of another. Modern statutes define the offense similarly to the way done y the common law, but now it is referred to as criminal mischief or vandalism. Modern criminal mischief statutes include damage to both personal, real, and tangible property (physical property). Criminal mischief is often graded based on the value of the property destroyed. Most statutes consider that criminal mischief is at the most a minor felony. Under the Model Penal Code criminal mischief includes destruction or damage to tangible property including damage by fire, explosion, flood, or other harmful force; tampering with property so as to endanger a person or property (for example, removing a stop sign or one-way road sign); and deception or threat that causes financial loss. The MPC requires that the acts be committed purposely or recklessly, except for damage by catastrophic means, which may be committed negligently.

Other Cases – Malicious Mischief

People v. Nicholas Y., 102 Cal Rptr. 2d 511 (Cal Ct. App 2000).
Nicholas Y appealed a finding that he vandalized the property of a theater (and holding him accordingly to be a ward of the court). What

Nicholas did was to write on the glass window of a projection booth at the theater with a Sharpie Marker. He admitted that he had written "RTK" on the window. Police testified to seeing 30 incidents of red magic marker throughout the theater including the one on the glass. Nicholas said the initials stood for "The Right To Crime."

Defense counsel argued to the court, "It's a piece of glass with a marker on it. You take a rag and wipe it off. End of case. It's ridiculous." The prosecution argued that Nicholas had trespassed and left fresh marks on the window, thus defacing the window with graffiti. The trial court held that he violated the vandalism statute, a misdemeanor. The appellate court had to decide whether writing with a marker on a glass surface constitutes defacing property.

The Court held,

"Graffiti may be, and regularly is, created with marker pens. It would be irrational to hold that use of a marker pen on, for example, a painted or stucco surface constitutes vandalism . . .while the use of a marker pen on glass is not. Each mars the surface with graffiti which must be removed in order to restore the original condition. This pragmatic fact is consistent with the primary meaning of the word deface . . . "to mar the face, features, or appearance of; to spoil or ruin the figure, form, or beauty of; to disfigure." This definition does not incorporate an element of permanence. Thus, it appears that a marring on the surface is no less a defacement because it is more easily moved.

Osmar v. City of Orlando, No. 6:12-cv-185 Orl-DAB (M.D. Fla. 2012).
Court held that defendant's (a participant in the Occupy Wall Street movement) political message written in chock on a public sidewalk or street near the Orlando City Hall did not violate the Orlando ordinance making it criminal to "write, print, make, paint, stamp, or paste any sign, notice, or advertisement upon the surface of any sidewalk or paved street in the city." The Federal Magistrate wrote,

"Osmar's chalk message did not violate the Orlando ordinance. A chalk message "as opposed to painting or posting a sign . . . is not permanent or long-lasting and can be washed away with water or . . . by wind or rain.. . . The City may not selectively interpret and enforce the Ordinance based on its own desire to further the causes of particular favored speeches."

WRAP UP

When others target our homes, they impact our sense of security and personal safety to a greater extent than when they just take our money or steal things from us when we are out and about. Perhaps we expect to be more vulnerable when we interact in public, but we have a stronger sense of security in the protection of our own homes. The common law recognized two felony crimes against habitation-- burglary and arson—and two misdemeanor crimes against habitation—trespass and malicious mischief. Modern statutes and the MPC retain these crimes but have distinctly broadened their scopes.

Chapter Nine: Property Crimes

Overview

All societies recognize that wrongfully taking property from others is unlawful. Larceny was the common law felony against stealing another's property. It is the crime from which all other theft offenses developed.

Many technical and often subtle distinctions developed in the common-law crime of larceny. Perhaps one reason for this was the reluctance of courts to find a thief guilty of larceny because the penalty at early common law was death. As commerce became more significant in England, the crime of larceny was not adequate either to deal with those who obtained financial advantages through false pretenses or to deter or punish servants who fraudulently appropriated property that rightfully came into their possession. Consequently, by the late 1700s, the English Parliament created two supplemental misdemeanor offenses: false pretenses and embezzlement. The offense of false pretenses came into being in 1757, before the American Revolution. The offense thereby became a part of the common law of those states that had it with the statutory modifications made by Parliament before the American Revolution. Embezzlement, on the other hand, did not become a statutory crime until the enactment by Parliament in 1799. . . . [I]n 1827 Parliament enacted a statute making receiving stolen property a misdemeanor. Thus embezzlement and receiving stolen property became English laws too late to become part of the common law adopted by the new American states. By subsequent enactments, the English Parliament broadened the scope of embezzlement. ...

All states have enacted statutes expanding the common-law concept of larceny to include all types of tangible and intangible property. Historically, the states maintained numerous statutes basically adopting the concepts of common law larceny and false pretenses and the later English statutes proscribing embezzlement and receiving stolen property. As new problems developed, legislative bodies attempted to fill the gaps by creating new offenses. This resulted in the legislative creation of numerous statutory offenses proscribing various forms of stealing and dishonest dealings. Often these statutes were confusing and in many instances contradictory.

In recent years many states have replaced their statutes with a consolidated theft statute that proscribes stealing in very broad terms. These new statutes make it unlawful for a person to commit any of the common law theft offenses mentioned as well as other crimes, and penalties are based on the amount and character of the property stolen. Scheb and Scheb, at 187.

Larceny

At common law larceny was defined as the trespassory taking and carrying away of the personal property of another with the intent to permanently deprive the other of his or her property. Because common law larceny was a capital offense, each of these elements was applied strictly. The actus reus requirement of larceny at common law was the trespassory taking and carrying away of possession. Trespassory taking means a wrongful taking (taking without permission.) The taking requirement requires asserting dominion and control over the property, however briefly. Consent obtained by force, fraud or threat qualified as a trespassory taking, in the same manner that stealing by stealth did. Carrying away the property involves moving it—even a very slight distance. This is the asportation requirement (recall we saw this with kidnapping).

Possession meant physical control over property and the ability to freely use and enjoy the property. Possession is different than custody which is the temporary and limited right to control property. The difference between possession and custody played an important role in the holdings of common law cases as the law of larceny developed over time in England. In later cases, the law of larceny extended to employees who were said to have custody over the tools needed to do their jobs, but that rightful, constructive, possession still belonged to the employer. Possession is also different than ownership, and this distinction becomes important in sorting out larceny from the crime of false pretenses.

At common law only tangible personal property could be the subject of larceny. Tangible property means property over which a person can exercise physical control; lands, crops, real estate, minerals are not tangible property. At common law, one could not steal intangible personal property such as stocks, bonds, checks, or promissory notes, deeds representing real estate, contracts. The property taken must have been "of another." Larceny involved taking possession of property from another person who had a superior right to possess the object. If the defendant was the co-owner of the property it was not larceny.

Common law larceny was a specific-intent crime. The mens rea requirement of larceny is the intent to permanently deprive another of the property. At the time of the taking, the offender had to intend to unlawfully and permanently deprive the other of the property for the crime to be larceny—or to possess it for an unreasonable length of time, or to intend to use it in such a way that the owner would probably be deprived of his property. If the person took the property honestly, but mistakenly believing that the property was his own property, no one's property, or that he had permission to take the property, then he lacked the intent to steal required for larceny. This was true even though his mistaken, but honest, belief was unreasonable. If a person intended to borrow and return property and then changed his mind, and decided to keep it, it was not larceny. A person can commit larceny of lost or misplaced property, if at the time they seize the property, he or she decides to steal it and not return it when the person knows who the owner is or can easily ascertain who the owner is through reasonable efforts. (Property is lost when its owner is involuntary deprived of the object and has no idea where to find it; property is misplaced when the owner forgets where he or she intentionally placed an object; property is abandoned when the owner no longer claims ownership of it.) A person cannot commit larceny of abandoned property because the property is no longer considered the property of another.

Larceny By Trick At Common Law

Wrongfully taking another's property by using a trick or a lie to get him or her to turn over possession of the property is a type of larceny. Larceny by trick is similar to the common law crime of false pretenses—the difference being that larceny by trick involves getting possession of property whereas false pretenses involves getting title. "The distinction between obtaining possession and obtaining title—the principal dividing line is not always easy to draw." LaFave, 2000, at 799. The lies used for larceny by trick may be written or oral, they must be generally misrepresentations of some present or past fact. The offender must have the fraudulent intent to take the property, make it his own, and keep it permanently at the time that he made the misrepresentation for the crime to be larceny by trick.

Modern Larceny

Some modern statutes follow the Model Penal code and abandon the asportation/carrying away requirement and provide that a person is guilty of theft if he or she unlawfully takes or exercises unlawful control over property. Modern larceny statutes also relax the nature of the property taken, and larceny under modern statutes often includes both theft of tangible and intangible personal property. In addition, a number of states have larceny statutes which include theft of minerals, tress, crops, and fixtures to real estate. The trend is to include any sort of property of value which can be moved. LaFave notes that gas and electricity are now commonly considered property which can be stolen. Contraband can now be stolen. Theft of the labor of another is not considered larceny, but most modern statutes make it theft to steal labor or services or use of property.

Most modern larceny statutes distinguish between grand larceny and petit larceny depending on the value of the property. The trend has been for states to enact comprehensive theft statutes which encompass all varieties of stealing (see, consolidated theft statutes below).

People v. Olivo, (Gasparik, Spatzier)
52 N.Y.2d 309 (1981)

Chief Judge COOKE.

These cases present a recurring question in this era of the self-service store which has never been resolved by this court: may a person be convicted of larceny for shoplifting if the person is caught with goods while still inside the store? For reasons outlined below, it is concluded that a larceny conviction may be sustained, in certain situations, even though the shoplifter was apprehended before leaving the store.

I.

In People v Olivo, defendant was observed by a security guard in the hardware area of a department store. Initially conversing with another person, defendant began to look around furtively when his acquaintance departed. The security agent continued to observe and saw defendant assume a crouching position, take a set of wrenches and secret it in his clothes. After again looking around, defendant began walking toward an exit, passing a number of cash registers en route. When defendant did not stop to pay for the merchandise, the officer accosted him a few feet from the exit. In response to the guard's inquiry, defendant denied having the wrenches, but as he proceeded to the security office, defendant removed the wrenches and placed them under his jacket. At trial, defendant testified that he had placed the tools under his arm and was on line at a a cashier when apprehended. The jury returned a verdict of guilty on the charge of petit larceny. The conviction was affirmed by Appellate Term.

II.

In People v Gasparik, defendant was in a department store trying on a leather jacket. Two store detectives observed him tear off the price tag and remove a "sensormatic" device designed to set off an alarm if the jacket were carried through a detection machine. There was at least one such machine at the exit of each floor. Defendant placed the tag and the device in the pocket of another jacket on the merchandise rack. He took his own jacket, which he had been carrying with him, and placed it on a table. Leaving his own jacket, defendant put on the leather jacket and walked through the store, still on the same floor, by passing several cash registers. When he headed for the exit from that floor, in the direction of the main floor, he was apprehended by security personnel. At trial, defendant denied removing the price tag and the sensormatic device from the jacket, and testified that he was looking for a cashier without a long line when he was stopped. The court, sitting without a jury, convicted defendant of petit larceny. Appellate Term affirmed.

III.

In People v Spatzier, defendant entered a bookstore on Fulton Street in Hempstead carrying an attache case. The two co-owners of the store observed the defendant in a ceiling mirror as he browsed through the store. They watched defendant remove a book from the shelf, look up and down the aisle, and place the book in his case. He then placed the case at his feet and continued to browse. One of the owners approached defendant and accused him of stealing the book. An altercation ensued and when defendant allegedly struck the owner with the attache case, the case opened and the book fell out. At trial, defendant denied secreting the book in his case and claimed that the owner had suddenly and unjustifiably accused him of stealing. The jury found defendant guilty of petit larceny, and the conviction was affirmed by the Appellate Term.

IV.

The primary issue in each case is whether the evidence, viewed in the light most favorable to the prosecution, was sufficient to establish the elements of larceny as defined by the Penal Law. To resolve this common question, the development of the common-law crime of larceny and its evolution into modern statutory form must be briefly traced.

Larceny at common law was defined as a trespassory taking and carrying away of the property of another with intent to steal it. The early common-law courts apparently viewed larceny as defending society against breach of the peace, rather than protecting individual property rights, and therefore placed heavy emphasis upon the requirement of a *trespassory taking*. Thus, a person such as a bailee who had rightfully obtained possession of property from its owner could not be guilty of larceny. The result was that the crime of larceny was quite narrow in scope.

Gradually, the courts began to expand the reach of the offense, initially by subtle alterations in the common-law concept of possession (e.g., American Law Institute, Model Penal Code [Tent Draft No. 1], art 206, app A, p 101). Thus, for instance, it became a general rule that goods entrusted to an employee were not deemed to be in his possession, but were only considered to be in his custody, so long as he remained on the employer's. And, in the case of *Chisser*, it was held that a shop owner retained legal possession of merchandise being examined by a prospective customer until the actual sale was made. In these situations, the employee and the customer would not have been guilty of larceny if they had first obtained lawful possession of the property from the owner. By holding that they had not acquired possession, but merely custody, the court was able to sustain a larceny conviction.

As the reach of larceny expanded, the intent element of the crime became of increasing importance, while the requirement of a trespassory taking became less significant. As a result, the bar against convicting a person who had initially obtained lawful possession of property faded. In *King v Pear* (1 Leach 212, 168 Eng Rep 208), for instance, a defendant who had lied about his address and ultimate destination when renting a horse was found guilty of larceny for later converting the horse. Because of the fraudulent misrepresentation, the court reasoned, the defendant had never obtained legal possession. Thus, "larceny by trick" was born.

Later cases went even further, often ignoring the fact that a defendant had initially obtained possession lawfully, and instead focused upon his later intent. The crime of larceny then encompassed, not only situations where the defendant initially obtained property by a trespassory taking, but many situations where an individual, possessing the requisite intent, exercised control over property inconsistent with the continued rights of the owner. During this evolutionary process, the purpose served by the crime of larceny obviously shifted from protecting society's peace to general protection of property rights.

Modern penal statutes generally have incorporated these developments under a unified definition of larceny (see, e.g., American Law Institute, Model Penal Code [Tent Draft No. 1], § 206.1 [theft is appropriation of property of another, which includes unauthorized exercise of control]). Case law, too, now tends to focus upon the actor's intent and the exercise of dominion and control over the property. Indeed, this court has recognized, in construing the New York Penal Law, that the "*ancient* common-law concepts of larceny" no longer strictly apply.

This evolution is particularly relevant to thefts occurring in modern self-service stores. In stores of that type, customers are impliedly invited to examine, try on, and carry about the merchandise on display. Thus in a sense, the owner has consented to the customer's possession of the goods for a limited purpose. That the owner has consented to that possession does not, however, preclude a conviction for larceny. If the customer exercises dominion and control wholly inconsistent with the continued rights of the owner, and the other elements of the crime are present, a larceny has occurred. Such conduct on the part of a customer satisfies the "taking" element of the crime.

It is this element that forms the core of the controversy in these cases. The defendants argue, in essence, that the crime is not established, as a matter of law, unless there is evidence that the customer departed the shop without paying for the merchandise.

Although this court has not addressed the issue, case law from other jurisdictions seems unanimous in holding that a shoplifter need not leave the store to be guilty of larceny. This is because a shopper may treat merchandise in a manner inconsistent with the owner's continued rights — and in a manner not in accord with that of a prospective purchaser — without actually walking out of the store. Indeed, depending upon the circumstances of each case, a variety of conduct may be sufficient to allow the trier of fact to find a taking. It would be well-nigh impossible, and unwise, to attempt to delineate all the situations which would establish a taking. But it is possible to identify some of the factors used in determining whether the evidence is sufficient to be submitted to the fact finder.

In many cases, it will be particularly relevant that defendant concealed the goods under clothing or in a container. Such conduct is not generally expected in a self-service store and may in a proper case be deemed an exercise of dominion and control inconsistent with the store's continued rights. Other furtive or unusual behavior on the part of the defendant should also be weighed. Thus, if the defendant surveys the area while secreting the merchandise or abandons his or her own property in exchange for the concealed goods, this may evince larcenous rather than innocent behavior. Relevant too is the customer's proximity to or movement towards one of the store's exits. Certainly it is highly probative of guilt that the customer was in possession of secreted goods just a few short steps from the door or moving in that direction. Finally, possession of a known shoplifting device actually used to conceal merchandise, such as a specially designed outer garment or a false bottomed carrying case, would be all but decisive.

Of course, in a particular case, any one or any combination of these factors may take on special significance. And there may be other considerations, not now identified, which should be examined. So long as it bears upon the principal issue — whether the shopper exercised control wholly inconsistent with the owner's continued rights — any attending circumstance is relevant and may be taken into account.

V.

Under these principles, there was ample evidence in each case to raise a factual question as to the defendants' guilt. In People v Olivo, defendant not only concealed goods in his clothing, but he did so in a particularly suspicious manner. And, when defendant was stopped, he was moving towards the door, just three feet short of exiting the store. It cannot be said as a matter of law that these circumstances fail to establish a taking.

In People v Gasparik, defendant removed the price tag and sensor device from a jacket, abandoned his own garment, put the jacket on and ultimately headed for the main floor of the store. Removal of the price tag and sensor device, and careful concealment of those items, is highly unusual and suspicious conduct for a shopper. Coupled with defendant's abandonment of his own coat and his attempt to leave the floor, those factors were sufficient to make out a prima facie case of a taking.

In People v Spatzier, defendant concealed a book in an attache case. Unaware that he was being observed in an overhead mirror, defendant looked furtively up and down the aisle before secreting the book. In these circumstances, given the manner in which defendant concealed the book and his suspicious behavior, the evidence was not insufficient as a matter of law.

VII.

In sum, in view of the modern definition of the crime of larceny, and its purpose of protecting individual property rights, a taking of property in the self-service store context can be established by evidence that a customer exercised control over merchandise wholly inconsistent with the store's continued rights. Quite simply, a customer who crosses the line between the limited right he or she has to deal with merchandise and the store owner's rights may be subject to prosecution for larceny. Such a rule should foster the legitimate interests and continued operation of self-service shops, a convenience which most members of the society enjoy.

In each case: Order affirmed.

Obtaining Property by False Pretenses (False Pretenses)

As mentioned above, the crime of false pretenses was created by English Parliament as a way to plug loopholes left by larceny as English society developed. At common law, a person committed the crime of false pretenses when he or she made a false representation of a past or present material (important or significant) fact which caused the person to whom it is made to pass title to the property to the person making the misrepresentation when that person knew that his representation is false had the intent to defraud.

The crime of false pretenses occurs where the defendant uses fraud or deceit to obtain not only possession but also ownership. The crime of false pretenses differs from larceny with respect to what is obtained. In larceny, the defendant obtains possession only, not title. With false pretenses, the person obtains title.

The actus reus of the crime of false pretenses is making a false representation of a present or past fact. This can include failure to disclose or concealing information, or reinforcing false impressions. Silence was not normally considered enough, nor was making a false promise. The representation had to be material—meaning one that would play an important role in a reasonable person's decision to enter the transaction. The victim must have relied upon the representation, meaning the representation was what caused them to turn over title to the property. Whether title passed turns on what the victim intended to do. If the victim sold the property based on the representation, then title transferred and the crime of false pretenses would exist. If, however the victim intended only to lease or lend the property, then only possession would be transferred, so the crime would be larceny by trick rather than false pretense.

As with larceny and embezzlement, the crime of false pretenses involved theft of the property of another, and most courts held that no crime occurred when the defendant co-owned the property with the victim. Modern courts are increasingly likely to hold that a co-owner can commit false pretenses against another co-owner.

The mens rea for false pretenses is intentionally deceiving another. This intent requirement is met if the defendant knows that the representation is untrue, that the defendant believes but does not know for a certainty that the representation is untrue, or that the defendant knows that he does not know whether the representation is false. An example of false pretense would be the defendant telling the victim that a painting he is offering to sell is a Van Gogh when, in fact, the defendant knows it is not a Van Gogh, or believes it is not a Van Gogh. If defendant honestly (and even unreasonably) believes the representation is true (that the painting is a Van Gogh) then he is not liable for false pretenses.

It is not a defense to the crime of false pretenses that the misrepresentation is one that an ordinarily intelligent person would not be deceived by. It is also not a defense that the victim suffered no pecuniary loss or that the defendant had no real pecuniary gain. The crime is making the representation, so as long as defendant knowingly made the requisite material false representation which caused the victim to transfer property, the fact that the trade was an even trade is irrelevant.

Model Penal Code-False Pretenses

The MPC refers to false pretenses as "theft by deception."

MPC §223.3 Theft by Deception
A person is guilty of theft if he purposely obtains property of another by deception. A person deceives if he purposely:

(1) creates or reinforces a false impression, including false impressions as to law, value, intention or other state of mind; but deception as to a person's intention to perform a promise shall not be inferred from the fact alone that he did not subsequently perform the promise;

(2) prevents another from acquiring information which would affect his judgment of a transaction;

(3) fails to correct a false impression which the deceiver previously created or reinforced, or which the deceiver knows to be influencing another to whom he stands in a fiduciary or confidential relationship;

(4) fails to disclose a lien, adverse claim or other legal impediment to the enjoyment of property which he transfers or encumbers in consideration for the property obtained, whether such impediment is or is not valid, or is or is not a matter of official record.

The term "deceive" does not, however, include falsity as to matters having no pecuniary significance or puffing statements unlikely to deceive ordinary persons in the group addressed.

Under the MPC, the crime of false pretenses does not include a misrepresentation that has no significance in terms of the value of the property. One example that may highlight the difference between the MPC approach and the common law approach would be if John and Sally want to sell their home to Fred and they represent to Fred that the house, including the balcony, has passed inspection and is in perfect condition. In fact, the balcony was termite ridden and in bad shape. If Fred intends to tear down the balcony as soon as he purchases the house, at common law the crime of false pretenses may have been committed if in fact the representation about the house as a whole prompted Fred to buy the home. It would not be a defense that it was irrelevant what condition the balcony and that Fred suffered no pecuniary loss. Under the MPC false pretenses does not include a deception that would have no pecuniary significant—since Fred was going to tear down the balcony in any event, the misrepresentation won't cost Fred any more than if John and Sally had not lied about its condition.

Embezzlement

As enacted by English Parliament embezzlement was the fraudulent conversion of the property of another by one who was already in lawful possession of it. Embezzlement has no overlap with larceny. The crime will either be either larceny or embezzlement; it cannot be both. Either the property was taken unlawfully at the outset (and the crime would be larceny) or was held lawfully at the outset (and the crime would be embezzlement). The actus reus for embezzlement is converting property that the offender currently, lawfully possesses. (Recall the actus reus for larceny was trespassory taking and carrying away). Conversion means to treat the property as your own and thereby deprive the owner of a significant part of its usefulness. If the defendant merely uses the property for a short time, or moves it slightly, he is not guilty of embezzlement, regardless of whether he intended to convert it. For example, assume that defendant's boss lends D the company car to do an errand, and D decides to abscond with it or sell it. The police stop D after he has driven the car for one mile. D is not technically guilty of embezzlement because he has not deprived the company of a significant part of the car's usefulness, and thus has not converted it.

The main distinction between larceny and embezzlement is that embezzlement is committed by one who is already in lawful possession of the property before he appropriates it to his own use. Employees are the most common embezzlers. They misappropriate property which their employer has entrusted to them. "Through a series of enactments English Parliament brought servants, brokers, bankers, lawyers, and trustees within the scope of embezzlement. Thus, an embezzlement occurred when someone occupying a position of trust converted another's property to his or her own use." Scheb and Scheb, at 188.

PEOPLE v. CASAS
184 Cal.App.4th 1242, 109 Cal.Rptr.3d 811 (2010)

RAMIREZ, P. J.   Defendant, Jorge Jose Casas, a salesman at a car dealership, used a trade-in vehicle to follow a customer home to collect the downpayment, a process referred to as "chasing." However, he did not return to the dealership immediately with the downpayment or the trade-in vehicle, using the vehicle to drive nearly 400 miles in search of drugs to purchase using the cash portion of the downpayment. He was convicted of embezzlement following a jury trial.

BACKGROUND

On January 18, 2008, Clifford B. went to a Ford dealership to purchase a new F-150 truck. Defendant was the salesperson who assisted him in the transaction. Clifford B. was driving a 2004 F-150 truck, which he intended to use as a trade-in. In addition, the purchase agreement called for a downpayment of $1,500. At the time of the purchase, Clifford did not have the downpayment with him; in such situations, the practice is for the salesman to follow the buyer home to collect the downpayment and submit it to the finance officer upon return to the dealership. This is referred to as "chasing" the buyer.

On this occasion, after signing the purchase agreement, Clifford B. drove home in the newly purchased truck, followed by defendant who drove the trade-in vehicle. Normally, salespersons are supposed to drive their own vehicles to "chase" a customer. When they arrived at Clifford's residence, Clifford gave defendant a check in the amount of $1,000 and $500 in cash. However, defendant did not return immediately with the trade-in truck or the downpayment.

The next day, January 19, 2008, Clifford B. realized he had left something in the old truck that he had traded in, so he called the dealership to arrange to retrieve the item. An assistant sales manager took the call but the trade-in vehicle was missing, along with the keys to the vehicle. Defendant did not show up at the dealership that day, although he was scheduled to work. The sales manager then reported the vehicle as stolen. On January 21, 2008, defendant showed up at the dealership with the trade-in vehicle and the check from Clifford B., but without any cash. When the police arrived, defendant informed the officer he had driven the truck to numerous locations over the two-day period in search of drugs to

purchase. The odometer indicated defendant had driven the trade-in vehicle nearly 400 miles. According to defendant's wife, she drove the only vehicle owned by the couple.

Defendant was arrested and charged with embezzlement as well as driving or taking a vehicle without the owner's permission. It was further alleged that defendant had been previously convicted of a serious or violent felony, within the meaning of the "Three Strikes" law and one prior conviction for which he had served a prison sentence (prison prior). He was tried by a jury, which convicted him of the embezzlement charge, but deadlocked on the unlawful driving of the vehicle charge. A mistrial was declared as to the vehicle count.

DISCUSSION

In conducting our independent review of the record . . . we noted an incongruity and inconsistency in the law governing the elements of embezzlement. Our research revealed cases holding that embezzlement, a form of larceny, has the same theft elements. The offense is committed by every person who (1) takes possession (2) of personal property (3) owned or possessed by another (4) by means of trespass (5) with the intent to steal the property, and (6) carries the property away. The general rule, as stated by the *Davis* court, is that the intent to steal required for larceny is an intent to deprive the owner *permanently* of possession of the property.

However, there are decisions that have affirmed convictions for embezzlement after noting that an intent to temporarily deprive the owner of the property is sufficient. Some cases have affirmed embezzlement convictions reasoning that the gist of the offense is the appropriation to the defendant's own use of property delivered to him for a specified purpose other than his own enjoyment of it.

Recently, the First District Court of Appeals held that evidence of a defendant's intent to restore embezzled property was irrelevant because of fraudulent intent, that is, the intent to use the property for a purpose other than that for which the dealership intended. In that case, an employee took an envelope containing approximately $30,000, which had been caught in the hopper at the top of the safe of a car dealership, but returned the money two weeks later. The defendant contended that an intent to restore property is a defense to embezzlement if the restoration occurs before criminal charges are filed.

The reviewing court noted that the offense of embezzlement contemplates a principal's entrustment of property to an agent for certain purposes and the agent's breach of that trust by acting outside his authority in his use of the property. The court in *Sisuphan,* however, did not address the precise question of whether an intent to permanently deprive the owner is, or is not, an element of the crime, and did not discuss the decision in *Davis,* holding that such a mental state is an element of the crime.

It is difficult to reconcile the two lines of cases dealing with contradictory mental states. However, to the extent that the cases are consistent in holding that the gist of the offense of embezzlement is the appropriation to one's own use of property delivered to him for devotion to a specified purpose other than his own enjoyment of it, the necessary mental state may be found to exist whenever a person, for any length of time, uses property entrusted to him or her in a way that significantly interferes with the owner's enjoyment or use of the property.

Here, the owner's use and enjoyment of the trade-in vehicle and monetary deposit for the truck purchase was interfered with significantly by defendant's use of the vehicle to travel approximately 400 miles, over the course of two days, in search of drugs, which were purchased with the cash portion of the downpayment. Even if defendant had intended to eventually return both the trade-in vehicle and the money, his appropriation of both, for his own personal use, was significant in duration and incompatible with the owner's enjoyment or use of the property.

[T]the court's modification of CALCRIM No. 1806, instructing the jury that an intent to temporarily deprive was sufficient to prove the mens rea of the crime of embezzlement was not error.

The judgment is affirmed.

PEOPLE v. REDONDO,
19 Cal. App. 4th 1428 (Cal. Ct. App. 1993)

FACTS
In the early morning hours of July 14, 1991, Merced Police Sergeant Wallace L. Broughton was patrolling an area of commercial buildings when he saw a sheriff's department car backed up to the Small Engine Doctor repair shop. He saw defendant standing behind the vehicle and saw the handle of a lawnmower sticking out the driver's side of the trunk. It looked as if defendant was tying the trunk down. Sergeant Broughton recognized defendant, having known him for 10 years. Since a burglar alarm had gone off earlier in the area, Broughton thought defendant had caught a burglar. Broughton turned his car around to come back and talk to defendant.
Defendant was leaving the area when Broughton came back. Defendant took off speeding and Broughton pursued. He lost track of defendant and then saw headlights leaving an orchard. Broughton stopped defendant at 3:24 a.m. and asked him if he stole a lawnmower. Defendant denied all knowledge of the lawnmower and said he was on his way to a call at the hospital. The lawnmower was not in defendant's car when Broughton stopped him. He allowed defendant to leave.

Broughton called the chief of police. He and other officers found the lawnmower in an orchard later that morning. The lawnmower was one being repaired at the engine repair shop. The owner of the shop had left it outside the night before on the washpad.

The tread on the tires of defendant's car matched the tire tracks in the orchard where the lawnmower was found and the tire tracks at the engine repair shop. Dirt and paint chips were removed from the trunk of defendant's car. A comparison of dirt from the engine repair shop and the items removed from defendant's trunk were consistent with the mower having been in the trunk of defendant's car.

The vehicle driven by defendant was assigned to him by the Merced County Sheriff's Department. It was owned by the county and had a salvage value of $1,000.

DEFENSE
Defendant testified that he received a call at home directing him to go to Merced Community Medical Center (MCMC) to interview a rape victim who was en route to the hospital. He left his home about 2:54 a.m. He arrived at MCMC and took a walk through the emergency room. When he did not see the victim, he left. He drove to Planada to look for a suspect in another case he was investigating. After doing this he started to drive back to MCMC. He stopped on the side of the road to urinate. He returned to his car and drove away. Shortly thereafter he was stopped by Sergeant Broughton. He then went to MCMC and interviewed the rape victim. He talked to the victim several times. Defendant testified he was not at the engine repair shop on July 14 and did not steal a lawnmower.

Defendant had several witnesses testify regarding the lighting at the engine shop to show that it would have been very difficult for Sergeant Broughton to identify anyone on July 14. In addition, defendant had several witnesses testify to his reputation for honesty and truthfulness in the community.

The rape victim testified she checked into MCMC about 3 o'clock. She spoke to defendant once later in the morning. The patient registration clerk at MCMC clocked the victim in at 2:59 a.m. She saw defendant arrive around 3:45 p.m.

Jerry Brockman, an undersheriff at Merced County Sheriff's Department, testified. He stated that he did not believe defendant was honest. Prior to July 13, 1991, Brockman thought defendant was honest.

DISCUSSION
Defendant's conviction under section 504 was based on his fraudulent appropriation of his official vehicle to steal the lawnmower. Section 504 provides: "Every officer of this state, or of any county, city, city and county, or other municipal corporation or subdivision thereof, and every deputy, clerk, or servant of any such officer, and every officer, director, trustee, clerk, servant, or agent of any association, society, or corporation (public or private), who fraudulently appropriates to any use or purpose not in the due and lawful execution of his trust, any property which he has in his possession or under his control by virtue of his trust, or secretes it with a fraudulent intent to appropriate it to such use or purpose, is guilty of embezzlement."

(1) Defendant argues that his use of the vehicle was purely incidental to the target offense and such momentary use of property cannot constitute embezzlement of the property. Defendant contends that in order for the taking to be a violation of section 504, it must be made with the intent to permanently deprive the owner of the property for at least an extended period of time.

In order to prove a violation of section 504, it must be shown that the defendant "is (1) an officer of a city or other municipal corporation or subdivision thereof or a deputy, clerk, or servant of such an officer (2) who fraudulently appropriated property in his possession and control entrusted to him for a use or purpose not in a lawful execution of that trust. These elements `may be proved by circumstantial evidence and reasonable inferences drawn from such evidence.'

People v. *Harby* is most closely on point to the facts presented here. In *Harby*, a city councilperson used a city-owned automobile to travel more than 4,000 miles on a pleasure trip. He was charged with willful or corrupt misconduct in office in violation of section 504 and Los Angeles Municipal Code section 63.106. The appellate court found the defendant had embezzled property from the city. "To drive a city-owned automobile on a 4,000 mile pleasure jaunt was so clearly an appropriation of the vehicle to a private use that illustration and authority seem supererogatory. His only right to the Chrysler was to use it in performing the city's business." "Such a journey without authorization required a use of the car that was inconsistent with its owner's rights and inconsistent with the nature of the trust reposed in appellant and therefore it was an embezzlement." The appellate court commented that "a journey subjected the automobile to substantial detriment. It was therefore to the extent of its use an embezzlement of the property of the city."

Although defendant's journey here was substantially briefer than the defendant's journey in *Harby,* his use was without authorization and was clearly inconsistent with the owner's rights and inconsistent with the nature of the trust reposed in defendant. Defendant not only used the automobile to steal the lawnmower, but used it to evade Sergeant Broughton at high speeds. By doing so, he subjected the automobile to detriment.

In *People* v. *Dolbeer* (1963), the defendant enlisted the aid of a phone company employee to provide him with a daily list of new phone company subscribers. After defendant was given the list, he quickly copied and returned them to the employee. The appellate court found the lists were property because they were physical goods and had a value. The appellate court also found that, even though the lists were returned promptly, an embezzlement had occurred and the defendant appropriated the lists with the intent to defraud.

Here, defendant's use of the vehicle was for a very brief period of time, but defendant appropriated the property to a purpose not in the due and lawful execution of his trust. Section 504 defines a violation in broad terms as "*any* use or purpose not in the due and lawful execution of his trust." Defendant's utilization of the car, although brief, was an appropriation not in the public interest.

III. Felony or Misdemeanor Embezzlement:

The following stipulation was entered into by the parties: "Mr. Redondo was at the time of this offense, a Detective of the Merced sheriff's department, that he was a deputy of Sheriff Sawyer who's an officer of this county, that the vehicle that he was driving was the assigned his assigned vehicle, and it was the property of this county, and that the value of that vehicle was approximately a thousand dollars, which is based upon a salvage value from the county persons who keep track of that."

(2) Defendant asserts that the amount of the theft should be limited to the reasonable value of the temporary use of the vehicle between 3 and 6 a.m. Defendant argues that such use was less than $400, the amount necessary to prove grand theft, and therefore his conviction should be reduced to a misdemeanor. Defendant made the same argument at sentencing, and the court rejected it.

V

[The court rejected the idea that by using the car to steal the lawnmower the defendant had embezzled public funds]. . . .

...[I]n *People* v. *Harby,* in finding the defendant had embezzled government property by using the city-owned automobile for private purposes, the court held that there was an embezzlement of the property of the city "to the extent of its use." Where government property is used rather than taken in a more permanent sense, value of the use is the appropriate test for determining a monetary equivalent of what was embezzled. To hold otherwise would have some absurd results. For example, if an employee used a fax machine once for an unauthorized fax, should that employee be found to have embezzled the entire value of the machine? We think not. If so, an employee who used the fax machine hundreds of times or took the fax machine would be guilty of the same offense as the one-time user. This would ignore the differing culpabilities of the defendants recognized by the petty theft/grand theft dichotomy. Defendant did not by his acts expose the county to the loss of the automobile; the county's loss was the loss of the use of that automobile for a certain amount of time. The value of the loss of use suffered by the county must exceed $400 to make the offense a felony.

The only evidence presented at trial established the salvage value of the automobile at $1,000. No evidence was presented as to the value of the limited use of the automobile. It certainly had value, but we have no reason to believe the value is anything near $400. Because the evidence failed to establish either embezzlement of public funds in any amount or the embezzlement of public property to the extent of more than $400 in value, we reduce the embezzlement to a misdemeanor.

DISPOSITION
Defendant's embezzlement conviction is hereby

reduced to a misdemeanor, and the trial court shall resentence him accordingly. In all other respects, the judgment is affirmed.

Model Penal Code Approach To Larceny, Embezzlement, And False Pretenses

The MPC approach to larceny and embezzlement has been to create a crime called "Theft by Unlawful Taking or Disposition" See MPC §223.2 (1) ("A person is guilty of theft if he unlawfully takes or exercises unlawful control over movable property of another with the purpose to deprive him thereof"). The actus reus of the crime is either taking something unlawfully or exercising control over something unlawfully. The words "unlawfully takes" encompasses the crime of larceny and the words "exercises unlawful control" encompasses the crime of embezzlement. By combining larceny and embezzlement in one code, the confusing issue of whether the thief took custody or possession is avoided. The inclusion of immovable property shows that the MPC significantly broadens the scope of common law larceny and embezzlement. The MPC relaxes the asportation requirement of larceny and it is no longer necessary for the thief to "carry away" the property.

Receiving stolen property

Receiving stolen property was a misdemeanor crime passed by English Parliament in 1827. As such it became enacted too late to be part of the common law adopted by the states. However, states have enacted statutes against receiving the stolen property of another when the receiver knows that the property was stolen and done with the intent to permanently deprive the owner of the possession of such property criminal. Receiving stolen property is generally classified as a misdemeanor.

This crime targets "fences" who are middlemen who buy goods at a very low price from thieves and resell them to end-users. The actus reus of this crime is receiving stolen property, and the mens rea of the crime is "knowing that the property has been stolen and with the intent to deprive the owner of the property." It is enough if the defendant believes that the goods are stolen, but if he merely suspects the goods might be stolen, this is not sufficient to meet the knowledge requirement. Under the Model Penal Code a presumption exists that a dealer possesses the required knowledge or belief in some circumstances such as when he has been found in possession of property stolen from two or more persons on separate occasions.

Most statutes cover not only property taken by larceny, but also property that was taken by embezzlement or false pretenses. One particular "trickiness" with the crime of receiving stolen property is that the stolen property which has been recovered is no longer considered stolen property. Case law indicates that if property is stolen by thief who then cooperates with police or police, the fence who buys it is not guilty of receiving stolen property, even if he believes the property is stolen because the property is no longer, in fact, stolen, but rather, recovered. (The receiver could still, however, be charged with attempted receipt of stolen goods.)

Consolidated Theft Statutes

A number of states have consolidated larceny, embezzlement, and false pretenses into a single theft statute. The Model Penal Code and several state provisions also include within their theft statutes the property offense of receiving stolen property, blackmail or extortion, the taking of lost or mistakenly delivered property, theft of services, and the unauthorized use of a vehicle. . . .

The commentary to the Model Penal Code explains that each of these property offenses involves the "involuntary transfer of property, and in each instance, the perpetrator appropriates property of the victim without his consent or with a consent that is obtained by fraud or coercion. Lippman, 4th ed., at 424.

Robbery

At common law, robbery was a felony offense. Robbery is larceny committed with two additional elements: first, the property is taken from the person or presence of the owner and, second, the taking is accomplished by using force or putting the owner in fear of the use of force. Common law robbery was the taking of another's personal property of value, from another person's possession or presence, by force or by placing the person in fear, with the intent to permanently deprive the other person of that property.

Most robberies take place directly from the victim's person. But it is enough that the taking is from the victim's presence. The test for presence is whether victim, if he had not been intimidated or forcibly restrained, could have prevented the taking. For example, if defendant enters victim's house and bedroom, and while pointing a gun at the victim, takes the victim's purse and carried it away, this is considered to be in the victim's presence.

Robbery requires a taking by the use of violence or intimidation. For example, if the victim is walking down a street and is momentarily distracted by a near collision, and the defendant stealthily plucks the wallet out of the victim's half-open purse, it is not a robbery when the victim did not realize what happened until sometime later. This example highlights the difference between larceny and robbery, since this taking was without violence or intimidation. If instead, the defendant grabbed the victim's purse from her grasp, whether it is a robbery or larceny depends on whether the victim had a chance to resist. There still has been no violence or intimidation, but the threat of harm may suffice in lieu of the actual violence. If victim was placed in apprehension of harm, then the crime is robbery. So, if defendant points a gun at the victim and states, "Your money or your life," this is a robbery even though no actual force is used. With robbery, a subjective standard is used, and the reasonable person standard is not applied. Thus, if the victim was actually frightened so that he or she turns over the property, it is irrelevant that a reasonable person would not have been apprehensive of bodily harm.

The same transaction cannot result in both a conviction for larceny and a conviction for robbery. This is because robbery is a form of larceny with the additional element of force. If force is used, then the crime is robbery; if force is not used or threatened, then the crime is larceny. (Larceny is what is called a "lesser included offense" to robbery.)

Under modern statutes, robbery is generally graded based on whether weapons were used and the value of property taken. Aggravated robbery is defined as armed robbery in most states. With armed robbery, a deadly weapon is generally required, but it is not essential that the weapon actually be capable of causing death. For example, the gun need not be loaded, and even if the gun is a toy pistol, if it can be shown that the victim believed that the pistol was real, the defendant can be convicted of armed robbery.

PEOPLE v. ISLAS,
Cal. Rptr. Filed October 5, 2016.

BIGELOW, *P.J.*

FACTS
Michael Angeles and Alex Vargas worked as loss prevention officers for Superior Grocers in Long Beach. On March 25, 2015, both men were on duty when Islas and Priscilla McMichael entered the store. Officer Vargas watched Islas select a three-pack of beer from the refrigeration aisle and then walk several aisles over to where McMichael stood. Officer Angeles saw McMichael place several items in her purse, including shampoo and lotion

bottles. Officers Angeles and Vargas then watched Islas approach McMichael to hand her the beer, and McMichael placed the beer in her purse with the other items. Islas and McMichael exited the store without paying. Officers Angeles and Vargas followed them outside.

Officers Angeles and Vargas approached McMichael and Islas in the parking lot. The two men identified themselves as loss prevention officers, displayed their badges, and asked McMichael and Islas to come back inside the store. McMichael and Islas attempted to walk away, but Officer Vargas positioned himself in front of McMichael to prevent her from leaving. McMichael then became hysterical and screamed at Officer Vargas. Islas began walking down a nearby alleyway.

Officer Angeles testified McMichael began swinging her purse at Officer Vargas, yelling that he could have the merchandise back, and throwing the items from her purse in his direction. One of these items, a lotion bottle, hit Vargas in the chest and exploded on him. As Vargas grabbed McMichael's purse, Islas returned to the scene. He grabbed Officer Vargas's right forearm with his left hand, curled his right hand into a fist, and raised it above his right shoulder. Officer Angeles warned Islas that the situation would escalate to a robbery if he hit him or Officer Vargas. Islas then let go of Officer Vargas's arm, and both Islas and McMichael fled the scene.

Officer Vargas' testimony was similar, but varied slightly. Vargas testified he grabbed McMichael's purse as she attempted to leave the parking lot. Both individuals engaged in a "tug-of-war" over the purse. McMichael's purse had a cross-body strap, so the tug-of-war took place while she was wearing it. Islas then ran back, grabbed Vargas's hand, and raised his fist in the air at Vargas. Vargas told Islas that if he punched him or Angeles, the situation would be considered a robbery. Islas lowered his hands, Vargas released McMichael's purse, and McMichael began throwing the items at Vargas as she and Islas fled down an alleyway.

Officers Angeles and Vargas then called 911 and followed McMichael and Islas. McMichael tripped and fell in the alleyway, but Islas continued running and got on the Metro train. Officers Angeles and Vargas detained McMichael. Shortly thereafter, Long Beach Police Officer Timothy Redshaw arrived in the alleyway, handcuffed McMichael, and searched her purse. He found a can of beer in her bag, but did not note this on his police report.

Angeles testified that he believed that the items recovered from McMichael's purse were not all of the ones he saw McMichael put into her purse in the store.

The police sent out a radio dispatch informing officers that a robbery suspect was on board the Metro train. Officer Edmund Moscoso responded, located the train, and detained Islas and two other individuals. Angeles and Vargas then identified Islas as the robbery suspect in a field show up, and the police arrested Islas.

DISCUSSION

Islas contends the evidence is insufficient to support the robbery conviction. Specifically, he argues the evidence did not establish he used force or fear with the intent to retain the victim's property. We disagree.

When an appellant challenges the sufficiency of evidence supporting a jury's verdict, the reviewing court examines whether there was substantial evidence, considered as a whole, to permit a reasonable trier of fact to find the defendant guilty of the charged crime beyond a reasonable doubt. The court's standard for determining what is "substantial evidence" is whether the evidence is "credible and of solid value." One witness's testimony can be sufficient evidence to sustain a conviction.

California law defines a robbery as "the felonious taking of personal property in the possession of another . . . and against [the person's] will, accomplished by means of force or fear." The distinguishing factor that turns a larceny into a robbery is the application of force or fear to the victim to permanently deprive him of his property. *Any* amount of force or fear beyond the seizure of the property that occurs concurrently with the larceny is sufficient to elevate the charge to robbery. Since California's robbery jurisprudence divides the taking of property into two elements — gaining physical possession of the property ("caption") and the carrying away of the property ("asportation") — the application of fear or force in either stage of the crime is sufficient to transform larceny into robbery. Therefore, even if the perpetrator acquires wrongful possession peacefully, mere theft will become robbery if he or she uses force or fear while moving the property. Additionally, a defendant can be found guilty of robbery if he uses force or fear either to acquire original possession of the property or resist attempts to retake the property.

Islas concedes that he used force or fear against

Officers Angeles and Vargas during the incident, but claims that this force or fear should not elevate the charge from larceny to robbery. He contends Officer Angeles' testimony shows that all of the items stolen from the store had been thrown out of McMichael's purse at the time he grabbed Officer Vargas's arm and brandished a fist at him, and thus McMichael surrendered the stolen merchandise before Islas intervened. He contends that "[t]he act of abandonment completed and ended the theft, and the subsequent use of force could not complete a robbery." Islas argues that "[i]f a theft is not being accomplished — if no caption or asportation is occurring — then there is no ongoing theft to aggravate into robbery." We are not persuaded.

Islas correctly contends that if a defendant "truly abandoned the victim's property before using force, then, of course he could be guilty of theft, but not of an *Estes* type robbery." However, the prosecution presented evidence that all the stolen property had not been abandoned. Officer Vargas testified that he was certain that the throwing of the items from the purse occurred after the struggle for the purse. Further, Officer Redshaw testified that he saw a can of beer in McMichael's purse well after the incident ended. Officer Angeles testified that not all of the items McMichael stole from the store and concealed in her purse were recovered in the parking lot.

Islas is correct that Officer Redshaw did not note in his police report that additional items were recovered from the Islas and McMichael, but he did testify to that fact. The jury was entitled to believe his testimony, as "[r]esolution of conflicts and inconsistencies in the testimony is the exclusive province of the [jury]." It was the jury's prerogative to give greater credibility to Officer Vargas's testimony that the items had not been completely abandoned at the time force was used. Further, the jury could accept Officer Redshaw's testimony that he recovered a beer although he

did not report it. Also, the jury could believe Officer Angeles's testimony. The jury needed only to believe *one* of these witnesses on the matter to convict Islas of robbery.

Islas also argues that his conviction should be reversed because he lacked the intent to steal the property when he used force against Officer Vargas. Officer Vargas testified that Islas grabbed his arm *after* he engaged in a "tug-of-war" with McMichael over her cross-body purse. Islas contends his use of force was a "defensive response" to Vargas's "aggressive behavior" against McMichael. Islas claims that if he intended to steal, he would have grabbed the purse rather than Vargas's hand. Furthermore, he claims that McMichael would not have thrown the items at Vargas if their intent was to retain the items, nor would they have fled without the merchandise once Vargas let go of the purse. Therefore, Islas submits that the only "reasonable inference" in this situation was that he was protecting McMichael from Vargas.

However "reasonable" this inference might be, it is not the inference the jury adopted. "It is robbery if the defendant committed a forcible act against the victim motivated by the intent to steal. . . ." Even if the defendant did not intend to instill fear or use force against the victim, the court will still sustain a robbery conviction if fear or force existed. Robbery is not a crime that terminates with the taking, but continues until the defendant has "won his way to a place of temporary safety." Therefore, a defendant can be convicted of theft, even if the taking already occurred, if he or she uses force while attempting to escape. Violence at any point in the commission of the crime will negate any peacefulness in the process.
The jury's verdict demonstrates it found that Islas used force at some point during the taking, moving, or escape with the property with the intent to steal the property. The jury examined the same facts that Islas now presents and found it wanting. We must do so as well. The judgment is affirmed.

STATE v. CURLEY,
939 P.2d 1103 (New Mex. Ct. of App) (1997).

The prosecution arose out of a purse snatching. The evidence was that the victim was walking

out of a mall with her daughter when Defendant grabbed her purse and ran away. The victim described the incident as follows: "I had my purse on my left side . . . . and I felt kind of a shove f my left shoulder where I had my purse strap with my thumb through it and I kind of leaned—was pushed—toward my daughter, and this person came and just grabbed the strap of my purse and continued to run." The victim used the words "grab" or "pull" to describe the actual taking of the purse and "shove" or "push" to describe what Defendant did as he grabbed or "pulled [the purse] from her arm and hand." However, there was also evidence that the victim's thumb was not through the strap of the purse, but was rather on the bottom of the purse. The purse strap was not broken, and the victim did not testify that she struggled with Defendant for the purse in any way or that any part of her body offered any resistance or even moved when the purse was pulled from her arm and hand. Defendant presented evidence that he was drunk and did not remember the incident at all.

Robbery is theft by the use or threatened use of force or violence. Because the words "or violence" refer to the unwarranted exercise of force and do not substantively state an alternative means of committing the offense. . . . we refer simply to "force" in this opinion. The force must be the lever by which the property is taken. . . . Although we have cases saying in dictum that even a slight amount of force, such as jostling the victim or snatching away the property, is sufficient, ... we also have cases in which a taking of property from the person of a victim has been held not to be a robbery, see State v. Sanchez (wallet taken from victim's pocket while victim was aware that the defendant was taking the wallet).

Defendant contends that such evidence exists in that the jury could have found that Defendant's shoving of the victim was part of his drunkenness, and then the purse was taken without force sufficient to constitute robbery. We agree. We are persuaded by an analysis of our own cases, as well as cases from other jurisdictions, that the applicable rule in this case is as follows: when property is attached to the person or clothing of a victim so as to cause resistance, any taking is robbery, and not larceny, because the lever that causes the victim to part with the property is the force that is applied to break that resistance; however when

no more force is used than would be necessary to remove property from a person who does not resist, then the offense is larceny, and not robbery.

LaFave and Scott state:
The great weight of authority, however, supports the view that there is not sufficient force to constitute robbery when the thief snatches property from the owner's grasp so suddenly that the owner cannot offer any resistance to the taking. On the other hand, when the owner, aware of an impending snatching, resists it, or when, the thief's first attempt being ineffective to separate the owner from his property, a struggle for the property is necessary before the thief can get possession thereof, there is enough force to make the taking robbery. Taking the owner's property by stealthily picking his pocket is not taking by force and so is not robbery; but if the pickpocket or his confederate jostles the owner, or if the owner, catching the pickpocket in the act, struggles unsuccessfully to keep possession, the pickpocket's crime becomes robbery. To remove an article of value, attached to the owner's person or clothing, by a sudden snatching or by stealth is not robbery unless the article in question (e.g., an earring, pin or watch) is so attached to the person or his clothes as to require some force to effect its removal.

LaFave & Scott, *supra*, § 8.11(d)(1) at 445-46. Thus, it would be robbery, not larceny, if the resistance afforded is the wearing of a necklace around one's neck that is broken by the force used to remove it and the person to whom the necklace is attached is aware that it is being ripped from her neck. … On the other hand, it would be larceny, not robbery, if the resistance afforded is the wearing of a bracelet, attached by a thread, and the person to whom the bracelet is attached is not aware that it is being taken until she realizes that it is gone.

We now apply these rules to the facts of this case. Although the facts in this case are simply stated, they are rich with conflicting inferences. Either robbery or larceny may be shown, depending on the jury's view of the facts and which inferences it chooses to draw.

In the light most favorable to the State, Defendant shoved the victim to help himself relieve her of the purse, and the shove and Defendant's other force in grabbing the purse had that effect. This view of the facts establishes robbery, and if the jury believed it, the jury would be bound to find Defendant guilty of robbery.

However, there is another view of the facts. Defendant contends that the evidence that he was drunk allows the jury to infer that the shove was unintentional and that the remaining facts show the mere snatching of the purse, thereby establishing larceny. Two issues are raised by this contention that we must address: (1) is there a reasonable view of the evidence pursuant to which the shove was not part of the robbery? and (2) even disregarding the shove, does the remaining evidence show only robbery?

We agree with Defendant that the jury could have inferred that the shove was an incidental touching due to Defendant's drunkenness. Defendant's testimony of his drunkenness and the lack of any testimony by the victim or any witness that the shove was necessarily a part of the robbery permitted the jury to draw this inference. Once the jury drew the inference that the shove was independent of the robbery, the jury could have found that Defendant formed the intent to take the victim's purse after incidentally colliding with her. Alternatively, the jury could have found that Defendant intended to snatch the purse without contacting the victim and that the contact (the shove) was not necessary to, or even a part of, the force that separated the victim from her purse. The victim's testimony (that she felt "kind of a shove" and then Defendant grabbed her purse) would allow this inference. Thus, the jury could have found that the shove did not necessarily create a robbery.

The question would then remain, however, whether the grabbing of the purse was still robbery because more force was used than would have been necessary to remove the purse if the victim had not resisted. Under the facts of this case, in which the victim did not testify that she held the strap tightly enough to resist and in which there was some evidence that she was not even holding the strap, we think that there was a legitimate, reasonable view of the evidence that, once the shove is eliminated from consideration, Defendant used only such force as was necessary to remove the purse from a person who was not resisting. Under this view of the facts, Defendant took the purse by surprise from a person who was not resisting, and not by force necessary to overcome any resistance. Therefore, the trial court should have given Defendant's tendered larceny instructions.

COMMONWEALTH v. ZANGARI, 677 N.E. 2d 702 (Mass. Ct. of App) (1977)

About 7:30 P.M., June 10, 1994, two elderly women, Nancy Colantonio and Vera Croston, returned in Croston's 1981 Chevrolet Citation automobile to their home at 36 Webster Street, Haverill. Croston, upon entering the driveway located by the side of the stairs leading to the porch and front door, stopped the car to let Colantonio out. Colantonio walked up the stairs. She felt someone snatch her purse from under her arm. She was stunned. Turning, she saw the back of a man running down Webster Street in the direction of Summer Street. She said she couldn't believe what she was seeing. While Colantonio was making her way, before the purse snatch, Croston was easing the car up the rest of the short driveway and locking the car. Standing at the back of the car and looking over it, Croston saw a man walking diagonally across Webster Street toward the house. She saw him full face, then lost sight of him until she saw his back as he fled down Webster Street.

Cheryl Kiley, tending her flower garden on the opposite side of Webster Street, saw a man run up the stairs, snatch Colantonio's purse, run down the stairs and turn and run down Webster Street. Kiley had a side view of the man.

Upon testimony to the foregoing effect and

further identification evidence from selections of photographs, Zangari was tried to a jury in Superior Court and found guilty of violating . . . unarmed robbery from a person over the age of sixty-five. (Colantonio was eighty-six at the time.)

On the present appeal from the judgment of conviction, Zangari contends that the trial judge erred when he denied motions for a required finding of not guilty because, says Zangari, the force the thief applied in snatching the purse was, as a matter of law, insufficient to satisfy the "force and violence" denounced in the statute. Zangari intimates that he could have been found guilty of larceny from the person. . . where force is not made part of the offense.

Zangari is complaining that the force applied to Colantonio was no more or little more than that used by a pickpocket who is chargeable only with larceny; hence some substantial force should be required to convict of armed robbery. The point of our leading case of Commonwealth v. Jones . . . was that "where the snatching or sudden taking of property from a victim is sufficient to produce awareness, there is sufficient evidence of force to permit a finding of robbery."

In pickpocketing, which is accomplished by sleight of hand, such evidence is lacking. The difference accounts for the perceived greater severity of the offense of unarmed robbery in contrast with larceny

---

ROCKMORE v. STATE,
114 So.3d 958 (2012)

TORPY, J.
Appellant challenges his conviction for robbery with a firearm, asserting that the trial court should have granted his motion for judgment of acquittal because he "abandoned" the stolen merchandise before he threatened a pursuing store employee with a firearm. Appellant also challenges the trial court's modifications to his proffered special jury instruction. We affirm.

The robbery conviction arose from Appellant's theft of clothing from a Wal-Mart store. A store employee confronted Appellant as he attempted to exit the store. Appellant fled with the merchandise, and the store employee pursued him. During the pursuit, the store employee grabbed Appellant's jacket, causing him to drop some or all of the merchandise. The employee continued to pursue Appellant until Appellant reached his get-away car. Before entering the car, Appellant displayed a firearm that had been concealed in his waistband and warned the employee to stop the pursuit. At that point, the employee retreated, and Appellant escaped.

Appellant was apprehended by police and charged with robbery. He admitted stealing the merchandise, but denied that he had committed robbery because he claimed that he had not possessed a firearm. He asserted as an alternative defense to the robbery charge that even if he had displayed a firearm, he had abandoned the merchandise before the display. He argued that this defense entitled him to a judgment of acquittal or, at the very least, a jury instruction that he should be found not guilty if he "abandoned" the stolen property before he threatened force. We conclude that this case was a proper one for the jury to determine whether the threatened violence was used "in the course of taking," as defined in the robbery statute. We also conclude that Appellant was not entitled to his proffered special instruction because it was an incorrect statement of the law, confusing, and was already covered in the standard instruction. One of the court's modifications to the special instruction was not erroneous. The other was invited error and harmless error nevertheless.

We start our analysis with *Royal v. State* (Fla. 1986) because *Royal* sparked a statutory amendment to the robbery statute.
In *Royal*, when the defendants were confronted by a store detective, they pushed him, fled from the store, and attempted to escape in a vehicle with the detective and other store employees in hot pursuit. After an employee attempted to grab the ignition key to prevent the defendants from escaping, one of the defendants punched him. Then, the other defendant pointed a gun at the employees, causing them to retreat. Our

high court held that the defendants could not be convicted of robbery because the acts of pushing the detective, punching an employee, and displaying the firearm in a threatening manner did not constitute a taking "by force," because the violence occurred "after the taking."

In response to *Royal,* in 1987 the Legislature amended section 812.13(1), Florida Statutes, to change the definition of robbery from a taking by force (or threat) to a taking where force (or threatened force) was used "in the course of the taking." Ch. 87-315, § 1, at 2052, Laws of Fla. (emphasis added). The amendment added a definition for the phrase "in the course of the taking," to include acts that are either "prior to, contemporaneous with, or subsequent to the taking," provided that the acts and the taking "constitute a continuous series of acts or events."
§ 812.13(3)(b), Fla. Stat. (1987). The statute retained a definition of "in the course of committing the robbery" for purposes of applying statutory enhancements. § 812.13(3)(a), Fla. Stat. (1987). The revised statute provides in material part as follows:

> (1) "Robbery" means the taking of money or other property which may be the subject of larceny from the person or custody of another, with intent to either permanently or temporarily deprive the person or the owner of the money or other property, when in the course of the taking there is the use of force, violence, assault, or putting in fear.
>
> . . . .
>
> (3)(a) An act shall be deemed "in the course of committing the robbery" if it occurs in an attempt to commit robbery or in flight after the attempt or commission.
> (b) An act shall be deemed "in the course of the taking" if it occurs either prior to, contemporaneous with, or subsequent to the taking of the property and if it and the act of taking constitute a continuous series of acts or events.

§ 812.13(1), (3), Fla. Stat. (1987).

The intent of this change was to expand the common law crime of robbery to include, among other circumstances, where the force is used after the taking, provided it is used during a "continuous series of acts or events." Clearly, in a case like *Royal,* the Legislature intended the use of force or threatened force during flight to fall within the statutory definition of robbery. *Messina v. State* (Fla. 1999) is analogous to *Royal.* There, the victim chased the defendant thief through a parking lot and sat on the hood of his car to prevent his escape with her stolen purse. The defendant started and stopped his car abruptly and then made a sharp turn, causing the victim to fall off the car and suffer injuries. Our sister court concluded that the use of force presented a jury question as event under the robbery statute. In *Royal,* *Messina,* and *Thomas,* the thieves retained possession of the stolen merchandise throughout the subsequent pursuit, arguably a fact that distinguishes this case.

On the other side of the coin are cases like *Baker* and *Simmons v. State,* wherein the courts held, as a matter of law, that the chain of events was broken by "abandonment" of the stolen property, precluding robbery convictions. In *Baker,* upon seeing store security personnel approaching, the defendant put down the stolen video recorder inside the shopping mall and began to flee. During the ensuing chase, he used force to evade capture. In affirming the dismissal of the robbery charge, our sister court concluded that, because the defendant did not use force as part of a "`continuous series of acts or events' involved with taking the property," the charge was properly dismissed. In *dicta,* however, the *Baker* court stated that "[t]he defendant would have to have been in continuous possession of the property during the escape and the subsequent flight or resisting of arrest in order for the act to fall within the amended statute."

Similarly, our Court in *Simmons* addressed a situation where the defendant discarded the merchandise before using force to resist capture. There, store employees confronted the defendant outside a department store after observing her remove merchandise without paying for it. They escorted her back inside the store, where she removed the merchandise and threw it to the floor. When the employees instructed her to accompany them to the security office, the defendant forcibly resisted. This Court, citing *Baker,* reversed the robbery conviction because "the property [had been] abandoned before any force was employed."

Appellant urges that this case is like *Baker* and *Simmons,* and unlike *Royal* and its progeny, because he dropped the merchandise before he made the alleged threat. Even assuming for the sake of discussion that dropping merchandise when grabbed by a pursuing merchant is the same as "abandonment" — as that term was intended in *Baker* and *Simmons,* and assuming that the *Baker dicta* was a correct pronouncement of the law — a factual dispute at trial precluded a judgment of acquittal here. Although Appellant testified that he had discarded all of the stolen merchandise before he allegedly brandished the firearm, the employee testified that he had not.

Our conclusion that a factual issue was presented does not end our labor, however, because Appellant argues in the alternative that he was entitled to a special instruction consistent with his version of the facts and urges that his proffered instruction was a correct statement of the law under *Baker* and *Simmons* and should not have been modified by the trial court. Appellant's argument and proposed jury charge presents the question of whether the "abandonment" of stolen goods by a thief who is being pursued is a sufficient break in the "continuous series of events" such that a robbery conviction cannot be sustained. Consistent with the *dicta* in *Baker,* Appellant contends that *Baker* and *Simmons* apply anytime an escaping thief discards or drops the ill-gotten-gains before employing force or threatened force to evade capture by someone in pursuit. We think *Baker* and *Simmons* can be distinguished.

Simmons can be distinguished because the defendant there had been apprehended and escorted by employees back inside the store This was an intervening event that interrupted the defendant's volitional course, thereby negating the continuity requirement of the statute. *Baker* is also distinguishable. There, the property was discarded in the shopping mall before the ensuing flight began. Arguably, the "taking" ended before the next act of flight began. Thus, the series of acts was not continuous because the defendant ceased the crime of theft before he began the flight. The *dicta* in *Baker* — that a fleeing thief must be in continuous possession of the stolen item(s) until the point of violence to constitute robbery — was unnecessary to the holding and in contravention of the plain language of the statute. Under this construction, if a fleeing thief drops the merchandise to retrieve a gun and shoot the pursuer, it is not robbery. We specifically reject the *Baker dicta* because it is repugnant with the plain and unambiguous language of the statute and legislative history outlining the reason for the statutory amendment.

Under the statutory definition of "in the course of taking," there is no question that the violent act (or threat) necessary for a robbery conviction may occur subsequent to the taking. The more difficult question is when do the subsequent violent act and the taking "constitute a continuous series of acts or events." A "series of acts or events" is simply a sequence of related acts or events. Section 812.13(3) in no way suggests that these sequential acts or events must be in furtherance of an effort to retain the stolen property, or, as the *Baker* court put it, "involved with taking property." Thus, flight upon detection, for example, is an "act" that is sequential to and related to the act of taking. Discarding the stolen goods would also be such an act. The further qualifier that these series of acts be "continuous" means only that the sequential acts are not interrupted.

Applying this statute to the facts in *Royal* illustrates what was intended. There the series of related acts were the taking, the push, the flight, the struggle at the car, the punch, the threat with the gun, and the escape by vehicle. The possession of merchandise during these acts was not an "act," any more than wearing a hat while walking is an act distinct from the act of walking. They were continuous acts because they happened one after the other without any significant temporal void. They were all related to the taking because the taking and the flight were part of the same episode. The escape is as much a part of the crime as is the taking itself. Whether the act of violence was motivated by a desire to retain the goods, avoid capture, or both, is of no moment. See Kearse v. State, ... (robbery conviction proper even if taking and subsequent murder not motivated by desire to steal property but to escape apprehension). The emphasis should be on whether the entire chain of acts is a part of a continuous series of events. That is all the statute requires.

This interpretation is consistent with and bulwarked by other language in the statute and the legislative history for the amendment. The statute defines "in the course of committing the robbery" to expressly include the "flight" after a robbery or attempted robbery. § 812.13(3)(a), Fla. Stat. [Our interpretation] evinces a legislative recognition that the actions of the thief during the flight are related to, and considered a part of, the underlying crime. Our interpretation is also consistent with a legislative staff analysis of the proposed amendment, which states that the purpose of the amendment is "to expand robbery to include force occurring in an attempt to take money or property, or in flight after the attempt or taking." The emphasized language plainly connotes that force during flight constitutes robbery, even after a mere "attempt" to take property.

AFFIRMED.

Blackmail-extortion

[The] common law misdemeanor of extortion consists of corrupt taking of a fee by a public officer, under color of his office, where no fee is due, or not so large a fee is due, or the fee is not yet due. Modern statutes continue to make such conduct by public officials criminal, generally under the name of extortion; the crime is generally classified as a crime against the administration of justice or against the conduct of government rather than as a crime against property. LaFave, 2000, at 880.

Extortion or blackmail statutes vary greatly in their wording and coverage. Many states require the defendant acquire the victim's property because of a threat. Some states require only that the defendant make a threat with intent to acquire the victim's property. Some statutes require the threats be written; but in most states oral threats suffice. All statutes cover the demand for money; many statutes add "property" or "chattel"; a few statutes broadly include "any pecuniary advantage" or "anything of value". Some states do not discuss the types of property at all and instead cover threats to induce the defendant to do "any act against his will"—for example, in one case the defendant's threats induces the victim to sign a statement admitting an illicit affair with the defendant's wife. Most statutes cover threats to cause bodily harm to the person or to injure the property of the victim or some other person, threats to kill the victim in the future, or threats to accuse the victim of a crime (it does not matter whether the threat is to file a formal complaint charging the victim with the crime or simply to publicize the fact that he has committed a crime). Statutes may, under some circumstances, treat threats to cause economic harm to another as a threat to injure another's property and therefore extortion/blackmail. Most extortion statutes include threats to expose some disgraceful defect or secret of the victim which would subject him to public ridicule or disgrace. A minority of statutes specifically include threats to publish defamatory matter about the victim or to injure his personal character or business reputation. It is not a defense to extortion/blackmail that the victim is in fact guilty of the act or possess the defect that the defendant threatened to expose. See, LaFave, 881-882.

Extortion/blackmail is closely related to robbery, but the crimes differ in that robbery by intimidation requires the defendant acquire the victim's property as a result of the threat, whereas extortion most statutes do not require the result. Robbery also requires that the property be taken from the person or presence of the victim while extortion does not. Some statutes require that the defendant must take the property against the will of the victim, while with extortion the defendant must have taken the property with the consent of the victim induced by an unlawful threat. (LaFave points out that this difference is merely a matter of semantics in that it is the defendant's threats which induce the victim to give up his property, something which he would not have otherwise done.)

Forgery and Uttering a Forged Instrument

Common law forgery is the "fraudulent making or alteration of a writing (the "instrument") to the prejudice of another man's right." An essential element of the crime of forgery is the intent to defraud. Uttering a forged instrument is a common law offense that was distinct from forgery. To utter means to "publish," so uttering a forged document means passing a forged instrument. Common law treated both forgery and uttering a forged instrument as misdemeanors.

Federal and state statutes tend to classify forgery as a felony. All states have extended the crime of forgery to any type of public or private legal document. (thus expanding the list of instruments that can be forged.) Some states combine the crimes of forgery and uttering a forged instrument into one statute. For example, the Arizona code makes forgery a felony and says that a "person commits forgery if, with intent to defraud, the person: falsely makes, completes or alters a written instrument; or knowing possesses a forged instrument; or offers or presents, whether accepted or not, a forged instrument or one which contains false information.

Among the more common examples of forgery today are:

➢ Signing another's name to an application for a driver's license
➢ Printing bogus tickets to a concert or sports event
➢ Signing another's name to a check on his or her bank account without authority
➢ Altering the amount of a check or note
➢ Signing another's name without authority to a certificate transferring shares of stock
➢ Signing a deed transferring someone's real estate without authorization
➢ Altering the grades or credits on a college transcript

PEOPLE v. CUNNINGHAM,
813 N.E.2d 891 (NY 2004)

ROSENBLATT, J.

Defendant was convicted of forgery in the second degree (Penal Law § 170.10) for signing his own name to a corporate check, in excess of his authority. Because defendant's conduct does not constitute forgery under our statute, we reverse his conviction.

I. As the owner of a logging operation, Peter Morat planned to open a sawmill business in Madison County, under the name Herkimer Precut, Inc. He engaged defendant as a consultant to arrange for financing and related activities. In exchange for his services, defendant was to receive a 20% interest in the new venture. As the project progressed, Morat turned over various financial aspects of the business to defendant, entrusting him with control over the corporate checkbook. Because defendant was responsible for paying bills, Morat would sometimes provide defendant with blank, signed checks. At no time, however,

did Morat authorize defendant to sign any checks.

After Morat discovered that corporate bills were not being paid, he examined the company's bank records and found unauthorized payments, some on checks he had signed in blank and others bearing a signature he did not recognize. Morat alleged that by improperly signing or issuing checks, defendant stole thousands of dollars from Herkimer Precut.

In two indictments consolidated for trial, a Montgomery County grand jury charged defendant with one count of grand larceny in the second degree, 15 counts of forgery in the second degree and 15 counts of criminal possession of a forged instrument in the second degree. A single count survived the trial: the forgery conviction before us, stemming from a $195.50 Herkimer Precut check defendant wrote to Nancy Herrick for work performed by

Northeast Woodcraft. In Montgomery County, defendant signed his own name to that check, telling Herrick that he owned Herkimer Precut. Herrick was acquainted with defendant personally and professionally and knew that he was affiliated with Herkimer Precut. She did not know, however, that Morat owned the company and that defendant lacked authority to sign checks. The check was for defendant's personal expenses.

We agree with the dissenters that forgery was not proved.

II. In *People v. Levitan*, we held that "[w]hile it is true that in certain rare instances one may commit a forgery by signing one's own name, this is so only where the signing is done in such a way as to deceive others into believing that the signer is in fact some third party." Levitan signed her name to deeds purporting to convey real property she did not own. In reversing her forgery conviction, we noted that "no pretense was ever made that the signatory was anyone other than defendant" We also observed that "[u]nder our present Penal Law, as under prior statutes and the common law, a distinction must be drawn between an instrument which is falsely made, altered or completed, and an instrument which contains misrepresentations not relevant to the identity of the maker or drawer of the instrument"

Although the Legislature has updated the statute to cover credit cards and certain other technological advances, it has not abrogated *Levitan*'s classic approach to forgery. In defining forgery, Penal Law § 170.00 (4) provides, in pertinent part, that "[a] person 'falsely makes' a written instrument when he makes or draws a complete written instrument . . . which purports to be an *authentic creation of its ostensible maker or drawer,* but which is not such . . . because the ostensible maker or drawer . . . did not authorize the making or drawing thereof" (emphasis supplied).

The terms "authentic creation" and "ostensible maker" are pivotal. In most prosecutions, the forger, acting without authority, signs someone else's name. Thus, in a typical case, the forger, John Doe, wrongfully signs Richard Roe's name, (mis)leading the payee into believing that the check is the authentic creation of

Richard Roe, its ostensible maker. Roe, of course, has not granted Doe any such authority and in many such instances has never even met Doe. In this simple formulation, the ostensible maker (Roe) and the actual maker (Doe) are two different people. If, however, the ostensible maker and the actual maker are one and the same, there can be no forgery under the statute.

Not surprisingly, the parties here disagree as to who is the ostensible maker. The prosecution argues that it is Herkimer Precut; defendant argues that he, the actual maker, is also the ostensible maker. They also disagree as to whether the check was the authentic creation of its ostensible maker.

The People contend that Herkimer Precut is the ostensible maker because its name appears on the check as owner of the account. Further, they argue that because defendant lacked authority to sign company checks, the check in question was not the authentic creation of the company, and a forgery is made out. Defendant counters that the check was an authentic creation of its ostensible maker and that because he signed his own name, he cannot be guilty of forgery: as the ostensible maker, he did not pretend to be anyone other than himself the actual maker. Moreover, defendant argues that even if Herkimer Precut was the "ostensible maker" of the check, defendant's relationship with Herkimer Precut was sufficient to make the check the "authentic creation" of the company. In *People v. Briggins* we observed that "when an individual signs a name to an instrument and acknowledges it as his own, that *person* is the `ostensible maker.'" Although *Briggins* involved a slightly different setting (and not a corporate check, as here), its language along with the statute's history and purpose, informs our analysis and supports defendant's position.

Forgery is a crime because of the need to protect signatures and make negotiable instruments commercially feasible. In its common-law roots, forgery had little to do with abstract questions of authority.[4]… As one treatise explains, "it is not forgery for a person to sign his own name to an instrument, and falsely and fraudulently represent that he has authority to bind another by doing so" and "the signer is guilty of false pretenses only"

As the court noted in *United States v. Young*, "[t]he majority of state law cases hold that signing one's own name on one's own check without sufficient funds to cover the amount of the check does not constitute forgery. In these cases, the person writing the check is not trying to pass himself off as someone else. . . . The same principle applies when an agent signs a company check without actual authority to do so."[6] We conclude that authority and authenticity are not the same thing. Defendant did not commit forgery merely by exceeding the scope of authority delegated by the corporation.[7] Our interpretation leaves no gap in the Penal Law. Although embezzlers who use their own names to sign checks beyond their authority are not guilty of forgery in New York, their conduct would ordinarily fall within our larceny statutes

Moreover, importing issues of authority into the statute, without express legislative language, would create vexing problems in adjudging forgery cases. If, for example, a corporate officer authorized to sign corporate checks does so for a personal purchase, is that forgery? Would an officer authorized to sign checks up to $20,000 who signs a check for $25,000 be guilty of forgery? While the prosecution argues that we should read our statute to justify convictions in those instances, it has not identified any New York decision interpreting the statute that expansively.

Accordingly, the order of the Appellate Division should be reversed and the indictment dismissed.

Negotiating a Bad Check (NSF)

People are writing fewer and fewer checks-- relying instead on wireless transfers of money (Smart Cash, for example). Still, checks are a relatively frequent method of transferring money, and many people continue to maintain checking accounts from which they occasionally write checks. Most checks bounce as the result of negligence, mistake or bad bookkeeping. "No sufficient funds checks" or "insufficient funds checks" are generally "made good" within the permissible statutory period and thus passing those checks are not criminal acts. Early statutes treated passing insufficient funds checks as false pretenses, but due to the widespread use of commercial and personal banking system, legislatures enacted worthless check statutes to cope with the problem of check fraud committed by professionals and organizations. These laws usually classify the offense as a misdemeanor and include restitution remedies and fees associated with bad checks.

Bribery

Bribery is a crime where money or valuables are exchanged, but there is no force or threat of force. Instead a gift, a favor, or a contribution is voluntarily made "coupled with a particular criminal intent". Although it often involves the transfer of money, bribery is not really considered a property crime, but rather a crime against public order.

Other Property-Related Crimes

There are several other crimes that could qualify as crimes against property in that they do not create physical harm to the victim. These include:

➢ Identity Theft
➢ Check Kiting
➢ Computer Crimes
➢ Consumer Fraud
➢ Government Fraud
➢ Fraudulent Use of Credit Cards
➢ Tax Fraude
➢ Intellectual Property Offenses (Copyright and Patent Infringement)
➢ Mail and Wire Fraud

- ➤ Money Laundering
- ➤ Securities Fraud
- ➤ Racketeering and Organized Property Crime

These crimes are all statutory with no common law equivalent. As you have learned so far, state statutes vary tremendously. Test your understanding and see if you can locate one or two of these crimes in a statute from a state of your choice. Can you identify the mens rea and actus reus elements? Are there attendant circumstances? Are there grades of offenses? See if you can find an appellate opinion discussing the crime.

WRAP UP

At English common law, the only property crimes were larceny and robbery which were felonies and thus capital offenses. As commerce and society developed, new legislation was needed and embezzlement and receiving stolen property laws were passed by English Parliament and by the new state legislators. States have more recently adopted consolidated theft statutes following the lead of the MPC to both simplify and broaden liability for actions which deprive others of their property. This chapter has only scratched the surface of the wide variety of crimes against property. Other property related crimes include a variety of white collar crimes, corporate crimes, and banking crimes such as check kiting.

Chapter Ten: Justifications

Overview

As mentioned earlier, the defendant may challenge the constitutionality of the law he is charged with breaking (i.e., is it too vague, does it violate the Equal Protection Clause, is the penalty too severe?). By taking the case to trial, the defendant is essentially challenging the state to prove all the elements that are required in the statute. Also at trial, the defendant is able to raise defenses. Defenses are either perfect defenses—if believed by the jury, perfect defenses result in the acquittal of the defendant—or they are imperfect—if believed by the jury, imperfect defenses result in conviction for a lesser charge, or the imposition of lesser punishment. The defenses in this and the next chapter are considered affirmative defenses. Affirmative defenses are those for which the defendant has the burden of producing evidence and persuading the jury. Those two burdens combined are what we refer to as "the burden of proof." The defendant never has the ultimate burden of proof, because it is the government which must ultimately prove beyond a reasonable doubt every aspect of the case to the jury in order to overcome the "presumption of innocence." Sometimes it is difficult to ascertain whether the defendant is making a "you didn't prove it defense" or a "I have an affirmative defense-defense." This is particularly true with regard to defenses that call into question the defendant's state of mind at the trial (mostly involving excuses such as insanity, intoxication, and mistake of fact or law).

Justifications

Sometimes doing the right thing results in harm. Society recognizes the utility of doing some acts in certain circumstances that unfortunately result in harm. In those situations, the defendant can raise a justification defense. Justification defenses allow criminal acts to go unpunished because they preserve an important social value or because the resulting harm is outweighed by the benefit to society. For example, if a surgeon cuts someone with a knife to remove a cancerous growth, the act is a beneficial one even though it results in pain and a scar. In raising a justification defense, the defendant admits he did a wrongful act (such as taking someone's life), but argues that the act was the right thing to do under the circumstances. At times, the state's view differs from the defendant's view of whether the act was, in fact, the right thing to do. In those cases, the state files charges to which the defendant raises a justification defense.

Justifications are affirmative defenses. As such, defendants must produce some evidence in support of these defenses. In most cases, the defendant must also convince the jury that it was more likely than not (a preponderance of the evidence) that his or her conduct was justified. For example, the defendant may claim that he or she acted in self-defense and at trial would need to call witnesses or introduce physical evidence that supports the claim of self-defense--that it was more likely than not that his or her actions were ones done in self-defense. State law may vary about how convinced the jury must be (called the standard of proof) or when the burden switches to the defendant to put on evidence, but all states generally require the defendant to carry at least some of the burden of proof in raising justification defenses.

Execution of Public Duties

Sometimes individuals must, in the course of their official duties, use force against others. For example, arrests involve physical force. Even in the least confrontational of arrests, police officers must use a certain amount of force to place the defendant in handcuffs. During war, some soldiers must kill or wound the enemy in a premeditated fashion. In order to carry out a death sentence in states that use the death penalty, some person or persons deliberately and intentionally act to take the life of the condemned. All of these situations involve individuals who harm or kill others, yet none of these individuals are routinely charged with crimes. Even if they were charged, they would escape conviction by raising the execution of public duties defense.[22] Because prosecutors rarely spend resources prosecuting cases that are easily defensible we don't often hear about this defense being raised.

Interestingly, MPC §3.08 provides individuals with a duty to care, discipline, or supervision a defense when they use force upon another in their capacity as parent, teacher, guardian, doctor, warden, etc.[23]

---

[22] MPC § 3.03 Execution of Public Duty.
(1) Except as provided in Subsection (2) of this Section, conduct is justifiable when it is required or authorized by:
(a) the law defining the duties or functions of a public officer or the assistance to be rendered to such officer in the performance of his duties; or
(b) the law governing the execution fo legal process; or
(c) the judgment or order of a competent court or tribunal; or
(d) the law governing the armed services or the lawful conduct of war; or
(e) any other provision of law imposing a public duty.

(2) The other sections of this Article apply to:
(a) the use of force upon or toward the person of another for any of the purposes dealt with in such sections; and
(b) the use of deadly force for any purpose, unless the use of such force is otherwise expressly authorized by law or occurs in the lawful conduct of war.

(3) The justification afforded by Subsection (1) of this Section applies:
(a) when the actor believes his conduct to be required or authorized by the judgment or direction of a competent court or tribunal or in the lawful execution of legal process, notwithstanding lack of jurisdiction of the court or defect in the legal process; and
(b) when the actor believes his conduct to be required or authorized to assist a public officer in the performance of his duties, notwithstanding that the officer exceeded his legal authority.

MPC § 2.10 Military Orders.
It is an affirmative defense that the actor, in engaging in the conduct charged to constitute an offense, does no more than execute an order of his superior in the armed services that he does not know to be unlawful.

MPC § 3.07 Use of Force in Law Enforcement.
(1) Use of Force Justifiable to Effect an Arrest. Subject to the provisions of this Section and of Section 3.09, the use of force upon or toward the person of another is justifiable when the actor is making or assisting in making an arrest and the actor believes that such force is immediately necessary to effect a lawful arrest.
(2) Limitations on the Use of Force.
(a) The use of force is not justifiable under this Section unless:
(i) the actor makes known the purpose of the arrest or believes that it is otherwise known by or cannot reasonably be made known to the person to be arrested; and
(ii) when the arrest is made under a warrant, the warrant is valid or believed by the actor to be valid.
(b) The use of deadly force is not justifiable under this Section unless:
(i) the arrest is for a felony; and
(ii) the person effecting the arrest is authorized to act as a peace officer or is assisting a person whom he believes to be authorized to act as a peace officer; and
(iii) the actor believes that the force employed creates no substantial risk of injury to innocent persons; and
(iv) the actor believes that:
(A) the crime for which the arrest is made involved conduct including the use or threatened use of deadly force; or
(B) there is a substantial risk that the person to be arrested will cause death or serious bodily injury if his apprehension is delayed.

[23] § 3.08 Use of Force by Persons with Special Responsibility for Care, Discipline or Safety of Others.
The use of force upon or toward the person of another is justifiable if:

(1) the actor is the parent or guardian or other person similarly responsible for the general care and supervision of a minor or a person acting at the request of such parent, guardian or other responsible person and:
(a) the force is used for the purpose of safeguarding or promoting the welfare of the minor, including the prevention or punishment of his misconduct; and
(b) the force used is not designed to cause or known to create a substantial risk of causing death, serious bodily injury, disfigurement, extreme pain or mental distress or gross degradation; or

Resisting Arrest

English common law recognized the right to resist an unlawful arrest by reasonable force except in cases in which the defendant was charged with murder of the officer. Any citizen could arrest a felon, and citizens could also use deadly force where needed to stop a fleeing felon, and if such force should kill the felon, the homicide was considered justified. The citizen took his chances as to the accuracy of his judgment, however. If it turned out that the person he had killed was not a felon, then his use of deadly force (and any resulting homicide) was not justified -- even when it was reasonable to believe that the person being arrested had committed a felony. With the development of the metropolitan police force in the nineteenth century, the law governing citizen's arrest gradually changed, restricting the general authority of citizens to arrest and use deadly force. *See*, Kerper, *supra* at 133.

---

(2) the actor is a teacher or a person otherwise entrusted with the care or supervision for a special purpose of a minor and:
(a) the actor believes that the force used is necessary to further such special purpose, including the maintenance of reasonable discipline in a school, class or other group, and that the use of such force is consistent with the welfare of the minor; and
(b) the degree of force, if it had been used by the parent or guardian of the minor, would not be unjustifiable under Subsection (1)(b) of this Section; or

(3) the actor is the guardian or other person similarly responsible for the general care and supervision of an incompetent person and:
(a) the force is used for the purpose of safeguarding or promoting the welfare of the incompetent person, including the prevention of his misconduct, or, when such incompetent person is in a hospital or other institution for his care and custody, for the maintenance of reasonable discipline in such institution; and
(b) the force used is not designed to cause or known to create a substantial risk of causing death, serious bodily injury, disfigurement, extreme or unnecessary pain, mental distress, or humiliation; or

(4) the actor is a doctor or other therapist or a person assisting him at his direction and:
(a) the force is used for the purpose of administering a recognized form of treatment that the actor believes to be adapted to promoting the physical or mental health of the patient; and
(b) the treatment is administered with the consent of the patient or, if the patient is a minor or an incompetent person, with the consent of his parent or guardian or other person legally competent to consent in his behalf, or the treatment is administered in an emergency when the actor believes that no one competent to consent can be consulted and that a reasonable person, wishing to safeguard the welfare of the patient, would consent; or

(5) the actor is a warden or other authorized official of a correctional institution and:
(a) he believes that the force used is necessary for the purpose of enforcing the lawful rules or procedures of the institution, unless his belief in the lawfulness of the rule or procedure sought to be enforced is erroneous and his error is due to ignorance or mistake as to the provisions of the Code, any other provision of the criminal law or the law governing the administration of the institution; and
. . .

(6) the actor is a person responsible for the safety of a vessel or an aircraft or a person acting at his direction and:
(a) he believes that the force used is necessary to prevent interference with the operation of the vessel or aircraft or obstruction of the execution of a lawful order, unless his belief in the lawfulness of the order is erroneous and his error is due to ignorance or mistake as to the law defining his authority; and
. . .

7) the actor is a person who is authorized or required by law to maintain order or decorum in a vehicle, train or other carrier or in a place where others are assembled, and:
(a) he believes that the force used is necessary for such purpose; and
(b) the force used is not designed to cause or known to create a substantial risk of causing death, bodily injury, or extreme mental distress.

The U.S. Supreme Court recognized that the right to resist unlawful arrest had been incorporated into the common law of the United States. In 1963, 45 states still recognized the right of an individual to resist an unlawful arrest with force since imprisonment, even for brief periods, subjected individuals to a abysmal conditions. As jail conditions improved, approval of the defense dwindled. Currently, only 12 states allow individuals to forcefully resist an unlawful arrest by a law enforcement officer. In other states, a person who is unaware that the aggressor is a police officer may possibly be successful in raising this defense. Also, a person may use force to resist arrest when faced with an officer's use of excessive force. (Generally the defense raised under those circumstances is self-defense.)

Necessity or Choice of Evils

Sometimes breaking the law is necessary or, at least, the better option. In those situations, the defendant may raise the justification known as either "necessity" or "choice of evils." Necessity defenses are found either in state statutes or state common law. The central elements of the necessity defense are: the defendant was faced with immediate or imminent harm; the defendant was not substantially at fault in creating the emergency; the harm created by defendant's criminal act is less than the harm he or she confronted; the defendant had no legal alternatives to violating the law; and the legislature had not already identified and chosen the lesser evil.

Common Law Necessity

The common law recognized the defense of "necessity" (but referred to it as "justification") in those cases where the accused acted in the reasonable belief that perpetration of the offense would prevent the occurrence of a greater harm or evil. Perhaps the most well-known and cited case of common law necessity is the English case of *Queen v. Dudley and Stephens* 14 QBD 273 DC. (1884)—a case in which the defendants were unsuccessful in raising the defense but ultimately prevailed after receiving a pardon from the Queen after sixth-months of incarceration.

> The three crew members of the yacht, the Mignoenette, along with the seventeen-year-old cabin boy were forced to abandon ship when a wave smashed into the stern. The four managed to launch a thirteen-foot dinghy with only two tins of turnips to sustain them while they drifted sixteen hundred miles from shore. On the fourth day, they managed to catch a turtle that they lived on for a week; they quenched their thirst by drinking their own urine and, at times, by drinking seawater. On the nineteenth day, Captain Thomas Dudley murdered young Richard Parker with the agreement of Edwin Stephens and over the objection of Edmund Brooks. The three only survived by eating Parker's flesh and drinking his blood until rescued four days later.

> Lord Coleridge, rejected the defense of necessity, stating,

> "The temptation to act . . . here was not what the law ever called necessity. Nor is this to be regretted. . . .

> To preserve one's life is generally speaking a duty, but it may be the plainest and the highest duty to sacrifice it. War is full of instances in which it is a man's duty not to live, but to die.. The duty, in case of shipwreck, of a captain to his crew, of the crew to the p passengers, of soldiers to women and children. . . ; these duties impose on men the moral necessity, not of the preservation but of the sacrifice of their lives for others . . . . It is not correct, therefore, to say that there is any absolute or unqualified necessity to preserve one's own life. . . .

> It is not needful to point out he awful danger of admitting the principled contended for.

> Who is to be the judge of this sort of necessity? By what measure of the comparative value of lives to be measured? Is it to be strength, or intellect, or what? It is the

plain that the principle leaves to him who is to profit by it to determine the necessity which will justify him in deliberately taking another's life to save his own. In this case, the weakest, the youngest, and the most unresisting was chosen. Was it more necessary to kill him than one of the grown men? The answer must be "No". . . .

Lord Coleridge sentenced the defendants to death but expressed his hope that Queen Victoria would pardon them. She did not pardon them, but she did commute their death penalty to a six-month prison sentence.

Modern Necessity Statutes

The test of necessity (whether the choice was the right one) is an objective test, and it is up to the court, not the defendant, to make the final determination on whether the harm sought to be avoided was greater than that committed by the defendant's criminal act. Most courts refuse to allow the necessity defense in intentional homicide cases, reasoning that one life cannot be weighed against another. Courts will examine the text or legislative history of a statute in order to determine whether the legislature disallows the necessity defense and will not give a jury instruction on the defense of necessity when it is clear that the legislature has already weighed the evils. For example, if the legislature had debated whether to enact a medicinal marijuana statute, but chosen not to, then a defendant charged with possession of marijuana could not claim medical necessity when charged with possession.

The Model Penal Code – Choice Of Evils

The Model Penal Code choice of evils provision lays out three steps for the defense: 1) identify the evils; 2) rank the evils; 3) choose the lesser evil to avoid the greater evil that is on the verge of happening.[24] Unlike the common law, the MPC defense is also available where the source of the emergency is coercion by another person rather than an event. The MPC also does not rule out the necessity defense in intentional homicide cases. The MPC identifies the following as appropriate choices:

> ➤ Destroying property to prevent spreading fire
> ➤ Violating a speed limit to get a dying person to a hospital
> ➤ Throwing cargo overboard to save a sinking vessel and its crew
> ➤ Dispensing drugs without a prescription in an emergency
> ➤ Breaking into and entering a mountain cabin to avoid freezing to death.

STATE v. OWENBY,
996 P.2d. 510 (Ore App 2000)

FACTS
Jack Ownbey is a veteran of the Vietnam War. He has been diagnosed with Post–Traumatic Stress Syndrome (PTSD). In his defense to the charges against him, Ownbey intended to show that "his actions in growing marijuana and possessing marijuana were as a result of

---

[17]MPC §3.02 Choice of Evils

(1) Conduct that the actor believes to be necessary to avoid a harm or evil to himself or another is justifiable, provided that:

(a) the harm or evil sought to be avoided by such conduct is greater than that sought to be prevented by the law defining the offense charged; and

(b) neither the Code nor other law defining the offense provides exceptions or defenses dealing with the specific situation involved; and

(c) a legislative purpose to exclude the justification claimed does not otherwise plainly appear.

(2) When the actor was reckless or negligent in bringing about the situation requiring a choice of harms or evil or in appraising the necessity for his conduct, the justification afforded by this Section is unavailable in a prosecution for any offense for which recklessness or negligence, as is the case may be, suffices to establish culpability.

medical necessity or choice of evils."

ORS 161.200, codifies that defense in Oregon. It provides:
(2) Unless inconsistent with . . . some other provision of law, conduct which would otherwise constitute an offense is justifiable and not criminal when:
(a) That conduct is necessary as an emergency measure to avoid an imminent public or private injury; and
(b) The threatened injury is of such gravity that, according to ordinary standards of intelligence and morality, the desirability and urgency of avoiding the injury clearly outweigh the desirability of avoiding the injury sought to be prevented by the statute defining the offense in issue.
(3) The necessity and justifiability of conduct under subsection (1) of this section shall not rest upon considerations pertaining only to the morality and advisability of the statute, either in its general application or with respect to its application to a particular class of cases arising thereunder.

HOLDING
Ownbey fails to recognize that the defense of necessity is available only in situations wherein the legislature has not itself, in its criminal statute, made a determination of values. If the legislature has not made such a value judgment, the defense would be available. However, when, as here, the legislature has already balanced the competing values that would be presented in a choice-of-evils defense and made a choice, the court is precluded from reassessing that judgment.

PEOPLE v. JOHN GRAY et al., 150 Misc.2d 852 (1991)

FACTS (Summary)
John Gray and others were charged with disorderly conduct for participating in a demonstration organized by Transportation Alternatives on October 22, 1990. Their actions blocked one of the NY bridges, and they were protesting that the bridge had opened traffic to cars during rush hour, when it had been reserved for pedestrians and bicycles.

They stipulated that they were ordered to move, didn't comply, and didn't resist. The state stipulated to not objecting to their presenting a defense of necessity.

OPINION
It was clear that these defendants' actions were motivated by the desire to prevent what they called the "asphyxiation of New York" by automobile-related pollution. Specifically, the harm they seek to combat is the release of ever higher levels of pollution from vehicular traffic, and the unnecessary death and serious illness of many New Yorkers as a result.

Defendants . . . testified that they also acted to prevent serious injuries to those individuals who continued to use alternative forms of transportation on the bridge.

Certainly, neither of these harms could be said to have developed through any fault of these defendants.

LEGISLATIVE PREEMPTION
There is no issue of legislative preemption in this case. In fact, in a departure from the usual situation in citizen intervention cases, it is clear that it is the defendants' point of view concerning air pollution and its accompanying dangers that has been confirmed and adopted by the Legislature.

Nor is this a case where the defendants are acting against what the courts have already recognized as a fundamental right, as in the abortion protests which have asserted a necessity defense. There is no corresponding fundamental right to contribute to life threatening air pollution. ...

THE NECESSITY DEFENSE AND CITIZEN INTERVENTION
The necessity defense is fundamentally a balancing test to determine whether a criminal act was committed to prevent a greater harm. The common elements of the defense found in virtually all common-law and statutory definitions include the following:

(1) the actor has acted to avoid a grave

harm, not of his own making;
(2) there are not adequate legal means to avoid the harm; and
(3) the harm sought to be avoided is greater than that committed.

A number of jurisdictions, New York among them, have included two additional requirements-- first, the harm must be imminent, and second, the action taken must be reasonably expected to avert the impending danger.

…

There is only one element of the necessity defense to which a standard more stringent than reasonable belief must be applied--that is the actor's choice of values, for which he is strictly liable. An actor is not justified, for example, in taking human life to save imperiled property. No matter how real the threat to property is, by making the wrong choice in placing the value of property over human life, the actor loses the defense. Thus, the choice of values requirement ensures that the defense cannot be used to challenge shared societal values.

THE CHOICE OF EVILS REQUIREMENT
As stated earlier, defendants' value choice is the one area where they must be held strictly liable. A Judge must decide whether the actor's values are so antithetical to shared social values as to bar the defense as a matter of law. As part of this objective inquiry, the requirement that a Judge also determine whether or not the defendant's value choice has been preempted by the Legislature has sometimes been read into the statute. New York provided that defendants must not be protesting only against the morality and advisability of the statute under which they are charged.

A reading of the cases in this area reveals that it is seldom the correctness of defendants' values which is at issue. Courts have generally recognized that the harms perceived by activists protesting nuclear weapons and power and United States domestic and foreign policy-- nuclear holocaust, international law violations, torture, murder, the unnecessary deaths of United States citizens as a result of environmental hazards and disease--are far greater than those created by a trespass or

disorderly conduct.

In this case, as well as in most necessity cases, it is clear that defendants chose the correct societal value. It is beyond question that both the death and illness of New Yorkers as a result of additional air pollution, and the danger to cyclists and pedestrians posed by vehicles on the south outer roadway, are far greater harms than that created by the violation of disorderly conduct.

The more difficult issue in many of the necessity defense cases has been whether the actors' perception of harm was reasonable. …

THE IMMINENCE OF GRAVE HARM REQUIREMENT
In evaluating whether defendants' perceptions of the harm they sought to avoid in this case were reasonable, the court must decide whether they had a well-founded belief in imminent grave injury. Such determination is almost always a question for the trier of fact. Defendants in the instant case presented several witnesses, as well as submitting studies, to establish the existence of a grave and imminent harm. …

Defendants clearly articulated their belief that encouraging automobiles at a rush hour traffic "choke-point" while discouraging walkers and cyclists produces a specific, grave harm that is not only imminent, but is occurring daily. This belief was supported by the testimony of expert witnesses and studies submitted into evidence. Former Commissioner of Transportation Sandler gave undisputed testimony that New York City would have to reduce vehicular traffic in order to come into compliance with the minimum standards set by the Environmental Protection Agency for air pollution. Indeed, recent litigation corroborates defendants' claim that New York's failure to comply with EPA standards is due, in substantial measure, to automobile-related pollution.

. . .The EPA's 1989 assessment concluded that motor vehicles were the single largest contributor to cancer risks from exposure to air toxics. Motor vehicles, said the EPA, are responsible for 55% of the total cancer incidence from air contaminants, five times greater than from any other air pollution source.

Unlike many of the cases in this area, where the harm sought to be prevented was perceived as too far in the future to be found "imminent", the grave harm in this case is occurring every day. ...
In light of all the evidence of grave and imminent harm cited by these defendants, the court finds that it would be improper to hold as a matter of law that they had not met their burden of production on this element of the defense, i.e., that no reasonable juror could find that defendants had a reasonable belief that grave and imminent harm was occurring. The inquiry therefore becomes whether the People have disproved this element beyond a reasonable doubt.

This court rejects the contention that proof of the imminent death of New Yorkers as a result of high levels of air pollution or accidents on the south outer roadway is required before the finding of an emergency can be made to uphold this defense. The medical evidence connecting air pollution and disease--namely, cancer and heart disease--is too well established for such a position to be logical.

In recent cases, it has become evident that the lesser evil sometimes must occur well in advance of the greater harm. In *People v Harmon* the defendants escaped from prison one evening after threat of assault, although there was no present or impending assault. The court ruled that imminency is "to be decided by the trier of fact taking into consideration all the surrounding circumstances, including defendant's opportunity and ability to avoid the feared harm." In this case, the threatened harm of increased deaths and illness through air pollution is a uniquely modern horror, very different from the fires, floods and famines which triggered necessity situations in simpler days. However, the potential injury is just as great, if not greater.

Pursuant to the foregoing discussion, this court finds the prosecution has failed to disprove the element that defendants in this case had a reasonable belief in a grave and imminent harm constituting an emergency, beyond a reasonable doubt.

THE NO LEGAL ALTERNATIVE REQUIREMENT
A key requirement of the necessity defense is that no reasonable legal option exists for averting the harm. Once again, the proper inquiry here is whether the defendant reasonably believed that there was no legal alternative to his actions. The defense does not legalize lawlessness; rather it permits courts to distinguish between necessary and unnecessary illegal acts in order to provide an essential safety valve to law enforcement in a democratic society.

Defendants in this case testified to a long history of attempts to prevent the harm they perceived. Although Transportation Alternatives is a group that is regularly consulted by the Department of Transportation and meets often with agency officials to propose measures to encourage walking, cycling and the use of mass transit, and to relieve traffic congestion with its accompanying pollution, they received no advance warning that the closing of the bicycle and pedestrian lane on the Queensboro Bridge was being considered.

THE CAUSAL RELATIONSHIP REQUIREMENT
New York is among the jurisdictions that require a defendant's actions to be reasonably designed to actually prevent the threatened greater harm. As with the other elements of this defense, the test consistent with the purposes of this defense is one of reasonable belief. Defendants' initial burden is to offer sufficient evidence of a reasonable belief in a causal link between their behavior and ending the perceived harm. The New York statute and most common-law formulations use the term "necessary" rather than "sufficient". In the opinion of this court, a defendant's reasonable belief must be in the necessity of his action to avoid the injury. The law does not require certainty of success.

Defendants testified that they had participated in two short-term campaigns in the recent past which only became successful when civil disobedience was employed. One of these campaigns resulted in the defeat of Mayor Koch's attempt in 1987 to ban bicycles from Manhattan streets. The second involved their attempts during the 1980's to obtain access to a roadway along the river in New Jersey for cyclists and walkers. All efforts at letter writing and petitioning had been rebuffed, and it was only after members of Transportation Alternatives were arrested for acts of civil disobedience that a three-month trial period of access to the roadway for walkers and cyclists was instituted.

Pursuant to the foregoing opinion, this court finds that the People have not disproved the elements of the necessity defense in this case beyond a reasonable doubt. Defendants are therefore acquitted.

PEOPLE v. DOVER,
790 P.2d 834 (Colo. 1990)

FACTS (Summary)
The prosecution proved beyond a reasonable doubt by the use of radar readings that James Dover was driving 80 miles per hour in a 55 mile-per-hour zone. However, the court also found that the defendant, who is a lawyer, was not guilty on the grounds that his speeding violation was justified because he was late for a court hearing in Denver as a result of a late hearing in Summit County, Colorado.

A Colorado statute, § 42-4-1001(8)(a) provides:
The conduct of a driver of a vehicle which would otherwise constitute a violation of this section is justifiable and not unlawful when: It is necessary as an emergency measure to avoid an imminent public or private injury which is about to occur by reason of a situation occasioned or developed through no conduct of said driver and which is of sufficient gravity that, according to ordinary standards of intelligence and morality, the desirability and urgency of avoiding the injury clearly outweigh the desirability of avoiding the consequences sought to be prevented by this section.

OPINION
In this case, the defendant did not meet the foundational requirements of § 42-4-1001(8)(a). He merely testified that he was driving to Denver for a "court matter" and that he was late because of the length of a hearing in Summit County. No other evidence as to the existence of emergency as a justification for speeding was presented. The defendant did not present evidence as to the type or extent of the injury that he would suffer if he did not violate § 42-4-1001(1). He also failed to establish that he did not cause the situation or that his injuries would outweigh the consequences of his conduct.

STATE v. CELLI,
263 N.W.2d 145 (S.D. 1978)

FACTS (Summary)
On a cold winter day, William Celli and his friend, Glynis Brooks, left Deadwood, South Dakota, hoping to hitchhike to Newcastle, Wyoming, to look for work. The weather turned colder, they were afraid of frostbite, and there was no place of business open for them to get warm. Their feet were so stiff from the cold that it was difficult for them to walk.

They broke the lock on the front door, and entered the only structure around, a cabin. Celli immediately crawled into a bed to warm up, and Brooks tried to light a fire in the fireplace.

They rummaged through drawers to look for matches, which they finally located, and started a fire. Finally, Celli came out of the bedroom, took off his wet moccasins, socks, and coat; placed them near the fire; and sat down to warm himself. After warming up somewhat they checked the kitchen for edible food. That morning, they had shared a can of beans but had not eaten since. All they found was dry macaroni, which they could not cook because there was no water.

A neighbor noticed the smoke from the fireplace and called the police. When the police entered the cabin, Celli and Brooks were warming themselves in front of the fireplace. The police searched them but turned up nothing belonging to the cabin owners.

OPINION
The trial court convicted Celli and Brooks of fourth-degree burglary. The appellate court reversed on other grounds, so, unfortunately for us, the court never got to the issue of the defense of necessity. But, this is the case frequently cited as an example of necessity.

Not everyone agrees that necessity should be a defense. Some argue that individuals should obey the law and should not be encouraged to violate legal rules. They note that society suffers when individuals make the wrong choice. Finally, some argue that the defense has been exploited and politicized when invoked by anti-abortion and anti-nuclear activists or other individuals who have broken the law in the name of various political causes.

Other Cases—Necessity/Choice of Evil

Commonwealth v. Kendall, 883 N.E.2d 269 (Mass 2008).
Kendall and girlfriend walked to a nearby bar/restaurant and drank heavily. They returned home; defendant's girlfriend busted her head open, and they couldn't stop the bleeding. There was no phone in their trailer and neither had cell phone. Although there were many neighbors in the trailer park who were home at the time, the defendant did not contact them to use their phone or request they call assistance. Additionally, there was a fire station 100 yards from their neighbor's home. The defendant, still drunk, got into their car and drove the profusely bleeding girlfriend to the hospital. Judge refused to give necessity instruction. The Court stated,

"The only issue here is whether the defendant presented some evidence on the third element of the necessity defense, namely that there were no legal alternatives that would be effective in abating the danger posed to . . . [girlfriend from her serious head wound.] . . . When viewing the evidence in the light most favorable to defendant, we conclude that he failed to present evidence to support reasonable doubt that his operation of a motor vehicle was justified by necessity.

State v. Salin, (Delaware, Kent County Ct. Common Pleas, June 13, 2003).
Defendant was an emergency medical services technician who was arrested for speeding while responding to a call to assist a 2-year-old who was not breathing. The court held that Salin reasonably assumed that the child was in imminent danger and did not have time to use his cell phone to check on child's progress. Salin was confronted by a choice of evils that his slightly harmful conduct was justified in order to prevent a greater harm.

State v. Warshaw, 410 A.2d. 1000 (Vt. 1979).
Defendants were part of a group of demonstrators that traveled to Vermont to protest at the main gate of a nuclear power plant. The plant had been shut down for repairs and refueling, and these protestors joined a rally designed to prevent workers from gaining access to the plant. They were told to leave the private premises; they refused and were charged with unlawful trespass. They were convicted at a trial in which the trial judge refused to allow any evidence of their claim of the defense of necessity. The majority of the appellate court ruled

"Low-level radiation and nuclear waste are not the types of imminent danger classified as an emergency sufficient to justify criminal activity. To be imminent, a danger must be, or must reasonably appear to be, threatening to occur immediately, near at hand, and impending. We do not understand the defendants to have taken the position in their offer of proof that the hazards of low-level radiation and nuclear waste buildup are immediate in nature. On the contrary, they cite long-range risks and dangers that do not presently threaten health and safety. Where the hazards are long term, the danger is not imminent, because the defendants have time to exercise options other than breaking the law."

Justice Hill filed a concurring opinion in which he wrote,
"While I agree with the result reached by the majority, I am unable to agree with their reasoning.. . . The defense of necessity proceeds from the appreciation that, as a matter of public policy, there are circumstances where the value protected by the law is eclipsed by a superseding value, and that it would be in appropriate and

unjust to apply the usual criminal rule.. The balancing of competing values cannot, of course, be committed to the private judgment of the actor, but must, in most cases, be determined at trial with regard being given for the crime charged and the higher value sought to be achieved.

Determination of the issue of competing values, and therefore, the availability of the defense of necessity is precluded, however, when there has been a deliberate legislative choice as to the values at issue. The common law defense of necessity deals with imminent dangers from obvious and generally recognized harms. It does not deal with non-imminent or debatable harms, nor does it deal with activities that the legislative branch has expressly sanctioned and found not to be harms. . . . Since defendant's defense of necessity was foreclosed by a deliberate legislative policy choice, there was no error on the trial court's part in not allowing the defense to be presented.

Justice Billings dissented, writing,
"Here, the trial court prevented the introduction of any evidence on the issue of necessity in spite of the offer of proof. . . . It is reversible prejudicial error for the trial court to exclude a whole line of material evidence tending to support a defense even though deficiencies in the admissibility of the evidence might have later appeared. Furthermore, it is not for the trial judge to rule on the ultimate credibility and weight of the evidence. . . . While the offer made by the defendants was laced with statements about the dangers they saw in nuclear power generally, it is clear that they offered to show that the . . . facility. . . was an imminent danger to the community on the day of the arrests, that if it commenced operation, there was a danger of meltdown and severe radiation damage to persons and property.. . . Furthermore, the defendants offered to show that, in light of the imminent danger of an accident, they had exhausted all alternative means of preventing the start up of the plant and the immediate catastrophe it would bring. I am of the opinion that the defendants are entitled to present evidence on the defense of necessity as it exists at common law.

State v. Aguilar, 883 F.2d 662 (9th Cir. 1989).
Defendants were convicted of masterminding and running a modern-day underground railroad that smuggled Central American natives across the Mexican border with Arizona. Several individuals worked with several churches which operated as "sanctuaries" and refugees were sent to Chicago and other places from Arizona. INS investigated the alien smuggling and infiltrated the sanctuary movement with several undercover informers. In January 1985 the government filed indictments which led to the convictions of the defendants. At trial the government sought to exclude evidence that the defendants believed that the 1980 Refugee Act entitled the Central American aliens to enter or reside in the United States lawfully. The district court granted the motion and excluded from trial "evidence of the defendant's belief that those aliens involved were refugees based on their interpretation of immigration laws. The Court stated,

"As a matter of law, a defendant must establish the existence of four elements to be entitled to a necessity defense:
(1) that he was faced with a choice of evils and chose the lesser evil;
(2) that he acted to prevent imminent harm;
(3) that he reasonably anticipated a causal relation between his conduct and the harm to be avoided; and
(4) that there were no other legal alternatives to violating the law."

The court found that the appellants' offer [presentation of evidence] was "legally deficient in at least one respect: They failed to establish that there were no legal alternatives." They claimed that the INS continuously has frustrated the present legal way of obtaining refugee status, that immigration judges deny the due process rights of those granted an asylum hearing and make incorrect determinations of credibility concerning the danger faced in the aliens' homelands. They argued that they established the sanctuary movement only after trying all these other methods and concluding there was "no other safe alternative."" The court, however, noted that the only other alternative they mentioned was "attempts at working with and through the INS" The defendants failed to look for a provisional remedy in the courts, filing class actions, etc. It thus concluded that the trial court did not err in excluding evidence and denying the defense.

Prisoners And The Necessity Defense

Prisoners, threatened with assaults or homosexual rape by other prisoners (or by guards) have raised the necessity defense when charged with escape. The necessity defense may be successful in these cases, subject to several conditions. Additionally, prisoners have also claimed the excuse of duress—a similar—but different defense which will be discussed in the next chapter. Below is an excerpt from a law review article discussing the justification of necessity and the excuse of duress as was applied in earlier cases of prison escape.

> In recent years, however, the violent atmosphere of the modern prison has attracted growing public attention, which has been reflected in a corresponding judicial involvement in penal affairs. Yet, while the courts increasingly have held that intolerable and inhumane conditions may be unconstitutionally cruel and unusual punishment, there has been, until very recently, no comparable acknowledgment of a prisoner's right to escape from such conditions.
> ....
> . . . Escapees from prison rarely have been able to invoke successfully common law defenses, including duress and necessity. The courts have feared that endorsement of any defenses to escape would lead to a "rash of escapes" rationalized by allegations of threats, assaults, and other prison horrors.
>
> Within the last few years a number of courts have abandoned the orthodox majority position, and have held that some defense may be available to those defendants charged with escape from prison. The first few courts to do so acknowledged the availability of the defense of duress; the more recent cases have focused on necessity.
> ....
> The epidemic of homosexual assaults and rapes in prisons and the inability of prison officials to contain this problem have forced the courts to devote increasing attention to this aspect of prison life. While no case yet has held that a prisoner has a constitutional right to be free from homosexual assault, the courts have begun to recognize an inmate's right to personal security. . . .
>
> While the court did not specifically delineate the boundaries of its notion of personal security, the implication is clear that such a right may include freedom from sexual attack. . . . The court noted that since the prisoners had a civil right to personal security, a correlative duty was imposed upon the prison administration to protect the inmates' rights. Whether the state's failure to provide that protection offers the prisoner a constitutional justification for escape has not yet been determined.
>
> Defendants who attempt to justify their escapes on such constitutional grounds face two imposing obstacles: the courts' lingering reluctance to scrutinize prison operations, and their aversion to deciding constitutional issues.
>
> The United States Supreme Court so far has declined to address this problem. Presently, prisoners are more likely to defend their escapes successfully with common law defenses such as duress and necessity, rather than constitutional arguments, particularly where homosexual assaults which prompt the escape occur merely as isolated incidents and thus are less likely to be considered to reach the level of cruel and unusual punishment.
>
> DURESS AND NECESSITY
> Confusion and misunderstanding have surrounded the common law defenses of necessity and duress. The courts and state legislatures have been inconsistent in their enunciation and application of these defenses. Numerous states have duress statutes, while only a few states provide a distinct codification of the necessity defense.

The defense of duress generally excuses one from criminal punishment for performing unlawful conduct if he was coerced to do so by the use of, or threat to use, unlawful force against himself or another, which a person of reasonable firmness would have been unable to resist. Necessity, in contrast, provides a defense for otherwise unlawful conduct if the actor reasonably believed the conduct necessary to avoid a greater harm to himself or another.

The two defenses have three significant features in common. First, neither defense is applicable to murder; thus, both are distinguishable from self-defense. Second, the actor must not have been at fault in creating the situation from which the threat arises. Finally, the threat must be present, imminent, and impending; a threat of future harm is insufficient.

Two important factors distinguish the two defenses. The first is that duress traditionally involves another human being who coerces the actor to perform certain conduct, whereas necessity has been limited historically to such non-human forces as acts of God and unavoidable accidents. Because of this requirement, most prison escapees, until very recently, have grounded their defenses upon duress and have disregarded necessity.

The second, and more significant, distinction between duress and necessity emerges from the basic nature of each defense. Duress is founded upon the theory that some compulsion excuses the actor from blame in a particular case, although the actor admits the wrongfulness of his act. In effect, the actor is excused, but the act itself is not condoned. Indeed, the coercer is criminally responsible for that act.

Necessity, however, involves no actual coercion; there is merely a choice between two evils, one of which is the commission of the unlawful act. Because society prefers to avoid the greater evil, public policy sanctions the choice of the lesser of the two evils. In such a case, the actor is still responsible for the deed, but because of special circumstances society holds that the act is not wrongful, morally or legally. The act is not merely excused, it is justified.

Thus, a successful duress defense proves a lack of criminal intent, but a necessity defense establishes that there was no criminal act. While a judicial decision regarding duress focuses on the state of mind of a particular defendant and thus establishes no general rule, a recognition of the necessity defense creates a new rule of law, because the issue is the act itself. Necessity, in contrast to duress, acknowledges a right to escape. Wayne Michael, Have the Prison Doors Been Opened—Duress and Necessity as Defenses to Prison Escape. Chicago-Kent Law Review, Volume 54 Issue 3 (1978) pages 913-919.

PEOPLE v. LOVERCAMP,
43 Cal. App.3d 823 (1974)

OPINION
Defendant and her codefendant, Ms. Wynashe, were convicted by a jury of escape from the California Rehabilitation Center

Defendant and Ms. Wynashe were inmates of the California Rehabilitation Center. They departed from that institution and were promptly captured in a hayfield a few yards away. At trial, they made the following offer of proof:

They had been in the institution about 2 1/2 months and during that time they had been threatened continuously by a group of lesbian inmates who told them they were to perform lesbian acts—the exact expression was 'fuck or fight.' They complained to the authorities several times but nothing was done about their complaints. On the day of the escape, ten or fifteen of these lesbian inmates approached them and again offered them the alternative—'fuck or fight.' This time there was a fight, the results of which were not outlined in the offer of proof. After the fight, Ms. Wynashe and defendant were told by this group of lesbians that they 'would see the group again.' At this point, both defendant and Ms. Wynashe feared for their lives. Ms. Wynashe was additionally motivated by a protective attitude toward defendant Lovercamp who had the intelligence of a twelve year old. It was represented that a psychiatrist would testify as to defendant's mental capacity. On the basis of what had occurred, the threats made, the fact that officials had not done anything for their protection, Ms. Wynashe and defendant felt they had no choice but to leave the institution in order to save themselves.

. .. [T]the court rejected the offer of proof. The defendants then offered no evidence. The case was submitted to the jury and to the surprise of no one the jury found both defendants guilty.

. . . .

Some preliminary observations are in order. When our culture abandoned such unpleasantries as torture, dismemberment, maiming and flogging as punishment for anti-social behavior and substituted in their place loss of liberty, certain problems immediately presented themselves. As a 'civilized' people, we demanded that incarceration be under reasonably safe and humane conditions. On the other hand, we recognized that the institutional authorities must be afforded a certain firmness of program by which the malefactors be kept where sentenced for the allotted period of time. Realizing that a certain percentage of penal inmates are going to be uncooperative, disruptive and, in some cases, downright dangerous, we invested our institutional officials with disciplinary powers over inmates far above any such powers granted to governmental authorities outside prison walls. It is hardly earth shattering to observe that prisons are not Brownie Camps and that within the inmate population are those who, if given the opportunity, will depart without due process of law. Therefore, as an aid to prison authorities and to discourage self-help release from incarceration, the offense of escape was born. Simply stated, if an inmate intentionally leaves lawful custody, he commits a new crime.

However, rather early in the legal history of the offense of escape, it became clear that all departures from lawful custody were not necessarily escapes or, to put it more accurately, there was a possible defense to an escape charge, to wit, necessity. In 1 Hale P.C. 611 (1736), it was written that if a prison caught fire and a prisoner departed to save his life, the necessity to save his life 'excuseth the felony.' So, too, we may assume that a prisoner with his back to the wall, facing a gang of fellow-inmates approaching him with drawn knives, who are making it very clear that they intended to kill him, might be expected to go over the wall rather than remain and be a martyr to the principle of prison discipline.

However, the doctrine of necessity to 'excuseth the felony' carried with it the seeds of mischief. It takes little imagination to conjure stories which could be used to indicate that to the subjective belief of the prisoner conditions in prison are such that escape becomes a necessity. Inevitably, severe limitations were affixed to this defense and the general rule evolved that intolerable living conditions in prison afforded no justification for escape. A reading of the cases invoking this rule presents a harsh commentary on prison life in these United States of America, revealing (with proper consideration of the sources of the complaints), prison life which is harsh, brutal, filthy, unwholesome and inhumane. A fair sampling of the authorities indicate that the defense has been rejected in cases involving unsanitary conditions in jail—'a filthy, unwholesome and loathsome place, full of vermin and uncleanliness,'; fear of being shot; unmerited punishment at the hands of the custodian; or escape from solitary confinement when the cell was infested with bugs, worms and vermin and when the toilet was flushed the contents ran out on the floor; extremely bad food, guard brutality, inadequate medical treatment and inadequate recreational and educational programs. Under the above general rule, none of these situations excused the felony.

Traditionally, the courts have balanced the interests of society against the immediate problems of the escaping defendant. This has tended to focus attention away from the immediate choices available to the defendant and the propriety of his cause of action. Thus, reprehensible conditions have been found to be insufficient to justify the escape, the public interest outweighing the defendant's interest.

In a humane society some attention must be given to the individual dilemma. In doing so the court must use extreme caution lest the overriding interest of the public be overlooked. The question that must be resolved involves looking to all the choices available to the defendant and then determining whether the act of escape was the only viable and reasonable choice available. By doing so, both the public's interest and the individual's interest may adequately be protected. In our ultimate conclusion it will be seen that we have adopted a position which gives reasonable consideration to both interests. While we conclude that under certain circumstances a defense of necessity may be proven by the defendant, at the same time we place rigid limitations on the viability of the defense in order to insure that the rights and interests of society will not be impinged upon. We have not formulated a new rule of law but rather have applied rules long ago established in a manner which effects fundamental justice.

In California, the two leading authorities are *People v. Richards*, and *People v. Whipple*.

Mr. Whipple escaped because he was the victim of 'brutal treatment of extreme atrocity.' The opinion was written at a time (1929) when writers, legal or otherwise, with a fine feeling for the delicacy of their readers left much to the imagination. Therefore, we are left to speculate as to the specific nature of the 'brutal treatment of extreme atrocity' to which Mr. Whipple had been subjected. However, whatever treatment Mr. Whipple had received, it had occurred in a remote mountain camp where a complaint was useless.[1] He departed. His sole defense was that the conditions existing at the camp together with his brutal and inhumane treatment made his imprisonment intolerable and therefore justified the escape. The trial court instructed the jury that an escape founded on any alleged unsanitary condition or alleged harsh, brutal or inhumane treatment received by him at the hands of his custodian would constitute no defense to the charge.

On appeal, the court recognized that, generally speaking, 'absolute necessity' would excuse the commission of a crime but insofar as an escape from jail was concerned, the authorities were in 'practical accord' in holding that ordinary adverse circumstances did not afford such a defense. The court concluded that even if the conditions of imprisonment were so

unwholesome as to seriously imperil the health and life of the prisoner or that prison guards might subject him to unjustifiable abuse or even serious physical injury, he escapes for those reasons 'at his peril.' Therefore, it was 'with very great reluctance' that the judgment of conviction was affirmed.

Turning to the more specific problem of escape based on an alleged threat of forcible sexual attack, the reported cases reflect an attitude of the courts which might charitably be characterized as viewing it with alarm but with results varying from benign neglect to dynamic inertia.

In *Richards*, an offer of proof was made that acts of sodomy had been inflicted on the defendant, that he complained but the guards would do nothing about it, that he had been threatened with death and that he had exhausted every possible remedy short of escape to avoid the threat of death. The trial court refused the offer of proof and refused an instruction on necessity.

Richards, affirmed, rejecting the claim of necessity and observed that the principle of justification by necessity, if applicable, involved a determination that the harm or evil sought to be avoided by such conduct is greater than that sought to be prevented by the law defining the offense charged. So viewed, the court concluded that the crime of escape was a greater harm than the threat of sexual assault, and that the prisoner '. . . should be relegated to relief through established administrative channels, or, that failing, through the courts.'

. . . [D]icta in *Richards* . . . suggests that if a prisoner were in immediate fear of his life or significant bodily injury and if no alternative course was availing, then perhaps the evidence might form a sufficient defense. Unfortunately for Mr. Richards, the court did not feel that the evidence was such that such a defense could be presented to the jury.

Three out-of-state cases on the subject of sexual attack against prisoners are of note.

In *State v. Green*, 470 S.W.2d 565, cert. den., 405 U.S. 1073, 92 S.Ct. 1491, 31 L.Ed.2d 806, the Supreme Court of Missouri rejected the defense of necessity based on threats of homosexual advances, citing a previous opinion of that court and Richards. In Green, the defendant had been a victim of a series of forceful acts of sodomy committed on him by numerous inmates. He had attempted to complain to the authorities who merely told him to "fight it out, submit to the assaults, or go over the fence." (470 S.W.2d P. 566.) On the day of escape, a group of four or five inmates told him that they would be at his cell that night and he would submit to their homosexual desires or they would kill or seriously harm him. He did not report this threat to anyone and escaped that evening. The court held that the defense of necessity was not available to him mainly on the basis that he was not 'being closely pursued by those who sought by threat of death or bodily harm to have him submit to sodomy.' (P. 568.) The court pointed out that the threatened consequences of his refusal to submit could have been avoided that day by reporting the threats and the names of those making the threats to the authorities and that the defendant had several hours in which to consider and report these threats. The court relied on the general principle '(d)efendant's defense resolves itself into the simple proposition that the conditions of his confinement justified his escape. Generally, conditions of confinement do not justify escape and are not a defense.

One Justice dissented, pointing out that the possibility of complaint to the authorities was illusory in view of his previous experience in which he had been told to 'fight it out, submit to the assaults, or go over the fence,' adding, 'The majority opinion does not recommend submission, and as a practical matter, self defense was impossible. All that was left was escape, and under these circumstances, the coercion and necessity were not remote in time, but present and impending. Escape or submission (and I do not believe defendant was unreasonable in not being willing to submit to five-fold sodomy) were literally all this defendant had left.'

In *People v. Noble* (1969), 18 Mich.App. 300, 170 N.W.2d 916, the Michigan Court of Appeal followed the same rationale in a case in which the defendant fled a prison work camp in desperation to avoid homosexual attacks by other prisoners. The court stated: 'The problem of homosexuality in the prisons is serious and perplexing, and never more so than in a case such as this where such activity is forced upon a young man against his will. However, the answer to the problem is not the judicial sanctioning of escape. While we have no reason to doubt the sincerity of this defendant, it is easy to visualize a rash of escapes, all rationalized by unverifiable tales of sexual assault. The solution must rather come from some kind of penological reform.' (P. 918.)

However, in *People v. Harmon* (1974), 53 Mich.App. 482, 220 N.W.2d 212, another panel of the Michigan Court of Appeal declined to follow Noble. In Harmon, the defendant offered evidence that his departure from prison was done under duress in order to avoid threatened homosexual attacks by other inmates. Evidence was adduced that the defendant had been accosted by other inmates who demanded sex from him, that he refused and had been beaten and kicked. Subsequently, he was again approached by a group of inmates who started hitting him, saying they would continue to do so until he gave them some sex. The group dispersed without having achieved their expressed goal and the next night the defendant escaped. He stated that he did not report these episodes because of fear of reprisals and a deputy warden confirmed that his fears in this respect were not unfounded. The trial court instructed the jury that even if they did find that the defendant fled to avoid homosexual attacks, such a claim would not serve as a defense to a charge of prison escape. The Court of Appeal reversed, holding that the facts were sufficient to require the submission of the defense of duress to the jury, and stated: 'The time has come when we can no longer close our eyes to the growing problem of institutional gang rapes in our prison system. Although a person sentenced to serve a period of time in prison for the commission of a crime gives up certain of his rights, 'it has never been held that upon entering a prison one is entirely bereft of all of his civil rights and forfeits every protection of the law.' Indeed, the State has a duty to assure inmate safety. The persons in charge of our prisons and jails are obliged to take reasonable precautions in order to provide a place of confinement where a prisoner is safe from gang rapes and beatings by fellow inmates, safe from guard ignorance of pleas for help and safe from intentional placement into situations where an assault of one type of (sic) another is likely to result. If our prison system fails to live up to its responsibilities in this regard we should not, indirectly, countenance such a failure by precluding the presentation of a defense based on those facts.'

While agreeing with *Noble* that prison reform by the legislature was the best solution, Harmon concluded: '. . . we should not, because of that fact, preclude a defendant from presenting available defenses in the courts of this state.' (*People v. Harmon*, Supra, 220 N.W.2d 212, 215.)

We, therefore, conclude that the defense of necessity to an escape charge is a viable defense. However, before Lovercamp becomes a household word in prison circles and we are exposed to the spectacle of hordes of prisoners leaping over the walls screaming 'rape,' we hasten to add that the defense of necessity to an escape charge is extremely limited in its application. This is because of the rule that upon attaining a position of safety from the immediate threat, the prisoner must promptly report to the proper authorities.

In *People v. Wester*, the court approved a jury instruction to the effect that even though a prisoner escapes to save his life, ". . . a further, continued, wilful and intentional departure from the limits of custody by him will constitute the crime of escape." The court held that such a prisoner escaping against his will would owe a duty to use reasonable efforts to render himself again to the custody of the law enforcement agency at the first available opportunity. Thus, the defense becomes meaningless to one who would use it as an excuse to depart from lawful custody and thereafter go his merry way relieved of any responsibility for his unseemly departure. A prisoner cannot escape from a threat of death, homosexual attack or other significant bodily injury and live the rest of his life with an ironclad defense to an escape charge.

From all of the above, we hold that the proper rule is that a limited defense of necessity is available if the following conditions exist:
(1) The prisoner is faced with a specific threat of death, forcible sexual attack or substantial bodily injury in the immediate future;
(2) There is no time for a complaint to the authorities or there exists a history of futile complaints which make any result from such complaints illusory;
(3) There is no time or opportunity to resort to the courts;[2]
(4) There is no evidence of force or violence used towards prison personnel or other 'innocent' persons in the escape; and
(5) The prisoner immediately reports to the proper authorities when he has attained a position of safety from the immediate threat.

Applying the above rules to the offer of proof in the instant case, we find the following:
(1) The prisoners were faced with a specific threat of forcible sexual attack in the immediate future. While we must confess a certain naivete as to just what kind of exotic erotica is involved in the gang rape of the victim by a group of lesbians and a total ignorance of just who is forced to do what to whom, we deem it a reasonable assumption that it entails as much physical and psychological insult to and degradation of a fellow human being as does forcible sodomy.

(2) There existed a history of futile complaints to the authorities which made the results of any belated complaint illusory.

(3) Between the time of the fight and the time the ladies went over the wall, there obviously existed no time for resort to the courts by the filing of a petition for an extraordinary writ.

(4) No force was involved in the escape.

(5) Because the defendants were apprehended so promptly and in such close proximity to the institution, we do not know whether they intended to immediately report to the proper authorities at the first available opportunity. Obviously, even though the defendant may have the mentality of a twelve-year-old, on retrial it must be

anticipated that she will so testify. Whether that testimony is believable under the facts and circumstances of this case, will be a question of fact addressed to the jury.

Whether any of the conditions requisite to this defense exist is a question of fact to be decided by the trier of fact after taking into consideration all the surrounding circumstances. The offer of proof in the instant case was sufficient to require the submission of this defense to the jury in an appropriate manner. The trial court erred in not submitting this matter to the jury.

In summary, simply alleging an escape to avoid homosexual attack will not suffice to prevent a conviction. This defense is one with severe limitations and it must be established by competent evidence in a trial where the testimony of witnesses is subject to scrutiny by the trier of fact. The credibility to be accorded to such a proposed defense lies solely within the function of the trier of fact and is to be determined by the facts and circumstances of each case as they arise.

We do not conceive that we have created a new defense to an escape charge. We merely recognize, as did an English Court 238 years ago, that some conditions 'excuseth the felony.' Judgment reversed.

Other Cases – Prisoners and Necessity/Choice of Evils/Duress

State v. Gomez, 92 F.3d 770 (9th Cir 1996). Gomez was about to be released from prison. He was contacted by Mir (convicted of international drug conspiracy), and asked to murder six witnesses for $10,000 a piece. Gomez contacted authorities when he got out, Mir indicted for solicitation and Gomez' identity revealed. Later a man with a gun threatened to kill Gomez, and Gomez learned there was a contract out on his life. He sought, unsuccessfully, assistance from U.S. Customs, his parole officer, Sac County Sheriff, Catholic and Protestant churches, newspapers. Scared, he started sleeping in the park and living on the streets, riding buses at night. Finally, Gomez armed himself with a shotgun. He was charged as a felon in possession.

The Ninth Circuit Court found that the threats were more than vague promises of future harm and that he had good reason to believe that he was in harm. Court held that the situation satisfied the present and immediate requirement of the necessity defense, that the government's actions placed Gomez in precarious position, and that Gomez had exhausted reasonable alternatives. The court noted that there was no evidence that Gomez possessed the shotgun for any other purpose than self-defense and, in fact, had dropped firearm when confronted with customs agents to demonstrate his cooperation.

Consent

Because crimes are harms against society and not specific individuals, consent by the "victim" does not negate the state's interest in denouncing and deterring certain conduct. Thus, the fact that the victim has given consent does not bar the defendant from being found guilty of the crime. That said, some crimes are defined in a way that lack of consent is an element of a crime (see, e.g., rape), and the state must prove beyond a reasonable doubt that no consent was given under those statutes. There are three exceptions to rule that consent is not a defense to criminal liability. In these three situations, the law recognizes consent as a defense to criminal conduct: 1) incidental contact (acts that do not cause serious injury or harm—being bumped on a bus); 2) sporting events (ordinary physical contact or blows are incident to sports such as football, boxing or wrestling); and socially beneficial activity. See, e.g., MPC §2.11[25]

---

[25] MPC § 2.11 Consent.

In cases in which consent could be a defense it must be freely and voluntarily given. That said, some victims are deemed incapable of giving consent--for example due to immaturity (age of consenter) mental incapacity, or intoxication. In cases where the "consenter" is deemed incapable of giving consent, the defendant will certainly not be able to raise consent as a defense. Similarly, when the defendant obtained consent by fraud, then the consent is not valid and will not provide a defense.

Finally, the fact that the victim forgives the perpetrator does not constitute consent and does not provide the defendant a defense to criminal liability.

STATE v. SHELLEY,
929 P.2d 489 (Wash.App. 1997)

FACTS

On March 31, 1993, Jason Shelley and Mario Gonzalez played "pickup" basketball on opposing teams at the University of Washington Intramural Activities Building (the IMA). (Pickup games are not refereed by an official; rather, the players take responsibility for calling their own fouls.) Gonzales was playing aggressively and fouled Shelley several times. At one point he hit the ball away and scratched Shelley's face. Shelley left and then returned to the game. ...Later in the game, Shelley threw a punch at Gonzalez and ended up breaking G's jaw.

During the course of the trial, defense counsel told the court he intended to propose a jury instruction that: "A person legally consents to conduct that causes or threatens bodily harm if the conduct and the harm are reasonably foreseeable hazards of joint participation in a lawful, athletic contest or competitive sport." Although the trial court agreed that there were risks involved in sports, it stated that "the risk of being intentionally punched by another player is one that I don't think we ever do assume." The court noted, "In basketball you consent to a certain amount of rough contact. If they were both going for a rebound and Mr. Shelley's elbow or even his fist hit Mr. Gonzalez as they were both jumping for the rebound and Mr. Gonzalez's jaw was fractured in exactly the same way then you would have an issue."

Reasoning that "our laws are intended to uphold the public peace and regulate behavior of individuals," the court ruled "that as a matter of law, consent cannot be a defense to an assault." The court indicated that Shelley could not claim consent because his conduct "exceeded" what is considered within the rules

---

(1) In General. The consent of the victim to conduct charged to constitute an offense or to the result thereof is a defense if such consent negatives an element of the offense or precludes the infliction of the harm or evil sought to be prevented by the law defining the offense.

(2) Consent to Bodily Injury. When conduct is charged to constitute an offense because it causes or threatens bodily injury, consent to such conduct to the infliction of such injury is a defense if:
(a) the bodily injury consented to or threatened by the conduct is not serious; or
(b) the conduct and the injury are reasonably foreseeable hazards of joint participation in a lawful athletic contest or competitive sport or other concerted activity not forbidden by law; or
(c) the consent establishes a justification for the conduct under Article 3 of the Code.
(
3) Ineffective Consent. Unless otherwise provided by the Code or by the law defining the offense, assent does not constitute consent if:
(a) it is given by a person who is legally incompetent to authorize the conduct charged to constitute the offense; or
(b) it is given by a person who by reason of youth, mental disease or defect or intoxication is manifestly unable or unknown by the actor to be unable to make a reasonable judgment as to the nature or harmfulness of the conduct charged to constitute the offense; or
(c) it is given by a person whose improvident consent is sought to be prevented by the law defining the offense; or
(d) it is induced by force, duress or deception of a kind sought to be prevented by the law defining the offense.

of that particular sport:

Consent is a contact that is contemplated within the rules of the game and that is incidental to the furtherance of the goals of that particular game. If you can show me any rule book for basketball at any level that says an intentional punch to the face in some way is a part of the game, then I would take another look at your argument. I don't believe any such rule book exists.

Later, Shelley proposed jury instructions on the subject of consent:

An act is not an assault, if it is done with the consent of the person alleged to be assaulted. It is a defense to a charge of second degree assault occurring in the course of an athletic contest if the conduct and the harm are reasonably foreseeable hazards of joint participation in a lawful athletic contest or competitive sport.

The trial court rejected these, and Shelley excepted. The trial court did instruct the jury about self-defense.

HOLDING

First, we hold that consent is a defense to an assault occurring during an athletic contest.

Logically, consent must be an issue in sporting events because a person participates in a game knowing that it will involve potentially offensive contact and with this consent the "touchings" involved are not "unlawful." The rationale that courts offer in limiting consent as a defense is that society has an interest in punishing assaults as breaches of the public peace and order, so that an individual cannot consent to a wrong that is committed against the public peace.

Urging us to reject the defense of consent because an assault violates the public peace, the State argues that this principle precludes Shelley from being entitled to argue the consent defense on the facts of his case. In making this argument, the State ignores the factual contexts that dictated the results in the cases it cites in support. When faced with the question of whether to accept a school child's consent to hazing or consent to a fight, or a gang member's consent to a beating, courts have declined to apply the defense. Obviously, these cases present "touchings" factually distinct from "touchings" occurring in athletic competitions.

If consent cannot be a defense to assault, then most athletic contests would need to be banned because many involve "invasions of one's physical integrity." Because society has chosen to foster sports competitions, players necessarily must be able to consent to physical contact and other players must be able to rely on that consent when playing the game. ...

There are, however, situations in which consent to bodily injury should be recognized as a defense to crime.

There is the obvious case of participation in an athletic contest or competitive sport, where the nature of the enterprise often involves risk of serious injury. Here, the social judgment that permits the contest to flourish necessarily involves the companion judgment that reasonably foreseeable hazards can be consented to by virtue of participation.

The more difficult question is the proper standard by which to judge whether a person consented to the particular conduct at issue. The State argues that when the conduct in question is not within the rules of a given sport, a victim cannot be deemed to have consented to this act. The trial court apparently agreed with this approach.

...

Instead, we adopt the approach of the Model Penal Code which provides:

(4) Consent to Bodily Injury. When conduct is charged to constitute an offense because it causes or threatens bodily injury, consent to such conduct or to the infliction of such injury is a defense if:

(c) the conduct and the injury are reasonably foreseeable hazards of joint participation in a lawful athletic contest or competitive sport or other concerted activity not forbidden by law.

... The correct inquiry is whether the conduct of defendant constituted foreseeable behavior in the play of the game.

Additionally, the injury must have occurred as a byproduct of the game itself.

Although in "all sports players consent to many risks, hazards and blows," there is "a limit to the magnitude and dangerousness of a blow to which another is deemed to consent." This limit, like the foreseeability of the risks, is determined by presenting evidence to the jury about the nature of the game, the participants' expectations, the location where the game has been played, as well as the rules of the game. Here, taking Shelley's version of the events as true, the magnitude and dangerousness of Shelley's actions were beyond the limit. There is no question that Shelley lashed out at Gonzalez with sufficient force to land a substantial blow to the jaw, and there is no question but that Shelley intended to hit Gonzalez. There is nothing in the game of basketball, or even rugby or hockey, that would permit consent as a defense to such conduct. Shelley admitted to an assault and was not precluded from arguing that the assault justified self-defense; but justification and consent are not the same inquiry.

STATE v. HIOTT,
987 P. 2d 135 (Wash App 1999)

FACTS (Summary)
Richard Hiott and his friend Jose were playing a game of shooting at each other with BB guns. During the game, Jose was hit in the eye and lost his eye as a result. Richard was charged with third-degree assault. His defense was consent.

OPINION
Hiott argues that the game they were playing "is within the limits of games for which society permits consent." Hiott compares the boys' shooting of BB guns at each other to dodgeball, football, rugby, hockey, boxing, wrestling, "ultimate fighting," fencing, and "paintball." We disagree.

The games Hiott uses for comparison, although capable of producing injuries, have been generally accepted by society as lawful athletic contests, competitive sports, or concerted activities not forbidden by law. And these games carry with them generally accepted rules, at least some of which are intended to prevent or minimize injuries. In addition, such games commonly prescribe the use of protective devices or clothing to prevent injuries.

Shooting BB guns at each other is not a generally accepted game or athletic contest; the activity has no generally accepted rules; and the activity is not characterized by the common use of protective devices or clothing.

Moreover, consent is not a valid defense if the activity consented to is against public policy. Thus, a child cannot consent to hazing, a gang member cannot consent to an initiation beating, and an individual cannot consent to being shot with a pistol. Assaults are breaches of the public peace. And we consider shooting at another person with a BB gun a breach of the public peace and, therefore, against public policy.

STATE v. FRANSUA,
510 P.2d 106 (N.Mex.App. 1973)

FACTS
Daniel Fransua and the victim were in a bar in Albuquerque. Fransua had been drinking heavily that day and the previous day. Sometime around 3:00 p.m., after an argument, Fransua told the victim he'd shoot him if he had a gun. The victim got up, walked out of the bar, went to his car, took out a loaded pistol, and went back in the bar. He came up to Fransua, laid the pistol on the bar, and said, "There's the gun. If you want to shoot me, go ahead." Fransua picked up the pistol, put the barrel next to the victim's head, and pulled the trigger, wounding him seriously.

OPINION
It is generally conceded that a state enacts criminal statutes making certain violent acts crimes for at least two reasons: One reason is to protect the persons of its citizens; the second, however, is to prevent a breach of the public peace. While we entertain little sympathy for either the victim's absurd actions or the defendant's equally unjustified act of pulling the trigger, we will not permit the defense of consent to be raised in such cases. Whether or not the victims of crimes have so

little regard for their own safety as to request injury, the public has a stronger and overriding interest in preventing and prohibiting acts such as these. We hold that consent is not a defense to the crime of aggravated battery, irrespective of whether the victim invites the act and consents to the battery.

Other Cases – Consent

State v. Djarlais,
Ms. Shupe got an order of protection against her husband, defendant, then continued to have contact with him despite the order. Shupe found out about an affair the defendant was having and told him that she did not want anything more to do with him. He then threw her on the bed and had sex with her twice over her protests. Trial court refused to give instruction on consent.

"Even if consent were a defense to the crime of violating a protection order, it is far from clear that the contact in this case was consensual. Ms. Shupe does not appear to have invited or solicited the defendant's presence on the night in question. More importantly, the jury found the defendant guilty of rape in the third degree….(which essentially means they found non-consensual sexual contact.) "We nevertheless reach the issue defendant raises because he seems to suggest that Ms. Shupe's repeated invitations and ongoing acquiescence to defendant's presence constituted a blanket consent or waiver of the order's term. We disagree. …"

Self-Defense

State laws governing the use of force in self-defense vary. The general rule concerning self-defense is that a person may use reasonable force, including deadly force, to defend against the unlawful use of imminent force. The law traditionally looked at three factors in determining whether the defendant's acts were justified by self-defense: (1) whether defender's belief that he had to use force to save himself was reasonable, (2) whether the defender had an opportunity to retreat in safety, and (3) whether the defender was the initial aggressor in the circumstance that lead to the use of deadly force. Scheb notes that the use of deadly force also requires that the person using such force is in a place where he or she has a right to be, acts without fault, and acts in reasonable fear or apprehension of death or great bodily harm. Scheb, *supra* at 433

The defense applies only when the defendant resists *unlawful force*. In general, this means that the aggressor must be attempting to commit a crime or a tort against the defendant. If the aggressor is entitled to act, then the defense may not be raised. If the aggressor is entitled to use some force but exceeds the force he or she is allowed to use, then the defendant may resist by also using force. If the defendant makes a reasonable mistake about whether the force being used against him is legal or not, he will nonetheless be protected by the defense. Emanuel, *supra* at 110.

The defense allows only proportional force. When acting in self-defense the defendant may use only the degree of force necessary to repel the unlawful force. The defense allows the use of deadly force, when necessary, but "[a] minor attack not dangerous to life or limb should not be met with an annihilating response." Id. For example, if Bob came at Tom with a plastic knife, Tom could only use non-deadly force to protect himself. People may use non-deadly force to resist virtually any kind of unlawful force, and the common law retreat rule (discussed below) is not applicable when a defender only uses non-deadly force. Deadly force is usually defined as force that is intended or likely to cause death or serious bodily harm. Note that the actual amount of harm that occurs is irrelevant to determining whether a particular force qualifies as deadly force. If defendant used a gun and points it at his assailant and shoots this is deadly force, even though he missed or inflicted merely a flesh wound. If, on the other hand, the defender used force that would not necessarily cause death or serious bodily injury, but in this instance it did, the force will be treated as non-deadly even if death or serious bodily harm results. A threat to use deadly force does not by itself constitute deadly force.

Because one may use self-defense only against unlawful force, an initial aggressor cannot generally raise the defense. There are two exceptions to this general rule. First, if the defendant provoked the exchange but did not use force or used only non-deadly force and the other responded with deadly force, then the defendant may resort to force (even deadly force) to defend himself against that use of deadly force. In this situation the "victim's" use of force is unlawful since it was excessive to defendant's initial use of force. Second, when the defendant-aggressor withdraws from the conflict and the other party initiates a second conflict, the initial aggressor may use force to defend against the other.

When the defendant is charged with homicide and raises a claim of self-defense, the defendant, to be successful, must show that he or she had a reasonable belief of unlawful harm being used, that the force he or she used was in response to imminent harm, and that the deadly force used was proportionate to the force used by the murder victim. In some states, the defendant must also show that he or she was not required to, or was unable to, safely retreat.

In determining whether a defender's belief as to the need for deadly force was reasonable, a fact-finder (usually the jury) must consider a variety of factors. These include the comparative size of the defender and the attacker, whether the attacker was armed, whether the attacker had a reputation as a vicious fighter etc. The fact-finder must also recognize that the defender is under extreme emotional stress in responding to an attack. He cannot be expected to draw fine lines as to the degree of force needed to repel a threat of serious bodily harm. As Justice Holmes once noted, "detached reflection cannot be demanded in the presence of an uplifted knife." The law does, however, place certain limits on what can be deemed reasonable. For example, the defender's belief must have related to immediate harm. One cannot respond with . . . force presently because he believes his assailant intends to ambush him several hours from now. The law also requires that the defender be in reasonable fear of possible death or serious bodily injury [to use deadly force.] If he fears no more than minor injuries, he cannot use deadly force. One who feels that the attacker will do no more than knock him to the ground cannot respond with deadly force simply because he does not want to suffer any kind of humiliation or injury. On the other hand, if he reasonably fears that the attacker will break his bones or disfigure him, this is sufficient without actually fearing death. Deadly force (i.e., force readily capable of causing death) can be used to respond to a serious bodily injury as well as loss of life.

The second factor in evaluating a self-defense claim--the opportunity to retreat in safety--is given somewhat different treatment in different states. In some jurisdictions, there is no special rule on retreat. On the one hand, the courts have said that there is no absolute duty to escape danger by retreating; the law will not require a non-aggressor to act in a humiliating or cowardly way. On the other hand, the judge or jury is not barred from considering the possibility of retreat as one of the many factors examined in determining the reasonableness of the defender's decision to use deadly force. Thus, under this approach, the significance of opportunity to retreat will vary with the facts of the particular case and the weight of the other circumstances supporting the reasonable use of deadly force, but the failure to retreat will not, by itself, automatically negate a claim of self-defense. Moreover, the possibility of retreat is given no weight whatsoever unless the retreat clearly could be accomplished with complete safety. Thus, retreat rarely is a factor when the attacker threatens the defender with a weapon such as a gun. No matter how fast the defender can flee, he is unlikely to be able to escape from such a threat with complete safety.

A majority of jurisdictions today, following the lead of the Model Code, have imposed an absolute requirement of retreat under some circumstances. These states reason that, though the defender is not at fault, the embarrassment he suffers in being forced to retreat is a small price to pay for saving the life that he otherwise would have to take. They accordingly hold that if the defender could have avoided the threat to himself with complete safety by retreating, and knew that he could do so, then his use of deadly force cannot be justified on the ground of self-defense. These jurisdictions do recognize certain exceptions to this rule, however. A defender is not forced to retreat from his home. At least in this respect, a man's home is still his castle and he cannot be forced to flee it by an attacker. In some jurisdictions, this exception has been carried to the defender's place of business, except where the attacker was a fellow employee who also had a right to be on the premises.

If the defender in a particular case originally was an aggressor—the initiator of the fight that resulted in the homicide—then a duty of withdrawal may make the availability of self-defense even more complex. To be an aggressor, a person ordinarily must deliver the first blow or directly challenge his opponent to fight. Simply using foul language or otherwise starting a verbal dispute is not sufficient. If the aggressor initiates the dispute with deadly force, then he ordinarily cannot reclaim a right of self-defense unless he effectively withdraws from his original position as an aggressor. In some jurisdictions, he can do this only by getting across to his opponent the message that he no longer desires to fight. In others, a reasonable attempt to communicate such a message is sufficient even if the other party refuses to recognize it. Once withdrawal is achieved, if the other party persists in the battle, the former aggressor now has a restored right of self-defense. If the aggressor began the battle using non-deadly force, then he may not have to communicate his withdrawal although he may bear some special burdens in claiming self-defense. Since he limited his aggression to non-deadly force, his opponent should not have escalated to the use of deadly force. Both he and his opponent are at fault, and a completed withdrawal therefore may not be needed to restore the right of self-defense. However, the defender still has a special responsibility as the person who started it all, and he therefore may be required to retreat (when physically possible) even in a state that ordinarily does not require retreat. Moreover, in the case of the aggressor, that duty to retreat may include retreat from the home. Kerper, *supra* at 135

The trend has been for states to reject the common law doctrine requiring persons to retreat before meeting force with force. Instead laws now permit individuals to stand their ground and use any force reasonably necessary to prevent harm. Many courts adopted the retreat rule but recognize a "castle exception" to the rule. The castle exception allows individuals to stand their ground (and not retreat) when they are faced with imminent, unlawful force in their homes--even when they could retreat safely. Domestic assault scenarios where both parties are "at home" and neither party has a duty to retreat raise interesting questions for the courts. A few courts have held that the castle exception is inapplicable in domestic violence situations where the assailant and defendant were both residents of the dwelling. However, the majority position (in states with a retreat rule) is to require retreat even in those cases.

Model Penal Code And Self-Defense

The MPC §3.04 (1) provides a justification for the use of self-defense stating, "the use of force upon or toward another person is justifiable when the actor believes that such force is immediately necessary for the purpose of protecting himself against the use of unlawful force by such other person on the present occasion." The MPC puts some restrictions on this justification in paragraph (2).[26]

---

[26] (2) Limitations on Justifying Necessity for Use of Force.

(a) The use of force is not justifiable under this Section:

(i) to resist an arrest that the actor knows is being made by a peace officer, although the arrest is unlawful; or

(ii) to resist force used by the occupier or possessor of property by another person on his behalf, where the actor knows that the person using the force is doing so under a claim of right to protect the property, except that this limitation shall not apply if:

(A) the actor is a public officer acting in the performance of his duties or a person lawfully assisting him therein or a person making or assisting in a lawful arrest; or

(B) the actor has been unlawfully dispossessed of the property and is making a re-entry or reception justified by Section 3.06; or

(C) the actor believes that such force is necessary to protect himself against death or serious bodily injury.

UNITED STATES v. PETERSON,
483 F.2d 1222 (D.C. Cir. 1973)
I

SPOTTSWOOD W. ROBINSON, III, Circuit Judge.

The events immediately preceding the homicide are not seriously in dispute. The version presented by the Government's evidence follows. Charles Keitt, the deceased, and two friends drove in Keitt's car to the alley in the rear of Peterson's house to remove the windshield wipers from the latter's wrecked car. While Keitt was doing so, Peterson came out of the house into the back yard to protest. After a verbal exchange, Peterson went back into the house, obtained a pistol, and returned to the yard. In the meantime, Keitt had reseated himself in his car, and he and his companions were about to leave.

Upon his reappearance in the yard, Peterson paused briefly to load the pistol. "If you move," he shouted to Keitt, "I will shoot." He walked to a point in the yard slightly inside a gate in the rear fence and, pistol in hand, said, "If you come in here I will kill you." Keitt alighted from his car, took a few steps toward Peterson and exclaimed, "What the hell do you think you are going to do with that?" Keitt then made an about-face, walked back to his car and got a lug wrench. With the wrench in a raised position, Keitt advanced toward Peterson, who stood with the pistol pointed toward him. Peterson warned Keitt not to "take another step" and,

when Keitt continued onward shot him in the face from a distance of about ten feet. Death was apparently instantaneous. Shortly thereafter, Peterson left home and was apprehended 20-odd blocks away.

This description of the fatal episode was furnished at Peterson's trial by four witnesses for the Government. Peterson did not testify or offer any evidence, but the Government introduced a statement which he had given the police after his arrest, in which he related a somewhat different version. Keitt had removed objects from his car before, and on the day of the shooting he had told Keitt not to do so. After the initial verbal altercation, Keitt went to his car for the lug wrench, so he, Peterson, went into his house for his pistol. When Keitt was about ten feet away, he pointed the pistol "away of his right shoulder;" adding that Keitt was running toward him, Peterson said he "got scared and fired the gun. He ran right into the bullet." "I did not mean to shoot him," Peterson insisted, "I just wanted to scare him."

At trial, Peterson moved for a judgment of acquittal on the ground that as a matter of law the evidence was insufficient to support a conviction. The trial judge denied the motion. After receiving instructions which in two respects are challenged here, the jury returned a verdict finding Peterson guilty of manslaughter. Judgment was entered

---

(b) The use of deadly force is not justifiable under this Section unless the actor believes that such force is necessary to protect himself against death, serious bodily injury, kidnapping or sexual intercourse compelled by force or threat; nor is it justifiable if:

(i) the actor, with the purpose of causing death or serious bodily injury, provoked the use of force against himself in the same encounter; or

(ii) the actor knows that he can avoid the necessity of using such force with complete safety by retreating or by surrendering possession of a thing to a person asserting a claim of right thereto or by complying with a demand that he abstain from any action that he has no duty to take except that:

(A) the actor is not obliged to retreat from his dwelling or place of work, unless he was the initial aggressor or is assailed in his place of work by another person whose place of work the actor knows it to be; and

(B) a public officer justified in using force in the performance of his duties or a person justified in using force in his assistance or a person justified in using force in making an arrest or preventing an escape is not obliged to desist from efforts to perform such a duty, effect such arrest or prevent such escape because of the resistance or threatened resistance by or on behalf of the person against whom such action is directed.

(c) Except as required by paragraphs (a) and (b) of this Subsection, a person employing protective force may estimate the necessity thereof under the circumstances as he believes them to be when the force is used, without retreating, surrendering possession, doing any other act that he has no legal duty to do or abstaining from any lawful action.

conformably with the verdict, and this appeal followed.

II

III

Peterson's consistent position is that as a matter of law his conviction of manslaughter — alleviated homicide — was wrong, and that his act was one of self-preservation — excused homicide. The Government, on the other hand, has contended from the beginning that Keitt's slaying fell outside the bounds of lawful self-defense. The questions remaining for our decision inevitably track back to this basic dispute.

Self-defense, as a doctrine legally exonerating the taking of human life, is as viable now as it was in Blackstone's time, and in the case before us the doctrine is invoked in its purest form. But "[t]he law of self-defense is a law of necessity;" the right of self-defense arises only when the necessity begins, and equally ends with the necessity; and never must the necessity be greater than when the force employed defensively is deadly. The "necessity must bear all semblance of reality, and appear to admit of no other alternative, before taking life will be justifiable as excusable." Hinged on the exigencies of self-preservation, the doctrine of homicidal self-defense emerges from the body of the criminal law as a limited though important exception to legal outlawry of the arena of self-help in the settlement of potentially fatal personal conflicts.

So it is that necessity is the pervasive theme of the well defined conditions which the law imposes on the right to kill or maim in self-defense. There must have been a threat, actual or apparent, of the use of deadly force against the defender. The threat must have been unlawful and immediate. The defender must have believed that he was in imminent peril of death or serious bodily harm, and that his response was necessary to save himself therefrom. These beliefs must not only have been honestly entertained, but also objectively reasonable in light of the surrounding circumstances It is clear that no less than a concurrence of these elements will suffice.

Here the parties' opposing contentions focus on the roles of two further considerations. One is the provoking of the confrontation by the defender. The other is the defendant's failure to utilize a safe route for retreat from the confrontation. The essential inquiry. . . is whether and to what extent the rule of necessity may translate these considerations into additional factors in the equation. To these questions. . . we now proceed.

V

The trial judge's charge authorized the jury, as it might be persuaded, to convict Peterson of second-degree murder or manslaughter, or to acquit by reason of self-defense. On the latter phase of the case, the judge instructed that with evidence of self-defense present, the Government bore the burden of proving beyond a reasonable doubt that Peterson did not act in self-defense; and that if the jury had a reasonable doubt as to whether Peterson acted in self-defense, the verdict must be not guilty. The judge further instructed that the circumstances under which Peterson acted, however, must have been such as to produce a reasonable belief that Keitt was then about to kill him or do him serious bodily harm, and that deadly force was necessary to repel him. In determining whether Peterson used excessive force in defending himself, the judge said, the jury could consider all of the circumstances under which he acted.

These features of the charge met Peterson's approval, and we are not summoned to pass on them. There were, however, two other aspects of the charge to which Peterson objected, and which are now the subject of vigorous controversy. The first of Peterson's complaints centers upon an instruction that the right to use deadly force in self-defense is not ordinarily available to one who provokes a conflict or is the aggressor in it. Mere words, the judge explained, do not constitute provocation or aggression; and if Peterson precipitated the altercation but thereafter withdrew from it in good faith and so informed Keitt by words or acts, he was justified in using deadly force to save himself from imminent danger or death or grave bodily harm. And, the judge added, even if Keitt was the aggressor and Peterson was justified in defending himself, he was not entitled to use any greater force than he had reasonable ground to believe and actually believed to be necessary for that purpose. Peterson contends that there was no evidence that he either caused or contributed to the conflict, and that the instructions on that topic could only misled the jury.

It has long been accepted that one cannot support a claim of self-defense by a self-generated necessity to kill. The right of homicidal self-defense is granted only to those free from fault in the difficulty; it is denied to slayers who incite the fatal attack, encourage the fatal quarrel or otherwise promote the necessitous occasion for taking life. The fact that the deceased struck the first blow, fired the first shot or made the first menacing gesture does not legalize the self-defense claim if in fact the claimant was the actual provoker. In sum, one who is the aggressor in a conflict culminating in death cannot invoke the necessities of self-preservation. Only in the event that he communicates to his adversary his intent to withdraw and in good faith attempts to do so is he restored to his right of self-defense.

. . . [K]illing in self-defense is excusable only as a matter of genuine necessity. Quite obviously, a defensive killing is unnecessary if the occasion for it could have been averted, and the roots of that consideration run deep with us. A half-century ago, in *Laney v. United States*, this court declared that, before a person can avail himself of the plea of self-defense against the charge of homicide, he must do everything in his power, consistent with his safety, to avoid the danger and avoid the necessity of taking life. If one has reason to believe that he will be attacked, in a manner which threatens him with bodily injury, he must avoid the attack if it is possible to do so, and the right of self-defense does not arise until he has done everything in his power to prevent its necessity.

....

In the case at bar, the trial judge's charge fully comported with these governing principles. The remaining question, then, is whether there was evidence to make them applicable to the case. A recapitulation of the proofs shows beyond peradventure that there was.

It was not until Peterson fetched his pistol and returned to his back yard that his confrontation with Keitt took on a deadly cast. Prior to his trip into the house for the gun, there was, by the Government's evidence, no threat, no display of weapons, no combat. There was an exchange of verbal aspersions and a misdemeanor against Peterson's property was in progress but, at this juncture, nothing more. Even if Peterson's post-arrest version of the initial encounter were accepted — his claim that Keitt went for the lug wrench before he armed himself — the events which followed bore heavily on the question as to who the real aggressor was.

The evidence is uncontradicted that when Peterson reappeared in the yard with his pistol, Keitt was about to depart the scene. Richard Hilliard testified that after the first argument, Keitt reentered his car and said "Let's go." This statement was verified by Ricky Gray, who testified that Keitt "got in the car and ... they were getting ready to go;" he, too, heard Keitt give the direction to start the car. The uncontroverted fact that Keitt was leaving shows plainly that so far as he was concerned the confrontation was ended. It demonstrates just as plainly that even if he had previously been the aggressor, he no longer was.

Not so with Peterson, however, as the undisputed evidence made clear. Emerging from the house with the pistol, he paused in the yard to load it, land to command Keitt not to move. He then walked through the yard to the rear gate and, displaying his pistol, dared Keitt to come in, and threatened to kill him if he did. While there appears to be no fixed rule on the subject, the cases hold, and we agree, that an affirmative unlawful act reasonably calculated to produce an affray foreboding injurious or fatal consequences is an aggression which, unless renounced, nullifies the right of homicidal self-defense. We cannot escape the abiding conviction that the jury could readily find Peterson's challenge to be a transgression of that character.

....

… We think the evidence plainly presented an issue of fact as to whether Peterson's conduct was an invitation to and provocation of the encounter which ended in the fatal shot. We sustain the trial judge's action in remitting that issue for the jury's determination.

V

The second aspect of the trial judge's charge as to which Peterson asserts error concerned the undisputed fact that at no time did Peterson endeavor to retreat from Keitt's approach with the lug wrench. The judge instructed the jury that if Peterson had reasonable grounds to believe and did believe that he was in imminent danger of death or serious injury, and that deadly force was necessary to repel the danger, he was required neither to retreat nor to consider whether he could safely retreat. Rather, said the judge, Peterson was entitled to stand his ground and use such force as was reasonably necessary under the circumstances to save his life and his person from pernicious bodily harm. But, the judge continued, if Peterson could have safely retreated but did not do so, that failure was a circumstance which the jury might consider, together with all others, in determining whether he went further in repelling the danger, real or apparent, than he was justified in going.

Peterson contends that this imputation of an obligation to retreat was error, even if he could safely have done so. He points out that at the time of the shooting he was standing in his own yard, and argues he was under no duty to move. We are persuaded to the conclusion that in the circumstances presented here, the trial judge did not err in giving the instruction challenged.

Within the common law of self-defense there developed the rule of "retreat to the wall," which ordinarily forbade the use of deadly force by one to whom an avenue for safe retreat was open. This doctrine was but an application of the requirement of strict necessity to excuse the taking of human life, and was designed to insure the existence of that necessity. Even the innocent victim of a vicious assault had to elect a safe retreat, if available, rather than resort to defensive force which might kill or seriously injure.

In a majority of American jurisdictions, contrarily to the common law rule, one may stand his ground and use deadly force whenever it seems reasonably necessary to save himself. While the law of the District of Columbia on this point is not entirely clear, it seems allied with the strong minority adhering to the common law. In 1856, the District of

Columbia Criminal Court ruled that a participant in an affray "must endeavor to retreat, ... that is, he is obliged to retreat, if he can safely." The court added that "[a] man may, to be sure, decline a combat when there is no existing or apparent danger, but the retreat to which the law binds him is that which is the consequence." In a much later era this court, adverting to necessity as the soul of homicidal self-defense, declared that "no necessity for killing an assailant can exist, so long as there is a safe way open to escape the conflict." Moreover, the common law rule of strict necessity pervades the District concept of pernicious self-defense, and we cannot ignore the inherent inconsistency of an absolute no-retreat rule. Until such time as the District law on the subject may become more definitive, we accept these precedents as ample indication that the doctrine of retreat persists.

That is not to say that the retreat rule is without exceptions. Even at common law it was recognized that it was not completely suited to all situations. Today it is the more so that its precept must be adjusted to modern conditions nonexistent during the early development of the common law of self-defense. One restriction on its operation comes to the fore when the circumstances apparently foreclose a withdrawal with safety. The doctrine of retreat was never intended to enhance the risk to the innocent; its proper application has never required a faultless victim to increase his assailant's safety at the expense of his own. On the contrary, he could stand his ground and use deadly force otherwise appropriate if the alternative were perilous, or if to him it reasonably appeared to be. A slight variant of the same consideration is the principle that there is no duty to retreat from an assault producing an imminent danger of death or grievous bodily harm. "Detached reflection cannot be demanded in the presence of an uplifted knife," nor is it "a condition of immunity that one in that situation should pause to consider whether a reasonable man might not think it possible to fly with safety or to disable his assailant rather than to kill him."

The trial judge's charge to the jury incorporated each of these limitations on the retreat rule. Peterson, however, invokes another — the so-called "castle" doctrine. It is well settled that one who through no fault of his own is attacked in his home is under no duty to retreat therefrom. The oft-repeated expression that "a man's home is his castle" reflected the belief in olden days that there were few if any safer sanctuaries than the home. The "castle" exception, moreover, has been extended by some courts to encompass the occupant's presence within the curtilage outside his dwelling. Peterson reminds us that when he shot to halt Keitt's advance, he was standing in his yard and so, he argues, he had no duty to endeavor to retreat.

Despite the practically universal acceptance of the "castle" doctrine in American jurisdictions wherein the point has been raised, its status in the District of Columbia has never been squarely decided. But whatever the fate of the doctrine in the District law of the future, it is clear that in absolute form it was inapplicable here. The right of self-defense, we have said, cannot be claimed by the aggressor in an affray so long as he retains that unmitigated role. It logically follows that any rule of no-retreat which may protect an innocent victim of the affray would, like other incidents of a forfeited right of self-defense, be unavailable to the party who provokes or stimulates the conflict. Accordingly, the law is well settled that the "castle" doctrine can be invoked only by one who is without fault in bringing the conflict on. That, we think, is the critical consideration here.

We need not repeat our previous discussion of Peterson's contribution to the altercation which culminated in Keitt's death. It suffices to point out that by no interpretation of the evidence could it be said that Peterson was blameless in the affair. And while, of course, it was for the jury to assess the degree of fault the evidence well nigh dictated the conclusion that it was substantial.

The only reference in the trial judge's charge intimating an affirmative duty to retreat was the instruction that a failure to do so, when it could have been done safely, was a factor in the totality of the circumstances which the jury might consider in determining whether the force which he employed was excessive. We cannot believe that any jury was at all likely to view Peterson's conduct as irreproachable. We conclude that for one who, like Peterson, was hardly entitled to fall back on the "castle" doctrine of no retreat, that instruction cannot be just cause for complaint.

VI

As we have stated, Peterson moved for a judgment of acquittal at trial, and in this court renews his contention that the evidence was insufficient to support a conviction of manslaughter. His position is that the evidence, as a matter of law, established a right to use deadly force in self-defense. In considering that contention, we must accept the evidence "in the light most favorable to the Government, making full allowance for the right of the jury to draw justifiable inferences of fact from the evidence adduced at trial and to assess the credibility of the witnesses before it." We have already concluded that the evidence generated factual issues as to the effect, upon Peterson's self-defense claim, of his aggressive conduct and his failure to retreat. By the same token, the ultimate question of guilt or innocence of culpable homicide was one for the jury to decide. The jury resolved the question in favor of guilt, and we perceive no basis for disturbing its decision. Nor, in the circumstances here, is there a ground for impugning its verdict that the grade of Peterson's offense was manslaughter.

The judgment of conviction appealed from is accordingly. . . Affirmed.

STATE v. THOMAS,
673 N.E.2d 1339 (1997 Ohio)

FACTS
On September 15, 1993, Teresa Thomas, defendant-appellant, shot and killed Jerry Flowers, her live-in boyfriend. At her trial for murder, Thomas admitted to shooting Flowers, but asserted that she had shot Flowers in self-defense, basing the defense on the battered woman syndrome.

Thomas and Flowers had known each other for most of their lives when they first began dating two years prior to the shooting. By the end of 1991, Flowers and Thomas began living together. In July 1993, they moved into a new mobile home.

Thomas testified that the relationship was marked by violence and intimidation, including incidents of Flowers pushing her against a wall, injuring her shoulder enough for her to go to the emergency room, and punching her in the abdomen, rupturing an ovarian cyst. She stated that he would purposely soil his clothes and then order her to clean them. He controlled the couple's money, and eventually ordered Thomas to quit her jobs. He did virtually all of the grocery shopping. On the two occasions when he permitted her to do the shopping, he required her to present to him the receipt and the exact change. At times, he would deny her food for three to four days. He also blamed his sexual difficulties on her.

Approximately three weeks before the shooting, Flowers's behavior became more egregious. In the middle of the night, almost every night, he would wake Thomas up by holding his hands over her mouth and nose so that she could not breathe. Flowers had trouble sleeping and on several occasions accused Thomas of changing the time on the clocks. He often told her how easy it would be to kill her by snapping her neck, shooting her with a gun, or suffocating her, and then hiding her body in a cave. This discussion occurred almost every time they awoke.

Three days prior to the shooting, Thomas fixed a plate of food, which Flowers refused to eat or to let her clear from the table. He put cigarette butts in the food and played with it. Thomas testified that if she had cleaned up the food he would have beaten her.

Thomas testified that Flowers forced her into having sexual relations against her wishes, that he blamed her for his periodic impotency, and that two days prior to the shooting, he anally raped her.

The night before the shooting, Flowers yelled at Thomas and threw flour, sugar, cider, and bread on the floor. They argued all night, and before Flowers went to work on Wednesday morning, he ordered Thomas to clean up the mess, told her he would kill her if she did not do it by the time he came home, and struck her on the arm.

After he left, Thomas went to see her mother and they returned to Thomas's and Flowers's mobile home. Thomas testified that her mother seemed entirely uninterested in Thomas's situation. When Thomas's mother left, Thomas went to see Flowers's father, and then she returned to her mobile home. Thomas started to clean up the kitchen but stopped to eat a sandwich, sitting at the kitchen table.

At 12:45 p.m., Flowers came home from work early and, according to Thomas, he sneaked to the mobile home so that she wouldn't see him. She did see him, however, and when she did not get up to meet him at the door, he started yelling. When Flowers moved to the kitchen door, Thomas ran to the bathroom. Thomas testified that she could not get out of the tiny bathroom window and that she was afraid that Flowers was going to kill her.

She then ran to Flowers's closet and grabbed his gun out of the holster. She ran back to the kitchen and Flowers continued to yell at her and threaten to kill her. According to Thomas, she fired two warning shots and when Flowers continued to threaten her, she shot him in the arm twice. Each of these two bullets also entered his torso. Flowers fell and then started to get up again, continuing to threaten Thomas. Thomas shot Flowers two more times, while he was bent over; the shots entered Flowers in the back.

Dr. Larry Tate, a pathologist with the Franklin County Coroner's Office, testified that Flowers had two bullet wounds in the arm, one in the chest, one in the abdomen, and two in the back. In support of her self-defense argument, Thomas presented the testimony of Dr. Jill Bley, a clinical psychologist who has extensive experience in treating and diagnosing women with the battered woman syndrome. Dr. Bley explained the classic symptoms and signs of the battered woman syndrome and then described her examination of Thomas. Dr. Bley stated that she diagnosed Thomas as suffering from the battered woman syndrome and that Thomas reasonably believed that Thomas was in danger of imminent death or serious bodily harm at the time of the shooting.

On September 22, 1993, the grand jury indicted

Thomas for aggravated murder, a violation of R.C. 2903.01(A), with a firearm specification, a violation of R.C. 2941.141. From December 7 through 17, 1993, the case was tried to a jury. At the close of the state's case in chief, Thomas moved for an acquittal. The court denied the motion in part, but finding that the element of "prior calculation and design" had not been proved, dismissed the charge of aggravated murder, allowing the case to proceed on the lesser included charge of murder with a firearm specification, in violation of R.C. 2903.02(A) and 2941.141. On December 20, 1993, the jury found Thomas guilty of murder with a firearm specification.

Upon appeal, Thomas argued that the trial court erred by not instructing the jury that she had no duty to retreat from a cohabitant and that the court's instructions to the jury on the battered woman syndrome were incomplete. The court of appeals affirmed the conviction. The cause is now before this court pursuant to the allowance of a discretionary appeal in case No. 95-1837.

ALICE ROBIE RESNICK, Justice.

This case presents issues involving the duty to retreat between cohabitants and jury instructions in trials in which the criminal defendant asserts the battered woman syndrome as support for the defense of self-defense.

I

We first consider whether there is a duty to retreat when one is attacked in one's own home by a cohabitant with an equal right to be in the home. In Ohio, the affirmative defense of self-defense has three elements:

(1) the defendant was not at fault in creating the violent situation,
(2) the defendant had a bona fide belief that she was in imminent danger of death or great bodily harm and that her only means of escape was the use of force, and
(3) that the defendant did not violate any duty to retreat or avoid the danger.

Because of the third element, in most cases, a person may not kill in self-defense if he has available a reasonable means of retreat from the

confrontation. This requirement derives from the common-law rule that the right to kill in self-defense may be exercised only if the person assaulted attempted to "retreat to the wall" whenever possible.

However, there is no duty to retreat when one is assaulted in one's own home. This exception to the duty to retreat derives from the doctrine that one's home is one's castle and one has a right to protect it and those within it from intrusion or attack. The rationale is that a person in her own home has already retreated "to the wall," as there is no place to which she can further flee in safety. Thus, a person who, through no fault of her own, is assaulted in her home may stand her ground, meet force with force, and if necessary, kill her assailant, without any duty to retreat.

In Ohio, one is not required to retreat from one's own home when attacked by an intruder; similarly one should not be required to retreat when attacked by a cohabitant in order to claim self-defense. Moreover, in the case of domestic violence, as in this case, the attacks are often repeated over time, and escape from the home is rarely possible without the threat of great personal violence or death. The victims of such attacks have already "retreated to the wall" many times over and therefore should not be required as victims of domestic violence to attempt to flee to safety before being able to claim the affirmative defense of self-defense.

There is no rational reason for a distinction between an intruder and a cohabitant when considering the policy for preserving human life where the setting is the domicile, and, accordingly, we hold that there is no duty to retreat from one's own home before resorting to lethal force in self-defense against a cohabitant with an equal right to be in the home.

II

We next consider the issue of whether, when a defendant presents the defense of self-defense based on the theory of the battered woman syndrome, the judge's instructions to the jury regarding self-defense must include a detailed definition of the syndrome. The trial court did not include in the jury charge the defendant's proposed instruction that would define battered women as those women in intimate relationships that have gone through the battering cycle at least twice. The defendant's proposed instructions would further state that if the cycle occurs a second time and the victims remain in the situation, they are defined as battered women.

As stated above, the second element of the affirmative defense of self-defense requires the defendant to prove that she had a bona fide [honest] belief that she was in imminent danger of death or great bodily harm and that her only means of escape was the use of force.

The trial court's instructions correctly emphasized to the jury that the second element of self-defense is a combined subjective and objective test. Self-defense is placed on the grounds of the *bona fides* of defendant's belief, and reasonableness therefor, and whether, under the circumstances, he exercised a careful and proper use of his own faculties. The jury instructions given by the trial court properly instructed the jury to consider all the circumstances when determining if appellant had an objectively reasonable belief of imminent danger and whether she subjectively honestly believed she was in danger of imminent harm.

Accordingly, we reverse the court of appeals as to the duty to retreat between cohabitants and affirm as to the jury instruction regarding the battered woman syndrome.

Judgment reversed in part and affirmed in part.

STRATTON, J., concurring

This case poses a troubling issue of a balancing of societal interests. There are strong public policies for preserving the sanctity of life on one hand and, on the other hand, for allowing one to protect oneself from harm in one's own home.

However, the issues involved in domestic violence complicate any attempt to consider a duty to retreat from one's own home. Domestic violence is the result of the abuser's need to dominate and control. Often the risk of violence against a woman is heightened when she attempts to *leave* the abusive relationship. Research demonstrates that the battered woman's attempt to retreat often increases the

immediate danger to herself. Statistics show that a woman is at the greatest risk of death when she attempts to leave a relationship. The abuser may perceive his mate's withdrawal, either emotionally or physically, as a loss of his dominance and control over her, which results in an escalation of his rage and more violence.

PFEIFER, Justice, dissenting.

The sanctity of human life must pervade the law. Accordingly, a cohabitant should be required to attempt to retreat before resorting to lethal force in self-defense against another cohabitant. I respectfully dissent.

There are dramatically more opportunities for deadly violence in the domestic setting than in the intrusion setting. Thus, to hold that cohabitants do not have to retreat before resorting to lethal force is to invite violence. Cohabitants should be required to retreat before resorting to lethal force in self-defense whenever it can be done safely. Such a duty would encompass leaving the home if that is necessary to prevent the destruction of life. It would also encompass retreating to the wall.

Finally, whatever you think about the first four shots, it is unconscionable to suggest that the last two shots were fired in self-defense. The law of self-defense has hitherto always been a shield. In this case, the majority is allowing the defendant to use the law of self-defense as a sword. I dissent.

COOK, Justice, dissenting.

I respectfully dissent. Contrary to the fears expressed by the majority and concurring opinions, imposing the duty to retreat upon cohabitants would not leave the occupant of a home defenseless from attacks. First, a person is relieved of the duty where there is no reasonable or safe means to avoid the confrontation. Accordingly, the use of deadly force is justified and the failure to retreat is of no consequence where retreat would increase the actor's own danger of death or great bodily harm.

For these reasons, I would hold that a person assaulted by another cohabitant in the home is obliged to "retreat to the wall" before defending with deadly force, provided that a reasonable and safe means of avoiding the danger exists.

New Stand Your Ground Laws

Arizona, Colorado, and Texas had previously enacted, "Make My Day" statutes allowing the use of deadly force in defense of habitation. In 2005, Florida went even futher and enacted a new law significantly expanding the right of self-defense for individuals. This law allows individuals to use deadly force in public places without the duty to retreat. The difference between the Florida "stand your ground" statute and the common law "castle exception" is that the Florida law does away with the need to retreat not just in one's home but also in public. Significantly, and problematically, Florida's law states that when a person claims to have used force in self-defense, the police may not arrest, detain, or initiate prosecution against them. Additionally, the person against whom they used force is prohibited from suing them civilly. Critics of the new law dubbed it the "shoot first" law and predicted it would lead to preemptive shootings. This law has been controversial and presents difficulty for law enforcement officers. Nevertheless, by 2009 twenty-five states had adopted some form of "stand your ground" laws.

Battered Woman's Syndrome And Self-Defense

Self-defense claims frequently arise in cases where a woman kills her partner or spouse after ongoing battering and abuse. When relationships involve constant, ongoing abuse with high levels of violence, victims are in "present danger" but may not necessarily be in imminent danger. Because the offender may strike out at any time, the victim lives in constant fear of unlawful harm. Courts generally apply the same rules of self-defense requiring proof of imminent harm in these situations, but they have increasingly attempted to allow defendants a fair chance to assert self-defense claims by presenting evidence on battered woman's syndrome. Still, even almost forty years since the first use of the battered woman syndrome defense, only two states have relaxed the requirement that the threat must be imminent and not just ever-present. Although most courts now admit expert testimony concerning battered woman syndrome, they limit the testimony to showing why the defendant, as the victim of ongoing assaults, simply did not leave the abuser rather than result to violence. The court may allow the syndrome evidence to explain why the defendant had a genuine and reasonable fear of imminent danger. But courts have not allowed evidence of ongoing violence to substitute for proof that the defendant was faced with an attack that required an immediate use of force to repel. Emanuel notes, "In these clearly non-confrontational situations, the defendant generally loses." Typically, trial judges either do not give the jury a self-defense instruction or they give one that makes it clear that the defense only applied if physical danger was imminent. These trial courts' refusals to give instructions are rarely reversed by the appellate courts.

STATE v. STEWART,
763 P.2d. 572 (Kans. 1988)

FACTS (Summarized)

Mike Stewart married Peggy Stewart, the defendant, in 1974 and subjected her and her two daughters, and one daughter, Carla, in particular to horrendous and consistent abuse over a long period of time. His violence and intimidation escalated over time; he abused drug and alcohol, beat Peggy with a bat, shot one of the pets, held a gun against Peggy's head and threatened to pull the trigger. Peggy had told friends that Mike would probably make good on his threat to blow off her head with a shot gun. Peggy ran away in 1986 to Oklahoma; was hospitalized for toxic psychosis, and so

Mike found her. He came to Oklahoma to the hospital to take her home. He drove Peggy back to Kansas, threatening to kill her if she ever ran away again; as soon as they arrived at the house, he forced her into the house and forced her to have oral sex several times. The next day, Peggy discovered a loaded .357 magnum. She hid the gun under the mattress of the bed in the spare room because, as she testified, she was afraid of it. As she cleaned the house, Mike stated that she should not bother because she would not be there for long. She testified she was afraid he was going to kill her. That night, Mike went to sleep around 8:00 p.m., and Peggy thought about suicide, she testified hearing voices in her head repeating "kill or be killed." At 10:00 p.m., she went to the spare room, retrieved the gun, walked back to the bedroom, and shot and killed Mike as he slept. At trial experts testified that Peggy was suffering from battered women syndrome and Post-traumatic stress syndrome. One psychologist testified that Peggy had repressed knowledge that she was in grave lethal situation (due to Mike's preparing to escalate the violence in retaliation for her running away, the loaded guns, veiled threats, and increased sexual demands which were indicators of the escalation of the cycle of violence). The state's psychiatrist did not believe in the batter woman syndrome, learned helplessness about why women don't leave, he did not believe that repeated demands for oral sex were sufficient to trigger post-traumatic stress disorder; he also discredited her diagnosis of toxic psychosis. At defense counsel request, judge gave self-defense instruction, and the jury found Peggy not guilty.

[Although state cannot appeal an adverse decision (not guilty finding), the government can appeal and ask for a legal determination – this does not overturn Peggy's acquittal — and will only be used for future clarification. The Appellate court discussed the elements of self-defense law in Kansas.]

OPINION

The traditional concept of self-defense has posited onetime conflicts between persons of somewhat equal size and strength. When the defendant claiming self-defense is a victim of long-term domestic violence, such as a battered spouse, such traditional concepts may not apply. Because of the prior history of abuse, and the difference in strength and size between the abused and the abuser, the accused in such cases may choose to defend during a momentary lull in the abuse, rather than during a conflict. However, in order to warrant the giving of a self-defense instruction, the facts of the case must still show that the spouse was in imminent danger close to the time of the killing.

A person is justified in using force against an aggressor when it appears to that person and he or she reasonably believes such force to be necessary. A reasonable belief implies both an honest belief and the existence of facts which would persuade a reasonable person to that belief.. A self-defense instruction must be given if there is any evidence to support a claim of self-defense, even if that evidence consists solely of the defendant's testimony.

Where self-defense is asserted, evidence of the deceased's long-term cruelty and violence towards the defendant is admissible. In cases involving battered spouses, expert evidence of the battered woman syndrome is relevant to a determination of the reasonableness of the defendant's perception of danger.

In order to instruct a jury on self-defense, there must be some showing of an imminent threat or a confrontational circumstance involving an overt act by an aggressor. There is no exception to this requirement where the defendant has suffered long-term domestic abuse and the victim is the abuser. In such cases, the issue is not whether the defendant believes homicide is the solution to past or future problems with the batterer, but rather whether circumstances surrounding the killing were sufficient to create a reasonable belief in the defendant that the use of deadly force was necessary.

. . .

Here. . . . there is an absence of imminent danger to the defendant."

Other Cases – Self-Defense

State v. Good, 1006 (1917).
Son threatened to shoot his father with a shotgun. The father went to a neighbor's, borrowed the neighbor's shotgun and came back. Son told dad to "stop.". When the father shot, the son turned and ran and the dad pursued him. The son then turned and shot his father, killing him. Trial court refused to give jury the instruction concerning withdrawal, and the Supreme Court of Missouri reversed holding that the judge's instruction "ignores and excludes the defendant's right of self-defense. Although he may have brought on the difficulty with the intent to kill his father, still, if he was attempting to withdraw from the difficulty, and was fleeing from his father in good faith for the purpose of such withdrawal, and his father, knowing that defendant was endeavoring

to withdraw from such a conflict, pursued defendant and sought to kill him, or do him some great bodily harm, the defendant's right of self-defense revived."

Harshaw v. State, 39 S.W.3d 753 (Ark. 2001).
Defendant acting in an honest, but unreasonable belief is entitled to claim imperfect self-defense. Defendant and deceased were arguing and deceased threatened to get his gun. They both retreated to their cars, and the defendant grabbed his shotgun in time to shoot the deceased as he was reaching in his car. Arkansas Supreme Court held that the trial court should have instructed the jury on manslaughter because the jurors could have reasonably found that Harshaw acted "hastily and without due care" and that he merited a conviction for manslaughter rather than murder. (Note, imperfect defenses are ones in which the defendant may not totally evade liability, but will instead be able to be convicted on a lesser charge. Manslaughter differs from murder in that it does not require a finding of "malice aforethought."

State v. Norman, 378 N.E. 2d 8 (NC 1989).
This was a case of egregious domestic violence. The North Carolina Supreme Court overruled the court of appeals which had held that the trial court had improperly declined to instruct the jury on self-defense. The supreme court ruled that the evidence did not "tend to show that the defendant reasonably believe that she was confronted by a threat of imminent death or great bodily harm." The court noted that if it adopted a relaxed requirement for self-defense this would legalize the opportune killing of abusive husbands by their wives solely on the basis of the wives' subjective speculation as the probability of future felonious assaults by their husbands.

State v. Hundley, 693 P.2d 475 (Kans. 1985).
Another case of egregious domestic violence. On the night defendant shot her abusive victim he had come to her hotel room, raped her, threatened her, choked her, hit her, forced her to shower with him, thrown a beer bottle at her, and continued threatening her with beer bottles (he had hit her many times with beer bottles). When defendant pointed a gun at him and told him to leave, he said "You are dead bitch, now. He reached for a beer bottle, turning his back to her, and she closed her eyes and fired again. She had not been physically blocked from going to the door. The question for the court was whether the jury could consider his past violence toward her. The Kansas Supreme Court stated,

"This is a textbook case of the battered wife, which is psychologically similar to hostage and prisoner of war cases . . . Battered women are terror stricken people whose mental state is distorted and bears a marked resemblance ot that of a hostage or prisoner of war. The horrible beatings they are subjected to brainwash the into believing there is nothing they can do. They live in constant fear of another eruption of violence. They become disturbed persons from the torture.

. . . An aggressor who is customarily armed and gets involved in a fight may present an imminent danger, justifying the use of force in self-defense, even though the aggressor is unarmed on the occasion. In other words, the law of self-defense recognizes one may reasonably fear danger but be mistaken."

State v. Janes, 850 P.2d495 (Wash. 1993).
Defendant was a 17-year-old who had been abandoned by his alcoholic father at age 7 and had endured 10 years of horrific abuse at the hands of his mother's boyfriend. He had been beaten with a belt and a wire hanger, hit in the mouth with a mop, punched in the face for failing to do his homework, knocked out by a piece of firewood, subject to frequent verbal threats, physical threats including threats to nail his hands to a tree, brand his forehead, break his fingers, be hit in the head with a hammer. Defendant shot the boyfriend twice as he walked into the home after work.. The night before the boyfriend had yelled at the defendant and his mother, and spoke in low tones which were generally reserved for threats. Defendant's mom had warned him that the boyfriend was still mad that day, and after returning from school, defendant loaded the pistol, drank some whiskey and smoked marijuana. The trial court refused to instruct the jury to consider whether he was entitled to invoke self-defense.

Commonwealth v. Moreira, 447 NE2d 1224 (Mass, 1983).
This case discusses the traditional and modern view concerning whether an individual may claim self-defense when he or she uses force to resist an unlawful arrest. The court stated,

"Accordingly, we conclude that in the absence of excessive or unnecessary force by an arresting officer, a person may not use force to resist an arrest by one who he knows or has good reason to believe is an authorized police officer, engaged in the performance of his duties, regardless of whether the arrest was unlawful in the circumstances." . . . "Our conclusion does not apply to cases in which the police officer uses excessive force in his attempt to subdue the arrestee. In such a situation the disposition of the case depends on the application of the rules pertaining to self-defense. Thus, we conclude that where the officer uses excessive or unnecessary force to subdue the arrestee, regardless of whether the arrest Is lawful or unlawful, the arrestee ay defend himself by employing such force as reasonably appears to be necessary. Moreover, once the arrestee knows or reasonably should know that if he desists from using force in self-defense, the officer will cease using force, the arrestee must desist. Otherwise he will forfeit his defense."

State v. Shaw, 185 Conn. 382 (1981).

James Shaw, Jr. rented one of two bedrooms in Wilson's owner-occupied house. Off the kitchen of this house were doors leading to both bedrooms, to a bathroom, to the hallway, and to the back door-fire escape. Wilson called Shaw to the common area of the house, where a discussion escalated first to an argument and then a physical altercation. Each claimed that the other initiated the "tussle." Wilson went to his bedroom and grabbed his .30-30 Winchester rifle, intending to order Shaw to leave. Shaw went to his bedroom and got his .22 revolver. Weapons in hand, they both entered the kitchen from their bedrooms. Shaw fired five or six shots hitting Wilson three times. The court had to decide whether co-tenants have a duty to retreat when faced with force in their home. The court held that the law in Connecticut required co-tenants to retreat. It stated,

"The question before us is whether General Statutes § 53a-19 imposes a duty to retreat upon a person in his dwelling when threatened by another person who also dwells in the same place. We have not addressed this question …

When faced with the problem of violence between two persons entitled to occupancy of the same dwelling, American jurisdictions have gone both ways on the issue of a duty to retreat. The majority of jurisdictions have adopted the rule that there is no difference created by the status of the assailant: there is no duty to retreat in one's dwelling whether one's assailant be an intruder or a co-dweller.

The rationale behind the no-retreat jurisdictions... was inherited from those periods when retreat from one's dwelling was necessarily attended with increased peril. In a civilized country a person's leaving his dwelling does not automatically ordain that he is forsaking a place of safety for one wrought with danger....

In recognition of the demise of the solitary fortress and the great value of human life the drafters of the Restatement (Second) of Torts have adopted the minority view. "The privilege [to defend oneself against another by force intended or likely to cause death or serious bodily harm] exists although the actor correctly or reasonably believes that he can safely avoid the necessity of so defending himself by (a) retreating if he is attacked within his dwelling place, which is not also the dwelling place of the other .... The privilege ... does not exist ... in a place which is also the dwelling of the other...."

We adopt the co-dweller retreat rule. . . A minority of jurisdictions have long recognized it. This rule is in line with a policy favoring human life over the burden of retreating from the home, and the usual self-defense principles would still apply to allow defense at the wall or where retreat is impossible. In the great majority of homicides the killer and the victim are relatives or close acquaintances. We cannot conclude that the Connecticut legislature intended to sanction the reenactment of the climactic scene from "High Noon" in the familial kitchens of this state."

Howard v. United States, 656 A.2d 1106 (D.C. 1995),

This case examines whether defendant's belief about the amount of force and the imminency of the force was reasonable. "It is a question for the jury to satisfy itself of all the evidence in the case whether the defendant was in imminent and manifest danger either of losing his own life or suffering grievous bodily harm…. or that it appeared so to the mind of a reasonable man."

Defense of Others

At common law a person had the right to use reasonable force to either prevent the commission of a felony or to protect members of his or her household. Many jurisdictions have codified this "defense of others" defense.

States have adopted one of two approaches to this defense: the more recent and prevalent modern view—the reasonable perception approach or the traditional view—the alter ego approach. The reasonable perception approach allows a person to use force to defend another from what he or she reasonably believes is the unlawful and imminent use of force by a third person. Under this approach, the defendant should be found not guilty if the defendant erroneously, but reasonably, believed that the person they were protecting was justified in using force. The alter ego approach places the defender in the shoes of the person they are seeking to protect. Under this approach, the defendant should be found not guilty only if the person being aided or protected could lawfully use force to defend him or herself—the defendant's reasonable belief that the other is in danger is not sufficient. If the defender is wrong in believing the person being defended was entitled to use force, there is no defense.

Some states had limited the defendant's right to use deadly force to defend another to those cases where the defendant came to the defense of a person with whom he or she had a special protective relationship (e.g., spouse, child, relative, employee). The trend has been to permit the use of deadly force to protect any other person. As with self-defense, the degree of force must be proportional--a person defending the other can use deadly force only when he reasonably believes the other is in immediate danger of serious bodily harm. A person is not justified in using more force than is necessary to repel the unlawful force.

MPC §3.05 provides the defense of force in defense of others and adopts the reasonable perception approach—with a main difference: it uses a subjective standard. If the person believes his intervention is necessary, the MPC allows the defense; there is no requirement that such a belief be reasonable.[27]

STATE v. BEELEY,
653 A.2d 722 (1995)

MURRAY, Justice.   The record reveals that on Sunday, May 19,

---

[27] MPC § 3.05 Use of Force for the Protection of Other Persons.
 (1) Subject to the provisions of this Section and of Section 3.09, the use of force upon or toward the person of another is justifiable to protect a third person when:
(a) the actor would be justified under Section 3.04 in using such force to protect himself against the injury he believes to be threatened to the person whom he seeks to protect; and
(b) under the circumstances as the actor believes them to be, the person whom he seeks to protect would be justified in using such protective force; and
(c) the actor believes that his intervention is necessary for the protection of such other person.

(2) Notwithstanding Subsection (1) of this Section:
(a) when the actor would be obliged under Section 3.04 to retreat, to surrender the possession of a thing or to comply with a demand before using force in self-protection, he is not obliged to do so before using force for the protection of another person, unless he knows that he can thereby secure the complete safety of such other person; and
(b) when the person whom the actor seeks to protect would be obliged under Section 3.04 to retreat, to surrender the possession of a thing or to comply with a demand if he knew that he could obtain complete safety by so doing, the actor is obliged to try to cause him to do so before using force in his protection if the actor knows that he can obtain complete safety in that way; and
(c) neither the actor nor the person whom he seeks to protect is obliged to retreat when in the other's dwelling or place of work to any greater extent than in his own.

1991, Beeley was working as a bartender at a social club in East Providence. Beeley's friend and codefendant in the Superior Court trial, John Perry (John), was a patron at the club that evening. After the club closed, Beeley and John went to a friend's house to play cards until approximately two-thirty on the morning of Monday, May 20, 1991. Beeley drove John to 80 Evergreen Drive in East Providence where, John testified, he lived in an apartment with his wife, Julie Perry (Julie). By then it was approximately four o'clock in the morning. John invited Beeley to spend the night at the apartment since it was so late. Beeley dropped off John at the entrance to the apartment building and then went to park his car.

The testimony in the record is contradictory as to what occurred next. John testified that he used his key to gain entry into the apartment through the front door, which was locked. Upon entering the apartment, John walked toward the bedroom and came face-to-face with his wife, Julie, in the hallway. Julie turned on the hallway light and John observed a man sleeping in the bed. John began screaming at Julie and asked her "Who was in the bed?" Julie responded "You know who it is." John recognized the man as Robert Harding (Harding). Harding was not wearing any clothes. The two men began wrestling and moved toward the door of the apartment. Harding attempted to force John out of the apartment through the door. John yelled out to Beeley who was waiting outside the apartment. Beeley entered through the doorway and pulled John out of the apartment. John testified that he waited outside of the apartment with Beeley for the police to arrive who had been called by Julie. John then went around to the window of the apartment, opened it, yelled to Julie "How could you do this to me?" and threw a plant on the ground.

Julie and Harding offered a different version of the events. Julie testified that on May 20, 1991, Harding was sleeping on the couch in the living room of the apartment. At approximately four o'clock in the morning she was awakened by "noise." From her bedroom she observed John standing in the hallway. Julie testified that she was sure that John had gained entry into the apartment through a living-room window because plant pots located on the window sill

were broken. Julie and John began arguing and Harding woke up. John kicked Harding in the face several times as he sat on the couch. As the two men struggled Julie called the police. John hollered to Beeley "somebody is in here" and then unlocked the door. Beeley entered the apartment, punched Harding in the face, and then left with John.

Harding corroborated Julie's testimony and indicated that as he was locked in combat with John, both tried to open the door. Harding testified that as he attempted to push John out the door, John unlocked the door. Initially Harding testified that John had opened the door, but later on cross-examination he recalled that he opened the door after John had unlocked it. John then called out to Beeley and Beeley entered and hit Harding in the face. Harding indicated that this was the first time he had ever met Beeley. Harding sustained facial injuries; however, it is unclear from the record whether Harding's injuries were caused by the single punch executed by Beeley or by the altercation with John.

Beeley testified that as he waited outside the apartment he could hear John and Julie yelling. He walked to the door and banged on it but did not attempt to open it. The door opened and then slammed shut. When the door opened again Beeley could see Harding who was naked grabbing John by the waist. Beeley did not know Harding and did not know what Harding was doing in the apartment. John was crying, and he yelled to Beeley, "This is the guy." Beeley hit Harding once to break his hold on John. Beeley observed Julie on the telephone, talking to the police. He then grabbed John and pulled him out of the apartment. Beeley and John waited outside for the police to arrive. Beeley further testified that he did not know how John gained entry into the apartment.

. . . .

Beeley contends that the trial justice erred in instructing the jury that one acting to defend another has only a derivative right of self-defense, and that his or her actions are not judged by the reasonableness of his or her own conduct and perceptions.

It is undisputed that Beeley hit Harding as Beeley entered the apartment. Beeley's defense to the charge of simple assault upon Harding was that when he entered the apartment, he saw John being held by a naked man (Harding) and speculated that the latter was an intruder who may have raped Julie. Beeley, in an attempt to break Harding's hold on John, executed a single punch at Harding. Beeley contends that he was therefore justified in assaulting Harding.

In instructing the jury on the charge of assault against Beeley, the trial justice stated:

> "[T]he state must prove by evidence and proof beyond a reasonable doubt the following facts: One, that on May 20, 1991 James Beeley assaulted Robert Harding. Two, that at the time James Beeley was not justified in coming to the assistance of John Perry."

The trial justice later instructed the jury with respect to defense of another and explained that

> "one who comes to the aid of another person must do so at his own peril and should be excused only when that other person would be justified in defending himself. Thus, if you find that Mr. Perry was not the aggressor and was justified in defending himself from the acts of Mr. Harding, then Mr. Beeley is then excused from any criminal responsibility for coming to the aid of Mr. Perry if Mr. Beeley in so doing did not use excessive force. However, if you find that Mr. Perry was in fact the aggressor and was not justified in his actions and was inflicting punches and kicks on Mr. Harding, then Mr. Beeley acted at his own peril and his actions would not be justified. In short, if Mr. Perry was justified in his actions, then so was Mr. Beeley in coming to his assistance. If Mr. Perry was not justified in his actions, then neither was Mr. Beeley. Our Supreme Court has said on repeated occasions, an intervening person stands in the shoes of the person that he is aiding."

The issue before us is whether an intervenor in an altercation between private individuals should be judged by his or her own reasonable perceptions or whether he or she stands in the shoes of the person that he or she is defending.

This court has addressed the issue of defense of another on several occasions. The cases have involved a defendant-intervenor aiding another in the context of an arrest situation. In State v. Small, we held that the defendant did not have the right to use force against a police officer in circumstances in which it was obvious that the third person had no such right. Thereafter, in *State v. Gelinas*, this court adopted the rule that "one who comes to the aid of an arrestee must do so at his own peril and should be excused only when the individual would himself be justified in defending himself from the use of excessive force by the arresting officer." Id. at 1386. Later in *State v. Aptt*, this court, faced with facts involving an arrest, and relying on Gelinas and Small, reached the same conclusion that a defendant who attacks a police officer in an effort to assist a third person in avoiding arrest is not entitled to an instruction on defense of a third person.

A review of the relevant authorities reveals that there are two rules followed by American jurisdictions. The first rule, adopted by the trial justice in the instant case, is sometimes referred to as the "alter ego" rule, and it holds that the right to defend another is coextensive with the other's right to defend himself or herself. The other view, which follows the Model Penal Code, is that as long as the defendant-intervenor reasonably believes that the other is being unlawfully attacked, he or she is justified in using reasonable force to defend him or her.

The Model Penal Code § 3.05, entitled "Use of Force for the Protection of Other Persons," provides in pertinent part as follows.

> "(1) Subject to the provisions of this Section and of Section 3.09, the use of force upon or toward the person of another is justifiable to protect a third person when:
>
> (a) the actor would be justified under Section 3.04 in using such force to protect himself against the injury he believes to be threatened to the person whom he seeks to protect; and
>
> (b) under the circumstances as the actor believes them to be, the person whom he

seeks to protect would be justified in using such protective force; and

(c) the actor believes that his intervention is necessary for the protection of such other person." Model Penal Code § 3.05(1) (Adopted 1962).

Under this section in order for the defense to be raised successfully, three conditions must be met. First, the force must be such as the actor could use in defending himself or herself from the harm that he or she believes to be threatened to the third person. In other words, the actor may use the same amount of force that he or she could use to protect himself or herself. Second, the third person must be justified in using such protective force in the circumstances as the actor believes them to be. Thus, if the third person was resisting an arrest by a known police officer, he or she would have no defense and, if the circumstances were known to the actor, the actor would have no defense either. Finally, the actor must believe that his or her intervention is necessary for the protection of the third party.

This view, which has been adopted in the new state criminal codes, is in our opinion the better view. We favor the doctrine which judges a defendant upon his or her own reasonable perceptions as he or she comes to the aid of the apparent victim. The justification should, of course, be based upon what a reasonable person might consider to be the imminence of serious bodily harm. As one court expressed it, not only as a matter of justice should one "not be convicted of a crime if he selflessly attempts to protect the victim of an apparently unjustified assault, but how else can we encourage bystanders to go to the aid of another who is being subjected to assault?" Moreover, to impose liability upon the defendant-intervenor in these circumstances is to impose liability upon him or her without fault.

In sum it seems to this court preferable to predicate the justification on the actor's own reasonable beliefs. We are of the opinion that an intervenor is justified in using reasonable force to defend another as long as the intervenor reasonably believes that the other is being unlawfully attacked. This rule is "predicated on the social desirability of encouraging people to go to the aid of third parties who are in danger of harm as a result of unlawful actions of others." . . . . [T]here is an "important social goal of crime prevention, a duty of every citizen."

Applying the foregoing to the instant case, we conclude that the trial justice incorrectly instructed the jury with respect to the charge of assault against Beeley. . . . Accordingly we vacate Beeley's conviction on the assault charge.

Other Cases—Defense of Others

State v. Aguillard, 883 F.2d 662 (9th Cir. 1990)
Protestors argued they had the right to prevent abortions by violating the law because they were defending the right of unborn children to live. In rejecting the defense of others, the court stated,

"The "defense of others" specifically limits the use of force or violence in protection of others to situations where the person attacked would have been justified in using such force or violence to protect himself. In view of *Roe v. Wade* and the provisions of the Louisiana abortion statute, defense of others as justification for the defendants' otherwise criminal conduct is not available in these cases. Since abortion is legal in Louisiana, the defendants had no legal right to protect the unborn by means not even available to the unborn themselves."

People v. Young, 183 N.E.2d 319 (N.Y. 1962).

Detectives not in uniform observed an argument taking place between a motorist and McGriff in the street in Midtown Manhattan. Detective Driscoll attempted to chase McGriff out of the roadway in order to allow traffic to pass, but McGriff refused to move back and his actions caused a crowd to collect. Driscoll identified himself, and then placed McGriff under arrest. As McGriff resisted, the defendant came out of the crowd from Driscoll's rear and struck the other detective on the head with his fist. Driscoll's kneecap was injured when defendant fell on top of him. At the station, Defendant said he did not know or think that Driscoll and Murphy were police officer. He said that he observed two white men who appeared to be 45 or 50 years old, pulling on a 'colored boy' (McGriff) who appeared to be a lad about 18 whom he did not know. The men had nearly pulled McGriff's pants off, and he was crying. Defendant admitted he knew nothing of what had transpired and made no inquiries of anyone; he just came there and pulled the officer away from McGriff. Defendant was convicted of assault in the third degree. The appellate division held that one is not "criminal liable for assault in the third degree if he goes to the aid of another who he mistakenly, but reasonably believes is being unlawfully beaten, and thereby injures one of the apparent assaulters."

The court held that whether one, who in good faith aggressively intervenes in a struggle between another person and a police office in civilian dress attempting to effect the lawful arrest of a third person, may be properly convicted of assault in the third degree was a question of law of first impression.

While the doctrine espoused by the majority of the court below may have support in some States, we feel that such a policy would not be conducive to an orderly society. We agree with the settled policy of law in most jurisdictions that the right of a person to defend another ordinarily should not be greater than such person's right to defend himself.

In this case . . . defendant intended to assault the police officer in civilian dress. The resulting assault was forceful. Hence motive or mistake of fact is of no significance as the defendant was not charged with a crime requiring such intent or knowledge. To be guilty of third degree assault "It is sufficient that the defendant voluntarily intended to commit the unlawful act of touching." Since in these circumstances the aggression was inexcusable the defendant was properly convicted.

Foster v. Commonwealth, 412 S.E.2d 198 (Va 1991)

In 1986 Foster was an inmate in a correctional center in Southampton County, Virginia. He was playing horseshoes with several others in the prison's recreational yard. Two other inmates (Robinson and Hooks) began arguing over whose turn it was to play. There was conflicting evidence about what happened then, but in essence, Foster hit Robinson in the head with a horseshoe to protect Hooks from being hit by Robinson. Foster was indicted for malicious wounding, and at trial he offered a jury instruction on self-defense and defense of others; the trial court refused to give the instructions, and the jury

found Foster guilty. Foster appealed. The court addressed both Foster's claims concerning self-defense and also his claim concerning defense of others. The Court, discussed the defense of others law in Virginia,

The (Virginia) Supreme Court has clearly recognized that one is privileged to use force in defense of family members. We find no Virginia cases, nor have any been cited to us, determining whether and when a person can use force to protect or defend a third person. Generally, however, this privilege is not limited to family members and extends to anyone, even a stranger who is entitled to claim self-defense. Like self-defense, the circumstances in which the protection of others may be raised as a defense are carefully circumscribed so as to preclude such a claim in situations where one has instigated the fray in order to provide an excuse for assaulting or murdering his enemy. In a majority of jurisdictions, a person asserting a claim of defense of others may do so only where the person to whose aid he or she went would have been legally entitled to defend himself or herself. The right to defend another is "commensurate with self-defense."

Consequently, in those jurisdictions which recognize the defense, the limitations on the right to defend one's self are equally applicable, with slight modifications, to one's right to defend another. One must reasonably apprehend death or serious bodily harm to another before he or she is privileged to use force in defense of the other person. The amount of force which may be used must be reasonable in relation to the harm threatened.

Jurisdictions which recognize the defense are split on the question whether the person to whose aid one comes must be free from fault in order to claim the defense of protection of others. The majority of those courts which have addressed the question have adopted an objective test so that one "may act on and is governed by the appearance of conditions when he arrives upon the scene, provided he acts honestly and according to what seems reasonably necessary in order to afford protection." Thus, under the majority view, in order to justifiably defend another, the defendant must reasonably believe that the person being defended was free from fault; whether the defended person was, in fact, free from fault is

Defense of Property and Habitation

The general rule concerning defense of property is that a person may use force, but not deadly force, to protect his or her property. The rules concerning the defense of habitation (one's home) are less clear.

Deadly force cannot be used against a mere trespasser. Neither may it be used against a thief. If a thief steals a car, the owner cannot use deadly force to stop him even if there is no other way to gain the immediate return of his property. Simply put, the law values the protection of life, including that of a thief, over the protection of property. There are, however, various other avenues through which property can be indirectly protected with the use of deadly force. Thus, . . . the law authorizes the use of deadly force to prevent some dangerous felonies, including several involving the taking of property. ... Finally, the common law drew a distinction between the protection of property generally and the protection of a dwelling. Because of the special importance of the home as a place of security and shelter, deadly force could be used to prevent forcible entry. Kerper, *supra* at 132.

The common law placed great emphasis on the security of a person's dwelling and permitted the use of deadly force against an intruder. The castle doctrine allowed the inhabitant to use all the force necessary to repel any invasion of the home when it appeared that people were in danger, but did not justify the use of deadly force to repel a mere trespass. Today, states vary in how much force they allow a person to use in defending his or her home. Some courts permit the use of deadly force to prevent a forcible entry into the habitation in circumstances where the occupant is threatened, or reasonably fears death or great bodily harm to self or other occupants, or reasonably believes the assailant intends to commit a felony. But many states treat the home like property and hold that deadly force may not be used to defend it. When the occupants feel threatened, then the general rules of self-defense apply, and deadly force may be justified. In several complex provisions, MPC §3.06, provides a defense when a person uses force int the protection of property.

PEOPLE v. CEBALLOS, 526 P.2d 241 (Cal. 1974)

BURKE, J.

Defendant lived alone in a home in San Anselmo. The regular living quarters were above the garage, but defendant sometimes slept in the garage and had about $2,500 worth of property there.
In March 1970 some tools were stolen from defendant's home. On May 12, 1970, he noticed the lock on his garage doors was bent and pry marks were on one of the doors. The next day he mounted a loaded .22 caliber pistol in the garage. The pistol was aimed at the center of the garage doors and was connected by a wire to one of the doors so that the pistol would discharge if the door was opened several inches.

The damage to defendant's lock had been done by a 16-year-old boy named Stephen and a 15-year-old boy named Robert. On the afternoon of May 15, 1970, the boys returned to defendant's house while he was away. Neither boy was armed with a gun or knife. After looking in the windows and seeing no one, Stephen succeeded in removing the lock on the garage doors with a crowbar, and, as he pulled the door outward, he was hit in the face with a bullet from the pistol.

Stephen testified: He intended to go into the garage "[f]or musical equipment" because he had a debt to pay to a friend. His "way of paying that debt would be to take [defendant's] property and sell it" and use the proceeds to pay the debt. He "wasn't going to do it [i.e., steal] for sure, necessarily." He was there "to look around," and "getting in, I don't know if I would have actually stolen."

Defendant . . . admitted having set up the trap gun. He stated that after noticing the pry marks on his garage door on May 12, he felt he should "set up some kind of a trap, something to keep the burglar out of my home." When asked why he was trying to keep the burglar out, he replied, "... Because somebody was trying to steal my property ... and I don't want to come home some night and have the thief in there ... usually a thief is pretty desperate ... and ... they just pick up a weapon ... if they don't have one ... and do the best they can."

When asked by the police shortly after the shooting why he assembled the trap gun, defendant stated that "he didn't have much and he wanted to protect what he did have."

. . . [T]he jury found defendant guilty of assault with a deadly weapon. An assault is "an unlawful attempt, coupled with a present ability, to commit a violent injury on the person of another."

Defendant contends that had he been present he would have been justified in shooting Stephen since Stephen was attempting to commit burglary, that under . . . *United States* v. *Gilliam,* defendant had a right to do indirectly what he could have done directly, and that therefore any attempt by him to commit a violent injury upon Stephen was not "unlawful" and hence not an assault. The People argue that the rule in *Gilliam* is unsound, that as a matter of law a trap gun constitutes excessive force, and that in any event the circumstances were not in fact such as to warrant the use of deadly force.

The issue of criminal liability where a trap gun or other deadly mechanical device . . . [is used] . . . appears to be one of first impression in this state,[1] but in other jurisdictions courts have considered the question of criminal and civil liability for death or injuries inflicted by such a device.
. . .
In the United States, courts have concluded that a person may be held criminally liable under statutes proscribing homicides and shooting with intent to injure, or civilly liable, if he sets upon his premises a deadly mechanical device and that device kills or injures another. However, . . . [there may be an exception to that rule whenthe person, were he present] . . . would be justified in taking the life or inflicting the bodily harm with his own hands. . . .

Allowing persons, at their own risk, to employ deadly mechanical devices imperils the lives of children, firemen and policemen acting within the scope of their employment, and others. Where the actor is present, there is always the possibility he will realize that deadly force is not necessary, but deadly mechanical devices are without mercy or discretion. Such devices "are silent instrumentalities of death. They deal death and destruction to the innocent as well as the criminal intruder without the slightest warning. The taking of human life [or infliction of great bodily injury] by such means is brutally savage and inhuman."

It seems clear that the use of such devices should not be encouraged.

Furthermore, even if that rule were applied here, as we shall see, defendant was not justified in shooting Stephen. Penal Code section 197 provides: "Homicide is ... justifiable ... 1. When resisting any attempt to murder any person, or to commit a felony, or to do some great bodily injury upon any person; or, 2. When committed in defense of habitation, property, or person, against one who manifestly intends or endeavors, by violence or surprise, to commit a felony...." (2) Since a homicide is justifiable under the circumstances specified in section 197, a fortiori an attempt to commit a violent injury upon another under those circumstances is justifiable.

By its terms subdivision 1 of Penal Code section 197 appears to permit killing to prevent any "felony," but in view of the large number of felonies today and the inclusion of many that do not involve a danger of serious bodily harm, a literal reading of the section is undesirable. *People* v. *Jones,* in rejecting the defendant's theory that her husband was about to commit the felony of beating her and that therefore her killing him to prevent him from doing so was justifiable, stated that Penal Code section 197 "does no more than codify the common law and should be read in the light of it." *Jones* read into section 197, subdivision 1, the limitation that the felony be "`some atrocious crime attempted to be committed by force.'" *Jones* further stated, "The punishment provided by a statute is not necessarily an adequate test as to whether life may be taken for in some situations it is too artificial and unrealistic. We must look further into the character of the crime, and the manner of its perpetration *When these do not reasonably create a fear of great bodily harm,* as they could not if defendant apprehended only a misdemeanor assault, *there is no cause for the exaction of a human life.*"

Jones involved subdivision 1 of Penal Code section 197, but subdivision 2 of that section is likewise so limited. The term "violence or surprise" in subdivision 2 is found in common law authorities and . . . developed so. . . that killing or use of deadly force to prevent a felony was justified only if the offense was a forcible and atrocious crime. . . .

Examples of forcible and atrocious crimes are murder, mayhem, rape and robbery. In such crimes "from their atrocity and violence human life [or personal safety from great harm] either is, or is presumed to be, in peril" However, . . . in our opinion it cannot be said that under all circumstances burglary under section 459 constitutes a forcible and atrocious crime.[2]

Where the character and manner of the burglary do not reasonably create a fear of great bodily harm, there is no cause for exaction of human life or for the use of deadly force The character and manner of the burglary could not reasonably create such a fear unless the burglary threatened, or was reasonably believed to threaten, death or serious bodily harm.

In the instant case the asserted burglary did not threaten death or serious bodily harm, since no one but Stephen and Robert was then on the premises. A defendant is not protected from

liability merely by the fact that the intruder's conduct is such as would justify the defendant, were he present, in believing that the intrusion threatened death or serious bodily injury. There is ordinarily the possibility that the defendant, were he present, would realize the true state of affairs and recognize the intruder as one whom he would not be justified in killing or wounding.

We thus conclude that defendant was not justified under Penal Code section 197, subdivisions 1 or 2, in shooting Stephen to prevent him from committing burglary. Our conclusion is in accord with dictum indicating that there may be no privilege to use a deadly mechanical device to prevent a burglary of a dwelling house in which no one is present.

. . .[I]n view of the supreme value of human life we do not believe bodily force can be justified to prevent all felonies of the foregoing type, including ones in which no person is, or is reasonably believed to be, on the premises except the would-be burglar.

Defendant also argues that had he been present he would have been justified in shooting Stephen under subdivision 4 of Penal Code section 197, which provides, "Homicide is ... justifiable ... 4. When necessarily committed in *attempting,* by lawful ways and means, *to apprehend* any person for any felony committed...." (Italics added.) The argument cannot be upheld. The words "attempting ... to apprehend" contain the idea of acting for the purpose of apprehending. An attempt to commit a crime includes, inter alia, the specific intent to commit a particular crime and "In statutes and in cases other than criminal prosecutions an `attempt' ordinarily means an intent combined with an act falling short of the thing intended." Here no showing was made that defendant's intent in shooting was to apprehend a felon. Rather it appears from his testimony and extrajudicial statement heretofore recited that his intent was to prevent a burglary, to protect his property, and to avoid the possibility that a thief might get into defendant's house and injure him upon his return.

. . . .

Defendant also does not, and could not

properly, contend that the intrusion was in fact such that, were he present, he would be justified under Civil Code section 50 in using deadly force. (13) That section provides, "Any necessary force may be used to protect from wrongful injury the person or property of oneself...." This section also should be read in the light of the common law, and at common law in general deadly force could not be used solely for the protection of property. Thus defendant was not warranted under Civil Code section 50 in using deadly force to protect his personal property.

. . . .

At common law an exception to the foregoing principle that deadly force could not be used solely for the protection of property was recognized where the property was a dwelling house in some circumstances. "According to the older interpretation of the common law, even extreme force may be used to prevent dispossession [of the dwelling house]." Also at common law if another attempted to burn a dwelling the owner was privileged to use deadly force if this seemed necessary to defend his "castle" against the threatened harm. Further, deadly force was privileged if it was, or reasonably seemed, necessary to protect the dwelling against a burglar.

Here we are not concerned with dispossession or burning of a dwelling, and, as heretofore concluded, the asserted burglary in this case was not of such a character as to warrant the use of deadly force.

. . .

LAW v. STATE,
318 A.2d 859 (Md. 1974)

LOWE, J., delivered the opinion of the Court.

When James Cecil Law, Jr. purchased a thirty-nine dollar shot gun for "house protection," he could not possibly have conceived of the ordeal it would cause him to undergo.

Mr. Law, a 32-year-old black man, had recently married and moved to a predominantly white middle-class neighborhood. Within two weeks his home was broken into and a substantial amount of clothing and personal property was taken.

The investigating officer testified that Mr. Law was highly agitated following the burglary and indicated that he would take the matter in his own hands. The officer quoted Mr. Law as saying: "`I will take care of the job. I know who it is.'" The officer went on to say that Law told him "... he knew somebody he could get a gun from in D.C. and he was going to kill the man and he was going to take care of it." Two days later he purchased a 12 gauge shotgun and several "double ought" shells.

The intruder entered the Law's home between 6:30 and 9:00 in the evening by breaking a windowpane in the kitchen door which opened onto a screened back porch. The intruder then apparently reached in and unlocked the door. Law later installed "double locks" which required the use of a key both inside and outside. He replaced the glass in the door window in a temporary manner by holding it in place with a few pieces of molding, without using the customary glazing compound to seal it in.

One week after the break-in a well meaning neighbor saw a flickering light in the Law's otherwise darkened house and became suspicious. Aware of the previous burglary, he reported to the police that some one was breaking into the Law's home. Although the hour was 8:00 p.m., Mr. Law and his bride had retired for the evening. When the police arrived, a fuse of circumstances ignited by fear exploded into a tragedy of errors.

The police did not report to or question the calling neighbor. Instead they went about routinely checking the house seeking the possible illegal point of entry. They raised storm windows where they could reach them and shook the inside windows to see if they were locked. They shined flashlights upon the windows out of reach, still seeking evidence of unlawful entry. Finding none, two officers entered the back screened porch to check the back door, whereupon they saw the windowpane which appeared to have been temporarily put in place with a few pieces of molding. These officers apparently had not known of the repair or the cause of damage.

Upstairs Mr. and Mrs. Law heard what sounded like attempts to enter their home. Keenly aware of the recent occurrence, Mr. Law went downstairs, obtained and loaded his newly acquired shotgun and, apparently facing the rear door of the house, listened for more sounds.

In the meantime, the uniformed officers found what they thought to be the point of entry of a burglar, and were examining the recently replaced glass. While Officer Adams held the flashlight on the recently replaced pane of glass, Officer Garrison removed the molding and the glass, laid them down and stated that he was going to reach in and unlock the door from the inside to see if entry could be gained. Officer Adams testified that they "were talking in a tone a little lower than normal at this point." Officer Adams stated that Officer Garrison then tested the inside lock, discovered it was a deadlock and decided no one could have gotten in the door without a key. A law enforcement student, riding with Officer Garrison that evening, testified that he then heard a rattling noise and someone saying "if there was somebody here, he's still in there." As Officer Garrison removed his hand from the window he was hit by a shotgun blast which Law fired through the door. Officer Garrison was dead on arrival at the hospital.

Officer Potts, the officer next to arrive at the scene, saw Officer Adams running to his car to call for reinforcements. He heard another shot and Officer Adams yell "they just shot at me."

The tragedy of errors had only begun. The officers, having obtained reinforcements and apparently believing they had cornered a burglar, subjected the house to a fusillade of gun fire evinced by over forty bullet holes in the bottom of the kitchen door and the police department transcription of a telephone conversation during the ensuing period of incomprehensible terror.

Mr. Law testified that while he stood listening to the sounds and voices at the door, fearful

that someone was about to come in "... the gun went off, like that, and when it went off like that it scared me and I was so scared because I had never shot a shotgun before and then I heard a voice on the outside say that someone had been shot." Mr. Law was not able to hear who had been shot but he then "... hollered up to my wife, call a police officer, I think I shot a burglar."

His wife called the police and most of her conversation was recorded.
. . . .

The appellant, James Cecil Law, Jr. was found guilty of murder in the second degree and of assault with intent to murder. He was convicted by a jury in the Circuit Court for Charles County following removal from Prince George's County. Judge James C. Mitchell sentenced him to concurrent ten year terms.

* * *

There is a dearth of Maryland authority upon the question of what constitutes justifiable homicide in the defense of one's home.
. . . .

The defense of habitation is explained by text writers and treated . . . as an extension of the right of self-defense. The distinction between the defense of home and the defense of person is primarily that in the former there is no duty to retreat. "A man in his own home was treated as `at the wall' and could not, by another's assault, be put under any duty to flee therefrom."

The regal aphorism that a man's home is his castle has obscured the limitations on the right to preserve one's home as a sanctuary from fear of force or violence.

". . . [I]f an assault on a dwelling and an attempted forcible entry are made under circumstances which would create a reasonable apprehension that it is the design of the assailant to commit a felony or to inflict on the inhabitants injury which may result in loss of life or great bodily harm, and that the danger that the design will be carried into effect is imminent, a lawful occupant of the dwelling may prevent the entry even by the taking of the intruder's life

The felonies the prevention of which justifies

the taking of a life "are such and only such as are committed by forcible means, violence, and surprise such as murder, robbery, burglary, rape or arson." It is "essential that killing is necessary to prevent the commission of the felony in question. If other methods would prevent its commission, a homicide is not justified; all other means of preventing the crime must first be exhausted."

The right thus rests upon real or apparent necessity. It is this need for caution in exercising the right that has been relegated to obscurity. The position espoused by appellant typifies the misunderstanding of the extent of the right to defend one's home against intrusion. He says:

> "The defendant is not required to act as a reasonable, prudent and cautious individual, nor was he required to limit his force to only that that was required under the circumstances — not when *28 the defendant was in his own home, and believed he was being set upon, or about to be set upon by would be robbers or burglars who were in the act of breaking into his home at the time."

The judgment which must usually be made precipitously under frightening conditions nevertheless demands a certain presence of mind and reasonableness of judgment. Although one is

> "not obliged to retreat ... but ... may even pursue the assailant until he finds himself

or his property out of danger ..., this will not justify a person['s] firing upon everyone who forceably enters his house, even at night." . . . [T]he taking of life is not justified "unless unavoidable.... Beyond this the law does not authorize the sacrifice of human life or the infliction of serious bodily hurt."

In 1894 Mr. Justice Harlan redefined the scope of the rule within its permissible limits:

> `A man may repel force by force, in defense of his person, habitation, or property, against one who manifestly intends and endeavors, by violence or surprise, to commit a known felony, such as murder, rape, robbery, arson, burglary, and the like, upon either. In these cases he is not obliged to retreat, but may pursue his adversary until he has secured himself from all danger; and if he kill him in so doing it is called justifiable self-defense; as, on the other hand, the killing by such felon of any person so lawfully defending himself will be murder. But a bare fear of any of these offenses, however well grounded, as that another lies in wait to take away the party's life, unaccompanied with any overt act indicative of such an intention, will not warrant in killing that other by way of prevention. ...'"

Other Cases – Defense of Habitation and Property

People v. Guenther, 740 P. 2d 971 (Colo 1987)
Neighbors pounded on David and Pam Guenther's door. Pam went outside and got into a struggle with one of the neighbors. David shot and killed two neighbors outside the front door with four shots from his .357 Magnum 6-inch revolver. The court had to decide whether Colorado's "make my day" statute allowed Guenther to use deadly force under these facts. The Colorado Supreme Court stated,

"In accordance with the explicit terms of the statute, we hold that the [make my day] statute provides the home occupant with immunity from prosecution only for force used against one who has made an unlawful entry into the dwelling and

that this immunity does not extend to force used against non-entrants.

Falko v. State, 407 So. 2d. 203 (Fl. 1981)
Another spring-gun case. Florida Supreme Court held that it was not a justifiable use of deadly force. It stated,

"Appellant erroneously presumes that the use of a deadly mechanical device, such as a trap gun, in defense of any property is a justifiable use of force based on the reasonable belief of its necessity. We agree with the state's argument that the use of such a device is fundamentally unnecessary and unjustifiable.

A trap gun or spring gun is absolutely incapable of exercising discretion or reason. Rather, it sentences its victim to death or great bodily injury in a split second explosion of deadly force. Such arbitrary brutality should necessarily be prohibited under any circumstance . . . .

WRAP UP

Justification defenses allow individuals to be acquitted when their actions would otherwise be a criminal but under circumstances that indicate it was the right thing to do: because they chose the path of less harm, because the act was consented to, because they were following their public duty, or because they were protecting themselves, others, or their property.

Chapter Eleven: Excuses

Overview:

Excuses, like justifications, are affirmative defenses, and the defendant will need to raise them and prove them (generally this means that they will give notice to the government that they intend to rely on the defense). Excuses focus on some characteristic of the defendant. With excuses, the defendant is essentially saying, "I did the crime, but I am not responsible because I was . . . insane (or too young, intoxicated, mistaken, or under duress)."

Insanity

Inanity is a legal determination that, at the time of the crime, the individual had a mental disease or defect that warrants either a finding of not guilty, a finding of guilty but insane, or a finding of not guilty by reason of insanity. Insanity is not a term used by psychiatrists or psychologists who, instead, discuss mental diseases or disorders. Instead "insanity" is a legal defense allowed by all but four states. Each state has grappled with the "test of insanity" they will adopt and have jurors apply. Three main tests of insanity exist today; one test, the *Durham* Rule, is still used only in one state; and one eighteenth-century test, the "Wild Beast Test" has been abandoned.[28] Idaho, Kansas, Montana, and Utah have abolished the defense of insanity.[29] The following case of State v. Johnson discusses these tests.

STATE v. JOHNSON,
399 A.2d 469 (1979)

DORIS, Justice.

The sole issue presented by this appeal is whether this court should abandon the M'Naghten test in favor of a new standard for determining the criminal responsibility of those who claim they are blameless by reason of mental illness. For the reasons stated herein, we have concluded that the time has arrived to modernize our rule governing this subject.

Before punishing one who has invaded a protected interest, the criminal law generally requires some showing of culpability in the offender. The requirement of a mens rea, or guilty mind, is the most notable example of the concept that before punishment may be exacted, blameworthiness must be demonstrated. That some deterrent, restraint, or rehabilitative purpose may be served is alone insufficient. It has been stated that the criminal law reflects the moral sense of the community. "The fact that the law has, for centuries, regarded certain wrongdoers as improper subjects for punishment is a testament to the extent to which that moral sense has developed. Thus, society has recognized over the years that none of the three asserted purposes of the criminal law rehabilitation, deterrence and retribution is satisfied when the truly irresponsible, those who lack substantial capacity to control their actions, are punished." The law appreciates that those who are substantially unable to restrain their conduct are, by definition, incapable of being deterred and their punishment in a correctional institution provides no example for others.

---

[28] The "wild beast test" was developed by the English courts by the middle of the eighteenth century, the courts said, "a man . . . totally deprived of his understanding and memory, . . . and doth not know what he is doing, no more than an infant, than a brute, or a wild beast is never the object of punishment. (*Rex v. Arnold*, 16 Howell's State Trials 695 (Engl. 1724). Persons excused by this rule were the so called, "raving maniacs." Lesser states of mental illness were not deemed sufficient to excuse criminal responsibility. In the case of mental defect, the test was whether the person was so retarded as to be an idiot—one who could not county twenty pence, identify his parents, or know his age.
[29] *Id.*

The law of criminal responsibility has its roots in the concept of free will.

Our law proceeds from this postulate and seeks to fashion a standard by which criminal offenders whose free will has been sufficiently impaired can be identified and treated in a manner that is both humane and beneficial to society at large. The problem has been aptly described as distinguishing between those cases for which a correctional-punitive disposition is appropriate and those in which a medical-custodial disposition is the only kind that is legally permissible

Because language is inherently imprecise and there is a wide divergence of opinion within the medical profession, no exact definition of "insanity" is possible. Every legal definition comprehends elements of abstraction and approximation that are particularly difficult to apply in marginal cases. Our inability to guarantee that a new rule will always be infallible, however, cannot justify unyielding adherence to an outmoded standard, solely at variance with contemporary medical and legal knowledge. Any legal standard designed to assess criminal responsibility must satisfy several objectives. It must accurately reflect the underlying principles of substantive law and community values while comporting with the realities of scientific understanding. The standard must be phrased in order to make fully available to the jury such psychiatric information as medical science has to offer regarding the individual defendant, yet be comprehensible to the experts, lawyers, and jury alike. Finally, the definition must preserve to the trier of facts, be it judge or jury, its full authority to render a final decision These considerations are paramount in our consideration of the rule to be applied in this jurisdiction in cases in which the defense of lack of criminal responsibility due to a mental illness is raised.

I.

The historical evolution of the law of criminal responsibility is a fascinating, complex story. For purposes of this opinion, however, an exhaustive historical discussion is unnecessary; a brief sketch will therefore suffice. The renowned "right-wrong" test had antecedents in England as early as 1582. In that year the Eirenarcha, written by William Lambard of the Office of the Justices of Peace, laid down as the test of criminal responsibility "knowledge of good or evil." During the 1700's the language of the test shifted its emphasis from "good or evil" to "know." During the eighteenth century, when these tests and their progeny were evolving, psychiatry was hardly a profession, let alone a science. Belief in demonology and witchcraft was widespread and became intertwined with the law of responsibility. So eminent a legal scholar as Blackstone adamantly insisted upon the existence of witches and wizards as late as the latter half of the eighteenth century. The psychological theories of phrenology and monomania thrived and influenced the development of the "right and wrong" test. Both of these compartmentalized concepts have been soundly rejected by modern medical science which views the human personality as a fully integrated system. By historical accident, however, the celebrated case of Daniel M'Naghten froze these concepts into the common law just at the time when they were beginning to come into disrepute.

Daniel M'Naghten attempted to assassinate Sir Robert Peel, Prime Minister of England, but mistakenly shot Peel's private secretary instead. This assassination had been preceded by several attempts on the lives of members of the English Royal House, including Queen Victoria herself. When M'Naghten was tried in 1843 the jury was charged with a test heavily influenced by the enlightened work of Dr. Isaac Ray who was severely critical of the "right and wrong" rule. After the jury acquitted M'Naghten the public indignation, spearheaded by the Queen, was so pronounced that the Judges of England were summoned before the House of Lords to justify their actions. In an extraordinary advisory opinion, issued in a pressure-charged atmosphere, Lord Chief Justice Tindal, speaking for all but one of the 15 judges, reversed the charge used at trial and articulated what has become known as the M'Naghten rules. The principal rule in M'Naghten's Case, 8 Eng.Rep. 718 (1843) states:

"To establish a defense on the ground of insanity it must be clearly proved that, at the time of committing the act, the party accused was laboring under such a defect of reason, from disease of the mind, as not to know the nature and quality of the act he was doing, or if he did know it, that he did not know that what he was doing was wrong."

This dual-pronged test, issued in response to the outrage of a frightened Queen, rapidly became the predominant rule in the United States.

This jurisdiction has long adhered to the M'Naghten standard for determining criminal responsibility. In *State v. Quigley*, this court intimated that the dual-pronged test of M'Naghten was the prevailing view in Rhode Island. Yet, in State v. Andrews where we expressly adopted M'Naghten, reference was made only to the knowledge of "right and wrong" portion of that test. Although it has not always been clear whether the "nature and quality" component of M'Naghten is included as part of the formal rule in this jurisdiction, as a matter of practice expert witnesses testify concerning both parts of the rule. Unlike several other jurisdictions, Rhode Island has never augmented M'Naghten with the "irresistible impulse doctrine."

II.

The M'Naghten rule has been the subject of considerable criticism and controversy for over a century. The test's emphasis upon knowledge of right or wrong abstracts a single element of personality as the sole symptom or manifestation of mental illness. M'Naghten refuses to recognize volitional or emotional impairments, viewing the cognitive element as the singular cause of conduct.   One scholar has stated that:

"[t]he principle behind M'Naghten, namely, that defect of cognition as a consequence of mental disease is the primary exculpating factor in the determination of legal insanity, has probably never been other than a legal fiction."

M'Naghten has been further criticized for being predicated upon an outmoded psychological concept because modern science recognizes that "insanity" affects the whole personality of the defendant, including the will and emotions. One of the most frequent criticisms of

M'Naghten has been directed at its all-or-nothing approach, requiring total incapacity of cognition. We agree that:

"Nothing makes the inquiry into responsibility more unreal for the psychiatrist than limitation of the issue to some ultimate extreme of total incapacity, when clinical experience reveals only a graded scale with marks along the way. * * * "The law must recognize that when there is no black and white it must content itself with different shades of gray." Model Penal Code, § 4.01, Comment at 158 (Tent.Draft No. 4, 1955).

By focusing upon total cognitive incapacity, the M'Naghten rule compels the psychiatrist to testify in terms of unrealistic concepts having no medical meaning. Instead of scientific opinions, the rule calls for a moral or ethical judgment from the expert which judgment contributes to usurpation of the jury's function as decision maker.

Probably the most common criticism of M'Naghten is that it severely restricts expert testimony, thereby depriving the jury of a true picture of the defendant's mental condition. This contention has been seriously questioned by some commentators who find no support for the argument that M'Naghten inhibits the flow of testimony on the responsibility issue. As a matter of practice in this jurisdiction, expert testimony under M'Naghten has been unrestricted and robust. Nevertheless, we are convinced that this testimony would be more meaningful to the jury were it not for the narrow determination demanded by M'Naghten.

That these criticisms have had a pronounced effect is evidenced by the large and growing number of jurisdictions that have abandoned their former allegiance to M'Naghten in favor of the Model Penal Code formulation. We also find these criticisms persuasive and agree that M'Naghten's serious deficiencies necessitate a new approach.

III.

Responding to criticism of M'Naghten as a narrow and harsh rule, several courts supplemented it with the "irresistible impulse" test. Under this combined approach, courts inquire into both the cognitive and volitional components of the defendant's behavior. Although a theoretical advance over the stringent right and wrong test, the irresistible impulse doctrine has also been the subject of widespread criticism. Similar to. M'Naghten's absolutist view of capacity to know, the irresistible impulse is considered in terms of a complete destruction of the governing power of the mind. A more fundamental objection is that the test produces the misleading notion that a crime impulsively committed must have been perpetrated in a sudden and explosive fit. Thus, the irresistible impulse test excludes those "far more numerous instances of crimes committed after excessive brooding and melancholy by one who is unable to resist sustained psychic compulsion or to make any real attempt to control his conduct."

The most significant break in the century-old stranglehold of M'Naghten came in 1954 when the Court of Appeals for the District of Columbia declared that, "an accused is not criminally responsible if his unlawful act was the product of mental disease or mental defect." *Durham v. United States*. The "product" test, first pioneered by the Supreme Court of New Hampshire in *State v. Pike* (1869), was designed to facilitate full and complete expert testimony and to permit the jury to consider all relevant information, rather than restrict its inquiry to data relating to a sole symptom or manifestation of mental illness. Durham generated voluminous commentary and made a major contribution in recasting the law of criminal responsibility. In application, however, the test was plagued by significant deficiencies. The elusive, undefined concept of productivity posed serious problems of causation and gave the jury inadequate guidance. Most troublesome was the test's tendency to result in expert witnesses' usurpation of the jury function. As a result, the court . . . took the extreme step of proscribing experts from testifying concerning productivity altogether. Finally, . . . the court abandoned Durham, decrying the "trial by label" that had resulted. . . .

Several commentators have advocated abolition of the separate defense of lack of criminal responsibility due to a mental illness. Proponents contend that abolition would result

in the responsibility issue being more properly considered as. . . [one of]. . . mens rea. Under a common proposal the criminal process would be bifurcated: first, the jury would resolve the question of guilt, and second, a panel of experts would determine the appropriate disposition. Arguably, abolition of the separate defense is subject to constitutional objections because it potentially abrogates the right to trial by jury and offends the guarantee of due process. We believe that such a drastic measure, if advisable at all, is appropriately left to the legislative process.

IV.

Responding to the criticism of the M'Naghten and irresistible impulse rules, the American Law Institute incorporated a new test of criminal responsibility into its Model Penal Code.[5] The Model Penal Code test has received widespread and ever-growing acceptance. It has been adopted with varying degrees of modification in 26 states and by every federal court of appeals that has addressed the issue. Although no definition can be accurately described as the perfect or ultimate pronouncement, we believe that the Model Penal Code standard represents a significant, positive improvement over our existing rule. Most importantly, it acknowledges that volitional as well as cognitive impairments must be considered by the jury in its resolution of the responsibility issue. The test replaces M'Naghten's unrealistic all-or-nothing approach with the concept of "substantial" capacity. Additionally, the test employs vocabulary sufficiently in the common ken that its use at trial will permit a reasonable three-way dialogue between the law-trained judges and lawyers, the medical-trained experts, and the jury.

Without question the essential dilemma in formulating any standard of criminal responsibility is encouraging a maximum informational input from the expert witnesses while preserving to the jury its role as trier of fact and ultimate decision maker. As one court has aptly observed:

"At bottom, the determination whether a man is or is not held responsible for his conduct is not a medical but a legal, social or moral judgment. Ideally, psychiatrists much like experts in other fields should provide grist for the legal mill, should furnish the raw data upon which the legal judgment is based. It is the psychiatrist who informs as to the mental state of the accused his characteristics, his potentialities, his capabilities. But once this information is disclosed, it is society as a whole, represented by judge or jury, which decides whether a man with the characteristics described should or should not be held accountable for his acts."

Because of our overriding concern that the jury's function remain inviolate, we today adopt the following formulation of the Model Penal Code test:

A person is not responsible for criminal conduct if at the time of such conduct, as a result of mental disease or defect, his capacity either to appreciate the wrongfulness of his conduct or to conform his conduct to the requirements of law is so substantially impaired that he cannot justly be held responsible. The terms "mental disease or defect" do not include an abnormality manifested only by repeated criminal or otherwise antisocial conduct.

There are several important reasons why we prefer this formulation. The greatest strength of our test is that it clearly delegates the issue of criminal responsibility to the jury, thus precluding possible usurpation of the ultimate decision by the expert witnesses. Under the test we have adopted, the jury's attention is appropriately focused upon the legal and moral aspects of responsibility because it must evaluate the defendant's blameworthiness in light of prevailing community standards. Far from setting the jury at large, as in the majority Model Penal Code test the defendant must demonstrate a certain form of incapacity. That is, the jury must find that a mental disease or defect caused a substantial impairment of the defendant's capacity to appreciate the wrongfulness of his act or to conform his conduct to legal requirements. Our new test emphasizes that the degree of "substantial" impairment required is essentially a legal rather than a medical question. Where formerly under M'Naghten total incapacity was necessary for exculpation, the new standard allows the jury to find that incapacity less than total is sufficient. Because impairment is a matter of

degree, the precise degree demanded is necessarily governed by the community sense of justice as represented by the trier of fact.

Several other components of our new test require elucidation. Our test consciously employs the more expansive term "appreciate" rather than "know." Implicit in this choice is the recognition that mere theoretical awareness that a certain course of conduct is wrong, when divorced from appreciation or understanding of the moral or legal impact of behavior, is of little import. A significant difference from our former rule is inclusion in the new test of the concept that a defendant is not criminally responsible if he lacked substantial capacity to conform his conduct to the requirements of law. As we noted at the outset, our law assumes that a normal individual has the capacity to control his behavior; should an individual manifest free will in the commission of a criminal act, he must be held responsible for that conduct. Mental illness, however, can effectively destroy an individual's capacity for choice and impair behavioral controls.

The drafters of the Model Penal Code left to each jurisdiction a choice between the terms "wrongfulness" and "criminality." We prefer the word "wrongfulness" because we believe that a person who, knowing an act to be criminal, committed it because of a delusion that the act was morally justified, should not be automatically foreclosed from raising the defense of lack of criminal responsibility.

The second paragraph of our test is designed to exclude from the concept of "mental disease or defect" the so-called psychopathic or sociopathic personality. We have included this language in our test to make clear that mere recidivism alone does not justify acquittal. We recognize that this paragraph has been the source of considerable controversy. Nevertheless, we believe that its inclusion in our test is necessary to minimize the likelihood of the improper exculpation of defendants who are free of mental disease but who knowingly and deliberately pursue a life of crime.

V.

As we have emphasized previously, preserving the respective provinces of the jury and experts is an important concern. Consonant with modern medical understanding, our test is intended to allow the psychiatrist to place before the jury all of the relevant information that it must consider in reaching its decision. We adhere to Dean Wigmore's statement that when criminal responsibility is in issue, "any and all conduct of the person is admissible in evidence." Nevertheless, the charge to the jury must include unambiguous instructions stressing that regardless of the nature and extent of the experts' testimony, the issue of exculpation remains at all times a legal and not a medical question. In determining the issue of responsibility the jury has two important tasks. First, it must measure the extent to which the defendant's mental and emotional processes were impaired at the time of the unlawful conduct. The answer to that inquiry is a difficult and elusive one, but no more so than numerous other facts that a jury must find in a criminal trial. Second, the jury must assess that impairment in light of community standards of blameworthiness. The jury's unique qualifications for making that determination justify our unusual deference to the jury's resolution of the issue of responsibility. For it has been stated that the essential feature of a jury "lies in the interposition between the accused and his accuser of the commonsense judgment of a group of laymen, and in the community participation and shared responsibility that results from that group's determination of guilt or innocence." Therefore, the charge should leave no doubt that it is for the jury to determine: 1) the existence of a cognizable mental disease or defect, 2) whether such a disability resulted in a substantial impairment at the time of the unlawful conduct of the accused's capacity either to appreciate the wrongfulness of his conduct or to conform his conduct to the requirements of the law, and consequently, 3) whether there existed a sufficient relationship between the mental abnormality and the condemned behavior to warrant the conclusion that the defendant cannot justly be held responsible for his acts.

VI.

So there will be no misunderstanding of the thrust of this opinion, mention should be made of the treatment to be afforded individuals found lacking criminal responsibility due to a mental illness under the test we have adopted. Unquestionably the security of the community must be the paramount interest. Society withholds criminal sanctions out of a sense of compassion and understanding when the defendant is found to lack capacity. It would be an intolerable situation if those suffering from a mental disease or defect of such a nature as to relieve them from criminal responsibility were to be released to continue to pose a threat to life and property. The General Laws provide that a person found not guilty because he was "insane" at the time of the commission of a crime shall be committed to the Director of the State Department of Mental Health for observation. At a subsequent judicial hearing if he is found to be dangerous, the person must be committed to a public institution for care and treatment. This procedure insures society's protection and affords the incompetent criminal offender necessary medical attention.

NOTES

[5] "(1) A person is not responsible for criminal conduct if at the time of such conduct, as a result of mental disease or defect, he lacks substantial capacity either to appreciate the criminality [wrongfulness] of his conduct or to conform his conduct to the requirements of law. "(2) As used in this article, the terms 'mental disease or defect' do not include an abnormality manifested only by repeated criminal or otherwise antisocial conduct." Model Penal Code, § 4.01 (Final Draft, 1962).

Mens Rea And Insanity

The interplay between mens rea and insanity is complex. Someone who is legally insane, may very well have the ability to form the mens rea required by the criminal statute. Conversely, a defendant who has a mental impairment not rising to the level of legal insanity may still not have the requisite mens rea required by the statute (and thus should be found not guilty). Kerper wrote,

> Whenever a certain state of mind is an element of the offense, a mental condition which would render the accused incapable of that state of mind will negate the presence of the

necessary mens rea. This is true even though the defendant's mental condition is not so severe as to relieve him from general criminal responsibility. Thus, an unsoundness of mind which would not meet the test of legal insanity may nevertheless establish the absence of the mens rea for a particular crime. This possibility is especially significant for the crime of murder, where first degree murder requires the element of premeditation. Very often the kind of deliberate decision-making required for premeditation will not be possible due to a mental illness that falls short of establishing legal insanity. The mentally ill (but not legally insane) accused will not be liable for first degree murder, although he will still be liable for second degree murder, which requires a lesser mens rea. Kerper, *supra*, at 17.

The Federal Approach To Insanity

The federal government was following the MPC approach when John Hinkley, Jr. attempted to assassinate U.S. President Ronald Reagan in March 1981. Hinkley's motivation for shooting at President Reagan, his press secretary, and two law enforcement officers was to impress actress Jodie Foster. At trial, he successfully claimed insanity and pointed to his obsessional fixation on her. The public outcry following the verdict of not guilty by reason of insanity in Hinckley's federal trial resulted in a change of the test of insanity in the federal court system. In 1984 Congress enacted the Insanity Defense Reform Act of 1984, 18 U.S.C. §4241 (1984), which eliminated the volitional prong of the federal test of insanity and essentially embraced the M'Naghten test. In addition to re-adopting the M'Naghten test, the Act changed the burden of proof in asserting insanity. The federal standard now requires the defendant to prove the defense of insanity by clear and convincing evidence rather than preponderance of the evidence—the earlier and lower standard. There has been some controversy in placing the burden of proof of insanity on the defendant, but the Court has held that this burden-shifting does not violate the defendant's right to due process under the constitution. *See, Leland v. Oregon*, 343 U.S. 790 (1954), and *Patterson v. New York*, 432 U.S. 197 (1977).

The Act also limited psychiatrists' ability to present evidence concerning the defendant's inability to control his or her behavior. It was unclear whether the Act prohibited the use of psychiatric evidence concerning the defendant's lack of specific intent to commit an offense. But, the Eleventh Circuit Court of Appeals noted in 1990, "Both Congress and the courts have recognized the crucial distinction between evidence of psychological impairment that supports an "affirmative defense," and psychological evidence that negates an element of the offense charged." It ruled that the language of the Act does not bar the use of psychiatric evidence to negate specific intent where that level of intent is an element of the offense charged by the government. *United States v. Cameron*, 907 F.2d 1051 (1990).

State Developments To Insanity[30]

The federal constitution does not require that states allow defendants to present an insanity excuse. Some states classify insanity as an affirmative defense and require the defendant to bear the burden of persuasion on insanity--generally using the 'preponderance of the evidence' standard. Some states have adopted the higher, 'clear and convincing' standard. In some states, when the defendant raises the defense of insanity and presents some evidence of insanity, the burden of production and persuasion then reverts to the state that must then prove defendant is not insane—usually beyond a reasonable doubt.

A defendant who claims insanity may be found "not guilty." In these cases, the defendant is like any other defendant who has been acquitted. In some states, the defendant may be found "not guilty by reason of insanity." In these cases, the defendant is institutionalized indefinitely in a mental institution. In some states, the defendant is found "guilty but mentally ill." In these states the defendant is generally sentenced in the criminal courts as other guilty defendants are, but there may be provisions for institutionalization in a mental institution or a special ward or wing in a criminal institution (prison).

---

[30] For a state-by-state analysis, see, "*The Insanity Defense Among the States*" at criminal.findlaw.com/criminal-procedure/the-insanity-defense-among-the-states.html.

Robert Black, Senior Fellow of the National Constitution Center, reported on the recent Supreme Court oral arguments *in Kahler v. Kansas*, ___ U.S. ___ (2020). He stated,

> There have been any number of precise formulations of the standard for an insanity defense, but the common thread, until recently, is that insanity operated as an "affirmative defense." An affirmative defense negates a defendant's criminal liability, even if it is proven that the defendant committed the alleged acts. So even if the prosecution proves that the defendant had the requisite criminal intent, or "*mens rea*," as well as having committed the act or crime itself—the "*actus reus*"—the defendant could still escape conviction by demonstrating insanity.

> This is still true in almost every state today, but Kansas is one of several that has abolished insanity as a separate defense. Instead, a mentally ill defendant may try to argue that, because of their mental illness, they lacked general criminal intent, and therefore that the prosecution has failed to prove its case—but that's it. James Kahler was convicted of murder and sentenced to death after he shot and killed his ex-wife, her mother, and two of their three children. Kahler raised his mental illness—chiefly depression, but also several personality disorders—at trial. But under Kansas law he could only argue that his conditions left him incapable of forming criminal intent, meaning in this context that he knew he was killing another person. His lawyers challenged that law as unconstitutional, and after the Kansas courts rejected his arguments the Supreme Court took the case to consider whether abolishing the insanity defense violates the 14th Amendment's Due Process Clause or the Eighth Amendment's Cruel and Unusual Punishment Clause.

> What makes this case so fascinating is that the Court has never before held, or even been asked to consider, whether the states may abolish traditional pillars of criminal law like the insanity defense. Broadly speaking, this is something the states simply haven't done. There is therefore no established framework for evaluating Kahler's claim, and oral argument showed a Court deeply uncertain how to approach the matter. Unsurprisingly, arguments from history took center stage, with Kahler's lawyer arguing that the insanity defense is deeply rooted in our nation's history and tradition. (In fact, they contend, it traces back even further in English common law, to the 1500s at least.) The irreducible constitutional minimum, she suggested, requires states to recognize that those who are incapable of moral judgment and cannot tell the difference between right and wrong—a standard drawn from the 1843 British case *R. v. M'Naghten*—cannot be held criminally responsible for their actions.

> Kansas, with the support of the U.S. Department of Justice, begged to differ. Even if the law has recognized insanity defenses in one form or another since time immemorial, they contended, no single formulation of the defense has ever been so uniformly adopted to be "deeply rooted" in our history. Furthermore, recognizing insanity as a separate defense, rather than an implicit result of general *mens rea* standards requiring criminal intent, is a relatively modern development. Kahler's counsel responded that the ancient understanding of criminal intent was different from, and broader than, our *mens rea* rules, and it included the very notion of moral judgment that today is only considered through an affirmative insanity defense. The case therefore may require the Court to parse not only our Constitution, but centuries-old common law rules as well.

> However, history was not the Court's only concern. Justice Elena Kagan tried to probe the limits of Kansas's argument, asking if a state could abolish other venerable defenses such as duress. Could states go so far as to make murder, or other crimes, into strict-liability offenses, where the defendant's mental state would be irrelevant once it was proven that they

committed the act of homicide? The state's counsel largely avoided the question, saying that it would turn on the historical record and that they had not done the research to provide a definitive answer.

Conversely, the Justices pressed Kahler's lawyer to specify exactly what standard she believed the Constitution required, and to confront earlier statements by the Court that it would not get into the business of formulating a standard as a matter of constitutional law. She responded that, while the Court should not choose one of the competing formulations to impose uniformly on the states, it should recognize a bedrock constitutional minimum above which the states are free to experiment.

Justice Stephen G. Breyer wanted to focus on the policy rationale behind Kansas's system. He provided a hypothetical of two individuals, both insane, who each killed a man, one of whom believed they were killing a dog and one of whom believed they had been ordered to kill by a dog. The traditional insanity defense would excuse both killings, while Kansas's law would excuse the former but not the latter, and Breyer wanted to hear why it made sense to treat these two defendants differently. Once again, clear responses were not forthcoming. Instead, both Kansas and the federal government argued that these are difficult questions whose answers are the states' responsibility, not the Court's.

Finally, Kahler's lawyer sounded an interesting note in her rebuttal, saying that Kansas had gone against "what we believe as a country." Consciously or otherwise, she was echoing Chief Justice Earl Warren, who would famously lean forward from the bench and ask, "But is it fair?" Professor Philip Bobbitt has cited Chief Justice Warren as a leading practitioner of argument from *constitutional ethos*, the bedrock American values—like fundamental fairness—embodied in our Constitution. The Court rarely relies on such arguments, but with text, history, and precedent offering such little guidance, perhaps *Kahler* is a chance for these considerations of basic values to shine.

It is difficult to predict how the Court will come out in this case, largely because the issue it presents is so novel. The Justices did not seem to line up as clearly hostile to one side or the other; instead, they each seemed to be trying to get a purchase on the case, to figure out how they should even go about analyzing this sort of constitutional claim. Whichever way the Justices go, however, *Kahler* looks to be a true landmark decision for generations to come. See, https://constitutioncenter.org/blog/kahler-v-kansas-can-states-abolish-the-insanity-defense

Model Penal Code—Insanity

MPC § 4.01 provides the substantial capacity test of insanity. It states, "A person is not responsible for criminal conduct if at the time of such conduct as a result of mental disease or defect he lacks substantial capacity either to appreciate the criminality of his conduct or to conform his conduct to the requirements of the law." The MPC does not include antisocial conduct in its definition of mental disease or defect. ("The term "mental disease or defect' do not include an abnormality manifested only by repeated criminal or otherwise antisocial conduct."). The MPC allows evidence of mental disease or defect when it is relevant to prove the defendant did not have the state of mind required as an element of the defense. See MPC §4.02 (1). According to the MPC, claiming mental disease or defect is an affirmative defense. See, MPC §4.03 (1).

Insanity versus Fitness-to-Proceed

Some individuals are so mentally disturbed that they may not be able to stand trial at which they would raise an insanity claim. The defendant's attorney may, after interviewing his or her client, determine that the defendant has a mental defect or is of such limited intelligence or understanding that he or she is not able to aid in his or her legal defense. In these cases, the attorney must inform the court that the defendant is incompetent or not fit to proceed. Unlike the insanity defense, which looks at the defendant's mental condition at the time of the offense, the fitness-to-proceed inquiry looks at defendant's mental condition at the time he or she is charged and prosecution commences. Courts will generally order a "competency" or "aid and assist" evaluation be done. If evaluators determine that the defendant is able to aid and assist, then the prosecution continues; if defendant is unable to aid and assist, then due process prohibits the states from continuing the criminal prosecution. State statutes control the fitness-to-proceed process and determine who has jurisdiction over a defendant who is unable to proceed. Often, if the defendant is found not fit to proceed, he or she will be institutionalized for treatment. Prosecution may continue, if and when the defendant, through medical or mental treatment, regains the ability to aid and assist in his or her own defense.

MODEL PENAL CODE FITNESS TO PROCEED

MPC §4.04 Mental Disease or Defect Excluding Fitness to Proceed.
No person who as a result of mental disease or defect lacks capacity to understand the proceedings against him or to assist in his own defense shall be tried, convicted or sentenced for the commission of an offense so long as such incapacity endures.

MPC § 4.06 Determination of Fitness to Proceed; Effect of Finding of Unfitness; Proceedings if Fitness Is Regained
(1) When the defendant's fitness to proceed is drawn in question, the issue shall be determined by the Court. If neither the prosecuting attorney nor counsel for the defendant contests the finding of the report filed . . . the Court may make the determination on the basis of such report. If the finding is contested, the Court shall hold a hearing on the issue. If the report is received in evidence upon such hearing, the party who contests the finding thereof shall have the right to summon and to cross-examine the psychiatrists who joined in the report and to offer evidence upon the issue.

(2) If the Court determines that the defendant lacks fitness to proceed, the proceeding against him shall be suspended, except as provided in Subsection (3) of this Section, . . .

(3) The fact that the defendant is unfit to proceed does not preclude any legal objection to the prosecution that is susceptible of fair determination prior to trial and without the personal participation of the defendant.

Other Cases—Insanity and Fitness to Proceed

State v. Armstrong, 671 So.2d307 (La. 1996).
Defendant went to the mortuary to get a copy of his father's death certificate. Police responded to the mortuary and found him standing over the Reverend with a bloody butcher knife. One officer drew his gun, and the defendant severed the reverend's head and held it up by the ears. He placed the headless body in a chair and walked up stairs and put the head into a toilet. He placed the knife in his briefcase, but on his cap, and walked out the door as if in a trance. He displayed no concern or awareness of the police. He had been evaluated as acute paranoid schizophrenic, medically discharged from military during

Vietnam War. Defendant had been committed 8 times to a mental institution from 1969-1992, and had been released only three days prior to killing the reverend. Grossly psychotic, off his meds, believed that the reverend was the antichrist, put head in toilet to prove it would not bleed.

Louisiana used the "right and wrong" test, and defendant was convicted by jury. The appellate court upheld his conviction.

State v. Odell, 676 N.W. 2d 646 (Minn 2004).
On April 23, 2000 Darren Odell attended Easter dinner at his great aunt's house. While his father was seated at the dining room table, Odell

retrieved a 9 mm Beretta handgun from his truck. When he returned, he waited until some of the guests cleared the dining room area. He fired three bullets into his father's chest which resulted in fatal wounds. Immediately following the shooting, Odell fled but returned shortly thereafter and peacefully surrendered himself to police.

He was indicted on one count of first-degree murder for shooting his father. In May, 2001 two doctors concluded that as a result of his mental illness, Odell was incapable of understanding the proceedings or participating in his defense, so he was committed to a Minnesota hospital for treatment and in fall 2002 was found competent to proceed to trial.

At trial he plead not guilty and not guilty by reason of mental illness under a Minnesota statute embracing the M'Naghten Rule. Extensive evidence relevant to appellant's mental state was introduced. All the experts agreed that Odell was suffering from schizophrenia at the time of the murder. They felt that he understood the nature and wrongfulness of shooting his father, yet elected to engage in criminal behavior regardless of the consequences. There was disagreement from the experts whether Odell did, or did not, meet the "wrongfulness" standard of M'Naghten.

"The narrow question before this court is whether the evidence presented at trial was sufficient to prove, by a preponderance of the evidence, that appellant did not understand the wrongfulness of his acts on April 23, 2000. The parties do not dispute that appellant suffered from a mental illness at the time of the offense. Further, it is undisputed that appellant knew that he was shooting his father and that such a shooting would result in his father's death. Therefore, appellant concedes that he knew the nature of his actions."

Ultimately the appellate court upheld the trial court's conviction, finding there was sufficient evidence to support it. The appellate court gave

State v. Wilson, 700 A.2d 633 (Conn 1997)
This case held that "wrong" should mean "morally wrong"

Finger v. State, 27 P.3d 66 (Nev. 2001).
This case shows the state abandoning the insanity defense altogether and holds that just looking at defendant's mens rea violates due process

State v. Bethel, 66 P.3d 840 (Kan. 2003).

deference to the trial court's decision to give greater weight to two of the doctors and to discredit or hold less persuasive the testimony of the other two experts. The trial court did not err in finding that, although Odell had proved by a preponderance of the evidence that, at the time of the murder, he was suffering from a severe mental illness, he had failed to prove that because of his mental illness he did not understand the nature of his act or that the act was wrong.

People v. Skinner, 704 P. 2d. 752 (1985).
Skinner strangled his wife while he was on a day pass from the Camarillo State Hospital at which he was a patient. He suffered from classical paranoiac schizophrenia. A delusional product of his illness was his belief that the marriage vow, "till death do us part" bestowed on a marital partner a God-given right to kill the other partner who has violated or was inclined to violate the marital vows, and that because the vows reflect the direct wishes of God, the killing was with complete moral and criminal impunity (i.e., not wrongful). He believed his act was not wrongful because it was sanctified by the will and desire of God.

The court examined the history of California's test of insanity from its initial adoption of the M'Naghten test, to the case of *People v. Drew* in which the court held the legal test of insanity was that of the MPC, Subsequent to Drew, the California legislature adopted an initiative which established a statutory definition of insanity. The question before the court was what the people of California (through initiative) and the California legislature (which adopted the initiative) intended in enacting the new standard. Did it intend to eliminate the Drew test and reinstate the M'Naghten test which required both prongs (a stricter test of insanity). The trial court concluded that the legislation adopted the much stricter test, but the appellate court found that the statute reinstated the M'Naghten test and directed a judgment of not guilty by reason of insanity.

This case held that abandoning inanity defense does not violate due process.

Foucha v. Louisiana, 504 U.S. 71 (1992).
Court used the Not Guilty By Reason of Insanity standard and held that the state could not institutionalize for reasons other than dangerousness due to insanity. Found that defendant's impairment that caused his acquittal.

Jones v. United States, 463 US. 354 (1983).

This case held that the defendant could be institutionalized based on NGRI verdict.

Dusky v. United States, 362 U.S. 402 (1960).
Fitness to proceed case

Extreme Emotional Disturbance (Diminished Capacity)

The excuse of diminished capacity (also called extreme emotional disturbance) is recognized in approximately fifteen states. This defense allows experts to testify that the defendant suffered from a mental disturbance that diminished his or her capacity to form the required criminal intent necessary to commit the crime. Diminished capacity is a compromise between finding the defendant not guilty by reason of insanity and finding the defendant fully liable. In some states, defendants may only raise diminished capacity/EED defenses when they are charged with intentional murder. When the defense is successful, the accused may still be convicted of second-degree murder. Indeed, the principal use of diminished capacity is to reduce first-degree murder to either second degree murder or manslaughter by showing defendant was not capable of premeditation, by showing lack of malice aforethought, or by showing that the offender he acted in the sudden heat of passion. Many states reject diminished capacity as a defense feeling it places too much reliance on psychiatrist testimony or may be too confusing for jurors.

The Model Penal Code allows a diminished capacity defense--although not labeling it as such. The MPC admits evidence that a defendant suffers from a mental disease or defect whenever relevant to prove defendant did or did not have a state of mind that is an element of the offense. Under the MPC, the defendant may introduce psychiatric evidence that refutes the state's evidence that he had the required mens rea--the crux of the diminished capacity defense.

Other Cases—Diminished Capacity

People v. Gorshen, 51 Cal. 2d 716 (1959).
Defendant was a dock worker who acted violently when ordered to "get to work and then started a fight when he was told that he was drunk and should go home. He later returned to work and shot and killed his foreman. The California Supreme Court affirmed trial court decision to convict Gorshen of second rather than first degree murder, which required premeditated intent to kill. Psychiatric testimony indicated that he suffered from chronic paranoiac schizophrenia, a "disintegration of mind and personality . . involving trances during which he hears voices and experiences visions, particularly devils in disguise." Gorshen believed that his foreman's remarked demeaned his manliness and sexuality and that this sparked enormous rage and anger. He was out of control and blamed the foreman. He developed an obsession with him and had an overwhelming desire to kill him.

State v. Dan White (Twinkie Defense!).
In 1979 a San Francisco jury convicted city official Dan White of manslaughter (instead of murder) for the killing of his co-worker Harvey Milk and Mayor George Moscone. Defendant argued that his depression was exaggerated by junk food, diminishing his capacity to form a specific intent to kill. When jurors returned a manslaughter verdict, nodding their acceptance of White's twinkie/diminished capacity defense, many members of the homosexual community marched in protest to San Francisco City Hall and had a violent confrontation with police there. After this case, Californians abolished the diminished capacity defense.

In October, 1985, Dan White committed suicide. His attorney said he had been troubled since his release after serving five years, one month and nine days in jail for the killings. Mr. White's layer argued that his client was mentally unstable and had a diminished capacity at the time of the shooting, in part, he argued, because Mr. White had an addiction for sugary junk foods.

People v. Noah, 5 Cal. 3d 469 (1971).
Court held that diminished capacity limited to specific intent crimes.

People v. Saille, 54 Cal. 3d 1103 (1991) Gil 105.
Court held that legislation abolishing Wells/Gorshen rule does not violate Due process

Automatism

The criminal law requires the state prove that defendant committed a voluntary act (or omission to act). Certain mental or physical conditions may prevent a defendant's act from being considered voluntary. When the defendant argues that some physical condition prevented his act from being voluntary, he is asserting the defense of automatism. Automatism is a negative defense (the defendant asserts that the state failed to prove something it was required to prove). But it also qualifies as an excuse because the defendant is, in essence, saying, "I did the act, but I am not responsible because some physical condition (such as a seizure) made my act involuntary."

Some courts have refused to allow the defense of automatism on the grounds that this defense is superseded by the insanity defense. They reason that if a condition affects the defendant's mind to the extent that the defendant's conduct is involuntary, it constitutes a mental disease or defect; and any defense involving mental disease or defect may be asserted only by the use of an insanity defense. *In Regina v. Quick*, 3 W.L.R. 26 (Engl. 1973), however, the court allowed the automatism defense when the defendant attacked another person and lapsed into unconsciousness because of low blood sugar. The court noted that the attack could have been prevented if the defendant had eaten a lump of sugar beforehand, and that the case was "not the sort of disease for which a person should be detained in a hospital rather than be given an unqualified acquittal. Insanity is only applicable where there is a malfunctioning of the mind caused by disease. A mental malfunctioning of transitory effect caused by the application to the body of some external factor such as violence, drugs . . . cannot be said to be due to the disease." The majority of American courts allow the automatism defense as distinct from the insanity defense. Emanuel, *supra* at 85-86. Recall from chapter two that MPC §2.01(1) and (2) precludes liability for an involuntary acts and excludes reflexes, convulsion, movement during unconsciousness from its definition of what constitutes a voluntary act.

Age/Infancy

At early common law, young and old alike could be found guilty of committing a crime. "Neither age, sex, nor unsoundness of mind could be offered as an excuse, and neither were these factors generally considered in mitigation of punishment." Kerper, *supra* at 112. Once the Church declared that a child under the age of seven could not be guilty of sin, it followed that ecclesiastic (church) courts would find that a child under seven years old could not be guilty of a crime. The church rule found its way to the king's courts and into common law. If the child was under the age of seven it was presumed (an irrebuttable presumption) that the child was not responsible. No matter how much evidence the prosecutor had about the sophistication of the child, if the child hadn't yet reached his or her seventh birthday, he or she could not be found guilty of a crime. If the child was between the age of seven and fourteen it was still presumed that the child was not criminally responsible, but the government could rebut the presumption by putting on evidence that child understood the nature and quality of the act and knew that it was wrong. Once a child reached the age of fourteen, no presumption existed, and defendants could not raise an "infancy" defense.

Although the common law rules about age were originally adopted by all of the states, today many states have discarded them. Some states have adopted an absolute minimum age for responsibility. Some states have no minimum age of responsibility. All states have developed juvenile court systems to balance the desire to hold children responsible and yet treat them differently than adults. Some states allow juveniles to be "waived" or "transferred" into the adult system. Some states have "legislative exclusions" (statutes) that exclude the juvenile court from having jurisdiction over some children or some offenses. The question of juvenile court jurisdiction is a different question than whether a child of a certain age can be responsible for his or her actions. But, because the discussion stems from the same concern (not wanting to treat children as adults) these issues frequently get lumped together.

The MPC deals with age as a defense by saying that those individuals who were less than sixteen years of age at the time of the commission of a crime cannot be tried and convicted of an offense. Sixteen and seventeen year olds were to be tried in Juvenile Court or be waived into adult court or they could not be tried and convicted for the offense.[31]

---

[31] MPC §4.10 Immaturity Excluding Criminal Conviction: Transfer of Proceedings to Juvenile Court
(1) A person shall not be tried for or convicted of an offense if:
(a) at the time of the conduct charged to constitute the offense he was less than sixteen years of age, in which case the juvenile court shall have exclusive jurisdiction; or

PEOPLE v. WOLFF,
61 Cal. 2d 795, 40 Cal. Rptr 271; 394 P.2d. 956 (1964)

FACTS

[Defendant was convicted of first degree murder for killing his mother when he was 15 years old.]

"In the year preceding the commission of the crime, defendant "spent a lot of time thinking about sex." He made a list of the names and addresses of seven girls in his community whom he did not know personally but whom he planned to anesthetize by ether and then either rape or photograph nude. One night about three weeks before the murder he took a container of ether and attempted to enter the home of one of these girls through the chimney, but he became wedged in and had to be rescued. In the ensuing weeks defendant apparently deliberated on ways and means of accomplishing his objective and decided that he would have to bring the girls to his house to achieve his sexual purposes, and that it would therefore be necessary to get his mother (and possibly his brother) out of the way first.

The attack on defendant's mother took place on Monday, May 15, 1961. On the preceding Friday or Saturday defendant obtained an axe handle from the family garage and hid it under the mattress of his bed. At about 10 P.M. on Sunday he took the axe handle from its hiding place and approached his mother from behind, raising the weapon to strike her. She sensed his presence and asked him what he was doing; he answered "it was nothing," and returned to his room and hid the handle under his mattress again. The following morning the defendant arose and put the customary signal (a magazine) in front of the window to inform his father that he had not overslept. Defendant ate the breakfast that his mother prepared, then went to his room and obtained the axe handle from under the mattress.

He returned to the kitchen, approached his mother from behind and struck her on the back of the head. She turned around screaming and he struck her several more blows. They fell to the floor fighting. She called out her neighbor's name and the defendant began choking her. She bit him on the hand and crawled away. He got up to turn off the water running in the sink, and she fled through the dining room. He gave chase, caught her in the front room, and choked her to death with his hands. Defendant then took off his shirt and hung it by the fire, washed the blood off his face and hands, read a few lines from a Bible or prayer book lying upon the dining room table, and walked down to the police station to turn himself in. Defendant told the desk officer, I have something I wish to report, I just killed my mother with an axe handle. The officer testified that the defendant spoke in a quiet voice and that "His conversation was quite coherent in what he was saying and he answered everything I asked him right to a T."

OPINION

[The court found that the defendant was too immature to commit first degree murder—that because of his age and experience he did not have fully developed sense that an adult would have needed to fulfill what the legislature intended by its words, willful, deliberate, and premeditated.

[The court found that the jury could find the defendant legally sane at the time of the murder.]

Certainly in the case now at bench the defendant had ample time for any normal person to maturely and appreciatively reflect upon his contemplated act and to arrive at a cold, deliberated and premeditated conclusion. He did this in a sense—and apparently to the full extent of which he was capable. But indisputably on the record, this defendant was not and is not fully normal or mature, mentally

---

(b) at the time of the conduct charged to constitute the offense he was sixteen or seventeen years of age, unless:

(i) the Juvenile Court has no jurisdiction over him, or

(ii) the Juvenile Court has entered an order waiving jurisdiction and consenting to the institution of criminal proceedings against him.

well person. He knew the difference between right and wrong; he knew that the intended act was wrong and nevertheless carried it out. But the extent of his understanding, reflection upon it and its consequences with realization of the enormity of the evil, appears to have been materially as relevant to appraising the quantum of his moral turpitude and the depravity vague and detached. We think that . . . the use by the legislature of "willful, deliberate, and premeditated" in conjunction indicates its intent to require as an essential element of first degree murder . . . substantially more reflection; i.e., more understanding and comprehension of the character of the act than the mere amount of thought necessary to form the intention to kill. ... Dividing intentional homicides into murder and voluntary manslaughter was a recognition of the infirmity of human nature. Again dividing the offense into murder into two degrees is a further recognition of that infirmity and of the difference in the quantum of personal turpitude of the offenders.

Upon the facts, upon the law, . . . we are satisfied that the evidence fails to support the finding that this murder by this defendant, in the circumstances of his undisputed mental illness, was of first degree, but that it amply sustains conviction of second degree murder.

Other Cases—Age/Immaturity

State v. KRL. 840 P.S. 210 (Washington 1992). KRL was 8 years and 2 months old when he and his friends were playing behind a building. Victim advised the boys to leave the area because it was dangerous. KRL talked back, Victim told him to leave "now." Boys ran off. 3 days later, KRL entered the victim's home without permission, removed goldfish from a fishbowl and chopped it into several pieces with steak knife and smeared it all over the counter. He clamped a plugged in curling iron onto a towel. KRLs mother testified at trial that he admitted to her that entering victim's home was wrong after she had eaten him "with a belt, black and blue." Mom said that KRL told her that the devil was making him do bad things. He was charged with burglary. There was trail testimony about defendant's capacity and he was described as "very normal intelligence" and "lower age academically"

Washington law said that children less than 8 were incapable of criminal intent. Those children between eight and twelve years of age were presumed to be incapable of committing crime. Presumption may be overcome that they have "sufficient capacity to understand that act or neglect and to know that it was wrong.

State made valiant effort to show that KRL's acts were so bad, but court concluded that his behavior was not uncommon to many young kids. Not enough evidence to prove that state had met its burden.

State v. Ramer, 86 P.3d 132 (Wash, 2004). Defendant was an 11-year-old juvenile charged with two counts of first degree rape. Defendant was in the bathroom with his arm around 7-year-old ZPG. When they came out of bathroom, ZPG's mom asked what happened, Ramer said, "basically nothing." Later ZPG said that Ramer had "rubbed his butt." ...and later he said that Ramer had also "placed his penis inside of ZPG's butt." When asked, Ramer freely admitted doing this.

Ramer told detective that he had sexual contact with ZPG approximately twice a week, and had also had contact with him several years earlier when the family had lived with them. He said "it was kind of sort of wrong." Ramer later said, "it wasn't wrong because he was into it too." When asked about what things were wrong, Ramer said to steal, murder, or poach. Ramer testified that he had also had sexual contact with his sister. There was a capacity hearing with lots of experts...

"We review the record for evidence sufficient to support the superior court's finding. When the superior court finds capacity, we review the record to determine whether there is substantial evidence that the state met its burden of overcoming the statutory presumption that children under 12 years of age are incapable of committing crime by clear and convincing evidence......

We have identified seven factors to consider in determining capacity: (1) the nature of the crime, (2) the child's age and maturity, (3) whether the child evidenced a desire for secrecy, (4) whether the child told the victim (if any, "not to tell"), (5) prior conduct similar to that charged, (6) any consequences that attached to that prior conduct, and (7) whether the child had made an acknowledgement that the behavior is wrong and could lead to detention.

Capacity requires the actor to understand the nature or illegality of his acts. …He must be able to entertain criminal intent. A sense of moral guilt alone. . . is not sufficient…."

[The court concluded that there was sufficient evidence to support trial court's holding that state had failed to prove by clear and convincing evidence that Ramer understood that his conduct was wrong.]

Intoxication

Voluntary Intoxication

Generally, defendants cannot escape liability for the crimes they commit after voluntarily becoming intoxicated with alcohol or some other substance. However, when a person is so intoxicated that he does not know what he was doing at the time of the crime, he may raise the imperfect defense of voluntary intoxication.

Where a crime requires an intention to cause a certain result and the defendant lacked that intention due to intoxication, he will not be liable for that crime. A person who killed another but was so intoxicated that he did not realize what he was doing would not be liable for the level of homicide (usually first degree murder) that requires an intent to kill. He would, however be liable for lesser degrees of homicide that do not require such an intent (unless the intoxication was involuntary and met the applicable standard for total excuse from responsibility). Intoxication may also negate a mens rea of knowledge. Thus, if a person is so intoxicated that he does not realize he is taking the property of another, he will not be liable for theft since that crime requires knowledge.

The two levels of mens rea not negated by intoxication are negligence and recklessness. Since negligence does not require awareness of an unjustifiable risk, the intoxicated person may be negligent even though he was so intoxicated that he could not appreciate the presence or nature of the risk taken. Recklessness, on the other hand, does require an awareness of the risk, at least as defined by the Model Penal Code. Yet the law will not recognize voluntary intoxication as a defense to a crime requiring recklessness even if the defendant was so intoxicated he did not know what he was doing. Using intoxicating substances is considered, in itself, a very risky business, automatically establishing the presence of recklessness on the part of the actor. Kerper, *supra* at 117.

State legislatures have begun limiting the defendant's ability to raise the defense of voluntary intoxication. In 1996, the Court upheld a Montana law that did not allow the jury to consider the defendant's voluntary intoxication in determining whether defendant possessed the mental state necessary for the commission of a crime. *Montana v. Egelhoff*, 518 U.S. 37 (1996). In 1996 the Florida Legislature enacted a statute that eliminated the defense, specifying that, except for controlled substances taken as prescribed by a doctor, evidence of voluntary intoxication is not admissible to show a lack of specific intent or to show insanity at the time of the offense. The trend is for states to disallow the defense on the theory that a defendant who voluntarily deprives herself of the ability to distinguish between right or wrong should be criminally responsible for her actions.

Involuntary Intoxication

Society expects people to be aware that alcohol and various drugs can cause intoxication. But when intoxication is not self-induced, the person should not be blamed. People who commit crimes after becoming intoxicated contrary to their own will or actions may raise the defense of involuntary intoxication. These defendants must show either that they were coerced by others into consuming an intoxicating substance or were tricked into taking such a substance by misrepresentation. Defendants may also raise the involuntary intoxication defense after mistakenly consuming a narcotic different than their prescribed medicine. Finally, some courts have allowed individuals who have had an extreme and unanticipated reaction to medication prescribed by a doctor to raise this defense. Acts committed by defendants who ingest intoxicating (non-prescribed) substances knowing what they are, but unaware of their full intoxicating capacity--for example, unwittingly smoking marijuana laced with LSD-are generally viewed as committing voluntary acts and the defense is unlikely to succeed. Similarly addicts who claim they cannot keep themselves from drinking or ingesting drugs are generally unsuccessful in raising the defense of involuntary intoxication.

Model Penal Code–Intoxication

The Model Penal Code[32] recognizes involuntary intoxication as a defense where "by reason of such intoxication the actor at the time of his conduct lacks substantial capacity either to appreciate its criminality or to conform his conduct to the requirements of law." Thus, the involuntary intoxication defense excuses responsibility with a standard quite similar to that applied with the insanity defense.

STATE v. STASIO, 396 A.2d 1129 (1979)

FACTS (Summary)
Defendant was convicted for assault with intent to rob and assault while armed with a dangerous weapon after he had been drinking at a bar from around 12:00 a.m. until around 5:00. Klimek, the bar-tender showed up on shift at 5:00 p.m. and at 5:40, the defendant entered and walked in a normal manner to the bathroom. Shortly thereafter he returned to the front door, looked outside and approached the bar. He demanded that Klimek give him some money. Upon refusal, he threatened Klimek. The defendant went behind the bar toward Klimek and insisted Klimek give him $80 from the cash register. When Klimek persisted in his refusal, the defendant pulled out a knife. Klimek grabbed the defendant's right hand and Colburn [defendant's drinking buddy], who had jumped on top of the bar, seized the defendant's hair and pushed his head toward the bar. The defendant then dropped the knife.

Stasio's defense at trial was that he was "so intoxicated that he could not form the intent to rob."

OPINION
It is generally agreed that a defendant will not be relieved of criminal responsibility because he was under the influence of intoxicants or drugs voluntarily taken. This principle rests

---

[32] MPC § 2.08 Intoxication.

(1) Except as provided in Subsection (4) of this Section, intoxication of the actor is not a defense unless it negatives an element of the offense.

(2) When recklessness establishes an element of the offense, if the actor, due to self-induced intoxication, is unaware of a risk of which he would have been aware had he been sober, such an unawareness is immaterial.

(3) Intoxication does not, in itself, constitute mental disease within the meaning of Section 4.01.

(4) Intoxication that (a) is not self-induced or (b) is pathological is an affirmative defense if by reason of such intoxication the actor at the time of his conduct lacks substantial capacity either to appreciate its criminality [wrongfulness] or to conform his conducts to the requirements of law.

(5) Definitions. In this Section unless a different meaning plainly is required:

(a) "intoxication" means a disturbance of mental or physical capacities resulting from the introduction of substances into the body;

(b) "self-induced intoxication" means intoxication caused by substances that the actor knowingly introduces into his body, the tendency of which to cause intoxication he knows or ought to know, unless he introduces them pursuant to medical advice or under such circumstances as would afford a defense to a charge of crime;

(c) "pathological intoxication" means intoxication grossly excessive in degree, given the amount of the intoxicant, to which the actor does not know he is susceptible.

upon public policy, demanding that he who seeks the influence of liquor or narcotics should not be insulated from criminal liability because that influence impaired his judgment or his control. The required element of badness can be found in the intentional use of the stimulant or depressant.

If a person casts off the restraints of reason and consciousness by a voluntary act, no wrong is done to him if he is held accountable for any crime which he may commit in that condition. Society is entitled to that protection. . . .

Our holding today does not mean that voluntary intoxication is always irrelevant in criminal proceedings. Evidence of intoxication may be introduced to demonstrate that premeditation and deliberation have not been proven so that a second degree murder cannot be raised to first degree murder or to show that the intoxication led to a fixed state of insanity. Intoxication may be shown to prove that a defendant never participated in a crime. Thus it might be proven that a defendant was in such a drunken stupor and unconscious state that he was not a part of a robbery. His mental faculties may be so prostrated as to preclude the commission of a criminal act. Under some circumstances intoxication may be relevant to demonstrate mistake. However, in the absence of any basis for the defense, a trial court should not in its charge introduce that element. A trial court, of course may consider intoxication as a mitigating circumstance when sentencing a defendant.

DISSENT

"Just as the lack of premeditation, willfulness, or deliberation precludes a conviction for first-degree murder; so should the lack of intent to rob or steal be a defense to assault and battery with intent to rob, or breaking and entering with intent to steal. The principle is the same in both situations. If involuntary intoxication negates an element of the offense, the defendant has not engaged in the conduct proscribed by the criminal statute. . . ."

[The dissent opines that the jury should have been allowed to decide whether Stasio was so drunk that he could not have formed the intent to rob.]

STATE v. HALL,
214 N.W.2d 205 (1974)

FACTS

[According to the state, Hall murdered and robbed Gilford Meacham in cold-blood.] Defendant was hitchhiking in the West, and Meacham offered him a ride from Oregon to Chicago, with defendant to drive. Defendant was then to split off and hitchhike to his home in North Carolina, while Meacham was to drive on to Connecticut to get married. According to the State, after defendant had passed Des Moines, Iowa, he shot Meacham in the head, robbed him of $208, dumped his body on a side road, drove on to Davenport, Iowa, took a bus from there to Chicago, Illinois, and then hitchhiked to the Southwest. Defendant's story was different. He testified that casual acquaintances in California gave him a pill and told him it was a "little sunshine" and would make him feel "groovy." He met Meacham in Oregon and they made the arrangement for the trip east. Meacham had a pistol. Defendant drove all the way to Iowa without rest and was exhausted. He testified he took the pill at Des Moines, it made him feel funny, and the road turned different colors and pulsated. Meacham was sleeping on the passenger side. Defendant testified he heard strange noises from Meacham's throat, like growling. Meacham's face grew and his nose got long, and his head turned into a dog like the one defendant's stepfather had shot. Defendant testified he got scared, picked up Meacham's gun, and shot him three times.

The County Attorney of Jasper County, Iowa, charged defendant with murder. A separate trial was held on the question of defendant's sanity to stand trial. A jury found him sane. Defendant pleaded insanity at the time of the act and stood trial on the murder charge; a jury found him guilty of first-degree murder. After the trial court overruled defendant's motion for new trial and sentenced him, he appealed.

OPINION

The case is different from the usual one in which the accused contends only that use of alcohol or other drugs prevented him from forming specific intent. Here defendant first contends the drug caused temporary insanity, which constitutes a complete defense. Defendant is right that insanity, if established, is a complete defense. Under our law the test of insanity is "whether defendant had capacity to know the nature and quality of his acts and [the] distinction between right and wrong." In addition to himself as a witness, defendant introduced testimony by two physicians who opined the drug was LSD and answered hypothetical questions about defendant's mental condition. By himself and those witnesses, defendant adduced substantial evidence which would meet the Harkness test in an ordinary case of an insanity defense. This evidence assumed the truth of defendant's testimony that he ingested the drug and sustained hallucinations as a result.

Defendant requested an instruction on insanity as a complete defense, tailored to include temporary insanity induced by drugs. The trial court refused it, and instructed that the jury should consider the claimed mental condition in connection with intent, as reducing the offense but not as exonerating it.

This court has held that a temporary mental condition caused by voluntary intoxication from alcohol does not constitute a complete defense. Is the rule the same when the mental condition results from voluntary ingestion of other drugs? We think so, and the cases so hold. Commonwealth v. Campbell ("there should be no legal distinction between the voluntary use of drugs and the voluntary use of alcohol in determining criminal responsibility"); State v. Christie (alcohol and phenobarbital); State v. Church (glue sniffing); State v. Clark (tranquilizer).

Defendant does not contend that extended use of drugs caused him "settled or established" insanity. He does argue that he did not take the pill voluntarily. But assuming he did take a drug, according to his own testimony no one tricked him into taking it or forced him to do so. Such is the language of defendant's own citations involving involuntary intoxication Defendant did not take the pill by mistake, thinking, for example, it was candy. If his own testimony is believed, he knew it was a mind-affecting drug.

We hold that the trial court properly refused the requested instruction.

Other Cases—Intoxication

State v. Cameron, 514 A.2d. 1302 (NJ 1986).
Intoxication is a defense to crimes requiring state prove specific intent when defendant is so intoxicated as to not be able to form the requisite mens rea.

Brancaccio v. State, 698 So.2d 597 (Fla. 1997).
Defendant was convicted of murder after the trial judge refused to instruct jury on defense of involuntary intoxication as a result of medication he was taking pursuant to a prescription. He had been confined recently to a mental hospital for threatening to kill his parents and himself. He was given Zoloft to treat depression. He was diagnosed as suffering from alcohol abuse, A.D.D., O.D.D. Hospital staff noted a personality change after the shift to Zoloft.

> Generally speaking an accused may be completely relieved of criminal responsibility if, because of involuntary intoxication, he was temporarily rendered legally insane at the time he committed the offense. And against speaking generally, the courts have considered one to be involuntarily intoxicated when he has become intoxicated through the fault of another, by accident, inadvertence, or mistake on his own part, or because of a physiological or psychological condition beyond his control.

People v. Low, 732 P.2d.622 (Colo. 1987).
Low ingested 40-50 cough drops a day for several months. He initially took them to combat a cold, and then to help him quit smoking and chewing. On one trip he consumed 120 cough drops within 24 hours. Psychiatrist testified that drops contain a drug that causes a psychotic disorder known as "organic delusional syndrome" or "toxic psychosis." Low had requested an instruction on involuntary intoxication. Defendant's conviction was overturned on other reasons.

Burrows v. State, 297 P. 1029 (1931).

Defendant was an 18-year-old who was traveling with an older man across the desert. The man insisted that defendant drink some whiskey with him and became abusive when defendant declined. Fearing that the older man would put him out of the car in the middle of the desert without any money, went ahead and drank the whiskey. He became intoxicated and killed the man. The court rejected his involuntary intoxication defense finding the older man had not compelled the defendant to "drink against his will and consent."

Duress

People who commit crimes because they have been threatened with death or harm can claim the excuse of duress (also referred to as coercion or compulsion). The duress defense excuses the crime when the defendant could only escape the threatened harm by committing a crime. Defendants must show that they exhausted all reasonable and available alternatives to violating the law. To successfully raise the defense, four further requirements must be met. First, the defendant must be threatened with serious bodily injury or death. Second, the threat must have been so substantial that a person of "reasonable firmness" would have been unable to resist it. The jury will decide what a reasonable person would have done under the circumstances and not necessarily what the defendant, ideally, could have done. Third, the threat must have been immediate or imminent. If there was ample time or opportunity to avoid the threatened harm, the defendant should have avoided it. Fourth, the defendant must not have placed himself in a situation where it was probable that he would be subjected to a threat.

Recall from the discussion in the previous chapter, prisoners who escape and claim their lives were in danger due to threats from other prisoners frequently raise the duress defense. In these cases, the defendant must show that he or she had taken reasonable, but unsuccessful steps to report the threats, that he or she did not use force or violence toward prison personnel or other innocent people, and that he or she surrendered or return to custody as soon as the claimed duress had ended or lost its coercive force.

As with most defenses, state statutes vary in their requirements and approaches to the defense of duress. Some states permit the defendant to raise the defense when he or she negligently (rather than recklessly or purposely) placed himself or herself in a potentially threatening situation. Some states follow the common law approach and limit the defense to defendants who have responded only to threats against themselves or members of their immediate families; other states permit the defense only when the defendant was threatened. Most states do not permit the defense to be raised in cases of intentional homicide. Some states do not require that the threat involve serious bodily injury if the offense committed is only a misdemeanor.

Some courts look to duress as negating the element of the offense charged and classify it as a negative defense (the defendant raised a reasonable doubt as to whether he acted in the exercise of free will). Most courts, however, classify duress as an affirmative defense and require the defendant prove the defense by the preponderance of the evidence.

Model Penal Code-Duress

The MPC[33] significantly extended the common law standard in the following ways: it does not require threats of death or serious injury; it does not require imminent threats; unlike most states' laws and

---

[33] MPC §2.09 Duress

(1) It is an affirmative defense that the actor engaged in the conduct charged to constitute an offense because he was coerced to do so by the use of, or a threat to use, unlawful force against his person or the person of another, that a person of reasonable firmness in his situation would have been unable to resist.

(2) The defense provided by this Section is unavailable if the actor recklessly placed himself in a situation in which it was probable that he would be subject to duress. The defense is also unavailable if he was negligent in placing himself in such a situation whenever negligence suffices to establish culpability for the offense charted.

common law, the defense of duress is permitted even in the case of intentional homicide; it extends to situations in which the threats were made to people other than the defendant or the defendant's immediate family members; and the MPC disallows defense if defendant recklessly or negligently placed himself in a situation where is was probable that he would be subjected to duress."

Other Cases—Duress

State v. Toscano, 74 N.J. 421 (1977).
"At common law the defense of duress was recognized only when the alleged coercion involved a use of threat of harm which is present, imminent and pending and of such a nature as to induce a well grounded apprehension of death or serious bodily harm if the act is not done.

It was commonly said that duress does not excuse the killing of an innocent person even if the accused acted in response to immediate threats.
…..

Duress shall be a defense to a crime (in NJ) other than murder if the defendant engaged in conduct because he was coerced to do so by the use of, or threat to use, unlawful force against his person or the person of another which a person of reasonable firmness I his situation would have been unable to resist."

People v. Unger, 362 N.E. 2d 319 (Ill. 1977).
A 22-year-old man was serving three years for theft in Statesville Penitentiary in Joliet. He was threatened by an inmate wielding a six-inch knife with sex. He was transferred to an honor farm and was beaten and sexually assaulted by a gang of inmates. Unger was warned against informing authorities and several days later he received a phone call informing him that he would be killed in retribution for having allegedly contacted correctional officials. Unger escaped from the dairy farm and was apprehended two days later while still wearing his prison clothes. He claimed he intended to return to the institution.

"The correctional system is dominated by gangs that were too powerful to be controlled by prison officials. Unger was entitled to a jury instruction on duress because he may have reasonably believed that he had no alternative other than to escape or to be killed or to suffer sever bodily harm. It was unrealistic to require a prisoner wait to escape until the moment that he was being "immediately pursued by armed inmates" and it was sufficient that Unger was threatened that he would be dead before the end of the evening."

People v. Anderson, 50 P.3d 368 (Cal 2002).
Defendant and others had suspected victim of molesting two small girls, one of whom was this friend's daughter. Defendant stated that his friend had threatened to "beat the shit out of him" if he did not kill the victim. A California statute permitted the use of the defense of duress except where the crime charged is one that is "punishable with death." At the time that statute was passed, all first degree murders were punishable by death, so duress was never available for a first degree murders. Defendant argued that he should get to present a duress defense, even though under the existing California law, first degree murder was no longer punishable by death.

The court held that the defense of duress was not available in any murder prosecution today, even in cases where the death penalty no longer applies. "There is no evidence that the legislature ever intended the substantive law to fluctuate with every change in death penalty law." The California court noted that California is tormented by gang violence, and if duress was recognized as a defense to the killing of innocents, then a street or prison gang need only create an internal reign of terror and murder can be justified, at least by the actual killer. Persons who know they can claim duress will be more likely to follow a gang order to kill instead of resisting than those who would know they must fact e the consequences of their acts.

(3) It is not a defense that a woman acted on the command of her husband, unless she acted under such coercion as would establish a defense under this Section. (The presumption that a woman acting in the presence of her husband is coerced is abolished.)
(4) When the conduct of the actor would otherwise be justifiable under § 3.02, this Section does not preclude such a defense.

State v. Riedl, 807 P.2d 697 (1991).
Riedl and his friend were drinking beer at a bar for about two hours. They left the bar and were confronted by three people in the parking lot, one of whom shouted threats at Riedl. Riedl testified that he reached for his keys, was punched by one of the three, ran for his car, got in, and stated the vehicle. He hit another car while attempting to get away. He sped away towards his home, when Officers Costello and Bowmen saw him five miles from the site of the confrontation. Riedl testified that he had two friends who had been killed in bar fights, and he had worked in a hospital and that knowledge contributed to his state of mind and compulsion to act as he did. The trial court was not convinced and he was convicted of speeding.

Riedl challenged the trial court's determination that the compulsion defense, as a matter of law, was not available for the charge of speeding. The case was "one of first impression" in Kansas.

"In the case before us, our threshold question is whether the defense of compulsion is available to a defendant charged with a strict liability offense. We conclude that it is." The court concluded that compulsion would apply to these types of charges and then went on to apply the compulsion defense to the facts of this case. "Once we accept the availability of the compulsion defense to absolute liability traffic offenses, we must examine the record carefully to determine whether there was sufficient evidence to invoke the compulsion defense."

The court concluded that he evidence failed to demonstrate that the compulsion was "continuous." Riedl testified, "When I left out of there, I thought there was a possibility that the guys in the parking lot would chase us." There was no evidence to indicate he was followed; he drove for approximately five miles without stopping or seeking assistance. "This lack of continuous threat is fatal to any attempt to assert the compulsion defense."

United States v. Calley, 46 CMR 1131 (1973).
"During midmorning on 16 March 1968, a large number of unresisting Vietnamese were placed in a ditch on the eastern side of My Lai and summarily executed by American soldiers." Lieutenant Calley was ultimately charged and convicted of murder arising out of the killing of those Vietnamese. He himself had shot into the ditch and had ordered several under his command to shoot at the Vietnamese in the ravine.

At trial he claimed that he committed no murder at My Lai because he was void of mens rea and that he acted in obedience to orders from Captain Medina. Essentially he claimed that he was not free to disobey the orders and thus he was not responsible for the My Lai massacre. He argued he was coerced into killing. The court rejected this defense and ruled that every person must accept responsibility for killing. No one who obeys the order to kill can transfer that responsibility. Despite the need for military discipline, which is admittedly great, the court held that officers must disobey clearly illegal orders, particularly when they lead to death.

"An order of the type appellant says he received is illegal. Its illegality is apparent upon even cursory evaluation by a man of ordinary sense and understanding.

Necessity And Duress

The excuse of duress and the justification of necessity are similar but distinct. The necessity defense applies to situations in which an actor, to avoid significant harm, must commit a less significant crime. The need to commit a crime may arise because of a situation, and the defense is not limited to circumstances involving threats from other people. The duress excuse applies to situations in which the threat is from a person or persons and the threat is serious--involving serious physical injury or death to the defendant unless the defendant commits a crime. With the necessity defense, the harm the defendant seeks to avoid must be greater than, not merely equal to, the harm caused by the defendant's conduct. The duress excuse does not require that the defendant prove that the harm from the threat was greater than the harm of the crime committed.

Mistake of Fact/ Mistake of Law

With strict liability crimes being the exception, criminal responsibility is always tied to culpable, blameworthy conduct. Sometimes people make mistakes and end up violating the law. But, since only morally blameworthy individuals should be punished, the law excuses individuals whose mistakes display a lack of intent.

Some courts require that the defendant's mistake of fact must be objectively reasonable—meaning a reasonable person would have made the same mistake. For example, Sam walks into an office and drops his wet umbrella off at the door. Upon leaving, Sam takes Frank's umbrella, believing it to be his. Sam would have made a mistake about the fact of the umbrella's true owner. Because the law excuses only reasonable mistakes, the jury will want to consider what Frank and Sam's umbrellas looked like when deciding whether Sam stole Frank's umbrella. Was Frank's umbrella the same size, color, and shape as Sam's? Was it in the same general location that Sam had left his umbrella? Was Frank's umbrella colorful and unique while Sam's umbrella was a generic looking black umbrella? Other facts may also be important. Was Sam color blind? What if Sam took Frank's umbrella without really paying much attention to color because he was in a hurry?

States must grapple with policy questions in determining whether mistake of fact should be permissible defense. Should an honest and good faith mistake of fact, however misguided, negate criminal intent? Should the law insist that the mistake be a reasonable one? If Sam can show that he truly believed he was taking his own umbrella (even if that belief was unreasonable), shouldn't that be enough to show he didn't have the type of guilty mind that we require before punishing people?

If Sam knew that he was taking Frank's umbrella but thought that the law allowed him to take other people's property he found preferable to his own, Sam would assert a mistake of law defense. Courts generally do not excuse these types of mistakes. Society is prepared to condemn those people who are willfully ignorant of the law and those who try to understand the law but are mistaken as to what it says.

The common saying, "ignorance of law is no defense," is generally, but not one hundred percent, accurate. Ordinarily, a mistake of law arises in a setting in which defendants intend to do an act that is prohibited, but claim that they should not be held liable because they honestly believed that they were not committing a crime. There are several problems with excusing defendants' behavior in these cases. First people are expected to know the law. Second, defendants may falsely claim that they were unaware of the law, and this claim would be difficult for the prosecution to overcome. Third, enforcing the laws promotes the public policy of social stability. (Consider a society where people avoid learning the law so they can honestly state that they were ignorant of it, and will thus have an excuse if ever brought to court.) Finally, individuals should not be permitted to define for themselves the legal rules that govern society. Because of these considerations, the common law rule, "ignorance of the law is not an excuse" developed.

Critics of the "mistake of law is no defense" approach note that because of the complexities of modern society, some people who violate some laws should not be considered morally blameworthy. The courts have, in fact, begun to relax the rigid application of the general mistake of law rule when (1) the law is one which would not have come to the defendant's notice and application of the law would violate the due process requirement of notice, (2) when the law required a showing of willful intent but the average person might not know all the laws because of how vast, complex, and highly technical they are (for example certain provisions of the tax code), and (3) when an individual relied to their detriment on the advice of a person, such as a chief of police, concerning the legality of their action.

Model Penal Code—Mistake

The MPC recognizes an ignorance of the law defense where the defendant does not know the law and the law has not been published or made reasonably available to the public. The MPC defense also applies where the defendant relies on official statements of the law (reliance).[34]

STATE v. SEXTON,
311 N.J. Super 70 (1998)

FACTS

On the evening of May 10, 1993, Ronald Sexton and Alquadir Matthews, who had been friends and neighbors for several years on Fairmount Avenue in Newark, were standing on the sidewalk near a house owned by defendant's mother. At some point the boys walked to a nearby vacant lot, where they both handled a handgun. As we will discuss below, the jury did not hear that the gun was registered to Matthews' grandmother, with whom he lived. Matthews assured Sexton that the gun was not loaded. Matthews repeated that assurance after Sexton asked whether he was "sure." Sexton pulled the trigger. The gun fired one bullet that hit Matthews. After the shot, each boy ran off. Matthews ran to his grandmother's apartment, where he collapsed. An ambulance soon arrived and took him to the hospital, and he died soon after. Sexton ran to his sister's apartment in the three-family house owned by his mother.

Later that night Sexton left his sister's apartment, returning to rented quarters in Montclair where he and his mother resided and from which he attended school. The next day, Sexton went to stay with his father in Philadelphia. There is contradictory evidence as to precisely when Sexton realized that Matthews had been shot, and when he learned that Matthews had died. In any event, defendant remained in Philadelphia with his father for eight months, long after learning of Matthews' death and after learning that the police were looking for him. Apparently his father advised him not to return to New Jersey. In January 1994, one of Sexton's uncles accompanied him to turn himself in to the police in Philadelphia.

OPINION

The primary issue for the jury was whether this shooting was the result of a tragic accident, or whether defendant acted recklessly and therefore was guilty of manslaughter.... At trial, as on appeal, the defense theory of the case was that at the time of the shooting, Sexton was under a reasonable though mistaken belief that the gun was not loaded. In *Wilson*, defendant's conviction of reckless manslaughter was reversed because the jury had not been charged that the State

---

[34] MPC § 2.04 Ignorance or Mistake.

(1) Ignorance or mistake as to a matter of fact or law is a defense if:

(a) the ignorance or mistake negatives the purpose, knowledge, belief, recklessness or negligence required to establish a material element of the offense; or

(b) the law provides that the state of mind established by such ignorance or mistake constitutes a defense.

 (2) Although ignorance or mistake would otherwise afford a defense to the offense charged, the defense is not available if the defendant would be guilty of another offense had the situation been as he supposed. In such case, however, the ignorance or mistake of the defendant shall reduce the grade and degree of the offense of which he may be convicted to those of the offense of which he would be guilty had the situation been as he supposed.

 (3) A belief that conduct does not legally constitute an offense is a defense to a prosecution for that offense based upon such conduct when:

(a) the statute or other enactment defining the offense is not known to the actor and has not been published or otherwise reasonably made available prior to the conduct alleged; or

(b) he acts in reasonable reliance upon an official statement of the law, afterward determined to be invalid or erroneous, contained in (i) a statute or other enactment; (ii) a judicial decision, opinion or judgment; (iii) an administrative order or grant of permission; or (iv) an official interpretation of the public officer or body charged by law with responsibility for the interpretation, administration or enforcement of the law defining the offense.

 (4) The defendant must prove a defense arising under Subsection (3) of this Section by a preponderance of evidence.

carried the burden of refuting the defense of mistake of fact. Although the State seeks to distinguish *Wilson v. Tard* on the facts, we find those facts to be on all fours with this case.

In *Wilson* the defendant claimed that he aimed the gun at the victim only to frighten him, and that he had first removed the magazine of bullets. He claimed he was unaware that one bullet remained in the chamber when he fired the gun. The victim was killed. Wilson argued that his mistaken but reasonable belief that he gun was unloaded negated the recklessness necessary for a manslaughter conviction. The District Court Judge, applying New Jersey law, agreed.

Here defendant's argument is even stronger. Sexton testified that Matthews invited him to the empty lot in order to show him "something." The something turned out to be the handgun.

Detective Gary Prystauk, a firearms examiner for the Newark Police Department Ballistics Laboratory, testified with respect to the gun that was recovered. According to him, the weapon's sealed chamber design required a person to pull the slide back in order to see whether a bullet was chambered. Detective Prystauk agreed that an inexperienced person easily might assume that once the magazine had been removed, no bullet remained in the chamber. In fact the gun can hold a chambered bullet with or without the magazine in place.

The failure to charge the jury that it was the State's burden to disprove defendant's reasonable belief that the gun was not loaded deprived defendant of a fair opportunity for the jury properly to weigh the evidence of an essential element of the crime: defendant's state of mind at the time of the shooting. We cannot ignore plain error in the jury charge.

N.J.S.A. 2C:2-4a(1) provides that "mistake as to a matter of fact ... is a defense if the defendant reasonably arrived at the conclusion underlying the mistake and ... [i]t negatives the culpable mental state required to establish the offense...." Where a mistake of fact would negate the mental state that is an element of a crime, the burden of disproving the mistake must fall on the State.

While we find no decision by a New Jersey court adopting the holding of *Wilson v. Tard,* this case calls for such a ruling before any retrial. The critical holding of *Wilson* is that once the defendant, as here, presents evidence of a reasonable mistake of fact that would refute an essential element of the crime charged, the State's burden of proving each element beyond a reasonable doubt includes disproving the reasonable mistake of fact.

In the case before us, in advancing the argument that he had reasonably believed that the gun was unloaded when he pulled its trigger, petitioner had raised a defense whose proof would negate the mental element necessary to constitute manslaughter. Thus, under Mullaney he should have borne only the burden of raising the issue, not that of proving it. The state was required to refute this defense beyond a reasonable doubt as an inseparable part of proving beyond a reasonable doubt that petitioner had acted recklessly and thus was guilty of manslaughter.

The State's burden with respect to the mistake of fact defense to negate the reckless state of mind for a manslaughter conviction is no less compelling than the burden of disproving a reasonable perception of risk to justify a homicide. The burden is comparable to that required where a defendant presents credible evidence of diminished capacity to negate mens rea.

Of course, the judge here did not expressly place the burden of proving the mistake on defendant, as did the judge in *Wilson.* Nevertheless, it is axiomatic that accurate jury instructions in a criminal case are essential to the defendant's constitutional right to a fair trial. . . . The judge did explain to the jury that it should acquit defendant of manslaughter if it found defendant to have acted upon a reasonable mistake that the gun was not loaded. The judge also made it clear that the State had to prove each element of the offense beyond a reasonable doubt. However, the judge did not make it clear to the jury that in order to prove the element of recklessness, the State had to prove beyond a reasonable doubt either that defendant did not actually believe the gun to be unloaded, or that his belief was unreasonable. In other words, the jury should have been instructed that the State had the burden of disproving the mistake of fact defense.

. . .

We cannot conclude that the jury understood that it was the State's burden to disprove defendant's mistake beyond a reasonable doubt.. . . Because the evidence of a reckless shooting rather than an accident was not strong, the failure to explicitly place upon the State the burden of disproving defendant's reasonable mistake of fact cannot be deemed harmless error. . . .

We affirm the conviction for unlawful possession of a handgun and the sentence for that offense. We reverse the conviction for reckless manslaughter

Other Cases—Mistake

People v. Snyder, 32 Cal. 3d 590, 186 Cal. Rptr 485 (1982).
Snyder appealed her conviction of felon in possession of a weapon charge. She claimed that she had plea bargained a marijuana possession charge which did not result in jail or prison, and had been told by her attorney that she was pleading to a misdemeanor. Believing she had not been convicted of a felony, Snyder also registered to vote and had voted. Police had already come to her home and found a gun registered to her husband and did not file any charges against her. The trial court refused to admit evidence of her mistaken belief that her prior conviction was a misdemeanor and that she was not a felon.

The court ruled that the statute for which Snyder was convicted was one of "general intent" and no specific intent was required. That is, in order to be found guilty, the state did not have to prove that Snyder knew of her status as a convicted felon.

"Lack of actual knowledge of the provisions of Penal Code §12021 is irrelevant; the crucial question is whether defendant was aware that she was engaging in the conduct.

In the present case, defendant was presumed to know that it is unlawful for a convicted felon to possess a concealable firearm. She was also charged with knowledge that the offense of which she was convicted was, as a matter of law, a felony.

Thus, regardless of what she reasonably believed, or what her attorney may have told her, defendant was deemed to know under the law that she was a convicted felon forbidden to possess concealable firearms. Her asserted mistake regarding her correct legal status was a mistake of law, not fact. It does not constitute a defense to §12021."

People v. Marrero, 507 N.E.2d 1068 (NY 1986).

The court held that "Mistake of law is a viable exemption in those instances where an individual demonstrates an effort to learn what the law is, relies on the validity of that law and later, it is determined that there was a mistake in the law itself."

The modern availability of this defense is based on the theory that where the government has affirmatively, albeit unintentionally misled an individual as to what may or may not be legally permissible conduct, the individual should not be punished as a result. "

The court discussed the policy reasons why mistake of law should not include situations where, as in this case, the defendant misinterprets a potentially ambiguous statute about whether he could carry a gun in New York City without a permit.

Lambert v. California, 355 U.S. 225 (1957).
Exception to the usual rule that ignorance or mistake of law is no excuse. Court held that due process was violated by convicting Lambert of a registration offense when it was unlikely to have come to his attention. Lack of awareness/mistake of law can be a crime when state fails to put people on notice of what the law says.

Cheek v. United States, 498 U.S. 192 (1991).
Exception to the usual rule that ignorance or mistake of law is no excuse. Defendant was counseled by anti-tax activists and came to believe that his wages did not constitute income so he owed not taxes. He was convicted of willfully attempting to evade. U. S. Supremes held that Congress required a citizen might innocently fail to be informed. showing of willful intent because the vast number of tax statutes made it likely that he average

Cox v. Louisiana, 379 U.S. 559 (1965).
U.S. Supreme Court overturned the convictions of students charged with picketing a courthouse

with intent of interfering with administration of justice. The Chief of Police had instructed them they could legally picket at a location 101 feet from courthouse steps, and they relied upon that representation.

"Appellant was convicted for demonstrating not "in," but "near," the courthouse. It is undisputed that the demonstration took place on the west sidewalk, the far side of the street, exactly 101 feet from the courthouse steps and, Judging from the pictures in the record, approximately 125 feet from the courthouse itself. The question is raised as to whether the failure of the statute to define the word "near" renders it unconstitutionally vague It is clear that there is some lack of specificity in a word such as "near." While this lack of specificity may not render the statute unconstitutionally vague, at least as applied to a demonstration within the sight and hearing of those in the courthouse, it is clear that the statute, with respect to the determination of how near the courthouse a particular demonstration can be, foresees a degree of on-the-spot administrative interpretation by officials charged with responsibility for administering and enforcing it. It is apparent that demonstrators, such as those involved here, would justifiably tend to rely on this administrative interpretation of how "near" the courthouse a particular demonstration might take place. Louisiana's statutory policy of preserving order around the courthouse would counsel encouragement of just such reliance. This administrative discretion to construe the term "near" concerns a limited control of the streets and other areas in the immediate vicinity of the courthouse, and is the type of narrow discretion which this Court has recognized as the proper role of responsible officials in making determinations concerning the time, place, duration, and manner of demonstrations. . . . Nor does this limited administrative regulation of traffic which the Court has consistently recognized as necessary and permissible, constitute a waiver of law which is beyond the power of the police. Obviously, telling demonstrators how far from the courthouse steps is "near" the courthouse for purposes of a permissible peaceful demonstration is a far cry from allowing one to commit, for example, murder, or robbery.

The record here clearly shows that the officials present gave permission for the demonstration to take place across the street from the courthouse. Cox testified that they gave him permission to conduct the demonstration on the far side of the street. This testimony is not only uncontradicted, but is corroborated by the State's witnesses who were present. Police Chief White testified that he told Cox "he must confine" the demonstration "to the west side of the street." James Erwin, news director of radio station WIBR, agreed that Cox was given permission for the assembly as long as it remained within a designated time. When Sheriff Clemmons sought to break up the demonstration, he first announced, "now, you have been allowed to demonstrate." The Sheriff testified that he had "no objection" to the students "being assembled on that side of the street." Finally, the State . . . conceded that the officials gave Cox and his group some time to demonstrate across the street from the courthouse. This agreement by the State that, in fact, permission had been granted to demonstrate . . . for seven minutes -- was confirmed.

The record shows that at no time did the police recommend, or even suggest, that the demonstration be held further from the courthouse than it actually was. The police admittedly had prior notice that the demonstration was planned to be held in the vicinity of the courthouse. They were prepared for it at that point, and so stationed themselves and their equipment as to keep the demonstrators on the far side of the street. As Cox approached the vicinity of the courthouse, he was met by the Chief of Police and other officials. At this point, not only was it not suggested that they hold their assembly elsewhere or disband, but they were affirmatively told that they could hold the demonstration on the sidewalk of the far side of the street, 101 feet from the courthouse steps. This area was effectively blocked off by the police, and traffic rerouted.

Thus, the highest police officials of the city, in the presence of the Sheriff and Mayor, in effect told the demonstrators that they could meet where they did, 101 feet from the courthouse steps, but could not meet closer to the courthouse. In effect, appellant was advised that a demonstration at the place it was held would not be one "near" the courthouse within the terms of the statute.

. . . The Due Process Clause does not permit convictions to be obtained under such circumstances.

Regina [Deputy Director of Prosecutions] v. Morgan, 2 WLR 913 AC 182.

This is a frequently cited case in which defendant invited the three co-defendants home to have sexual relations with his wife. He led them to believe that she would consent to this group activity. He cautioned them that she was "kinky" and may struggle a bit in order to enhance her sense of excitement. They held her down and each engaged in intercourse with her in the presence of one another. The three were convicted of rape. The facts and result of this case are peculiar (no rape), but can be attributed to the law of rape in England which required that the government prove that the defendant knew the victim did not consent to rape. Here if they were wrong about her consent (which they were), it did not matter if was reasonable that they were wrong (it wasn't, but that did not matter).

The trial court had instructed the jury that they must have reasonably believed that despite Mrs. Morgan's resistance, she consented to the rape. The Law Lords overturned the conviction and ruled that a male who acts on an unreasonably mistaken belief in the female's consent does not possess the criminal intent and should be acquitted. "Either the prosecution proves that the accused had the requisite intent, or it does not." As a result of this case, Parliament enacted a statutory amendment providing that the mistake of fact defense requires an honest and reasonable mistake.

State v. Bougneit, 294 N.W.2d 675 (Wis. 1980). Requirement that mistake must be reasonable may violate due process.

People v. Vogel, 46 Cal. 2d 798 (1956). Defense of reasonable mistake.

State v. Sawyer, 110 A. 461 (Conn 1920). Mistake of law negates the specific intent to deprive for theft.

Post-traumatic Stress Disorder

Post-traumatic stress disorder (PTSD) refers to the unique stresses suffered during combat (or more recently, any exceptionally traumatic experience). PTSD often manifests itself in flashbacks, outbursts of anger, blocked-out memories. PTSD is not a legal defense in itself, but in some instances PTSD may affect a defendant's understanding so severely that is allows him or her to raise an insanity defense. Courts may allow defendants to introduce PTSD evidence for its bearing on defendant's intent or during sentencing hearing to mitigate punishment. Following World War II, "combat fatigue" was used to describe these anxiety disorders. Present generations have heard these conditions described as PTSD. Because of the bizarre type of warfare that service personnel endured in Vietnam, the unpopularity of the war, the availability of drugs, and the difficulties encountered in adjusting to civilian life, many veterans suffered severe psychological reactions. To a lesser extent, the stress of combat in Operation Desert storm also caused delayed traumatic stress disorder. Current military operations in Afghanistan, Iraq, and elsewhere can be expected to cause similar results.

Entrapment

When defendants claim entrapment they assert that the government wrongly caused them to commit their crimes. As with other excuses, entrapment is a claim by the defendant that although they did the crime, they are not responsible.

The entrapment defense developed in the United States in the 1930s. In *Sorrells v. United States*, 287 U.S. 435 (1932), an undercover agent posed as a thirsty tourist and ultimately overcame Sorrell's resistance and persuaded him to locate some illegally manufactured alcohol. The Court reversed Sorrells' conviction, finding that the officer induced Sorrells--a person who otherwise would not have committed the crime--to commit the crime. The Court held that entrapment occurs when criminal conduct is the product of "creative activity of law enforcement officers." "Entrapment is the "conception and planning of an offense by an officer, and his procurement of its commission by one who would not have perpetrated it except for the trickery, persuasion, or fraud of the officer."

Since *Sorrells* the courts have adopted one of two approaches in deciding whether police have gone too far--both of which were discussed in *Sherman v. United States,* 356 U.S. 369 (1958). In *Sherman* a government informant (facing criminal charges) befriended the defendant, and confided to him his addiction to narcotics and the difficulty in overcoming it. The government agent eventually convinced Sherman to obtain and split the cost of illegal narcotics. Although the entire Court found Sherman was entrapped, five justices supported what is now known as the "subjective test of entrapment," and four justices supported what is now known as the "objective test of entrapment."

Subjective Test Of Entrapment

The subjective test of entrapment focuses on the defendant and asks whether he or she was predisposed to commit the crime. Did the government created the intent to commit the crime in someone who would otherwise not intend to commit a crime, or did the government do no more than plant a trap for the unwary criminal? If it is the former, then the defendant was entrapped under the subjective approach. This approach, embraced by the federal courts and majority of the states, excuses the defendant from criminal liability because it is wrong for the government to punish the defendant when it was the state that prompted the defendant to act in the first place. With this approach, the jury must first decide whether the idea of committing the crime originated with the government agent, and if so, did the agent use tactics that induced the defendant to commit the crime. Merely providing an opportunity to commit a crime does not constitute an inducement. Rather, inducement involves appeals to friendship, promises of sexual favors, promises of economic or material gain, appeals to compassion, or requesting assistance in carrying out the crime. A person who is predisposed to commit the crime is someone who is ready and willing to engage in conduct in the absence of government inducements. Factors the court considers in determining whether the defendant was induced include:

➢ The character or reputation of the defendant, including prior criminal arrests and convictions for the type of crime involved.
➢ Whether the accused suggested the criminal activity.
➢ Whether the defendant was already engaged in criminal activity for profit.
➢ Whether the defendant was reluctant to commit the offense.
➢ Whether the defendant seemed to be familiar with the culture surrounding the criminal endeavor.
➢ The attractiveness of the inducement.

One critique of the subjective test of entrapment is that it fails to provide police with any bright line rules since it is factually specific and focuses on characteristics of the individual defendant.

Objective Test Of Entrapment

The objective test, followed by a substantial minority of the states, focuses on keeping police from engaging in inappropriate activities designed to manufacture crime. "The crucial question" according to Justice Frankfurter's opinion in *Sherman*, "is whether the police conduct revealed in the particular case falls below standards to which common feelings respond, for the proper use of governmental power." Frankfurter noted that the government agent in *Sherman* took advantage of Sherman's susceptibility to narcotics and manufactured Sherman's response by his repeated requests to get him drugs. One question courts ask in applying the objective test of entrapment is whether police activity went beyond judicial tolerance--is this something we want police to be doing?

Entrapment And Due Process

Defendants sometimes argue that entrapment tactics violate the Due Process Clause of the Constitution claiming that the government's conduct was so unfair and outrageous that it would be unjust to convict them. The Court has rejected this argument in several cases finding that due process is violated only when law enforcement tactics violate fundamental fairness or were shocking to the universal sense of justice.

Model Penal Code–Entrapment

The MPC provides a defense of entrapment. MPC § 2.13 (1) holds that acgovernment official perpetrates an entrapment when he "induces or encourages another person to engage in conduct constituting such offense by either: a) making knowingly false representations designed to induce the belief that such conduct is not prohibited; or b) employing methods of persuasion or inducement that created a substantial risk that such an offense will be committed by persons other than those who are ready to commit it." Paragraph 2 provides that he defendant will be acquitted of the crime if he can prove by a preponderance of the evidence that his or her conduce was in response to the entrapment.. The defense is not available where the defendant's crime causes or threatens bodily injury. See MPC §2.13 (3).

OLIVER v. STATE,
703 P.2d 869 (Nev. 1985)

HISTORY
Ernest Oliver was convicted of larceny from the person in the Eighth Judicial District Court and sentenced to 10 years in prison. He appealed. The Supreme Court reversed.

FACTS
On the night of Oliver's arrest, three policemen undertook to conduct a "decoy operation" near the intersection of Main and Ogden in Las Vegas. That corner is in a downtown area frequented by substantial numbers of persons commonly characterized as "street people," "vagrants," and "derelicts." It appears Oliver, a black man, is one of these.

Disguised as a vagrant in an old Marine Corps jacket, the decoy officer slumped against a palm tree, pretending to be intoxicated and asleep. His associates concealed themselves nearby. The decoy prominently displayed a ten-dollar bill, positioning it to protrude from the left breast pocket of his jacket. This was done, the decoy later testified, "to provide an opportunity for a dishonest person to prove himself." Oliver, who had the misfortune to come walking down the street, saw the decoy and evidently felt moved to assist him. Shaking and nudging the decoy with his foot, Oliver attempted to warn the decoy that the police would arrest him if he did not move on. The decoy did not respond, and Oliver stepped away. Up to this point, Oliver had shown no predisposition whatever to commit any criminal act.

Then, Oliver saw the ten-dollar bill protruding from the decoy's pocket. He reached down and took it. "Thanks, home boy," he said. Thereupon, he was arrested by the decoy and the two other officers. Following the trial, a jury convicted Oliver of larceny from the person, and he has been sentenced to ten years imprisonment.

OPINION

Oliver's counsel contends he was entrapped into committing the offense in question. We agree. Government agents or officers may not employ extraordinary temptations or inducements. They may not manufacture crime.

We have repeatedly endorsed the following concept: Entrapment is the seduction or improper inducement to commit a crime for the purpose of instituting a criminal prosecution, but if a person in good faith and for the purpose of detecting or discovering a crime or offense, furnishes the opportunity for the commission thereof by one who has the requisite criminal intent, it is not entrapment.

Thus, because we discern several facts which we believe combined to create an extraordinary temptation, which was inappropriate to apprehending merely those bent on criminal activity, we feel constrained to reverse Oliver's conviction. We note, first of all, that the decoy portrayed himself as completely susceptible and vulnerable. He did not respond when Oliver attempted to wake him, urging him to avoid arrest by moving to another location. Moreover, the decoy displayed his ten-dollar bill in a manner calculated to tempt any needy person in the area, whether immediately disposed to crime or not.

In the case of Oliver, the police succeeded in tempting a man who apparently did not approach the decoy with larceny in mind, but rather to help him. Even after being lured into petty theft by the decoy's open display of currency and apparent helplessness, Oliver did not go on to search the decoy's pockets or to remove his wallet.

On this record, then, we think the activities of the officers, however well intentioned, accomplished an impermissible entrapment. Through the state's own witnesses at trial, Oliver's counsel established a prima facie showing that Oliver's criminal act was instigated by the state. There was no countervailing evidence whatever. Accordingly, on this record, we must conclude as a matter of law that Oliver was entrapped, and we reverse his conviction.

DEPASQUALE v. STATE, 757 P.2d 367 (1988)

FACTS

Four officers on the LVMPD's S.C.A.T. Unit (Street Crime Attack Team) were performing a decoy operation near the intersection of Fremont Street and Casino Center Blvd. in Las Vegas on April 30, 1983, at 11:45 p.m. Officer Debbie Gautwier was the decoy, and Officers Shalhoob, Young, and Harkness were assigned to "back-up." Officer Gautwier was dressed in plain clothes and was carrying a tan shoulder bag draped over her left shoulder.

Within one of the side, zippered pockets of the bag, she had placed a $5 bill and $1 bill wrapped with a simulated $100 bill. The money, including the numbers of the simulated $100 bill, were exposed so as to be visible to persons nearby; however, the zipper was pulled tight against the money so as to require a concentrated effort to remove it.

Officer Young, also in plain clothes, was standing approximately six to seven feet away from Officer Gautwier (the decoy), near the entrance of the Horseshoe Club, when Randall DeBelloy approached Officer Gautwier from behind and asked if he could borrow a pen. Officer Gautwier stated that she did not have a pen, and DeBelloy retreated eight to ten feet. Within a few seconds he approached a second time, asking for a piece of paper. Again the response was "no." During these approaches Officer Young observed DeBelloy reach around Officer Gautwier toward the exposed cash.

DeBelloy again retreated eight to ten feet from Officer Gautwier. He then motioned with his hand to two men who were another eight to ten feet away, and the trio huddled together for 15 to 30 seconds. As DeBelloy talked with the two men, he looked up and over in the direction of Officer Gautwier. Vincent DePasquale was one of the two men who joined DeBelloy in this huddle.
While this trio was conversing, Officer Gautwier had been waiting for the walk signal at the intersection. When the light changed, she crossed Fremont Street and proceeded southbound on the west sidewalk of Casino Center Blvd. DePasquale and DeBelloy followed her, 15 to 20 feet behind. After crossing the street, Officer Gautwier looked back briefly and saw DeBelloy following her. DePasquale was four to seven feet behind DeBelloy and to his right.

As they walked in this formation, DePasquale yelled out, "Wait lady, can I talk to you for a minute." As Officer Gautwier turned to her right in response—seeing DePasquale whom she identified in court—DeBelloy took a few quick steps to her left side, took the money with his right hand and ran.

DeBelloy was arrested, with the marked money in his possession, by Officers Harkness and Shalhoob. DePasquale was arrested by Officers Gautwier and Young. Both were charged with larceny from the person and convicted by a jury.

OPINION

DePasquale argues that he was entrapped, that the district court erred in its instruction to the jury on the law of entrapment, that the evidence fails to support the verdict, and that the sentence of ten years is disproportionate and, therefore, cruel and unusual.

Upon these facts, the decoy simply provided the opportunity to commit a crime to anyone who succumbed to the lure of the bait. Entrapment encompasses two elements:

(1) an opportunity to commit a crime is presented by the state
(2) to a person not predisposed to commit the act.

Thus, this subjective approach focuses upon the defendant's predisposition to commit the crime. In the present case, the cash, although exposed, was zipped tightly to the edge of a zippered pocket, not hanging temptingly from the pocket of an unconscious derelict. Admittedly, the money was exposed; however, that attraction alone fails to cast a pall over the defendant's predisposition. The exposed valuables (money) were presented in a realistic situation, an alert and well-dressed woman walking on the open sidewalks in the casino area.

The fact that the money was exposed simply presented a generally identified social predator with a logical target. These facts suggest that DePasquale was predisposed to commit this crime. Furthermore, the fact that DePasquale had no contact with the decoy but rather succumbed to the apparent temptation of his co-defendant to systematically stalk their target, evidences his predisposition.

Lastly, DePasquale complains that his sentence was disproportionate to the crime and, therefore, cruel and unusual punishment. A sentence is unconstitutional if it is so disproportionate to the crime for which it is inflicted that it shocks the conscience and offends fundamental notions of human dignity. While the punishment authorized in Nevada is strict, it is not cruel and unusual.

Other Cases—Entrapment

State v Doran, 5 Ohio St. 3d 187 (1983).
In this case Ohio courts chose to adopt the subjective test of entrapment in Ohio after evaluating both the advantages and difficulties inherent in the majority, subjective approach, and the minority view, the objective approach.

"Our sole reservation concerning the subjective test involves the scope of admissible evidence on the issue of an accused's predisposition. While evidence relevant to predisposition should be freely admitted, judges should be hesitant to allow evidence of the accused's bad reputation, without more, on the issue of predisposition. Rather, while by no means an exhaustive list, the following matters would certainly be relevant on the issue of predisposition: (1) the accused's previous involvement in criminal activity of the nature charged, (2) the accused's ready acquiescence to the inducements offered by the police, (3) the accused's expert knowledge in the area of the criminal activity charged, (4) the accused's ready access to contraband, and (5) the accused's willingness to involve himself in criminal activity. Under this approach, the evidence on the issue of an accused's predisposition is more reliable than the evidence of the nature of inducement by police agents under the objective test.

"Where the criminal design originates with the officials of the government, and they implant in the mind of an innocent person the disposition to commit the alleged offense and induce its commission in order to prosecute, the defense of entrapment is established and the accused is entitled to acquittal. However, entrapment is not established when government officials merely afford opportunities or facilities for the commission of the offense." and it is shown that the accused was predisposed to commit the offense."

United States v. Russell, 411 U.S. 423 (1973).
Joe Shapiro, and undercover federal agent met with defendant and two other co-defendants. Shapiro offered to provide them with a chemical essential to the manufacture of meth, in return for ½ of the drugs produced. The three provided Shapiro with a sample of their most recent batch and showed him their lab. Shapiro delivered the chemical and then watched as they began to manufacture.

Defendants argued that although they were predisposed to manufacture and sell drugs, the government violated due process by prosecuting them for a crime in which the government had been intimately involved. U.S. Supreme Court rejected the argument and stressed that, although the drug Shapiro provided was hard to get, it was not impossible (evidenced by the fact that the defendants were already manufacturing). "While we may someday be presented with a situation in which the conduct of law enforcement agents is so outrageous that due process principles would absolutely bar the government from invoking judicial process to obtain a conviction, this instant case is distinctly not of that breed." Law enforcement tactics were neither in violation of fundamental fairness nor shocking to the universal sense of justice.

Miller v. State, (110 P.3d 53 (Nev. 2005)).
This case involved another decoy operation in Las Vegas. The decoy operation was designed to combat an increase in street-level robberies occurring in downtown Las Vegas. In this case Las Vegas Metropolitan Police Department

detective Leavitt placed $21.00 in his pocket and allowed a little of the money to be seen. Enough was showing so that if someone got close they could see it, but it was also hidden enough that they didn't attract everyone. Detective appeared dirty and smelled of beer, walked with a limp and carried a can of beer so as to appear intoxicated. When the Miller approached Leavitt, he asked him for money, but the detective declined. Miller then put his arm around Miller and invited him to get a drink. The defendant pulled Miller close in to him, reached his hands into the detective's pocket, took the money, then loosened his grip and again asked for money. Miller then asked again for money, and detective said he couldn't because it was all gone. Team converged, arrested Miller. Charged Miller with larceny from a person and Miller was convicted. Miller argued on appeal that he was entrapped.

The Court concluded that Miller was not entrapped because he was predisposed to commit the crime. The court examined its prior cases and stated, "We have drawn a clear line between a realistic decoy who poses as an alternative victim of potential crime and the helpless, intoxicated, and unconscious decoy with money hanging out of a pocket. The former is permissible undercover police work where the latter is entrapment."

Cruz v. State, 465 So.2d 516 (Fla. 1985).
Defendant got caught up in a Tampa police decoy operation in a high-crime area. Officer posed as a smelly, inebriated, indigent wino. He leaned with his face toward the wall from which could plainly be seen $150.00 in currency hanging out his rear pant pocket. Defendant and a companion passed the officer at 10:00 p.m., said something to him, and then moved on. Ten to fifteen minutes later he returned, took the cash from the decoy's pocket without harming him in any way. Officers arrested Cruz as he walked from the scene. The court noted that the decoy situation did not involve the same modus operandi as any of the unsolved crimes which had occurred it he area. Police were not seeking a particular individual nor were they aware of any prior criminal acts by the defendant.

The court discussed the two approaches that had been enunciated by the court. The subjective standard, which defines entrapment as law enforcement conduct which implants in the mind of an innocent person the disposition to commit the crime is a defense only to those who were not predisposed to commit the crime induced by the government. "In recent years. . . this court has fashioned a second, independent standard for assessing entrapment. It recognizes that when official conduct inducing crime is so egregious as to impugn the integrity of a court that permits a conviction, the predisposition of the defendant becomes irrelevant."

"As the part played by the State in the criminal activity increases, the importance of the factor of defendant's criminal intent decreases, until finally a point may be reached where the methods employed by the state to obtain a conviction cannot be countenanced, even though a defendant's predisposition is shown Whether the police activity has overstepped the bounds of permissible conduct is a question to be decided by the trial court rather than the jury."

"To guide the trial courts, we propound the following threshold test of an entrapment defense: Entrapment has not occurred as a matter of law where police activity (1) has at its end the interruption of a specific ongoing criminal activity; and (2) utilizes means reasonably tailored to apprehend those involved in the ongoing criminal activity."

The court applied the test to the case before them and found that the drunken bum decoy operation fails. The court noted that the record did not show what, if any, specific criminal activity was targeted, and also that they had planted $150.00 to make sure that more than $100.00 was taken…the amount bumping the crime up to a felony.

The Cruz court, unlike most, applies both a subjective standard (whether Cruz himself was enticed into doing something he would otherwise not do AND the objective standard (whether reasonable persons would be enticed by the police decoy tactic used. Most states use one test or the other.

Henderson v. United States, 237 F.2d 169 (5th Cir. 1956).
Entrapment is not a defense to private (non-governmental) inducement

State v. Fiechter, 547 P.2d 1247 (N. M. 1976).
"Entrapment occurs when police conduct . . . . shakes public's confidence in fair and honorable administration of justice."

Hampton v. United States, 435 U.S. 484 (1976).

Supplying material for commission of offense is not entrapment under federal law	Sending child porn advertisements to defendant who then orders the magazines.
Jacobsen v. United States, 503 U.S. 540 (1992.)	

WRAP UP

Excuses are defenses that assert, "Although I did the act, I am not responsible because I was (fill in the excuse). Insanity, extreme emotional distress, age, intoxication, mistake, PTSD, PMS, and other syndromes are excuses in which the defendant asserts that, even though he or she committed the act, he or she is not blameworthy. States vary greatly in how (and if) they define and allow insanity as a defense. When insanity is a defense, some states allow a verdict of not guilty by reason of insanity, but the trend has been to substitute that verdict with a "guilty but mentally ill" verdict. Few states allow the defenses of diminished capacity and voluntary intoxication but when they do, these two defenses require the defendant prove that because of the disturbance (whether it be physiological or mental) that they lacked the higher mens rea requirements of purposeful or knowing actions and thus they deserve to be convicted only of lesser charges.

Index

Made in the USA
Las Vegas, NV
02 April 2021